Contents

KU-460-619

TRADE UNIONS

Selected Readings

Edited by W. E. J. McCarthy

Second Edition

Pen

Penguin Books Ltd, Harmondsworth, Middlesex, England
Viking Penguin Inc., 40 West 23rd Street, New York, New York 10010, U.S.A.
Penguin Books Australia Ltd, Ringwood, Victoria, Australia
Penguin Books Canada Limited, 2801 John Street, Markham, Ontario, Canada L3R 1B4
Penguin Books (N.Z.) Ltd, 182–190 Wairau Road, Auckland 10, New Zealand

First published 1972
Reprinted 1974, 1976, 1978
Second edition 1985
Reprinted 1986

Printed and bound in Great Britain by
Cox & Wyman Ltd, Reading
Set in Times Linotron

Introduction

Trade unions are always in the news, but this does not help them to be understood. This collection of readings, like its predecessor, is designed to provide the would-be student of the subject with a representative sample of the serious thought and study that is concerned with trying to understand these complex and diverse institutions. It is compiled from books, articles and reports published in Britain and the United States.

Since the publication of the first edition in 1972, the volume of specialist academic research devoted to union behaviour has greatly increased. The economic consequences of trade unions, and their presumed effect on employment, productivity and prices, has also become the subject of prolonged and controversial debate among economists. At the same time sociologists and students of politics have written at considerable length about the proper role of trade unions in the modern democratic state. More important still, their legal status and their relations with the government of the day have become major political issues – leading to a series of complex and at times contradictory statutes and legal decisions. As a result there has arisen a rapidly expanding race of labour law specialists, who have written a stream of books and filled the columns of many old and new periodicals.

These developments have meant that for this edition I have had to survey a much wider spectrum of publications dealing with a far greater range of issues than before. This is why the number of readings included is almost double that of the first, and why most of them are included for the first time. Fortunately it has proved possible to retain all but one of the first edition's subject-headings, and the book is still divided into seven sections or parts. The first deals with union objectives and methods; the second with industrial democracy. The next two concern forms of union government and structure. Subsequent parts describe and analyse the factors affecting union growth and the economic consequences of trade unionism. The final part deals with union relations with government and their status in law.

Unfortunately the flood of research, analysis and comment has not produced equally acceptable and well-established conclusions in all areas of the subject. In some ways the arguments have become increasingly complex and the level of debate more uneven. It is important to understand how this has happened and why the serious consideration of trade union behaviour can be said to have both advanced and retreated in recent years. This introduction is partly devoted to such an explanation. But it is also designed to provide a short guide to some of the more complex issues raised in subsequent readings.

It helps to proceed by first considering those areas where most progress has been made, i.e. those covered by Parts One, Three, Four and Five. There can be no doubt that over the last ten years progress has been most evident in the area of union growth (Part Five). In the first edition it was necessary to warn readers that 'there is no generally accepted theory of union growth'. It can be said that in terms of membership trends, at the level of the economy at least, this is no longer the case. In Reading 17 Bain and Price demonstrate that variations in the overall level of union membership can be broadly explained by the interaction of three related factors: economic activity rates, employer policies and government action. This explanation is not without its critics, who are well represented in Readings 18, 20 and 21, but for the most part the points they make are best regarded as qualifications, reservations and suggested extensions of Bain's theory. It remains true that in this field there has been real progress. In broad terms, we know why a trade union movement grows, declines or stagnates.

It is also true that in the more complex field of union government and structure (Parts Three and Four) considerable progress has been made. Readings 13 and 14 present some of the results of empirical studies based on a representative sample of British unions. In Reading 10 H. A. Clegg uses international data to argue that the shape a union takes is originally a function of technology and industrial organization, subject to the overriding qualification that what emerges does not prevent effective job-regulation.

What we know about the factors affecting union government and structure do not amount to a general explanation or theory. But it is now possible to talk much more sensibly about the importance and likely effects of various developments and trends, e.g. the growing use of 'reference back' procedures, different forms of balloting, or the emergence of so-called 'conglomerate' unions. It is also possible to discern the emerging shape of British unions as a result of the present spate of mergers (see Readings 11 and 12).

Finally, it is clear that in the area of union objectives and methods – the subject of Part One – we know much more than we did ten years ago. There have been a spate of case studies concerned with union bargaining behaviour and several comprehensive surveys of workshop relations. They have added greatly to our knowledge of union strategy and tactics, especially at workshop level. The relationship between shop stewards and their members was almost over-researched in the seventies, and Reading 4 contains a fascinating extract from one of the most perceptive of these studies.

This brings us to those areas of trade union studies where additional knowledge and generally acceptable conclusions have been rather more difficult to come by – even when the flow of articles and books has mounted year by year. What can be said about them?

In the case of trade unions and industrial democracy – the subject of Part Two – the problem has been the lack of data to be investigated. Until the mid-seventies the theoretical debate about whether trade union representation at board level would undermine the independence of collective bargaining appeared to have been won by Hugh Clegg (see Readings 5 and 6, retained from the first edition). In practical terms the British TUC adopted a position very similar to that of Clegg: they did not favour any form of boardroom representation in case it compromised their independence and freedom to negotiate with management. Yet Clegg was not without his academic critics – see Reading 7 by Paul Blumberg.

However, after Britain's entry into Europe the Heath government felt the need to do something about the EEC's Fifth Directive. This proposed legislation to encourage, or impose, worker directors in various forms. Partly in reaction to the Fifth Directive, and partly for reasons of its own which are summarized in the introduction to Part Seven, the TUC decided to adopt a more positive line: they sought to persuade an incoming Labour government to provide legislation imposing trade union representation at board level.

The result was the establishment of the Bullock Committee and its 1977 Report, which is the basis of Reading 8. This contains the substance of Bullock's argument for 'single channel representation', i.e. the use of existing union machinery to select worker directors. It also includes the nub of the Report's argument that 'there is no fundamental and irreconcilable incompatibility between board level

11

representation and collective bargaining': in effect, their answer to Clegg.

Unfortunately, at least for the advance of our subject, Bullock's proposals met with a combination of employers' resistance and trade union apathy, and were finally buried by a new and hostile government. As a result Britain has continued to be almost the only country in Western Europe where there is no legal right to worker representation at boardroom level, where the notion of industrial democracy has not been given any formal recognition by the state. Consequently, this aspect of the subject has remained very much a matter of theoretical debate, since there has been almost nothing to study and research.

The only exception of much significance occurred, for a time, in the Post Office. Here, for two years in the late seventies, an attempt was made to implement at least some of the principles behind the Bullock Report – most importantly parity of representation for union nominees at the corporate board level. Fortunately Eric Batstone and his colleagues were given the chance to study this unique experiment in considerable detail, and their main conclusions form the basis of Reading 9. Much light is thrown on the theoretical debate about industrial democracy. The authors conclude that the overall impact of the scheme was slight, and that the more drastic consequences foreseen by commentators did not occur. Once again, to paraphrase Hugh Clegg in another context, 'an ounce of fact has been found to be worth a pound of theory'.

In the case of the economic consequences of trade unionism, the subject matter of Part Six, the difficulties in the way of agreed advance have been quite different and much more complex. Yet they are worth exploring in some depth, partly as an introduction to the readings in Part Seven and partly because of their intrinsic importance for the future of the subject.

The first point to make is that much work has been done, and some progress has been made. A substantial measure of agreement exists among labour economists and students of industrial relations about a limited range of issues – most notably the effect of trade unions on money wages. It has also been widely accepted, at least in specialist academic circles, that further progress is difficult because of the complexity of the data and the problem of measurement.

However, over the last few years a number of economists have entered the field to express more dogmatic and unqualified views. Academic specialists have not known quite how to deal with this invasion of their territory for two main reasons. First, the new entrants are committed to what they call a 'free market economy'. In theoretical terms this means that they do not proceed on the assumption that the advantages and disadvantages of price competition within a particular market are a matter for empirical inquiry. They believe that one can proceed on the *a priori* assumption that additional price competition *must* be preferable to any form of restriction on what Adam Smith termed 'the invisible hand' of market forces. Second, and in its way still more frustrating, 'free market' men usually give no sign that they have even heard of the very considerable body of specialist literature in the field of industrial relations and labour economics.

Yet since 1979 it has not been possible to ignore the invaders, who are represented in Readings 27 and 28, if only because union – government relations have come to be dominated by their view of the world. This has led to substantial changes in government policy and trade union law, which are the subject of much of Part Seven. In the limits available to me I have tried to do justice to all sides of the ensuing debate. Thus in Readings 25 and 26 much of the area of agreement between labour economists and other specialists is summarized. The evidence shows that where collective bargaining is introduced wages tend to rise faster than would otherwise be the case during the upswing of the trade cycle. They also tend to slow down at a lower pace during periods of recession. In this sense it is agreed that there is almost always a positive trade union wage differential. What remains in dispute is its average size and the reasons for variations in particular cases. At the moment it looks as if the positive differential can be as low as a few per cent or as high as 40 per cent. Part of the problem lies in the inadequacy of all known ways of measuring union strength, e.g. the percentage of the labour force unionized, the numbers covered by collective bargaining, or those involved in industrial action. Different results are obtained by using each of these measures, none of which are entirely satisfactory.

Then there are the difficulties that arise out of the need to calculate what Charles Mulvey terms 'the adjustment vector'. The problem here is that many factors other than trade unionism are known to influence relative pay levels, e.g. the degree of skill involved, sex or race differences, the size and profitability of a firm or its geographical location. Anyone who sets out to calculate the union wage differential in a particular labour market or economy must try to allow for all these influences, so that they arrive at the appropriate net figure

13

which is the result of unionism. They also need to make assumptions about the effect of so-called 'market forces' on general and relative pay movements in the absence of collective bargaining – often in circumstances where it has existed for as long as recorded figures are available. Unfortunately, economists do not agree about the extent to which pay adjusts to what are termed the conditions of supply and demand in the 'external' labour market, although most labour economists believe that variations in the number of jobs available do not account for rates of increase in pay in particular firms, even where there are no trade unions. This is partly because, many studies suggest, movements in pay are much more affected by what is termed the conditions in the 'internal' labour market, i.e. the decisions taken in firms that affect pay levels and pay structures and the reasons for them. These show that in many firms pay rises at rates largely determined by the extent to which management has the pay system under effective control, or by the need to reward and encourage higher levels of performance, output, responsibility or flexibility. Factors of this kind are said to account for the persistence of wage improvements and earnings growth in firms which have a substantial labour surplus, and who may be declaring widespread redundancies.

In the specialist literature there is also no support for the view that there is an underlying tendency for wage rates to fall to the point where the market is 'cleared' and the unemployed are absorbed into work, or at least that this would happen if only union monopoly power were sufficiently reduced. In the first place, the demand for labour is a derived demand. It arises from a multiplicity of factors, including both demand in the product market and changes in technology. If factors of this kind are moving in a way which reduces the demand for any particular category of skill, or labour in general, no reduction in its relative price can hope to reverse this tendency. Secondly, there is no way to reduce the supply of labour, in overall terms, as the demand for it declines. Workers cannot be burnt, or stockpiled, to maintain their price. In the long run the numbers coming on to the market are largely a function of birth rates some fifteen years ago. Thirdly, to reduce wages at the 'port of entry' to a firm will almost certainly have unwelcome implications for the stability and acceptability of its internal wage structure, which in an increasing number of cases is based on systems of internally consistent job-evaluation. Fourthly, many studies suggest that a complex network of normative and cultural factors limit the extent to which pay is free to respond to changes in the level of demand. They also indicate that when people change jobs, or decide not to move, a complex of social and psychological factors affect their choice much more than differences in pay. Finally, the knowledge that workers have of alternative employment opportunities, and their ability to respond to them by moving house, or travelling longer distances to work, are severely limited. In all these ways the labour market differs from what is supposed to happen in the product market, or the market for money. And all these constraints have nothing to do with collective bargaining – although unions must take them into account.

The first three readings in Part Six are best regarded as different ways in which serious students of the subject have reacted to evidence of this kind. In Reading 22 a well-known American labour economist, Arthur Rees, accepts that labour markets cannot be expected to operate as other markets do: changes in price cannot hope to determine the long-term supply or demand for labour; inter-group comparisons or 'traditional parties' usually explain much more about differentials than the assumptions of neoclassical short-term marginal analysis. Yet Rees still believes that we can work towards a more adequate overall theory of pay determination by making some assumptions about 'profit maximization'. He therefore sets out to construct a modified economic model of union wage policy which can be tested against reality.

In Reading 23 a very different position is adopted by Arthur Ross, another American student of the subject, in his classic refutation of the utility of the neoclassical approach. Ross argues that progress depends on the abandonment of the notion of competitive equilibrium borrowed from the neoclassical theory of the firm. What is required is 'a broader frame of reference', since 'even the most primitive clichés of politics, sociology and psychology throw a good deal of light on this problem'. In particular, it must be appreciated that the key to union wage policy 'is not to be found in the mechanical application of any maximization principle'.

In Reading 24 Peter Mathias, a distinguished economic historian, takes a much more limited and pessimistic view. He shows no enthusiasm for multidisciplinary approaches or more advanced statistical techniques. As he sees it, the problem is that the phenomena to be examined and accounted for are too complex and immeasurable to be dealt with in a systematic or rigorous way. As a result, he poses a quite devastating question to students of the subject:

Are the variables too many, the 'frictions' too great, the elasticities so indeterminate, the competitive forces so lax, the public sector and public influence so powerful, reasons of equity so persuasive, exogenous factors so numerous and heterogeneous that economic theory can *never* say anything useful or operational about the influence of trade unions on the general level of wages?

Readers must decide for themselves. It is time to turn to the preoccupations of those economists committed to the restoration of the 'free market economy'.

As Henry Phelps Brown shows in Reading 25, there is little evidence from past studies that the union wage differential is accompanied by an equal ability to improve real wages in the long run. These would seem to depend much more on the rate of increase in productivity. Union action also seems to have left profit margins more or less intact, largely because employers have felt able to pass on negotiated wage increases via rising prices. As a result, however, it has to be admitted that union wage bargaining may well have become a significant factor in the generation of inflation. And where increases in unit labour costs cannot be offset by subsequent improvements in performance or output, the ultimate effect is likely to be some loss of sales. If these are significant enough, there must eventually be an effect on the overall demand for labour. Thus it is generally accepted among labour economists that the union wage differential may be responsible for at least some of the decline in Britain's economic position and part of the rise in unemployment. The problem is to decide whether it has been a significant influence. These questions are dealt with in the remaining five readings in Part Six, starting with the views of two leading 'market economists', F. A. Hayek and Patrick Minford.

In Reading 27 Hayek assumes that the only constraint on wages that prevents them falling to a point where more or less full employment is possible is union monopoly power. He also assumes that this power belongs to union leaders and that it derives from their ability to exploit legal immunities which have existed, with some interruptions and modifications, since 1906.

In Reading 28 Patrick Minford adopts a slightly more complicated theory of causation, but comes to similarly simple conclusions. Quite apart from the influence of union monopoly power, the responsiveness of the labour market to changes in price, and its ability to use price change to remove excess supply, may well be restricted by one other factor. This is the present flat rate of unemployment benefit, which is said to prevent unemployed non-unionists from accepting jobs at rates low enough to raise employment. Nevertheless, the fact that the percentage of workers in unions rose by 13 per cent from 1963 to 1979 is taken as proof that union power rose by a similar amount over the same period, leading to an identical increase in 'total real wages', an 8·5 per cent reduction in output and the destruction of a million jobs.

The two readings which follow have been chosen to present somewhat different and more complex views of union power and the factors which may also have influenced Britain's long-term decline. So far as possible they avoid a repetition of the kind of empirical objections to the 'free market' analysis which is to be found in other readings.

Thus, in Reading 29, Brian Burkitt concentrates on the relative lack of union power compared to the power of corporations, multinationals or owners of private wealth. He also stresses that where unions appear powerful it is because their members perform essential or irreplaceable services, which can be denied to employers or the community until their demands are met. Thus power, on the workers' side of the bargaining table, is the result of particular technological and operational requirements, which have little or nothing to do with general legal rules.

Finally, in Reading 30, Karel Williams and colleagues give reasons for supposing that since the 1960s at least Britain has actually been a relatively low wage economy with rates of increase in labour productivity comparable to that of its major competitors. On this evidence they consider it unreasonable to suggest that 'it's the bloody-minded workers and their unions who have ruined British industry'. Much more important has been a series of non-price factors, including defective marketing, inadequate financial institutions and the right kind of government assistance to industry.

It seems to me that we are now in a position to provide three explanations for the comparative lack of progress in this critical area of trade union studies. First, there has been the problem of causal attribution, made more difficult by the fact that so many of the important factors to be measured or estimated are not linked to satisfactory statistical series. Here the contrast with the problem of union growth and the work of Bain is most marked. This problem seems to me to be much more important than the absence of a suitable multidisciplinary theory or model to be tested against the data that is available. The absence of such a theory has not prevented considerable advances in areas such as union government or union structure.

Second, the obvious way of tackling a problem of this kind, which has been used most effectively in studies concerned with union objectives and methods, is to narrow the frame of reference. One proceeds by case studies of what happens in particular firms or unions. At this level of aggregation it is much more easy to observe and even quantify the impact of a large number of variables. Information is available that is not embodied in economy-wide series compiled on the basis of returns to the Central Statistical Office.

It is only fair to say that over the last ten years there have been a number of specialist studies of this kind dealing with factors affecting pay determination. Some of these have been concerned with evaluating the relative importance of wage bargaining by trade unions. By and large they support the more modest claims of labour economists about the size of the union wage differential, and some are referred to in the readings (others are listed in the bibliography). The problem is that case studies can always be challenged on grounds of their representativeness. They may well not be typical of what happens in other industries or in other sectors of the economy, much less the economy as a whole. This raises the third difficulty.

The fact is that what the public is interested in, and what politicians want to know about, is the overall or general impact of unions. They want an answer to the question: how far have unions been responsible for inflation and unemployment since, say, the mid-sixties? And if the answer is 'quite a lot', what can be done about it? The tragedy has been that the specialists, at their present level of knowledge, find it very difficult to answer questions of this kind: except to say that it is all very complex and hand round a book-list. Partly as a result, undue attention and credence has been given to the answers of those who have mistaken faith and conviction for the patient accumulation of all the relevant data.

So we come to the final section of the readings, concerned with trade unions and the state. It may appear that the central issue here is much the same as that considered in Part Six. In fact, the causes of disagreement are even wider and much more fundamental than those discussed in the first edition. It is true that, as England and Weekes demonstrate in Reading 31, the acceptance of trade unionism by government has tended to turn on their view of the economic impact of collective bargaining. It is also clear that since the mid-fifties successive governments have come to blame unions for their presumed economic consequences, e.g. the ineffective use of labour, wage-induced inflation, and so on. However, since the early seventies increasing emphasis has also been placed on the social and community costs of disruptive industrial action, most notably by so-called 'essential' workers in the public services.

Yet, as Lord Wedderburn makes clear in Reading 37, until recently government ill-will and resentment did not involve a denial of the social utility of trade unionism as such, nor a rejection of the general case for collective bargaining. On the contrary, to a varying extent and with different degrees of success all governments sought to engage trade union leaders in a dialogue, seeking to enlist their cooperation or acceptance of various attempts to 'reform' collective bargaining, usually involving different forms of pay restraint.

Thus even the 1971 Industrial Relations Act, which was seen by the unions as an attack on their legitimate rights, was said to be designed merely to prevent the 'abuse' of union power. Under its provisions, legal protection was made dependent upon the acceptance of state regulation of union procedures and rules. Those who accepted were offered aids to recognition and the right to bargain. Thus the Heath government claimed to be implementing the recommendations of the 1978 Royal Commission on Trade Unions and Employers' Associations, which proposed an extension of collective bargaining.

As Wedderburn shows, the fundamental rupture occurred in 1980. The Employment Act of that year set out to withdraw state support for collective bargaining, which had been accepted by all governments since the passage of the 1906 Trade Disputes Act. The 1982 Act continued this process, and a third Act was passed in 1984. The overt objective, as Wedderburn says, was to 'restrict the social power of unions'. The underlying aim was to 'break real wage resistance'.

It is important to note that these intentions are not denied by Ministers themselves. They are also embodied in other policies designed to abolish minimum wage standards, restrict the scope of industrial tribunals, or frustrate various EEC proposals for improving equal pay legislation and granting disclosure and consultation rights to worker representatives. The plain fact is that the present government is opposed to attempts to regulate the labour market – either by collective bargaining or by legally imposed rights which trade unions help to enforce.

In Reading 36 Richard Tur argues that in broad terms such policies are justified, at least so far as the detailed application of the 1980 and 1982 legislation is concerned. He disagrees with Wedderburn about the effect of union power and its continued necessity. But on the central purpose of the government they are as one. Tur puts it like this:

The political economy which informs current legislation is simplicity itself. Presupposed are rational individuals . . . constrained only by the hidden hand of market forces . . . On such a view the primary role of government is to free the economy from forces which obstruct or distort the operation of the hidden-hand mechanism. Thus restrictive practices, *unreasonable* restraint of trade, job protectionism and 'artificially' high wage settlements, born of union power and privilege, all contribute to the inefficiency of the economy and to imperfect competition. Such obstructions must therefore be eliminated. Viewed in this light, trade unions must be under severe attack because they inevitably distort the operation of the hidden-hand mechanism.

It may be said that identical assumptions lie behind the nostrums of Hayek and Minford. But when a government takes action to remove legal rights that have existed for almost a century, then many would wish to argue that more is at stake than the validation of a particular theory of the labour market.

This is the view taken in several of the readings in Part Seven, and we need to understand the extent to which the argument advanced has become political or social rather than economic. This can be seen most clearly in Reading 32, by Colin Crouch. He argues that few modern democratic states can afford the consequences of free collective bargaining. This poses a number of alternative policies, all of which are designed to constrain its effects. In the case of Britain, says Crouch, there are only two effective choices: *neo-laisser-faire* or *bargained corporatism*.

The first is very much the strategy of the present government and involves a tight monetary policy, reductions in public expenditure, privatization and the toleration of low levels of growth and employment. These policies need to continue until such time as reductions in taxation induce individuals and companies to increase effort and efficiency. Meanwhile, everything must be done to break the strength of the unions and lower 'real wage resistance'. Otherwise, if and when recovery comes, union-induced inflation will force a return to low growth and still higher unemployment.

Fortunately we are not concerned here with the feasibility of such a policy. The point is that it involves a range of political and social objectives which assume much more than that free collective bargaining creates economic problems for government. Underlying this view of society is the assumption that social and moral progress is to be achieved by the encouragement of individual responsibility and effort in circumstances where the 'invisible hand' of the market is free to distribute power and rewards in the best possible way. Given such a view of human motivation and the class structure it is difficult to see a role for trade unions. Their power and influence can be safely destroyed, since they have no worthwhile function to perform.

Crouch argues that the alternative – bargained corporatism – can take several forms, but that it is most likely to appeal to governments of the left. In the past it has been thought to be compatible with higher levels of public expenditure and government action to prevent unemployment from rising. But these features are not critical for our purposes. The central point for us to note is that bargained corporatism involves an entirely different way of dealing with the problem of free collective bargaining. Government has to seek an agreement with the unions on how to constrain its effects. This means there can be no frontal assault on the legal basis of union power. On the contrary, concessions may have to be made in these and other areas of social policy. As a result, union leaders must be allowed a substantial degree of political influence.

Once again we do not need to consider the viability of policies of this sort, or even whether other variants or options are available to British governments. The point at issue is that choices of this kind turn, in the end, on political, social and even personal value-systems, and that some of the most important relate to the value placed on trade unionism. These issues are discussed in various ways in Readings 31, 33 and 37. To appreciate the range and scope of the arguments advanced in favour of unions, it is necessary to consider them briefly under four heads.

The most common of all is the 'matching power' argument. This asserts that the individual worker is in a dependent relationship with even the best employer and in all but the tightest labour market. Only by combination in a union can the worker hope to match the employer's natural power. Once one accepts that there is even something in this argument, collective bargaining is seen as a way of avoiding extensive state regulation of the employment relationship. It was Otto Kahn-Freund who termed the elaboration of the matching power argument 'the doctrine of collective laisser-faire'.

Second, an argument is often advanced for trade unionism as being beneficial to industrial peace. It is said that given their dependent relationship workers are bound to develop genuine and deeply felt grievances, which they will eventually combine to remedy. Collective bargaining exists to channel and structure such demands, so that they can be considered and resolved without frequent and damaging recourse to industrial action. In view of this function union leaders have often been termed 'the managers of discontent'.

Third, more positive arguments for unions are put forward based on the right of workers to participate in management decisions. It is said that they can contribute to the quality of these decisions, and that their involvement in the aims of the organization will only be fully realized if they are consulted and informed. It is also suggested that such objectives can only be carried out by truly independent trade unions. A more extended version of this argument is used to justify the involvement of the TUC in government decisions and institutions – especially those of most direct concern to working people.

Finally, and with increasing frequency today, the legal status of trade unionism is linked to the preservation of democracy. It is argued that trade unions must be allowed to perform their essential functions free from legal liability and financial penalty in the interests of political pluralism. For, as Crouch observes, taken to extremes the doctrine of neo-laisser-faire is essentially authoritarian and centralist. It assumes a strong, if democratically elected, central government, powerful enough to resist sectionalist pressures for more jobs or higher levels of public expenditure. There is thus a sense in which it aims to place decisions 'beyond the reach of democratic politics' so that they can be regulated by the 'invisible hand' of the market. To this end, supporters of the doctrine must be willing to use 'the most coercive and least democratically responsible areas of state' – i.e. the police and the armed forces if need be – to break strikes in vital services. What the doctrine wishes above all to prevent, says Crouch, is 'detailed government interference with the rights of property owners, and if the cost of doing that is considerable interference with other kinds of liberty, then so be it'.

What should be clear by now is why generally acceptable conclusions have been most difficult to attain in the area of our subject covered by Part Seven. It is not just that experts are unable to agree on how to weigh the factors to be fed into the economists' adjustment vector. The problems are more difficult to overcome than those engendered by the race of scholars who insist on using a naive and non-empirical model while refusing to take note of the established literature. It is not merely that the position adopted by supporters of the government challenges assumptions that have been made by most writers on the subject for almost a century. It is that so many of the issues in dispute depend on differences of judgement and value, many of which can hardly be said to turn on the results of further study and research.

The reader should not understand by this that there is no role for fact and logic in this part of the subject. These requirements, and their limits, are well illustrated in the contents of Readings 34 and 35. Both are extracts from the present government's Green Paper on Proposed changes in union law. This discussed a whole series of ways of changing the then existing legal framework, most of which were included in the 1982 Employment Act. In the first excerpt, the Green Paper sets out the case for and against making unions liable for the 'vicarious acts' of their officials. The second considers whether or not British labour law should be changed from a system of 'negative immunities' to one of 'positive rights'.

As both extracts demonstrate, to understand what is involved in such changes it is necessary to appreciate the somewhat complex details of the existing legal position. It is also as well to understand, at least in outline, the arguments which have been adduced by the supporters and opponents of these reforms in the past. In the case of the argument against making unions liable, there is also some evidence about the effect of modifying the law to be drawn from the experience of the 1971 Industrial Relations Act. Most important of all, a careful reading of both extracts suggests that any move in either direction is neither simple nor predictable. Much is seen to depend on the precise words used in any future statute; even more on how judges choose to interpret them.

But it would be naive to assume that, in the end, attitudes towards changes of this kind will turn on matters of fact or logic. The government ultimately decided to impose a liability on unions for the unlawful acts of their agents, including shop stewards, according to a complex statutory code which provided for damages of up to £500,000. Given the new areas of illegality created by the two Employment Acts, this represented a significant reduction in the scope for legal industrial action open to unions and their members. Whether it will lead to a similar reduction in union power remains to be seen.

At the same time the government also decided not to embark on a move towards positive rights. For as Wedderburn rightly argues, and the Green Paper tacitly accepts, this is not a question which has significant implications for the crucial issue of union power and its legal limits. Consequently, the game was not thought to be worth the candle.

This survey of the reasons for the uneven development of our subject is now complete. What has been uncovered prompts three prognostications about its future. First, students will continue to refine and modify Bain on growth – especially if what happens to union membership during a prolonged recession appears to contradict his forecast of future trends. Second, a spate of case studies and occasional macro-surveys will seek to draw conclusions about the impact of the same recession on union government, structure and bargaining behaviour. This may well modify some of the generalizations and findings set out in these readings. For it should be remembered in studying them that much of what we know about these matters is based on evidence collected in the middle and late seventies.

Third, empirically-based labour economists will doubtless conduct an increasing number of micro-studies; for they are the only way to deal with the host of social, institutional, organizational and other non-market factors that affect wage movements. My guess would be that these studies will suggest that during periods of recession non-market and non-union factors are more significant in reducing the rate of increase in money wages than any loss of union density or strength. In other words, these factors will, taken together, turn out to be more important constraints on the fumbled gropings of the 'invisible hand' than trade union wage bargaining. If so, my third prognosis is that all these findings will continue to have little or no influence on 'free market' men or women. If the rate of increase in wages falls sufficiently, it will be said to be the consequence of the measures which have been taken to undermine union power. If the rate of wage advance remains stubbornly high, this will be taken as a sign that further measures are required. But the reader, like the editor, must wait and see.

Part One

Union Objectives and Methods

The first three readings consider how far unions have distinctive functions which set them apart from other organizations.

In Reading 1 Allan Flanders argues that the essential purpose of a trade unicn is 'participation in job regulation', which is mainly advanced by collective bargaining. Yet this aim is not incompatible with the pursuit of wider social purposes such as the attainment and preservation of full employment or a more egalitarian society. His view remains typical of a wide spectrum of British students of the subject. In broad terms it is probably shared by the majority of union activists.

In Reading 2, from a classic American study, R. F. Hoxie adopts a narrower approach. Unions exist to defend and advance the group interests of their members. They do this by seeking to impose on management common conditions of employment which limit wage and job competition. Hoxie's rejection of wider social purposes is more representative of union activists in the United States. But similar views are held by many union members and some officials in Britain, e.g. in white collar unions.

Reading 3, by Richard Hyman, is a Marxist view of union aims. It attacks the limitations of what is termed the 'institutional' approach of writers like Flanders and Hoxie. Unions must continue to work for the overthrow of capitalism. It they 'appear to retreat from their original purposes' they will face periodic 'rank and file revolt'.

In Reading 4, Eric Batstone and his colleagues are mainly concerned with the methods unions use to attain stated goals. In the case of shop stewards and other workshop representatives these are found to vary, not least in the emphasis given to 'leadership' and 'trade union principles'.

1 Allan Flanders

What are Trade Unions For?

From Allan Flanders, *Management and Unions*, Faber & Faber, 1970, pp. 37–47.

There is great confusion today about the purposes of trade unions. This affects attitudes to their future and what should be their legal and social rights and obligations in present-day society, as well as their own decisions on policy and organization. No less an authority than. Professor Galbraith has stated that unions in the future will 'have a drastically reduced function in the industrial system' and will 'retreat more or less permanently into the shadows'. And his is not a lone voice. Trade unions are increasingly made the target of many criticisms. Much of this may be unfair, but the unions themselves rarely bother to state their own case in persuasive terms.

I would like, first, to reject two views of union purpose which merely mislead. They are poles apart but they have this in common. Those who hold them believe they know more about what trade unions are for than the unions and their members know themselves.

The first is the Marxist view. Admittedly it has many different shades and variations and, since all its advocates claim to be offering the one true interpretation of the one true gospel, they are often violently at odds with each other. Most of them, however, would subscribe to a recent exposition by the editor of the *New Left Review*.

As institutions, trade unions do not *challenge* the existence of society based on a division of classes, they merely *express* it. Thus trade unions can never be viable vehicles of advance towards socialism in themselves; by their nature they are tied to capitalism. They can bargain within society but not transform it (Anderson, 1967, pp. 264–5).

From this it follows that the inevitable limits of trade union action must be overcome with the help of a revolutionary movement or party which – to continue quoting from the same essay – 'must include intellectuals and petit bourgeois who alone can provide the essential *theory* of socialism'. Why? Because 'Culture in a capitalist society is

. . . a prerogative of privileged strata; only if some members of these strata go over to the cause of the working class can a revolutionary movement be born' (Anderson, 1967, pp. 266–7).

Ignoring for a moment the conceit in this statement, I would not dispute the point that trade unions are not a substitute for political parties, be they revolutionary or reformist. Workers do not join unions because they think alike and share the same political outlook. They do so for the sake of gaining immediate improvements in their lot which can only come from collective action. Their unity, that completeness of the organization of trade unions which is the foundation of their strength, must always be imperilled when they import political faction fights. Unions may decide by a majority to support a particular political party – as many in this country have decided to affiliate with the Labour Party – but this is another matter. It reflects no more than a recognition that they must engage in political as well as industrial action to further their own objectives and that taking sides is the best strategy because it produces the best results.

What I find so objectionable as well as invalid in the Marxist view is its implicit contempt for 'pure and simple' trade unionism. Trade unions, by doggedly sticking to their immediate ends and refusing to be captured and exploited by any political party, have gradually transformed society. Only not according to the sacred texts or the dialectical laws! That they may be right in preferring reform to revolution and unity to discord never crosses the mind of those whose theory tells them all the answers.

I do not deny that socialism – as someone once said – has been 'the conscience of the labour movement' (Herberg, 1943). But this is socialism as a set of ideals, as a moral dynamic, not as a particular blueprint for an economic or political system. In this sense it has undoubtedly provided restraints against the emergence of the cruder forms of business unionism that can be found in the United States.

If the first mistaken view of the purposes of trade unions comes from the Left, then the second comes from the Right. The operative word for its expression is *responsible* trade unionism. Michael Shanks (1961, p. 115) has amusingly characterized, and only slightly caricatured, this view.

There has grown up in recent years a widespread superstition that a trade union leader is a sort of *ex officio* civil servant, responsible to the community at large. The trade union leader's main responsibility, to judge from the sort of comment one reads in the press and hears from middle-class lips, is to 'keep his chaps in line' or 'knock some sense into them' . . . In practical terms, the main function of a union leader according to this view is to deter his members from putting in ambitious wage claims, stop them from going on strike, and behaving in other antisocial ways, and encourage them to work harder and increase their productivity . . . Having done all that, he can gracefully retire with a peerage. He may even be introduced to the Queen and taken to dine in a West End club from time to time.

The essence of this view is that trade unions are there to act as a kind of social police force – to keep the chaps in order and the wheels of industry turning. To this there is only one answer. The first and overriding responsibility of all trade unions is to the welfare of their own members. That is their primary commitment; not to a firm, not to an industry, not to the nation. A union collects its members' contributions and demands their loyalty specifically for the purpose of protecting their interests as they see them, not their alleged 'true' or 'best' interests as defined by others.

Leadership is important, of course. Trade union leaders should be ahead of their members in thinking about their problems. It is their responsibility to point out the further and more far-reaching consequences of decisions which could be regretted later despite their strong immediate appeal. When union leaders seek only to court popularity and defend this on the grounds that they are the 'servants' of their members, they betray the responsibilities of their office. When the argument is over, however, their principal task must be one of representation. If they fail in this the trade union no longer serves its purpose. No other organization is there to do this job.

Obviously trade unions cannot reasonably behave as if they were not part of a larger society or ignore the effects of their policies on the national economy and the general public. No voluntary organizations can do that with impunity. If they do, they turn society against them and society can retaliate. In any case members of trade unions are citizens and consumers as well as producers. Even so, trade unions exist to promote sectional interests – the interests of the section of the population they happen to organize. As do professional associations and many other bodies! There is nothing selfish or slightly disreputable about this; it is an essential part of the democratic process. Indeed, once trade unions appear to be acting as servants of employers or servants of the government, they are bound to be written off by their own members who will turn, as they sometimes do already, to unofficial leaders to take up their demands.

Both of the views I have been attacking belittle the democratic function of trade unions: their function of representation. That is why each in its different way claims to know better than the trade unions themselves where the interests of their members lie. My starting point in defining union purpose is the opposite premise: that the best way of finding the right answer is to look at the behaviour of trade unions, to infer what they are for from what they do.

Here one thing is at once certain, and it applies to all trade unions and has applied throughout the greater part of their history. The activity to which they devote most of their resources and appear to rate most highly is collective bargaining. So the question we have to ask is: what purposes do unions pursue in collective bargaining? The conventional answer is that they defend and, if possible, improve their members' terms and conditions of employment. They are out to raise wages, to shorten hours and to make working conditions safer, healthier and better in many other respects.

This answer is right as far as it goes, but it does not go far enough. Collective bargaining may be what the words imply – that depends on how we define bargaining – but it is also a rule-making process. The rules it makes can be seen in the contents of collective agreements. In other words, one of the principal purposes of trade unions in collective bargaining is regulation or control. They are interested in regulating wages as well as in raising them; and, of course, in regulating a wide range of other issues appertaining to their members' jobs and working life.

Why do they have this interest in regulating employment relationships and what social purpose does such regulation serve? It is certainly not a bureaucratic interest in rules for their own sake. Unions and their members are interested in the effect of the rules made by collective bargaining, which is to limit the power and authority of employers and to lessen the dependence of employees on market fluctuations and the arbitrary will of management. Stated in the simplest possible terms, these rules provide protection, a shield, for their members. And they protect not only their material standards of living, but equally their security, status and self-respect – in short, their dignity as human beings.

One can put the same point in another way. The effect of rules is to establish rights, with their corresponding obligations. The rules in collective agreements secure for employees the right to a certain rate of wages; the right not to have to work longer than a certain number of hours; the right not to be dismissed without consultation or compensation, and so on. This surely is the most enduring social

29

achievement of trade unionism; its creation of a social order in industry embodied in a code of industrial rights. This, too, is the constant service that unions offer their members: daily protection of their industrial rights.

Such rights could be, and to some extent are, established by law. But collective bargaining serves yet another great social purpose. Apart from providing protection, it also permits participation. A worker has more direct influence through his union on what rules are made and how they are applied than he can ever exercise by his vote over the laws made by Parliament. We hear a lot these days about participation, including workers' participation in management. I have yet to be convinced that there is a better method than collective bargaining for making industry more democratic, providing its subjects and procedures are suitably extended. Putting a few workers or union officials on boards of directors only divorces them from the rank and file. In collective bargaining, trade unions must continually respond to and service their members' interests.

The constant underlying social purpose of trade unionism is, then, participation in job regulation. But participation is not an end in itself; it is the means of enabling workers to gain more control over their working lives. Nothing has happened over the post-war years to change that basic purpose or to lessen its importance. The really remarkable thing about this period has been the slow rate of progress made by trade unions in advancing their social purpose, in spite of incessant activity on wage claims and the seemingly more favourable circumstances resulting from full employment. To account for this we must consider another equally fundamental aspect of trade unionism.

Trade unions are a mixture of movement and organization, and the relationship between the two is the key to an understanding of the dynamics of their growth. Movement in the words of G. D. H. Cole (1937, p. 12), 'implies a common end or at least a community of purpose which is real and influences men's thoughts and actions, even if it is imperfectly apprehended and largely unconscious'. The members of a movement combine because, sharing in some measure the same sentiments and ideas, they want to achieve the same things. The bonds of organization are different. An organization must have effective means for ensuring that its members comply with its decisions. These means are its sanctions: the rewards it can offer and the penalties it can impose to uphold its internal discipline. On the strength of its sanctions, rather than on the appeal of its objectives, the unity and power of an organization depends.

One problem which has always confronted trade unions is how to convert temporary movement into permanent organization. In their early days they often counted their membership by supporters during a strike rather than the number paying regular contributions. To evolve from loose groups that could be destroyed when the economic tide flowed against them, they had to acquire sanctions strong enough to sustain continuous membership. One way, usually the most important, was to secure recognition from employers, so as to build up enduring relations with them in the form of collective bargaining. They could then provide their members with the constant service of advancing their industrial rights. More than that, they could then prevent employers from penalizing union membership, perhaps getting them to penalize non-membership instead, as under 'closed shop' agreements.

While movement had to be converted into organization if trade unions were to flourish, they could not subsequently allow it to languish and disappear. Trade unions by their very nature have to be dynamic organizations. They must constantly renew their vigour by keeping the spirit of a movement alive in their ranks. In this respect they differ, for instance, from business organizations. The latter can grow and expand if they have sufficient money to buy command over the material and human resources they need. People will join them, that is to say enter their employment, for the sake of the remuneration offered. Trade unions cannot be run simply as businesses. Many members may join who wish to play no active part in union affairs, who see their contribution, perhaps, as nothing more than payment for a service. Even so, every union must have at least a core of active members who feel some deeper loyalty. A trade union that had none of the characteristics of movement, which was thrown back entirely on the bonds of organization, would be in a sorry state. To sum up, trade unions need organization for their power and movement for their vitality, but they need both power and vitality to advance their social purpose.

With this conclusion in mind, how are we to assess the position of trade unions in our society over the past two decades, the period since the war? Until recently there was only one word to describe it – it has been by and large a period of stagnation. Only now can one discern important signs of change. Looked at from the point of view of organization there was no overall union growth. True, total membership figures increased slowly but they have not kept pace with the growing size of the labour force. Density of union organization, the proportion of actual to potential membership, has declined. This decline was greatest among male manual workers because of the contraction of industries – coal, cotton, railways – that had long been the citadels of union strength. But even among the far less well-organized sections of women and white-collar workers, in spite of some impressive increases in membership, their overall density of organization has only barely increased.

This has had its counterpart in an absence of movement. Given the inflationary background, unions may have been constantly busy putting in claims for wage increases and negotiating settlements. They had to run fast in order to stay on the same spot. This has become almost a routine, a response to pressures rather than the outcome of campaigns. Where were the new objectives directed towards a further fulfilment of the unions' social purpose, which alone could have generated a genuine movement to capture interest and arouse enthusiasm?

Yet over the post-war years there has been at the same time a great upsurge of union activity *in the workplace*. Bargaining between shop stewards and management has developed on a scale previously unknown. This bargaining is not only about money, though that is an important feature. It is equally associated with demands for a greater say in managerial decisions in such matters as discipline and redundancy, control of overtime and fringe benefits. In general, for a variety of reasons, workers are raising their sights; their level of aspirations and expectations is rising. The increase in workplace bargaining has undermined the regulative effect of industry-wide agreements in many industries, so that much of the old formal system of collective bargaining has become a pretence and is in a state of decay.

This has very important implications for trade unions. In terms of their basic social purpose, the upsurge of workplace bargaining represents at once a danger, an opportunity and a responsibility. It is a danger because, although they now rely heavily on the workplace activity of their stewards, this activity in its present form threatens their discipline, cohesion and strength. At the same time it is an opportunity for the trade unions to make the most of a movement already in being. Properly led and directed it could result in a considerable extension of the subjects of collective bargaining and, therefore, a greater fulfilment of their basic purpose of job regulation. Their responsibility is self-evident once the danger and opportunity has been stated. [. . .]

There is, however, another contemporary facet of the question of what trade unions are for, which the controversy over incomes policy throws into sharp relief. Many trade unionists sincerely believe that support for an incomes policy is virtually a betrayal of union purpose. They argue that trade unions should always be fighting for higher wages and, therefore, should not be confined and crippled by 'norms' or restrictions of any sort. In their eyes restraint and militancy are incompatible. On the other hand, a large section of the general public seems to think that union power and militancy are the main stumbling blocks in making an incomes policy work. These it sees as one of the chief causes of inflation in conditions of full employment and the reason why we will continue to have rising costs and prices until the power of the unions is curbed. Both of these positions I believe to be mistaken.

If the basic social purpose of trade unions is job regulation and control, then the pursuit of this purpose does not stop short at the boundaries of an industry. Regulation is now needed on a national scale, because full employment has generated intense competition among trade unions to get more for their members at the expense – let us face it – of members of other unions. Some attempt must be made to tame this industrial jungle war. There is no prospect of bringing more order and justice into our national pay structure, or even of improving the position of low-paid workers unless we have some national rules or guidelines to regulate the 'free for all'.

This is what an incomes policy is about. It is not just a device to get us out of our present balance-of-payments difficulties. Even when we are out of pawn to foreign bankers, the need for regulation will remain. We may have a long way to go in producing a viable policy, but it is not an objective which trade unions can spurn and remain true to their own purpose. Only those who hold the Marxist view can brush it aside until – on some glorious but unspecified date in the future – we enter the promised land and the day of a fully socialist planned economy dawns.

The opposite position, which sees the country's salvation in curbing the power of trade unions, is just as untenable. One of the problems in making an incomes policy work is the weakness, not the strength, of our trade unions. Many people who assert that unions have too much power go on to blame them, when they fail to prevent unofficial strikes, for not exercising enough control over their members. They cannot have it both ways. These same people are usually advocates of responsible trade unionism, in the sense that I have attacked this view of union purpose. They believe that trade unions should subordinate union claims and policies to the national interest, as they define it. They are crying for the moon. The only restraints that trade unions will ever voluntarily accept on the use of their bargaining power are *those which they have agreed*. Incomes policy cannot be treated as if it were simply an exercise in economic engineering. It is pre-eminently a social problem, a problem of finding agreement on national rules which are accepted as reasonable and fair, at least for the time being, and preferable to a continuation of the present 'free for all'.

References

ANDERSON, P. (1967), 'The limits and possibilities of trade union action', *The Incompatibles*, ed. R. Blackburn and A. Cockburn, Penguin.

COLE, G. D. H. (1937), *Short History of the British Working Class Movement 1789–1937*, Allen & Unwin.

HERBERG, W. (1943), 'Bureaucracy and democracy in labour unions', *Antioch Rev.*, Autumn.

SHANKS, M. (1961), *The Stagnant Society*, Penguin.

2 R. F. Hoxie

The Economic Programme of Trade Unions

From R. F. Hoxie, *Trade Unionism in the United States*, Appleton-Century-Crofts, 1917, 2nd edn 1923, reprinted 1966, pp. 279–93.

The union viewpoint and program is not solely economic. It is perhaps primarily so. But some of the union aims, principles and theories, and many of the union policies, demands, methods and attitudes are legal, political, ethical and broadly social. For this reason a study of the trade union program is difficult. The unions give no systematic statement of their aims, principles, policies, demands and methods. Not only do they not relate these things systematically – they do not even state them truly and clearly. The unionists do not usually independently understand the theory of their own demands or of their constructive program. They *feel*. But as always in working-class movements, the rationale of the demands and the movement has had to be worked out for them by middle-class minds.[1] To a large extent aims, principles and policies must be inferred from demands and methods. What one must do is to study constitutions, working rules, rules for discipline and, above all, agreements with employers which lay down the rules minutely covering incidents of work and pay, in order to discover demands and methods, and then with the help of declarations in constitutions and literature to try to build up policies, principles and aims – putting the whole thing finally into systematic shape.

The trade union program, or rather the trade union programs, for each trade union has a program of its own, is not the handful of unrelated economic demands and methods which it is usually conceived to be, but is a closely integrated social philosophy and plan of action. In the case of most union types, the program centers, indeed, about economic demands and methods, but it rests on the broad foundation of conceptions of right, of rights and of general theory peculiar to the workers, and it fans out to include or reflect all the economic, ethical, juridical and social hopes and fears, aims, aspirations and attitudes of the group. It expresses the workers' social

1. See, in confirmation, Webb and Webb (1894, p. 229).

theory and the rules of the game to which they are committed, not only in industry but in social affairs generally. It is the organized workers' conceptual world.

The union program may be classified conveniently under six heads:

1. There are what may be called general or ultimate aims.

2. There are the union principles and theories. These principles and theories seem to be the natural and probably inevitable outcome of the peculiar conditions under which the laborers live and work, and the peculiar problems which they have to face and solve. They cannot be judged as right or wrong individually or before the most careful study has been made of the conditions and circumstances which give rise to them. And they must be judged relatively to these conditions and circumstances.

3. There are the general policies. Here we have the general means by which the unionists, imbued with the principles and theories mentioned above, seek to control the concrete situation in the interest of their ultimate aims.

4. There are the demands. These represent the specific means by which the unionists try to put into effect their general policies.

5. There are the methods. These represent the specific modes which are employed to enforce the demands.

6. Finally, there are the attitudes. These concern mainly the broader economic and social ideas and ideals of the organized workers.

The program of each union type is an organic whole within which the specific items are closely related and mutually dependent. To understand fully the significance and causes of any one, the program must be comprehended as a whole. For example, suppose that it is a certain method which is in question. This is put in force in direct obedience to certain general union attitudes and to enforce demands. One cannot understand the why of it, cannot interpret it fairly, until one understands the attitudes and demands which bring about its use. But the demands which lie back of the methods are made, not merely for their own sake, but to enforce certain general policies and, therefore, to understand the why of the demands one must grasp the general policies which lie back of them. But we cannot stop there. Back of the general policies are the theories and principles, without a knowledge of which we are almost sure to go astray in any attempt to judge their significance. And, finally, the theories and principles have no sure significance apart from the general aims which they are intended to subserve.

No attempt will be made here to formulate separately the programs of the different types of unionism. Only a general compilation of the aims, principles and theories, general policies, demands, methods and attitudes of unions of all types is submitted [see appendix 2 of *Trade Unionism in the United States*]. It therefore contains many contradictory items and it reflects the diverse and contradictory character of the different union types. It exhibits the scope and character of union strivings and furnishes a basis for discussion. As the types have to a large extent different and sometimes contradictory aims, principles, theories, policies, demands, methods and attitudes, the program as a whole is incapable of clear-cut interpretation and causal explanation. What we need now is to try to separate this general mixed program into separate type programs and attempt to get an interpretation and causal explanation of each one. What we need is a study of each type separately to try to find out what it stands for and the peculiar problems, conditions and forces that have determined its program. We need, for example, a special study of guerrilla unionism as it developed in the case of the Bridge and Structural Iron Workers; of hold-up unionism as developed in the Chicago building trades, etc. This will be a starting point for further study of these groups and a guide to the study of other groups and to social action which we may be called upon to take.

But while the trade union program as a whole and as differentiated for each type of unionism is mixed and incomplete, the economic program has for all unions a single, definite, outstanding viewpoint. The economic viewpoint of unionism is primarily a group viewpoint and its program a group program. The aim of the union is primarily to benefit the group of workers concerned, rather than the workers as a whole or society as a whole; its theories which attempt to explain the determination of wages, hours, conditions of employment, etc., are not general but primarily group theories. They are attempts to explain how the wages, hours and conditions of employment are determined for a group of workers. The principles of action which it lays down are primarily group principles and its economic policies, demands and methods are primarily intended to protect and benefit the group of workers concerned.

It is necessary to emphasize all this because most of the fallacies which the economists claim to find in union theories, principles, policies, demands and methods result from the attempt to interpret these as applying to society as a whole, whereas they are intended to apply only to a particular group of workers. Much of the misunderstanding and controversy between scientific management and unionism, for example, results from the fact that scientific management argues in terms of the welfare of the individual worker or of society as a whole, while the unions argue primarily in terms of group welfare. The economists declare rightly that unions by their methods cannot raise wages – meaning wages as a whole – and assume wrongly that this indicates a fallacy in the union theories and methods. The scientific managers declare rightly that limitation of output must lower wages – meaning wages as a whole – and assume wrongly that this also indicates a fallacy in the union policies and methods. They make both statements because they do not understand that the unions are not primarily concerned with wages as a whole, but with the wages and standards of living of particular groups. To understand and to judge the union aims, theories and program, then, we must always bear in mind that, so far as they are economic, they are not general in their scope but are applied primarily to the situation and welfare of the particular group of workers.

The principal economic aims of the union are to prevent the lowering and, if possible, to raise the wages of *all* the members of the group: to shorten the hours of work of the group; to increase the security and continuity of employment of the members of the group and, if possible, *to secure steady and assured work for all in it*; to prevent the deterioration and, if possible, to better the general conditions of employment of all the members of the group – especially to better the conditions of safety and sanitation in the shop and to prevent arbitrary discipline, demotion and discharge of workers, and arbitrary fining and docking of wages.

The fundamental assumptions and theories upon which the unionists base their principles and program of action in support of these aims, we have already considered. In brief, they are these:

1. The interests of the employers and workers of the group are generally opposed; the employer is seeking the greatest possible output at the least possible cost; he is, therefore, constantly seeking to lower the wage rate, to lengthen the hours of work, to speed up the workers, to lower the wages by fining and docking, to weed out the least efficient workers, to maintain the poorest and least costly

conditions of safety and sanitation compatible with the efficiency of the workers in the shop from day to day (regardless of the long-time effects upon the workers or their efficiency, since, if they are injured or made ill, there are plenty more outside to take their places); to lay off and discharge workers whenever it is temporarily economical; to degrade highly skilled and high-priced workers or to displace these by less skilled and lower-priced workers, and to lessen the number of workers employed to do a given amount of work wherever possible by the introduction of new machinery and new processes, etc. The union which represents the working group is seeking the continuous employment of all its members at the highest possible wage rates and under the best possible conditions as respects hours, security and continuity of work, safety, comfort and sanitation, etc. All the efforts of the employer just stated, in the interest of greatest possible output at least possible cost, are thus seen to be directly opposed to the interest and welfare of the working group.

2. The wage dividend of the group of workers is determined by bargaining between the employer and the workers over the division of the group product. The relative bargaining strength of the employer and the workers being determined, the workers stand frequently to lose in wage rates or in the amount of wages through increased effort and output of the group, since the increased output of the group means generally lower prices for the unit of the product, rarely or never an increase of the value of group products proportional to the increased effort and output and may mean simply increased effort and output for the same or even less value of product. Under these circumstances, increased effort and output of the group never mean a proportionate increase of wages for the group, but always a lowering of the wage rate, in the sense of the wages for a given amount of work and output, and they may mean more work for the same or even less pay. Thus the group which increases output generally benefits other groups at its own expense in wage rates or wages. Moreover, this increase of output of the group where the demand for the goods is not extremely elastic, tends to weaken the bargaining strength of the workers and so still further to lower wage rates, since where it is the result of increased effort of the workers it means increased supply of labor without a correspondingly increased demand for it, and where it is the result of new machinery and new processes it means lessened demand for the labor without

any lessened supply of it, speaking always in group terms. In the one case it especially exposes the workers to lower wage rates, in the other to unemployment.

3. The group dividend being determined, the wages and conditions of employment of the workers in the group depend upon the relative bargaining strength of the employers and the workers.

4. The bargaining strength of the employer is always greater than that of the individual worker, owing to circumstances which we have already discussed.

5. The full bargaining strength of the employer will always be exerted against the individual worker because of the opposition of interest and other circumstances already discussed.

6. Therefore, individual bargaining between the employer and the worker, that is, competition between the individual workers in the group for work and wages, will tend to result in lowering wages and conditions of employment and keeping them down to what can be demanded and secured by the weakest bargainers of the labor group.

7. This tendency applies not only to the case of the original bargain but tends to result whenever, after the workers of the group are employed, they allow the employer to pit them one against the other. This occurs whenever in the course of the work they enter into individual bargaining or whenever, as in the case already considered, individual workers of the group are forced or allow themselves to be tempted by bonuses or premiums to speed up, and thus to compete with one another.

The result of these assumptions, which are the workers' interpretation of group experience, is the positive economic program of unionism, the broad outline of which may be put into two propositions: (a) if the wages and conditions of the group are not to sink to what can be commanded by its weakest labor bargainer, they must make the strength of the weakest bargainer equal to the strength of the group; (b) if the wages of the group are to be kept from falling or to be increased and the conditions of employment maintained or bettered, they must constantly attempt to increase the bargaining strength of the group as against the employers of the group and as against other groups.

How, then, can the unions carry this program into effect? First, how can they make the strength of the weakest bargainer of the group equal to the bargaining strength of the group? If we accept the position of the workers as so far tenable, it is evident that this can be done only by removing the possibility of all competition between the individual workers of the group. The general method devised by the unions for accomplishing this is to substitute collective bargaining for individual bargaining between the employers and the workers. This, however, tells us little. In order to understand what it means, we must ask, what are the principles which the unionists seek to establish by collective bargaining and what are the policies, demands and methods which they find it necessary to adopt in order to maintain these principles?

The unionists say that it can be done only by the establishment and maintenance of two principles: (a) the principle of uniformity in regard to all conditions of work and pay where competition between the workers can take place; and (b) the principle of standardization or restriction on changes in the conditions of work and pay over considerable periods of time. That is, wherever the workers are doing the same kinds of work, the conditions governing their work and pay must be uniform for all, and wherever changes in the conditions might threaten conditions of uniformity of work and pay of all such workers, these changes must be made only on such terms as the union shall agree to. To get at the main union policies, then, we have only to ask, where might lack of uniformity in conditions of work and pay, or unrestricted changes in these, result in individual competition between the workers? And to get the rest of their program in this connection we have only to ask, what demands and methods are necessary to prevent competition and the violation of these principles, where all the assumptions of the unions are considered to hold?

It is evident, then, that competition can easily take place between worker and worker in regard to the wage rate. Therefore, in order to uphold the principle of uniformity, *a standard rate of wages* must be established for each subgroup of workers, at least as a minimum. Even with a standard wage rate, competition can take place with respect to the amount of work and output that shall be done. Hence, to uphold the principles in question, *a standard hour's or day's work* must be established for each subgroup – at least as a maximum – and all speeders must be eliminated. Competition can also take place in regard to the number of hours worked per day or week. Hence, if the principle is to be upheld, the necessity of *a standard day or week*. But it is evident that if these standards are established we have practically *a standard wage as a maximum*. It is evident, also, that nothing conduces so much to speeding by individuals and the violations of the standards previously mentioned as secret bonuses and premiums or any form of 'efficiency payments'. This is one reason why the unions look askance at piece work where they are not in a position to control its operation and why they abhor premium and bonus systems of all kinds.

But competition or underbidding is possibly not only in regard to wage rates, hours, and the exertion and output, but also in regard to the safety and sanitation of the shop, the comfort and convenience of working conditions, the men one is willing to work with, the times of beginning and ending work, the convenience of shifts, the time, place, mode and character of payment, the materials and tools used, and all the minor details and conditions of work and pay. Hence, to secure uniformity, the necessity from the union's standpoint of minute specification of standards in regard to all the incidents of work and pay, from which no deviation can be allowed. This explains the multitude of petty and harassing restrictions of which employers complain.

It is evident that these standards cannot persist if they are violated with impunity; yet successful enterprise demands some degree of flexibility. Hence a long list of irregularities and violations which the unions are forced to allow but which they seek to punish so that they may not become habitual and so break down the principle of uniformity. This is accomplished by charging enough extra so as not to allow of underbidding or of extra profit to the employer, such as extra pay (time and a half or rate and a half) for overtime, for doing extraordinary kinds of work, for work in irregular ways, at irregular times (Sundays and holidays) or under irregular circumstances.

It is evident that these standards cannot be maintained effectively so far as *all* the workers are concerned if the employer is allowed to adopt at will changes in methods and processes of work. Such changes make it possible for the employer to create new tasks and jobs for which no standards or uniformities have been established, to lop off parts of the work from the old standardized classes, along with laying off the workman himself, and in both ways to create new classes of workers with new conditions of work and perhaps lower rates of pay. Hence, if the workers are to maintain their old standards of work and pay for *all* the members of the group, to prevent the degradation of skilled workers and the introduction into their midst of subgroups in which competition exists, they must prevent the introduction of such new conditions of work – the creation of new tasks and jobs and new classification of workers – except under their control and under conditions that will secure on the new jobs conditions of work and pay uniform with the old. Generally this means that they cannot allow these changes except when a new collective bargain is made, unless they can foresee and provide for them. They must restrict the change of conditions of work and pay over considerable periods of time if the principle of standardization or uniformity is to be upheld. This means that *they must carefully delimit the field of work of the group and keep it the same*. Hence, in part, the union tendency to resist new trades, new machinery, new methods and processes, and hence a part of their opposition to time study.

But under all these circumstances, with the constant menace of industrial change, the constant effort of the employer to induce individual workers to compete with their fellows for their own advantage by pressure, or by the holding out of immediate advantages in work and pay, competition cannot be kept out and these principles upheld unless there is a high degree of solidarity of the working group. The union must *control the working personnel* of the group – and all the members in the group must feel that their interests are common rather than individual and must be willing to sacrifice individual advantages to the common good. Hence, to maintain these principles, the union must determine who shall be members of the group and must be able especially to determine who shall come into the shop. *This is the real basis of the demand for the closed shop and the abhorrence of scab or non-union workers*.

Furthermore, they must be able to exercise constant oversight in respect to the conditions of work and the workers in the shop. Hence one reason for the demand of union representatives on the job, stewards and business agents, and for the coming into the situation at any time of other union officials to pass upon conditions, to present complaints, to discipline workers and to settle disputes. They have learned from experience that non-union men in the shop will not ordinarily live up to the rules of the union, and even union men who are dependent upon the employer dare not make full complaints and resist the demands of the employer. They require to be backed by the official representatives and to complain and negotiate through them.

But, further, the unionists have found that even in a closed shop where all the workers are unionists the solidarity of the group cannot be maintained where the workers are too highly specialized and lack a considerable degree of craft training. Under such circumstances it is easy for the employer to pit worker against worker, arouse jealousies and induce individual competition. Hence, in part, the union *abhorrence of specialization* and their demand for the apprenticeship system.

So much for uniformity and standardization in order to make the strength of the weakest member of the group equal to the bargaining strength of the group as a whole. The methods by which they try to enforce these policies are in general *anything that works,* strikes, boycotts, legislation where necessary, violence, etc. It is to be noticed that these policies, while intended primarily to uphold the principles claimed, do generally result in the *restriction of output and industrial progress*. They are not so intended consciously but they do have these effects. All this also implies the necessity of a large control of all the conditions of industry, work and pay in the shop by the organized workers. This is what they call industrial democracy, displacing the complete authority of the employer in matters of hiring, discharge, discipline, promotion, demotion and so on.

I pointed out that the broad outline of the program may be put into two propositions: (*a*) if the wages and conditions of the group are not to sink to what can be commanded by its weakest bargainer, the workers must make the strength of the weakest equal to the strength of the group: (*b*) if the wages of the group are not to fall and are to be increased and the conditions of employment bettered, the workers must constantly endeavor to increase the bargaining strength of the group as against the employers of the group and as against other groups. In general, the principles, policies and methods used to make the bargaining strength of the weakest equal to the bargaining strength of the group also have the effect of strengthening the bargaining power of the group as against the employer. In general, therefore, the program for the first purpose is also employed in the attempt to force the employers to advance wages and to improve conditions of employment, that is, to force a larger share of the output to be devoted to bettering wages and conditions.

These methods, however, so employed, are not so much in the interest of uniformity as in opposition to industrial changes which allow the substitution of less skilled for more skilled workers, of specialized workers for trained craftsmen, of machinery for hand labor and, so, the elimination of workers in the group. It can readily be seen that, if these changes were allowed, wages and conditions of employment could hardly be advanced and unemployment within the group, with greater competition and lower wages, might result even were the group dividend increased and the closed shop maintained, provided the union assumptions be maintained that wages and conditions are determined by bargaining under conditions which make the interests of the employer and the worker opposed. For these changes would constantly create what is virtually an increasing supply of labor in the group and would enable the employer more readily to substitute less skilled and low-priced labor for more skilled and high-priced labor. The open shop would obviously aggravate these adverse conditions. Degradation of skilled workers, increased competition among the workers in the group, and greater uncertainty and discontinuity of employment inevitably result from unregulated changes in industrial conditions. The bargaining strength of the group against the employer cannot be increased or even maintained if they are allowed. In the attempt to increase this bargaining strength, the union recognizes the advantage of a monopolistic control of the labor supply. Hence another reason for apprenticeship demands and the closed shop.

Moreover, the bargaining strength of the group is almost always bound to be weak compared with that of the employer. Inimical changes cannot be prevented, the closed shop cannot be maintained, advantage cannot be taken of favorable opportunities for advances, and losses in wages and conditions cannot be staved off under unfavorable conditions, granting the union assumptions, if the group is not *recognized* as the bargaining entity and if it is not at least as acute a bargainer as the employer. This requires that the bargaining for the unions be carried on by skilled specialists – men who know all the conditions of the trade and the market. But the men in actual employ cannot have this knowledge and skill. Hence the union demand that the employer bargain with the group through *representatives* of the workers not in his employ. Thus we have representative bargaining. But the union still is not so strong a bargaining entity as the employer if it cannot enforce the terms of the bargain on the employer and its own members. Hence the necessity of a strong union with strong disciplinary powers and hence again, the necessity for group solidarity and the closed shop and apprenticeship.

The other part of the program which aims to strengthen the group against other groups is closely related to the group wage theory which we have discussed. Believing that wages and conditions of employment of the particular group depend on strengthening its economic position or bargaining power in the sale of its products as against other groups, the unionists naturally seek directly to limit the output of the group and directly to limit the labor supply of the group through apprenticeship regulations and the closed shop, on the basis of the same reasoning employed by capitalistic monopolies. From all this it can readily be seen why unionists object so strenuously to working with non-unionists or scabs and to handling any work that has been done by scabs.

Reference

WEBB, S., and B. WEBB (1894), *The History of Trade Unionism*, Longman.

3 Richard Hyman

A Marxist Approach to Union Objectives

From Richard Hyman, *Industrial Relations: A Marxist Introduction*, The Macmillan Press, 1975, pp. 16–20, 85–93 and 199–203.

Trade unionism provides a good example of the way in which a purely institutional perspective can be dangerous and misleading. It is very common to meet such statements as 'the union has reached an agreement with the employers'; but what precisely does this mean? A trade union is in many ways a very peculiar kind of organization. Its main work does not involve the production of identifiable goods or services, but rather the attempt to influence the actions and decisions of *others*: employers and legislators, for example. Only a fraction of union organization and activity is represented by full-time employees based on a union office; trade unionism 'exists' wherever workers are unionized, yet most members are engaged in identifiably trade union functions only infrequently. Hence a trade union is not a physical entity in the same way that factories, hospitals or prisons are. So what does it mean to say that 'the union' adopts a particular policy or carries out a certain action? This is a clear instance of what was earlier termed reification: treating an impersonal abstraction as a social agent, when it is really only people who act.

Sometimes the term 'the union' is used to refer to the various workers who are members of the organization in question. But this is unsatisfactory, for it is not uncommon for policies to be adopted or agreements signed without any involvement of the mass of a union's membership, and perhaps without their knowledge. Conversely, the notion of 'the union' may be applied to the actions or decisions of official union spokesmen, representatives or leaders, or to membership activities which are initiated or endorsed by them. But this too is unsatisfactory; for if a union is not simply the sum of its members, neither is it merely the property of its leaders. To identify a union with its officials is to imply that the latter need not be differentiated from the membership as a whole. But, on the contrary, the *situations* of union leaders differ significantly from those of the members they represent; and this leads in turn to differences in

47

attitudes, interests, objectives and conceptions of what is good for the members and for 'the union'.[1]

Any analysis of industrial relations which takes as its starting-point the trade unions and other formal institutions can scarcely avoid coming to grief over problems such as this. The approach adopted in this book is thus to focus not only on trade unions as organizations, but also on *workers* and their problems and aspirations. Those employed in industry or commerce or in public services naturally devise strategies to satisfy their aspirations or to redress their grievances, and such strategies involve in part the attempt to control the work relations in which they are involved. Official trade union action is at times central to such strategies. But the effects of trade union involvement in job control are often ambiguous, for reasons which are discussed later; so in some circumstances, workers may view the official union as irrelevant to their objectives or even as an obstacle.

If workers' grievances and aspirations are to form the starting-point of industrial relations analysis, it is clearly necessary to investigate what these are. What do workers want? There is no simple answer to this question; and indeed, intense controversy surrounds the whole issue of what men and women expect from their employment, and what their work means to them. Any attempt to survey attitudes to work would draw an immense variety of responses. Most of these would normally focus on aspects of the job other than the work tasks themselves. A typical employee would probably say that what he looks for in a job is a decent level of pay with increases at the going rate; reasonable working conditions; sociable mates and a chance to talk to them; a foreman who isn't a bastard . . . If asked to consider the job itself, most people would hope for work which is neither too exhausting physically or emotionally, nor so routine as to be monotonous; they would also seek some opportunity to control their own

---

1. The perceptive reader may argue that precisely the same objections could be made to the use of abstractions like 'capital', 'management' or 'the state'; yet these are employed throughout this book. Two justifications may be offered. Firstly, management and state bureaucracies are explicitly *authoritarian* control structures where far greater uniformity of practice is imposed than is the case within trade unions. Secondly, conflicts of interest and objective among governmental and managerial bureaucrats are not of central relevance to the issues discussed in this book; nor are they normally salient for workers in industry, whose perspective forms its analytical starting-point.

work, rather than being subject to constant instructions and supervision.

In almost every case, some work aspirations can be easily and clearly expressed, while others are confused and perhaps scarcely recognized in a conscious manner. The patterns of job expectations which people hold tend to be affected by the character of their occupation, their social background and similar factors. Expectations are also shaped by broad societal influences. Where men and women are encouraged – by general cultural values and by costly and sophisticated means of mass persuasion (such as TV advertising) – to aspire to every latest consumer gimmick, it is not surprising that pay is often given top priority; that many workers seem less concerned with what happens to them during working hours than with what their job allows them to buy outside work. Moreover, most people before starting employment undergo a process of schooling which seems primarily designed to teach them that it is natural to obey orders from those in authority without question, while more diffuse pressures generate the widespread assumption that any job is likely to be fairly uninteresting and unpleasant. Thus it is not surprising that aspirations for creative work, and for control over work, tend to be below the surface of everyday job discussion. But even if suppressed, such aspirations nevertheless exist and can erupt to make their mark on the processes of industrial relations.

To say that employees have certain expectations and aspirations, and that these necessarily affect industrial relations, is not to provide any concrete information about the character of industrial relations. To do this it is necessary to add information about the *context* of work and industry. Any succinct statement of this broader social and economic context involves selective emphasis on a few key characteristics. From a Marxist perspective, the crucial fact about the economies of Western Europe and North America – where most studies of industrial relations have had their focus – is their *capitalist* character. This means that much of the productive system is privately owned, with ownership concentrated in a very small number of hands;[2] that *profit* – the pursuit of economic returns to the owners

---

2. In Britain, surveys have shown that only 4 per cent of the adult population hold shares in industrial or commercial companies, while 1 per cent own 81 per cent of all privately-owned shares. Yet gross profits account for roughly 20 per cent of the national income.

49

– is the key influence on company policy (whether or not top management actually possesses a financial stake in the firm); and that control over production is enforced *downwards* by the owners' managerial agents and functionaries.[3] In most countries, it is true, the state owns a growing sector of industry; but almost invariably, the operation of this sector is modelled on private capitalism in terms both of its hierarchy of control and of its respect for the constraints of profit. (Arguably, in Eastern Europe – where state ownership of industry is almost total – these same features of capitalism are maintained. Possibly this could help explain many aspects of *their* industrial relations. But this is too large an issue to pursue here.)

A capitalist environment has consequences with important implications for the nature of industrial relations. Most fundamentally, work has the status of wage-labour. Jobs are located within a labour *market*; the prospective worker must find an employer willing to pay a wage or salary in return for the disposal of his skill, knowledge or physical strength. The capacity to work is thus bought and sold, rather like fruit or vegetables (though unlike fruit and vegetables, workers can band together – and at times stand up and fight).

From the fact that labour is treated as a commodity stem many of the fundamental conflicts in industry. The wages and conditions which the worker naturally seeks as a means to a decent life are a *cost* to the employer, cutting into his profits, and he will equally naturally recognize that certain minimum standards of wages and conditions are necessary in order to recruit and retain labour, and to sustain the 'morale' thought essential to encourage hard work. But this normally gives employers only a limited motive for generosity.) Because the employer must regard labour as a cost to be minimized, it is in his interest to retain a worker in employment only while it is profitable to do so. This means that workers' jobs are always at the mercy of economic and technological vagaries. If there is a slump in demand for the goods or services produced, or if new techniques are devised which can allow them to be produced more cheaply and profitably, men and women will find themselves unemployed. [. . .]

In similar fashion, those who treat union democracy as an issue of limited moment often regard the goals of trade unionism as unproblematic. The conception of industrial relations in the narrow terms of job regulation encourages the assumption that union objectives are

3. Some writers have exaggerated the significance of the growth of professional management, arguing that this alters the capitalist character of modern industry.

relatively uncontroversial. Thus Flanders insists that collective bargaining must be recognized as the invariable central purpose. 'All the other activities which the trade unions have undertaken and all the other purposes they have acquired must be regarded as a by-product and auxiliary to this their major activity and purpose, since success in it has been the condition for their survival and the basis of their growth.' Yet if the sole important function of unionism is to join with employers in negotiating and administering rules governing wages and working conditions,[4] then the business of union decision-making is indeed largely technical. If unions have to accept the capitalist arrangements of industry – the structure of ownership, of economic priorities and of managerial authority – then they can be expected to provide no more than a limited range of improvements in the worker's situation. The reasonable member, in turn, will view his union as no more than a fairly narrow service agency; so long as it delivers the goods he has no cause to worry about its internal government. It would be as pointless to tell his full-time official how he should go about his job as it would be to tell his green-grocer.[5]

Such a definition of trade union purposes is sometimes presented as a simple description of – or deduction from – what trade unions actually *do*. But in fact it incorporates assumptions which are intensely political in character. What is involved is a restrictive specification of the *legitimate* functions of trade unions: functions which exclude any serious challenge to the existing social order and the structure of control in industry. This moralizing standpoint is made explicit in the recent comments of an eminent labour lawyer:

Management can legitimately expect that labour will be available at a price which permits a reasonable margin for investment, and labour can equally legitimately expect that the level of real wages will not only be maintained but steadily increased. Management can claim a legitimate interest in obtaining for each job the most qualified worker available; labour can claim a legitimate interest in obtaining a job for each worker who is unemployed. Management can and must always expect that the arrangements of society (through law or otherwise) ensure that labour is as mobile as possible in the geographical as

4. In fact, Flanders recognized a wider social and political purpose for trade unionism; but this could not be comfortably accommodated within the theoretical framework of 'job regulation' (Flanders, 1968).
5. The American economist Hoxie, who classified trade unions according to their objectives, noted a connection between the narrow aims of 'business' unionism and a lack of democracy in government (Hoxie, 1923, p. 47).

well as in the occupational sense; labour must always insist that workers enjoy a reasonable measure of job security so as to be able to plan their own and their families' lives. Management expects to plan the production and distribution of goods or supply of services on a basis of calculated costs and calculated risks, and requires society to guarantee the feasibility of such planning by protecting it against interruption of these processes; labour well realises that without the power to stop work collectively it is impotent, and expects to be able to interrupt the economic process if this is necessary in order to exercise the necessary pressure. Management's interest in planning production and in being protected against its interruption is the exact equivalent to the worker's interest in planning his and his family's life and in being protected against an interruption in his mode of existence, either through a fall of his real income or through the loss of his job. All this is palpably obvious, except for a person blinded by class hatred either way (Kahn-Freund and Hepple, 1972, p. 52).

What is taken for granted in this catalogue of 'legitimate expectations' is the existence of a society in which capital dominates over labour. Briefly translated, the argument is that the pursuit of profit by the owners of capital (though remarkably, profit is not explicitly mentioned) is 'the exact equivalent' of workers' dependence on wages. Employers have a natural right to exploit workers and disrupt their lives; workers have a highly qualified right not to be *excessively* exploited or disrupted. Hence the legitimate functions of trade unions extend no further than the protection of their members against the more extreme consequences of their subordination to capital; the *fact* of this subordination they are not entitled to challenge.

However self-evident such assumptions may appear to employers and establishment politicians, it is *not* inevitable that unions' objectives should be so narrowly defined. Trade unionists have often proclaimed far more radical aims: the reconstruction of the social order; the abolition of the dominating role of profit; the establishment of workers' control of industry; the reorganization of the economy to serve directly the needs of the producers and the general members of the society; the humanization of work; the elimination of gross inequalities in standards of living and conditions of life; the transformation of cultural richness from the privilege of a minority to the property of all. Time and again, the case for these broader social goals has been argued within the trade union movement; and the cogency of the argument is reflected in the rule-books of many unions (including the TGWU and AEU), which prescribe objects ranging far beyond the narrow confines of collective bargaining.

If the objectives which are in practice pursued by trade unions are confined to the negotiation of limited improvements within the frame-work of capitalist work relations, this represents a restrictive *policy* which is in turn the outcome of a specific set of power relationships both inside and outside the unions. The effect of powerful external pressures on the definition of trade union objectives is too rarely considered in the study of industrial relations. It is obvious that those with positions of power and privilege in industry and society have a strong interest in the goals espoused by trade unions. Their purely economic objectives, if ambitious, conflict with the capitalist's desire to minimize costs of production; involvement in a struggle for control challenges his managerial prerogatives; while any connection with socialist politics is a potential threat to his very existence. Govern-ments, having as their major priority the stability and success of the prevailing economic system, have a similar interest in the goals of trade unionism. It is not surprising, then, that socializing influences (in Allen's terms) bear heavily on the selection of union policy.

The actual behaviour of unions results from the action of a complex of secondary processes which modify and distort the basic economic features of union activity and bring it to terms with society at large. This is what is called socialization. It is not possible for unions which arose in opposition to the dominant effects of capitalism to operate within the system as permanent bodies without taking on some of the characteristics of the system itself (Allen, 1966, p. 24).

Some of these pressures are ideological. The terms of discussion in the media and in everyday political debate – both of which are profoundly affected by the power of capital – encourage trade union-ists to disavow as 'subversive', 'irresponsible' or 'economically disas-trous' any but the most modest of objectives. To embrace more ambitious aims is to challenge everyday language and assumptions, which presuppose that capitalist economic relations are natural, permanent and morally unassailable; and this requires a highly devel-oped consciousness and determination. Reinforcing such ideological pressures are more material forces. The cruellest of the contradictions facing trade unionists is that those in positions of economic and social dominance – resistance to whom is the fundamental purpose of collec-tive action – can readily apply their power to threaten the very secu-rity and survival of union organization. Historically, judges and legislators have regularly combined to impose the most rigorous restrictions on employee combination and union action. Employers have used an armoury of weapons, including victimization, lockouts, and outright physical violence, to undermine or destroy unionism. The possibility of repression can never be wholly ignored, therefore, when trade unionists formulate their objectives.

Faced with such massive external power, the pressures are intense for unions to engage in a tacit – indeed sometimes explicit – trade-off. When Flanders writes that collective bargaining 'has been the condition for their survival and the basis of their growth' he underlines (perhaps unintentionally) these pressures. For the more ambitious and extensive a union's objectives, the more likely are the politically and socially powerful to express their hostility through acts of repression. Conversely, if it curbs those objectives which seriously threaten the *status quo* it may be able to win the acquiescence and even goodwill of employers and the state. Historically, unions which have become firmly established have been drawn inexorably towards policies which are relatively acceptable to these significant others. Thus it is rare indeed for trade union commitment to major social change to be an operational one, in the sense of influencing day-to-day industrial tactics or serious long-term strategies: the socialist attachments of British unions are in general confined to the rhetoric of rule-book preambles and conference speeches. Similar pressures normally affect industrial policies in such manner that interference with managerial control does not go 'too far', while economic demands are characterized by 'moderation'. Evidently, then, the central role of collective bargaining in union policy should be interpreted as an *accommodation to external power*.

Where unions are willing to confine their aims within these comparatively innocuous limits, far-sighted managements have little reason to resist, and some reason to welcome, the unionization of their employees. By making explicit the many discontents which work in capitalist industry generates, unions help to make workers' behaviour more predictable and manageable. Resentment is not permitted to accumulate explosively, but is processed in a manner which facilitates at least temporary solution; and union involvement in any settlement increases the likelihood that the members will feel committed to the agreed terms. At the level of government, similar considerations apply. The legalization of unions may in itself mute some of the radicalism associated with their former 'outlaw' status. Involvement in various consultative and administrative committees generates a degree of identification with government economic policy on the part of union leaders, and encourages them to tailor their own strategies accordingly. More generally, once trade unions acquire a recognized social status they tend 'to integrate their members into the larger body politic and give them a basis for loyalty to the system' (Lipset, 1959, p. 113).

The process involved in this domestication of union goals is often viewed as a reflection of 'institutional needs'. The tendencies just described may be attributed to unions' institutional interest in establishing stable bargaining relationships with those controlling significant reserves of social power, and in avoiding aims and actions which might arouse strong hostility and hence jeopardize organizational security. Such institutional concerns affect not only the basic orientation towards collective bargaining, but also the content of what is collectively agreed. Thus Ross has called attention to what he terms 'union-oriented provisions' in agreements. These, he suggests, 'are intended to define the status of the union in the enterprise' and 'cover such crucial matters as union security and managerial prerogatives, and such minor matters as the use of bulletin boards. They often provide for the checkoff of union dues, the right to participate in all grievance negotiations . . .' (Ross, 1948, p. 23). As another American author comments, 'the union shop, or other forms of compulsion, are highly important to the strength and stability of labor unions. It is the union as an organization, not the worker directly, that needs the "job control"' (Olson, 1965, p. 87). Conceding terms which consolidate a union's membership and reinforce its organizational security may involve little direct cost to the employer; but such concessions may be traded against more material improvements in workers' conditions, and more crucially they are usually dependent on the adoption of conciliatory and accommodative policies on the part of the union.

The notion of 'institutional needs' is a useful piece of shorthand; but it is highly misleading if it conceals the fact that what is at issue is not merely a set of pressures *internal* to trade unionism, but more importantly the impact of *external* agencies with which unions are engaged in continuing power relations. Both pressures are particularly salient for the full-time official, who is specifically concerned with the union's internal strength and integrity, and is also engaged in day-to-day relations with the representatives of capital. Hence commitment to stable and cordial bargaining relationships is particularly strong at the level of the full-time official.

This concern with externally-generated institutional needs is a potent influence on the relationship within trade unionism between power for and power over. This subtle point was grasped succinctly half a century ago by Gramsci, the profound Italian theorist and revolutionary. The essence of trade union achievement, he argued, is the winning of a form of 'industrial legality' which guarantees certain concessions by capitalists to their employees. Such concessions represent 'a great victory for the working class'; yet they do not end the domination over workers and their organizations by employer power. 'Industrial legality has improved the working class's material living conditions, but it is no more than a compromise – a compromise which has to be made and must be supported until the balance of forces favours the working class.' The development of cohesive and aggressive organization at the point of production is a precondition of a significant shift in the balance of forces and a serious challenge to the power of capital. But the attitude of the official to such a development, Gramsci argued, is ambivalent or even hostile. 'The union bureaucrat conceives industrial legality as a permanent state of affairs. He too often defends it from the same viewpoint as the proprietor . . . He does not perceive the worker's act of rebellion against capitalist discipline as a rebellion; he perceives only the physical act, which may in itself and for itself be trivial' (Gramsci, 1969, pp. 15–17).

The union official, in other words, experiences a natural commitment to the existing bargaining arrangements and the terms of existing collective agreements. This commitment, moreover, is attributable less to any personal characteristics of the official than to his *function*: the negotiation and renegotiation of order within constraints set by a capitalist economy and a capitalist state. Yet if the union official sees orderly industrial relations as essential for stable bargaining relationships with employers and ultimately for union security, his viewpoint in many respects parallels that of management. The union leader, wrote Wright Mills in an often quoted passage, 'is a manager of discontent. He makes regular what might otherwise be disruptive, both within the industrial routine and within the union which he seeks to establish and maintain' (Mills, 1948, p. 9). Job control, as it primarily concerns the 'union-as-an-organization' (and hence the official as the main guardian of 'organizational interests') is therefore concerned more with stabilizing the detail of the relationship between labour and capital than with conducting a struggle *against* the domination of capital. Such control may thus involve the *suppression* of irregular and disruptive activities by the rank and file which challenge managerial control. In this way, *union* control and *workers'* control may face in opposite directions, and the element of power over the members inherent in union organization may be turned against them.

Conclusion

External constraints – the power of employers and the state – impose forceful limits on the purposes adopted by trade unions. They find themselves accorded legitimacy, recognized and even encouraged, only when their aims and actions do not seriously challenge the continuation of capitalism. Union officials, directly concerned with organizational stability, are particularly susceptible to these pressures; but the membership at large is also subject to ideological influences which narrowly define the legitimate goals of unionism. The possibility of the democratic determination, by trade unionists collectively, of objectives best serving their own interests in the struggle against capital is subverted or suppressed.

The institutionalization of trade union functions has historically accompanied a more general attenuation of internal democracy; and the two processes are indeed intimately related. For the more limited the objectives pursued, the less central to the worker's life interests is his union; and the less, therefore, his incentive to become actively involved in the machinery of internal decision-making. The more exclusive the focus on collective bargaining, then, the less likely it is that most members will seek to control either the means or the ends of union action. At the same time, the pressures on the official to maintain control *over* the rank and file in order to support stable and orderly industrial relations are further corrosive of internal democracy.

Thus the historical development of trade unionism has revealed strong and mutually reinforcing obstacles to democratic control. Yet it would be over-simple to conclude that an irresistible and irreversible 'iron law of oligarchy' is involved in this process. The variations between organizations in terms of both policy and internal democracy demonstrate that counter-pressures can in some circumstances prove significant. And most crucial among these is the *practice* of workers themselves. The deprivations and aspirations which drive workers to create collective organizations, to seek to exert control over work relations, lead them naturally to react forcibly when their unions appear to retreat from their original purposes. The 'rank-and-file revolt', experienced in almost every industrialized nation in recent years, is clear evidence of this.

References

ALLEN, V. (1966), *Militant Trade Unionism*, Merlin.
FLANDERS, A. (1968), *Trade Unions*, Hutchinson.
GRAMSCI, A. (1969), *Soviets in Italy*, Institute of Workers' Control.
HOXIE, R. F. (1923), *Trade Unionism in the United States*, 2nd edn, Appleton-Century-Crofts.
KAHN-FREUND, O., and B. HEPPLE (1972), *Laws Against Strikes*, Fabian Society.
LIPSET, M. (1959), in *Sociology Today*, ed. R. K. Merton, Basic Books.
MILLS, C. W. (1948), *The New Men of Power*, Harcourt Brace.
OLSON, M. (1965), *The Logic of Collective Action*, Harvard.

4 E. Batstone, I. Boraston and S. Frankel

Union Principles and the Role of Shop Stewards

From E. Batstone, I. Boraston and S. Frankel, *Shop Stewards in Action: The Organization of Workplace Conflict and Accommodation*, Blackwell, 1977, pp. 27–40.

It is difficult to define clearly the nature of union principles. The principles or goals, which trade unionists pursue, clearly vary. But there are certain elements in the day-to-day behaviour of many shop stewards which can be described as embodying the basic principles of trade unionism. The first of these is an emphasis upon unity and the collectivity. While the definition of the collectivity may vary, for shop stewards it implies at the least the prevention of the fractionalization of the domestic organization. A second important element is some idea of social justice. That is, those within the collectivity are to be treated both fairly and equally (Brown, 1973, p. 133; Batstone *et al.*, 1976). This involves, on the one hand, ensuring that members of the collectivity are not subject to managerial whim. On the other hand, the notion of fairness requires that union members look after each other. There should be no discrimination against the less fortunate, while the unbridled pursuit of self-interest should be minimized.

The goals and principles which are enunciated in Joint Shop Stewards' Committee (JSSC) meetings indicate how far stewards espouse union principles. Table 1 shows how stewards defined union principles in these meetings. Such principles are more frequently referred to on the shop floor. On the staff side, certain principles – fairness and justice, protection from managerial whim – receive no expression in steward meetings. All of the themes outlined above are referred to in stewards' meetings on the shop floor. But, even in meetings of stewards, a third of the references to values and goals on the staff side are to the maintenance of individualism rather than union principles; that is, staff stewards were keen to preserve certain areas where the individual worker could pursue his own interests irrespective of the collectivity. There are, then, limits to the pursuit of collective interests on the staff side. Over half of the staff stewards,

Table 1 Primary principles expressed at JSSC meetings

	Staff %	Shop floor %
The maintenance of unity	18	26
Fairness and justice	–	7
Protection from managerial whim	–	13
Helping the less fortunate	36	22
Concern for the interests of others	13	33
Increasing individual incomes	13	–
Protecting individual opportunities	20	–
Total references	100%	101%
No. of references	22	162

Source: Observation

compared with only one in ten of those on the shop floor, agreed with the view that 'Generally you can't act according to union principles – they don't feed the family.'

The first broad contrast between our two steward organizations is, then, the contrasting goals which are pursued and the perspectives which inform them. On the shop floor, stewards more consistently adopt a conflict image of industry and, along with this, express a stronger and more consistent commitment to union principles. On the staff side, there is a greater degree of ambivalence over the nature of relationships in industry, and a less certain commitment to union principles. Staff stewards, as a group, more readily espouse a belief in industrial harmony and individualism. These differences between our two groups of stewards are associated with differences in ideas concerning the proper role of stewards and steward organization in relation to the membership.

Stewards' relations with their members

Within most democratic organizations there is disagreement as to the amount of freedom which officials should have. It is seldom argued that such officials should ignore the wishes of their members. This is important, for it means that the debate on the role of the official relates to a limited range of possible patterns of behaviour. Debate concentrates primarily upon the extent to which the official should merely carry out the wishes of his members rather than exercising his own discretion in pursuing their interests. The idea of a delegate is that he should be mandated by his members and do no more or less than carry out their wishes. In contrast, the representative is often expected to adopt much more of a leadership role, taking initiatives and playing a major part in the development of policies as well as in their execution. The British Member of Parliament is a classic example of the representative role.

Trade unions and domestic organizations are no exception to this debate on the role of the official. Considerable differences of view existed between our two groups of stewards. For the moment we confine ourselves to pointing out that in describing their role half of the staff stewards emphasized a delegate style. That is, they described their task as carrying out members' wishes and simply acting as a channel of communications between members and management. Only 16 per cent of stewards on the shop floor described their role in these terms.

The broad contrasts between our two domestic organizations are shown by stewards' views on the relationship between the steward collectivity and the membership. In the questionnaire we asked stewards what made a domestic organization a good one. The replies showed that on the shop floor there was a stronger emphasis upon a representative role, involving leadership. About three-quarters of shop-floor stewards' comments were of this kind, compared with less than half of those from the staff side. A greater emphasis upon a leadership role for the steward was also found on the shop floor when we raised the question of the extent to which stewards should carry out the wishes of their members or of the steward community. Less than half of the staff stewards agreed with the view that 'A steward should support JSSC resolutions even if these are against his own members.' Three-quarters of the stewards on the shop floor supported this view. The contrast is confirmed by informal interviews with stewards. Typical of the staff view is the following: 'I wouldn't tell the chaps they weren't on. I don't run the members, they run me . . . They're there to tell me what to do, not the other way round.' In contrast, many shop-floor stewards argued: 'You've got to be willing and able to tell the men that they're on a non-winner and to tell them they're just not on . . . A steward's got to be able to stand up to his section.'

This difference in emphasis upon a delegate or representative role is also reflected in how the conveners and other stewards define their

Table 2 How conveners saw their role

	Staff %	Shop floor %
References to convener leadership	39	77
References to conveners carrying out members' wishes	61	23
Total responses	100%	100%
No. of responses	72	79
No. of respondents	2	3

Source: Informal interviews

role. Table 2 shows how the conveners saw their role. A strong contrast can be seen in the extent to which the different conveners emphasized a representative role, as indicated by an emphasis upon leadership,[1] or delegate role, as indicated by a concern with carrying out the wishes of the membership. On the shop floor, such leadership by the conveners receives general support from other stewards. Similarly, the staff conveners' greater concern with a delegate role finds favour with the majority of staff stewards. In the questionnaire we asked stewards how they saw the role of convener. Only 28 per cent of staff replies made any reference to leadership; in contrast, 59 per cent of shop-floor replies did so. A similar pattern is found when we consider responses obtained from informal interviews of both a general and issue-specific nature with stewards. Only 3 per cent of comments on the staff side support the idea of convener leadership, compared with 35 per cent of comments on the shop floor.

At the level of the domestic organization as a whole, then, there is a considerably greater emphasis on the shop floor upon leadership by stewards, conveners, and JSSC. On the staff side a delegate role finds greater support with its emphasis upon simply carrying out the wishes of the membership. Such differences relate to variations in commitment to union principles. These principles stress that on occasion it may be wrong to pursue the demands of a particular group of members, for such demands may be the expression of sectional self-interest which would operate to the disadvantage of other groups. Accordingly, if union principles are to be pursued, it may be necessary to oppose, or at least to attempt to change, the expressed wishes

---

1. Only statements which support the idea of leadership are included in the classification 'references to leadership'.

of the membership (Fox, 1971, chapter 4). On the shop floor, therefore, stewards tend to be concerned with leadership in the pursuit of union principles.

Staff stewards place greater emphasis upon a delegate role, as might be expected from their greater ambivalence concerning union principles. For, if these or any other type of ideology consistent with collective organization are not fully accepted, there is less of a base upon which leadership can rest. Goals have to be defined much more in terms of members' expressed wishes, and accordingly steward action has to be seen rather more in terms of a delegate role.

This discussion has been concerned with broad contrasts in the views expressed by stewards in our two domestic organizations. They are, however, merely tendencies, and accordingly we need to go on to look at how attitudes vary between stewards within each organization. If, for example, particular shop-floor stewards tend to reject union principles and a representative role, then it suggests that what we have termed ideological forms of power are more effective in some areas than in others. This is indeed the case, and after looking at individual variations in role conceptions, we go on to consider how it is that within the same organization some stewards accept a role definition which others less fully espouse.

Differences in role definition between individual stewards

The distinctions which can be made between stewards are numerous. We concentrate here upon two dimensions since these appear to be powerful explanations of differing patterns of behaviour. They are distinctions which are relatively crude, and there is little doubt that they could be further refined and that in some situations other dimensions might be usefully added.

Our categorization of stewards derives largely from the ideas of stewards themselves, and in particular from the expectations of the conveners and the more experienced stewards. It may therefore be useful briefly to outline their views before going on to discuss the distinctions which we make. Central to their view of the steward role is a concern to protect the union organization. It is important, therefore, that problems should be handled by the union rather than by individual workers. This is not simply a concern with the institutional interests of the organization, for the conveners believe that it is through the union that workers can best protect their interests. Hence, the conveners and the experienced stewards on the shop floor are especially critical of those workers who make individual bargains with management, and, in their view, invariably run into problems which they then bring to the union. However, views differ between the staff and shop-floor conveners as to how stewards should handle problems. The shop-floor conveners and experienced stewards stress that stewards should be able to handle the great bulk of issues by themselves. A common criticism made by the conveners is that some stewards use them as 'whipping boys' and fail to bargain hard themselves or to tell their members 'they're not on'. As a shop-floor convener explained to a steward, 'The union is protection for the members. A steward should deal with problems himself and give the convener strength. He shouldn't just moan . . . A steward cannot support his section when they're wrong.'

The staff conveners would like to be able to achieve such a leadership role, but they believe they are unable to do so. One of them argued, 'On the shop floor workers have stronger class loyalty. They'll follow the conveners much easier than our members will follow us. Our members often think they're middle-class.' Accordingly, the staff conveners are keen that stewards should bring problems to them so that they can possibly achieve success and thereby foster commitment to the union. On the shop floor, the conveners have a more permissive model of domestic organization. They do not want direct involvement in many problems. Rather, they want to see certain norms and principles pursued by stewards on their own initiative. These values are maintained through discussions with stewards; stories are told of successes and major errors by other stewards, and the dangers of the present activities of certain of them are emphasized (Turner, 1971, pp. 111–14).

The shop-floor conveners are particularly concerned that stewards should not be fooled or pushed around either by their own members or by management. For example, one steward was forced to resign because he was 'conned' by management. A convener said the steward had been stupid to be fooled and 'soft' to resign: 'He's resigned several times before.' Another steward had received a good deal of criticism from some of his members because he was often away from the job. Under member pressure he ceased attending steward meetings. Several of the more experienced stewards told him it was 'ridiculous to let the blokes push you around like that'.

At the same time, the steward must always be committed to the interests of his members. There is a danger, in emphasizing leadership, that stewards may become distanced from those they are meant to represent and begin to pursue their own individual interests. Shop-floor stewards who become foremen are the subject of a good deal of criticism. Some stewards have on occasion been suspected of using their union role to avoid work or gain special advantages for themselves. For example, on one section there were a number of difficult problems, and a convener and an experienced steward from another section discussed these and agreed that they resulted from the section's steward 'feathering his own nest. It gives the organization a bad name.'

Finally, stewards should not pursue sectional interests to the detriment of other groups. A steward must take into account the interests of others. This was often seen as involving 'facing the facts of life'. Often groups will not be able to achieve their aspirations, and some compromise will be necessary. One steward insisted on pursuing a claim which was about to result in the lay-off of many other workers. The conveners agreed, 'It's all right for him to argue that way. His view would be different if he had to explain to the mass [meeting] why they were being laid off.' Such compromise and balancing of interests require that stewards achieve room for manoeuvre from their members, and do not commit themselves totally to achieving certain things (Walton and McKersie, 1965, pp. 312–13). For example, in discussing some difficult piecework negotiations, the conveners and several experienced stewards agreed that the steward had 'put himself on the hook because he's promised the men' that he would negotiate a certain rate for them, and 'now he's stuck'.

These expectations of individual stewards and marked differences in patterns of behaviour suggested to us a categorization of stewards in terms of two cross-cutting dimensions, both of which we have discussed in the previous section. The first is the extent to which emphasis is placed upon a delegate or representative role, the second the pursuit of union principles. Using these two dimensions we can distinguish a number of ideal types as shown in Figure 1.

The leader is a steward who is able to play a representative role in relation to his members, as he attempts to implement union princi-ples. He not merely demonstrates a commitment to such goals but is generally able to achieve them. The 'nascent leader' is often spon-sored by a leader; he is committed to union principles but, without the support of other stewards, he is unable to maintain the necessary representative role. The 'cowboy', by contrast, is able to play a representative role at least in the short-term, but is not committed to union principles as we have defined them. He is typically concerned

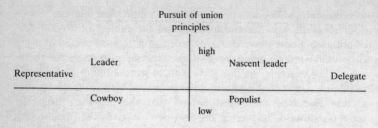

Figure 1 Steward types

with maximizing the short-run earnings of his own particular group of members. Finally, the 'populist' lacks both a commitment to union principles and the ability or desire to be a representative; he acts as a delegate. Accordingly his activities are generally much more determined by the expressed wishes of his members.

In our discussions we are primarily concerned with leaders and populists. In the organizations we studied, the number of nascent leaders and cowboys was small.[2] In part, this is because these two types tend to continue as stewards for relatively short periods of time. The nascent leader either achieves the necessary resources and becomes a leader or, without the support of other stewards, returns to the role of populist. The cowboy frequently faces opposition from other stewards whose members are adversely affected by his activities; when, therefore, he ceases to achieve gains for his members and their support wanes, he is likely to be rapidly replaced.

Our classification of stewards is based upon observation. Stewards are classified as representatives rather than delegates if they shape the majority of issues which they deal with, either by initiating issues themselves or by amending or squashing issues raised by others, and if they tend to handle issues themselves without resort to the conveners or other experienced stewards. Stewards are defined as pursuing union principles if their systems of argument to all audiences more frequently refer to the norms of steward leadership than to members' wishes. Such a classification is relatively easy for stewards with whom we had a good deal of contact, even though we were not systematically observing them. For a small number of stewards, less than 10 per cent, our data are less complete, and accordingly our classi-

2. This need not be typical: certainly it is possible to envisage organizations where cowboys dominate.

fication is less reliable. The classification of these stewards is based upon both observation and their reputations among other stewards. However, for this reason we can only estimate the distribution of stewards between types, as shown in Table 3.

Populists form the largest single type of steward in both our domestic organizations, and total over three-quarters of all staff stewards. On the shop floor the 38 per cent of stewards who are leaders cover almost half of all the membership, compared with only 15 per cent on the staff. Nascent leaders and cowboys total only 17 per cent of stewards on the shop floor, and only 4 per cent on the staff side.

We concentrated our observation upon stewards who were generally seen by others to be typical of the two extremes of leader and populist. Here we are concerned with the extent to which our distinction between these two types of stewards, based upon observation of their *behaviour*, is reflected in differences in their commitment to union principles and a representative role at the *attitudinal* level, as obtained through interviews. The differences we note therefore reflect merely broad tendencies, for not only does an interview often present stewards with choices abstracted from specific issues and problems, but also stewards may not in reality have the resources to achieve the role they would like. With these cautions in mind, we turn first to a consideration of stewards' differing degrees of commitment to union principles.

Table 3 *Distribution of stewards between types*

	Staff %	Shop floor %
Leaders	18	38
Nascent leaders	4	10
Cowboys	–	7
Populists	78	45
Total	100%	100%
No.	26	151
% *sections/areas* covered by:		
Leaders	n.a.	46
Populists and others	n.a.	54
% *members* covered by:		
Leaders	15	49
Populists and others	85	51

Source: Observation and interviews

Union principles and individual stewards

One indicator of commitment to union principles is why stewards believe workers should belong to a trade union. Those who espouse union principles may be expected to place a greater emphasis upon workers' rights and social justice rather than to express a concern simply with wages and conditions. They will define trade unionism as more than mere instrumentalism. Table 4 shows that while more than four in five leaders see the importance of union membership in terms of defending workers' rights and the pursuit of socialism, only a quarter of shop-floor populists and 12 per cent of staff populists do so.

Table 4 Main reason for being a member of a union

	Leaders %	Staff populists %	Shop-floor populists %
Improve wages and conditions	17	88	75
Defend workers' right/socialism	83	12	25
Total respondents	100%	100%	100%
No. of respondents	17 (3 staff)	16	17

Source: Steward questionnaire

This variation in commitment to union principles is also to be seen in stewards' views on the statement, 'Generally you can't act according to union principles – they don't feed the family.' Table 5 shows that about two in three leaders strongly disagreed with this view, compared with only one in five shop-floor populists. No staff populists expressed such strong disagreement with this statement, and indeed over half agreed with it. In other words, they demonstrated much less commitment to union principles than even their counterparts on the shop floor. However, for our present purposes we would stress that leader stewards demonstrate much greater commitment to union principles than do populists. In this respect, the evidence suggests that the observed differences between the two types of steward are associated with differing role perceptions on the part of the stewards themselves. We now move on to see whether this is equally true of the second dimension we used in defining different types of steward.

Table 5 Union principles as a guide to action

'Generally you can't act according to union principles – they don't feed the family.'	Leaders %	Staff populists %	Shop-floor populists %
Strongly disagree	59	–	18
Disagree	29	46	71
Agree	12	48	11
Strongly agree	–	6	–
Total respondents	100%	100%	100%
No. of respondents	17 (3 staff)	16	14
No answer	–	–	3

Source: Steward questionnaire

Individual stewards and commitment to representative or delegate roles

The second dimension by which we distinguished types of steward concerned whether they tended towards a representative or delegate role. Leaders were defined as actually achieving the former role, while populists tended to adopt the latter. Here we are concerned with the extent to which such differences in terms of action reflect, or are associated with, differences in attitudes.

In the questionnaire, we asked two questions of relevance to this point. The first of these sought respondents' views on the following statement: 'A steward is a representative, but he is also a leader; sometimes he has to tell his members they're not on, sometimes stir them to action.'[3] Table 6 shows that almost nine in ten leaders strongly agreed with this, compared with less than a third of the staff populists and less than half the shop-floor populists. Indeed, almost a third of the staff populists rejected this view.

The second relevant question concerned the greatest influences upon the respondent as a steward. Those favouring a delegate role were expected to emphasize their own members, while those who accepted a representative role were expected to make more frequent references to other stewards, particularly JSSC and the conveners. Table 7 supports this. In listing the two greatest influences upon them, nearly two-thirds of leaders' comments were to meetings or members

3. Pedler asks a similar question, but only one in five of the stewards asked saw themselves as 'a leader who often has to win his members over' (1973–4, p. 56).

Table 6 The steward as leader

'A steward is a representative, but he is also a leader; sometimes he has to tell his members they're not on, sometimes stir them to action.'	Leaders %	Staff populists %	Shop-floor populists %
Strongly agree	88	31	47
Agree	12	38	41
Disagree/strongly disagree	–	31	12
Total respondents	100%	100%	100%
No. of respondents	17 (3 staff)	16	17

Source: Steward questionnaire

Table 7 Two greatest influences upon respondent as steward

	Leaders %	Staff populists %	Shop-floor populists %
Steward body	65	45	35
Members	35	49	44
Other	–	6	21
Total respondents	100%	100%	100%
No. of respondents	17 (3 staff)	16	16
No. of responses	34	34	29
No answer	–	–	1

Source: Steward questionnaire

of the steward body, and only about one-third to the membership more generally. Among populists, more references were made to their members as major influences than were made to the steward body. In addition, a number of populists thought that other groups, including management and persons outside the domestic organization, significantly influenced their behaviour.

Our informal interviews with stewards also demonstrate, through general discussion and explanations of specific events, that leaders put a greater emphasis upon a representative role. Table 8 shows that in discussing the relationship between members and themselves, they placed greater stress upon leadership on their own part and by the JSSC and conveners. All of the shop-floor leaders' comments were of this kind, as were over four-fifths of staff leaders' comments. Less than a third of populists' references were to leadership, while at least two-thirds referred to the need for the stewards to carry out the wishes of their members. Shop-floor leaders made no reference to following members' wishes, and only 17 per cent of staff leaders' comments were of this kind.

Table 8 Stewards' references to aspects of their role

	Leaders		Populists	
	Staff	Shop floor	Staff	Shop floor
	%	%	%	%
Own leadership	63	79	–	17
JSSC/convener leadership	20	21	16	15
Follow members' wishes	17	–	84	68
Total responses	100%	100%	100%	100%
No. of respondents	3	9	9	9
No. of responses	30	135	102	127

Source: Informal interviews

Concerning the representative or delegate roles, a relationship exists between our classification, based on observation, and expressed attitudes. Our distinction between populists and leaders reflects differing degrees of commitment to the idea of union principles and a representative role; that is, to the norms of what we have termed leadership. The question therefore arises of how such contrasts in role definition develop not merely between the two organizations, but also within them.

References

BATSTONE, E., I. BORASTON and S. FRANKEL (1976), 'Bargaining in Action', *Industrial Studies*, 2, ed. E. Coker and G. Stottard, Arrow.

BROWN, W. A. (1973), *Piecework Bargaining*, Heinemann.

FOX, A. (1971), *A Sociology of Work in Industry*, Collier Macmillan.

GOODMAN, J., and T. WHITTINGTON (1973), *Shop Stewards*, Pan.

PEDLER, M., 'Shop Stewards as Leaders', *Industrial Relations Journal*, vol. 4, 1973–4.

TURNER, B. A. (1971), *Exploring the Industrial Sub-Culture*, Macmillan.

WALTON, R. A., and R. B. MCKERSIE (1965), *A Behavioural Theory of Labour Negotiations*, McGraw-Hill.

Part Two

Trade Unions and Industrial Democracy

The five readings chosen here illustrate stages in the continuing debate about the role of unions in advancing the somewhat elusive aim of 'industrial democracy'.

Reading 5, from an early work by G. D. H. Cole, sets out the traditional case for union involvement in management which formed the basis of the 'syndicalist' movement. If union structure can be reformed, and capitalist exploitation ended, unions should enter into partnership with the state to create effective industrial self-government. What stands out today is Cole's easy assumption that once state ownership of industry becomes the norm, collective bargaining can safely be allowed to wither away, so that 'wages would be determined by the native goodness of the consumers' hearts, as reflected in their rulers'.

In Reading 6 Hugh Clegg mounts his influential attack on the syndicalist position, originally published in 1951. It remains the most effective reply to Cole and all his latter-day disciples. Unions are seen as 'second grade' democracies, which are limited in their objectives but essential to hold management in check. If they were to participate in the management of private or public industry this would compromise their vital role as an 'independent opposition that did not seek to govern'.

Clegg's views remained the orthodoxy of the leaders of the British trade union movement until some time in the sixties. But this did not prevent his position being challenged by academics and others who considered it unduly negative. One of the best of the arguments against Clegg is to be found in Blumberg's *Industrial Democracy: The Sociology of Participation*, which is the basis of Reading 7. He argues that mere opposition is 'neither a necessary nor a sufficient condition of democracy'. In industry this must involve 'the accountability of leadership to an electorate which has the power to dismiss that leadership'. Clegg's fear that involvement in management selection would undermine the union's primary function of collective bargaining is dismissed by citing the example of the Histandrut in Israel. This confederation of unions owns large parts of industry and is responsible for the appointment of managers; yet collective bargaining over wages and conditions continues, even if 'management tends to be weak and timid, from the level of the foreman up'.

By the early seventies the EEC's Fifth Directive offered British unions the prospect of a legally-based form of industrial democracy. At the same time Jack Jones, the influential leader of the Transport and General Workers' Union, had come to favour trade union representation at board level as a means of exerting union control over top-level management decisions. The result was a revival of trade union interest in the traditional objectives of the syndicalists and an eventual change of TUC policy.

By 1974 a Labour government existed which was prepared to consider changes in company law in the direction now favoured by the TUC. To this end the Bullock Committee on Industrial Democracy was established to decide how industrial democracy could be best advanced by 'representation on boards of directors . . . accepting the essential role of trade union organization in this process'. Jack Jones was a prominent member of the Committee. Its majority report proposed 'parity of representation' for trade union worker directors in all enterprises employing more than 2,000 people.

Reading 8 consists of extracts from the majority report. It deals with Bullock's much-discussed plans for 'single channel communication', i.e. the use of existing union machinery to select board nominees. Non-unionists were to be denied any part in the selection process, although they were allowed to participate in a secret ballot to decide whether or not such a scheme should be adopted in their place of work. Also included is Bullock's reply to Clegg's objection that 'there is a fundamental and irreconcilable incompatibility between board level representation and collective bargaining'.

However, the CBI and other management organizations mounted a strong campaign against the implementation of the Bullock Report. Large parts of the trade union movement were also found to be unenthusiastic or even opposed. A limited experiment was tried, for a time, in the Post Office; but when Labour lost office in 1979 the incoming Conservative administration proved to be against all forms of worker participation based on legal rights. Thus Britain is now almost the only West European country where the notion of industrial democracy is given no legal support. Yet this is a debate which continues, and all opposition parties are committed to providing some kind of legal support if and when they form a government.

Fortunately for the progress of our subject, the experiment in the Post Office was studied in some depth by Eric Batstone and his colleagues. Their recently published book is the basis for Reading 9. Batstone shows that the more extreme assertions of both sides of the traditional debate were not borne out by the Post Office experience. The union-based worker directors made little impact on corporate decisions and the day-to-day running of the Post Office; yet they were not absorbed into management and their presence did not prevent the normal operation of collective bargaining.

5 G. D. H. Cole

Trade Unions as Co-Managers of Industry

From G. D. H. Cole, *The World of Labour*, Bell, 1913, pp. 352–67.

The first question usually asked of the syndicalist is whether he proposes that the workers should actually *own* the means of production. The answer given is practically unanimous: ownership, it is agreed, must be vested in the community as a whole. The difficulty arises when any attempt is made to define ownership. Generally, syndicalists mean, in vesting ownership in the community, not to surrender any share in control, but merely to do away with the idea of property altogether. Mr Graham Wallas has pointed out in a paper on syndicalism in the *Sociological Review*, July 1912, the essential ambiguity of the word 'ownership' and has advised that it should be dropped out of the controversy altogether. After all, the question is who is to control industry: if absolute control is placed in the hands of the unions, 'State' or 'common' ownership is merely a name.

The question, therefore, resolves itself purely into one of control. Here we may as well adopt Mr Webb's threefold distinction as a basis for argument.[1] The control of industry involves, first the decision what is to be produced, when and where it is to be produced, and in what quantities it is to be produced. Secondly, someone has to decide what the processes of production shall be, *how* production shall be carried on. Thirdly, the question of conditions, including all the matters now covered by the Factory Acts, at least some matters of 'discipline', pay, hours and the like have to be determined by some authority.

What share can producer and consumer have in deciding all these matters? The syndicalist, where he denounces the State and expresses his determination to sweep it away, has to give the producer control in everything. Even the community which owns is, to his mind, merely an abstraction, a convenient way of shelving the vexatious question of ownership. But even the syndicalist of this type does not propose to hand over absolute control to the particular class of producers engaged in each industry. He suggests that in the adjustment of supply

1. Mr Webb in a recent course of lectures on the subject.

to demand, the Trade Union Congress or its Executive and the local Trades Councils (*Bourses du Travail*) should take the place of the State and tell each section of producers what to produce. But the question what is to be produced is a matter either for the workers who actually produce it or for the community; it is not a matter for all the producers as producers, no matter what they produce. The Trade Union Congress and the Trades Councils, with their enlarged functions, are in fact merely the State and the municipality in disguise. They are (for this purpose) imperfect organizations of consumers and not real producers' organizations at all.

Thus, we find at the outset a part of the control of industry which cannot be handed over to the producer. Obviously, the consumer, the person *for* whom the goods are made, and not the person *by* whom they are made, must decide what is to be produced, when it is to be produced and in what quantities. Whether the consumer must also decide where it is to be produced is another matter and does not seem to be equally evident.[2] This, however, is of less importance, and the solution will emerge as the discussion proceeds.

This answer, however, simple and self-evident as it may at first sight appear, really begs the question. It presupposes the absolute irresponsibility of the producer to the individual consumer as well as to the State. The capitalist of the present day is theoretically in just such a position as this argument tries to prove absurd: he can produce what he likes, when, where and in what quantities he pleases. Only, the public, on its side, can refuse to buy and the refusal of the public is the capitalist's loss. The consumer controls the capitalist through his pocket. We cannot, therefore, say how far a trade union could safely be given a similar power, until we know what the trade union in question would be like. If it were a trading body exercising a monopoly, but selling its goods for its own profit, would not the consumer have on it exactly the check he has now on the trusts? And the trusts are not accused of making the wrong articles, but of charging too much for them. There may be other objections to such a body as the trade union would then be, but it would not be in the least likely to make the wrong sort of articles, or the wrong quantity or to manufacture them at the wrong time. Like the trust, it would be out to meet the demand of the market.

If, on the other hand, the trade union is not a trading body, if its members are to be paid at a fixed rate independent of the selling price

2. If the consumer gets his goods, it does not concern him *where* they are made.

77

of their produce, if, that is to say, profiteering is to be eliminated, then clearly the consumer must have some other means of directing their production. They must, in such a case, find out what to make by consultation with a body representing the consumers: they must negotiate with the State and be guided by the organized, instead of by the unorganized, will of the consumer.

There is, of course, a third possibility. The trade union may trade, not directly with the consumer, but with the State. The State may give its order and pay the union as a whole for the produce and this might well be in itself a sufficient measure of control. But enough has been said to make it clear at least that not even in this first sphere of control can an immediate answer be given. It will be necessary, then, to return to the question later on.

The second type of decision, according to Mr Webb's classification, has to do with the processes of production and it is round these that the dispute really centres. Trade unions have, no doubt, shown themselves in the past bad and partial judges of new industrial processes. Confronted with an irresponsible employing class, which thrust upon them exactly such processes as it chose, with regard solely to commercial value and heedless of the effect on the workers, they have come to regard every innovation with mistrust. They resisted the first introduction of machinery and they have been apt to rebel at every extension of its use. They have tried to bolster up the old system of apprenticeship and to perpetuate out-of-date methods of production; and they have done all this, not from any deep sense of the value of craftsmanship, but merely from a fear that wages would be lowered and men thrown out of employment. All these reproaches are habitually levelled at the unions when it is proposed to invest them with any degree of control over industrial methods. [...]

The opposition of labour to new processes arises from the use to which new processes have been put: where an invention in the hands of a capitalist employer is unwelcome, it will be very welcome when the workers, as a whole, are enabled to use it for the lightening of the daily task. The failure of modern trade unionism to accept new inventions is no reason for supposing that, were the danger of exploitation removed, the hostility would remain unaltered.

The producer, then, is clearly entitled to a very considerable share in the control of this second industrial sphere. Clearly, the trade union of the present, a 'fighting' or a 'friendly' organization devoted to 'collective bargaining' or 'mutual insurance', is not structurally fitted to take over such control. That is not the question at issue and the unfitness of actual trade unions to control processes will be generally admitted. The question is whether, could trade union structure be adapted to the purpose, it would be desirable to place such power in the hands of the producer.

Processes are, generally speaking, decided by experts. Under capitalism, invention is generally carried on, for profit, by independent investigators, working in the hope of hitting on a success, while the normal work of management, including the application of inventions, is carried on by a salaried manager. But, more and more, great firms are retaining their own inventors and paying them a fixed salary to experiment and give the firm the benefit of the results. The control of industrial processes and inventions may, then, be classed together as functions of 'management' – functions with which trade unions organized on the 'craft' basis of the present can, at the most, interfere only occasionally and, in the main, in a negative fashion. The question at issue is not whether 'management' should be conducted by mob rule, by its transference to the trade union as a whole, but whether the managers, who are also producers, should be responsible to, and elected by, the rest of the producers in the particular industry or by an external authority representing the consumers. Clearly, if the consumers elect, the managerial staff will remain independent of the workers, who will be organized against them as a trade union; if the producers elect, the managerial staff will be absorbed into the union, which will take on, to some extent, a hierarchical form.

The right to elect the rulers is a recognized principle of democratic political theory. Is there any reason why such a principle should not be applied to industry also? Indeed, is 'industrial democracy' possible unless it is so applied? In politics, we do not call democratic a system in which the proletariat has the right to organize and exercise what pressure it can on an irresponsible body of rulers: we call it modified aristocracy; and the same name adequately describes a similar industrial structure. If democracy can be applied to the workshop, the workers must elect and control their managers, in so far as those managers are concerned with the processes and not with the what, when and how much of production. [. . .]

It is often maintained that the producer's interest in these matters will be looked after well enough by the benevolent State and that, with his organization behind him, he need not fear the adoption of the more economical and less pleasant process unless it is really just, in the interests of the whole community, that it should be adopted.

Such a view would not be tenable in the case of a thoroughly democratic State of democratic men; still less is it true of the State of today or tomorrow. For the ordinary individual, the State is so far and the workshop so near. The strike moves the emotions and Parliament fails to do so just because a man cannot miss the governing class in the workshop, while few even realize its existence in the State. Could the workers elect and remove the governing members of industry, they would begin to exercise a real democratic control.

We may admit, however, that the State must to some extent share in the control of processes. This it can do by preserving an ultimate right to intervene in the control of the management with the producers. Even if the whole personnel of the industry, including foremen and managers of every grade, from the highest to the lowest, be elected, and re-elected at intervals, by the workers, the guild-socialist solution, as we shall see, still provides a safeguard whereby the State can secure the community against exploitation. To this also we shall have to return shortly.

The third sphere of control is that of conditions of labour, including the regulation of hours and wages. By those who envisage the trade union of the future as a purely independent body, engaged in negotiating with the State in a nationalized industry, much as it deals now with the private capitalist or trading concern, this has always seemed the chief sphere for control by the producers. They have, in fact, regarded the producer's part in control as confined, for good and all, to collective bargaining. But as they have, in many cases, combined this view with an urgent demand for the extension of trade boards, dealing with hours as well as wages, over the whole of industry, it would seem that they desire to make the share of the producer in control altogether illusory; for the method of trade boards amounts, essentially, to determination of wages and hours by the consumer, in accordance with a standard of life laid down by consumers' morality. It would seem, then, that such persons give with one hand only to take away with the other and that, while paying lip-service to the ideal of joint control by producer and consumer, they still leave all the power and all the authority on one side and, on the other, only a mere semblance of representation. [. . .]

The power of the trade union, as an external organization, to force up wages would certainly tend to disappear when nationalized industry became the rule; under the State, unless competitive industry remained beside it, wages would be determined by the native goodness of the consumers' hearts, as reflected in their rulers. A strike against a manager on a particular question would still be possible; strikes concerned with wages or hours would be strikes against the moral standard of the community – and, in the community's eyes, the lowness of the standard would in no way condone the offence.

Moreover, it is essential now for the unions to control wages and hours because their members are underpaid and overworked. The demand for the control of industry is something quite different from a demand for higher wages or shorter hours; it is essentially a demand to control industrial conditions and processes. It is in this sphere, if at all, that the demand must be met and it is useless to try to get round it by the promise of workshop committees and strong independent trade unions under collectivism.

In fact, at the close of our examination of the three spheres of industrial control, we have come back to what is, in the end, the crucial question. There are two opposing alternatives to capitalism, which we may call roughly syndicalism and collectivism. Is there a third in which they can be reconciled? [. . .]

The guild socialism of the *New Age* is a proposal for the co-management of industry by the State and the trade unions. Ownership of the means of production is to rest with the community, but the unions are to be definitely recognized by the State as the normal controllers of industry. They are to be statutory bodies exercising a monopoly, but admitting of free entry on reasonable conditions. The amount and character of their production are to be determined for them by demand,[3] but the methods and processes are to be left entirely in their hands; they are to elect their own officials and to be self-governing corporations with the widest powers. In fact, they are to resemble in their main characteristics the self-governing professions, the doctors and the lawyers, of the present. As the guilds will include everyone concerned in the industry, from general manager to labourers, they will be in essence 'guilds', i.e. associations not of *dependent*, but of *independent*, producers. [. . .]

There is no space here to enter fully into the guild socialism of the *New Age*,[4] which, indeed, is ultimately less important in its details than in the general ideal illumination which it sheds. Accepting the general idea of 'national guild' or trade union control, let us try to see a little more clearly exactly what it implies. Above all, let us ask ourselves whether the guild or trade union ought to be a trading body

3. Demand would be made articulate through the consumers' organizations, national and local, i.e. the State and the municipality.

4. See Orage (1914). See also the publications of the National Guilds League.

or to sell at prices fixed jointly with the State. We have seen that it would be dangerous to delegate absolute control of methods to any corporation which had not an interest in satisfying the consumer's needs and satisfying them at a reasonable price. Is there not a danger that the 'guild', if its members have nothing to gain by producing commodities as cheaply as possible, will tend to perpetuate anti-quated methods and processes? The doctors are hindered in doing this because they have a high standard of their own and also because they compete one with another; but can the guild be relied on to have a similar public spirit and public motive?

Advocates of control by the producers are more than a little apt to give the producer even more than his due and to make the share of the State in control to some extent illusory. The objections to union profiteering are as overwhelming as the objections to profiteering generally and the argument against the trust holds equally when every worker in it is a shareholder. The pay of the members of the guild must, then, not be of the nature of profit. The State must have a share in determining it and preserve some control. This it will preserve partly in the right to withhold supplies; but it will be necessary in addition to have some regular means of friendly cooperation. The State and the unions must not come into contact only as enemies and when they disagree; they must have some common body of general negotiation, in which the heads of the guilds may meet the heads of the State to arrange the production and services to be demanded of the guilds. In addition to the National Executive of each National Guild and to the Guild Congress, which represent the producers alone, there must be a joint board, equally representative of both parties. This body must be linked up, on the side of the consumers, with Parliament and with a government department; but it must not be directly under a government department and a cabinet minister. Normally, the guild must be left to administer its own internal affairs and to produce, by such methods as may seem to it best, the commodities required by this joint board and, ultimately, by the consumer. Producer and consumer together must control ends, while the guild looks after means.

Reference

ORAGE, A. R. (ed.) (1914), *National Guilds*, Bell.

6 H. A. Clegg

Trade Unions as an Opposition Which Can Never Become a Government

From H. A. Clegg, *Industrial Democracy and Nationalization*, Blackwell, 1951, pp. 19–28.

Our trade unions claim to be democratic institutions and, indeed, the claim must be allowed if trade unions are compared with many other institutions which make the same claim. But few of those who know them would be prepared to declare that their democracy is full and complete. Their constitutions present a great variety: some prefer to elect their officers, others choose to have them selected by an elected executive; some elect their executives and general secretaries by national ballot, others prefer to have them chosen by an annual conference; in all of them an annual or biennial conference is the supreme arbiter of policy, but some prefer to leave the executive free to act between conferences, whereas others check their executives by forcing them to have recourse to the ballot before action can be taken on certain matters. Despite this variety, two generalizations may be made, at least about our larger trade unions. The first, that their chief officials and most important executive members are wellnigh irremovable and that their policies, put forward as agreed proposals on a principle of 'executive solidarity', are generally supported by their conferences. Those who effectively govern the union rarely come before their members as a body to secure confirmation of their power and where they do there is no effective alternative body to choose to make the votes of the members fully effective. The most that the disgruntled member can do is to vote for an opposition candidate in an election to an official position or in an electoral division, whether by area or by trade, for one place in the executive. The opposition candidate may well be unknown and so stand little chance, and even if elected, is not in a position to effect, by himself, great changes in policy. The result is that very many trade union members may grumble about their unions' policy, but do not take the trouble to attempt the very difficult task of changing it.

The second generalization is that when there is something of an effective opposition, it does not show itself to be an asset. The checking devices popular in some of the older unions, when put into use, may do nothing more than make leadership weak and ineffective. Besides this, organized opposition in the British trade unions over the last twenty or thirty years has been largely communist. Before 1920, and particularly in the period 1910–20, 'unofficial reform movements' were common – for instance, among miners, railwaymen, engineers and building workers – but the experience of the shop stewards' movement in the First World War and of the communist-inspired 'Minority Movement' in the twenties has inclined union leaders – often rightly – to see communist influence behind any opposition movement and to take disciplinary action. In many unions this has not ousted the communists, but since power cannot be won by a single open contest at the polls, they have had to work by steps, marshalling block votes and capturing a place on a committee here and an official position there. Where this method begins to achieve success the result is that the leadership of the unions, nominally united in carrying out the agreed policy of the union, is split into bitter factions. When it has achieved complete success, leadership becomes united and effective, but even more solidly entrenched than ever, so that there is even less opportunity for organized opposition, and democracy is more remote than before.

These criticisms must not be exaggerated. A strong and sustained effort on the part of the membership of any union can change policy and leadership. If such efforts are rarely made, it may be assumed that the membership is tolerably contented. To those who argue that the explanation is apathy rather than contentment, the reply may be made that union members can still vote with their feet. This opportunity is limited in establishments where the closed shop or the 100 per cent union rule apply, but the field for its application is still wide and union leaders are sensitive to losses in membership. It is always open to the union leader to ask the man who criticizes the democracy of his union's institutions whether he could devise better. Trade union democracy is limited, but it is still democracy. If trade unions had no internal democracy there would be, at least where anything approaching a closed shop was in force, trade union despotism.

The main defence of this limited form of democracy, however, is the same as that of the limited democracy of our political parties. The primary task of a union is to protect its members and to protect them against someone – the employer. The trade union is thus industry's opposition – an opposition which can never become a government. This explanation fits well. There is need for an opposition in industry. Not only would industry be autocratic without it, but we must remember that industrial units are not voluntary associations and autocracy, therefore, becomes all the more dangerous. It is true that the involuntary nature of industry cannot be compared with that of the State, but, on the other hand, most men are tied more closely to their job than to their bowls' club, slate club or political party. Full employment has done much to reduce these ties, but the housing shortage has worked the other way. The main activities of the union can well be interpreted as opposition, as opposition to the wages the employer pays, the conditions of the establishment, the way he and his agents treat his men, in the endeavour to obtain improvements. And the union has the incentive to oppose, to discover, if possible, the shortcomings of the employer. For if employers had no short-comings there would be no need for trade unions – as we know them. The defence of the second-grade democracy of the trade unions is, then, that they must present a united front to the employers; that if their internal democracy were more perfect, industry would be less democratic, since its opposition would be too weak. This interpre-tation is attractive, but we must remember that there are important differences between politics and industry, and no analogy drawn from political democracy can be applied direct to industry without refer-ence to them.

In the first place, managers and workers are engaged in a common enterprise whose success depends on working together, even if unwillingly. This is true also of a nation, but the bonds uniting the members of a single enterprise or industry, and their common interest in its success, are much more clearly visible. Many, perhaps most, electors think of their part in politics as passive. The worker must take an active, if grudging, part in the work of the enterprise in which he is employed.

Secondly, there is no industrial equivalent to the electorate. Indus-trial managements elected by workers alone might well exploit the consumer. Workers are in much the same position in relation to their industry as the civil service is to the State. Civil servants are still only a small minority of the nation and the workers of most industries are greatly outnumbered by the consumers. Yet the consumers of most commodities are far too scattered and difficult to identify to form an electorate. Only the State itself has the organization and power to protect their interests. And if the State does regulate industry in their interest we have, in private industry, three parties – workers, managers and government.

The methods of governments and of the civil service are often thought to be too slow and bureaucratic to provide satisfactory industrial management. Industry is said to require more flexibility and greater speed of action. This is given as one of the main reasons for the adoption of the device of the public corporation in nationalized industry. In so far as it is valid, the forms of parliamentary democracy are unsuitable to industry.

If, then, the trade union is industry's opposition, it must pursue its ends by methods different from those of a parliamentary opposition. The aim of a parliamentary opposition is to defeat and replace the government. A trade union can never hope to become the government of industry, unless the syndicalist dream is fulfilled. It can never hope to do so by such constitutional means as present a broad and inviting path to the parliamentary opposition. Just because the trade union cannot attain its ends, revolution excepted, by replacing the industrial government which it faces, the industrial equivalent of legislation – the collective agreement – differs vitally from parliamentary laws. In Parliament, bills are normally proposed by the government and passed because of its majority. The opposition, if it can see any profit thereby, attacks the government's proposals, seeks to show that their effects will be harmful, and votes against them. It may, indeed, seek to amend some aspects of a bill and claim credit for any amendments which the government accepts; but the final act is the responsibility of the government alone, and the greater its unpopularity, the more obvious its failure, the more is the opposition pleased, for the failure of the government is the victory of the opposition. The collective agreement, however, is a joint affair which commits both parties equally. The trade union may accept certain clauses or even the whole agreement, because the alternative is the posting of terms which its members will have no alternative but to accept, but the signature of its officers is appended to the agreement and they are responsible for seeing that its terms are honoured by their members, until and unless it is revised.

The process of joint consultation, of which so much is heard today, has similar results. Joint consultation may be any exchange of views between workers or their representatives and employers or managers on matters of common interest, but it is usual for discussions which precede collective agreements to be called 'collective bargaining' and for the words 'joint consultation' to be reserved for discussion on other matters. It may go no further than an exchange of views and that in itself may be useful to both parties; but the purpose of joint consultation, in most instances, is to come to some understanding, short of a signed agreement with all that entails in responsibility and as a precedent, which is nevertheless a *joint* understanding; the one party is morally bound to carry it out and the other to give its support. Thus we can see that the essential difference between parliamentary and industrial opposition is this: the parliamentary opposition attacks the government in order to discredit the government and thereby to bring nearer the day when it shall be given the responsibility for doing better; the industrial opposition attacks the employer in order to force him to accept an agreement more favourable to its members, for which it will take, along with the employer, a share of responsibility.

Out of this arises one of the most difficult problems of industrial democracy – the problem of trade union responsibility. The trade union opposes the employer in order to secure from him more favourable treatment for its members, but the wider the scope of its collective agreements and the more inclusive the coverage of the understandings arising out of joint consultation, the more probable it is that any individual action taken by the employer or his agents, which has an effect upon the workers, is taken within the terms of an agreement or under the shelter of an understanding. If any worker or group of workers feels a grievance arising out of the act, the union cannot give support and is even bound to use its influence to persuade acquiescence. Admittedly, there arise under any collective agreement or understanding a host of debatable issues in which the union may seek to show that the action of the worker is justified and the action of the employer wrong, but however wide the contested frontier, each agreement or understanding makes more ample the territory in which the action of the employer is unchallengeable, unless it breaks the agreement and until the agreement is revised. An employer may pay pensions to his workers. The union may contest every pension paid – without effect, for what right has it to interfere in a scheme drawn up by the employer and financed by his generosity? To achieve its ends, the union may then propose a better scheme, discuss it with the employer, modify its proposals and finally come to an agreement, which is drawn up and signed. Thereafter it can challenge only those cases in which there are reasonable grounds for claiming that the employer has infringed the agreement.

Despite agreements, grievances arise and the function of the union is then violently changed. From being champion of the workers, it must change to acting as policeman for a joint agreement with the employer. This function is admittedly necessary, in the interest of the union and in the interest of the workers themselves; but it is not so popular, nor so satisfactory a role, as that of champion of the oppressed. It is out of this necessity that there arises much of the discontentment that leads to unofficial strikes; and in so far as this is the cause of unofficial strikes, the communists or other malcontents on whom the blame is laid are carrying out the function of opposition. They may misrepresent, they may exaggerate grievances, but is it not the task of an opposition to do so? This is not, of course, the only cause of difference between 'rank-and-filers' and union executives. In any large-scale organization the different viewpoints of those at the centre and those at the periphery must cause some trouble; and in a trade union, in which the means at the disposal of the executive to discipline its members are not usually of great strength, the trouble is likely to come to the surface; trade unions are not less democratic because of that.

We can see at once that there is an overwhelming case against trade union control of industry. If the trade union became the government of industry it would be transformed from a largely voluntary to a largely involuntary association. All the shortcomings of its internal democracy, which may be justified when its primary function is one of opposition, would become powerful engines of oppression; and there would be no recourse to help against that oppression, for with trade union government of industry, trade union opposition would have ceased. Similar objections can be made to joint control; in so far as the joint control was effective, it would work in the same way as trade union control, and in so far as opposition remained, industrial government would become a weak and unhappy coalition. It is unnecessary to mount a heavy attack against ideas which live on only as the pale ghosts of the enthusiasms of the crude but heroic army of the early syndicalists. The point to be made is that, even whilst it avoids these obvious pitfalls, a trade union, by binding the employer, and therefore itself, over an even wider field of industrial activity, may find itself in an almost equally dangerous position.

It would, however, be of no assistance to the union to advise it to avoid responsibility at all costs. For by avoiding responsibility the trade union condemns itself to the easy but largely ineffective role of permanent opposition. [...]

Can this be called industrial democracy? It has already been pointed out that trade unions have not yet entirely accepted this interpretation even in the establishments where it is carried out most fully and most sincerely by the employer. The task of opposition becomes very different from that of parliamentary opposition. Parliamentary opposition assumes and seeks to reveal that the government is wrong; but the assumption of this interpretation is that the management of industry is fundamentally sound and requires independent opposition only to guide it into the right course, which the employer is only too eager to discover. Dare we make this assumption?

In some ways industrial paternalism comes closer to the theories of the syndicalists than does the interpretation which makes opposition the primary function of industrial democracy. To explain this, we must digress into political theory. Political theorists have always differed as to whether the cooperation necessary to any stable and happy society is 'natural' or 'artificial'. The theorist of parliamentary democracy must believe that the device of government, resting ultimately upon the coercive powers of the State, is necessary to produce sufficient cooperation; and yet that, to preserve freedom under such a government, the essentially disintegrating force of opposition must be permitted and even encouraged. A free society must depend on a balance between disintegrating and unifying forces. The anarchist, and with him the syndicalist, believes that a unified society would arise 'naturally' if only the restraints of coercive government and class distinctions were removed. The paternalistic theory, based on the analogy of the family, also accepts a 'natural' unity, but makes it dependent, not on equality and liberty, but on the functioning of society as an organism in which the various members carry out their different duties, whatever they may be. The theory which lies behind the modern progressive employer's approach to industrial democracy is not pure paternalism, for he accepts independent trade unionism. But it contains, and must contain, elements of paternalism. Leadership in the common effort comes from above. The pressure is not from below. Progressive management seeks to draw its employees into an intelligent cooperation in its undertaking. Independent trade unions are accepted in the hope that they may play their part in achieving this end. But since unions must remain outside the undertaking to maintain their independence, since they must remain a permanent opposition, they cannot take the lead in this and they must, for the same reasons, avoid complete assimilation to the management's purpose.

The progressive employer and the syndicalist, then, have this in common, that they wish to make industry work through genuine cooperation in a common purpose. Moreover, both of them can argue that their primary object is human happiness; and the argument that working together to a common end is productive of happiness may be readily accepted. It is much harder to demonstrate that deliberate opposition leads to happiness. [...]

There have long been two schools of democrats, the one seeking to interpret democracy passively, as a means of ensuring as far as possible that governments act according to the wishes of the people, and the other arguing that democracy must mean more than that, must mean the active participation of the people in the work of government. The first school have replied that 'active participation' slips so easily into the assumption of a common purpose and thence to some mystical 'general will'. Then those whose actions and ideas seem contrary to the 'general will' are regarded as evil and soon suppressed as disrupters of the common purpose. So that the last state of the democracy of active participation is indistinguishable from totalitarianism. Admittedly, this danger would be avoided if the active participation was in the work of an anarchist society; but few of us today have the courage to be anarchists. Although working in industry involves active participation in industry, we cannot, for these reasons, accept 'active participation', based as it must be, if anarchism is avoided, on managerial leadership, as a full and adequate definition of industrial democracy. We must also include the trade union as an opposition body which, however beneficent the employer, however eager he may be to carry his workers along with him in everything that affects them, can never be absorbed into an organic industrial order; for if it is absorbed, where is the guarantee of democracy? Progressive management, in accepting trade unionism, goes beyond a purely paternalistic 'active participation', but its view of industrial democracy remains necessarily a managerial view. Trade unionism, while desirous of intelligent cooperation, sees its primary function as protection of workers against employers and managers, and has an equally valid approach to industrial democracy.

We may well, however, accept progressive management as part of industrial democracy, and as the more important part the smaller the industrial group we are considering. To deserve the name democratic it must be management which accepts and comes to terms with trade unionism, for, although without that it may be a paternalism which cares satisfactorily for the welfare and happiness of its workers, there is no independent barrier against degeneration into autocracy. No internal scheme of representation can deserve to be called independent and there is a firmer foundation for democracy in trade union opposition to the most autocratic employer than in the undertaking of the most benevolent of paternalists without trade unionism. The more autocratic the employer and the larger the group we consider, the more necessary it is to stress the element of opposition in democracy. For we have learned to believe that in a large, and particularly in an involuntary association, an organic conception of democracy is likely to be a cover for coercion and oppression in the service of a mystical common purpose and general will.[1]

As soon as we reject any simple and unique definition of industrial democracy we can see that a number of combinations of its elements – trade union opposition and willing participation of workers with management in a common enterprise – is possible and that there may be ample room for argument about which combination is the most democratic. This need not disturb us; surely it needs no elaborate argument to show that democracy is a relative matter and that the determination of more or less is in large measure dependent on the frailties of human judgement and on the field in which it is to work. In fact, there exist many combinations of the elements of industrial democracy in different establishments and in different industries, and different combinations may seem to give equally satisfactory or unsatisfactory results.

1. It is worth noting that the currently popular study of 'human relations in industry' has concentrated its attention mainly on inquiry into relations within small industrial groups and has also, perhaps because of this, neglected the importance of power relations within industry. When its exponents talk of industrial democracy they therefore tend to stress the importance of common endeavour to the exclusion of the need for independent checks to power.

7 Paul Blumberg

The Case against Clegg's View of Industrial Democracy

From Paul Blumberg, *Industrial Democracy: The Sociology of Participation*, Constable, 1967, pp. 139, 144–6 and 153–4.

The recent discussions of industrial democracy by Hugh Clegg – one of Britain's leading industrial-relations experts – are extremely important for the entire subject of workers' management [Clegg, 1951 and 1960]. In essence, Clegg's views represent the culmination of an ideological and political retreat from the idea of workers' control, an idea which reached the peak of its influence in Britain in the period between 1910 and 1922 with the influence of syndicalism in British unions, the rise of guild socialism and the development of the shop stewards' movement. What Clegg offers is the latest, most contemporary, and most sociologically sophisticated refutation of workers' management, a refutation which has been embraced by the Centre and Right of the British Labour party and used as a justification for opposing any extension of workers' management in the nationalized sector. Clegg directs his theses both at and beyond the British industrial scene and stresses that his arguments against workers' management have near-universal applicability. It is therefore crucial to assess these arguments here. [. . .]

Clegg argues that any attempt by modern-day 'industrial democrats' or enthusiasts of workers' control to extend the influence of workers or their unions or other workers' representatives into the realm of management threatens to destroy the very basis of industrial democracy as it exists today: the autonomous trade unions. Advocates of workers' control would create an industrial despotism, not an industrial democracy, because they would destroy independent trade unions which are the bulwark of industrial pluralism which in turn is the essential component of industrial democracy. Clegg believes that the kind of complete workers' control envisaged by those firm believers in total industrial self-government is possible only 'if industry is operated by small independent groups of free associates'. Unfortunately, however, such workers' control is incompatible with the irreversible large-scale organization of industry today. But this should not be a cause of concern. Rather, Clegg advises that, like Molière's *bourgeois gentilhomme* who never realized he had been speaking prose all his life, those contemporary worshippers of workers' control should realize that industrial democracy need not be a remote aspiration, but rather is an accomplished fact, and lies in the existence of a free trade union movement whose activities are accepted by modern management. [. . .]

I find Clegg's arguments both logically and empirically weak, and thus desperately in need of correction. First of all, his definition of democracy is simplistic and inadequate, for he tends to believe that the mere existence of an opposition has certain magical properties which guarantee democracy wherever it is found. The truth of the matter, however, is that opposition, though one means of achieving democracy, is neither a necessary nor a sufficient condition of democracy. For example, there are historically many circumstances where opposition has existed but where political democracy was completely absent. Medieval society saw conflicts between rival royal and aristocratic elites for power and was thus partially pluralistic, but certainly not democratic in any meaningful sense. In England before the second Reform Act which extended the suffrage widely, there was political opposition, political rivalry between Whigs and Tories, but little democracy as far as the vast majority of the population was concerned.

On the other hand, there are numerous examples of democracy, mainly on a small scale, which have flourished without any organized opposition – the town meeting, the dissenting chapel, the trade union lodge, the consumers' cooperative. And modern Mexico has achieved a measure of political democracy without the presence of a meaningful opposition political party.

I believe, therefore, that to define democracy exclusively in terms of opposition is a mistake; democracy is much more appropriately defined as the *accountability* of leadership to an electorate which has the power to remove that leadership. In this sense, the role of opposition is to make accountability effective by facilitating the selection of alternate sets of leaders. It should be made clear, however, that the mere existence of political opposition, without accountability, does not assure democracy.

Clegg himself realizes the importance of accountability to democracy when he discusses nationalized industry, and he argues correctly that industries must, if they are to be democratically organized at all, be accountable in some fashion to the public. With respect to the socially owned sector, he argues that 'we must have some means of public accountability and control'.

Now, if we are correct in arguing that democracy is best defined in terms of accountability, rather than in terms of opposition, then surely one must conclude that there is very little democracy – industrial or otherwise – in the ordinary trade-union-organized factory, as Clegg claims there is. For although the trade unions do constitute an opposition, nevertheless the employer is only minimally accountable to the union or the workers for decisions which lie outside the immediate job area. Thus, trade union opposition in itself does not constitute a sufficient condition for genuine industrial democracy.

But suppose we grant Clegg's definition of democracy as being synonymous with the existence of organized opposition. Even if we do so, his argument fails and the analogy he has made from politics to industry will not stand. Remember that Clegg has argued that in government the 'essence' of democracy is organized opposition and that in industry the same is true, so that the existence of trade union opposition is sufficient to guarantee industrial democracy. However, the crucial condition of any true multi-party system, or any system where political opposition exists, is that one or more parties is always ready and able to *replace* the party in power. An 'opposition' whose role is confined to protesting, making suggestions or criticizing, but which can never itself *assume power*, is not an effective or a genuine opposition at all.

Now, it is obvious that British trade unions, in the public as well as the private sector, can never 'replace' their employer and become the ruling power in industry as, for example, the Labour party may replace the Conservative party in government. Clegg himself is quite aware of this, for as he admits parenthetically, 'The trade union is thus industry's opposition – *an opposition which can never become a government*.' Further on, he states the idea again, but this time more explicitly.

The aim of a parliamentary opposition is to defeat and replace the government. A trade union can never hope to become the government of industry, unless the syndicalist dream is fulfilled [which Clegg believes is impossible].

What Clegg does not seem to realize is that with this admission his analogy between political and industrial democracy completely breaks down and his entire argument lies in ruins. If trade unions have no power to replace the present government of industry but are merely able to challenge management in a carefully delineated sphere of its activity – the job area – then, in terms of Clegg's own definition, there is no pluralism, no choice, no alternative and no opposition – in short, no democracy. Nowhere does Clegg meet this issue.

In summary: (a) Clegg's definition of democracy is faulty. He defines it in terms of the formal existence of an opposition rather than in terms of the accountability of leadership to the led. As employers are not accountable to their employees or to trade unions for the vast majority of their decisions, industrial democracy cannot be said to exist in the ordinary trade-union-organized enterprise; (b) even if we accept Clegg's definition of democracy as synonymous with the existence of opposition, industrial democracy is still absent in public and private enterprise, for the trade union does not constitute a genuine opposition in the full sense of the word, i.e. one that is ready and able to assume power and replace the present leadership. If this is true, then industrial democracy is something still to be attained and not, as Clegg argues, something to be cherished as an accomplished fact. [. . .]

Clegg fears that trade union management would lead to a new form of industrial despotism, not to industrial democracy, because, by taking responsibility for management, the unions would be unable to protect their workers' interests. This has also been contradicted by the Histadrut experience. First, workers in Histadrut firms are organized into an autonomous National Organisation of Workers in Histadrut Enterprises and, at the plant level, relations between management and the workers' committee are characterized by a genuine 'two-sided bargaining approach'. In brief, a healthy conflict of interest exists between the two groups. Second, there is regular grievance machinery in *Koor* firms to settle differences which arise between the union and management. It is significant that most of the levels through which grievances pass are weighted in favour of the trade union, and Derber found that *Koor* personnel managers thought that this grievance procedure was unfair to management. But workers had their complaints, too, and believed that management usually came out on top. Third, at least one study has shown that Histadrut managers tend to think like managers in the private sector, and, more important, trade union leaders representing workers in the Histadrut sector tend to think like trade union representatives in private enterprise, i.e. they have worker-oriented attitudes and have not been coopted by management in any sense.

Fourth, the trade unions in Histadrut plants have *more* power and influence over management than they do in private establishments. Especially regarding discipline, transfers, promotions and the like, the Histadrut management regularly consults the workers' representatives, and to a degree unknown in the private sector. Fifth, wages and conditions in *Koor* plants are generally superior to those in private industry and are recognized as such by the workers who regard an appointment in a *Koor* factory as a privilege: job security is much greater, wages are as high or higher, and fringe benefits are 10–20 per cent better.

Finally, management's authority in Histadrut enterprises does not take the form of despotic, arbitrary, and unchecked rule over groups of docile workers who have been abandoned by their trade union, as suggested by Clegg's thesis, but, on the contrary, management tends to be weak and timid, from the level of the foreman upwards.

References

CLEGG, H. A. (1951), *Industrial Democracy and Nationalization*, Blackwell.
CLEGG, H. A. (1960), *A New Approach to Industrial Democracy*, Blackwell.

8 The Bullock Committee on Industrial Democracy

The Role of Trade Union Representatives on Management Boards

From The Dept of Trade, *Industrial Democracy: Committee of Inquiry Report*, chmn A. Bullock, HMSO, 1977, pp. 160–77.

The role of trade unions

Many of those submitting evidence suggested to us that employee representation on the board should be based, not on trade union machinery, but on works councils or consultative committees which are separate from collective bargaining and which represent all employees, whether union members or not. Such councils and committees, it has often been argued, are an essential preliminary to representation on the board, encouraging participation below board level and providing the machinery through which employee representatives are appointed and can report back.

We are surprised that so many people in this country have placed so much emphasis on works councils and similar consultative committees. For, as a senior official of the International Labour Organization has pointed out:

A rapid survey of the role played by works councils around the world shows that there is often disenchantment with their functioning. There is a broad consensus in many countries that works councils have not lived up to the expectations that were placed in them when they were first initiated. Many examples could be given from various parts of the world to show that the works council is not, perhaps, an ideal means of handling employer–employee relations at enterprise level. One of the reasons for this seems to be the lack of real decision-making powers possessed by most councils. Experience has shown that a purely advisory arrangement under which workers are given information and may express an opinion, but have no influence on whether this opinion is taken into account or not is not likely to create much enthusiasm or even interest (Schregle, 1976, p. 8).

At least one major association of employers in the United Kingdom has taken this point. The Coventry and District Engineering Employers' Association has concluded on the basis of a survey which it undertook on the European experience of worker participation that:

The procedures, systems and institutions which have been established in most European countries for providing joint consultation or decision-making have been, until recently, largely alternatives to collective bargaining or varying forms of it. This is particularly true of works councils or committees which are a common feature of the European scene apart from Ireland and Great Britain. This factor has been overlooked in the debate on worker participation and industrial democracy, which has tended to assume rather more for the works council system than the facts justify. It is doubtful whether employees in companies with obligatory works councils have had any more sense of involvement than their British counterparts and the survey suggests that works councils have rarely inhibited managements' freedom to decide and act accordingly. This view is substantiated by the growing shop steward movement in Europe, increasing resistance to national or district bargaining in favour of plant bargaining and the pressure for increased industrial democracy (Perry, 1974, p. 119).

Indeed, as the Coventry and District Engineering Employers' Association implies, works councils have generally tended to decline in importance and, in spite of recent attempts in some European countries to strengthen them, they are increasingly being overshadowed by the growth of shop steward organization and workplace bargaining. Germany may be considered an exception to this generalization because there works councils have extensive statutory powers; but it would be singularly inappropriate to introduce German-style works councils into the United Kingdom because their functions are generally performed here by shop stewards' organizations[1] in workplace bargaining.

In general, the growth of shop steward and equivalent trade union organization and workplace bargaining has proceeded much further in the United Kingdom than in Europe. The number of shop stewards and the incidence of workplace bargaining in the United Kingdom have increased dramatically over the past twenty years and have resulted in a decline in consultative committees. Research undertaken ten years ago for the Donovan Commission concluded that consultative committees

cannot survive the development of effective shop-floor organisation. Either they must change their character and become essentially negotiating committees carrying out functions which are indistinguishable from the processes of shop-floor bargaining, or they are boycotted by shop stewards and, as the influence of the latter grows, fall into disuse (Royal Commission on Trade Unions and Employers' Associations (The Donovan Commission), 1968, p. 54).

1. The phrase 'shop steward' is used generically throughout the report to refer to trade union lay representatives at the place of work.

98

The growth of workplace bargaining and the decline of joint consultation has, of course, taken place unevenly across the private sector, and it is still possible to point to companies with consultative committees which are the sole form of representation within the plant or which exist independently alongside the negotiating machinery. But, even where the form of the old consultative system remains, for the great majority of large companies the employee representatives are always shop stewards or equivalent representatives and the consultative machinery is closely integrated with the negotiating machinery.

Given the rapid and continuing development at the workplace of a representative structure based on trade union machinery, any attempt to bypass this structure would be seen as an attack on trade unions and collective bargaining and would be fiercely resisted. The dangers of proceeding with industrial-relations legislation without trade union support have been amply demonstrated, and we think it is impractical to contemplate a system of representation on the board which does not have the support of the trade union movement.

Even if it were practical in the United Kingdom to attempt to erect an alternative structure to trade unionism on which board level representation could be based, it would be undesirable. For the policy of successive governments over the course of the twentieth century, and particularly in the last ten years, has been to encourage and strengthen trade unionism and the collective bargaining which it makes possible. We have no wish to deviate from this trend. For we agree with the Donovan Commission that, over a wide range of issues, 'collective bargaining is the most effective means of giving workers the right to representation in decisions affecting their working lives, a right which is or should be the prerogative of every worker in a democratic society' (The Donovan Commission, 1968, p. 54). To put it another way, since trade unions are necessary to ensure that employees have an effective voice in decision-making both within the company and within the wider society, we wish to ensure that board level representation is designed in such a way that it does not undermine the unions' representative capacity.

There are also other reasons why employee representatives on the board should be based on a single channel of representation through trade union machinery. Such machinery would provide the expertise

and independent strength necessary to support employee representatives and to enable them to play an effective role in decision-making
on the board. It would also provide an established and trusted channel
of communication to and from the shop floor through which employee
representatives could keep in touch with their constituents. Perhaps
most important, integrating employee representatives into a wider
system of representation based on trade union machinery would be
the most effective way of ensuring that board level representation did
not conflict with collective bargaining but that the two processes
operated in a mutually supportive way.

What we propose in this chapter, therefore, is a system of employee
representation on the board which is based on trade union machinery.
In practice, we think that the trade union machinery which most
employees will wish to use is that which is internal to their company,
the shop steward organization and its equivalent, rather than that
which is external to it, the branch, the district committee, and the
national executive. We see considerable value in shop stewards being
the key figures in a system of board level representation. They are
almost invariably elected by trade union members at the workplace
and because their constituencies are small (generally between fifty and
sixty employees) they are kept in close touch with those they represent; indeed, the extent to which members are involved in the election
of shop stewards and equivalent representatives and in the activities
of those representatives on behalf of their constituents is probably
greater than in most other bodies which are organized on democratic
lines. Moreover, as the Donovan Commission has pointed out, and
the workplace industrial-relations surveys of 1972 and 1973 have
confirmed, shop stewards are 'rarely agitators pushing workers
towards unconstitutional action' (Parker, 1975, p. 98). Rather, they
are generally 'supporters of order exercising a restraining influence
on their members in conditions which promote disorder ... more
of a lubricant than an irritant' (The Donovan Commission, 1968, pp.
28–9). We think that companies in this country will find it useful
to have such people on their boards.

It follows from our support of the principle of a single channel of
employee representation through trade union machinery that our
proposals in this chapter do not provide any special rights for
employees who are not members of a trade union. As we demonstrated in Chapter 2, the proportion of non-unionists is generally small

in the large companies in the private sector to which our proposals apply, and most of these are white-collar employees, the group among whom unionization is increasing most rapidly. Nevertheless, we have carefully considered the arguments put to us about the position of non-unionized employees in general; the position of particular groups of non-unionized employees; and a different but related problem, the position of employees who are represented by staff associations and professional associations which are not affiliated to the TUC.

Although our proposals do not make any special provisions for non-unionized employees, we do not wish to create a system whereby a trade union representing a minority can force the majority, whether unionized or not, to accept board level representation against its will. Hence we have built into our proposals a ballot in which all employees will have the right to show whether they wish to be represented on the board of their company through trade union machinery. If the ballot is favourable, we do not see how or why we should make special provision for those who have chosen not to join a trade union and who are thus unable to speak with a collective voice. We believe that if employees wish to be represented on the board, they must be prepared to organize at lower levels to make representation on the board effective. In taking this view we are not introducing a new principle into industrial relations. When unions engage in collective bargaining, they generally determine the terms and conditions of employment for everyone employed in the grades for which they are recognized, not just for those who happen to be union members. Employers would find it highly disruptive if this principle were not followed in collective bargaining. And we think they would find it highly disruptive if the same principle were not followed in employee representation on the board.

Some people have suggested to us that managers and other professional groups play a particularly important role in the running of companies and often occupy a unique position between the board and other employers – at one point representing the company in discussions with employees and at another being employees themselves – and they have argued that a special seat on the board should be reserved for these groups. Provided that professional and managerial employees are organized collectively, as increasingly many of them are, we can see no reason why they should not be represented on the board among the employee representatives. But we do not think that

101

a special seat should be reserved for them on the board by law. It would be unfortunate for legislation on industrial democracy to give the impression that certain employees had a special and presumably higher status in the eyes of the law than other employees. In any case, we find it difficult to accept that any group of employees should be able to demand a seat on the board by right unless they constitute a significant proportion of the company's total employment. The Federal Republic of Germany's Codetermination Act of 1976 illustrates the problem which arises if board seats are reserved for small groups. This Act gives the right to at least one of the employees' seats to the senior executives of the company. The provision was included at the insistence of the minority partner in the West German coalition government. As has been pointed out by its opponents, the result has been to give a group of employees constituting on average five per cent of total employment in West German companies, the right to 16 per cent of employee representation on company boards.

Nothing in our proposals prevents a staff association, a professional association, or any other employee organization which is not affiliated to the TUC from being represented on a company's board. To play a role in such representation an employee organization has only to satisfy two conditions: it must be 'independent' of the company but 'recognized' by it. The Employment Protection Act 1975 provides procedures by which trade unions may claim recognition and establish their independence.[2] If an employee organization cannot meet these requirements, then we do not think it should be granted any rights in a law on industrial democracy.

Triggering the system

Regardless of what role trade unions play in a system of employee representation on the board, the system itself must first be set in motion. We have considered three main ways in which the system can be introduced: by making it mandatory, by requests from recognized trade unions, and by ballots of all employees.

West Germany provides the best known example of a mandatory system. There, regardless of whether trade unions, works councils or employees are interested in being represented, companies of a certain

2. Employment Protection Act 1975: for recognition, see sections 11–16; for independence, see sections 7–8.

size and type must put employee representatives on their supervisory boards. In the various statutes there is no trigger mechanism as such; the law simply requires board level representation on an appointed day. In contrast, the Swedish system is optional: board representation can be requested by one or more recognized trade unions which represent over 50 per cent of the company's employees. The relevant section of the 1973 Act stipulates that

decisions on the establishment of employee representation shall be taken by a local trade union which is bound by a collective agreement in relation to the enterprise and represents more than half of the enterprise's employees, or similarly bound trade unions which taken together are of that extent.[3]

The third method may be linked with the previous two and incorporates a secret ballot. Denmark provides an example of how it may work. Danish law requires that before representation on the board becomes mandatory on companies there should be a secret ballot of all employees in the company to see if a majority of them wish to be represented on the board. The right to request a ballot rests with the company's consultation committee or with one or more unions representing over 10 per cent of the workforce, or with 10 per cent of the workforce itself.

We think that the first of these methods is undesirable because it forces board representation on employees whether they want it or not. To operate a system of board representation for the benefit of employees who are interested in it is a recipe for ensuring that it will become moribund. The second method, a request from one or more recognized trade unions representing more than half of a company's employees, seems a more viable proposition: it ensures that board level representation is not introduced against the wishes of the company's major trade unions, without whose support it could not be a success. This method does not directly assess the wishes of the employees themselves, however, and many individuals and organizations have suggested to us that employees, as distinct from the unions to which they may belong, are often indifferent, if not hostile, to the notion that they should be represented on company boards.

We believe that the most effective way of meeting this argument

3. Act relating to Board representation of employees in joint stock companies and cooperative associations. Adopted by Swedish Parliament December 1972, Section 7.

is to put it to the test by asking all the employees in a company what they think. More specifically, before a company would be required to accept employee representatives on its board, a secret ballot would be held. Unless otherwise agreed by all the parties concerned, the ballot would be held at the company's expense and in company time and on company property, thereby giving employees every chance to vote should they wish to do so. All full-time employees would be eligible to vote, including those on short time or laid off, but not part-time employees. In industries with very high labour turnover, unions and employers might wish to stipulate that employees should also have a minimum period of service with the company before being eligible to vote. We think it important, however, that as few people as possible are disfranchised, and that if a minimum period of service were stipulated, it should be quite short, say six months.

The question of what majority should be required in such a ballot proved to be a difficult one. We consider that in a matter of such importance to a company's employees, it is reasonable to require not only that a majority of the eligible employees who vote should be in favour of the proposals but also that such employees should constitute a sizeable proportion of the electorate. It would be possible, and not altogether unusual, to require a minimum turn-out as a precondition of the effectiveness of the ballot, but this could result in an abstention being as significant and, in certain circumstances, even more significant, than a vote against. In other words, abstention would be ambivalent: it could equally indicate apathy or boycott. To overcome this difficulty, we propose that, in addition to the requirement for a simple majority to vote in favour of the proposals, such majority should represent at least one-third of the eligible employees. It may be objected that this further requirement erects an additional hurdle for employees to overcome before employee representation becomes effective. We do not deny this, but consider that the provision for the ballot to be held in company time on company property should produce a high turn-out. It may be objected that the appropriate proportion should be one-half, rather than one-third, of the work-force. We believe that because of illness and the geographical dispersal of employees in many large enterprises it is wrong to assume that, for any practical purposes, the effective electorate is more than about 80 per cent of all eligible employees. On this basis, we believe that the affirmative vote of one-third strikes the right balance between these competing objections. Thus, if the *turn-out* was only one-third of the electorate, every vote cast would need to be in favour. For a 40 per cent turn-out a majority of 5:1 would be required (i.e. $33\frac{1}{3}$ per cent of the electors voting 'yes' to $6\frac{2}{3}$ per cent voting 'no'). Even for a 50 per cent turn-out at least a 2:1 majority (i.e. $33\frac{1}{3}$ per cent of the electors voting 'yes' and $16\frac{2}{3}$ voting 'no') would be required.

The balloting process which we have recommended would give unions which were opposed to employee representation on boards an opportunity to campaign against it. It would also give all employees, whether unionized or not, the right to be involved in the decision. Where most of them were opposed to employee representation through trade union machinery, they could prevent it being introduced. We believe then that the secret ballot will be an important democratic check. We hope also that it will have the effect of involving everyone in the company in the debate about employee representation on the board. For the ballot to be a success the trade unions will have to explain to employees what is involved in board representation and employees will have to be sufficiently interested to turn out to vote. We noted in Chapter 5 the widespread belief that most employees do not want to be represented on the board and that trade unions are not democratic enough to speak on behalf of their members. The ballot we propose will allow both of these propositions to be tested.

Reporting back

We emphasized in Chapter 8 the importance of employee representatives keeping in touch with their constituents; if they do not, they will be of little use to the board or to those they represent, for they will not provide the necessary communication link between the two. Here we briefly discuss what reporting back may involve.

Reporting back to the membership is generally a central feature of trade union organization, and hence the law does not need to require that a system of reporting back should be created. It need only emphasize the desirability of this practice and leave it to the recognized unions to work out how employee representatives can best be included in the existing union communication network within the company. Indeed, one of the reasons we have opted for a single channel of representation through trade union machinery is that it provides an excellent means by which employee representatives can keep in touch with their constituents.

An obvious starting-point for any system of reporting back would be the Joint Representation Committee. It would provide a continuing reference point for employee representatives, and they would be expected to report regularly to it. The members on the JRC would then have the task of making reports to other parts of the trade union structure – the branches of individual unions, joint shop steward committees, or other joint union committees – which in turn would have the job of disseminating information more widely to the union membership and to employees as a whole. The employee representatives themselves might occasionally make reports to these lower-level parts of the trade union structure and on occasions to groups of employees, so that the hierarchical system does not cut them off from those on the shop floor.

This is only one way in which a system of reporting back might be developed. There are numerous other options open to the unions. If they wished, they could create a special structure to deal with reports from employee representatives on the board, or, where a company has a works council system which formally involves trade unions, they might decide to use it as one of the channels of communication. The form of the reporting back machinery will no doubt vary from one company to another. But whatever form the machinery takes, it must enable employee representatives to keep in touch with those they represent.

Employee representation and collective bargaining

We noted in Chapter 6 that the view has been expressed that there is a fundamental and irreconcilable incompatibility between board level representation and collective bargaining. The clearest statement of this view came from the Electrical, Electronic, Telecommunication and Plumbing Union (EETPU), which argued that the job of trade unions is through collective bargaining 'to consider, contest, and oppose, if necessary, the exercise of managerial prerogatives'. 'It is not the responsibility of work people to manage the enterprise'; indeed, 'it is essential that trade unions retain their independence' (EETPU, 1976, paragraph 24 et seq.).

We agree with the EETPU that trade unions must retain their independence. But we do not see why this independence need be compromised by representation on the board. If, as we propose in Chapter 9, the employee representatives on the board are equal in number to the shareholder representatives, and if the former are backed by the strength of the trade unions in the company, they will carry both weight and influence on the board. Indeed, they will be able where necessary to oppose a policy not only on the board but also in collective bargaining.

More generally, we see no necessary contradiction between board level representation and collective bargaining. Rather, we believe that they are similar and complementary processes. Both contain elements of cooperation and conflict, harmony and discord. Both by their very natures involve the mutual dependence of union and management. Perhaps most important, both have the same basic objective: to enable employees to participate in decision-making in the enterprise in which they work. And hence both involve participation in 'management', not in the sense of participating in the executive tasks which must be performed to implement major company policies, but in the sense of participating in the formulation of these strategic policies. As the TUC has pointed out in its report on industrial democracy, 'the extension of joint control or joint regulation in any form, including collective bargaining, is a *de facto* sharing of the management prerogative' (TUC, 1976, p. 37). In short, board level representation does not raise any new issues of principle for trade unions which already engage in collective bargaining. It simply creates an additional means by which they may influence the managerial process, particularly those aspects of this process which collective bargaining is inadequate to handle by itself.

Some people have suggested to us that one way of avoiding any confusion and conflict between board level representation and collective bargaining would be to require employee representatives to relinquish all other union offices, such as being a shop steward, once they are on the board. We think this is an unrealistic and unhelpful proposal which, by reducing the coordination of trade union policy in collective bargaining and at board level, might produce the very confusion and conflict which it was attempting to avoid. The only example we know of employee representatives at board level being required to relinquish office was in the British Steel Corporation when the original board representation scheme was introduced in 1968. It had the effect of alienating employee representatives from the unions and the union membership, and when the scheme was revised, the requirement that employee representatives on the board should not be union office-holders was dropped.

References

Employment Protection Act, 1975, HMSO.

EETPU (1976), *Evidence of the EETPU to the Bullock Committee*, HMSO.

PARKER, S. (1975), *Workplace Industrial Relations, 1973*, HMSO.

PERRY, A. P. (ed.) (1974), *Workers' Participation – The European Experience*, Coventry and District Engineering Employers' Association, 1974.

ROYAL COMMISSION ON TRADE UNIONS AND EMPLOYERS' ASSOCIATIONS (The Donovan Commission) (1968), *1965–8 Report*, HMSO.

SCHREGLE, J. (1976), 'Workers' Participation in Decisions Within Undertakings', *International Labour Review*, vol. 113.

TUC (1976), *Evidence of the TUC to the Bullock Committee*, HMSO.

9 E. Batstone, A. Ferner and M. Terry

Unions on the Post Office Board

From E. Batstone, A. Ferner and M. Terry, *Unions on the Board,* Blackwell, 1983, pp. 160–77.

Institutional form and practice

The Bullock Committee (unless otherwise stated, we refer to the majority of the Committee) argued that, if a strong form of board representation was introduced, the difficulties in decision-making at the board which might arise from differences of view between worker directors and other board members would be more than compensated for by the easier implementation of jointly agreed decisions. This led the Committee to put forward proposals that were more radical than any existing scheme of board representation in this country, or elsewhere in Western Europe. Even in West German industry where a form of parity representation exists, the role of the board is limited and the links between worker directors and the unions are weak. In other countries, such as Sweden, worker directors form only a minority of the board and their links with the unions are seriously constrained, not least by rules concerning the confidentiality of board matters. The British Steel Corporation worker directors studied by Brannen *et al.* were a minority sitting on an advisory board and had virtually no formal and continuing links with their unions.

The Post Office worker director experiment bore greater resemblance to the Bullock proposals than any other scheme of board representation, despite the fact that the Bullock Committee was solely concerned with large companies in the private sector. As in the Bullock proposals, all Post Office board members had identical formal responsibilities, which included some recognition of worker and union interests. The democratized Post Office board was also of the size envisaged by the majority of the Bullock Committee. (It was therefore somewhat larger than the average board in companies employing over 50,000 staff: Bullock, 1977, p. 63.)

The Post Office experiment operated on a 2X + Y formula similar to the one proposed by Bullock. That is, there were an equal number of management and union representatives and an additional, smaller, third group. The Post Office scheme differed, however, in certain respects. First, all board members were formally appointed by the Minister. In practice, he did not reject any union nominee, even though tempted to do so on one occasion. Second, the Chairman was formally separate from the management 'X' group. Third, the 'Y' group was not determined by the two 'X' groups, and included two 'consumer representatives': this had been a condition of crucial Liberal support for the proposals in Parliament.

The Post Office experiment was also firmly union-based, as had been proposed by the majority of the Bullock Committee. All the 'worker directors' were selected by and through the trade unions. In this process, COPOU [Council of Post Office Unions] played a role comparable with that of Bullock's Joint Representation Committee. Individual Post Office unions selected their nominees, and it is likely that a similar arrangement would have occurred in the private sector had Bullock been implemented. Again, however, there were a number of differences. The Bullock majority proposed a 'triggering' process in which unions opted for a ballot of workers; if this achieved the requisite level of support, then worker directors would be introduced. No such ballot figured in the Post Office scheme, although formal ratification was a condition of the experiment. Second, Bullock had envisaged that worker directors would be lay union members, typically shop stewards. A number of the Post Office union nominees were full-time officials. This difference largely reflects the distinctive nature of much of the public sector including the Post Office and its unions. [...]

Despite a number of differences, then, the Post Office experiment was quite similar to the scheme of board representation proposed by the majority of the Bullock Committee. Most importantly, it employed the 2X + Y formula and was firmly union-based. The question which must now be asked is, how significant were these features for the operation of the scheme? In seeking to answer this question we will concentrate upon a comparison of the Post Office and the British Steel Corporation (BSC) schemes. This allows us to sidestep any problems associated with making international comparisons (Marsden, 1978), although, where relevant, reference will be made to the experience of other countries. More importantly, the British Steel experiment provides a useful contrast in that, at least in the period studied by Brannen and his colleagues, it lacked both parity representation and a strong union base.

A common finding of previous studies of worker directors is that they have rarely introduced major conflicts into the boardroom.

Worker directors have tended to adopt a managerial approach, although there are some signs that this may be changing in the face of widespread redundancy and rationalization. But in British Steel large-scale closures and redundancies were not associated with a more radical approach on the part of the worker directors. They accepted the financial logic of management, and confined themselves to the communication of views between workers and the board and to trying to minimize social hardship. Brannen *et al.* explain the managerial orientation of the worker directors partly in terms of union strategy more generally (1976, pp. 205–9), but they also stress that the structure of the BSC scheme made the worker directors particularly susceptible to managerial influence.

It might have been expected, *a fortiori*, that the Post Office union nominees would adopt a similarly managerial approach, given that there was not the same immediate threat to job security as in the steel industry, and that the Post Office had a very long history of industrial peace and cooperation. In addition, like the BSC worker directors, the Post Office union nominees had to learn, and adapt to, the norms of board conduct; they were dependent upon managerially structured information and proposals at the board; and they became embedded in a network of informal management contacts.

Nevertheless, the Post Office union nominees did not act like their BSC counterparts. They tried to manipulate boardroom norms, to challenge management assumptions and to exploit their network of management contacts. They appeared less dependent upon management for information than the BSC worker directors; they were much more critical of management; and they were more likely to try to change management proposals and to take initiatives in the boardroom (Brannen *et al.*, 1976, pp. 178–84).

Despite these differences, the experience in the Post Office was similar to that in BSC and other worker director schemes in three important respects. First, the union nominees tended to focus upon matters of relevance to worker and union interests and industrial relations. This reflected both their areas of expertise and their preoccupations (although the emphasis was even stronger in the Post Office than BSC). Second, the union nominees had relatively little impact upon the outcome of board discussions. Again, they probably had rather more effect than did the BSC worker directors, but what is striking is how marginal it was. Third, the extent to which the union nominees influenced worker and union attitudes, though greater in the Post Office case than in BSC, was still remarkably limited.

In short, compared with BSC (and with most other schemes of board representation), the Post Office experiment was distinctive in that the union nominees were less prepared to accept management's definitions and perspectives, and this contributed to expressions of conflict at the board. But, despite this, their general impact was not significantly greater than that of most worker directors. Few board decisions were different as a result of the union nominees' pressure, and the extent to which they affected management and union behaviour was limited. In seeking to explain these similarities and differences, we look first at the particular institutional arrangements.

2X + Y

It is generally accepted that if worker directors have equal representation with management on the board, then they will have a significant impact upon decisions. At first sight, the Post Office experience casts doubt upon this view. A number of factors serve to explain the limited influence of the union nominees.

First, they did not act as a caucus, and therefore did not exploit to the full the power which they formally possessed. This failure was in part due to the agreement setting up the scheme. But it is open to question how far the union nominees could have acted in a united way given substantial differences of interest between the unions. Furthermore, the evidence indicates no greater level of success when the union nominees were united on an issue.

A second possible explanation concerns the 'Y' element. For if this group tended to support management, then the union nominees would consequently be outnumbered. This was indeed the case: consumer representatives generally favoured management policies, as did most of the other members of the third group. This pattern reflected the biases associated with the origins of part-time members, embodied within dominant notions of 'expertise' which part-time board members were meant to represent. In addition, most of them accepted that the primary responsibility for the Post Office lay with the full-time members and, in particular, the Chairman. Part-timers normally deferred to the full-timers' views.

Third, the union nominees themselves tended to accept the notion of the full-timers as *primi inter pares*. In part they did so because it was part of the board ethos. But, also, to have done otherwise would have been to endanger union independence. Accepting the primary role of full-timers at the board was consistent with the traditional oppositional role of trade unions.

Nevertheless, the union nominees did attempt to change policies. The number of union nominees meant that there was a greater possibility than at BSC of full-time members' views failing to gain acceptance from the board as a whole. This possibility led full-time members to highlight conflicts of interest and to question the 'good faith' and representativeness of the union nominees, particularly when faced by criticism from the union nominees which exploited rhetorics of unity. These conflicts could on occasion dominate board meetings and there were some signs that this tendency was increasing. As a result, board discussions were sometimes inconclusive and the full-time members in particular became less 'open' at the board and kept some issues away from board meetings.

The $2X + Y$ formula of board representation may not have led to dramatic changes of policy but it did complicate board discussion considerably. Suspicions of 'bad faith' increased as the experiment progressed and full-time members had to adopt a variety of strategies to ensure that their views generally won through. In assessing the experiment, therefore, most full-time members argued that the union nominees had obstructed the effective operation of the board, while the union nominees claimed that the full-time members had failed to understand the implications of the board's 'democratization'.

Both of these views are quite correct given their respective sets of assumptions. Experience in the boardroom reflected, rather than resolved, the fundamental differences in management and union rationales concerning industrial democracy. In this respect – and despite the apparent overarching consensus on basic corporation goals – the Post Office experience casts doubt upon whether the high-lighting of different interests in the boardroom by means of a $2X + Y$ formula can lead to mutually satisfactory outcomes.

The union base and the pattern of union–management relations

We have seen that the Post Office union nominees were less suscep-tible to incorporation into a managerial perspective than other worker directors have been. This had much to do with the structure of the scheme, which encouraged a close link between the union nominees and their unions, and reflected the view that the nominees should put a union viewpoint to the board. The selection of union representatives on the board was controlled by the unions, and they were able to ensure that neither management nor Minister influenced who was selected. Those selected as union nominees were on the whole considerably more senior than were the BSC worker directors, and they were more likely to have played a significant role in their unions nationally as well as locally. The traditional depth and scope of consultation and negotiation in the Post Office, and the strong emphasis on service and administrative issues in board discussions, meant that the union nominees' entry into the Post Office boardroom was less of a 'culture shock' than had been the case for the BSC worker directors.

Despite the fact that they were not formally allowed to negotiate, the union nominees were deeply embedded in union affairs. Some of them were full-time officials; all of them sat on various union committees, including the executive. All of them regularly discussed board matters with other officials of their unions. They spent more time with other union members than with other board members or managers. There was, therefore, a stronger check upon any tendencies towards incorporation into a managerial perspective than in other worker director schemes. At the time of Brannen et al.'s study, for example, the BSC worker directors had no regular contact with key union officials; the same is true of most worker directors in West Germany whose primary links are with a non-union-based works council which operates under the requirement of cooperation; in other cases, norms of confidentiality limit the significance of contact (see Batstone and Davies, 1976).

Our findings provide us with some basis for speculating briefly on what would have happened if the union link had been even stronger; for example, if the union nominees had been key negotiators. Certainly, it would have been more difficult for other board members to doubt the union nominees' views. The nominees would also have been much more influential within the unions since they would have had a considerable monopoly of knowledge and contacts. In other words, such union nominees would have had considerably greater 'clout' both at the board and within the unions. But this may well have exacerbated the problems of negotiation at the board that we have already discussed. Moreover, if senior negotiators were seen to be tied or constrained by board decisions rather than collective agreements, this could well have led to major challenges to their position within the unions. The presence of senior negotiators on the board could, therefore, have created serious problems for the unions.

A second form of tighter link between the unions and their nominees would be for the former to mandate the latter. This would have made little difference – the union nominees generally pursued union policy. Moreover, it is unlikely that conflict at the board would have been greater if the union nominees had been mandated, for two further reasons. First, the unions often had no set policy on issues that were not normally matters for negotiation or joint consultation, and this served to reduce the degree of boardroom conflict. Second, the unions did not see board representation as the primary means of pursuing their demands and interests. They placed greater emphasis upon strong bargaining relationships and the long-standing system of consultation and negotiation.

An important strand of argument in the Bullock recommendations was that the presence of worker directors would facilitate the implementation of decisions. The union base was seen as important for this process. We have suggested that in the Post Office there were few indications that implementation of board policy was facilitated by the experiment or that it was likely to become so had the scheme continued. In part, this follows from the fact that the union nominees were unable to influence board decisions to any great degree. In addition, however, the greater understanding of management thinking derived from board involvement could just as easily lead to greater opposition to management as to greater cooperation. Our evidence suggests that there were cases of both, but many managers and union officials believed that the industrial democracy experiment was increasingly being used to further the unions' own bargaining position rather than to promote cooperation.

In view of the deterioration in industrial relations in the Post Office and the level of conflict at the board, it is perhaps surprising that industrial democracy did not lead to a further heightening of industrial conflict. A number of factors explain why this was not the case. First, there were occasions when board representation did lead the unions to a more sympathetic view of management or to an appreciation of the balance of power which counselled moderation. Second, the unions supported many of the broad aims of management even though they were frequently opposed to its more detailed policies. Third, since they operated in the public sector, union leaders were acutely aware of the need to maintain political credibility: industrial action could damage member interests both directly, and indirectly through adverse political reactions. Fourth, Post Office industrial relations had traditionally been dependent upon strong bargaining relationships between key management and union negotiators. Through these contacts the union leadership had always had a relatively good understanding of management and its strategies. Those relationships had also generally permitted some form of accommodation between management and unions and had typically discouraged aggressive tactics by both parties. While there were signs that these bargaining relationships were becoming more strained, they nevertheless continued to permit a degree of accommodation.

In summary, then, the union base was crucial in limiting the extent to which the union nominees adopted a managerial approach. By the same token, it served to highlight conflict at the board. However, board representation did not lead to significant changes in board policy, with the consequence that there was little likelihood of greater union cooperation in the implementation of that policy. Conflict might well have been further exacerbated by the industrial democracy experiment if it had not been for the unions' limited horizons, the marginality of the experiment for both unions and management, and the degree of consensus over the general goals of the Post Office. This conclusion highlights the importance of looking at worker directors in their specific context.

The nature and role of the board

An important assumption underlying proposals for worker directors is that the board plays a strategic role in corporate policy-making. Several studies have questioned the validity of this assumption (see Batstone and Davies, 1976). If these studies are correct, then the extent to which workers and unions can affect management policy through board representation is limited; the impact of worker directors is therefore likely to be reduced.

More recent studies, however, have pointed to variations between companies in the significance of boards (e.g. Gustavsen, 1976; Brookes, 1979; Cressey et al., 1981, pp. 12–13). Several factors may explain these variations. First is the role of dominant shareholders who may choose to make the board a central mode of control or may choose to by-pass it. The impact of a dominant shareholder – the government – upon the Post Office was complex: formally it placed great emphasis upon the responsibilities of the board, but it could also severely constrain the freedom of the board by issuing specific ministerial instructions. At the time of our research the government had insisted upon a structure of semi-autonomous businesses which limited the role that the board could play. In an attempt to defend the corporation from unpredictable intrusions by government, management had developed a centralized structure (cf. NEDO, 1976; Burns, 1977), but the importance of the board was still uncertain.

Second, the role of the board is related to the pattern of corporate organization: the importance of the introduction of semi-autonomous businesses in the Post Office has just been noted. A board can therefore make organizational decisions which serve to limit its own direct impact. Moreover, the power of the board may be limited by the decisions of managerial groups with delegated powers within the company.

Third, the precise organizational form and the nature of the production process may provide subordinate groups with considerable power which they can use against higher levels, including the board. We have suggested that the scale and complexity of the Post Office gave many managers a considerable degree of power (see also Batstone, 1976, pp. 19–20).

Fourth, it is necessary to make a distinction between the board as a collectivity which meets and makes decisions, and individual board members. In many companies, particular board members, notably chairmen and managing directors, appear to have very considerable power (e.g. Francis, 1980; Nyman and Silberston, 1978; Burns and Stalker, 1961). They are likely to be the primary link with shareholders, and at the same time be intimately involved in the detailed operation of the company. They therefore play key 'boundary' roles which, we have noted, are recognized by other board members who are unlikely to use their constitutional powers against them unless major crises occur.

Strategically powerful board members are, of course, constrained by shareholders and other members of the organization. But they can play a central role in determining the scope of the board and the pattern of corporate organization. The Post Office experience demonstrates this clearly: the full-time members were committed to changing the corporation's structure and altering the role of the board. Similarly, in the light of their assessment of the industrial democracy experiment, they reduced their reliance upon the board. The union nominees were generally unable to counter these moves.

The full-time board members and other key members of management also sought to change the pattern of organization more generally. Organization has been defined as 'the embodiment of purpose'

117

(Selznick, 1957; see also Batstone, 1978). Purpose was determined in the Post Office case not only by government but also by this key internal group. They set about creating a framework of rules, sanctions and rewards to guide and constrain the actions and decisions of other organization members. Thus, one cannot conclude simply from an analysis of routine activities that boards or key board members do not play a significant role in decision-making. If they have successfully structured the activities of others, they have little need to make decisions on a day-to-day basis. Only when things are going wrong will they need to play a more manifest role, which may or may not involve the board. In the Post Office, much organizational rule-making occurred outside the board, although it was clearly controlled by individual full-time board members. The board itself acted primarily to ratify decisions and subsequently to play a relatively passive, although significant, monitoring role.

Finally, it is important to consider how the broad thrust of board activities can be guided by the interests identified as central by a powerful managerial group. Emery and Thorsrud (1969) have argued that boards of directors in private companies tend to focus upon those matters which are of primary interest to shareholders, and hence reflect a central preoccupation with the preservation and growth of the company as a body of capital assets. In publicly-owned companies such as the Post Office, however, the central preoccupations may be qualitatively different, in that they frequently derive from political rather than market concerns; moreover, the often contradictory political requirements of public corporations may make their objectives much less clear-cut than those of private sector firms. The key infrastructural public services have imposed upon them a variety of service requirements as well as financial rules. These politically-constrained goals are important for the survival of public corporations and hence figure as items of central importance in boardroom debate. For example, the falling standards of service were a major concern in the Post Office during the course of the research. At the same time, governments have been concerned to develop a more commercial and market-oriented approach for public corporations, including the Post Office. As we have seen, key members were appointed to the Post Office board to pursue this particular strategy. This involved significant changes in the structure of board activity and information. 'Commercialism' implied a greater devolution of decision-making and a new emphasis at the board and within the businesses upon market-related issues. Again, the central group of key managers sought to shape board issues and structures to achieve the required aims. In particular, within the requirements of the new commercialism, the board was to become less of an administrative body and to approximate more closely the board in a private company.

This attempt by the key group to change board priorities and activity complicated the role of the union nominees. Their efforts to pursue worker and union interests meant that what management members increasingly saw as minor matters of detail were of central importance to them. Similarly, the embodiment of these new priorities in board papers led the union nominees to question the assumptions upon which management wished to operate. In other words, conflict in the board was intensified by the new strategies of the managerial elite, which saw the union nominees as obstructing the proper role of the board at a time when obstruction could be both commercially and politically damaging. Management therefore felt it necessary to reduce its reliance upon the board. But this in turn exacerbated the problems of the union nominees (since it kept certain issues off the board agenda) and thus tended to intensify conflict, as the board's agenda and role themselves became topics of disagreement. At the same time, management action prevented the board from becoming the catalyst for a more 'democratic' approach in the corporation as a whole.

We conclude, then, that the board tended to play a limited role. This was in part the result of government control and the scale and complexity of the Post Office. But we have also stressed the way in which the role of the board was the product of the policies of a managerial elite which included key board members, and of the resultant conflict between it and the union nominees.

Other studies have recognized that topics typically discussed by boards may make it difficult for worker directors to play a full role. Some have also made reference to changes in the content of board proceedings as a result of the presence of worker directors. What we have emphasized is the need for analysis to link the role of the board to a dynamic conception of corporate strategy as well as to the minutiae of tactics relating to industrial democracy.

In this section we have considered a number of key institutional features of the Post Office scheme of board representation and have attempted to draw out their more general relevance. The arguments we have presented suggest that the institutional details proposed by the majority of the Bullock Committee do indeed affect importantly the operation of a worker director scheme. They both serve to foster and maintain a union perspective on the part of worker directors and make it more difficult for other board members to ignore their views. The Post Office experience suggests, however, that this does not facilitate the implementation of mutually-agreed decisions. Although accommodation was reached on occasion, more typically the full-time members were able to prevent the union nominees from having any significant effect on policy. The $2X + Y$ formula complicated the process of board debate, but it did not stop the full-timers from controlling the board agenda and decision-taking. At the same time, there was little evidence to suggest that – beyond occasional instances – the experiment did much to improve relations between management and unions.

The impact of board representation

In Chapter 1 we outlined four different views concerning the impact and effects of worker representation at board level. The Post Office experience confirmed none of the arguments put forward by the two extreme schools of thought. There was no evidence that the experiment was leading to any greater incorporation of the unions into the philosophy and practices of management than might already have occurred through collective bargaining; board representation was not weakening the unions' bargaining strength or autonomy, or their ability to oppose management in the interests of their members. Similarly, the 'property rights' argument gains little support from the Post Office experience. The industrial democracy experiment did not impose any significant additional constraints upon management, and managerial autonomy was not noticeably undermined by the union nominees: there was little sign of powerful and well-informed trade unions exercising a veto right at the board over the decisions of a gravely weakened management.

The two 'intermediate' views – that board representation can under certain circumstances lead to gains for workers or for management – can be less easily discounted. The union nominees were prevented, either by inter-union differences or by the intervention of the independent directors, from effectively challenging management proposals. Further, the unions proved unable to elaborate coherent alternative policies. Management was also able to control the content and procedures of board debate to a high degree, so that the union nominees found themselves outflanked or out-argued on many issues. Thus the unions' procedural victory – securing a 'strong' scheme of board representation – did not lead to a substantive one, in the shape of increasing worker influence over strategic management decisions. It should, however, be noted that unions did gain small but significant negotiating advantages on one or two issues through the experiment.

If the union nominees had such a limited impact, it is at first sight difficult to understand why management should have been opposed to the experiment. Management's resistance to the scheme reflected the fact that it had been created by political intervention and union pressure, and had not arisen out of managerial strategy for accommodating to, or incorporating, the unions. It was thus not a particularly suitable vehicle for the pursuit of managerial ends. Moreover, the operation of the experiment provoked growing managerial hostility, for it introduced into the boardroom the conflict that was increasingly characterizing labour–management relations in the Post Office at the time. The political pressures for commercialism were forcing management to try to extend its own freedom and prerogatives in order to be able to react flexibly to its new environment. The 'administrative' ethos of the civil service was thus formally no longer an appropriate model. Equally, the traditional emphasis upon winning union consent and cooperation was reduced.

While the unions accepted in principle that the Post Office should adopt a more commercial strategy, they demonstrated a growing hostility to many of the implications of management's new approach. For the changes associated with commercialism endangered both the traditional role and influence of the various unions and traditional norms concerning the wage–effort bargain. Union dissatisfaction was particularly strong during the period of the industrial democracy experiment. Incomes policies, along with changes in payment systems, had served to intensify dissatisfaction over absolute and relative pay levels. There were growing pressures at union conferences for the unions to adopt more aggressive strategies towards management over pay and other benefits, and to exert greater control over the major technical and organizational changes planned by management.

The institutional arrangements of parity representation and the maintenance of close links between the union nominees and their unions meant that the nominees, far from being incorporated, acted as a transmission belt bringing these wider management–union conflicts into the boardroom.

If the preceding argument is correct, and the particular context of board representation is crucial, then it follows that one cannot predict *a priori* whether worker directors will serve managerial or worker interests. Moreover, as we argued in Chapter 1, analyses of industrial democracy cannot stop with the investigation of institutions. Statements based on generalized notions of conflictual or consensual interests and static concepts of organizations and institutions can have only limited usefulness. In order to understand the operation of particular schemes, it is necessary to identify the specific roots of conflict and consensus, and to examine the changing strategies of management and unions. We develop these more general themes in a further volume, *Legitimacy and Labour in State Enterprise*.

Nevertheless, our analysis suggests that schemes that are sufficiently 'strong' to minimize the risk of worker 'incorporation' are likely to be opposed by management, and hence are likely to occur on any large scale only in a political climate favourable to the extension of worker and union power. But even under such auspicious circumstances, industrial democracy may offer no more than marginal advantages to workers and unions.

It is precisely on these grounds that it is often argued that an extension of collective bargaining is a more effective union strategy. Collective bargaining is seen as more desirable because it does not endanger union independence; it is more consistent with existing union practice; it permits unions to select the issues on which they bargain and does not impose constraints upon the demands which they make (e.g. Ogden, 1982). We believe that this view is too simplistic. First, it has been widely argued that collective bargaining does not guarantee union independence but can, like industrial democracy, lead to the incorporation of unions and workers (e.g. Hyman, 1975). Second, there is a danger of comparing the rather mundane experience of industrial democracy schemes with an idealized picture of collective bargaining which exaggerates the gains workers have achieved by it. Moreover, the unions have shown only a limited interest in gaining greater control over management strategy through collective bargaining. Third, there might well be attractions – for example, when unions are weak – in being able to employ the sorts of institutional sanctions and pressures associated with board membership. Again, therefore, the specific context assumes importance.

In conclusion, then, the Post Office experience provides little support for the more extreme arguments concerning board representation. The overall impact of the union nominees was marginal. They can best be seen as an irritant rather than as a major obstruction for management, while for the unions, they brought only limited gains.

The optimistic Bullock thesis does not, then, receive much support from the Post Office experiment. The Bullock model pays insufficient attention to the specific contexts in which board representation is located. 'Strong' schemes of worker directors tend to reflect, rather than resolve, the underlying patterns of conflict and cooperation in industry.

References

BATSTONE, E. (1976), 'Industrial Democracy and Worker Representation at Board Level: A Review of the European Experience', in E. Batstone and P. L. Davies, *Industrial Democracy: European Experience*, HMSO.

BATSTONE, E. (1978), 'Management and Industrial Democracy', *Industrial Democracy: International Views*, SSRC.

BATSTONE, E., and P. L. DAVIES (1976), *Industrial Democracy: European Experience*. HMSO.

BRANNEN, P., E. BATSTONE, D. FATCHETT and P. WHITE (1976), *The Worker Directors: A Sociology of Participation*, Hutchinson.

BROOKES, C. (1979), *Boards of Directors in British Industry*, Research Paper no. 7, Department of Employment.

BULLOCK, A. (chmn) (1977), *Industrial Democracy: Committee of Inquiry Report*, Cmnd 6706, HMSO.

BURNS, T. (1977), *The BBC: Public Institution and Private World*, Macmillan.

BURNS, T., and G. M. STALKER (1961), *The Management of Innovation*, Tavistock.

CRESSEY, P., *et al.* (1981), *Industrial Democracy and Participation: A Scottish Survey*, Research Paper no. 28, Department of Employment.

EMERY, F., and E. THORSRUD (1969), *Form and Content in Industrial Democracy*, Tavistock.

FRANCIS, A. (1980), 'Company Objectives, Managerial Motivations and the Behaviour of Large Firms: An Empirical Test of the Theory of "Managerial" Capitalism', *Cambridge Journal of Economics*, IV, p. 4.

GUSTAVSEN, B. (1976), 'The Board of Directors, Company Policy and Industrial Democracy', *Handbook of Work Organization and Society*, ed. R. Dubin, Rand McNally.

HYMAN, R. (1975), *Industrial Relations: A Marxist Introduction*, Macmillan.

MARSDEN, D. (1978), *Industrial Democracy and Industrial Control in West Germany, France and Great Britain*, Research Paper no. 4. London: Department of Employment.

NATIONAL ECONOMIC DEVELOPMENT OFFICE (NEDO) (1976), *A Study of the UK Nationalized Industries*, HMSO.

NYMAN, S., and A. SILBERSTON (1978), 'The Ownership and Control of Industry', *Oxford Economic Papers*, March.

OGDEN, S. G. (1982), 'Trade Unions, Industrial Democracy, and Collective Bargaining', *Sociology*, 16, p. 4.

SELZNICK, P. (1957), *Leadership in Administration: A Sociological Interpretation*, Harper and Row.

Part Three

Trade Union Structure

By union structure is meant those sections of the labour force which a given organization seeks to recruit. Most unions aim to recruit members in particular parts of the labour force, defined by reference to specific occupations, industries or sectors. A few relatively large unions organize over a very wide spectrum and have been termed 'conglomerates'.

In Reading 10 Hugh Clegg advances a theory of the determinants of union structure which helps to explain its relative stability and absence of 'rational principles'. Structure emerges at the foundation of a given union, where it is largely determined by the level of technology and industrial organization during the period of early growth. However, if this historically-determined structure is to survive it must not prevent the development of effective job regulation. Fortunately for most unions in most countries, this now takes the form of participation in collective bargaining, which is compatible with almost any existing structure. Clegg's views appear deceptively simple, but he has provided by far the best explanation so far for the relatively unchanging and apparently chaotic structure of the British trade union movement.

Both remaining readings deal with recent merger movements, which have produced a limited degree of structural change. In Reading 11 Robert Buchanan estimates the extent of the movement and compares it to similar developments in earlier periods. He concludes that change has been influenced by the impact of inflation, inter-union competition and technological change. There may also be a link between company mergers and union amalgamations.

In Reading 12, by Roger Undy and his colleagues, the results of a study of merger activities in major unions since 1960 are summarized. Mergers are said to be of three different types: defensive, consolidatory or aggressive. Different causal factors influence each type, but in all cases the role of national officials has been crucial.

Speculating about the impact of their findings on future union structure, the authors suggest the possibility of 'four surviving predators' engaged in 'a series of battles for supremacy', a prospect 'not altogether unlike Orwell's vision of 1984'.

10 H. A. Clegg

A Theory of Union Structure

From H. A. Clegg, *Trade Unionism under Collective Bargaining*, Blackwell, 1976, pp. 29–39.

Technology, legitimacy and ideology

Few ideas about trade unionism have enjoyed such widespread support as the notion that industrial unionism – a single union for all workers in each industry – is the best trade union structure. While syndicalists, communists, and socialists have argued for it, it has also found favour among conservatives; and captains of industry have championed it as well as shop stewards and union leaders. But many trade unions are still shaped to different patterns.

The enemy of industrial unionism is occupational unionism. Organization by occupation divides trade unionism within industries, and many occupational unions straddle industrial boundaries. Furthermore, occupational unionism breeds general unions, for where favourably situated occupations are strongly organized in their separate unions there is an incentive for the remaining group of workers to huddle together for support regardless of occupational and industrial boundaries.

Two types of occupational union have already been described in some detail: craft and promotion unions. They flourished in the many nineteenth-century industries which relied on skilled hand-operations. A third type of occupational union has grown apace in the twentieth century, especially since the Second World War. This is white-collar unionism which divides white-collar employees from manual workers, often divides one white-collar occupation from another, and in many instances disregards industrial boundaries.

These and other trade union types are the products of technological change and the new forms of industrial organization which it brings. The industrial revolution called forth new skilled occupations suited to craft and promotion unions. Increasing mechanization led to mass production with its easily learned, repetitive tasks which did not equip individual occupations with the resources to build powerful unions on their own. Mass-production workers therefore turned to industrial

127

and general unions. But mass production also brought increasingly large industrial undertakings which required large administrative, financial, planning, and sales departments staffed by white-collar employees who eventually formed their own unions. In their early years, craft unions made great use of unilateral regulation; so did the promotion unions, although they could not push it as far as the craftsmen did. Industrial and general unions had to rely mainly on collective bargaining. And most white-collar unions were especially dependent on recognition from employers in order to operate effectively. Unilateral regulation is entirely dependent on internal union discipline to maintain its rules. Union members must refuse employment except in accordance with the rules and, once employed, they must watch for and resist any attempt at infringement by the employer who is under no obligation to respect the rules. Under collective bargaining the employer accepts responsibility for applying the rules which he or his association has agreed, and this greatly eases the burden on union discipline. Union discipline may, of course, be tested by a strike to change the agreement, but fewer demands are made on union members by an occasional strike, called at a favourable moment after a campaign has aroused enthusiasm, than by continuous daily enforcement of union regulations. It is this characteristic of collective bargaining which has allowed trade unionism to spread far beyond those privileged occupations which have the resources to enforce unilateral rules.

Consequently, whereas unilateral regulation requires that unions adopt the structure which, given existing industrial organization and technology, enables them to impose their rules most effectively, collective bargaining is compatible with any form of union organization so long as the union is recognized by the employer. Craft unions, promotion unions, white-collar unions, industrial unions, and general unions all find it possible to operate by means of collective bargaining. In addition, recognition by the employer gives a trade union a legitimacy which it could not otherwise enjoy. The claim of the union to represent its members no longer rests on its own strength alone. Consequently, collective bargaining supports and preserves union structure as it existed at the time of recognition; and, for each trade union movement, that structure was shaped by the state of industrial organization and technology during the period of its birth and development.

Paradoxically, however, collective bargaining also permits ideology to have some impact on union structure. So long as occupational unions rely on unilateral regulation, they are not likely to be persuaded of the virtues of merging their identities in industrial unions, for the consequential weakening of their power to enforce their rules would be too evident. But since unions with almost any structure can regulate by means of collective bargaining – so long as they are recognized by the employers – industrial unionism is no longer ruled out under collective bargaining, even for craft unions. If the advocates of industrial unionism can win sufficient support to carry through the reorganization required by their doctrine, the new union structure may turn out to be as effective as the old, if not necessarily more effective.

It is, however, much easier to persuade unions to come together by amalgamation than to prevail upon them to split themselves up or to transfer groups of members to other unions. Consequently advocates of industrial unionism may succeed in persuading occupational unions within a given industry to amalgamate into an industrial union, but they must expect strong resistance from general unions and occupational unions which straddle industrial boundaries.

The exception to this generalization is a catastrophe which destroys a trade union movement. If and when an opportunity to reconstruct the movement occurs, the movement can be reconstructed to taste. So long as collective bargaining is the method of regulation, it places no limits on the new structure; and there are no existing unions to bar the way to it.

Existing structures

This statement of the theory must now be tested against the existing structures in the six countries.

The British trade union movement is the oldest in the world because the industrial revolution began in Britain; and because it is the oldest movement it is also the most complex. Its complexity can be seen in the large number and varied types of occupational unions, and also in the size of its general unions which developed as a consequence of the strength of occupational unionism. Besides the two avowed general unions – the Transport and General Workers, and the General and Municipal Workers – some of the major occupational unions have acquired many of the characteristics of a general union by recruiting in new areas and absorbing other occupational unions. They include the Amalgamated Union of Engineering Workers, and the Electrical, Electronic, Telecommunication and

Plumbing Union. There are few important industries in the country which do not employ members of all four unions. All four of them have white-collar sections, those of the Transport and General Workers and the Engineers being among the major white-collar unions in the private sector. Besides these four, there are a number of other unions which can be found in dozens of different industries, including the Shop Distributive and Allied Workers, the Construction Workers, and the Boilermakers. There are some industrial unions, such as the Mineworkers, but it is also common to find a so-called industrial union working alongside separate maintenance unions and separate white-collar unions, and perhaps other specialist unions as well. The railways and the steel industry are two examples, and in the steel industry the two major general unions also have substantial groups of members. Although the doctrine of industrial unionism has more than once come close to acceptance as the official policy of the Trades Union Congress, it has had little practical effect. There have been waves of amalgamation – one after the First World War and another since 1964 – which have greatly reduced the total number of unions but have done nothing to simplify the overall pattern. Instead they have strung together groups of members and areas of recognized bargaining rights in ever more incomprehensible confusion.

The Australian unions come next to the British in the complexity of their structure. This cannot be explained by the date of Australia's industrial revolution, for in that respect Australia was not ahead of Germany or the United States. It is due to two other features of Australian industrial relations. Firstly, nineteenth-century emigrants to Australia carried the structure of British craft unionism with them. One of the most important Australian unions, the Engineers, was a branch of a British union, and many others were copies of their British counterparts. Secondly, the arbitration system brought stability to Australian union structure before collective bargaining was generally established anywhere else. Once recognized by the arbitration tribunals, the legitimacy of existing Australian unions was firmly established, and, after that, further structural development came only through amalgamation.

Trade unionism was established early in the United States, but for a variety of reasons, including the continued large-scale entry of immigrants from all over Europe with their differing languages and customs, it failed to establish itself outside a fairly narrow range of occupations and industries until after 1937. Consequently the American movement consists of two parts, indicated by the hyphenated title of its central confederation, the AFL-CIO. Broadly speaking, the American Federation of Labor brought together the occupational unions of the nineteenth century on what was called a craft basis – using the term loosely; whereas the Congress of Industrial Organizations was a confederation of industrial unions of the twentieth century, established in areas which the occupational unions had failed to conquer. Accordingly the American movement has more regard for industrial boundaries than either the British or Australian movements. Nevertheless, it is an elementary error to regard America as a country of industrial unionism, or of well-defined union boundaries. Although the statutory procedures for securing recognition have helped to stabilize the overall structure of American trade unionism as it was in 1937, they have also complicated the detail of American union structure. Because recognition is achieved by ballot, generally on a plant-by-plant basis, many American unions have been tempted to expand into weakly organized industries and occupations with little regard for the neatness of union boundaries. Any union is entitled to ask for a ballot if it can give the requisite indication of support, and winning the ballot confers legitimacy. In this way the Teamsters have branched out from road haulage into a number of services and manufacturing industries; and the Laborer's Union and the former District 50 of the Mineworkers (now an independent union) are well on their way to general unionism – although on a modest scale when compared with the Transport and General Workers, and the Australian Workers' Union.

If German unions cannot trace their history back earlier than American unions, they were able to establish themselves more quickly and effectively. By 1914 German unions had achieved a much higher density than American unions had, and after 1918 their lead increased further. By that time the overall structure of German trade unionism had much in common with the modern American pattern. Powerful occupational unions vied with strong industrial unions, although in Germany they did not establish separate confederations. In 1922 the main German confederation committed itself to industrial unionism, but the occupational unions refused to accept the new policy, and the 1925 conference was forced to modify it by resolving that industrial unionism was to be achieved only by consent. Since there was no likelihood of the occupational unions agreeing to their dismemberment, it seemed that stalemate had been reached.

No one can say how the structural controversy would have been settled by the German unions if they had been left to work it out for themselves. In 1933 they were wiped out by Hitler, and when the time came for reconstruction in 1945 the organizational obstacles to industrial unionism had disappeared. Consequently the leaders were able to redraw union boundaries according to the neatest and most simplified industrial plan which has ever been achieved. They created sixteen large unions, each covering a major industry or a group of industries.

The doctrine of industrial unionism also carried the day in France, but for rather different reasons. After a period of growth under the Second Empire, French unions were shattered in the suppression of the Paris Commune of 1871, and the process of reconstruction began to gather speed only towards the end of the century. Consequently occupational unions – with the exception of the printers – had little opportunity to build themselves up as effective regulatory bodies, and there was no system of collective bargaining to give external legitimacy to existing union structures. At the beginning of the twentieth century the movement was captured by syndicalist doctrine which included industrial unionism as one of its principles. The central confederation, the CGT, was therefore committed to reconstructing the unions along industrial boundaries, and, with no powerful organizational barrier to reform, the task had been accomplished by 1914.

However, a structure built on one doctrine was not proof against the attack of other doctrines. France is a Catholic country, and many Catholic employees were not receptive to the Marxism of the CGT. By 1945 a separate Catholic trade union movement of some strength had emerged in France, and two years later the anti-communist minority pulled out of the CGT to constitute the CGT-FO. More recently the Catholic unions have split into a doctrinally pure minority (the CFTC) and a non-confessional majority (the CFDT), left-wing but non-communist. Each of these confederations consists mainly of 'industrial' unions, although special arrangements are made for white-collar sections. Thus most French workers have a choice of three or four unions within the plant which are divided, not according to any structural principle, but on political and religious grounds. Indeed, some have an even wider choice because of the existence of independent unions and other tiny confederations devoted to more rare and esoteric creeds. And now that collective bargaining – of a limited kind – has become established in France, it gives legitimacy to these political and religious divisions.

Provided that the reconstruction of trade unionism in 1945 in Germany is not regarded as the birth of a new movement, Sweden is the youngest of the six trade union movements. There was little trade unionism in Sweden until the end of the nineteenth century, but thereafter growth was rapid. By 1912, when the LO adopted the principle of industrial unionism, a number of occupational unions had already achieved some strength; but since then the LO has continued by slow and methodical pressure to reduce the number of affiliated unions by amalgamation within industries and has even persuaded a small general union, the Amalgamated Unions, to transfer its members to the appropriate industrial unions.

Accordingly the LO now consists largely but not entirely of 'industrial' unions, but it does not follow that the Swedish trade union movement is industrially organized, for white-collar unionism is more developed in Sweden than anywhere else. Some white-collar unions cover the relevant occupations within a single industry, but the two largest unions affiliated to the TCO, one of clerical workers and technicians and the other of foremen and supervisors, both organize across the whole range of manufacturing industry and beyond. To complicate the picture, a number of LO unions also recruit white-collar occupations. LO and TCO unions compete for insurance employees and for shop assistants.

Efforts to organize manual and white-collar employees into the same unions have not met with complete success in any of the six countries. In France the teachers' unions are federated together in the independent FEN, and there is also the CGC which organizes white-collar employees in the private sector. In Germany there are separate confederations for civil servants and for white-collar employees in the private sector. Many predominantly manual unions in Australia and Britain have their white-collar sections, but most white-collar trade unionists belong to separate unions. White-collar unions are least in evidence in the United States. There are few white-collar unions of any importance outside the relatively ill-organized public sector. But that is because there are few white-collar trade unionists in private employment. Although many manual unions seek to include white-collar employees as well, few of them have achieved much success.

Confederal structure

The confederal structures[1] of some of the six countries have already

1. The word 'confederation' is here used to denote nationwide groupings of trade unions, whether called federations, confederations, congresses, or given some other title. The same usage is followed in referring to employers' organizations.

been mentioned, and the comparisons can now be drawn together. Britain and the United States each have a single central confederation, the TUC and the AFL-CIO. The TUC is the more comprehensive of the two, for there are now few British unions of any size and importance which remain unaffiliated, whereas the two largest unions in the United States are outside the AFL-CIO. The Teamsters were expelled on grounds of corruption, and the Auto Workers withdrew because of policy differences. In West Germany there are separate confederations for private white-collar employees and civil servants, but they are dwarfed by the DGB which includes many more white-collar and public employees than they do. The independent confederations are relatively more important in Sweden, and there are three of them: the TCO, a confederation for senior civil servants and professional employees, and a small syndicalist confederation. In Australia the ACTU occupies the place of the LO, and the ACSPA that of the TCO, but there are separate confederations for federal servants, for state servants, and for professional employees. Finally, France has not only its separate white-collar organizations in education and private industry, but also its confederations divided on political and religious grounds. Consequently, whereas the other five countries have either a single confederation or one which easily outnumbers all the rest put together, the CGT accounts for no more than half of French trade unionists, and perhaps less than that.

There is one obvious reason why Sweden and West Germany have independent white-collar confederations whereas Britain and the United States have not. The main confederations of the first two countries are committed to industrial unionism. White-collar employees can be organized under their aegis only if they join one of their industrial unions. If white-collar employees want their own unions, therefore, they must stay outside, and if they want their independent unions to belong to a confederation, they must found their own. In Britain and the United States, by contrast, the single confederations acknowledge no over-riding principle of organization, and white-collar occupational unions are free to join. But this is not the whole story. Until a few years ago many British white-collar unions including the largest – the Teachers, and the National and Local Government Officers – remained outside the TUC, and at one time plans for a white-collar confederation were far advanced. They were abandoned when the government made it clear that they would not recognize the proposed body on the same terms as the TUC, or allow it separate representation on joint union–government consultative and planning bodies, thus refusing to legitimize it. In the anti-union atmosphere of the United States, most separate white-collar organizations have until recently sought to demonstrate that they were exclusively professional associations with no interest in union activities. But the spread of collective bargaining legislation covering state and local authority employees has tempted many of them away from their professional purity to compete in ballots for statutory recognition to represent their members in collective bargaining. It is by no means inconceivable that a white-collar confederation may emerge if these bodies continue to grow in strength and to extend their trade union activities.

The experience of Australia emphasizes the point that the willingness of a central confederation to accept occupational unions is not enough to prevent white-collar unions forming a separate confederation. The ACTU recognizes no organizational principle, but it has been no more effective in winning the adherence of white-collar employees than the industrial unionist LO. The difference between Britain and Australia appears to be that the TUC has wooed the white-collar unions for nearly fifty years, setting up arrangements for co-operation with major white-collar unions which would not take the final step of affiliation, whereas the ACTU, perhaps reflecting a more proletarian ethos in Australian manual trade unionism, has begun to show an equivalent interest in white-collar unions only in recent years. Before that, the ACSPA and the public-service confederations were more eager to cooperate with the ACTU than the ACTU with them.

It seems, therefore, that there is a widespread tendency of white-collar trade unionists to want their own unions, and even their own confederations. This preference does not arise from the requirements of a method of regulation as it did in the craft and promotion unions of the nineteenth century, for most white-collar unions rely on collective bargaining which does not entail any particular union structure. It must therefore be due to a conviction that the interests of white-collar employees differ from those of manual workers, and cannot be effectively represented in a unified organization. It is outside the scope of this study to speculate whether this conviction rests mainly on class mythology or on a realistic assessment of privilege and income distribution.

Regulating union structure

All the central confederations have power to intervene in jurisdictional disputes in which two or more affiliated unions claim the right to recruit a given group of workers, and these powers could be employed to change trade union boundaries according to some principle of organization. But that does not happen very much. Where confederations have espoused industrial unionism, as in France, Sweden, and West Germany, boundaries between affiliated unions are generally clear-cut and there are not many disputes. Where boundaries are complex and obscure, as in Australia, Britain, and the United States, it is because there is no single recognized organizational principle, and disputes are usually settled 'on their merits', which means the manner calculated to cause the least trouble. It is true that the TUC disputes committee has adopted rules, which are known as the 'Bridlington principles', and developed a body of case-law. But the rules are principles of good relations, not of structural design, and the case-law is intended to preserve established rights. Regulation of union structure on these lines does not provide a means of reform; it reinforces the tendency of collective bargaining to stabilize union structure.

Where the state has taken powers to promote or enforce union recognition, these too can be used to regulate structure. But the American legislation has left the decision on recognition to a ballot. The union of the voters' choice is recognized, and this arrangement has complicated union structure by acting as an incentive to competition, although, like most other methods of regulating recognition, it stabilizes structure once recognition has been achieved. From time to time the Australian arbitration tribunals have refused to register a union, but this has almost always been done to preserve the rights of registered unions. The tribunals therefore stabilize, but do not simplify, union structure. It is doubtful whether they could succeed in reforming union structure by deregistering established unions. Deregistration has generally been used as a penalty for flouting the authority of the tribunals; and in most instances it has not been effective. The tribunals have subsequently allowed the offending union to return not much the worse for the experience.

French law also regulates collective bargaining, and recognizes 'the most representative organizations' as having a statutory right to bargain if the employers are willing to meet them, but this power has not been used to reform trade union structure in France any more than in other countries. On the contrary the French authorities seem to have shown a delight in recognizing minuscule unions, splinter-groups, and breakaways, and France is an exception to the general rule that the power to recognize is generally used to stabilize union structure. Because of the proliferation of confederations divided on political and religious grounds, all of which have been recognized as 'most representative organizations', French union structure has now become far more complex than it was when collective bargaining was first introduced. One reason for multiplying recognition is that if the French had espoused either the preservation of existing rights, or the American method of exclusive recognition for the majority union, the CGT would have emerged the victor.

A theory of union structure

The theory's account of union structure can be summarized in the following propositions. The structure of many unions reflects the state of technology and industrial organization at the time of their birth and growth; the new skills of the industrial revolution led to craft and promotion unions; mass production favoured industrial and general unions; white-collar employees have multiplied, and their unions have grown with the large-scale organizations of the present century. But methods of trade union regulation are also relevant. Before the development of collective bargaining, unilateral regulation required organization by occupation. As collective bargaining developed, the existence of strong occupational unions promoted general unions; but, in the absence of strong occupational unions, industrial unions predominated. Collective bargaining is compatible with any union structure, and recognition by employers or the state for the purpose of bargaining stabilizes and legitimizes existing structures; collective bargaining also permits the ideology of industrial unionism to have an effect on structure. This ideology, however, has its greatest opportunity where unions have acquired little regulatory power, or where a trade union movement has been wiped out and the destruction of established obstacles to industrial unionism permits reconstruction to a predetermined pattern. White-collar employees tend to see their interests as different from those of manual workers and to prefer their own separate occupational unions.

11 Robert T. Buchanan

Mergers in British Trade Unions: 1949–79

From Robert T. Buchanan, *Industrial Relations Journal*, vol. 12, no. 3, May–June 1981, pp. 40–49.

Since the early 1960s there has been a steady increase in trade union mergers, the movement reaching a peak in the early 1970s and since then declining steadily. This paper examines the main features and effects of this movement and identifies the main reasons for it, taking account of a similar movement that began in 1911 and became particularly prominent between 1917 and 1922. An earlier study of union mergers in these two periods explained them in terms of the competitive recruitment conditions existing in these periods, the changes occurring in technology that affected the growth and financial strength of some unions, and the weak bargaining position of some unions; company amalgamations were also thought to have some influence (Buchanan, 1974).[1] It was suggested that the concentration of mergers into the two periods noted may be due to the mergers in companies occurring also during these periods and due also to the rapid rise in prices occurring at that time which affected differentials and encouraged a wider base for bargaining. Since the earlier study, however, the character of the merger movement has changed; white-collar unions have become much more important in the process, and the reasons for amalgamations appear now to be much more in terms of inflation and the size of an effective trade union.[2]

The information used in this study has been the annual figures of membership of unions recorded by the Department of Employment.[3] The method of classification used is similar to that in the earlier study. Most mergers are of the form of one union absorbing another, and

1. Similar reasons are given for mergers in US trade unions in Chitayat (1979).
2. Other studies of union mergers are: Graham (1970); Ulman (1955) (see also articles on US union mergers in the *Monthly Labour Review*, March 1967 and June 1971); Freeman and Brittain (1977); comments on this article by Seltzer, G., and by Chaison, G. N., and a reply by Freeman, J., and Brittain, J., in *Industrial Relations*, vol. 17, 1978.
3. Access to Department of Employment records for this purpose is gratefully acknowledged.

it was assumed that the larger union absorbed the smaller. Where a number of unions were involved, the amalgamation was classified as the largest absorbing the others.[4] In a few cases, the amalgamating unions retained their own identity, as in the case of the four sections of AUEW or the amalgamation of the printing, bookbinding and paper workers (NUPBPW) which amalgamated with SOGAT but remained a separate union till the arrangement was legally dissolved in 1972.

Membership figures used for unions involved in mergers are those for the year prior to the amalgamation.

Post-war trends in union mergers

The post-war trends in trade union mergers are given in Table 1; this shows the total number of unions, and membership absorbed, and also gives estimates for white-collar unions. The figures show a fairly stable level of mergers until the early 1960s, then a rising trend which reached a peak in membership and number of unions by the early 1970s. The trend now appears to be towards a decline, though by 1979 the position had not completely returned to the 1949–62 level. From 1963 till the early 1970s, the merger movement was primarily manual, but during the 1970s it became more of a white-collar movement.

Table 1 *Number and membership of trade unions absorbed by merger 1949–79*

| | Number | | | Member-ship | | | Number |
	Manual	white collar	Total	Manual	white collar	Total	merger cases
1949–50	6	8	14	4,249	8,369	12,618	13
1951–3	9	3	12	16,784	2,247	19,031	9
1954–6	14	2	16	9,519	6,120	15,639	16
1957–9	6	—	6	11,023	—	11,023	6
1960–62	15	4	19	12,951	3,137	16,088	17
1963–5	25	7	32	51,775	36,776	88,551	32
1966–8	27	7	34	225,759	40,131	265,890	33
1969–71	40	21	61	261,997	167,026	429,023	54
1972–4	36	33	69	123,798	56,870	180,668	54
1975–7	17	25	42	8,045	97,930	105,975	41
1978–9	11	12	23	26,616	16,751	43,367	22

4. The number of persons in various occupational groups 1911–17 is given in Price and Bain (1976).

The normal pattern of amalgamations occurring up till about 1962 was mainly concerned with manual unions, and about one-third of all unions acquired were small textile unions reorganizing in the light of falling demand for textile labour. Thus many of the small beamers', twisters' and drawers' unions amalgamated among themselves, a number of the sailmaker societies merged and some of the narrowly defined textile unions amalgamated, becoming broader-based unions like the Yorkshire Society of Textile Craftsmen, formed in this way in 1952.

Other mergers in this period reflected contraction in demand in other trades; and the National Society of Coppersmiths merged in the National Union of Sheetmetal Workers in 1959 for this reason, the National Cutlery Union accepted the same fate in 1957 and the Blacksmiths merged with the Boilermakers in 1962 for essentially this reason.

The range of trades involved in mergers in this period was wide, and unions in the glass industry, the building trade, printing, boots and shoes and other trades were involved. These were often small specialist unions – like the Amalgamated Society of Boot and Shoe Makers and Repairers, the Scottish Associated Tilefixers or the Manchester Umbrella Makers.

Some white-collar unions merged during this period. These were mainly small unions of post office workers, unions of customs and excise staff or small unions representing specialist civil service staff, all of which tended to merge with each other. The largest white-collar merger at this time was the creation of the London Typographical Society, of approximately 20,000 members, from two smaller unions, the Society helping to form the National Graphical Association in 1963 by merging with the Typographical Association.

But the unions acquired during the 1949–62 period were primarily fairly small in size as well as being mainly manual; the average size was about 1,000 members, though most were much smaller. Table 2 shows the size distribution of acquired unions and shows the years 1963–79 divided into periods each with a roughly similar number of acquired unions to that in 1949–62 and a roughly similar number of merger cases; the periods are thus roughly comparable. Table 3 then analyses the same material by size of receiving union, with 1960–62 being taken to represent the period of normality. These tables show that, prior to 1963, mergers were either among relatively small unions or small unions were absorbed by very large unions. With the development of the merger movement, the average size of union acquired

Table 2. Trade unions acquired by merger 1949–79 (shown by size of union acquired)

Size group of TUs acquired	1949–62		1963–8		1969–71		1972–4		1975–9	
	No. of TUs acquired	Membership acquired	No. of TUs acquired	Membership acquired	No. of TUs acquired	Membership acquired	No. of TUs acquired	Membership acquired	No. of TUs acquired	membership acquired
< 100	19	779	11	584	6	230	25	1,112	9	537
100 < 500	22	4,753	19	4,294	13	3,274	17	3,996	10	2,584
500 < 1,000	9	6,955	9	6,560	9	6,466	9	6,298	16	11,356
1,000 < 2,500	11	20,577	13	22,581	15	25,720	4	5,993	16	23,550
2,500 > 5,000	2	1,400	3	11,688	3	9,092	5	16,800	6	20,851
5,000 < 10,000	3	21,590	–	–	6	40,099	6	37,382	5	38,236
10,000 < 15,000	1	12,345	4	53,140	2	25,667	1	10,293	1	14,809
15,000 < 25,000	–	–	4	86,574	3	59,280	1	19,500	2	37,419
25,000 < 50,000	–	–	1	47,535	1	32,764	–	–	–	–
50,000 < 100,000	–	–	2	121,382	2	121,013	1	79,294	–	–
100,000	–	–	–	–	1	105,418	–	–	–	–
Total no. of TUs acquired	67	74,399	66	354,441	61	429,023	69	180,668	65	149,342
No. of white-collar TUs acquired	17	19,873	14	76,907	21	167,026	33	56,870	37	114,681
No. of merger cases	61		65		54		54		63	

Table 3 Trade unions acquired by merger (shown by size of acquiring trade unions)

	1960–62		1963–8		1969–71		1972–4		1975–9	
	No.	Membership	No.	Membership	No.	Membership	No.	Membership	No.	Membership
< 100	3	86	1	25	2	40	4	105	1	87
100 < 500	2	411	5	539	3	328	16	1,162	1	119
500 < 1,000	2	610	3	135	1	553	4	1,494	5	1,616
1,000 < 2,500	1	202	6	2,472	5	3,501	4	1,469	5	3,047
2,500 < 5,000	2	902	2	462	3	3,378	10	6,473	5	4,962
5,000 < 10,000	1	98	3	2,958	2	401	1	114	1	746
10,000 < 15,000	1	1,928	3	6,980	4	14,489	1	5	–	–
15,000 < 25,000	–	–	–	–	1	769	2	3,546	2	17,993
25,000 < 50,000	–	–	2	24,649	1	6	–	–	4	6,129
50,000 < 100,000	1	9,835	16	80,713	16	72,302	5	14,641	12	49,249
100,000	6	2,016	25	235,508	23	333,256	22	151,659	29	65,394
	19	16,088	66	354,441	61	429,023	69	180,668	65	149,342

rose four- or fivefold and the proportion acquired by very large unions increased greatly. The very large unions then became much more prominent in the merger process than during 1949–62.

In the changes that occurred among manual unions after 1963, the amalgamation of small textile unions among themselves again continued to be an important part of the total merger movement. And although the larger unions in the textile industry (National Union of Dyers and Bleachers, National Union of Hosiery Workers, and Tailor and Garment Workers) have had merger negotiations with each other, no amalgamations among them have taken place so far, nor have they been greatly involved in the absorption of the smaller unions. In textiles, the merger process has largely been confined to the smaller unions. But amalgamations occurred among larger-sized unions after 1963 in a number of other industries. In the printing industry, the National Union of Printing, Bookbinding and Paper Workers, which organised mainly in the printing and bookbinding industry, merged in 1966 with NATSOPA, which organized mainly in printing to form SOGAT, and the NGA absorbed a number of other print unions during the 1960s, raising its membership significantly. (The original SOGAT amalgamation was dissolved early in 1972, the National Union of Printing, Bookbinding and Paper Workers retaining the SOGAT name as part of the dissolution agreement.) In shipbuilding, the absorption in 1963 of the Ship Constructors and Shipwrights by the Boilermakers was a sizeable amalgamation, and the amalgamation of the National Union of Sheetmetal Workers and the Heating and Domestic Engineers was also a significant merger. But the largest mergers are probably the absorption by the AEU of the Amalgamated Union of Foundry Workers in 1967 and of DATA and the Constructional Engineering Union in 1971 to form AUEW into a federal union of four sections.

In the building industry, the Scottish Plasterers Union, with about 4,000 members, was taken over in 1966 by the National Association of Operative Plasterers, the EETU absorbed the plumbing trade unions with over 50,000 members in 1968 and, in 1970 and 1971, there were sizeable mergers between the Amalgamated Society of Woodworkers, the Associated Society of Painters and Decorators and the Amalgamated Union of Building Trade Workers, resulting in the appearance of UCATT in 1972.

In the case of white-collar unions, some mergers among these had occurred during the 1960s in printing, in the insurance industry, in the gas industry, in teaching and in entertainment and in some other industries. But the main expansion came in the late 1960s with the creation of ASTMS in 1968 from ASSET and the Association of Scientific Workers, with mergers among the various nursing bodies in 1968 and 1970 and with the movement towards amalgamation among the bank and insurance organizations that began in 1968 and 1969. These trends continued during the rest of the 1970s. A number of small civil service unions amalgamated during the 1970s covering post office employees, customs and excise officers and similar groups, and in 1973 CPSA absorbed the roughly 20,000 members in the Ministry of Labour Staff Association. A number of unions representing teachers amalgamated between 1973 and 1978, covering teachers in different types of institutions, school inspectors, women teacher organizations and headmasters. And throughout the 1970s mergers in banking, insurance and finance have been dominated by competition between ASTMS and NUBE, the latter in April 1979 becoming the Banking, Insurance and Finance Union. ASTMS, although only formed in 1968, established itself in the insurance field in 1970 with the absorption of the Union of Insurance Staff and three small Prudential Staff Associations, giving it more than 20,000 members in the insurance industry. It continued to absorb small insurance staff organizations with the Royal Group Guild in 1971, Stamford Mutual in 1973 and the Pearl Insurance and other groups in 1974 and 1975. At the same time it absorbed the Midland Bank Staff in 1974, an organization of approximately 10,000 members, giving it a foothold in banking. It also took in the larger-sized United Commercial Travellers Association in 1976. For NUBE, the trend has been in the opposite direction. It continued to absorb small bank staff organizations during the 1970s, absorbing the Royal Bank of Scotland Staff in 1975 and a small Lloyds Bank organization in 1976. By the early 1970s NUBE had decided to widen its area of recruitment to take in insurance and finance house staff organizations, and this led it to accept the 1971 Industrial Relations Act and to seek the jurisdiction of NIRC in achieving recognition with some finance houses. It also led to the absorption by NUBE of the Guardian Royal Exchange Staff Association in 1978 and the Phoenix Staff Union in 1979, NUBE then changed its name to BIFU in order to emphasize its wider interests.

Although large unions were responsible for many of the mergers during the 1960s, they appear to have been even more important in the 1970s. The TGWU's absorption of the Scottish Commercial Motormen in 1971, of the Scottish Transport and General Workers and the NUVB in 1972 and of other smaller unions in 1974 and 1975 are typical cases. The NUGMW, the Society of Civil and Public Servants and APEX are other unions with over 100,000 members who were active in absorbing smaller unions in the 1970s, as well as AUEW and ASTMS.

Reasons

1. Competitive recruitment and technical change

The earlier study suggested that competitive recruitment conditions and technical change were two important reasons for the rise in mergers during the 1960s. Both reasons seem to have been important in the case of textile mergers, technical and organizational change reducing the membership of some unions and the TGWU's standing invitation to absorb all remaining textile unions providing an encouragement to amalgamation among themselves. These trends have continued into the 1970s, and the unsuccessful attempts at a merger between the three main textile unions have not helped to overcome the competitive recruitment situation. Other examples of technical change bringing mergers are the absorption of the blacksmiths and shipwrights in 1962 and 1963 by the boilermakers, encouraged by the establishment of prefabrication in shipbuilding and the replacement of rivetting by welding. Also, the merging of the moulders, instrument makers and, in 1967, the foundry workers with the engineers are further examples.

In printing, technical change has been important in producing at least one union merger virtually each year throughout the 1960s and 1970s, with larger mergers in 1963, the creation of the NGA, the (later abortive) merger of NUPBPW and NATSOPA in 1966 and, in 1969, when NGA absorbed the Amalgamated Society of Lithographic Printers. NGA has now absorbed the National Union of Wall Covering, Decorative and Allied Trades, is discussing a merger with SOGAT and has reorganized its trade group structure to allow white-collar workers to be taken into membership, as a response to the problems created by technical change in printing. The use of computer machinery and other changes in printing has meant that more and more work in the industry is being done by people without craft training or a traditional apprenticeship. This has allowed non-print, white-collar unions to expand their activities in the printing industry, especially since the existing blue-collar unions have offered no membership facilities to white-collar workers. As a result, APEX and ASTMS now have an established membership in printing, and other unions are also attempting to gain a foothold. Attempts to regulate recruitment through the TUC have not been entirely successful, and NGA saw that it must either accept a declining influence in determining future conditions in the industry or widen its base to include white-collar workers. Recent amalgamations and a change in NGA's trade group structure have been steps to achieve this. However, the case of printing shows that technical change, by offering new opportunities for recruitment, often creates competitive recruitment conditions at the same time. The banking, insurance and finance industries, discussed later, have had a broadly similar experience, though technical change has been less important in creating the conditions of competitive recruitment.

Another case where recruitment conditions brought union mergers is seen in the white-collar unions of the steel industry. Here, the Steel Industry Management Association, with about 12,000 middle and senior managers as members, found itself by the mid-1970s in direct competition for members with the mainly blue-collar Iron and Steel Trades Confederation, which wished to extend its own white-collar section of clerks and supervisors into management grades. Attempts at merger here have failed since SIMA feared loss of identity by being absorbed into ISTC. But, in any case, the TGWU's white-collar section has some members in supervisory grades in the steel industry, and competition for members also exists there. It now seems likely that the TGWU will move into the management field by absorbing SIMA.

Something of a similar case existed with the Electrical Power Engineers Association, which represented senior management in the electricity industry until the mid-1970s. The union then decided to broaden its recruitment base and enter the lower- and middle-management field in general engineering and related industries, representing professional engineers and managers generally; it changed its name to the Engineers and Managers Association to reflect its wider interests. EMA then attempted to achieve a merger with UKAPE and with the Association of Supervisory and Executive Engineers in 1976 and 1977 in order to widen its membership. While the merger negotiations in the UKAPE were unsuccessful, agreement with ASEE was achieved, and EMA at the same time absorbed the Shipbuilding and Allied Industries Management Association at the end of 1977. And in 1979 it entered the aerospace industry by absorbing the British Aerospace Staffs Association. This policy has brought it into conflict with TASS, APEX, ASTMS and other unions already recruiting in this field, who argue that representation by a separate union is unnecessary and that existing unions like TASS and NALGO are quite sufficient. The policy has also led EMA into conflict with ACAS over recruitment rights and also into conflict with the TUC over rulings of TUC dispute committees made under the Bridlington rules. But the EMA case illustrates more than competitive recruitment conditions. Though affiliated to the TUC, EMA is politically neutral, like BIFU (formerly NUBE). Both claim that this is an important part of their appeal to white-collar workers and hence that it separates them from the other large, politically committed unions. The same factor exists in the merger now planned between the First Division Association, organising about 10,000 senior civil servants, and IPCS, also representing senior civil servants; both are non-political in character.

In a number of the cases already noted, the influence of technical change in promoting mergers is fairly clear; in other situations it is perhaps less so. Clearly, the number of scientific and technical employees, working often at managerial level, has increased in recent years, and technical change in this wider sense has given this group significant industrial power (see Price and Bain, 1976). Union mergers appear in some cases to be attempts to consolidate or extend that power. An indication of the power was given in 1977, when manual workers in power stations took industrial action, but its effectiveness was reduced by the engineers operating the grid system. If, however, the engineers had initiated action, the manual workers would have been largely powerless to influence its effects. It would seem that some union mergers have been pursued in order to make the power and influence of such groups more effective.

2. Growth in membership

A further reason for mergers has been that the growth in membership in some cases has begun to slow up, and with a low level of subscriptions existing in most unions, financial problems are then not far away, especially under conditions of rapidly rising prices. Mergers are then seen as a means of obtaining new bargaining rights and of widening the field of recruitment as well as improving the financial position of the union.

The changing trends in membership appear to have had some influence in promoting mergers, particularly in the 1960s and 1970s. Total union membership has risen slowly in the post-war years. Manual membership has risen, in total, at least until 1970, and density of manual unionism has increased at about 2 per cent per annum throughout the post-war years. White-collar density, however, by the early 1960s had begun to increase at about 5 per cent per annum and has continued at that level into the 1970s (see Price and Bain, 1976). It is within these trends that membership in some sectors has been stable and, in other sectors, expanding rapidly; this has provided conditions for mergers, particularly of white-collar unions.

Changes in employment have brought a decline in the membership of many small unions and encouraged mergers among them throughout the post-war years. These changes have also brought mergers of some small unions of moulders with the engineers between 1963 and 1968, the blacksmiths and shipwrights with the boilermakers in 1962 and 1963 and similar mergers in later years. Stable membership and fixed union funds have also prevented some unions from pursuing an aggressive union wage policy; it also creates financial problems if income is stable and union commitments are rising with rising prices. The lack of an aggressive union wage policy by the Amalgamated Scientific Workers was an important issue in its merger negotiations with DATA in the late 1960s and was one reason why these negotiations failed and ASW merged with ASSET in 1968 to form ASTMS.

The trend in membership has been an important factor in promoting mergers in a number of other cases. Thus APEX has always organized clerical, computer and managerial staff in both the private and public sectors. More recently, however, it has tried to widen its field of recruitment by taking in senior and technical management, particularly in the oil industry, by absorbing some widely different staff organizations, and by entering the insurance field. This was done by absorbing the General Accident Staff Association, an action which brought it into conflict with ASTMS and the TUC. It seems probable that without a continuing rise in membership, APEX could find itself in a more difficult financial position; it would then be in a weak bargaining position itself and would be open to a possible takeover by another large white-collar union.

NUBE seems to have been another case where the original recruitment field of the union provided limited potential growth in membership, and the rules of the union were amended by 1971 to allow it to recruit on a wider basis. The whole field of banking, insurance and finance then gave NUBE a potential membership of possibly 500,000 members rather than one of perhaps 200,000 by being restricted to banking alone. It also allowed NUBE to deal with its difficult financial position around 1970 by a planned expansion in membership and income. It had been asked by some small insurance unions, at that time, to accept them into membership, but had been obliged to refuse them since its rules prevented such mergers. ASTMS accepted them in 1970 and NUBE met the situation by changing its rules in 1971.

NUBE, at this time, also tried to improve its position by proposing a merger with the Council of the Bank Staff Association, each organization having a membership of 70,000 to 80,000 members. Since 1968 a system of national negotiations operated between the five London Clearing Banks and NUBE, along with the Council of the Bank Staff Associations representing the staff side in the national negotiation Council. However, the Staff Associations tended to be the stronger of the two organizations on the staff side, and their control of this side during negotiations led to difficulties during the 1970s and the failure of a merger to be agreed. In addition, the expulsion of NUBE from the TUC over its acceptance of the 1971 Act, and the consequent suspension of Bridlington rules in banking, allowed ASTMS to accept the Midland Bank Staff in a merger arrangement in 1974 and gain a substantial footing in the recruitment of bank personnel. NUBE continued to try to get a merger with the remaining staff associations in a new federal union of employee organizations, even though it was likely to remain in an unsatisfactory position in any such organization. No merger of this kind has been possible during the 1970s, and the failure to achieve it seems to have encouraged NUBE to pursue mergers with small building society staff associations and among similar organizations in insurance. The unsatisfactory position of NUBE in the staff side of the national negotiating arrangements led it to withdraw from those arrangements in 1977.

This encouraged NUBE to move strongly into the insurance field with its absorption of the Guardian Royal Exchange Staff Union in 1978 and the Phoenix Staff Union in 1979.

But the problem of stable or declining membership is more significant for craft unions, like AUEW, operating in the manufacturing industries, where employment trends have been unfavourable by contrast with service industries, and where the future for skilled workers is not encouraging. Thus where TGWU has increased its membership significantly during the 1970s, the AUEW engineering section has remained static. This has been reflected in a weakened

149

financial position, and if membership cannot be increased financial problems are likely to continue. [...]

3. The problem of size and structure

For a number of reasons, union size and structure has also become increasingly important to union mergers. Under conditions of rapidly rising pay and prices it would seem that medium- and large-sized unions have significant benefits over small unions. Only unions with perhaps 200,000 members and over may appear to have the membership and income to provide the services now required of any viable union, i.e. regional as well as national offices, legal and other specialist services, research, publicity and similar commitments. And with low subscription rates in many British unions, the provision of these services has become increasingly difficult in the last decade and seems to have forced some unions – banking seems to be an example – to seek mergers to help resolve this problem. This may be particularly true of unions recruiting on a narrow single-craft, or single-industry basis. The larger-sized unions also have the benefit of being able to finance strikes more easily since only a very small proportion of their members are likely to be on strike at any one time. They are also likely to be able to carry the problem of turnover and the retention of members more easily than a small union. And for unions in some industries, like UCATT in construction or FTAT (the Furniture, Timber and Allied Trades) in the 'finishing trades' of construction, turnover is important and mergers may be a way of dealing with this. In addition, the more widely based the union, the more easily can it deal with turnover and survive a recession in which members may move into contiguous industries and retain their membership.

But although mergers may be pursued in order to achieve the size necessary for an effectively operating union, the experience of AUEW in trying to make mergers effective seems to have had a widespread influence. AUEW has tried since 1971 to change its federal structure linking the four sections of the union into a full amalgamation with no success. Despite proposals made at Worthing in 1974, modified in 1976, and further changes since then, no full agreement has yet been made. This has discouraged other merger discussions between AUEW and EETPU and encouraged the Boilermakers to begin merger discussions with GMWU. This may have encouraged other unions to seek mergers with small unions who can be fully integrated rather than with large unions whose identity, rules and structure might need to be maintained. Thus it is noticeable that ASTMS, which has been more actively involved in mergers than most unions, has almost invariably absorbed small unions who have not created obstacles to their full integration.

Size and structure have created a further problem in that the dominant size and position of the TGWU has encouraged merger discussions with the aim of creating a union of equivalent countervailing power. Certainly the powerful position of the TGWU and its leadership of the semi-skilled and unskilled workers has allowed it to negotiate a narrowing of the pay differential for skill in recent years, and the need for skilled unions to be organized into equally large organizations has been behind some recent merger discussions.

Other influences

The importance of the political views of merging unions, or the lack of them, has already been briefly noted and is an important precondition to favourable negotiations. Some unions or staff organizations are consciously non-political, like the Civil Service Union, with approximately 50,000 members in the lower grades of the civil service. CSU has been unwilling to discuss a merger with CPSA since it does not wish to become actively involved in political issues in the same way that CPSA has in recent years. And many white-collar staff associations have the same view. Others, like BIFU, have a very limited involvement in political affairs. This union does not take part in political debates at TUC conferences and has a political adviser from both the main political parties. In other cases, the political views of the merging parties have been an important pre-condition to a successful merger. Thus, while an important difficulty preventing full amalgamation by the four sections of AUEW has been the problem of finding an acceptable constitution, the issue has also been one of merging the politically different views of TASS with the engineering section.

The case of engineering also illustrates the further problem of finding an acceptable organizational structure and constitution. The central problems here have been the creation of a national committee giving satisfactory representation to each section and also the existence of elected officials in the case of the politically right-wing engineering section and appointed officials in the politically left-wing TASS. A similar structural problem existed when NUPBPW and

NATSOPA attempted an amalgamation in the early 1970s the former having a very loose structure with elected branch officials and power concentrated at the branch level, whereas NATSOPA is more centrally organized with appointed area officials and a General Secretary with strong powers. In printing, the main merger at present being planned is between NGA and SOGAT. The former has been able to change its structure in recent years. This ability to adapt allowed it recently to absorb the National Union of Wall Coverings, Decorative and Allied Trades and seems likely to make a merger with SOGAT successful.

A further factor encouraging mergers seems to be the attempt to improve the bargaining position of some groups by amalgamations. The obvious examples here have been nurses, teachers and bank employees. In nursing, the amalgamation between 1968 and 1970 of the Student Nurses Association, the Royal College of Nursing and the National Association of State Enrolled Nurses created a single organization of over 70,000 members. In teaching there have been a number of mergers, particularly since 1974, involving smaller unions, though the process of concentrations has not gone as far as among nurses or bank employees. In the case of banking, BIFU has been attempting to create a merger with the Confederation of Bank Staff Associations, as indicated earlier.

General reasons for mergers

If trade union mergers in pre-war years are considered, it is clear that a period of intense merger activity existed between 1917 and 1922, although some increase in mergers occurred from 1911 (see Buchanan, 1974). Prior to 1917, any union amalgamation required each of the unions to get a majority of its membership to vote in favour. But as G. D. H Cole has observed, these stringent conditions were often dealt with by the unions concerned dissolving with a recommendation to their members to join another particular union (see Cole, 1953). The 1917 legislation changed the conditions necessary for a union merger to a majority of those voting, in a vote of at least half of the total membership.[5] This change seems to explain the big increase in mergers from 1917, although, as already noted, the figures suggest that the increase really began in 1911.

How are the two periods of union mergers in the UK to be explained? One common feature of the two periods was rapidly rising

5. The Trade Unions (Amalgamation) Act.

prices, which tend to create financial difficulties for small unions, make the size and efficiency of large unions more important and may also emphasize the need to protect living standards by a powerful union negotiating with employers or government. Prices in the first period rose from 1910 and increased very rapidly from 1915, reaching a peak in 1920. In the second period prices began to rise more rapidly from the mid-1960s, and from the late 1960s the annual rise became much greater. Both periods have contained years of stable or falling real incomes and union mergers might be seen partly as a response to this weak bargaining position.

Much of the stress in recent years on achieving trade unions of sufficient size to be able to provide satisfactory services seems to have arisen in conjunction with a rapid rise in prices and wages. These trends in wages and prices thus seem to be important pre-conditions to the growth in union mergers.

A further pre-condition seems to be changes in the growth and pattern of union membership. Both periods have shown evidence of this and recent examples have already been quoted. Here, some avenues of growth in membership appear to have reached a limit and new ones are opening; growth, at least for some unions, may have been more through merger than by the enrolling of new members. At the same time, mergers have allowed access to expanding areas of recruitment and brought competitive recruitment conditions, typical of recent years.

A third general influence may have been a desire to improve union concentration and the bargaining power of unions in their dealings with employers and government. But although mergers may improve concentration it is only possible to make a broad indication here of their effects; any accurate estimation of their effects on union concentration would require a separate study.

Any mergers involving transfers of members within one size group of unions would have no effect on the size distribution and concentration of unions; only gains and losses in membership arising from inter-group transfers will affect the size distribution, assuming that a merger, by itself, did not put the receiving union into a new size class, and disregarding the effects of growth or decline in membership over a period of time after the unions are merged. The gains and losses arising from mergers and the resulting net balance for each size group of unions, for the period 1963–79, are given in Table 4; these gains and losses are then compared with the change in total membership for 1963–78 (latest figures available). The figures appear to suggest that while mergers explain some of the change in membership of most groups, they explain little of the growth in the largest-size group. Here membership increased by 3·8 million over the period, whereas membership acquired by the trade union giants through merger amounted to 680,000. But this makes no allowance for the continued growth of unions absorbed by merger or shifts between different-size groups and does not give an accurate indication of the contribution of mergers to the concentration process.[6] Nevertheless, at a time of rising prices, stable or falling real incomes and increased company concentration through mergers, it seems likely that increased bargaining power is sought by trade unions, and mergers are one way of achieving this.

It might be questioned how far these general conditions conducive to mergers, and also the reasons for amalgamations discussed earlier, provide conditions for a continuation of union mergers in future years. Technological changes and competitive recruitment conditions have already been mentioned as important reasons, and these seem likely to be continuing influences. So also is the rapid rise in wages and prices, as this creates increasing financial problems for small and medium-sized firms. [. . .] And any trend toward a demand for better services by trade unions at the same time as wages and prices are rising is likely to put continuing pressure on unions to amalgamate.

A further factor which may affect the trend in union mergers is the future trend in company mergers. Company and union mergers do not tend to rise and fall at exactly the same time. But there is something of a similarity in trend; union mergers were significant between 1917–22, while company mergers expanded from 1918 till 1931; again, company mergers increased from the early 1950s till the mid 1970s, while union mergers were prominent from the mid 1960s to the mid 1970s.[7] Many company mergers tend to react on trade unions and both are obviously affected by technical change.[8]

If there is a broad connection between these two trends, are company mergers likely to continue at a high level in the near future, encouraging a similar trend in unions? A recent study has suggested that increasingly competitive conditions in international trade,

6. The contribution of mergers to the process of union concentration has generally been considered much less important than that of internal growth. This is the view held by Phelps Brown and Hart (1957) and Simpson (1972). But this analysis has itself been questioned by Hannah (1976) and Hannah and Kay (1977).

7. See Hannah (1976), Appendix 1; also Dept of Trade and Industry, *Annual Abstract of Statistics and British Business*, August 1980, HMSO.

8. See Hughes (1970 and 1972).

Table 4 *Membership involved in mergers 1963–79*

Size group of TU membership	By Size of TU acquired (thousands)	By size of acquiring TU (thousands)	Net Balance (thousands)	Change in total membership 1963–78 (thousands)	Change in number of unions 1963–
< 99	2·5	0·2	-2·3	-3·0	-58
100 < 499	14·2	2·2	-12·0	-4·0	-20
500 < 999	30·6	3·8	-26·8	-11·0	-15
1,000 < 2,499	77·9	10·5	-67·4	-63·0	-40
2,500 < 4,999	58·5	15·3	-43·2	-71·0	-24
5,000 < 9,999	115·7	4·2	-111·5	-61·0	-8
10,000 < 14,999	103·9	21·5	-82·4	157·0	-13
15,000 < 24,999	202·8	22·3	-180·5	-154·0	-8
25,000 < 49,999	80·3	30·8	-49·5	+46·0	+1
50,000 < 99,999	321·7	216·9	-104·8	-311·0	-4
100,000	105·4	785·8	+680·4	+3,834·0	+8
	1,113·5	1,113·5	0·0	+3,045·0	-181

increased takeover bidding and similar trends suggest continued company concentration, though at a slower rate than the company mergers of the 1960s.[9] If this is so, a continuation of union mergers seems likely in the future.

9. Hannah (1976).

References

BUCHANAN, R. T. (1974), 'Merger Waves in British Unionism', *Industrial Relations Journal*, vol. 5, no. 2, Summer.

CHITAYAT, G. (1979), *Trade Union Members and Labour Conglomerates*, Praeger.

COLE, G. D. H. (1953), *An Introduction to Trade Unions*, Allen & Unwin.

Department of Trade and Industry, The (1970), *A Survey of Mergers, 1958–68*, HMSO.

FREEMAN, J., and J. BRITTAIN (1977), 'Union Merger Process and Industrial Environment', *Industrial Relations*, vol. 16, no. 2, May.

GRAHAM, H. (1970), 'Union Mergers', *Industrial Relations* (Quebec), vol. 25, pt 3.

HANNAH, L. (1976), *The Rise of the Corporate Economy: The British Experience*, Johns Hopkins University Press.

HANNAH, L., and J. A. KAY (1977), *Concentration in Modern Industry*, Humanities Press.

HUGHES, J. (1970), 'Giant Firms and British Trade Unions' Response', *Trade Union Register 1970*, ed. K. Coates *et al.*, Merlin Press.

HUGHES, J. (1972), 'The Trade Union Response to Mergers', *Readings on Mergers and Takeovers*, ed. J. M. Samuels, Elek.

PHELPS BROWN, E. H., and P. E. HART (1957), 'The Size of Trade Unions', *Economic Journal*, vol. 67, March.

PRICE, R., and G. S. BAIN (1976), 'Union Growth Revisited: 1948–74 in Perspective', *British Journal of Industrial Relations*, vol. 14, no. 3, November.

SIMPSON, D. H. (1972), 'An Analysis of the Size of Trade Unions', *British Journal of Industrial Relations*, vol. 10, no. 3, November.

ULMAN, L. (1955), *The Rise of the National Trade Union*, Harvard University Press.

12 R. Undy, V. Ellis, W. E. J. McCarthy and A. M. Halmos

Recent Merger Movements and Future Union Structure

From R. Undy, V. Ellis, W. E. J. McCarthy and A. M. Halmos, *Changes in Trade Unions*, Hutchinson, 1981, pp. 214–20, 339–43.

Features that facilitate mergers

All the unions examined, regardless of their systems of government, were led into mergers by their national full-time officials. No union experienced anything that could be described as a general membership drive for amalgamations. The 1960s and 1970s mergers were thus distinctly different from those, like the AEU [Amalgamated Engineering Union], that received their impetus in the 1920s from local-level, rank-and-file amalgamation committees. Agents for change that promoted mergers hence made themselves felt at the national level mainly through those processes that by-passed the constitutionally-prescribed policy-making channels. The existence of constitutionally-processed policy decisions urging the formation of an industrial union did, however, play a part in some unions in shaping the direction of this merger activity.

The *change agents* that promoted mergers were themselves largely the product of previous developments in the areas of change. All the merging unions examined tended to react initially in the merger field in response to changes that affected some aspect of size, which produced in turn *defensive, consolidatory* and *aggressive* approaches to mergers.

Size change agents were of two, not mutually exclusive, kinds. First, there were absolute changes in size and, second, relative size developments. Significant and adverse absolute changes in size provoked the most marked *defensive merger* activity. All the unions forming UCATT [Union of Construction, Allied Trades and Technicians] and the minor AUFW [Amalgamated Union of Foundry Workers] in the AUEW [Amalgamated Union of Engineering Workers] merger were primarily stimulated in their merger search by a decline in their absolute membership, as were a number of the minor unions joining ASTMS [Association of Scientific, Technical and Managerial Staffs] and the TGWU [Transport and General Workers' Union]. A significant and continuous decline in membership in an inflationary period threatened the financial viability of many of the above unions, unions that had already attempted within the confines of their existing and traditional job territories to mitigate or reverse their numerical and financial decline. Their common problem was that they could not independently maintain or improve their existing levels of services and benefits over the short or medium term. In extreme cases even the unions' survival was brought into question. Such defensive unions, as a member of the AUEW commented, thus paradoxically 'amalgamate in order to remain independent'.

A similar kind of adverse absolute change created a defensive posture among some of the white-collar unions and associations which merged with ASTMS. Several small white-collar organizations maintained a bargaining presence, such as the Engineer Surveyors' Association, on a membership of 1,000 to 2,000 members. In their case the absolute change came from the increased demands on the organization and not from the decline in membership. Industrial relations legislation, innovations in bargaining, such as job evaluation and incomes policy, and the general increased demands on the organization exposed such unions' and associations' inability to service membership effectively from a narrow base. A belief developed in this situation that such a union could survive only with a much higher level of membership if it was to continue to provide the services needed by its membership in the 1970s. The small white-collar unions and associations found themselves, as one official remarked, needing 'full-time experts'. Unable to afford such experts from their own limited resources, the very minor white-collar unions opted as a defensive measure to merge with ASTMS. They needed a larger absolute membership in order to survive as a viable organization.

Secondly, relative size developments produced, in some unions, *consolidatory* and *aggressive* mergers. Major and minor merging unions in the AUEW merger came into an amalgamation primarily intended to *consolidate* the AEU's position as the premier union in the engineering industry. Through this amalgamation the AEU and the more minor merging unions expected to preserve the craftsmen's hegemony in the industry. The relative size changes that brought about such a consolidatory merger were those that challenged the individual union's growth expectations and/or adversely influenced its position in some sphere of inter-union competition. The AUEW's component unions were affected in both these ways. DATA

[Draughtsmen's and Allied Technicians' Association], the AUFW and the AEU itself all experienced lower growth rates than past experience had led them to expect. Moreover, in DATA's and the AEU's cases competitor unions also had relatively and significantly higher growth rates than either union.

In ASTMS and the TGWU, mergers were pursued more *aggressively* than in the other major merging unions. In the numerous mergers entered into by these unions minor merging unions driven by defensive motives joined major unions seeking to enhance their relative positions vis-à-vis other competitor unions. Led from the top, ASTMS and the TGWU generally outbid their competitors for the privilege of rescuing minor unions from extinction. This was not, however, an altogether altruistic act. Both major unions expected to make effective inroads into the minor merging unions' new and relatively unorganized job territories – or, on the other hand, to prevent the better organized areas of job territory falling to some other competitor organization.

The *direction of change* given by the above changes in some aspect of size did nothing to produce a more logical or planned inter-union structure in Britain. The TUC's efforts to create certain patterns of unionism through its industrial committees were not successful, although its promotion of legislative changes, which made mergers considerably easier, opened the way for the merger movement. Inter-union structures were therefore primarily affected in an *ad hoc* manner by the mergers encouraged by the legislative changes.

The mergers, however, gathered considerable momentum of their own as the past absolute and relative size changes, mentioned above, interacted with the existing structure of UK unions to produce a scramble for mergers that developed its own dynamic. The individual merger was turned by this combination of circumstances into a merger movement. In the first instance, a merger stimulated by absolute size reasons disturbed other unions' relative size considerations. These disturbed unions, in turn, sought mergers in order to restore the status quo in respect to their relative size or to reduce the competitor unions' recently-gained relative size advantage.

The mergers were encouraged to develop in this way by the existing structure of UK unions. There were in the engineering and building industries in the 1960s, for instance, no clear boundaries to the various unions' recruiting territories. Prior to the merger movement, several formerly exclusive craft unions had extended vertically within their original industrial and craft bases while the general unions had

159

spread themselves horizontally across several blue-collar occupations in a number of industries. ASSET [Association of Supervisory Staffs, Executives and Technicians] also achieved, mainly through mergers, a similar multi-industrial base in white-collar employment. A minor union seeking a merger was thus faced by a number of options, even if it narrowed its search to its industrial base or related occupations. Only the highly craft-conscious minor unions, in practice, rejected outright the option of joining a general union, such as the TGWU. Minor merging unions such as the NAOP [National Association of Operative Plasterers], the NUVB [National Union of Vehicle Builders] and the AScW [Association of Scientific Workers] were thus all in a position to assess competitive bids for their membership and job territories, from more than one union.

In this environment the merger proposals made, for instance, by the ASW to the ASPD [Associated Society of Painters and Decorators] and AUBTW [Amalgamated Union of Building Trade Workers] threatened to weaken the relative strength of the TGWU in the building industry. Similarly, the AEU's merger talks with the AUFW, NUVB and the other minor engineering unions could, if successful, have undermined the TGWU's relative position in engineering in general and in the highly competitive vehicle industry in particular. Outside these industries the TGWU's relative position in the TUC and its committees was also likely to be adversely influenced if the ASW [Amalgamated Society of Wood Workers] and/or the AEU were successful in creating two new craft-dominated industrial unions. Also, ASSET faced an intense inter-union recruiting contest with DATA if that union, and not itself, was successful in merging with the AScW.

Competition for merger partners in the industries examined, and in the ASSET's, and later the ASTMS's, bid for rapid growth, was thus intense. Jones's and Jenkins's ascendancy in their respective and highly concentrated unions, the TGWU and ASTMS, and their own commitments to an aggressive merger policy, made their unions 'the predators' of the merger movement. Any misunderstanding or difficulty between the AEU or the ASW and its potential merger partners was fully exploited by the TGWU. Similarly, ASSET took advantage of DATA's inability to complete a merger with the AScW. Through this kind of competitive merger action and the widespread belief that a minimum size of union was necessary to remain efficient and effective, a feeling of 'we must go somewhere' developed among the minor unions and heightened their awareness of the costs of remaining fully independent.

In the competitive merger searches parameters were set by a combination of factors. Normally the causes of the size changes, the perceived solutions to the adverse effects of such changes, the historical growth objectives and existing membership affinities between merging unions interacted to set the parameters of the search. If the causes of the adverse absolute or relative size changes were perceived to be irreversible, largely because they arose from exogenous factors, the affected unions reacted by seeking mergers that could, in a quantitative manner, immediately compensate for the previous perceived adverse size changes. The parameters of many of the unions joining the AEU, TGWU and ASTMS were influenced by such ideas.

On the other hand, if the merger search was stimulated by adverse size developments arising largely from endogenous factors, the merger search parameters were influenced by different considerations. If, for instance, adverse size changes were perceived as the product of shifts in actual or potential members' attitudes to unionization, as in the ASW's, ASPD's and AUBTW's situation, the search parameters were influenced by the unions' attempt to change those attitudes. In the ASW's case, the mergers were not intended primarily to provide an instant change in job territory; the ASW merged with the other unions in the same predicament in order to change the qualitative nature of union activity in the building industry. There was an assumption that the separate unions' original members could be retained and potential members recruited through a restructuring of unions in the building industry. It was thought, in the ASW, that the combined merged unions could 'deliver the goods' which independently they had failed to provide. A number of small white-collar unions that later joined the ASTMS appeared to be influenced by similar reasons. The perceived causes of the adverse size changes thus influenced the parameters of unions' merger searches.

However, for unions led by highly craft-conscious national officials, historical growth objectives and membership affinities were the most important factors determining the merger search parameters. Even though the conditions that originally spawned ideas of industrial unionism had changed somewhat by the 1960s, it still remained a powerful influence on the parameters of the ASW's and AEU's merger searches.

By contrast, the leaders of the TGWU and the ASTMS faced no

such historical and internal constraints on their merger activities. The TGWU's and ASTMS's existing members had affinities across many industries in, respectively, blue-collar and white-collar occupations. But even if they, the existing membership, had objected to their leaders' merger activities breaking into new job territories, the concentrated and highly flexible systems of government safeguarded the national full-time leadership's discretion in this field of activity. The TGWU and ASTMS were therefore operating within a wider merger area than were the more craft-oriented unions.

Generally, a union seeking a merger remained clearly within the above search parameters until its originally identified options had been exhausted. It was normally only as a last resort that a minor merging union sought a merger outside its immediate job territory. On the odd occasion that minor unions broke prematurely out of their natural territories, the personal preferences and antagonisms of the leading merger negotiators played an important part in the decision.

The TGWU and ASTMS therefore had in certain situations *features that facilitated mergers*. They both had wider parameters of merger searches than any other unions. If a blue-collar or white-collar union was moved by either absolute or relative size changes to increase its membership by a merger, the TGWU and ASTMS respectively were the most pro-merger unions likely to have an affinity with the minor union's existing membership. And, unlike the other interested unions, the TGWU and ASTMS provided minor merging unions with the trade group structures that guaranteed a high degree of industrial autonomy within the larger organization. Unions merging in order to retain at least a vestige of independence were allocated a degree of autonomy by the TGWU and ASTMS which could not be matched by most other unions. [. . .]

Thus mergers were not only shaped by existing systems of government, but also, in turn, influenced the form of government adopted by major merging unions. In the scramble for new job territories the major merging unions sought to make themselves more attractive to the minor merging unions. Hence there was a move, for instance in the AEU, to sectionalization (a policy also previously followed by the Boilermakers in their amalgamation), and an adjustment to acknowledge industrial interests in the GMWU [General and Municipal Workers' Union], while ASTMS had a proliferation of industrial groups.

Finally, it can be concluded that, given existing membership affinities, systems of government and the factors promoting change, the merger movement of the 1960s and 1970s appears as a somewhat random process. Certainly it appears to lack direction, or movement in any preordained conscious form. The only observable 'trend' or 'pattern' is towards fewer and larger unions; there are no 'models' or overall policies designed to 'rationalize' or 'improve' the structure and/or government of British trade unionism. Indeed, it is difficult to see how attempts by the TUC or others to shape British unions according to some overall plan, even if concerned with 'relating union structures to changing patterns of industrial organization', could have produced a movement towards industrial unionism or some other theoretically orderly construct. For in the competitive and internally directed merger movement of the 1960s and 1970s the pursuit of numbers, however defined, came to overshadow all other objectives. [. . .]

Future merger change

To begin with, it is surely reasonable to suppose that, given the absence of easily available natural growth, the post-1964 merger movement will quicken and extend. So far as the smaller unions are concerned, there are over 250 with less than 1,000 members. Most of them organize in areas of stagnant or declining membership. It seems to us that most of them will survive only at the cost of rapid absorption into larger organizations.

At the other end of the scale come the thirty-nine unions with over 50,000 members, eleven of which were included in our study. Taken together they cover about 88 per cent of all union members. It seems to us that it is here that we will discover potential merger partners for most small unions that manage to survive into the 1990s. What is it possible to say about the merger objectives of the larger unions? From the viewpoint of their merger potential, they can best be considered in three groups.

The first consists of the twenty or so unions whose membership is confined to the public sector – the civil service, local government, education, the Health Service and the nationalized industries. In the anticipated climate of public sector retrenchment and expenditure cuts, the three and a half million trade union members covered by unions in this group would appear to be prime candidates for defensive or consolidatory mergers – especially those who are members of the ten or so unions with a membership less than 100,000.

In terms of its size and diversity NALGO [National and Local Government Officers' Association] might be thought to be in the strongest position to make an expansionist bid for one or more of these organizations, although it must be noted that the majority of unions involved actually organize in areas where NALGO's leadership has no direct experience and a very small membership. In this respect it is arguable that there is more support for a consolidatory merger between the CPSA [Civil and Public Services Association] and the SCPS [Society of Civil and Public Services] and a defensive merger involving the remainder of the non-industrial civil service. Similar alliances are discernible among teachers, or in respect of the NHS.

In other parts of the public sector there is probably less scope for amalgamations. In some nationalized industries – for example, mining and iron and steel – there is already one dominant union organized on industrial lines. In others, such as railways and the Post Office, several well-entrenched organizations guard their independence and show little desire for change.

But there are more possibilities among our second group of unions; those with more than 50,000 members whose job territories are largely confined to the private sector. There are about ten of these unions, organizing in fairly narrow sections of private industry – for example, clothing, textiles, baking, agriculture, printing and paper. Taken together the unions in this group represent about a million workers, who, with some notable exceptions are for the most part in poorly paid, under-organized and declining trades. In most cases the merger movement of the 1960s had produced one or two major unions, but there remains considerable scope for further consolidation. In some trades the major union is still surrounded by numerous small craft groups. In the well-organized printing and paper industry there have also been a number of relatively minor amalgamations, but the attempt to merge two of the three largest unions – SOGAT [Society of Graphical and Allied Trades] and NATSOPA [National Society of Operative Printers and Assistants] – had to be unscrambled during the early 1970s, partly for personal reasons.

And so we come to our third and final group, which is the most important of all from the viewpoint of future merger activity. This consists of the ten unions with more than 50,000 members, most of which organize in both the public and the private sector. The bulk of them have developed job territories across a wide spectrum of British industry, and naturally enough they include the five largest unions in our sample: the TGWU, the GMWU,[1] the AUEW, ASTMS and

1. Now the GMBATU: see below.

UCATT. Alongside these are five other unions with similar 'Intermediate–open' scope for recruitment, whose membership is as follows:

EETPU [Electrical, Electronic, Telecommunication and Plumbing Union]	420,000
USDAW [Union of Shop, Distributive and Allied Workers]	441,000
APEX [Association of Professional, Executive, Clerical and Computer Staff]	151,000
ASBSBSW [Amalgamated Society of Boilermakers, Shipwrights, Blacksmiths and Structural Workers][2]	128,000
NUSMWCHDE [National Union of Sheet Metal Workers, Coppersmiths, Heating and Domestic Engineers]	75,000

These ten unions represent between them more than 50 per cent of organized workers, or just over six million trade unionists. It seems evident that the merger ambitions and plans of their leaders will largely determine the future structure of the British trade union movement. What can we say about the options and opportunities open to them in the light of our study?

First, we may surely assume that only four of the ten have the organizational resources and membership base to operate as natural aggressors in a major merger battle: the AUEW, ASTMS, the TGWU, and the GMWU. The crucial question is which of these is likely to develop the most merger potential both in relation to the six remaining intermediate–open unions and in respect of the wider trade union movement.

At first glance the leadership of the AUEW might seem to be in the best position. At least three of the smaller organizations listed above are similar in origin – ex-craft unions, with similar histories, traditions and rule-books (the EETPU, the ASBSBSW and the NUSMWCHDE). Like the AUEW, they organize and recruit within the engineering industry and know its procedure and agreements.

However, we discovered in the study that structural similarities and membership consanguinity are not self-evident and sufficient arguments in merger discussions. It is even more important to be able to offer an attractive 'deal' to the established leadership in the minor

2. Subsequently amalgamated with the GMWU to form the General, Municipal, Boilermakers and Amalgamated Trades Union (GMBATU).

merging union. In this respect it helps if one's own decision-making structure is flexible, receptive and reasonably centralized on the non-bargaining side.

But our study demonstrated that from this viewpoint the national leadership of the AUEW are in a relatively weak position. They are also divided among themselves and are not agreed about the terms on which their existing alliance can continue. In some ways the present leaders of the AUEW(E), who wish to form future alliances on the basis of a common rule-book, might be thought to be better placed if they could escape from the confines set by one of their present merger partners, the 'left-wing' leadership of TASS [Technical and Supervisory Section]. It has been argued that, if TASS were to decide to separate itself from the present federal structure of the AUEW, the way would be clearer for the emergence of a more widespread and genuine amalgamation of craft and ex-craft unions extending beyond engineering (including unions such as UCATT and the bulk of the organizations in the TUC's Group 8: Iron and Steel and Minor Metal Trades).

But for this to happen the national leadership of the AUEW(E), who would need to take the lead in such a merger movement, would have to be prepared to develop and carry through their own constitutional modifications. These would need to include some provision for occupational and/or trade autonomy, within the context of a common rule-book. But they would also want to concern themselves with the consequences of any likely mergers on their own political position. And this would almost certainly involve preservation and extension of the present arrangements for postal ballots. Several potential merger partners might find it difficult to accept terms of this kind.

For all these reasons we would argue that both ASTMS and the TGWU are in a rather stronger starting position in the merger race. Both unions' decision-making systems might have been designed to facilitate merger 'deals'. In both cases the leadership has considerable experience of accommodating the wishes of a variety of merger partners. What can we say about their relative handicaps?

ASTMS starts with the advantage of impressive earlier form in the promising areas of non-TUC staff associations; particularly insurance, commerce and banking. It would also claim to be the natural home for the bulk of the unions in the TUC's Group 17: Professional, Clerical and Entertainment. (Included in this group are other intermediate–open unions like APEX and the broadcasting and television unions.) Other white-collar organizations that might reasonably be regarded as natural merger partners for ASTMS would appear to include both the NUJ [National Union of Journalists] and even the EMA [Engineers' and Managers' Association]. (In both instances, ASTMS already recruits alongside these organizations, and would claim to be gaining in relative importance.) In general terms it may be said that, if ASTMS were able to carry through a merger movement of this scope, it would virtually double its present membership – i.e. move to a base of one million members.

Clearly the main difference between ASTMS and the TGWU is that the latter can hope to advance across a somewhat broader front – that is, into adjacent job territories affecting both manual and non-manual workers. So far as manual workers are concerned the most obvious opportunities for future TGWU initiatives would seem to be outside the territories of other intermediate–open unions (for example, in the TUC's Group 3: Transport Workers), mainly concentrating on the non-railway unions. But they might also hope to attract one or more of the less financially stable and rather 'closed' unions in areas such as clothing, textiles, baking or agriculture.

So far as intermediate–open unions are concerned, the most promising medium-term target for the TGWU would seem to be USDAW, given the fact that its traditional base in the cooperative movement is rapidly declining. The possibility of a 'monster' merger between the TGWU and GMWU is a matter best considered after we have discussed the relative position and form of the GMWU.

Given their record among white-collar groups, the leaders of the TGWU would naturally claim that they could hope to at least match the performance of ASTMS in this area. This may well be the case so far as manufacturing industry is concerned, outside the area of middle-level and higher management. In this respect the most important struggle may well be over the future of APEX. If ASTMS were able to effect an early amalgamation with APEX the balance of advantage in manufacturing would clearly tip in their direction, but even on this basis it can be said that the immediate merger potential of the TGWU is likely to be somewhat larger than ASTMS.

Of course, relative growth potential would be transformed if the leaders of the TGWU would come to terms with their 'sister' general union. Which brings us to the future chances of the GMWU in the merger race.

The first point to make is that on past form the GMWU's immediate position is even weaker than that of the AUEW. It lacks the penumbra of smaller unions with similar origins and structural features. Yet its own admixture of regionalization and horizontal concentration allied to an absence of occupational autonomy has

167

helped to make it an even less attractive merger partner in the past. It also has the disadvantage of being in more or less open competition with the larger, and more constitutionally attractive, TGWU – often from a subordinate position at the bargaining table.

On the other hand, the GMWU could argue that it was in a relatively strong medium-term position, on several grounds. In the first place, it could hope to merge with one or two reasonably-sized organizations in the public sector, for example COHSE [Confederation of Health Service Employees], the Firemen and even the Greater London Council Staff Association. Second, given a modest degree of occupational autonomy, it still hopes to be able to attract one or more of the ex-craft unions with which it shares common bargaining rights – most notably the EETPU.[3] Third, the leaders of the GMWU might well argue that in time their apparently impregnable 'right-wing' image will make them the natural allies of other 'right-wing' leadership groups – those who more or less control unions as diverse as UCATT, USDAW and NALGO. But these are little more than hopes and speculations. At the moment of writing it must be said that the merger prospects for the GMWU are at least as dim as those facing the present leadership of the AUEW(E).

Yet it does not follow that the future leaders of the GMWU will wish to abandon their present independence and autonomy, merely to enable their own organization to be engulfed by an organization that is more than twice its size. There are no compelling reasons why they should enter what would be at best a consolidatory and at worst a defensive merger – least of all in association with an increasingly diffused and fragmented TGWU leadership. Indeed, there seems to be little reason why any of our four surviving predators should wish to merge with each other in the foreseeable future. On the contrary, they are likely to remain on the scene – whatever else changes – searching for minor partners, who can be more easily absorbed into an existing or barely modified government structure, in ways that are unlikely to threaten existing alliances and power groups.

In this respect, it might be argued, the prospect for British trade union structure is not altogether unlike Orwell's vision of 1984. There, it may be remembered, a series of battles for supremacy ends in the emergence of three super-states – Eurasia, Oceania and Lastasia – each unable, or unwilling, to overcome or absorb the other; each content to coexist, in a state of containable conflict, mitigated by periods of unity and cooperation in the face of a common threat. [. . .]

3. The boilermakers' amalgamation was an example of such a move.

Part Four

Trade Union Government

In Reading 13 Undy and his colleagues criticize previous ways of classifying union government, notably by means of the misleading distinction between degrees of 'democracy' or 'oligarchy'. Such categories do not help to analyse the quality or effectiveness of leaders and their decisions. They also cannot cope with how union decision-making structures change through time. A new typology is advanced, which plots degrees of 'decision dispersal' along two continuums termed 'vertical concentration' and 'horizontal diffusion'. The most important British unions are classified by reference to this typology.

In Reading 14 John Gennard and his associates summarize the results of a survey of admission, discipline and expulsion rules in seventy-nine TUC unions. Gennard concludes that they seldom reach standards proposed by the TUC or laid down during the period of the 1971 Industrial Relations Act. Yet he finds little evidence that the result is injustice or the abuse of power. In general, union officials turn out to be reluctant to use their rights under the rule-book – especially the ultimate sanction of expulsion for disobedience. Gennard's work has been much cited in the debate about the need for further legal regulation of union rule-books, especially in circumstances where unions operate union membership as a condition of employment. (These matters are discussed at greater length in Part Seven of the readings.)

Reading 15 comes from the work of two distinguished American students of industrial relations, Derek Bok and John Dunlop of Harvard. It is included for two reasons. First, it is the best short description of the factors constraining union leadership when deciding day-to-day issues: i.e. membership demands, the influence of subordinates and the effect of the wider environment. Second, it is all the more persuasive because what is said about unions in the United States is so obviously relevant to unions elsewhere, including Britain.

Reading 16, by Roderick Martin, is retained uncut from the first edition; it remains a classic of its kind. Martin argues that 'union democracy exists where union executives are unable to prevent opposition factions distributing propaganda and mobilizing electoral support'. He goes on to devise an explanatory framework for use in classifying the constraints that inhibit the use and abuse of power in unions. He draws attention to the importance of a wide variety of external and internal factors, most of which are still ignored or misunderstood by the great majority of economists, journalists and politicians of all parties.

13 R. Undy, V. Ellis, W. E. J. McCarthy and A. M. Halmos

A Typology of Union Government

From R. Undy, V. Ellis, W. E. J. McCarthy and A. M. Halmos, *Changes in Trade Unions*, Hutchinson, 1981, pp. 38–60.

It is common in studies of comparative union government to describe and classify unions according to their democratic or oligarchic tendencies (see Turner, 1962). This practice no doubt predominates owing to unions' own claims to be democratic and the influence of the seminal and pioneering works in this field by the Webbs (1901), Michels (1911) and Lipset *et al.* (1956). All these studies were centrally concerned with the extent to which unions could claim to be democratic. As a result, the direction of research into union democracy has tended to be almost solely concerned with such matters as participation rates, closeness of elections and the existence of factions or parties (see, for instance, Martin, 1968, and Edelstein and Warner, 1975).

Little has been written therefore about the quality or effectiveness of the leadership's decisions. In particular, the question of whether a factionalized or party-type system of union government actually contributes anything to the quality of national leadership decision-making has not been fully discussed. Moreover, there has also been an absence of comment in the 'democratic' literature regarding the extent to which a particular system of government allows the 'democratic' or 'oligarchic' national leadership the opportunity to carry out or execute the policy of the union or to achieve its organizational objectives. There is no discussion, for instance, of the question of whether or not a more or less democratic union survives or grows more effectively than any other union in a changing environment.

Therefore existing theories of union government, with their bias towards participatory aspects of democracy, do not offer any satisfactory methodological guide for a study that seeks to consider both the responsiveness of leaders to members and the comparative effectiveness of systems of government. They do not suggest a method of assessing the relative merits of those constitutional changes that both promote commonly accepted legitimate goals of unionism (for example, growth and hence more bargaining power) and produce a reduction in participatory opportunities. Yet such changes occurred in several small unions that sought defensive mergers with the TGWU [Transport and General Workers' Union], if only because such mergers replaced existing elections of full-time officials with appointment on the TGWU model. Also, the ASW [Amalgamated Society of Wood Workers] and the ASPD [Associated Society of Painters and Decorators], in forming UCATT [Union of Construction, Allied Trades and Technicians], changed some full-time officer positions from election to appointment in the hope, ultimately, of strengthening their bargaining opportunities. Yet it is obviously misleading to state that either of the above changes was positively undemocratic purely because they reduced participatory opportunities; for both changes were primarily intended to help the unions concerned achieve goals to which their members generally subscribed.

There are also considerable problems in applying participatory theories of democracy to unions as 'wholes'. These classificatory problems arise because unions may be governmentally divided in a way that makes such definitional generalizations as 'more or less democratic' largely meaningless. A union may, for instance, have two separate or vertically bifurcated channels of decision-making. It may also have different systems of decision-making and methods of choosing leaders at each of several horizontal levels of government. Its decision-making processes may, for example, be constitutionally vertically divided into bargaining and non-bargaining channels. A union could then be highly devolved and participative in the bargaining channel and highly centralized and non-participative in its non-bargaining control. Further, the nature of decision-making may be compounded, yet again, by variations in the location of issues and means of determining issues at national, regional, district, branch and shop floor levels of government. Hence to talk of such unions as 'more or less democratic' in an overall sense is to risk misleading generalizations with little or no concrete meaning.

Thus democratic constructs drawn from wider political theory present serious problems when used in relationship to unions. It is with these thoughts in mind that the following alternative typology is proposed.

Our typology is intended to promote an understanding of both comparative changes in unions' systems of government and the role national leadership in a changing environment. It provides a means of considering the effectiveness of union government and analysing participatory mechanisms. The typology facilitates these objectives by recognizing that unions' systems of decision-making are composed of different but interrelated parts. In particular, the typology recognizes this internal division of unions by analysing union decision-making along two main dimensions, vertical and horizontal (see Figure 1). It will be seen that the vertical dimension plots positions on a continuum from 'centralized' to 'decentralized'. Along the horizontal dimension we plot a similar continuum in terms of the degree of 'concentration' and 'diffusion'.

The *vertical dimension* of government refers to the various levels of government within a particular union, tor example regional and local (including district and shop floor) levels of decision-making. Within the vertical structure the typology distinguishes between those vertical channels of decision-making that deal primarily with questions of a collective bargaining nature and those that concentrate on other matters – such as political and administrative issues. Hence unions are seen as being vertically bifurcated into bargaining and non-bargaining channels of decision-making. This division is employed primarily for explanatory purposes. It can however be justified by reference to *de facto* union practices, although in some unions, for instance the TGWU, it is also written into their rule-books. Thus, as in other spheres of union study, a *de facto* and *de jure* distinction may be usefully made when referring to either the vertical or horizontal structures of decision-making. But we also have to note that issues to be

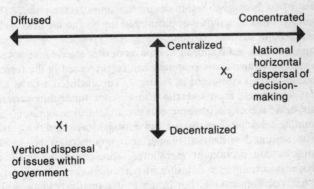

Figure 1 National union government: vertical and horizontal dispersal diagram. The hypothetical case of union X is shown. The position X_0 represents the centralized and concentrated non-bargaining decision-making of the union, while X_1 represents the decentralized and diffused bargaining decision-making of the union.

173

determined within the vertical structure of union government may be generally dispersed throughout the bifurcated vertical structure or largely located in any one level of government. In this sense a union can be said to be 'centralized' if it retains a greater degree of national control over a larger number of issues than other unions with which it is compared. Similarly, a union may be described as 'decentralized' if it devolves more issues than other unions down to its lowest level of decision-making. Finally a union can be said to be decentralized along one of its vertical channels of decision-making, for example, bargaining, yet centralized in its other vertical or non-bargaining channel. For example, union X in Figure 1 is shown as decentralized in the bargaining field X_1 but centralized in its non-bargaining activities X_0.

On the *horizontal dimension* a union can be similarly but less drastically dissected. A union may at each vertical level of government have different horizontal structures. For instance, the national level of government may be composed of a large heterogeneous lay biennial conference, a lay executive, a lay appeal body and appointed full-time officers. It may also be free from factionalism. On the other hand, it may have an elected full-time executive, elected full-time officers and a small homogeneous annual lay conference. It may also be riddled with factionalism. Thus unions may have different concentrations or diffusions of power over decisions taken at the level of government under discussion. The more people/committees actually share in decision-making, the more dispersed the power. Obversely, the fewer people/committees, the more concentrated the power. Thus in Figure 1 union X is shown as diffused in the bargaining field X_1 but concentrated in the non-bargaining field X_0.

Using the same basic approach, an overview of the relative government systems of two or more unions can be presented in the form of a diagram. This is contained in Figure 2. The enclosed area at each level of government represents the relative scope for decision-making. The top level is national government, the middle level represents any appropriate level between district and national level, and the bottom level is composed of district, branch and shop-floor levels. A small or large shaded portion at each level represents respectively the relative concentration or diffusion of participation in, and responsibility for, decision-making. For instance, if a relatively large area of government has only a dot, or small shaded area in it, the suggestion is that at that level there is large scope for decision-making but a concentration of power over the relatively large number of issues

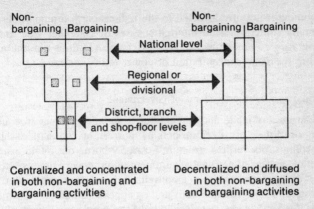

Figure 2 System of union government showing vertical and horizontal de facto dispersal of decision-making

resolved. It should also be noted that similar diagrams can also be used to show movement through time. They can, for instance, be used to compare the TGWU in 1960 with the TGWU in 1975. (N.B. In all uses of this figure the drawings represent *de facto* situations unless specifically identified as *de jure* descriptions.) [. . .]

Before turning to examine the continuum of national government, it can be concluded that a *de jure* vertically bifurcated union will, by virtue of its structure, tend to be more concentrated in its general national decision-making processes than single-channel unions. It would appear to need, in order to maintain itself as a union and avoid fragmentation, a 'strong counterpoise at the centre'[1] to bind together the semi-autonomous bargaining groups as in the TGWU and ASTMS [Association of Scientific, Technical and Managerial Staffs]; while, in contrast, *de jure* single-channel unions such as the AEU [Amalgamated Engineering Union] and the ASW will, through the encouragement they give to the formation of independent factions and parties, tend to have a far more diffused system of national government. Finally, somewhere between these extremes will be a union like the GMWU. Such an organization structurally needs to contain its semi-autonomous regions within the bounds of national government to maintain unity of purpose. However, because bargaining is constitutionally retained within the one system of government and non-

1. Bullock (1960), p. 205. Bevin was the founding father and first general secretary of the TGWU.

bargaining issues are devolved to the regions, such a union does not normally court the same internal stresses or gain the same growth advantages as the *de jure* bifurcated union. It does not therefore require the same concentration of power at the centre.

Comparison between systems of government

The suggestion made above regarding a union's tendency to concentrate or diffuse its decision-making powers at the national level according to its vertical structure is largely borne out by an examination of systems of national government in our chosen unions. At this level of government most unions have a national conference, an executive, a rules revision body and an appeals committee[2] or equivalents. General secretaries usually hold the most senior posts. (They hold this position, for instance, in the TGWU, ASTMS, the GMWU [General and Municipal Workers' Union],[3] the ASW and NALGO [National and Local Government Officers' Association]. In the AEU, however, the president is the most influential single figure.) Assistant or deputy general secretaries, national officers or, if full-time, national-executive councillors normally hold the next position in the national hierarchy. In the AEU and the ASW (UCATT) these national full-time positions are elected, whereas in the other unions studied they are, apart from the general secretary, nearly all appointed.

Although national positions and bodies are reasonably common across unions, their influence is not. All unions disperse some power constitutionally over several bodies and positions. The degree of concentration or diffusion nationally is influenced heavily, however, by the interaction between vertical structure, discretionary or non-discretionary leadership roles, flexible or non-flexible procedures for decision-making, the methods of choosing leaders and the absence or presence of factions or parties. Obviously, individual leaders are also important. But the extent of this individual influence will, by and large, be constrained by constitutional factors. An individual leader in a union where power is constitutionally concentrated in one position will, *ipso facto*, have potentially more influence on policy than

2. The appeals body was a later addition for unions, including the GMWU, which introduced one under the influence of the Industrial Relations Act 1971; see GMWU Report of 60th Congress (1975), Appendix 2, p. 519.

3. Now known as the General, Municipal, Boilermakers and Allied Trades Union (GMBATU)

if the same individual were the leader of another union where, *ceteris paribus*, power was more diffused because of a formal system of checks and balances.

Thus the potential for concentration of power, and hence dominance of national decision-making by one leader, will tend to be great in a union that both constitutionally provides such a role and structurally requires a strong figure-head. Such conditions are found in the TGWU. This vertically bifurcated multi-industry union has one elected position at the top of the full-time officer hierarchy, the general secretary. It also provides this position with a highly discretionary decision-making role within flexible national decision-making procedures. Moreover, appointments of all other full-time officials are made under the general secretary's guidance. Further, the lay GEC [General Executive Council] in the 1960s contained no opposition of any consequence. The TGWU therefore provides a combination of constitutional circumstances suitable for individual dominance, and therefore an extreme concentration of power.

Dominance, even in the TGWU, would however be only potential. Exercise of power would still depend on the abilities of the individual. If an individual is incapable, indolent or disinterested in using the potential for power, he or she is likely to achieve considerably less in terms of influencing policy than a far more able and ambitious person in a more constitutionally constricted role. Therefore a very able national leader in a single-channel and homogeneous union such as the AEU, which had a diffusion of power owing to the opposite constitutional factors – that is, little discretion in any one position, inflexible decision-making processes, election of all full-time National Executive and well-developed factions or parties – could still be of some importance in decision-making. However, it would have to be recognized that in most situations the potential for power would be far below that of the leader in a concentrated union.

The unions at the centre of this study thus resemble the two extremes of the national level concentrated – diffused continuum. The TGWU provides its general secretary with the potential for an extremely powerful role at the concentrated end of the continuum, while the AEU, and later the AUEW [Amalgamated Union of Engineering Workers] Engineering section, restricts its president within a far more diffused system of government. Between the two ranging from concentration to diffusion on the non-bargaining power continuum stood, in the 1960s, ASTMS, the GMWU and the ASW (UCATT).

Constitutionally, in 1960 the TGWU was still basically the same union as that formed in the amalgamation of 1922.[4] The thousand-strong regional trade group delegates to the Biennial Delegate Conference (BDC) were and still are constitutionally members of the premier decision-making body. The lay General Executive Council (GEC) was and still is responsible for governing the TGWU between conferences. Regional trade group delegates to the BDC are elected at the branches, and the thirty-nine-strong GEC, which meets quarterly, is composed of regional and national trade group representatives. A further body of major importance in the TGWU is however the eight-strong Finance and General Purposes Committee (F&GPC), elected from within the GEC. The GEC can delegate most of its power to this inner cabinet, which meets monthly. It is thus capable of taking virtually all major decisions between meetings of the BDC.

There is, however, within the formal structure of national government of the TGWU, a great deal of procedural flexibility which can enhance the influence of an able general secretary and limit the role of the BDC. Structurally, for instance, the rules in 1960 allowed for the formation, subject to GEC approval, of lay sectional committees to deal with the affairs of a particular section of a trade group. This flexibility was used by the leadership to accommodate and defuse, in a *de facto* and *ad hoc* manner, pressure for more wide-ranging constitutional change which they regularly faced and defeated at the BDCs. Between 1949 and 1965 there were, for instance, ninety-four motions at nine BDCs demanding the formation of separate and hence extra trade groups. The GEC opposed, successfully, all but one of these motions. The exception was a proposal in 1957[5] for an Oil Trade Group to be formed. Yet outside the conference, pressures for formal structural change were absorbed by more minor *ad hoc* and *de facto* adjustments sanctioned by the inner circle of national leaders. The overall structure of the TGWU's government was hence largely left untouched until 1967 despite numerous attempts by lay delegates at BDCs to alter its shape.

Similarly, the formal procedures for decision-making and the methods of appointing full-time officials and electing the general secretary went largely unchanged between 1949 and 1965. This was not due, however, to the absence of membership pressure for change. Various trade groups within the TGWU repeatedly pressed, for

4. See Bullock (1960) for comment on the formation of the TGWU.
5. See TGWU Report, 17th BDC (1957), minute 23.

instance, for permission at BDCs to hold lay trade group delegate conferences. They were almost equally regularly defeated at the BDCs by the 'platform' (the national leadership). Only the General Road Haulage Section's success in pressing a motion opposed by the platform at the 1953 BDC[6] broke the general rule of platform dominance at BDCs in this particular policy field.

However, apart from these two occasions the platform carried the day at the BDC on all other issues including general policy matters between 1949 and 1965. The national leadership achieved this dominance by making effective use of the concentration of power endowed in them and the General Secretary in particular by the union's constitution. Demands for constitutional change were softened by *ad hoc de facto* concessions and/or were defeated at Conference by bringing the weight of the representative of the 'common good', the general secretary, to bear against sectional demands. Tactically this was often achieved at the BDC not by opposing a motion outright, but by replacing it with what can be termed a 'negative composite', sponsored by the GEC, which, on 'being accepted by Conference, there would be no occasion to move the [original] motion'.[7] On the occasion quoted here it was used and passed to negate an attempt by several trade groups to establish new trade groups and enforce reference-back procedures in negotiations. Such tactics of the platform invariably succeeded. No 'Executive Policy Statement', whether a negative replacement for composite motions or a positive policy statement, was defeated between 1945 and 1965.

The influence of the national leadership in the TGWU was not, however, always a negative force preventing change. In fact, the best examples of the use of the concentrated power in the TGWU come from examples of change. Moreover, most of these changes came in the TGWU when either the general secretary proposed a change or after the general secretary himself had changed. In 1968, for instance, Frank Cousins, at the end of his period as general secretary, successfully proposed a motion to remove the 1949 ban on Communists holding office in the TGWU; the ban had itself been instigated by the former general secretary, Arthur Deakin. Morever, until Cousins moved against the ban in 1968 it had been repeatedly upheld by the platform despite repeated efforts at Rules Conferences to remove it.

6. See TGWU Report, 15th BDC (1953), minute 74.
7. See, for example, TGWU Report, 20th BDC (1963), minute 88.

Also, TGWU policy on the closed shop[8] and collective security[9] was changed under the influence of general secretaries who led the move to change a policy which the union's national leadership had previously constantly supported.

It may be, of course, that the general secretary of the TGWU is successful in promoting policy change because he does not make any proposals to the BDC, GEC, or F&GPC that are likely to be defeated. However, the consistency with which the TGWU's general secretaries have successfully sponsored changes that have previously been resisted, and have resisted others that have been repeatedly promoted, makes this appear doubtful. It is rather that the constitutional power endowed in the TGWU's general secretary permits him to innovate and persuade the BDC and other bodies that what he, the only nationally elected officer, proposes represents the union's best and non-sectional interests. It is from this position that he dominates the national non-bargaining decision-making process. Moreover, the procedural arrangements themselves help him to achieve this end. Senior full-time officers and particularly the general secretary speak for the lay GEC in BDC debates. This advantageous position arises at least partly because, according to rule, only three members of the lay GEC can actually attend the BDC in their official capacity. Furthermore, the BDC meets only every two years. It obviously cannot control policy between meetings. Also when it does meet, its size – some 1,000 delegates – and its composition – regional trade group representation – militates against the formation of an effective opposition. Organization across like-minded groups is not assisted by the division of delegates according to region and trade group or by the ban (until 1968) on Communists. The BDC is thus highly fragmented and dependent almost solely on the platform for a lead. In practice, on a platform largely without any leading lay members, the general secretary plays the major role provided by his constitutional right to speak on behalf of the lay GEC.

Again, at the lay GEC, the procedures place the general secretary in a predominant position. The GEC was, until at least 1975, largely untouched by effective factionalism. Like the union itself, it is divided by regional and trade group allegiances. Meeting quarterly, it cannot

8. See TGWU Report, 22nd BDC (1967), minute 63, and Report of 23rd BDC (1969), minute 43.
9. See TGWU Report, 18th BDC (1959), minutes 55 and 56.

closely monitor, let alone control, day-to-day operations. Moreover, for its operations it relies entirely on a system of detailed reports presented to it, up to 1968, almost solely by national officials. A similar method of business is also used at the inner cabinet, the F&GPC. Hence the general secretary, or other senior full-time officials, initiate most of the work of the national bodies of the TGWU through the constitutional procedures.

Full-time officials are themselves also influenced by the general secretary, if by no other means than through the patronage of that office. This arises through the general secretary's dominant role in the appointment of senior full-time officials. Although in rule the GEC make appointments, the responsibility has, in practice, been delegated to the F&GPC which tends to rely on the general secretary for advice in such administrative matters. Taken to its extreme, the general secretary can also, if he so wished, 'set up' his successor, even though this post is elected. Thus until 1978 all general secretaries had been assistant general secretaries or, in the case of Jack Jones, assistant executive secretary. In the absence of effective factionalism, and weak or non-existent unofficial canvassing, the power of the incumbent, if swung behind one of the contenders for office, can be electorally very influential. Moreover, without an effective oppositional grouping within the TGWU and in the absence of tolerance of unofficial electoral organizations, any official who does step outside the rules restricting canvassing can receive short shrift. Tony Corfield, for instance, found this out to his cost when, following his writing of a pamphlet, *Collective Leadership for the TGWU*, which was highly critical of the TGWU's leadership during the election for Cousins's successor in the mid-1960s, he was in consequence required to resign his post as secretary of TGWU's Political, Educational and International Department. Thus, not only can the established leadership of the TGWU promote and appoint to key positions within the union, but they can also enforce the rules to reduce the effectiveness of any unofficial opposition within the union.

Thus in the TGWU's national level of government the general secretary is provided, by the constitution, with extensive powers. If the general secretary is capable of exercising such powers he has ample opportunity to dominate the national level of government. The power available can be used to innovate or conserve. The TGWU therefore depends to a great extent for its ability to react to a changing environment on the competence of the general secretary and on whether or not he is an innovator or a conservationist. An innovating general secretary, Jones, used the power inherent in the TGWU to change quite radically the nature of that union.

The ASTMS, as it developed in the late 1960s and early 1970s, is somewhat similar to the TGWU. It is both *de jure* vertically bifurcated and multi-industry. There is also a great deal of flexibility in national government which can be exploited by the general secretary who has, under rule, a large degree of discretionary power. But in contrast to the TGWU, the general secretary of ASTMS is not uniquely legitimized as a unifying force. He is not elected: his post is only one of several full-time appointments made by the National Executive Council of the union. But in common with other unions' general secretaries, the general secretary of ASTMS innovates and persuades and uses the research facilities and journals to formulate objectives and elaborate strategies.

Unlike the general secretary of the longer-established TGWU, the premier officer of the new and fast-growing ASTMS does not have the TGWU's sophisticated procedures and structures of national government or its highly developed bureaucracy. ASTMS's NEC and its Annual Delegate Conference (ADC) do not always agree. The ADC, in contrast to its counterpart in the TGWU, has on several occasions rejected the NEC, and hence the general secretary's, advice. However the NEC 'formulates the policy of the Association'[10] in cooperation with the ADC. It is therefore not a a purely executive body. It is capable of legislative action which compensates it somewhat for its inability consistently to persuade the ADC to accept its advice – although the NEC cannot, with impunity, ignore the wishes of the ADC. In 1972, for instance, when the general secretary and the NEC decided to register under the Industrial Relations Act (IRA), they were prevented from doing so by the ADC which voted for de-registration of the union. Moreover, the rejection of the NEC's recommendation to register owed something to the efforts of appointed full-time officials who mobilized delegates against the NEC and the general secretary. Thus there has not existed in the ASTMS a continuous or consistent domination of the union's conference or full-time officials by the NEC and the general secretary such as occurs in the TGWU.

On the other hand, ASTMS's lay NEC and full-time general secretary do have a large degree of discretion outside of the lay

10. ASTMS Rule Book, rule 24 (6).

ADC's influence. Moreover, within this considerable sphere of influence the NEC is heavily dependent on and defers to the general secretary, who is an *ex officio* non-voting member of the NEC. This may well be because the twenty-two-member NEC is partly a mixture of notables, including a few MPs with no immediate shop-floor contact, and other largely inexperienced new members of the union. For instance, in 1975 only seven of the twenty-two members of the NEC had more than two years' experience on that body. In this respect it is therefore less stable than the GEC of the TGWU, where the 30–40 membership has a turnover of twelve to fifteen members every two years.

However, nascent factionalism can be identified in ASTMS. This may further limit the general secretary's influence in relation to the NEC. Over the 1960–75 period the normally unorganized mix of Labour Party, Communist and Roman Catholic groups has been joined by an ultra-left group of International Socialist (now Socialist Worker Party) origins. It is claimed that this latter faction shows signs of electoral organization.[11] Industrial groupings are also emerging within the unions. 'Insurance', with its concentration of members in large offices and closed branches, may signify a potentially high polling capability, and if so it could well upset the existing balance in ASTMS's NEC and ADC.[12]

It can be seen therefore that ASTMS is not as concentrated as the TGWU at the national level. Despite the *de jure* vertical bifurcation, discretionary rule-books and flexibility of procedures, ASTMS's general secretary is not as free to innovate and persuade or resist change as his counterpart in the TGWU. ASTMS does not have the organizational features found in the TGWU of highly developed but flexible procedures for dealing with business and selecting lay officials. It also lacks the mix of lay delegates and absence of faction, which underpins the general secretary of that union. The machinery of government that supported the general secretary's position in the TGWU around 1960 is thus somewhat less developed in ASTMS.

Moving towards the diffused end of the continuum but still tending to be a relatively concentrated union, the highly regionalized but *de*

11. See *Socialist Worker*, 11 May 1974 and 10 August 1974, for a leading IS member on the internal politics of ASTMS and his own dismissal from the NEC.

12. See, for instance, *The Times*, 22 September 1976, for comment on the vote on ASTMS's NEC against nationalization of banking and insurance, which owed much to the insurance section's opposition to the proposal.

jure single-channel GMWU maintains a viable national presence by bringing the key figures in the ten regions, the appointed regional secretaries, directly into national level government. They all sit on the GMWU's highest executive body, the General Council (GC).[13] Half of them sit on its Executive Committee (EC). In practice the EC tends to be more important as a national decision-maker than the GC. In the 1960s regional secretaries shared their national executive functions with the elected general secretary and fourteen regionally elected lay members. Again, in practice, the lay members tend to defer to their regional secretaries on the GC and EC of the GMWU.

At the GMWU's major policy-making body the Annual Congress (AC), regional secretaries again extensively influence the decision-making process. Delegates are elected to the Congress from the regions, by branch voting. These delegates attend regional pre-Congress mandating meetings in which regional secretaries are involved. In the absence of faction and with restrictions on communicating and organizing across branches,[14] the regional secretary is very well placed at mandating meetings to persuade the uncoordinated, and hence unorganized, delegates to accept guidance from himself as the acknowledged expert on which motions are worthy of regional support at the Annual Congress. Bearing in mind, as mentioned above, that the GMWU's regional secretaries also have the last word in appointment of other lesser regional officers, it can be reasonably stated that they are thus in an extremely powerful position in the union at regional and national level.

The GMWU's government at the national level is therefore mainly dependent on one major and a number of minor 'general secretaries'. The major figure is the general secretary and the minor generals are the regional secretaries. The resemblance to the relationship between a medieval king and his barons is sometimes noted by students of the GMWU. Power is not as concentrated nationally as in the TGWU or ASTMS, but it is still spread between individuals rather than factions or parties. The general secretary's job is thus primarily one of balancing the small number of regional interests rather than

13. This arrangement was changed in January 1975. The General Council was then disbanded and the National Executive Committee (now called Executive Council) was enlarged. This does not basically alter the above argument, as all regional secretaries are now on the new EC, plus twenty lay delegates and the general secretary. It would appear that the new structural changes had no impact on the GMWU's general system of government, which is dominated by the general and regional secretaries.

14. See GMWU Rule Book, rule 13.

unifying a large number of fragmented, non-factionalized, and hence relatively powerless interests of the TGWU and ASTMS.

The ASW, by comparison with the above unions, was closest, before the UCATT merger, to the AEU. In common with the AEU, and in contrast to the unions examined above, the ASW elected all its officials. Its rule-book was reasonably precise. The area of discretion constitutionally allocated to its senior official, the general secretary, was, by TGWU and ASTMS standards, not very large. Again in contrast to the TGWU, ASTMS and the GMWU, the ASW's Executive Council (EC) was full-time and elected by branch ballot vote, similar to the AEU of the 1960s. This is still the case in respect of UCATT.

However, two factors make the ASW somewhat less diffuse nationally than the AEU. First, the factions in the ASW and in UCATT are considerably less well developed than their counterpart, the parties, of the AEU. The ASW's mainstream establishment faction composed of Labour Party loyalists had a comfortable majority over the left opposition on the five-man EC of the ASW in the early 1960s. 'Rank and File', and later 'The Building Workers' Charter' group, both left-wing Communist-dominated organizations, did not seriously challenge the established leadership's hold in the ASW nationally in the 1960s although they had some impact at the local level: for example, the Barbican and Horseferry disputes.[15] Faced by a weaker faction than that found in the AEU, the ASW's general secretary and his supporters on the EC were in a stronger position to influence policy than their engineering counterparts.

Second, the rule-book of the ASW allowed, and still allows in UCATT, the EC and general secretary the opportunity to selectively implement the union's National Conference decisions. Under rule a joint council of the EC and the lay General Council, which is a much less influential body than the EC although it is a lay check on that body's activities, can refer a conference decision to the wider membership before it becomes union policy. This the joint council did, for instance, in 1976 in order to reverse a National Conference decision opposing the 'Social Contract'.[16] Hence the UCATT's national leadership does have some important discretionary elements in the

15. See 'Cameron Report', *Report of Court of Inquiry into Trade Disputes at the Barbican and Horseferry Road Construction Sites in London*, Cmnd 3396, 1976, HMSO.
16. See *Morning Star*, 21 June 1976, and *The Times*, 14 July 1976, on these events.

decision-making procedures which, as will be shown below, make it less diffused than the AEU. However, the inbuilt system of checks and balances on the EC and general secretary, the election of officers and the existence of factions all combine to make the UCATT more diffused than most of the other unions examined.

At the diffused end of the continuum stands the Engineers (AEU 1920–67, AEF [Amalgamated Union of Engineering and Foundry Workers] 1967–71 and AUEW(E) since 1971). Constitutionally the national government of the Engineers revolves around the president, general secretary, seven-man Executive Council (EC) and fifty-two-member National Committee (NC). The president, general secretary and EC are all full-time elected executive posts. The NC, on the other hand, is a lay legislative body elected annually. In addition, the Rules Revisions Meeting (the NC under another name) and the lay Final Appeal Court also play, periodically, a part in national government of the Engineers. There is therefore a constitutionally-prescribed division of powers between the full-time executive and the lay legislature. Voting for full-time officers took place at the branch until the introduction of postal ballots in 1972. The period of office for each individual position is three years in the first instance and five years thereafter until, 'being 60 years of age or over' and having fought at least two elections, 'he or she shall not be required to seek re-election but shall continue in office until the age of 65 years'.[17] The lay NC by contrast is elected annually and indirectly through the branch, district committee and divisional committee process.

Thus both senior national Engineers' bodies are much smaller than their equivalents in the TGWU. Also, and perhaps more importantly, all positions of importance in the Engineers are elected not appointed. The elected Executive virtually sits on a par with the elected president and in terms of actual decision-making is superior to the general secretary. The president only has, for instance, a casting vote on the EC and, since 1975, no vote at all on the lay NC, which is the major legislating body in the Engineers. Furthermore, the general secretary does not have any kind of vote at either body although he has the major full-time official role vis-à-vis the Final Appeals Court. He also controls the official internal communications system and edits the Journal. Hence the formal decision-making processes are, at the national level of the Engineers, considerably diffused. No one position in this craft-dominated, decision-making

17. AUEW Engineering Section, rule 2.

process has the unique prestige or unifying purpose found in the general secretary of the TGWU. The formal *de jure* system of national government in the Engineers is thus a complex arrangement of checks and balances based on multi-faceted electoral processes.

Underpinning the constitutionally prescribed checks and balances of the Engineers is an unofficial and uninstitutionalized two-party system. The two parties, ideologically divided into left and right electoral organizations, represent, primarily and respectively, Communist and Labour Party divisions within the Engineers. They also enforce the internal formal checks and balances on arbitrary government. Moreover they can act, through their elected supporters, as the coordinating agents across the diverse national decision-making bodies. They can hence help to make the union governable by creating a common identity of interest which can unite the major ideological groupings on the disparate parts of national government on controversial issues.

Thus the crucial relationship between national officials and committees in the Engineers, unlike the TGWU, is not primarily affected by a single office. Instead, the Engineers are much more affected by party politics and the interplay between organized groups on the EC and NC and the allegiance of the president and general secretary to either of the unofficial parties. Combinations of, for instance, left-wing president and left-wing NC members or right-wing general secretary and right-wing EC members are normally more important in the Engineers than the abilities or political affiliations of any one isolated individual national official of the union. A politically divided EC at odds with a president may, for example, give the legislating NC more influence within the union than it would otherwise enjoy if a majority of the EC were politically in tune with the president.

Internal divisions of a political nature thus dominate the Engineers' national decision-making processes. The balance of political interests largely determines the extent to which the ability of the president or other senior national officials can be brought to bear on controversial matters. For instance, in 1960 the president, Lord Carron, used his position to limit the impact of the NC at a time when it was under the influence of the so-called 'Progressives' – a predominantly Communist Party and Left Labour alliance. Carron was able to do this because he was backed by a consistent majority of 'moderates' on the EC. At both TUC and Labour Party Conferences Carron adopted what has been termed a 'Janus-like' posture on the question of unilateral nuclear disarmament (see Richter, 1973, pp. 100 and

156–8); this effectively negated the left-wing NC's earlier resolution on the subject.

Somewhat similarly, but obversely, the newly elected left-wing president, Hugh Scanlon, faced in 1968 the first of a series of rebuffs from the more right-inclined NC. Scanlon had urged the NC to sanction industrial action on the 'package deal' negotiated with the EEF [Engineering Employers' Federation]. The NC, dominated by the 'right' and backed by a number of EC members of a similar political persuasion, successfully rejected the president's proposals. Later the Labour moderates repeated this treatment. They rejected the proposals from Scanlon and the left on postal ballots in 1971. In 1974 and 1975 they also refused to accept the president's proposals on the restructuring of the new amalgamation. Thus no one body or official consistently dictates or dominates policy-making in the Engineers; government is, on all politically controversial issues, a party matter, rather than a function of organizational bureaucracy.

Thus, in summary, the Engineers stand at the diffused end of the horizontal continuum. Constitutionally prescribed diffusion and the not unconnected internal and unofficial two-party system make the Engineers' national government quite distinctly different from that of the concentrated TGWU. Between these two extremes, starting from the concentrated end of the horizontal continuum, stood, in the early 1960s (and for ASTMS the early 1970s), ASTMS. GMWU and ASW (later UCATT).

Other unions and relative positions within the typology

In addition to the unions described above we studied others in rather less detail – mainly from the viewpoint of particular aspects of their job territory and/or bargaining behaviour. As a result we generated much useful information on comparative systems of government, most notably in respect of unions such as the AUFW [Amalgamated Union of Foundry Workers], the NUM [National Union of Mineworkers], the ASBSBSW [Amalgamated Society of Boilermakers, Shipwrights, Blacksmiths and Structural Workers],[18] the POEU [Post Office Engineering Union], NALGO, NUBE [National Union of Bank Employees], the NUT [National Union of Teachers] and NUPE [National Union of Public Employees]. From this information it is possible to analyse all these unions from the viewpoint of our

18. Now part of the GMBATU.

typology, stating how far they exhibit characteristics similar to, or different from, the unions described above.

Of these unions the AUFW is closest to its craft partner in Engineering, the AEU, while the industrial NUM also has similar internal ideological divisions to the Engineers but with a federal system of government somewhat closer to that of the GMWU. Moving towards the middle ground between the TGWU and the Engineers or the horizontal continuum are the craft-dominated ASB and POEU. The ASB is highly decentralized like the Engineers but without its unofficial party system, and hence with considerably more power concentrated in the hands of its leading elected national full-time officials. By comparison, the POEU is highly centralized in both its bargaining and non-bargaining decision-making channels. It is also far less diffused than the Engineers in its national level of government, which is extensively influenced by its appointed officials, although the degree of factionalism in the organization is noticeably greater than that in the TGWU. Similarly the *de jure* vertically bifurcated NALGO, with its local government traditions, is also somewhat dependent on its appointed full-time officials, although not so reliant as are most other unions who also choose their officials by this process: for instance, NUBE, the NUT and NUPE. NALGO was, however, like these other unions in the public sector, highly centralized in 1960 in both its non-bargaining and bargaining channels.

It is possible to present the vertical dispersal of decision-making, and the degree of participation in and division of responsibilities at each level, in the form of a diagram which applies to all the unions referred to in this chapter. This is attempted in Figure 3 and Figure 4 (see pp. 190–91 for an explanation of the significance of the different levels and shadings used in the diagram). It should be noted that *the diagram represents the de facto position* in each union, so far as we are able to determine it on the basis of our investigations. Also, it should be stressed that it is a proximate model of the distribution of power within very different organizations; a heuristic device, the utility of which needs to be judged in use. It should not be taken to imply or assume more similarity between organizations than is necessary for the purpose of analysis and classification in the field of union government: thus we are not suggesting that there is no difference between the NUT, NUBE and NUPE; merely that, for our purposes, they can be usefully grouped together.

Finally, so far as non-bargaining is concerned, we show in Figure 4 the relative position of each of the eight models in Figure 3, by

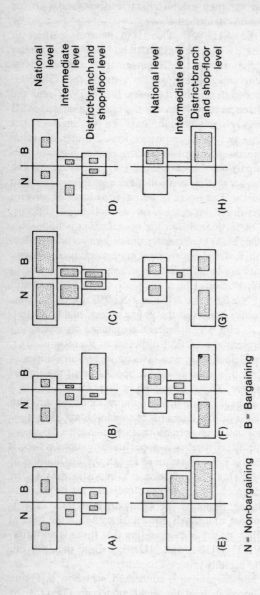

Figure 3 De facto systems of government, circa 1960 (ASTMS 1970). 'Intermediate' level refers to the regional or equivalent level, e.g. AUEW Division. A: TGWU – highly centralized and highly concentrated (the single-channel NUT, NUBE and NUPE, for non-bargaining systems of decision-making, were similar in 1960 to the TGWU: however, their bargaining systems were somewhat different) B: ASTMS; C: POEU, and similar to NALGO. D: GMWU – highly regionalized and concentrated: E: NUM – regionalized and diffused; F: ASB; G: UCATT (ASW); H: AUEW(E), and similar to AUFW – decentralized and diffused.

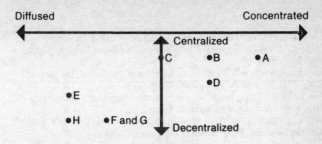

Figure 4 Relative vertical and horizontal dispersal of unions' systems of non-bargaining decision-making area, 1960 (ASTMS 1970): A–H as in Figure 3.

reference to both the vertical and the horizontal planes of government.

Summary and conclusions

In this section we found the democratic typologies commonly used for examining union government unsuitable for our analytical needs. In particular, they were not useful for examining the comparative effectiveness of unions' systems of government. Neither did the existing typologies offer a satisfactory means of separating, for analytical purposes, variations and movements within unions, for instance in the non-bargaining and bargaining channels of decision-making.

Our alternative typology overcomes these difficulties by distinguishing between certain aspects of union decision-making found to be important in our case studies of union change. Union government is, in our typology, divided into interrelated parts. The primary division is into vertical and horizontal dimensions of government. Within the vertical continuum unions can be described as being centralized or decentralized, while at each horizontal level of government, within the vertical structure, decision-making can be described according to its concentrated or diffused nature. Second, in order to facilitate an understanding of the separate movements that can take place in a union's non-bargaining and bargaining structures, the vertical continuum is presented as bifurcated. This division, either *de facto* or *de jure*, allows, for instance, separate and contrary movements in the non-bargaining and bargaining continuums of government to be analysed.

191

Trade Unions

References

BULLOCK, A. (1960), *The Life and Times of Ernest Bevin*, vol. 1, Heinemann.

EDELSTEIN, J. D., and M. WARNER, (1975), *Comparative Union Democracy*, Allen & Unwin.

LIPSET, S. M., M. TROW and J. COLEMAN (1956), *Union Democracy: The Internal Politics of the International Typographical Union*, Free Press.

MARTIN, R. (1968), 'Union democracy: an explanatory framework', *Sociology*, vol. 2.

MICHELS, R. (1911), *Political Parties*, Free Press.

TURNER, H. A. (1962), *Trade Union Growth, Structure and Policy*, Allen & Unwin.

WEBB, S., and B. WEBB (1901), *Industrial Democracy*, Longman.

14 J. Gennard, M. Gregory and S. Dunn

Union Rules and Union Discipline

From J. Gennard, M. Gregory and S. Dunn, 'Throwing the Book: Trade Union Rules on Admission, Discipline and Expulsion', *Department of Employment Gazette*, vol. 88, no. 6, June 1980, pp. 591–600.

[. . .] The importance of formal rules can be exaggerated unless consideration is given to how they are applied in practice. For example, absence of elaborate and detailed procedure by no means implies that the trade union concerned is likely to behave in an arbitrary manner towards its members.

It may be that the rules have remained vague in the specification of the powers and procedures that the union might use, precisely because there have been so few cases in which the rule-book has been tested.[1] In addition, some unions issue handbooks providing guidance to branch and full-time officials on the application of the rules in particular situations, which may establish further procedures and rights for the protection of individual members not specified in detail in the rule-book.

The present study is confined to the contents of union rule-books and is not intended to be a complete account of trade union procedures on admission and discipline. Rather, it is to be seen as a starting-point for further research into the operation of union rules, particularly where union membership is a condition of employment, and as providing some basic factual information in an area where there has been little recent empirical research.[2]

---

1. For example, the rule-book of the Amalgamated Textile Workers Union merely states that all disputes shall be decided by the Central Executive Council. No further procedures or members' rights are elaborated. However, a senior official of the union could only remember one instance of a disciplinary dispute in the many years he had been associated with the union (or part of it, as the union is the product of a recent amalgamation). Clearly in practice the procedural inadequacy of the rule-book is not a matter for great concern.

2. Other studies of the content of trade union rules relating to the admission and disciplining of members include: (*a*) Rideout (1965); (*b*) A survey of affiliated members conducted by the TUC in 1969. The results are briefly described in the General Council's Annual Report to the TUC's Annual Congress of 1969.

Legal requirements

Until 1971 the legal rights of a trade union member were based upon the rules of the trade union which the courts interpreted as the terms of a contract between the union and the individual member. The courts have imposed the further requirement that the application of trade union rules should conform with the principles of natural justice.[3] The statutory obligations imposed upon trade union rule-books were minimal. As a condition of registration under the 1871 and 1913 Trade Union Acts[4] the rules of registered unions were required to cover a limited range of topics including any fines and forfeitures for which the member might be liable. The rules of unregistered unions were not regulated by legislation.

In 1968 the Donovan Commission recommended the extension of the statutory requirements imposed on the rules of registered trade unions to cover a range of new issues.[5] On the subject of admission, union rules should state the qualifications that an applicant must possess to be eligible for membership, and rejected candidates should have a right of appeal against exclusion to the union's executive council or equivalent body. Disciplinary rules should specify, in detail, the offences for which a member might be disciplined, the appropriate penalty in each case and the procedure for appeal against disciplinary action. The Commission also recommended that an independent body be established to hear complaints against trade unions by individuals who had exhausted or did not have access to the trade union's internal procedures[6]. Legislation based on the Donovan proposals was dropped after the defeat of the Labour government in the general election of June 1970.

The next administration's Industrial Relations Act attempted far-reaching reform of the legal position of trade unions.[7] The main

3. For an analysis of the common law principles of natural justice see chapter 10 of Rideout (1979). Some idea of what the principles of natural justice are may be gathered from the discussion of the TUC's 1969 proposal on rule-book reform and section 65 of the 1971 Industrial Relations Act. Perhaps the principle can be summed up as the right to have a fair hearing before an impartial tribunal.

4. See the Trade Union Act 1971 s14.1 and Schedule 1. The provisions of the 1913 Act were confined to political funds which are outside the scope of this article.

5. See the *Report of the Royal Commission on Trade Unions and Employers' Associations*, Cmnd 3623, 1968, HMSO, especially chapter 11, paras. 650, 651 and 658–69.

6. See the *Report of the Royal Commission on Trade Unions and Employers' Associations*, paras. 658–9. It was envisaged that the independent review body would be composed of three members: two trade unionists and a lawyer acting as chairman. Awards of damages made by the review body would have been legally enforceable.

provisions relating to the admission and discipline of members were contained in section 65 of the Act. Appropriately qualified applicants were protected from arbitrary or unreasonable exclusion from membership. Members were protected from unfair or unreasonable disciplinary action. Disciplinary proceedings were subject to more stringent requirements. The accused member received the right to written notice of the charges; a reasonable time to prepare a defence; a full and fair hearing; a written statement of the finding and an opportunity for appeal if provided for by the union's rules. Termination of an individual's membership by the trade union was precluded unless the member received reasonable notice, and a statement of the grounds for expulsion. Section 65 established guiding principles that were intended to apply to all trade unions, but registered unions were also subject to the direct supervision of the registrar who could require that registered unions incorporate the principles of the Act into their rule-books.

The Industrial Relations Act was repealed by the Trade Union and Labour Relations Act of 1974. However, certain principles of the 1971 Act were continued by sections 5 and 6 of the new Act. Section 5 continued the individual's right not to be unreasonably or arbitrarily excluded or expelled from membership. Section 6 required that trade union rules firstly specify the offences for which a member might be expelled, and secondly establish a procedure for handling disciplinary cases in conformity with the rules of natural justice.

At present there are few statutory constraints on the formulation and operation of disciplinary rules as both sections 5 and 6 were repealed by the Trade Union and Labour Relations (Amendment) Act of 1976.[8] However, the position seems likely to change in the near future as Clause 3 of the present Government's Employment Bill revives the right not to be unreasonably excluded or expelled from membership where union membership is a condition of employment.[9]

8. After TULRA 1976 the Certification Officer's (replacement of the old Registrar of Friendly Societies) principal function was to ascertain the *bona fide* independence of trade unions from influence by employers or other outside sources.

9. Both the IRA 1971 and TULRA 1974 in effect permitted trade unions to exclude inappropriately qualified persons from membership, thus enabling unions to maintain apprenticeship systems and other restrictive entry practices. It is unclear what effect the absence of this provision in Clause 3 will have on the operation of such entry practices by trade unions.

7. For an analysis of the operation of the 1971 Act see Weekes *et al.* (1975). They concluded that, in practice, section 65 had very little impact on the rule-books of either registered or unregistered unions.

TUC initiatives

Following the Donovan report, in June 1969, the TUC published a series of its own proposals for the reform of the internal rules and procedures of affiliated members.[10] In substance they bear some similarity to the Donovan recommendations and to parts of the Industrial Relations Act. However, they differ in that they are only intended as guidelines for voluntary reform.

The TUC proposals are set out in some detail below. The principles outlined act as the basis for the discussion of the content of the rule-books set out later in the paper as they provide a useful guide as to what model rules and procedures might consist of.

On the issue of admission to membership the TUC made ten suggestions that should be incorporated into a separate rule or section of the rule-book. The rules should contain a clear statement of the qualifications necessary for admission to the union of specific categories of membership. There should be provision for a clear procedure for admission, and notification should be given to the applicant when the procedure is complete. It should be clearly stated which body in the union has the power to accept or reject applications. The rules should state the grounds on which an applicant might be rejected. A rejected applicant should be provided with a written statement of the reasons for exclusion. There should be a right of appeal against rejection. This right should be given to the applicant himself rather than the applicant's sponsors, as was common in many rule-books. The appeal should be to a higher body than the one that made the original decision. No individual involved in making the initial decision to reject the applicant should be involved in the appeals process. There should be a clear, detailed procedure for appeal, and the appeals body should have the power to enforce its decisions.

On the issue of discipline the TUC recommended that the rule-book should detail the offences for which a member might be disciplined by the union and should state the appropriate penalty in each case. In addition the rules should lay down a detailed procedure that complied with the principles of natural justice for the handling of disciplinary cases. Natural justice, as defined by the TUC, comprises three basic elements. The opportunity to be heard, a fair hearing, and a *bona fide* decision.

10. The TUC proposals were circularized to all affiliated unions in June 1969. They are stated in full in the General Council's 1969 Annual Report to Congress.

The necessary preconditions for the opportunity to be heard are: a reasonably convenient time and place for the hearing, sufficient notification of the hearing and sufficient information of the charges against the member for him to be able to prepare his defence. A 'fair hearing' requires firstly that a member has the opportunity to state his case and support that case with the testimony of witnesses, written documents, and so on, and secondly that he can hear and answer the case against him. A *bona fide* decision requires that the final judgement be honest, unbiased and in accordance with the union's rules.

The TUC further proposed that the union's rule-book should provide for the right of appeal against any penalty awarded against a member. The appeals procedure should also conform with the rules of natural justice. The appeals body should be higher in status than the one imposing the penalty and comprised of people with no personal involvement in the case. The aggrieved member should be informed in writing of his right to appeal and the procedure to do so. Where practicable an expelled member should remain a member until the appeals process was exhausted.

These proposals have remained the basis of TUC policy since 1969. In 1976 the TUC took a further initiative. In May of that year an independent review committee was established to consider appeals from individuals who have been dismissed from, or have given notice of dismissal from their jobs as a result of being expelled from, or have been refused admission to, a union where union membership was a condition of employment and where the individual had exhausted the internal procedures of the trade union.[11]

The survey

Our study covers the rule-books of seventy-nine affiliated unions with a membership of just under 12 million or 99 per cent of the TUC's total membership.[12] All but three of the eighty-one unions in the TUC with 5,000 or more members have been included.[13] One union with slightly

11. For an analysis of the operation of the independent review committee see 'The Independent Review Committee: the Success of Voluntarism?' *Industrial Relations Review and Report*, no. 208, September 1979.

12. Information relating to the number of members in trade unions, the TUC, etc., has all been taken from the TUC's Statistical Statement to Delegates for the 1979 Annual Congress.

13. The rule-books of three unions, NATKE, the National Union of Insurance Workers, and the Power Loom Carpet Weavers' Association, proved unobtainable within the short space of time available for preparing this article.

fewer than 5,000 members has also been included because a high proportion of its membership work under closed shop conditions.[14] The original purpose of the investigation was to examine the rule-books of unions with substantial numbers of members working in closed shops. However, because of the recent spread of compulsory unionism across many sectors of British industry the majority of trade unions now have members affected by the practice.[15] With certain exceptions[16], it is in general not possible to make a clear distinction between 'closed shop prone' and 'non-closed-shop prone' unions, so the study was extended to encompass the rule-books of all major trade unions.

Rules relating to the admission of members

Entry requirements

All but one of the unions studied mention some type of entry requirement in their rule-books, but the amount of detail with which such conditions are specified varies considerably. In general, craft unions are most precise in the elaboration of the occupational groups eligible for membership and the qualifications an applicant must possess to obtain entry into the union. The Sheet Metal Workers Union for example, specifies thirty-one separate occupational categories that are eligible for recruitment.[17] Frequently, unions catering primarily for craft employees specify an indentured apprenticeship as a necessary qualification for membership. These unions tend to have a separate category of membership for skilled workers, which usually has higher benefit and contribution levels than other categories of membership covering less-skilled employees within the same industries.

Three other groups of unions have clearly specified entry requirements. First, there are those unions which recruit from particular grades within particular industries. Many of these cater for white-collar public sector workers: for example, Civil and Public

14. BALPA with a membership of 4,457.

15. For an analysis of the spread of the closed shop across industries see J. Gennard *et al.* in *Employment Gazette*, January 1980.

16. There are certain unions that have specifically adopted an anti-closed-shop stance, such as the NUT and POEU, but in general most unions have members affected by some form of closed shop arrangement.

17. See Rule 3(*a*) of the National Union of Sheetmetal Workers, Coppersmiths Heating and Domestic Engineers.

Services Association, and Institution of Professional Civil Servants. Others in this category also require that applicants possess specialized qualifications: for instance, entry into National Association of Colliery Overmen, Deputies and Shotfirers (the supervisors' union in coal-mining) is dependent upon possession of a deputy's certificate; likewise membership of British Association of Airline Pilots (the commercial airline pilots' union) requires a commercial airline pilot's licence. Secondly, there are unions such as the Union of Post Office Workers or National Union of Mineworkers or National Union of Railwaymen that are open to all workers within a particular industry. In practice, the distinction between industrial unions and those only open to particular grades is not so great as might appear from reading the rule-books, as in many industries the spheres of recruitment are clearly defined by collective agreements with employers and arrangements between trade unions. Thirdly, there are some large unions such as the Transport and General Workers' Union, Association of Scientific, Technical and Managerial Staffs or Association of Professional, Executive, Clerical and Computer Staff which are not confined to particular industries but recruit applicants from broad, very loosely defined occupation groups. The TGWU is an interesting case because, along with a few other unions, the national rule-book empowers the branch (subject to ratification by the General Executive Council) to make local bylaws affecting entry requirements. Although in general membership is open to a wide range of different occupations, therefore, in certain areas or for particular jobs the entry requirements may be much stricter and are not specified in the national rule-book. Only the General and Municipal Workers claims to be entirely open. Rule 25(1) of the union states: 'All persons engaged in any kind of industry or service whether manual, clerical, technical or administrative shall be eligible to join the union.' In practice the union's recruitment areas will be restricted by collective bargaining arrangements, etc., not referred to in the rule-book. One union, the Ceramic and Allied Workers, mentions no entry requirements; the rules merely state that membership 'shall consist of an unlimited number of members'.[18]

It is common for union rule-books to provide the executive council or the annual conference with discretionary powers to accept other individuals or categories of worker into membership. In most instances, the power is unrestricted; in theory the authorized body can

18. Ceramic and Allied Workers Union Rule no. 1.

admit anybody it chooses into membership. However, in some unions the rule-book limits this discretionary power to workers in areas of employment closely associated with those normally eligible for recruitment. These discretionary powers are designed to give the union flexibility to adjust to changed circumstances. For example, the National Graphical Association has recently adopted the discretionary power to recruit new groups of workers so that the union can respond to the challenge of technological change which threatens to undermine the traditional basis of the union's membership.[19]

Other grounds for the rejection of applicants for membership

All the unions studied reserve the right to reject applicants for reasons other than failure to meet the basic occupational entry requirements. However, the grounds on which exclusion from membership may take place are generally not stated in detail. Reasons mentioned for rejection include bad health, previous expulsion from membership, a criminal record or previous dismissal from employment for misconduct. The United Road Transport Union has a general requirement that applicants be of steady habits and good moral character.[20] The National Union of Seamen has a comprehensive list of grounds for exclusion which are clearly related to the working environment of its members. For instance, the union can exclude 'Any person whose presence aboard ship would be prejudicial to the personal safety and well-being of others on board'.[21] The General and Municipal Workers are unique in having a rule to exclude an applicant from membership in order to conform with a decision of the TUC's independent review committee.[22]

Procedures for rejecting applicants to membership

There is provision in the rules of twenty-four unions with over 2·3 million members for an excluded applicant to be informed of the reasons for rejection. This figure probably understates the true position as, in practice, unions providing a right of appeal against rejection imply a right to be notified of the grounds for exclusion,

19. NGA; 3(4).
20. URTU; 2(2).
21. NUS; 2(13).
22. NUGMW; 43(13).

whether or not it is actually stated in the rules, as it would hardly be possible to mount an effective appeal if the appellant had no knowledge of the reasons for his exclusion. Provision for a right of appeal against rejection is made by thirth-three unions with a membership of over five million. Interestingly, three rule-books covering 450,000 members state that a rejected applicant should be given a statement of the grounds for exclusion, but do not mention any right of appeal. It is quite common for unions without a right of appeal against rejection is made by thirty-three unions with a effect that 'nothing in these rules shall preclude a rejected applicant from reapplying for membership'. So in practice rejected applicants have another chance to apply, though this falls short of a right of appeal as, in all probability, the second and subsequent applications will be dealt with by the same body of individuals that rejected the first application.

Where an opportunity of appeal against exclusion exists, the procedure almost invariably lays down that it is the individual concerned, rather than his sponsors who are already members of the union, that has the right to use the appeals procedure. In all but two unions the appeal is normally to a higher body than that which made the original decision. The most common provision (seventeen unions) is for an applicant rejected at branch level to have a right of appeal to executive council or equivalent level. However, this is by no means always the case. For example, in the Transport and General Workers' Union appeal against exclusion goes to district level. In the National Graphical Association final responsibility for admission rests with the National Council, which acts upon the recommendation of the branch. The individual has two opportunities of appeal against rejection; first, he can challenge the branch's recommendation, which is considered by an appeals and disciplinary committee composed of National Council members; second, he can challenge the committee's recommendation, which must be endorsed by the National Council.[23]

In some unions application for membership can be made to the branch, district, or the executive council. In these unions applicants rejected at lower levels can appeal to the executive council, but initial rejection by the executive council creates the difficulty that appeal to the executive council would involve the same group of individuals hearing the appeal as rejected the original application. Most of these unions avoid this problem by having a separate appeals procedure for

23. NGA; 17(1).

Table 1 Admission rules: the rights of applicants excluded from trade union membership

Admission rules providing for:	No. of unions	Percentage of all the unions studied	No. of members in union with rules mentioned below (thousands)	Percentage of the total membership
Notification to a rejected applicant of the grounds for exclusion from membership	24	**30**	2,346	20
Right of appeal against exclusion	33	**42**	5,056	42
Procedures for appeal:				
(*a*) a hearing at which the applicant has the opportunity to state his case	8	**10**	552	5
(*b*) appeal in writing only	10	**13**	198	2
(*c*) procedure left unspecified	15	**19**	4,302	35

Notes: 1. The categories outlined are not mutually exclusive, so the columns do not add up to the total no. of unions or members.
2. The total no. of unions studied = 79.
3. The total membership of the unions studied = 11,974,000.
4. Membership totals rounded to the nearest thousand.
5. Percentages rounded to the nearest whole number.

those rejected in the first instance by the executive council. In these circumstances, the appeal is a specially appointed appeals body, or in one case the union's annual general conference. However, in two of the unions studied, applicants rejected at executive council level can only appeal to the executive council, though in practice the problem rarely arises since applicants only apply direct to the national level for admission into the union where there is no appropriate branch. Cases of direct application to the executive level are uncommon and cases of appeal by rejected applicants rarer still.

In general, the procedure for appeal by rejected applicants is less clearly specified than that for disciplining union members. In sixteen unions involving 4·3 million members the procedure for appeal and the rights that the individual has at appeal are entirely unspecified, as only the right of appeal and the body to which the appeal should be made are specified. In a further four unions involving 400,000 members the appeal is made in writing only. In a further ten involving 420,000 members the rules permit the appellant to state his case in person. In three of these unions the procedure and the rights specified are the same or similar to those relating to the disciplining of members. One union rule-book, (the National Union of Agricultural and Allied Workers) mentions a further right of appeal to the independent review committee of the TUC in cases where a rejected applicant stands to lose his employment through the existence of a closed shop.

Disciplinary rules

General clauses

A very general or 'blanket' clause that empowers the union to take disciplinary action against a member for a wide range of unspecified offences is employed by sixty-nine unions with 11·2 million members. The wording of general clauses varies considerably; the most common is a rule that protects the union from 'action contrary or detrimental to the aims and interests of the trade union or its members'. Other common clauses guard against those who 'attempt to injure the interests of the union' or 'action likely to bring the union into disrepute' and against members who are 'not fit and proper persons' to be members of the union. In other cases the wording is less explicit. For example, the Annual General Meeting of the Educational Institute of Scotland is empowered to 'expel from the Institute any member whose expulsion appears to be expedient'.[24] The Post Office Management Staff's Association can discipline for any 'valid' reason.[25] In most cases a blanket clause is accompanied by other rules that specify particular offences in detail. The purpose of the general clause is to guard against unforeseen circumstances; for instance, the rule-book of the Transport and General Workers Union lists specific offences and then covers itself against other eventualities by laying down that a member may in addition be disciplined for 'other forms of

24. Educational Institute of Scotland; 2(8).
25. POMSA; 11.

misconduct'.[26] However, in nine rule-books covering 900,000 members the disciplinary section contains only a general clause; no specific offences are mentioned. And thirty-one unions with 5·7 million members have a double indemnity against the unforeseen, as some body within the union, usually the executive council, has discretion to act as it sees fit in cases where the rules are silent.

The second most common type of offence specified in rule-books is that of breaking or disregarding the rules, and forty unions covering 7·4 million members have such a rule. This rule is accompanied in twenty unions covering 3·4 million members, by a rule enabling the union to discipline a member who disobeys or disregards a lawful instruction of an official or member of the union empowered by the rule or an authorized body to make such an order. Another general rule found in seven rule-books, covering 2·1 million members, protects the union against members whose conduct is likely to lead to the break-up of the union.

Specific offences

The disciplinary offences listed in Table 2 are largely self-explanatory. However, clarification is necessary for three of the categories of offence mentioned. Rules against the unauthorized publication of information are designed to prevent confidential information concerning the union being leaked to outsiders, and to prevent branches or individual members circulating documents or pamphlets within the membership that undermine the union's authority or attack its policy.

Trade rules are used by craft unions to impose obligations or restrictions on the manner in which members behave. Such rules cover issues like the limitation of overtime or the prohibition of certain types of payment system. In some rule-books the exact nature of these restrictions is not clearly stated. In these cases the branches are empowered to make their own bylaws on trade practices, subject to ratification by a higher body within the union. Other unions, however, have detailed rules governing the working practices of members laid out in the rule-book itself. Examples of this type of rule can be seen in Rule 33 of the Sheet Metal Workers, which instructs members not to work under *Bedanx* systems of payment, or in Rule 43 of the National

26. TGWU; 11(19).

Table 2 Disciplinary offences

Types of offence mentioned in disciplinary rules	No. of unions	Percentage of all unions studied	No. of members in unions with rules of each category mentioned below (thousands)	Percentage of the total membership of unions studied
General 'blanket' clause	63	**80**	11,211	**94**
Breaking the rules in the rule-book	40	**51**	7,376	**62**
Disobeying the instruction of an authorized member or official	20	**25**	3,438	**29**
Attempting to 'break up' the unions	7	**9**	2,100	**18**
Rules concerning the misuse or misappropriation of union funds and property	35	**44**	4,990	**42**
Examples				
(a) Fraud/misappropriation of union funds	22		3,352	**28**
(b) Wrongfully obtaining or withholding union funds or property	10	**13**	243	**2**
(c) Damage or destruction of union property	3	**4**	187	**2**
(d) False claim to union benefits	14	**18**	2,740	**23**
Rules against members – blacklegging, assisting an employer or handling work during a dispute	15	**19**	2,656	**22**
Prohibition of the circulation of confidential or unauthorized or false information about the union	14	**18**	2,884	**24**
Rules prohibiting members from slandering, libelling or maliciously charging another member or official	12	**15**	1,663	**14**
Rules prohibiting from working at below the union wage rate	8	**10**	440	**4**

Table 2 (*contd*)

Types of offence mentioned in disciplinary rules	No. of unions	Percentage of all unions studied	No. of members in unions with rules of each category mentioned below (thousands)	Percentage of the total membership of unions studied
Rules for expelling a member wrongfully gaining admission	12	**15**	2,208	**18**
Rules for disciplining members assisting an applicant gaining admission under false pretences	3	**4**	456	**4**
Rules against fraud or impersonation in union ballots	2	**3**	486	**4**
Rules against the infringement of trade practices	10	**13**	800	**7**
Rules against unprofessional conduct	3	**4**	432	**4**
Rules for disciplining members failing to pay fines or levies	3	**4**	110	**1**

Notes: 1. There are no total figures for either the number of unions or the percentages covered as the categories are not exclusive or comprehensive. Most rule-books contain several of the types of offences listed.
2. The examples of rules relating to the misuse or misappropriation of union funds or property add up to more than the total for this category because several unions have more than one rule of this nature.
3. Percentages rounded to nearest whole number.
4. Total no. of rule-books studied = 79.
5. Total membership of unions studied = 11,974,000.

Graphical Association, which prohibits members from handling work that is going to or coming from an 'unrecognized source'.

Three unions catering for professional workers, the National Union of Teachers, the National Union of Journalists and the National Association of Schoolmasters and Union of Women Teachers, have a rule that constrains members from 'unprofessional conduct'. Two of these unions (NUJ and NUT) have detailed codes of conduct attached to the rules, which specify the nature of such conduct. Both of these unions also lay down a different procedure for handling cases of unprofessional conduct to that used for other types of disciplinary offence.

Disciplinary powers

Only three of the unions studied do not have the authority to expel for disciplinary offences. These are all small unions catering for specialized groups of white-collar workers, with a combined membership of less than 60,000.[27] In addition, fifty-nine unions have the power to suspend a member temporarily from some or all of the benefits of membership. Members are generally obliged to pay full subscriptions during the period of suspension.

Half the unions studied are empowered to levy fines. The level of fines that may be charged varies considerably between unions. The rules of nine unions do not mention a maximum limit to the fine that may be levied, but of the remaining thirty unions fourteen can only levy a fine of £10 or less.[28] On the other hand, eleven unions with 1·1 million members can charge fines of £50 and over. The highest permitted level is £250 specified by the Association of Cinematograph Television and Allied Technicans (ACTT). Unpaid fines and levies generally count as arrears of subscriptions and can so contribute towards expulsion from membership. Under SOGAT's rules the imposition of fines leads directly to the possibility of exclusion, as a member fined for disciplinary offences on these occasions is liable to expulsion. The rule-books of a small number of white-collar unions specifically state that there shall be no fines.

The number of unions listed in Table 3 as being empowered to remove or debar a member from union office is an understatement of the actual number of unions with this power. It includes only those unions that mention removal from office in the section of the rules relating to the disciplining of members. Some unions treat the

27. The Health Visitors' Association, the Association of University Teachers and the Greater London Staffs' Association have no disciplinary rules for the disciplining of members.

28. In 1965 Rideout pointed out that the maximum level of fine that many unions were empowered to levy was so low that, in practice, unions were obliged to expel from membership in all cases involving serious breaches of the rules. This would appear still to be the case for over one-third of the unions which specify a right to fine members.

Table 3 The disciplinary powers of trade unions

Disciplinary powers specified in the union's rule-book	No. of unions	Percentage of all unions studied	No. of members in union with the disciplinary powers mentioned below (thousands)	Percentage of total membership of unions studied
Expulsion	76	**96**	11,917	**99·5**
Suspension (from some or all of the benefits of membership for a limited period of time)	59	**75**	10,655	**90**
Fines	39	**49**	6,992	**58**
Removal/debarring from office	17	**22**	3,390	**28**
Reprimand	8	**10**	1,222	**10**
No disciplinary powers	3	**4**	57	**0·5**

Notes: 1. The categories mentioned above are not mutually exclusive, and many unions have more than one of the powers listed, therefore the columns do not add up to either the total number of unions studied or 100 per cent.

2. No. of unions studied = 79.

3. Total membership of unions studied = 11,974,000.

disciplining of officials as a separate issue, one that is outside the scope of this article.

A small minority of unions specify 'official reprimand' or 'admonition' before the branch or executive committee as a penalty. In addition, one small craft union, the National Union of Domestic Appliance and General Metal Workers, is empowered to publish the names of offenders to the trade. The names of members blacklegging or assisting an employer during a dispute are displayed in the union's offices and circulated at the annual conference.[29]

The extent to which appropriate penalties are specified for particular offences

In general, most rule-books leave considerable discretion to the disciplinary body in determining the penalty to be imposed for a

29. NUDAGMWU; 35.

particular offence. This is not surprising given the general way in which offences tend to be worded. However, this is not true in every case. For example, the National Graphical Association lays down that infringement of most of its disciplinary rules are punishable by a fine of up to £75 or expulsion. But for certain offences the penalty is more precisely specified; for example, the penalty for working in an unrecognized office is expulsion, but the maximum penalty for insulting or interfering with chapel or branch officials is £10.[30] Some unions, mostly catering for manual workers, state the appropriate penalty for minor misdemeanours such as disorderly conduct at a branch meeting.

Level within the union at which disciplinary jurisdiction lies

All unions with disciplinary powers indicate the body that has jurisdiction over such matters, even though in many cases disciplinary action can be initiated at several different levels. In thirty-eight unions it is the branch that has disciplinary power. In four cases the decision of the branch has to be ratified by a higher body, usually the executive council. In a further four unions the branch makes a recommendation that is taken into account when the executive council makes the final judgement. The rules of seventeen unions where disciplinary action against members is normally taken at branch level provide that all cases involving expulsion be ratified by a higher body, usually the executive committee, before expulsion takes effect. In twenty-seven unions the executive council is empowered to handle all internal discipline, but most of these are unions catering for non-manual workers. The list is by no means exhaustive. Three unions have some other procedure involving a specially-constituted body.

Members' rights during disciplinary proceeding

There is considerable variation in the detail with which members' rights during disciplinary proceedings are specified. Certain unions, such as the EETPU, NGA, NUJ and NUT, specify in great detail the procedure for hearing disciplinary cases. However, there are twenty-two unions with 2·6 million members that merely name the body that handles the case and make no mention of the procedure involved. [...].

30. NGA; 41 and 43.

Appeals procedures

Of the unions studied, seventy-five with a membership of 11·6 million provide a right of appeal against disciplinary action to a higher body than that which made the original decision. The larger unions tend to have several stages of appeal, often involving an initial appeal from branch to regional or district level, then to the executive council or a sub-committee of the executive council and finally to a specially-constituted appeals tribunal or the union's annual conference.

In the forty-six cases where the final appeal is heard by the executive council, the general council or a permanent appeals tribunal, decisions can be reached fairly rapidly. Nine unions ensure that no undue delay occurs by stating in the rules that the appeal must be heard within a specified time, often 21 or 28 days from the time of the original hearing or the date of the member's request for an appeal. Others achieve the same purpose by establishing that the appeal must be heard at the next convenient meeting of the appropriate body. However, in the union where final appeal is heard by the union's annual conference or an appeals body that only meets on an occasional basis, the member may have to wait a considerable length of time before a final decision is reached on his case. The delay can be even longer where the delegates' conference is held on a biennial or even triennial basis.

Appeals tribunals are generally composed of long-serving union members elected by the annual conference or appointed by the executive council. Frequently the rules exclude members of the executive council from participation in the appeals tribunal, so ensuring that no individual involved in making the original decision hears the appeal.

By and large, unions with detailed procedures at the first stage of the disciplinary process tend also to be the most detailed in their provision for appeal, though seven unions with 260,000 members have significantly more elaborate procedural requirements at appeal than at the original hearing. Most unions specify a period of time, commonly 14–28 days from the original hearing or notification of the result, within which the member must make his appeal. The TUC recommended that where practicable no penalty should be enforced before the appeals process is exhausted. Such a rule would be very difficult to operate where appeal is made to the annual conference because of the length of time that might elapse before the final appeal is heard. However, of the unions where the appeal goes before the executive council or a permanent appeals body, twenty-one with 2·4

Table 4 Final appeals body that hears members' appeals against disciplinary decisions

Final appeals body	No. of unions	Percentage of all unions with disciplinary rules	Membership (thousands)	Percentage of total membership of unions with disciplinary rules
Executive council (or equivalent body)	18	24	1,437	12
General council (or equivalent body)	5	7	687	6
Specially-appointed appeals tribunal	23	30	6,326	53
Specially-appointed appeals tribunal that meets annually	2	3	1,280	11
Annual conference (or equivalent body)	24	32	1,250	10
Arbitration	4	5	830	7
No provision for appeals	4	5	148	1
All	76	100	11,958	100

Notes: 1. Three of the unions studied have no disciplinary rules and have been excluded.
2. All percentages rounded to nearest whole number.
3. Membership rounded to nearest thousand.

million members provide that no disciplinary action be taken before the appeals process is exhausted. [...]

Exclusion for arrears

Little attention was paid to trade union rules relating to the exclusion of members for non-payment of dues until the case *Edwards* v. *SOGAT* came before the Court of Appeal in 1970.[31] At that time, as with many other unions, membership of SOGAT automatically lapsed after six weeks of failure to pay subscriptions. There was no provision for the member to be notified of impending exclusion or to have an opportunity of explaining why he might have failed to maintain

31. *Edwards* v. *SOGAT* [1971] ch. 354.

payments. Edwards paid his subscriptions through a check-off system, but due to an oversight of a union official the payments were not recorded and he appeared to be in arrears. After six weeks he was expelled according to the rules, and as union membership was a condition of employment, he lost his job as a consequence.

Following this case the TUC issued three recommendations relating to exclusion for arrears. Firstly trade unions should make the responsibility to maintain subscriptions clear to the member through the rules and any other available means. Secondly, the rules should state the period after which a member could or would be excluded, and, thirdly, they should specify the body or person within the union with power to exclude for arrears.[32] In 1971 the General Council considered a further recommendation that unions include a rule providing for notification to be given to a member before exclusion.[33] This proposal was rejected because of the administrative difficulty and high financial cost involved in keeping in touch with the subscriptions of every member that such a rule would entail, especially for the large general unions with a high membership turnover.[34]

Expulsion for arrears

Of the seventy-nine unions studied only the Association of University Teachers has no power to expel a member for financial default. However, the rule-books of three unions with 210,000 members refer to exclusion for arrears as 'suspension', and the individual is restored to full membership upon payment of his outstanding debt.[35]

All but three unions have separate rules for dealing with members out of compliance other than the general disciplinary procedure. The remaining seventy-six rule-books state a particular length of time, most commonly 13 or 26 weeks, after which membership may be terminated for non-payment of dues. The period varies considerably between unions; at one extreme the Bakers and the Wire Drawers and

32. Contained in the TUC General Council's Annual Report to the 1970 Congress. The recommendations were sent to affiliated members in April 1970.

33. See para. 57 of the TUC General Council's Annual Report to the 1971 Congress.

34. This poses a severe practical problem given the very high turnover in membership of many unions. The problem is exacerbated because few unions have their membership records computerized.

35. The unions that mention only suspension for arrears are: URTU; National Union of Hosiery and Knitwear Workers; the National Association of Schoolmasters and Union of Women Teachers.

Kindred Workers wait 52 weeks and at the other, the National Association of Licensed House Managers is authorized to expel after 4 weeks and the Educational Institute of Scotland can exclude as soon as the member goes into arrears. This final case is not as oppressive as it may sound because in common with some other non-manual unions the expectation is that members pay their subscriptions annually in a lump-sum payment. Two non-manual unions have alternative periods and procedures for exclusion according to the method of payment. Members making 'fractional' payments of their subscriptions have a longer period before exclusion than those who pay annually. In ten rule-books special mention is made of members who pay their dues through 'check off' systems. In these cases termination of union membership is immediate upon cancellation of the authorization to the employer to make deduction at source payments. [. . .]

Conclusion

Fifteen years ago Professor Rideout suggested that, with certain notable exceptions, the development of trade union rules and procedures had not kept pace with the increasingly sophisticated requirements imposed on them by the evolution of case law.[36] Since 1965 external pressure for the reform of trade union rules relating to admission and discipline has intensified with various attempts at legislation increasing the statutory requirements made upon trade union internal rules and proposals from the TUC for voluntary reform. It is difficult to measure the precise impact of these new influences without conducting a comparative survey of union rules as they stood in the mid 1960s, before attempts at legislative and voluntary reform, with the latest editions of the rules of the same unions. Our study is not strictly comparable with earlier studies, so any assessment of change that may have occurred in union rules must necessarily be tentative.

With certain exceptions, the admission and disciplinary rules of most of the unions studied do not reach the standards of procedural elaboration required by the 1971 Industrial Relations Act or recommended by the TUC's 1969 proposals. For instance, on the issue of admission to membership, only one-fifth of the unions studied provided notification of the reason for rejection to excluded applicants

36. See Rideout (1965).

for membership, and only two-fifths provided rejected applicants with a right of appeal.

Disciplinary rules tend to be more detailed, but here again the degree of sophistication varies greatly between unions. Many unions still rely primarily on general or 'blanket' clauses rather than a range of specific offences. It is unusual to find the appropriate penalties set out for particular offences apart from minor misdemeanours, though this is hardly surprising given the general way in which offences tend to be worded. Certain unions provide extensive rights to members facing disciplinary action. In some cases the principles of natural justice are explicitly mentioned in the rules. However, other unions are much less specific in the provision of procedural rights to the accused member. About half the unions studied require that a member should be given notice of the details of a disciplinary charge and the time and place at which it will be heard. The right of the member to state his case or answer the case against him is mentioned by the rules of about one-third of the unions. However, in a further quarter of the unions studied the rules refer to the right to attend a hearing. It seems likely that these unions in practice also provide the right to be heard. Other rights such as the right to call witnesses, produce documentary evidence, or be spoken for by a friend are mentioned by a significant minority of rule-books.

All but four unions expressly permit appeal by a member against disciplinary action. There are a few cases in which the procedure for appeal is more detailed at the appeal stage than at the initial hearing, but, in general, unions with elaborate appeals procedures tend also to have sophisticated procedures at the first stage of the disciplinary process.

The majority of unions have adopted the TUC's model rule that gives the union express power to terminate membership in compliance with a decision of a disputes committee of the TUC under the Bridlington Agreement. But few rule-books mention the TUC's independent review committee as the final source of appeal when a member works in a closed shop and thus faces dismissal from employment upon expulsion from the union. However, this does not mean that in practice unions ignore the TUC body, as frequently the role of the IRC is mentioned in closed shop agreements negotiated through collective bargaining. A third of the union membership agreements analysed in a recent survey by the Industrial Relations Department of the LSE specified that cases involving the possibility of dismissal from employment after expulsion from trade union membership should be referred to the independent review committee.[37]

Rules relating to expulsion for arrears of subscriptions often do not mention a right to notification before exclusion or an opportunity for the member to explain his arrears. In practice, however, it can be argued that it would be difficult to build such rights into rule-books without committing unions to the potentially high cost involved in keeping track of every member's subscription. The preliminary results of a programme of interviews with officials from sixty trade unions also undertaken by the LSE team[38] investigating the operation of the closed shop, indicate that in practice unions exercise a considerable degree of flexibility in dealing with members out of compliance. Usually the member is allowed a considerably longer period than that specified by the rule-book before exclusion occurs, and in most cases re-entry into the union is virtually automatic, although it may involve the loss of previously-established benefit rights or the payment of a higher entry fee than that normally charged.

There has been a dearth of recent research on the practical operation of union rules. The Donovan Commission found little evidence to suggest that there was widespread abuse of power by trade unions over members or would-be members.[39] It seems unlikely that the position has altered in the twelve years since the Commission's report was published. There are probably few instances of injustice to individual members. In general, the trade union officials interviewed in the survey expressed considerable reluctance to resort to disciplinary measures, especially the ultimate sanction of expulsion from membership, unless no other course of action was possible. In the first three years of its operation, the TUC's independent review committee received only twenty-eight cases that came within its terms of reference which indicates that individual grievances and disputes are generally settled satisfactorily within the internal procedures laid down by trade union rule-books.[40]

37. See Gennard (1979).

38. The programme of interviews with trade union officials, based on a questionnaire, is part of a research project covering all aspects of the operation and extent of the closed shop in Britain. As yet this aspect of the LSE team's work has not been published.

39. The *Report of the Royal Commission on Trade Unions and Employers' Associations*, paras. 619–31, especially para. 622.

40. See Appendix 1, p. 363, of the TUC General Council Annual Report to Congress, 1979.

References

GENNARD, J., *et al.* (1979), 'The Content of Closed Shop Agreements in Britain'. *Employment Gazette*, October.

RIDEOUT, R. W. (1965), 'The content of trade union disciplinary rules', *British Journal of Industrial Relations*, July.

RIDEOUT, R. W. (1979), *The Principles of Labour Law*, 3rd edn, Sweet and Maxwell.

WEEKES *et al.* (1975), *Industrial Relations and the Limits of the Law*, Blackwell.

15 D. Bok and J. Dunlop

How Trade Union Policy is Made

From D. Bok and J. Dunlop, *Labor and the American Community*, Simon & Schuster, 1970, as included in *Readings in Labor Economics and Labor Relations*, ed. Richard L. Rowan, Richard D. Irwin Inc., 1972, pp. 228–32.

At present, most commentators seem to assume that the future of the labor movement rests mainly in the hands of its leaders. This point of view is reflected in the constant criticism of labor leaders, and it is buttressed by a mass of opinion data to the effect that unions are run pretty much as the top officials see fit. Yet one must beware of such opinions, for each of the groups that most influence the public view of organized labor has its special reasons for misconceiving the role of the union leader and exaggerating his influence.

The businessman, for example, is accustomed to organizations where the leader enjoys considerable power (though not so much as the outsider tends to suppose). As a result, many executives assume instinctively that the union leader enjoys comparable authority; they overlook the fact that union officials must win office by election. Businessmen may also exaggerate the role of the union leader as a result of their natural tendency to assume a 'harmony of interests' between themselves and their employees. This assumption has suffused the literature of business for decades and stems, once again, from understandable motives. Few managements wish to harbor the thought that they are pursuing their own interests at the expense of their employees. It would be most disagreeable to concede that wages are kept unfairly low or that the quest for efficiency has led to harsh supervision or uncomfortable working conditions. As a result, when employees organize or protest or strike, many employers assume that harmonious relations within their plants have been disrupted by some opportunistic union leader who has succeeded in leading the workers astray. This reaction, once again, is not a simple matter of tactics; it springs naturally from a network of beliefs that help many executives to justify their behavior as businessmen and human beings.

Intellectuals also have their reasons for ascribing great influence to the union leader. As Bertrand Russell has pointed out, the liberal critic has traditionally been sentimental toward the underdog. He has been unable to champion the cause of the poor and the disadvantaged

217

without idealizing them as well. As a result – until recently, at any rate – these critics could seldom bring themselves to blame union shortcomings on the members; instead, they concluded that the leaders must somehow be responsible.

Other forces also helped to reinforce this bias. After the rush of organizing in the thirties, union members seemed to have become representative of the entire working class. Under these circumstances, it would have been most awkward to fault the members for labor's failure to press for social reform. How could the liberal justify his programs if the beneficiaries themselves were indifferent to them? Unless the rank and file were on his side, how could he urge the unions to reform and still keep true to his democratic principles? Above all, how could he harbor any optimism at all if the entire working class had to be persuaded to support his programs? With all these difficulties, it was far easier to assume that unions were made up of willing members who were held back by the stubbornness and selfishness of powerful leaders. These beliefs could begin to weaken only when union members were no longer seen as representative of the lower classes and unions were no longer the only organized force for social reform. Thus, it is no accident that intellectuals did not acknowledge the lack of liberal, reformist sentiments among the members until the 1960s, when students, black militants, and other groups had already begun to offer organized support for fundamental social reforms. (Characteristically enough, now that the pendulum has begun to swing, it has swung very far indeed in the minds of many critics. Union members are now viewed not only as apathetic and undisposed to social reform; they are erroneously perceived as a highly conservative force in the society.)

Because of these tendencies to exaggerate the influence of the labor leader, one must take pains to construct a more realistic picture of how union policy is actually made. Otherwise, society will often misdirect its energies by flailing away at union officials for actions that are not really within their power to change. In the process, deeper forces may be overlooked, forces that actually determine union behavior and must ultimately be changed if the conduct of unions is to change.

In the end, union behavior is the product of four broad influences that are constantly interacting upon one another: the desires of the members, the nature and abilities of the leadership, the capacities and opinions of subordinates, and the pressures of the environment. This book has been a series of illustrations showing how these forces interact in the most important areas of union activity. In the brief space remaining, it is possible only to distill these illustrations into a more succinct, more general statement.

What the members want

Starting first with the rank and file, a mass of data suggests that the members are primarily interested in their union as an agent for negotiating with the employer and administering the collective bargaining agreement. Where these functions are involved, the members exert influences through many different channels to impose certain restraints upon their leaders. Sometimes the demands of the members are very high, even impossibly so; sometimes they can be modified by the leaders through education and persuasion. Once formed, however, these demands can be ignored only at the risk of decertification, election defeat, refusals to ratify contracts, wildcat strikes, or other ways of withholding cooperation.

The members expect little and ordinarily demand even less in other areas of union activity, such as organizing, political action, or community service. Their main interest is simply that these programs do not require too large an expenditure of dues or demand too much time and attention from union officials. To enforce this interest, members exert pressure either by refusing dues increases and special levies to pay for the programs or by withholding their cooperation or participation, which is often essential if the programs are to succeed.

Throughout the entire range of union programs, the members tend to impose closer restraints upon local leaders than upon national officials, especially if the local organizations are small. At the national level, it is much more difficult to marshal an effective protest or to oust the incumbent officials, since opposition must be mounted in many widely scattered groups of members. But in the national as well as in the local union, the influence of the member expresses itself more insistently and through many more channels than most observers have been prepared to concede. On the whole, moreover, the influence has been much less salutary than critics of unions like to acknowledge. A candid appraisal compels the conclusion that the rank and file has contributed to most of the widely-condemned union shortcomings: racial discrimination, excessive wage demands, featherbedding, and – in many instances – irresponsible strikes. Corruption, of course, is one form of union misbehavior that cannot be attributed significantly to the membership. Critics may often respond to the above-mentioned arguments by asserting that autocratic unions can also indulge in featherbedding, racial discrimination, etc. This is undoubtedly correct, but one reason may be that democratic elections are only one way by which the views of the members are impressed upon the leader; there are other highly effective conduits for transmitting membership demands and values, even in seemingly autocratic unions.

Influence of subordinates

The union leader is also limited by his subordinates. In many cases, of course, the subordinate is simply a vehicle for pressures arising from the membership. Thus, local officials will resist advice or commands which, if carried out, would threaten defeat at the next local election. But subordinates can limit their superiors in ways quite independent of any rank-and-file sentiments. Local leaders may develop personal ambitions that can be furthered by resisting the international. Staff personnel may have views and priorities that conflict with those of the union leaders they serve. Local officials or staff can simply lack the ability to carry out orders effectively. In theory, of course, the higher official may have formal authority to order his subordinates about. In practice, however, the situation is not so simple. The leader must normally obtain genuine cooperation and even enthusiasm from his subordinates, and this cannot often be achieved if the leader does not accommodate himself, to some extent at least, to the abilities and desires of those whom he commands.

Effect of environment

The environment presses in upon the union from many directions: through the policies of employers, the market pressures affecting the firm, the industry and the entire economy, the attitudes of the public, and the provisions of the law. With all its endless variety, the environment affects the union in three essential ways.

To begin with, the environment acts upon the members and shapes their outlook, their expectations, and their preferences. For example, the openness of the society and the lack of class divisions have had much to do with the unwillingness of union members to support a labor party. The educational system and the gradual evolution of community values have produced large changes in the attitudes of union members toward the Negro. The restless disaffection of the young pervades the unions as it does so many other institutions. Advertising and the widespread emphasis on material success inflate the demands that members make in collective negotiations. As a general rule, influences of this sort play their most vital role in helping to determine union goals.

The environment also affects the methods unions can use to achieve their goals and the degree of success that they will achieve. Thus, the creation of vast conglomerate firms has impelled many different unions to join in 'coalition bargaining' to increase their bargaining power. In turn, the effectiveness of this strategy will be conditioned by the financial health and competitive position of the firm and its separate units, as well as by conditions in the economy as a whole. In similar fashion, labor's success in organizing mass-production industries in the thirties (after repeated failures in the past) was greatly helped by such factors as the impact of the Depression, the personnel policies of the firms involved, and the newly enacted federal law to protect union organization. Conversely, the inability of many of the same labor officials to organize the South ten years later was due to another set of social and community pressures that hampered the organizer and dulled the incentive of employees to join a union.

The environment affects the union movement in still another way by helping to shape the quality of labor leadership. The political traditions and the laws of this country insure that union leaders will be chosen by the members. This policy in turn implies that the leaders will be chosen from the ranks and will be generally representative of the membership. At the same time, the educational system, the programs of scholarships and student aid, the emphasis on social mobility, and the willingness to recognize talent whenever it appears, all create opportunities through which promising individuals can escape the shop floor and the assembly line from which tomorrow's labor leaders must be drawn. The low prestige that society accords to union leaders also helps to insure that many employees will take advantage of these opportunities instead of seeking a union post. In this way, environmental forces diminish the pool of talent available for union office.

The limits of leadership

What freedom of action remains to the union leader caught between the pressures of the environment and the demands of the rank and file? To begin with, he can experiment and innovate, at least on a modest scale. He may not always be able to launch new programs costing large sums nor will he be quick to experiment at the risk of failing to meet

221

the critical demands imposed by his members. Moreover, his innovations will eventually have to win acceptance by the rank and file in order to survive and flourish. Nevertheless, the activities and achievements of the union will ultimately reflect the capacity of its officials to offer up new goals, new programs, and new benefits for the members to consider.

Union leaders can also do something to alter the opinions of the members and affect their attitudes toward the goals and policies of the organization. On specific trade union issues – to accept or reject the contract, to strike or not to strike – the leader may have great influence, especially if he is popular and without vocal opposition. On more general matters of value, social attitude, and political choice, his opportunities for exerting influence may be sufficient to deserve attention, but they are not large. Where these issues are concerned, it is normally too difficult to reach the members, too hard to engage their attention seriously, too arduous to overcome all the competing messages reaching them through other media and other sources.

Finally, and perhaps most important, the leader can have the imagination to conceive of new strategies and new opportunities in the environment to help the union make fresh progress toward its goals. This capacity is partly a matter of knowing the environment well, but it is ultimately dependent on the intuition, the judgment, and the imagination of the leader. It is this type of influence and power that John L. Lewis demonstrated so tellingly in perceiving that the time was ripe for massive organizing in the thirties.

It is very hard to guess how much an able, imaginative leader could accomplish to make progress toward union goals. Nevertheless, it is safe to say that the process of selecting union officials – while admirably suited for certain purposes – is not likely to produce an unusual number of leaders with exceptional vision or imagination. Indeed, one would frankly expect less talent of this sort in unions than in most other major institutions. In addition, many of the forces that press upon the labor leader are strong indeed and leave him with much less freedom of action than many critics seem to recognize. For example, those who exhort the unions to exercise wage restraint, eliminate featherbedding, or refrain from strikes seem greatly to underestimate the pressures from the members. Although most union leaders have a degree of influence over the policies of their organizations, few would stay in office very long if they slighted their members' concern for safeguards against the loss of work or ignored their desire to seek pay raises – and go on strike if need be – to keep pace with wage and price increases they see occurring all around them.

One can readily sympathize with the visions of other critics who deplore the failure of union leaders to seize opportunities to turn their talents to new fields: organizing the poor, mobilizing the members to fight for consumer protection, and taking the lead in searching for a more meaningful life for workers caught between their television set and the tedium of a semiskilled, repetitive job. In one sense, unions seem naturally suited to such tasks in view of their experience in organizing mass movements, their large memberships, and their commitment to high social purposes. Yet, critics invariably overlook the enormous difficulties involved; the members' lack of interest in undertaking ventures outside the traditional union domain, their unwillingness to see their dues expended for such purposes, the shortages of talented leadership in labor's ranks, and the pressures on existing leaders, whose time and energy are already stretched thin attending to conventional union tasks. In the face of such limitations, even a leader as gifted and energetic as Walter Reuther has been unable to make noteworthy progress in organizing the poor, expanding union membership, altering Detroit politics, or expanding the skilled job opportunities for Negro members. By underestimating these problems, liberal critics have succeeded – after two decades of biting prose – in accomplishing virtually nothing except antagonizing the union leadership.

The critic's role

This sketch of union behavior has clear implications for the critic's role in assessing social institutions. In reality, union members, leaders, subordinates, and environmental forces interact in such an intimate way that it is treacherous to single out one set of actors in the drama and heap responsibility upon them. Union behavior must be seen as the product of a complex, interrelated process. In order to be effective and fair, the critic must seek to identify the various centers of initiative throughout this process and suggest the actions that can be taken by each of these groups to make it easier for unions to progress toward desirable goals.

16 Roderick Martin

Union Democracy: An Explanatory Framework[1]

From Roderick Martin, 'Union democracy: an explanatory framework', *Sociology*, vol. 2, 1968, pp. 205–20.

Introduction

Concern with the impact of bureaucratization upon the prospects for internal democracy in representative institutions, particularly trade unions, has been a prominent strain in sociological analysis since Roberto Michels's *Political Parties* (1911) first appeared in English in 1915.[2] His aphorism 'who says organization says oligarchy' has become a sociological commonplace. Yet, despite Michels and his pessimistic followers, democratic ideology and even democratic practice survive. The present paper provides an explanatory framework for the varying degrees to which British trade unions conform to Michels's pattern of bureaucratized oligarchy.

The framework comprises a classification of constraints inhibiting union executives from destroying internal opposition, together with tentative hypotheses to explain their operation. The hypotheses developed are derived mainly from a detailed comparative study of the Amalgamated Engineering Union (AEU) and the National Union of Railwaymen (NUR), and represent a first skirmish with the complexities of the problem, not its final conquest. Further empirical investigations will modify, and may refute, some of them. Despite this the 'constraint' approach is presented as the most appropriate approach to the study of union politics and the most likely to lead eventually to an adequate theory of union democracy.

In his comparative study of British trade union government V. L. Allen (1954) uses a 'weak' definition of union democracy, in terms of presumed leadership responsiveness to rank-and-file opinion. Unions are instrumental collectivities, established to protect and improve the living standards of their members; the only criterion of leadership effectiveness relevant for their members (and by implication for the investigator), is the extent to which they achieve this

1. I am grateful to Mr S. M. Lukes, Mr A. H. Halsey, Professor J. D. Edelstein and especially Mr A. Fox for their comments on an earlier draft of this paper.
2. Early works based upon his approach include Burnham (1943) and Kopald (1924).

end.[3] Autocratic union leaders are democratic in so far as they represent the economic interests of their members vis-à-vis the employers. Lack of democracy consists in failure to represent these interests and is reflected in declining membership, not electoral defeat. Union elections are unimportant because incumbent office-holders can always secure their re-election 'given rank-and-file indifference' (Allen, 1954, p. 63).

This definition and the subsequent analysis have serious inadequacies. It is impossible to assess the responsiveness of union leaders to their constituents except through the electoral process, for elections provide the only means of discovering majority opinion. Few British trade unions continue to use the referendum and, where they do, executive control of question formulation makes it into a tool for legitimating executive policy (Allen, 1954, pp. 103–8). The assumption that union membership fluctuates with the level of membership satisfaction with leadership performance is manifestly false. Union membership is not a purely voluntary action, like membership of a sports club; the closed shop and the apprenticeship system seriously inhibit the union member's freedom to resign, whilst the 'Bridlington Principles' seriously restrict transfers.[4] Furthermore, union membership declines gradually rather than catastrophically and it is unjustifiable to assume that the defection of a minority at any one time indicates majority dissatisfaction. Changes in the level of union membership are due to a complex of factors, including the general level of prosperity, the responsiveness of the leadership to *minority* interests, the growth or contraction of the industry covered, union and group sanctions, etc.[5] Finally, there have been occasions when union membership has actually increased despite membership dissatisfaction expressed through successful anti-executive conference resolutions.[6]

3. '. . . trade union organization is not based on theoretical concepts prior to it, that is on some concept of democracy, but on the end it serves. In other words, the end of trade union activity is to protect and improve the general living standards of its members and not to provide workers with an exercise in self-government' (Allen, 1954, p. 15).

4. As Allen himself recognizes; but instead of analysing the consequences of this fact he resorts to a normative plea for legal restrictions on compulsory union membership (Allen, 1954, p. 64). For the Bridlington Agreement and the limitation on transfers, see Lerner (1961).

5. See the table of textile union membership in Turner (1962, p. 125; also p. 300).

6. For example, during the period of wage restraint 1948–50. The Annual Conference of the Union of Shop, Distributive and Allied Workers early in 1950 repudiated its Executive's support for wage restraint, presumably indicating membership dissatisfaction. Despite this, USDAW's membership increased between 1949 and 1950 (Corina, 1961; TUC *Annual Reports*, 1949, 1950).

The merits of alternative definitions of union democracy are not discussed in Lipset, Trow and Coleman's classic study of the International Typographical Union, *Union Democracy* (1956); definitions are only mentioned in parentheses.[7] Thus, union democracy is defined as 'the institutionalization of opposition' (p. 13) and as 'the possibility that an official can be defeated for re-election' (p. 404) – although the two factors are not necessarily related, opposition can be institutionalized without ever achieving office, whilst office-holders can be defeated without the institutionalization of opposition. However, the definition implicit throughout the study is the institutionalization of opposition, preferably with a minimum turnover in union officials. The study relates the institutionalization of opposition to the nature of the occupation, the structure of the union, etc.

Although their substantive analysis cannot be faulted, their initial definition of union democracy is unsatisfactory. A definition which involves the classification of trade unions into the International Typographical Union and the rest is of limited usefulness. Moreover, the assumption that union politics can be analysed in terms of the two-party system of twentieth-century parliamentary democracy fails to do justice to the complexity of reality; as Mark Perlman (1962, p. 100) noted in his study of the International Association of Machinists, it is 'too mechanical, too insensitive to environmental problems'. Parliamentary terms require substantial modification before being applied to union politics. Instead of government and opposition, the opposition forming an alternative government, a permanent executive is usually faced by a very small, uninstitutionalized opposition, seeking to mobilize a large enough segment of the indifferent majority to influence the leadership in a certain direction or to infiltrate into it. The government disregards, conciliates or attempts to divide the opposition by taking its ablest members into the government. There is no union equivalent to the parliamentary electoral pendulum.

To avoid the difficulties posed by either definition, the present paper returns to an older, less precise conceptualization. 'The status of the opposition' is the distinguishing characteristic of democracy; democracy exists where organized opposition is tolerated, totalitarianism where it is not. Similarly with trade unions. Union democracy exists when union executives are unable to prevent opposition

7. The section on the theory of democracy (Lipset, Trow and Coleman, 1956, pp. 13–16) does not include a definition.

factions distributing propaganda and mobilizing electoral support.[8] It does not require that opposition should be institutionalized, nor that it should be democratic (in practice opposition groups usually vie with the executive in manipulating the indifferent majority) – merely that it should survive as a recognized form of political activity. The survival of faction limits executive ability to disregard rank-and-file opinion by providing the *potential* means for its overthrow (although the potential is rarely realized). Faction is an indispensable sanction against leadership failure to respond to membership opinion. Occasionally opposition factions will influence union leaders in a particular direction, occasionally they will defeat official candidates (and sometimes see their candidates assume official attitudes). But democracy can survive even if neither condition is met.

This view does not deny that faction can be dysfunctional; the disclosure of internal divisions may harm a union's bargaining position. But the view that public disagreement is necessarily damaging accepts the leadership perspective too readily. Faction is the life blood of democracy, not simply 'a luxury most unions cannot afford' (Taft, 1954, pp. 239–40). Behind the scenes compromises between influential groups on policy and personnel questions provide a better foundation for oligarchy than democracy.

What determines the status of union opposition? A step towards understanding the determinants of effective opposition has been taken in Edelstein (1967, esp. pp. 22–3). His elaborate theory specifies the characteristics of the formal structure of union government likely to create conditions of equality between incumbent and opposition candidates in union elections; the effectiveness of opposition, and thus the degree of union democracy, is measured by the frequency with

8. Howe and Widick quoted in Berger, Abel and Page (1954, p. 122): 'There is one decisive proof of democracy in a union (or any institution): oppositionists have the right to organize freely into "parties", to set up factional machines, to circulate publicity and to propagandize among the members . . . The presence of an opposition . . . is the best way of insuring that a union's democratic structure will be preserved . . . To defend the right of factions to exist is not at all to applaud this or that faction. But this is the overhead . . . of democracy . . . The alternative is dictatorship.'

The term 'faction' is used to designate comparatively unstructured conflict groups, whose membership fluctuates according to the issues in dispute. This usage accords with the characterization of faction in Nicholas (1965, esp. pp. 44–6). It differs from Pocock's (1957, p. 296) usage in emphasizing the positive role of faction in the functioning of the whole.

which incumbent candidates are defeated and the closeness of the voting. Democracy is most likely when the formal political structure facilitates the emergence of a small number of powerful candidates instead of a large number of weak ones.

Although the model may be appropriate, the measure is inadequate. Overwhelming leadership victories may be due to effectiveness in carrying out the wishes of the majority of union members, not to the lack of union democracy. Close election results and a high turnover in union officials are as likely to indicate incompetence as internal democracy. Indeed, a high turnover in union officials may indicate lack of leadership responsiveness to majority opinion, since removal from office is the ultimate sanction on executive disregard for membership opinion. Electoral rejection signifies the inadequacy of less drastic sanctions. Moreover, although Edelstein is right to emphasize formal organization and particularly the distribution of power between national district and local bodies, an organizational theory of union democracy is sociologically inadequate. It may provide a basis for prediction, but not for explanation. Formal organization is a dependent, not an independent variable, reflecting, *inter alia*, the union's history, membership spread (past, present and future), collective bargaining position and functional needs. An adequate theory of union democracy requires the integration of organizational variables into a wider conceptual framework.

The framework presented here focuses on the constraints upon union leaders to tolerate faction. It assumes that union leaders will not tolerate faction unless constrained to do so, since the existence of any opposition limits the range of alternative choices open. Although this is a logical not an empirical assumption, it is a justifiable one; most union leaders regard opposition as an aid to the economic enemy. The construction of a theory of union democracy, therefore, involves the classification of these constraints, and if possible their integration into a comprehensive theory.

Although the range of constraints upon union leaders is extremely wide and their relative importance varies from union to union, and possibly even from official to official, a preliminary attempt at classification is possible. Constraints can be classified into twelve categories: political culture; government attitudes and behaviour; pattern of membership distribution, past, present and future; industrial setting, including the degree of ownership concentration, and the collective bargaining system; economic environment; technology and rate of technological change; source of union bargaining power; membership characteristics; membership beliefs; opposition expertise and resources; leadership beliefs; and union structure. Each factor affects the chances for union democracy by increasing or reducing the executive's ability to destroy opposition.

Political culture (Beer and Ulam, 1962, pp. 32–42)

The political culture – the complex of values, beliefs and emotional attitudes surrounding political institutions – acts as a constraint upon union leaders directly, and indirectly through its influence upon membership beliefs about the legitimacy of particular political practices. A political culture emphasizing democratic values, including responsiveness to majority opinion, toleration of opposition and individual freedom, will obviously exert pressure upon union leaders to act accordingly both directly and indirectly by moulding membership expectations of the role behaviour of leaders. The British political culture, with its negative evaluation of expulsion and ballot rigging as political tactics, will influence union leaders to refrain from using them even when they may seem to provide the most effective means of defeating opposition. The furore created by the electoral malpractices in the Electrical Trades Union between 1955 and 1960 indicates the reality of this constraint.[9] Similarly, an authoritarian political culture, emphasizing obedience, the subordination of the individual to the group and the duty of private organizations to the State, will exercise a different constraint.

Government attitudes and behaviour

Government attitudes and behaviour have a dual impact upon the democratic potential of trade unions. On the one hand, government pressure for restraint during periods of war or economic crisis can create a division between the leadership and the rank-and-file, leading to the emergence of 'irresponsible' opposition groups, as in the Engineers and the Miners' Federation during the First World War. In this situation factional conflict, and thus democracy, is likely. On the other hand, the increasing scope of government influence, partic-

9. For an account of the ETU trial, see Rolph (1962).

229

ularly its concern to limit wage inflation and maintain satisfactory working conditions, increases pressure for centralization and bureaucratization, and hence the power of the executive. Union executives need authority and expert advice in negotiations with central government; both involve an increase in executive power.

Membership distribution

The distribution of union membership (past, present and future) conditions the likely pattern of economic interest group conflict between members and thus the likely form of anti-leadership groupings, and largely determines union structure. In general, 'the more homogeneous the interests of the members of the union, the greater chances for democracy', because economic conflict between union members reduces the likelihood of anti-leadership alliances, and thus reduces the threat opposition poses for the leadership (Lipset, Trow and Coleman, p. 414). However, the general statement requires elaboration. The basis of cleavage and the pressures making for bureaucratization, and consequently the democratic potential, vary between different types of unions.

In craft unions, like the AEU before the Second World War, occupational homogeneity and industrial heterogeneity provide a basis for both consensus and cleavage. Occupational solidarity, compounded of occupational interests, tradition and consciousness of difference from industrial workmates, provides a basis for consensus, whilst industrial differences provide a basis for cleavage. The destructive potential of cleavage is limited by the fact that wage conflict, reflecting knowledge of earnings differentials and wage reference groups, is more likely to be intra-industry than intra-union.[10] Industrial unions, with industrial homogeneity and occupational heterogeneity are less likely to be democratic, for wage rivalry is likely to be intra-union, inhibiting anti-leadership alliances and allowing the executive to play interest groups off against each other.

The impact of membership spread upon bureaucratization similarly varies between different types of unions. Bureaucratization is most highly developed in general unions with a diverse semi-skilled and

10. For 'compulsive comparison' in the motor industry, see Turner, Clack and Roberts (1967, esp. pp. 142–3). For a general statement of the utility of reference group theory to the analysis of wage comparisons, see Lipset and Trow (1957, esp. pp. 396–7).

unskilled membership, like the National Union of General and Municipal Workers. In unions like the NUGMW the lack of common interest between different groups of members and the unsuitability of settling particular industrial problems at annual representative conferences increases the power of the full-time officials as the only unifying element. The significance of this factor is reduced in craft and industrial unions (Clegg, 1954, p. 342).

Industrial environment

The degree of ownership concentration, the level of cooperation between employers, the range of products and product markets, and the collective bargaining system all exert pressure for centralization and bureaucratization, and thus oligarchy. Concentrated ownership, cooperation between employers and a limited range of products and product markets all exert pressure for centralized collective bargaining and national regulation, strengthening the position of the executive and reducing democratic potential. All are features of the railways industry. Similarly, dispersed ownership, rivalry between employers and a wide range of products and product markets, all characteristics of the engineering industry, minimize the pressures for national regulation and increase democratic potential.[11] The final relevant factor in the industrial environment is the attitude of the employers; employer hostility places a premium upon internal solidarity, lowering the constraints upon executive repression of opposition. (Indeed, external hostility as well as historical inevitability contributed to the development of oligarchic tendencies within the German Social Democratic Party analysed in Michels's classic account.)

Economic environment

The economic situation in the industry or industries covered by the union exercises a dual constraint, on the readiness of the executive to tolerate opposition and on the likelihood of the indifferent

11. For a fuller general discussion of the relation between factors in the industrial environment and union democracy, see Lipset (1954, pp. 83–7); for the influence of external pressures on the government of the United Automobile Workers, see Steiber (1962). For a detailed discussion of the factors influencing the development of one unofficial movement in the railway and engineering industries in Britain, see Martin (1964).

majority's listening to the proposals of opposition factions. The constraints work in opposite directions. Other things being equal, during prosperity or in a prosperous industry, the executive will be able to afford to tolerate opposition, but the impetus to oppose will be weak because discontent will be limited. Factional fights may be frequent, but manageable. During depression, executive ability to insist upon solidarity will increase, but the appeal of opposition will be greater.

Technology

Both the content of the industrial technology and the rate of technological change affect the potential for union democracy. Directly, the level of technology conditions the work setting and the work flow, the level of interaction possible between union members on the job and consequently the opportunities for the evaluation of union personalities and policies.[12] A 'craft' technology (as in printing), with a discontinuous work flow and ample opportunity for face-to-face contact between union members, provides opportunities for the creation of unofficial solidarity and for political discussion which a 'machine' technology does not.[13] The rate of technological change, independent of its content, increases or diminishes the chances that the executive will fall out of step with the rank and file. The faster the rate of technological change, the greater the likelihood of conflict between the executive and the membership (or within either group) and the greater the potential for democracy. Under pressure from the employers or the government the executive may prove too sympathetic to change; or under the domination of old-established power groups the executive may respond too slowly. Either increases the potential for faction.

Source of bargaining power

The source of union bargaining power, mass or workshop, affects the potential for opposition directly, by determining the distribution of power between the executive and substructural groups, and indirectly through the likelihood of unofficial stoppages and the emergence of

12. For the significance of the level of interaction between union members, see Raphael (1965).

13. For 'craft' and 'machine' technology, see Blauner (1964).

anti-leadership groups based on unofficial direct action. Mass bargaining power, as in general unions like the NUGMW, is likely to produce a strong executive; workshop bargaining power, as in the AEU, a weak executive.[14] In the AEU the constraint exerted by workshop bargaining is increased by the institutional separation between the union structure and the workshop, and the consequent creation of an independent power base for the shop stewards. Moreover, workshop power increases the likelihood of unofficial stoppages, as in the car industry, by rendering executive support superfluous (Turner, Clack and Roberts, 1967, ch. 7). The importance of this constraint varies with the level of unemployment; high unemployment reduces workshop power, the feasibility of unofficial action and thus opposition.[15]

Membership characteristics

Membership characteristics affect the potential for union democracy directly in so far as they include specific political skills, and indirectly through their impact upon the level of membership participation (Lipset, Trow and Coleman, 1956, pp. 415–16). Directly the educational level of the membership determines the level of literacy, the probability of members possessing verbal skills and thus the differential ability of officials and rank and file to utilize the union political system. The more educated the membership, the lower the differential and the greater the constraint on the executive. Indirectly, membership characteristics influence democratic potential through their effect upon the level of membership participation; although a low level of membership participation does not necessarily indicate the absence of democracy,[16] a high level is likely to provide a firmer basis for opposition than a low level. Membership participation is related to the following membership characteristics: the degree of informal association on or off the job; the degree of isolation from

14. In the International Association of Machinists the bargaining rights and powers of the local lodge underpin the diffusion of power between the executive and the rank and file (Perlman, 1962, p. 102).

15. As one opposition faction member said in 1921: 'A powerful shop steward movement can and only does exist in given objective conditions . . . How can you build factory organizations in empty and depleted workshops, while you have a great reservoir of unemployed workers?' (Quoted in Martin, 1964, p. 49).

16. Hence the irrelevance of Goldstein's (1952) documentation of membership apathy.

non-members (by work schedule, physical isolation or status marginality); the number of role relationships between members; the degree of identification with the occupation and the union; and the number of functions performed by the union.

Membership beliefs

Membership beliefs constrain the executive directly, where they concern the legitimacy of particular political practices, and indirectly, by limited executive interference in particular areas. Membership beliefs about the legitimate degree of executive interference with branch autonomy reduce executive ability to root out opposition. In the AEU for example, executive attempts to prevent the use of the Branch Local Purposes for affiliation fees to unofficial movements were successfully resisted in 1926 as an infringement of branch prerogatives. Similarly, membership beliefs regarding craft 'custom and practice' circumscribe executive freedom of action and provide a 'Sacred Books' basis for resistance to executive initiatives, as in the National Society of Operative Printers and Assistants at the present time.

Opposition expertise and resources

The level of opposition political expertise is determined by five factors: the number of former union leaders still active within the union; the number of politically experienced lay members; their level of education; their material resources; and their ideological commitment.

Lipset, Trow and Coleman relate the likelihood of former union leaders returning to the rank and file to the status of the occupation and to the chances of maintaining the status of union leader. However, the extremely low turnover in union leaders reduces the importance of this factor. When full-time union officials do leave office they either retire completely, enter another branch of the labour movement or go over to the other side. Moreover, few unionized occupations are likely to attract former union leaders on status or financial grounds; union leaders would return out of solidarity, habit or not at all. A more important determinant of the level of opposition political expertise is the number of politically experienced rank-and-file members, training either within the Labour or Communist Parties or within the union itself. The limited transferability of political skills, and the reluctance of Labour or Communist Parties to allow able activists to drop out (sometimes counterbalanced by the communist desire to infiltrate), increases the importance of intra-union training. Hence, the number of responsible posts open to rank-and-file members is of primary importance. In the AEU, for example, the shop stewards system provides a training ground for opposition members as well as an independent power base, whilst the Lay District Committees provide a means for lay members to acquire wide experience and to spread their name.

The advantages of a high level of education for union opposition has been discussed above, whilst the advantages of material resources to pay for meetings, propaganda and travelling is obvious. More complex is the nature of the relation between ideology and opposition. According to Lipset, Trow and Coleman, ideological cleavages are more likely to sustain democratic opposition than interest group cleavages. This view requires modification. Within British trade unions ideological cleavages make for permanent, but not for effective, opposition. Ideological, primarily communist elements form an important part of union opposition, but the majority of union members do not recognize this extra-union ideological commitment as legitimate.[17] Hence, although communist groups form an ideological nucleus around which fluctuating economic or policy groups cluster, the price of organizational expertise is compromised legitimacy. Opposition groups which are based upon policy or interest group differences, and which preserve their ideological virginity (or conceal its loss), are more likely to be effective than ideological opposition groups.

Leadership attitudes

Leadership attitudes can be conceptualized as an independent constraint, determined by individual political beliefs, membership beliefs, rationalization of the functional requirements of leadership roles and sensitivity to the surrounding political culture. Attitudes emphasizing internal democracy, moderation and craft custom are

17. The following incident at the NUR Annual General Meeting in 1926 illustrates the strength of union feeling against outside interference. Circulars from the Communist Party to union members fell into the hands of J. H. Thomas, the Political General Secretary, who read them aloud to the delegates. The disclosure of this attempt by an outside body to influence union policy effectively forestalled left-wing attempts to criticize Thomas's conduct during the General Strike.

235

more likely to restrict the repression of opposition than attitudes based upon the need . to 'trust the leadership'. Commitment to communism, or extreme anti-communism, is likely to reduce executive toleration of opposition by giving a lower priority to democratic procedure than to the need to keep the communists in (or out).

Union structure[18]

As the mechanism through which all other pressures operate, union structure is crucially important. The main determinants of the extent to which the formal structure facilitates or hinders the articulation of disagreement are the degree of substructural autonomy and conversely of centralization, the position of full-time vis-à-vis lay officials and the electoral system itself. Union democracy is most likely where substructural autonomy, particularly at regional level, is greatest and centralization least, where full-time officials are subject to effective lay supervision and where the electoral system exerts pressure for a small number of powerful rather than a large number of weak candidates. A high degree of national integration and centralization, only formal provision for lay supervision, and a completely 'open' electoral system reduce the chances for union democracy.

Each constraint discussed circumscribes executive freedom of action by restricting interference with opposition factions or by increasing the strength of the opposition. The relation between different constraints, and especially the mediation of external constraints through union structure, becomes clearer after systematic comparison between the AEU and the NUR.

To illustrate the potential utility of the constraint approach, Table 1 analyses the AEU[19] and the NUR[20] in terms of the constraints outlined. + indicates a relative not an absolute value, i.e. in comparison with the other union. The relevant category has been omitted where data is not available.

18. For a fuller discussion of the structural determinants of union democracy, see Edelstein (1967).

19. There is no sociological study of the Amalgamated Engineering Union, although a more than adequate history is in preparation. The most useful study is Marsh (1965); see also Jeffreys (1945).

20. Even less attention has been paid to railway unionism than to engineering unionism; however, Bagwell (1963) contains much information.

Table 1

	AEU	*NUR*
Membership spread		
industrial	heterogeneous	homogeneous
occupational	restricted	heterogeneous
Industrial structure		
ownership concentration	low	high
employer unity	low	high
product range	wide	narrow
collective bargaining	national/workshop	national
Economic environment	prosperous	declining
Technology		
work situation	unclassifiable	low-level interaction
rate change	rapid	slow
Membership characteristics		
leisure time	+	
income	+	
association on job	+	
isolation from non-members		+
Membership beliefs		
custom	+	
local autonomy	+	
Bargaining power	workshop	mass
Opposition expertise		
former TU leaders		
lay officials	+	
resources	+	
Union structure		
substructural autonomy	+	
lay authority	+	
centralization		+
electoral system	+	

External and internal constraints inhibit the AEU Executive's ability to destroy opposition. Power within the union is still largely in the hands of skilled groups, whilst membership is spread over a wide range of industries; a sound basis thus exists for both consensus and cleavage. Ownership within particular industries is dispersed, the degree of cooperation between employers is comparatively low and national agreements are supplemented by district and, more importantly, workshop agreements. The diversity of products and shop conditions severely limits the importance of external regulation. The varied and often rapid rate of technological change provides ample opportunity for the leadership and rank and file to fall out of step. External pressure for centralization within the union is comparatively low, whilst the workshop power of the union members is comparatively high. Internal constraints, reflecting external pressures, membership traditions and the functional needs of the organization, act in a similar fashion. Membership commitment to craft 'custom and practice' is combined with 'an almost fanatical attachment to local autonomy' (Clegg, Fox and Thompson, 1964, pp. 4–5; Webb and Webb, 1894, p. 97). The shop steward system, the plethora of branch offices and the District Committee system provide a training ground for lay members and a chance to build up independent power bases, whilst the absence of any appointed officials further limits Executive initiative.[21] These constraints are mediated through an almost excessively democratic political structure. A high degree of branch and district autonomy is accompanied by effective provision for lay oversight over full-time officials, the National Committee 'instructing' the Executive, whilst the system of indirect election of delegates to the annual conference reduces the advantages the Executive gains from its control of the union publicity machine.[22]

It is thus not surprising that the history of the AEU has been characterized by an unusual degree of factional conflict, reflected in well-publicized battles between the right and left wings.

Far fewer constraints inhibit the NUR Executive's power. Its membership is restricted to one industry, but covers a wide range of occupations; intergrade rivalry thus limits the possible construction of anti-leadership majorities. The extreme degree of ownership concentration, the narrow product range and union dependence upon mass bargaining power increase the pressure for centralization within the union. The work situation provides comparatively few chances for informal interaction between union members, and the consequent formation of unofficial solidarity, whilst the comparatively low level of wages and long working hours provide few chances for spare time political activity. Reflecting these pressures, the union's formal organization is highly centralized. There is a low degree of substructural autonomy; branches are subject to dissolution by the Executive whenever they are considered 'unnecessary or undesirable or prejudicial to the interests of the union or its members', whilst they can only

21. For shop stewards, see Marsh and Coker (1963).
22. For 'instructing', see Turner (1962, p. 228).

combine to form District Councils with the consent of the Executive. The District Councils themselves are weak: 'the powers of the District Councils shall be consultative and propagandist and such other work as may be delegated to them by the Annual or Special General Meetings or the Executive Committee ... (they) shall have no governing or controlling power over any members, branch or official'. Lay oversight over full-time officials is not very effectively provided for; there is no provision for the exclusion of full-time officials from the supreme governing body, the AGM. Finally, the electoral system places a premium upon the re-election of incumbent office-holders by providing for their direct election (NUR Constitution and Rules, *passim*).

The NUR Executive thus has greater freedom to act against opposition groups than the AEU Executive. Economic, social and constitutional factors combine to create a highly centralized organization, with a powerful full-time Executive. It is thus not surprising that the history of the NUR has been characterized by a dominant Executive and a comparatively quiescent rank and file, despite the long run-down of the industry.

Systematic comparison between the AEU and the NUR Executives in terms of the constraints inhibiting the destruction of opposition provides a framework for understanding the contrasting political histories of the two unions. The external environment, membership traditions and attitudes, and union structure have combined to make it likely that the AEU Executive would be unable to destroy opposition; the vicissitudes of history, particularly the strength of communist nuclei, transformed probability into certainty. Similarly, the external environment, membership characteristics and union structure have combined to reduce the chances of faction in the NUR.

In conclusion, constraint analysis suggests that union democracy, defined as the survival of faction, is associated with:

1. Democratic political culture.
2. Government indifference.
3. Occupational homogeneity, industrial heterogeneity.
4. A low level of ownership concentration, disagreement between predominantly friendly employers.
5. Decentralized collective bargaining.
6. Craft technology.

7. Rapid technological change.
8. Workshop bargaining power.
9. A highly educated membership, with a high degree of identification with the craft and the union.
10. A high level of membership participation.
11. Membership commitment to local autonomy and the preservation of customary rights.
12. An experienced, non-ideological opposition.
13. Executive commitment to democratic procedures.
14. A decentralized union structure, with substructural autonomy, extensive constitutional power in the hands of lay members and an indirect electoral system.

This set of propositions, based upon limited empirical investigation, constitutes only the first step towards the formulation of an adequate theory of union democracy. Detailed analysis of the internal politics of more unions is obviously necessary to test, modify and refute these hypotheses. Particular attention needs to be given to assessing the varying importance of different constraints. Are some factors, for example membership spread, level of technological development and union structure, more 'basic' than others? If so, under what conditions? Such questions cannot be answered in this initial, tentative formulation. Despite this, 'constraint' analysis is likely to provide greater insight than the formalism of organizational theory and may eventually provide the basis for a general theory of union democracy.

Concluding remarks

Union politics bear more resemblance to the politics of the Namierite House of Commons of 1760 than to the two-party politics of the 1960s. Instead of government and opposition, the opposition forming an alternative government, there is a permanent 'court' party opposed by a smaller, equally permanent, 'country' party; in between are the majority of union members, usually prepared to support the 'court' party through indifference or the hope of patronage, but willing on occasion to flirt with the 'country' party when the 'court' party fails to deliver the goods. The 'country' party is in turn partly composed of an illegitimate ideological nucleus very roughly analogous to the Tory Jacobites, partly of legitimate but traditional opponents of the administration (analogous to the backwoods Tory gentry, hostile to all taints of 'court corruption') and partly of careerists who see nuisance value as the best guarantee of promotion into the higher ranks of the 'court' party.[23]

23. Even the rhetoric has an eighteenth-century ring. One member of the 'court' party declared: 'A true, genuine, high-flying tantivy Tory is pretty akin to a Jacobite, and Jacobites and papists are first cousins' (quoted in Robson, 1949, p. 37). For Tory read socialist, for Jacobite read communist and for papist read Russian spy.

References

ALLEN, V. L. (1954), *Power in Trade Unions: A Study of their Organization in Great Britain*, Longman.

BAGWELL, P. S. (1963), *The Railwayman: A History of the NUR*, Allen & Unwin.

BEER, S. H., and A. B. ULAM (1962), *Patterns of Government*, Random House.

BERGER, M., T. ABEL and C. PAGE (1954), *Freedom and Control in Modern Society*, Van Nostrand.

BLAUNER, R. (1964), *Alienation and Freedom*, Chicago University Press.

BURNHAM, J. (1943), *The Machiavellians*, John Day.

CLEGG, H. A. (1954), *General Union in a Changing Society*, Blackwell.

CLEGG, H. A., A. FOX and A. F. THOMPSON (1964), *A History of British Trade Unions since 1889*, vol. 1, Clarendon Press.

CORINA, J. G. (1961), 'Wage restraint 1948–50', unpublished D. Phil. thesis, University of Oxford.

EDELSTEIN, J. D. (1967), 'An organizational theory of union democracy', *American Sociological Review*, vol. 32, pp. 19–39.

GOLDSTEIN, J. (1952) *The Government of British Trade Unions*, Allen & Unwin.

JEFFREYS, J. B. (1945), *The Engineers*, Lawrence & Wishart.

KOPALD, S. (1924), *Rebellion in Labor Unions*, Boni & Liveright.

LERNER, S. (1961), 'The TUC jurisdictional dispute settlement', in *Breakaway Unions and the Small Trade Unions*, Allen & Unwin, pp. 66–81.

LIPSET, S. M. (1954), 'The political process in trade unions', in M. Berger, T. Abel and C. Page (eds.), *Freedom and Control in Modern Society*, Van Nostrand, pp. 82–94.

LIPSET, S. M., and M. A. TROW (1957), 'Reference group theory and trade union wage policy', in M. Komarovsky (ed.), *Common Frontiers of the Social Sciences*, Free Press.

LIPSET, S. M., M. A. TROW and J. S. COLEMAN (1956), *Union Democracy*, Free Press.

MARSH, A. (1965), *Industrial Relations in Engineering*, Pergamon.

MARSH, A., and E. L. COKER (1963), 'Shop-steward organization in the engineering industry', *British Journal of Industrial Relations*, vol. 1, pp. 170–91.

MARTIN, R. (1964), 'The national minority movement: a study in the organization of trade union militancy in the inter-war period', unpublished D. Phil. thesis, University of Oxford.

MICHELS, R. (1911), *Political Parties*, Dover, 1959.

NICHOLAS, R. W. (1965), 'Factions: a comparative analysis', in *Political Systems and Distribution of Power*, Tavistock.

PERLMAN, M. (1962), *Democracy in the International Association of Machinists*, Wiley.

POCOCK, D. (1957), 'Factions in Indian societies', *British Journal of Sociology*, vol. 8, pp. 295–306.

RAPHAEL, E. E. (1965), 'Power structures and membership dispersion in unions', *American Journal of Sociology*, vol. 71, pp. 274–93.

ROBSON, R. J. (1949), *The Oxfordshire Election of 1754*, Clarendon Press.

ROLPH, C. H. (1962), *All Those in Favour: The ETU Trial*, Deutsch.

STEIBER, J. (1962), *Governing the UAW*, Wiley.

TAFT, P. (1954), *The Structure and Government of Labor Unions*, Harvard University Press.

TURNER, H. A. (1962), *Trade Union Growth, Structure and Policy*, Allen & Unwin.

TURNER, H. A., G. CLACK and G. ROBERTS (1967), *Labour Relations in the Motor Industry*, Allen & Unwin.

WEBB, S., and B. WEBB (1894), *Industrial Democracy*, Longman.

Part Five

Factors Affecting Union Growth

As was mentioned in the introduction, it was thought necessary in the first edition to include the disclaimer: 'There is no generally accepted theory of union growth.' But in the last ten years or so George Bain and his colleagues have striven mightily to develop and refine a theory of aggregate membership change which appears to fit the facts in most countries where there are comparable figures. It seems to me that in its broad outlines Bain's theory stands up to this test, but it has not been without its critics.

Reading 17 contains the most recent short statement of the theory, shorn of statistical elaboration and equations and confined to United Kingdom data. The reader is warned that the writers have been forced to simplify, but anybody who wishes to pursue the matter further should consult the bibliography for references to more extended work.

Bain and Price show that variations in the overall level of union membership over the last thirty years or so can be broadly explained in terms of the interaction of three related factors: economic activity rates (notably movements in prices and employment levels), employer policies and government action. Much less important has been the role of changes in union structure and the composition of the labour force. Unimportant, according to Bain and Price, has been the impact of union leadership or sex and age differences in potential membership. Predicting developments in the 1980s Bain and Price posit a gradual decline in existing densities; how far this goes will 'largely depend on how employers behave'.

There follow three short extracts from a lively debate between Bain and Ray Richardson, an early and persistent critic of his methodology and conclusions. In Reading 18 Bain is told that his theoretical analysis is 'shallow and *ad hoc*', and that the relationship he assumes between union growth and the business cycle may well be more complex. It is also possible that it is union growth that causes inflation, rather than the reverse. Most importantly, Richardson argued that Bain's results may derive, to some extent, from his preference for aggregative data and 'macro' explanations. This may have led him to downgrade the importance of changes in the composition of the labour force, which may be difficult to measure accurately at the macro level.

In Reading 19 Bain and Elsheikh are generally unrepentant, although they accept that theirs is an aggregate theory which seeks to explain relative rates of growth at the level of the national economy. They also complain that Richardson has not fully appreciated their distinction between the 'propensity' to organize and the 'opportunity' to organize.

In Reading 20 Richardson is even more unyielding. The focus on aggregate variables has led to a serious underestimation of the role of 'compositional' and 'structural' factors, e.g. the rise in the number of white-collar workers and the increasing size of the public sector. He remains convinced that 'there is too great a reliance on crude assertions about the behaviour of women workers and employers'.

Finally, in Reading 21, Undy's work is said to show that Bain's theory over-stresses the role of external factors and treats them in an unselective way. In particular, the study of British unions since the 1960s reveals that one of the primary conditions for achieving high growth was 'a national leadership oriented and committed to growth as a priority'. In time this had a contagion effect, as other leaders came to emulate the 'self-help activities of growth-oriented general secretaries in a number of large unions'. Thus the calibre of leadership in a minority of organizations helped ultimately to produce higher aggregate growth.

It should be noted that in Reading 17 Bain and Price consider Undy's arguments and reject them. They decide that 'only a very small amount of union growth can be unambiguously attributed to the independent influence of union leaders and their policies', and conclude: 'Undy and his colleagues surely dramatically overstate their case when they speak of "the critical role of leadership".'

Doubtless there will be further salvoes in this debate, but the student should not ignore the very considerable progress that has been made. No doubt the prolonged recession will require further modifications and elaborations of Bain's theory, but it is difficult to believe that it will be replaced.

17 G. S. Bain and R. Price

The Determinants of Union Growth

From *Industrial Relations in Britain*, ed. G. S. Bain, Blackwell, 1983, pp. 12–33.

The questions raised by data on union growth, though numerous, are broadly of two kinds. First, what factors account for variations in the rate of change of unionization from one year to the next, or, more generally, from one period to another? Second, what factors account for variations at any particular moment in the level of unionization between different groups, occupations, sectors and industries? The following discussion attempts to answer both types of question. In particular, why did union density decline slowly and slightly in the twenty years before 1968 and swiftly and sharply after 1979? In contrast, why did union density increase markedly not only in aggregate but also among males, females, manual workers, white-collar workers and in almost every industry in the period 1969–79? And why was the level of union density in, for example, 1979 higher among men than women, among manual than white-collar workers, in the public than the private sector of the economy, and in some industries than others?

These questions are not approached with a *tabula rasa*. The literature on union growth has listed most of the possible determinants of unionization. For the purpose of the following discussion, they can be conveniently grouped under six headings: the composition of potential union membership, the business cycle, employer policies and government action with respect to union recognition, personal and job-related characteristics, industrial structure and union leadership.

Composition of potential union membership

Since the level of union density is higher among men than women and among manual than white-collar workers, changes in the relative share of potential union membership held by each of these groups affect the level of aggregate union growth for purely arithmetical reasons. Similarly, changes in the industrial distribution of potential

Table 1 Union membership and density by industry in Great Britain 1948, 1968, and 1979

	1948			1968			1979			Change 1949–68			Change 1969–79		
	U.M. (thousands)	P.U.M. (thousands)	U.D. (%)	U.M. (thousands)	P.U.M. (thousands)	U.D. (%)	U.M. (thousands)	P.U.M. (thousands)	U.D. (%)	U.M. (thousands)	P.U.M. (thousands)	U.D. (%)	U.M. (thousands)	P.U.M. (thousands)	U.D. (%)
Food and drink	247·2	575·3	43·0	252·0	729·3	34·6	444·3	685·4	64·8	+ 4·8	+154·0	− 8·4	+192·3	− 43·9	+30·2
Tobacco	26·1	43·7	59·7	26·7	34·7	76·9	30·0	31·3	95·8	+ 0·6	− 9·0	+17·2	+ 3·3	− 3·4	+18·9
Chemicals	141·5	401·0	35·3	186·9	474·6	39·4	288·6	490·5	58·8	+ 45·4	+ 73·6	+ 4·1	+101·7	+ 15·9	+19·4
Metals and engineering	1,913·7	3,514·4	54·5	2,410·4	4,249·8	56·7	3,033·9	3,809·4	79·6	+496·7	+735·4	+ 2·2	+623·5	−440·4	+22·9
Cotton and man-made fibres	274·3	350·1	78·3	146·3	180·6	81·0	112·1	114·1	98·2	−128·0	−169·5	+ 2·7	− 34·2	− 66·5	+17·2
Other textiles	201·3	511·8	39·3	165·6	478·1	34·6	170·5	359·9	47·4	− 35·7	− 33·7	− 4·7	+ 4·9	−118·2	+12·8
Leather, leather goods and fur	23·5	71·6	32·8	14·8	52·1	28·4	11·6	41·0	28·3	− 8·7	− 19·5	− 4·4	− 3·2	− 11·1	− 0·1
Clothing	146·0	387·2	37·7	119·7	359·6	33·3	127·7	307·2	41·6	− 26·3	− 27·6	− 4·4	+ 8·0	− 52·4	+ 8·3
Footwear	92·8	120·0	77·3	75·6	106·4	71·1	65·2	80·3	81·2	− 17·2	− 13·6	− 6·2	− 10·4	− 26·1	+10·1
Brick and building materials	58·4	164·4	35·5	56·1	194·3	28·9	83·5	133·5	62·5	− 2·3	+ 29·9	− 6·6	+ 27·4	− 60·8	+33·6
Pottery	44·0	71·5	61·5	41·1	57·0	72·1	43·1	59·9	72·0	− 2·9	+ 14·5	+10·6	+ 2·0	− 2·9	− 0·1
Glass	29·8	66·7	44·7	40·2	76·7	52·4	46·6	71·4	65·3	+ 10·4	+ 10·0	+ 7·7	+ 6·4	− 5·3	+12·9
Timber and furniture	122·2	273·0	44·8	95·3	294·9	32·3	92·6	266·5	34·7	− 26·9	+ 21·9	−12·5	− 2·7	− 28·4	+ 2·4
Paper and board	60·8	163·9	37·1	98·4	244·0	40·3	116·2	205·3	56·6	+ 37·6	+ 80·1	+ 3·2	+ 17·8	− 38·7	+16·3
Printing and publishing	206·7	272·8	75·8	292·2	368·4	79·3	326·0	347·7	93·8	+ 85·5	+ 95·6	+ 3·5	+ 33·8	− 20·7	+14·5
Other manufacturing	89·6	228·8	39·2	95·7	331·2	28·9	143·0	330·4	43·3	+ 6·1	+102·4	−10·3	+ 47·3	− 0·8	+14·4
Coal mining	691·4	800·1	86·4	398·9	443·8	89·9	297·6	306·6	97·1	−292·5	−356·3	+ 3·5	−101·3	−137·2	+ 7·2

	1948 U.M. (thousands)	1948 P.U.M. (thousands)	1948 U.D. (%)	1968 U.M. (thousands)	1968 P.U.M. (thousands)	1968 U.D. (%)	1979 U.M. (thousands)	1979 P.U.M. (thousands)	1979 U.D. (%)	Change 1949–68 U.M. (thousands)	Change 1949–68 P.U.M. (thousands)	Change 1949–68 U.D. (%)	Change 1969–79 U.M. (thousands)	Change 1969–79 P.U.M. (thousands)	Change 1969–79 U.D. (%)
Other mining and quarrying	42.2	74.2	56.9	21.4	54.2	39.5	22.5	52.0	43.3	− 20.8	− 20.0	−17.4	+ 1.1	− 2.2	+ 3.8
Gas	101.1	137.6	73.5	90.5	129.5	69.9	95.5	105.8	90.3	− 10.6	− 8.1	− 3.6	+ 5.0	− 23.7	+ 20.4
Electricity	101.0	157.4	64.2	181.5	242.3	74.9	178.3	179.9	99.1	+ 80.5	+ 84.9	+10.7	− 3.2	− 62.4	+ 24.2
Water	16.7	29.3	57.0	33.5	47.5	70.5	61.4	66.2	92.7	+ 16.8	+ 18.2	+13.5	+ 27.9	+ 18.7	+ 22.2
Construction	611.2	1,325.8	46.1	472.0	1,570.7	30.1	519.7	1,415.2	36.7	− 139.2	+ 244.9	−16.0	+ 47.7	− 155.5	+ 6.6
Distribution	325.8	2,089.1	15.6	294.5	2,762.9	10.7	428.3	2,872.2	14.9	− 31.3	+ 673.8	− 4.9	+ 133.8	+ 109.3	+ 4.2
National government	375.3	709.1	52.9	457.1	602.7	75.8	583.8	639.5	91.3	+ 81.8	− 106.4	+22.9	+ 126.7	+ 36.8	+ 15.5
Local government and education	860.9	1,241.2	69.4	1,366.8	2,221.2	61.5	2,232.0	2,879.9	77.5	+ 505.9	+ 980.0	− 7.9	+ 865.2	+ 685.7	+16.0
Health services	222.5	521.9	42.6	369.8	976.3	37.9	971.2	1,317.9	73.7	+ 147.3	+ 454.4	− 4.7	+ 601.4	+ 341.6	+35.8
Post and telecommunications	283.1	324.1	87.3	400.6	408.5	98.1	427.6	428.1	99.9	+ 117.5	+ 84.4	+10.8	+ 27.0	+ 19.6	+ 1.8
Railways	474.6	535.3	88.7	228.9	274.5	83.4	204.2	208.9	97.8	− 245.7	− 260.8	− 5.3	− 24.7	+ 65.6	+ 14.4
Road transport[1]	481.8	520.3	92.6	432.6	521.0	83.0	451.0	449.6	100.3	− 49.2	+ 0.7	− 9.6	+ 18.4	+ 71.4*	+ 17.3
Sea transport	112.7	150.5	74.9	90.4	101.4	89.2	83.8	87.2	96.1	− 22.3	− 49.1	+14.3	− 6.6	+ 14.2	+ 6.9
Port and inland water transport	140.0	150.7	92.9	92.3	128.1	72.1	59.8	71.9	83.2	− 47.7	− 22.6	−20.8	− 32.5	− 56.2	+11.1
Air transport	11.9	30.7	38.8	41.1	62.5	65.8	78.5	92.5	84.9	+ 29.2	+ 31.8	+27.0	+ 37.4	+ 30.0	+19.1
Insurance, banking and finance	137.1	352.3	38.9	250.3	583.0	42.9	395.3	720.9	54.8	+ 113.2	+ 230.7	+ 4.0	+ 145.0	+ 137.9	+11.9
Entertainment[2]	96.4	135.6	71.1	97.7	113.7	85.9	128.7	114.8	112.1	+ 1.3	− 21.9	+14.8	+ 31.0	+ 1.1	+ 26.2

Table 1 (contd)

	1948			1968			1979			Change 1949-68			Change 1969-79		
	U.M. (thousands)	P.U.M. (thousands)	U.D. (%)	U.M. (thousands)	P.U.M. (thousands)	U.D. (%)	U.M. (thousands)	P.U.M. (thousands)	U.D. (%)	U.M. (thousands)	P.U.M. (thousands)	U.D. (%)	U.M. (thousands)	P.U.M. (thousands)	U.D. (%)
Fishing	11·0	23·0	47·8	5·7	13·1	43·5	2·3	11·2	20·5	− 5·3	− 9·9	− 4·3	− 3·4	− 1·9	− 23·0
Agriculture, horticulture and forestry	213·4	965·9	22·1	125·4	503·7	24·9	83·5	367·1	22·7	− 88·0	− 462·2	+ 2·8	− 41·9	− 136·6	− 2·2
Miscellaneous services	105·5	2,001·4	5·3	125·0	2,582·4	4·8	262·2	3,575·7	7·3	+ 19·5	+ 581·0	− 0·5	+ 137·2	+ 993·3	+ 2·5

Source: Price and Bain (1983: Table 6).

Notes: 1. The union membership and union density data for this industry are considerably overstated. The potential union membership data include only those employed in road haulage firms. But the union membership data include the entire membership of the commercial road transport group of the Transport and General Workers' Union, which contains not only workers employed in road haulage firms but also employees engaged in driving duties within firms in manufacturing and other sectors of the economy (e.g. in engineering and distribution).

2. The union membership and union density data for this industry are also considerably overstated. The pre-entry closed shop is widespread in this industry, and a large number of persons who are primarily employed elsewhere belong to entertainment unions so that they can seek employment within this industry.

union membership can affect aggregate union growth. For example, between 1948 and 1979 the share of potential union membership taken by the eighteen industries in Table 1 with a density level above 75 per cent in 1979 decreased from about 47 per cent to 43 per cent, whereas in the same period the five industries with a density level below 29 per cent in 1979 increased their share of potential union membership from about 26 per cent to 30 per cent. In short, the industrial tide was running against the trade union movement between 1948 and 1979, and this worked to undermine aggregate union membership and density.

One way to assess the impact of changes in the composition of potential union membership upon union growth is to measure how much larger aggregate union density would have been if these changes had not occurred (see Price and Bain, 1983). If the female share of potential union membership had remained constant since 1948, then total union density would have been higher by 0·7 percentage points in 1968 and by 1·8 percentage points in 1979; if the white-collar share of potential union membership had remained constant since 1948, then total union density would have been higher by 1·8 percentage points in 1968 and by 3·6 percentage points in 1979; and if the industrial distribution of potential union membership had remained constant since 1948, then total union density would have been higher by 2·4 percentage points in 1968 and by 3·7 percentage points in 1979. Since changes in the sexual, occupational and industrial composition of potential union membership are interrelated, the separate effect of each of these changes cannot simply be added together to obtain the total impact of the changing composition of potential union membership upon aggregate union growth. Nevertheless, the figures indicate that all three effects worked against the maintenance of aggregate union density; indeed, whereas the negative impact of the industrial effect was about the same throughout the whole of the period 1949–79, that of the sexual and occupational effects was greater in 1969–79 than in 1949–68.

The negative effects of these changes in the composition of potential union membership are probably sufficient in themselves to account for the slight downward trend in aggregate union density during the years 1949–68. By their very nature, however, they do not vary sufficiently to account for the year-to-year movements around the trend in union growth during this period. And since these negative effects persisted and, in most respects, were accentuated after 1968, there is a need to explain why union density nevertheless increased markedly during the next eleven years and then in 1980 began just as markedly to decline. To begin to answer these questions the focus of the analysis must turn to the business cycle, and, in particular, to such components of the cycle as retail prices, wages and unemployment.

The business cycle

An increase in the rate of change of retail prices is likely to encourage workers to become and to remain union members because of the threat which it poses to their standards of living. If workers think in real as distinct from money terms, however, they will not perceive their standards of living being threatened by rising prices if money earnings are rising even faster. Hence the relationship between prices and earnings is also likely to be important. But regardless of what is happening to prices, an increase in the rate of change of money earnings may encourage workers to unionize, for they may credit such an increase to the efforts of unions and become or remain union members in the hope of doing as well or even better in the future (Bain and Elsheikh, 1976, pp. 62–5).

The 'threat' and 'credit' effects associated with rising prices and earnings provide a good deal of the explanation for the contrasting experience of union growth between 1949–68 and 1969–79. As Price and Bain (1983, Table 7) have demonstrated, the behaviour of prices and wages also contrasts sharply between the two periods: both rose slowly in the first period and rapidly in the second. Moreover, although increases in earnings generally exceeded increases in prices in both periods, the gap between them narrowed considerably during the later period; in other words, real earnings increased much more slowly during 1969–79, and, in some years during the last half of this period, they actually declined as prices increased faster than earnings. White-collar workers were particularly hard hit. Whereas increases in white-collar earnings generally kept up with and even exceeded increases in manual earnings prior to 1968, the reverse was true during 1969 to 1979. The white-collar/manual earnings differential was severely squeezed, primarily as a result of the flat-rate characteristics of a series of incomes policies, and a non-indexed, progressive tax system produced 'fiscal drag' and a 'wage-tax spiral' which caused an even greater erosion of real disposable income during 1969–79, particularly for higher-paid white-collar workers (Wilkinson and Turner, 1972; Taylor, 1980, p. 38). Hence there can be little doubt that the behaviour of prices and earnings during the period 1969–79, encouraged large numbers of workers, particularly those in white-collar jobs, to unionize in an attempt to defend or to improve their standards of living. By the same logic, union density stagnated and declined in the period 1949–68 because the relative stability of earnings and prices meant that the positive impact of the 'threat' and 'credit' effects was not sufficiently large to counteract the negative impact of the changing composition of potential union membership.

The impact of unemployment upon union growth is less clear-cut than that of prices and earnings. There are several reasons for expecting unemployment to have a negative impact upon union growth. Unemployed workers may have little incentive to become or to remain members because there is usually little that a union can do to get them employment; also, the benefits of collective bargaining have little relevance for them, and the cost of union subscriptions is greater in relation to income. Moreover, when unemployment is high or increasing, employers may be more able and willing to oppose unionism; for in so far as unemployment reduces the level of aggregate demand, production lost as a result of strikes and other forms of industrial action will be less costly to employers. And if they wish to maintain production in the face of industrial action they can more easily do so by recruiting an alternative labour force from among the unemployed. Indeed, workers who are not unemployed may be reluctant to join unions in periods of high unemployment for fear of antagonizing their employers and thereby losing jobs which are in short supply. Finally, inasmuch as unemployment reduces the ability of unions to win collective bargaining advances, the benefits of membership are reduced even for members who are not unemployed, and some of them may come to feel that union membership is no longer worthwhile.

But there are contrary forces which may reduce the negative impact of unemployment on union growth. Some unemployed members may for social and political reasons be reluctant to cut their links with the union movement and, since many unions waive or at least reduce subscriptions for unemployed members, it often costs them little, if anything, to maintain their membership. There may also be economic reasons for workers, especially those in skilled trades, to remain union members when unemployed: they may obtain unemployment benefit, maintain their eligibility for other union 'friendly benefits', receive information about job openings, and acquire access to those which exist in closed trades. More generally, and probably of greater importance, as Hawkins (1981, pp. 84–85) has argued, the threat, as distinct from the experience, of unemployment may encourage employees to join a union for 'basic self-protection' in case they are faced with redundancy.

Given the conflicting influences which unemployment may produce, its overall impact upon union growth is difficult to predict. But it is probable that when the level of unemployment is low and changes in its level are small, it will have little impact one way or the other upon union growth, because its positive and negative effects are likely to be small and to cancel each other out. Another reason for expecting an insignificant relationship when unemployment is low is that most unions permit members to be in arrears for several months before dropping them from membership; hence, except in periods of severe recession, most unemployed members are likely to be re-employed within this period and to be back in 'good standing' before their membership has lapsed. When the level of unemployment is high and changes in its level are large, however, it is likely to have a significant negative impact upon union growth, primarily because unemployed non-members will have little incentive to join unions and unemployed members will have little incentive to remain in unions as their attachment to the labour force is broken and they endure long spells out of work.

The evidence is consistent with this reasoning (see Price and Bain, 1983, Table 7). During the period 1949–68, when the annual average level of unemployment was 1·9 per cent and the changes in its level varied from −0·9 to +0·9 percentage points, it appears not to have influenced union growth; as already indicated, union density stagnated and declined during this period, and this is adequately accounted for by the relative stability of earnings and prices and by unfavourable changes in the composition of potential union membership. Even during the period 1969–79, when the annual average level of unemployment was 4·1 per cent and the changes in its level varied from −1·1 to +1·6 percentage points, it appears to have had little influence upon union growth; at most it may have slightly dampened the growth-inducing effects of the accelerating pace of price and wage inflation during this period (Price and Bain, 1983). Unemployment appears to have had no significant impact upon union growth in the post-war period until 1980, since when its magnitude has increased substantially. Unemployment increased by 1·7 percentage points to 7·4 per cent in 1980 and by 3·9 percentage points to 11·3 per cent in 1981, and, in spite of large increases in earnings and prices in 1980 and, to a lesser extent, in 1981, union membership and density declined sharply in both years. There can be little doubt that unemployment is the major reason for this decline.

Employer policies and government action

Economic factors are clearly critical in determining whether workers decide to become and to remain union members. But how workers decide these questions will also be significantly influenced by the attitudes and behaviour of employers. The greater the degree of recognition which employers confer upon unions, the less likely employees are to jeopardize their jobs and career prospects by being union members, the more easily they can reconcile union membership with their 'loyalty' to the company, and, most important, the more effectively unions can participate in the process of job regulation and thereby offer employees services and benefits which will encourage them to become and to remain union members (Bain, 1970, pp. 122–3; CIR 1974, p. 68). In short, the greater the degree of union recognition, the more likely workers are to join unions and to remain in them. Union recognition and union growth are mutually dependent, however, because the degree to which employers are prepared to recognize unions is at least partly dependent upon their membership strength. Hence union recognition and union growth combine together in a 'virtuous circle' of cause and effect in which the more unions obtain recognition and succeed in participating in job regulation, the more they are likely to grow, and the more they grow, the more they are likely to increase their recognition and deepen their participation in job regulation.

One of the factors which affects the willingness and ability of employers to resist union organization and participation in job regulation – the extent of unemployment – has already been mentioned, and other factors will be referred to later in this chapter. But one factor – the government's role in promoting union recognition – needs to be dealt with here because it is important in accounting for the pattern of aggregate union growth in Britain since 1948. In World War II, as in World War I, the government fostered union growth by introducing policies which, directly and indirectly, tended to neutralize or at least contain employer opposition to unions (Bain, 1970, ch. 9). In the years following the end of World War II public support for union recognition and the extension of collective bargaining became much weaker. But the publication of the report of the Donovan

Commission, the White Paper *In Place of Strife* and the Labour Government's Industrial Relations Bill in 1968–9 greatly improved the climate for union recognition. All these documents affirmed the principles of freedom of association and union recognition, and the Commission on Industrial Relations, established in 1969, strongly reaffirmed these principles in a series of reports recommending the recognition of unions and the development of collective bargaining. Many of the Commission's recommendations were ignored by the firms to which they were directed, but its reports nevertheless had a significant impact upon union growth by encouraging employers and managers to attach more importance to industrial-relations principles and procedures and to view the growth of union organization among virtually all levels of employees as, if not desirable, at least inevitable. As a result, many employers recognized trade unions as part of a more general restructuring of industrial relations within their firms and industries.

With the defeat of the Labour Government in 1970 and the passage of the Industrial Relations Act in 1971 the climate for union recognition became less favourable. Although the Act provided a mechanism by which unions could obtain recognition from recalcitrant employers, only registered unions could make use of this mechanism and most TUC unions decided not to seek registration. Moreover the whole tenor of the legislation was restrictive rather than permissive. At no point did the Act or its accompanying Code of Practice stress the desirability of extending union recognition. Thus union growth received little help from the Industrial Relations Act (see Price and Bain, 1976, pp. 325–3), and it expanded less rapidly in 1971–3 than in 1969–70 and 1974–9.

The legislative framework for union recognition became more favourable again after the return of a Labour government in 1974, the consequent repeal of the Industrial Relations Act and the passage of the Employment Protection Act in 1975. The new Act provided both voluntary and statutory procedures for promoting union recognition, and by 1979 these had directly extended collective bargaining, in one way or another, to approximately 133,000 employees (Price and Bain, 1983). In addition, as the Advisory, Conciliation and Arbitration Service (1981, pp. 100–102) has pointed out, the Act indirectly promoted union growth and extended collective bargaining by making employees more aware of the feasibility of collective representation and by encouraging employers to recognize unions voluntarily in order to obtain orderly bargaining structures and to avoid the public scrutiny which would result from a reference under the statutory procedure.

This procedure was increasingly undermined after 1977 by a series of unfavourable legal decisions (see Lewis and Simpson, 1981, pp. 140–47), and in 1980 it was abolished by the newly elected Conservative Government. But the Employment Protection Act had other sections which indirectly promoted union growth. Its provisions for time off work for carrying out trade union duties and training, for facilities for union lay officers, and for disclosure of information by employers encouraged union growth, particularly in areas where unions were already recognized, by strenthening their organization at the workplace and increasing their depth of participation in job regulation. The provisions of the Health and Safety at Work Act 1974 providing for health and safety representatives had a similar effect. So did those provisions of the Trade Union and Labour Relations Act 1974 which, by removing the legal restrictions the Industrial Relations Act had placed on the closed shop, made possible a large increase in the number of formal union membership agreements, thereby helping to extend the closed shop among both white-collar and manual workers in both the public and private sectors of the economy (Brown, 1981, pp. 54–9; Gennard et al., 1980, pp. 16–22).

Nor were these the only pieces of legislation which promoted union growth by strengthening union organization at the workplace and increasing the depth of union participation in job regulation. Virtually all of the much-increased volume of government intervention into industrial relations in Britain throughout the whole of the period 1969–79 tended to have this effect. It did so – as is demonstrated elsewhere in this book – by directly and indirectly encouraging employers in both the public and private sectors to adopt a more professional approach to industrial relations. Among other things, this involved them in placing greater emphasis on collective bargaining as the preferred method of job regulation, reforming and formalizing bargaining structures and procedures, and underpinning these with greater union stability and security by supporting the spread of shop steward organization and facilities, the check off, the closed shop and other union membership arrangements. These processes were further encouraged in the private sector by the steady increase in the size of enterprises, and in the public sector by the reorganization of the health service and local government, and by an increased emphasis on productivity and efficient manpower utilization.

The above discussion leads to the conclusion that the impact of government action upon union growth during the period 1969–79 arose not only from public policies which were expressly designed to extend union recognition into areas where it was previously absent, but also from public policies which, by encouraging employers along the path of reforming, formalizing, and consolidating collective bargaining, helped to strengthen union organization at the workplace and to increase the depth of union participation in job regulation in areas where union recognition had been conceded many years earlier. The data presented above in Table 1 support this conclusion. Even allowing for the general framework of white-collar union recognition which had existed in engineering and newspaper publishing for many years before 1969–79 (Bain, 1967, pp. 31–73), the size of the increase in union membership and density among white-collar workers in manufacturing industries generally during this period suggests that unions must have expanded considerably in areas where they had previously lacked recognition and strength. A similar conclusion is suggested by the substantial increases in union membership and density among both white-collar and manual workers in such industries as food and drink, chemicals and, to a lesser extent, insurance, banking and finance. But about 50 per cent of the increase in union membership during this period occurred in the public sector – especially in health services and local government and education which between them added almost $1\frac{1}{2}$ million members to union ranks – where generally unions have been recognized for many years – and a further 20 per cent occurred in engineering and metals, where the recognition problem is confined primarily to small firms which are not members of the Engineering Employers Federation. Hence although unions were successful during 1969–79 in extending their representative base into areas in which they were previously unrecognized and weak, most growth during this period resulted from unions 'topping up' membership in areas where they were already recognized and moderately well-organized.

The data on the distribution of union growth during the period 1969–79 underline the duality which exists in the industrial pattern of unionization in Britain – between the well-organized sector of public services and manufacturing and the poorly organized sector of private services, construction and agriculture – and, by so doing, point to the important interrelationship which exists between the economic and political determinants of union growth. In both sectors price and wage inflation provided a common backdrop to union growth: the erosion of real incomes encouraged workers to turn to unions, and the unions' apparent success in defending their members' economic interests reinforced this process. In the well-organized sector, however, the unions were sufficiently well established to take advantage of the benefits offered by public policy, and, in doing so, they were frequently able to obtain the support of professional and relatively sophisticated personnel managers who seemed, in the context of the reforming and restructuring of collective bargaining which was going on in the 1970s, to have taken to heart Flanders's well-known aphorism that they could 'only regain control by sharing it' (1967, p. 32). In contrast, in the poorly organized sector there was much less scope for building upon existing union organization and recognition. Moreover, employer policies, relatively untouched by the new 'professionalism' and usually unchallenged by workers, remained generally hostile to collective bargaining, and public support for union recognition was not sufficiently strong to overcome them. In short, in the well-organized sector economic factors, employer policies and public support for union recognition combined to produce a major expansion and consolidation of union membership and organization. In the poorly organized sector neither economic factors nor public support for union recognition were felt sufficiently strongly to overcome an environment which was generally hostile to unionism; put simply, union density in this sector was below the level at which a 'virtuous circle' between union growth and union recognition could begin.

This conclusion raises the question of why some sectors and industries are more highly unionized than others. Greater public support for union recognition of the type discussed above tends to apply across all industries, and hence does not help to account for differences in unionization between industries. Similarly, an increase in the cost of living is a general factor which tends to be the same across industries. Earnings and unemployment do vary between industries, however, and as Bain and Elsheikh (1979, pp. 148–50) have shown, these factors account for some of the variation in the inter-industry pattern of union growth. But most of the variation is explained by other factors.

Personal and job-related characteristics

Several writers have suggested that the inter-industry pattern of union growth is significantly influenced by certain factors which are associated directly with individual workers and the jobs they hold. The

257

factors mentioned include age, sex, part-time employment, labour turnover and occupational status.

Age. Shister (1953, pp. 421–2) has claimed that younger workers are likely to show a greater propensity to unionize than older workers because, among other things, younger workers' shorter lengths of service will make them feel less 'loyalty' towards their employer, their greater mobility and relative lack of seniority and superannuation benefits will make employer victimization for union activities less costly to them, and their generally higher level of education will make them more resentful of arbitrary treatment by employers. There are other reasons, however, for expecting the reverse relationship to hold: for example, older workers have fewer opportunities than younger workers to improve their terms and conditions of employment by changing jobs, and, if they are in jobs in which productivity tends to decline with age, they may have more need of union protection as they get older. In any case, the level of unionization is determined not only by the propensity to unionize but also by the opportunity, and, in general, older workers will have had more opportunities to join unions, and unions will have had more opportunities to recruit them, because they will have been in the labour force for a longer period than younger workers. Hence, even if Shister is correct in asserting that younger workers have a greater propensity to unionize than older workers, the 'exposure effect' may result in a higher proportion of older workers actually being union members.

In fact, empirical studies in the United States (e.g. Blinder, 1972; Moore and Newman, 1975) have found that older workers are more likely to be unionized than younger workers. Similarly, in Britain Bain and Elsheikh (1979, p. 148) and Richardson and Catlin (1979, pp. 378–80) have shown that the higher the proportion of older workers in an industry, the higher its level of unionization. But more highly unionized industries may have a higher proportion of older workers because the benefits brought by unions reduce labour turnover. Moreover, many of the highly unionized industries are old and declining and have relatively few new entrants each year. Hence the direction of causation may run from unionization to age rather than from age to unionization and, as Richardson and Catlin point out, 'show more about the kind of industry that employs old workers than about the propensity of old workers to join unions'.

Sex. Many writers have argued that women have a lower propensity to unionize than men because of the nature of female employment: women do not participate continuously in the labour market because of marriage and family responsibilities, and they are often secondary earners whose pay is not the family's main source of income. This argument suggests that the higher the proportion of women and, in particular, married women in an industry, the lower its level of unionization is likely to be.

Bain and Elsheikh (1979) found little evidence to support this argument in an empirical study of the inter-industry pattern of unionization in Britain, a finding confirmed by Richardson and Catlin (1979). Similarly, Bain (1970, pp. 40–3) found that the proportion of women in the labour force does not exert a significant impact upon the inter-industry and inter-occupational patterns of white-collar unionism in manufacturing, a finding which agrees with that obtained in a later study of the inter-establishment pattern of unionization in manufacturing (Elsheikh and Bain, 1980). But this same study indicated that the proportion of women does have a significant negative impact upon the inter-establishment pattern of unionization among manual workers. The reason for this conflicting result is not clear, but it may be explained by the distribution of female employment: female manual workers are much less evenly spread across establishments than female white-collar workers, and the establishments in which female manual workers tend to be concentrated may have other characteristics, not controlled for in the study, which make them more difficult to unionize.

Be that as it may, differences in the way in which men and women are distributed across industries and occupations – differences which may partly result from discriminatory behaviour by employers and male-dominated unions – largely explains why women generally are not so highly unionized as men. The distribution of female employment is skewed to a greater extent than male employment in the direction of industries characterized by small establishments and of occupations characterized by small work groups, and these characteristics – which, as explained below, tend to inhibit unionization – rather than any intrinsic characteristics peculiar to women account for their lower degree of unionization. Similarly, changes in the distribution of female employment are largely responsible for the marked increase in female union membership and density during the period 1969–79. Almost 60 per cent of the increase in female potential membership in this period occurred in the public sector, and this sector contributed almost 50 per cent of the increase in total union membership and about 65 per cent of the increase in female union membership during 1969–79. Thus the factors which caused unionism to grow in this area – of which some have been discussed above and others will be discussed below – also account for a large part of the increase in female union membership and density during this period.

Part-time employment. This practice is closely associated with female employment and is rapidly growing. Work and such work-related matters as trade unionism are likely to be less central to the life interests of part-time workers than of full-time workers. Hence, other things being equal, the larger the proportion of part-time workers in an industry, the lower its level of unionization is likely to be.

But Bain and Elsheikh (1979) found that part-time employment is not a significant determinant of variations in the inter-industry pattern of unionization in Britain, a finding confirmed by Richardson and Catlin (1979). The explanation for this lack of significance is provided by the way in which part-time employees are distributed across industries. Of the five industries with the highest proportion of part-time employees, only two – distribution and miscellaneous services – are poorly unionized; the other three – health services, local government and education and entertainment – are well unionized. Distribution and miscellaneous services are poorly unionized not so much because of their high proportion of part-time employees as because they have other characteristics – in particular, a large number of small establishments – which are unfavourable to the organization not only of part-time employees but also of full-time employees. Similarly, the other three industries are well unionized because they have certain characteristics, for example, public employers, large employing units, and widespread closed shops, which are favourable to organizing not only full-time but also part-time employees. Indeed, as the success of such unions as the National Union of Public Employees in organizing part-time employees in the health service and in local government and education demonstrates, where the characteristics of an industry enable a substantial degree of unionization to be established among full-time employees, the organization of the part-time employees is likely to follow fairly readily.

But in areas where these characteristics do not exist, a large proportion of part-time employees is likely to impede unionization. In a study of the inter-establishment pattern of unionization in manufacturing, Elsheikh and Bain (1980) found that part-time employment had a significant negative impact upon white-collar unionism but not upon manual unionism. This difference probably occurs because union density is about half as great, whereas the proportion of part-time employment is about twice as great, among white-collar as among manual employees in manufacturing. Thus unions are much less able in white-collar than in manual areas in manufacturing to use prevailing social norms and closed shop arrangements to persuade part-time employees to become and to remain members. Similar considerations apply in sectors such as distribution and miscellaneous services. Thus although the extent of part-time employment does not help to account for the variation in unionization *between* industries, it may nevertheless be an important factor in explaining the low level of unionization *within* a particular industry or occupation.

Labour turnover. A high degree of labour turnover is another factor which is closely associated with female employment, but is also characteristic of male employment in certain areas. The higher the degree of labour turnover among employees the more difficult and more costly will unions find them to recruit and to keep in membership. Moreover, many of the advantages of unionization are only forthcoming after several years of continuous pressure upon employers, and hence workers may be reluctant to take the time and trouble to organize themselves into unions unless they expect to be employed in their present work long enough to enjoy these advantages. Indeed, a high degree of labour turnover may indicate that workers are leaving unsatisfactory work as an alternative strategy to improving it through unionization. Be that as it may, these arguments suggest that the higher the degree of labour turnover in an industry, the lower its level of unionization is likely to be.

Bain and Elsheikh (1979) found that labour turnover has a significant negative impact upon the inter-industry pattern of unionization when considered by itself, but not when the effect of other factors was controlled for, a finding which was confirmed by their inter-establishment study of manufacturing (Elsheikh and Bain, 1980). This result also appears to be explained by the way in which employment is distributed across industries. The industries in which employees have the highest degree of turnover – distribution, miscellaneous services, construction, timber and furniture, health services and clothing – are, with one exception – health services – characterized by small establishment size and private ownership, whereas industries in which

261

employees have the lowest degree of turnover – railways, water, port and inland water transport, coal mining, post and telecommunications, electricity and air transport – are characterized by large employing units and public ownership (Bain and Eksheikh, 1981: Tables 11 and 16). In short, although labour turnover appears to have a significant negative impact upon unionization, it tends to be associated with other, more powerful factors which overshadow its effect.

Occupational status. Although craftsmen have historically been the vanguard of the trade union movement, the extent of skilled status among manual workers no longer has a significant impact upon either the inter-industry or the inter-establishment pattern of unionization in Britain (Bain and Elsheikh, 1979; Elsheikh and Bain, 1980); the reason is that unskilled and semi-skilled workers now tend to be as well unionized as skilled workers. White-collar workers are generally less well unionized than manual workers, however, and, perhaps not surprisingly, the higher the proportion of white-collar workers in an industry or an establishment, the lower its level of unionization tends to be (Bain and Elsheikh, 1979; Elsheikh and Bain, 1980).

The question arises, however, as to why white-collar workers are generally less well unionized than manual workers. The answer most often advanced is that the different social positions which the two groups hold in the system of social stratification produce different ideologies: manual workers have an ideology which is favourable to trade unionism in that it stresses conflict and collectivism, whereas white-collar workers have an ideology which is inimical to unionism in that it emphasizes harmony and individualism. This answer has been shown to be deficient in several respects (Bain *et al.*, 1973). As indicated earlier in this chapter, there are many similarities in the way in which white-collar and manual unionism fluctuate over time, and the factors which affect their growth are also broadly similar. Some of these have already been mentioned above: the relationship between prices and earnings, and the relationship between employer policies and government action. The latter relationship is particularly important in explaining the generally lower level of unionism among white-collar employees: employers have generally been much more opposed to recognizing and negotiating with unions on behalf of such employees, and government action has often been necessary to help overcome this opposition (Bain, 1970, ch. 9). Another part of the explanation is provided by the lower degree of employment concentration among white-collar employees: in most firms they tend to be found in smaller numbers and in smaller work groups than manual workers. And, as is indicated below, the degree of employment concentration is of crucial importance in determining the extent of unionization among both white-collar and manual employees.

Industrial structure

The above discussion has made it clear that the impact of the various personal and job-related determinants of union growth is very much affected by the way in which employment is distributed across and within industries. Indeed, Bain and Elsheikh (1979, p. 153) concluded from an analysis of the inter-industry pattern of union growth in Britain over a twenty-year period that 'as unions are increasingly accepted as part of the structure of British society and union membership becomes increasingly widespread, it becomes less dependent upon the self-selection of individuals with similar personal characteristics and attitudes and more dependent upon the characteristics of the firms and industries in which individuals work'.

An important characteristic of an industry is the extent to which the employment of those who work in it is concentrated in large groups, and a number of studies in a variety of countries have demonstrated that this factor is closely related to the extent to which an industry is unionized. In Britain, Bain and Elsheikh (1979, p. 146) found that the degree of employment concentration, as measured by the average size of establishment, accounts by itself for about 40 per cent of the variation in the inter-industry pattern of unionization in production industries. It also accounts for a considerable amount of the variation in the occupational and industrial patterns of white-collar unionism in manufacturing (Bain, 1970, pp. 72–81). And within individual manufacturing industries it is significantly related to the inter-establishment pattern of both white-collar and manual unionism: in general, unionization tends to increase as establishment size increases, but it does so at a decreasing rate, so that an establishment which is twice as large as another does not, other things being equal, have twice the level of unionization (Elsheikh and Bain, 1980). Finally, although adequate data on employment concentration do not exist for the public and private services sectors of the economy, this factor is clearly important in explaining their very different degrees of unionization (see Lockwood, 1958, pp. 141–50).

The strong positive relationship between the size of establishments

263

and the extent to which they are unionized is fairly easy to explain. To begin with, the larger the establishment, the more interested unions are likely to be in organizing it, for the lower are the *per capita* costs of doing so and the greater the return in subscriptions and bargaining power. More important, the larger the establishment, the more interested its employees are likely to be in joining trade unions. For the larger the number of employees, the more likely they are to be treated not as individuals but as members of groups, to have their terms and conditions of employment determined not by the personal considerations and sentiments of their managers but by bureaucratic rules which apply impersonally to all members of the group to which they belong, and hence to come to the conclusion that the most effective way of modifying these rules in their favour is by collective rather than individual bargaining. In short, the larger the number of employees in an establishment, the more likely they are to feel the need to unionize because of the bureaucratic manner in which they are governed on the job, and the more easily trade unions can meet this need because of the economies of scale characteristic of union recruitment and administration.

Establishment size may also be linked to unionization by another causal mechanism: the impact which it has upon the willingness of employers to concede union demands for recognition. Initially, almost all employers, for reasons which are understandable if not commendable, are opposed to recognizing unions and bargaining with them. As unions develop in large, bureaucratically administered firms, however, employers may increasingly offer less resistance because they come to realize that 'if the bureaucratic rules are to be acceptable and friction in their operation is to be reduced to a minimum', they need to be 'formulated in consultation with organised groups representative of all the main interests involved' (Kelsall *et al.*, 1956, p. 322). In short, as Flanders (1974, pp. 355–6) has observed, large employers have an interest in obtaining union 'assistance in managerial control, in making and upholding rules to regulate work and wages for the sake of gaining employee consent and cooperation and avoiding costly strikes', and this interest may encourage them to extend recognition to unions and further their participation in job regulation.

Some employers also have an interest in obtaining union assistance in market control, in 'taking wages out of competition' by reducing disparities in labour costs between firms. Their interest in regulating wages is derived from their interest in regulating prices in competitive product markets, and the higher the proportion of labour costs to total costs, the greater is their interest in regulating wages and the more such regulation contributes to the regulation of prices and the control of competition. Thus, in industries where labour costs make up a large proportion of total costs *and* where unions can develop sufficient strength to enforce collective agreements, employer opposition to them is likely to be less severe and less sustained and hence the level of unionization is likely to be higher, other things being equal, than in industries where these conditions do not exist. The evidence for Britain is consistent with this reasoning: in production industries – the only sector with data on labour costs – the more labour intensive an industry or an establishment, the higher its level of unionization tends to be (Bain and Elsheikh, 1979; Elsheikh and Bain, 1980; Beaumont and Gregory, 1980).

Regardless of its size and labour intensiveness an establishment may be easier to organize if it is owned or controlled by a large enterprise than if it is a single independent unit. Even if the establishments within a large enterprise are administered in a decentralized fashion, they are in institutional, and perhaps physical, proximity to each other, and for all the reasons which Shister (1953, pp. 422–4) sets out, this proximity may make unionization easier. Its effect is likely to be much stronger, however, if the enterprise has a centralized personnel policy. In this case, regardless of how few employees there may be in a particular establishment, they are likely to become aware of their common interests because their terms and conditions of employment will tend to be determined in a bureaucratic fashion by formal rules which apply impersonally throughout the whole enterprise. Multi-establishment enterprises are also more likely to employ professional personnel managers (Brown, 1981, p. 30), and if they, rather than paternalistic managers in individual establishments, formulate the policy on union recognition, it is likely to be more favourable to trade unionism and collective bargaining. Indeed, if the enterprise wishes to bargain on a company-wide basis, a union may be recognized in an establishment where it has only a few members. Within a single independent establishment a paternalistic style of administration is more likely to be applied to white-collar than to manual workers, and, within a multi-establishment enterprise, company-wide bargaining and personnel policies are more commonly applied to white-collar than to manual employees (Brown, 1981, p. 14). And, interestingly, Elsheikh and Bain (1980) found that the level of unionization tends to be lower among white-collar employees,

265

but not among manual employees, in single independent establishments even when their size and labour intensiveness are controlled for, than in establishments which are part of a larger enterprise.

The above discussion of industrial structure has been largely based upon the private sector of the economy. But similar forces operate within the public sector. The large size of employing unit and the high degree of bureaucratization characteristic of the public sector have clearly fostered among employees, including those in managerial and executive positions, an awareness of their collective interests and of the need to advance them through collective organization (Lockwood, 1958, pp. 142–5). Bureaucratization has also made employers in the public sector more willing to recognize unions, and, indeed, to encourage employees to belong to them. For example, the Treasury informs new entrants to the civil service that

besides being a good thing for the individual civil servant . . . it is also a good thing for Departments and for the Civil Service as a whole that civil servants should be strongly organised in representative bodies . . . it is hopeless to try to find out the wishes of a scattered unorganised body of individual civil servants each of whom may express a different view. When they get together in representative associations, their collective wish can be democratically determined and passed on to the 'management' with real force and agreement behind it; the 'management' know where they stand and can act accordingly (cited by Bain, 1970, pp. 124–5).

Most local authorities and nationalized industries have made similar pronouncements. Indeed, the government has placed the various industries it has nationalized under a duty to recognize and bargain with appropriate trade unions. In short, the greater degree of employment concentration and bureaucratization and the greater degree of union recognition in the public as compared with the private sector of the economy go a long way to explaining its greater degree of unionization.

Union leadership

So far nothing has been said about union leadership. Shister (1953) has claimed that union leaders have an impact upon union growth through the organizing techniques which they devise for recruiting employees, the structural and governmental forms which they design for the union, and the nature of the collective bargaining relationships which they forge with employers and governments. Shister made this claim with respect to the United States, but Undy *et al.* (1981, pp. 163–6 and 349–50) have recently advanced a similar argument for Britain.

Few people would quarrel with the basic contention that union leadership has an impact upon union growth. Leadership is likely to be an important factor in determining the particular time and place of a union's emergence. And the importance of leadership style and policies for 'the union *incidence* of growth – that is, which union succeeds in organizing a given group of workers – is,' as Shister has pointed out, 'too obvious to need comment'.

But how important is leadership in influencing aggregate union growth? This is a difficult question to answer. When an attempt is made by examining the growth of unions in areas in which they have sharply demarcated spheres of organization and other unions are effectively prohibited from recruiting, the problem is to isolate the independent effect of leadership by controlling for all the other factors which directly, as well as indirectly through their impact on leadership style and policies, affect union growth. When an attempt is made to assess the importance of leadership by comparing the growth of unions in areas where they are competing with other unions to recruit the same group of workers, the other determinants of union growth are controlled for, but the problem is then to demonstrate that a particular union's growth in this area occurred at the expense of continuing non-unionism rather than at the expense of another union which, in spite of having different leaders and policies would, in the absence of the successful union, have recruited the workers in question; for workers who join one union rather than another when presented with a choice of leadership styles and policies might nevertheless have joined the other in the absence of such a choice.

These problems are well illustrated by the work of Undy *et al.* Even if they are correct in asserting that 'ASTMS's and the TGWU's selective recruitment efforts in areas of non-unionism . . . almost certainly positively affected their membership growth without depriving other unions of an immediate membership increase' – although, since both are general unions which generally recruit in competition with other unions, there is no way of knowing whether this is so – special recruitment campaigns depend for their success not only upon the way they are pursued and the charisma and policies of union leaders but also upon the determinants of union growth discussed above being broadly favourable. Special recruitment campaigns may have attracted a significant number of members when the climate for union growth was very favourable, as in the period

1969–79, but they generally do not appear to have done so when the climate for union growth has been unfavourable, as in the period 1949–68 (see Bain, 1970, pp. 92–100) and in the years since 1979. Similarly, although Undy and his colleagues are undoubtedly correct to claim that by adopting policies favourable to the extension of such practices as the closed shop and the check off, certain unions influenced their growth in areas in which other unions were not capable of recruiting, these practices cannot be attributed solely, or even mainly, to union leaders and their policies. While these practices would not exist if unions were opposed to them, their introduction and extension during the late 1960s and the 1970s was, as indicated above, critically influenced by employer policies and government action.

Since only a very small amount of union growth can be unambiguously attributed to the independent influence of union leaders and their policies, and would not have occurred in the absence of these leaders and policies, Undy and his colleagues surely dramatically overstate their case when they speak of 'the critical role of leadership'. Unions and their leaders basically act as catalysts in the recruitment process. Before a group of workers can be successfully organized there must be some irritant resulting in a widespread feeling of dissatisfaction. Unions and their leaders cannot create this antipathy, they can only discover where it exists, emphasize it, and try to convince the workers that it can be remedied by unionization. Their role in aggregate union growth is vigorously to exploit the opportunities which are generated by the determinants of union growth discussed above, but it is a role which is tightly circumscribed by these determinants. Indeed, given the other determinants of union growth discussed in this chapter, most of the increase in union membership and density during the period 1969–79 and most of the decrease in union membership and density since 1979 would have occurred regardless of which union leaders were in office, because 'union leadership is dependent upon and constrained by the same socio-economic forces which motivate or enable workers to join trade unions', and, 'as such, it is very much a secondary and derivative determinant of aggregate union growth' (Bain and Elsheikh, 1976, pp. 23).

The destiny of union growth

Now that the strategic determinants of union growth have been identified, an attempt can be made to predict its future course in Britain during the 1980s. Such an attempt has to start with the existing pattern of unionization. Despite the high density levels attained in the well-organized sector of public services and manufacturing, there are still substantial numbers of non-members, especially among white-collar workers in manufacturing, whose recruitment would greatly increase the strength of the trade union movement; indeed, if the 3·3 million non-members in this sector in 1979 had been unionized, aggregate union density would have been about 70 per cent rather than 55 per cent. But further union recruitment in this sector is likely to be constrained by the 'saturation effect': the greater difficulty of further increasing union membership as union density rises, partly because there are fewer workers left to recruit and partly because those who are left have less propensity and/or ability to unionize (see Bain and Elsheikh, 1976, pp. 67–8). For example, many of the non-members in manufacturing are located in small establishments and, in the case of white-collar workers, in managerial grades. The scope for further union growth in the well-organized sector is also likely to be limited by future employment trends: forecasts suggest that public employment will remain at roughly its present level throughout the 1980s, whereas both manual and white-collar employment in manufacturing will continue to decline substantially (Institute for Employment Research, 1982, Table 3.1).

The largest untapped potential for union growth in Britain is in the poorly organized sector and, in particular, among the more than six million unorganized workers in private services. Although union density increased in private services during 1969–79 – especially in insurance, banking, finance and, to a lesser extent, in distribution – in general the gains were very limited. They were limited primarily because private services are characterized by a large number of small establishments, part-time working and high labour turnover, and employer opposition to union recognition and collective bargaining. These characteristics are unlikely to change in the near future, and hence private services will remain a major obstacle to union growth for some time to come.

Even if unions are able to make modest membership gains in private services in the 1980s as they did in the 1970s, aggregate union density will probably still decline, other things being equal, simply because employment in this area is expanding so rapidly. This expansion is merely a particular example of the negative impact which the changing pattern of employment predicted for the 1980s will have upon union growth. Even if unions maintain throughout the 1980s the levels of union density reached in all areas in 1979, aggregate union density in 1990 will nevertheless be lower than in 1979 by, other things being equal, 0·7 percentage points as a result of the relative increase in women workers, 1·0 percentage points as a result of the relative increase in white-collar workers, and 2·0 percentage points as a result of changes in the industrial composition of the labour force (Price and Bain, 1983).

But the assumption that other things will remain equal does not hold for long in the real world. Many of the other determinants of union growth have already changed dramatically since 1979, and in such a way as to reinforce the negative impact of the changing composition of the labour force. The rate of wage and price inflation has moderated, and the earnings differential has widened in favour of white-collar workers (Price and Bain, 1983, Table 7). In addition, the Conservative Government elected in 1979 repealed those sections of the Employment Protection Act which enabled a union to make a unilateral reference under the statutory procedure for obtaining assistance with a recognition dispute. It has also passed legislation designed to curb the closed shop. Perhaps most important, unemployment has increased dramatically and, as the recession has deepened, some employers have adopted a much tougher stance towards trade unions.

Economic forecasts suggest that the decline in the rate of inflation and the increase in unemployment will continue, with both trends levelling off in the mid 1980s (Institute for Employment Research, 1982). Greater public support for union recognition is unlikely to be forthcoming until a Labour government is returned to power and the prospects of this happening in the next few years do not appear good at the moment. It remains to be seen how effective the Conservative Government's labour legislation will be, but, even if it does not undermine existing closed shops, it will almost certainly restrict the growth of new closed shops. And the changing composition of the labour force will continue to work against the trade union movement. Thus trade union density is likely to continue to fall over the next year or two, to stabilize when unemployment stops increasing and then, assuming inflation continues at a moderate rate, to fluctuate slightly around a declining trend as it did during the years 1949–68.

How steeply declining this trend will be, however, will largely depend upon how employers behave. As this chapter has made clear, union recognition was greatly extended and deepened during the 1970s, with the result that trade unionism and the collective bargaining which it makes possible are now more deeply embedded in the management process than ever before. This greater degree of union recognition may act as a ratchet which will prevent union membership slipping away on the scale which, for example, occurred during the mass unemployment of the inter-war years. But the present government is questioning the desirability of collective representation and is attempting by legislative and other means to shift the balance of power in industrial relations more firmly in favour of employers. If employers take full advantage of the opportunities with which they are now being presented to reduce the extent and depth of union recognition, then the relationship between union growth and recognition will be reversed and become a 'vicious circle', and the downward trend in union density will be much steeper. Hence union growth has reached a watershed, and its direction during the 1980s will depend, as in the previous decade, upon the crucial interrelationship between economic forces, employer policies and government action.

References

BAIN, G. S. (1967), *Trade Union Growth and Recognition*, HMSO.

BAIN, G. S. (1970), *The Growth of White Collar Unionism*, Oxford University Press.

BAIN, G. S., and F. ELSHEIKH (1976), *Union Growth and the Business Cycle*, Blackwell.

BAIN, G. S., and R. PRICE (1980), *Profiles of Union Growth*, Blackwell.

BLINDER, A. (1972), 'Who Joins Unions?', *Working Paper 36*, Princeton Industrial Relations Section.

BROWN, W. (1981), *Changing Contours of British Industrial Relations*, Blackwell.

COMMISSION ON INDUSTRIAL RELATIONS (1974), *Trade Union Recognition: CIR Experience*, HMSO.

ELSHEIKH, F., and G. S. BAIN (1980), 'Unionisation in Britain: An Inter-establishment Analysis Based on Survey Data', *British Journal of Industrial Relations*, vol. 18.

FLANDERS, A. (1974), 'The Tradition of Voluntarism', *British Journal of Industrial Relations*.

GENNARD, J., *et al.* (1980). 'The Content of British Closed Shop Agreements'. *Department of Employment Gazette*, vol. 88.

HAWKINS, K. (1981), *Trade Unions*, Hutchinson.

INSTITUTE OF EMPLOYMENT RESEARCH (1982). *Review of the Economy and Employment*, Warwick.

LEWIS, R., and B. SIMPSON (1981), *Striking a Balance*, Martin Robertson.

LOCKWOOD, B. (1958), *The Blackcoated Worker*, Allen & Unwin.

MOORE, W., and R. NEWMAN (1975), 'On the Prospects for American Trade Union Growth', *Review of Economic Statistics*, vol. 62.

RICHARDSON, R., and S. CATLIN (1979), 'Trade Union Density and Collective Agreement Patterns in Britain', *British Journal of Industrial Relations*, vol. 17.

SHISTER, J. (1953), 'The Logic of Union Growth', *Journal of Political Economy*, vol. 61.

TAYLOR, R. (1980), *The Fifth Estate*, Pan

WILKINSON, F., and H. A. TURNER (1972). *Are Trade Unions to Blame for Inflation?*, Cambridge University Press.

18 Ray Richardson

Defects in Bain's Theory of Union Growth

From Ray Richardson, 'Trade Union Growth: a Review Article', *British Journal of Industrial Relations*, vol. 15, no. 2, July 1977, pp. 279–82.

This book[1] is one of a projected series on aspects of trade union growth and is specifically concerned with aggregate patterns of union growth over time, with particular empirical reference to the UK, USA, Australia and Sweden. It is short (only 155 pages), lucidly written and has a particularly clear exposition of the relevant econometric problems, so that nobody, not even those who are innocent of the mysteries of statistical method, need have serious misgivings about being able to follow the discussion. [. . .] In my view, however, the theoretical analysis in the book is shallow and *ad hoc*.

For example, in the discussion of the effect on union growth of price inflation the authors point to two effects, both of which are held to suggest a positive relationship between the two variables. First, with money wages constant, higher inflation reduces real wages, thus causing workers to unionize in order to defend their standards of living. Secondly, inflation may imply business prosperity, when employers 'may be more prepared' to recognize unions, so as to avoid industrial action at a particularly damaging time and because wage increases are relatively easily passed on. Now, both of these arguments may be true, but each requires a more detailed defence than is presented in the book. Thus, why do workers wait for inflationary periods before they act on their belief that being a member of a union results in real wages that are higher than they would otherwise be? Is it (a) that unions are particularly effective in such periods, (b) that unions are always effective but workers perceive their benefits more acutely during inflationary periods, or (c) that unions are not then particularly effective but workers misguidedly believe that they are? These three possibilities do not have the same implications but they do raise interesting problems for empirical inquiry.

As for the second effect, is it so obvious that employers will agree to a change which they believe will cause them permanent damage

1. Bain and Elsheikh, 1976.

merely because the costs of resisting the change are temporarily high? This part of the discussion is reminiscent of the analysis of strikes, where it is well known that attempts to force clear and determinate predictions from the analysis require strong, and possibly misleading, assumptions. The authors do not recognize these, or any other, ambiguities, and so their analysis is arbitrary and unconvincing.

In discussing the relationship between union growth and changes in money wages the authors recognize that workers always have an incentive to join unions, so as to increase their real wages. However, they then make the extraordinarily *ad hoc* statement that 'when money wages are rising, workers may, rightly or wrongly, credit such rises to unions', and hence join. Workers may indeed make such a connection, but where is there even a hint of that integrated, comprehensive, interdisciplinary theory that would make such a connection plausible?

The discussion on unemployment uses familar arguments; when labour markets are slack, unionization falls, and vice versa. Here, however, the authors see contrary forces. In fact the forces are not contrary, that is, they do not work to make the relationship a positive one, they merely attenuate its negative size. Nevertheless, the authors suggest that the relationship is likely to be 'relatively weak', but relative to what? Do they mean that it is likely to be statistically insignificant? There is certainly nothing in the text that persuades the reviewer that the qualifications raised for this variable are more potent than those that could be raised for the others.

Thus in my view the model as presented is not convincing. In addition, there are two other theoretical problems that are worth discussing, even though the authors do not consider them at all seriously. First, the causal sequence is held to be exclusively from price inflation, money wage changes, etc., to union growth, never the other way around. Thus the authors presumably believe that union growth has no impact on unemployment, wage changes, etc. This strong and unusual position, together with its implications, might have been considered at some length.

Secondly, and more important, the explanatory variables are explicitly all aggregate variables (although they may have indirect structural effects). One implication of this is that all the workers not in a union in year t have the same probability of joining a union in year $t + 1$ (where that probability is given by the rate of inflation, the rate of unemployment, and so on). Female workers, white-collar workers, public sector workers, all have the same probability of joining a union as do male workers, manual workers or private sector workers. This implication is contrary both to the facts and to at least some theories of union growth. Bain and Elsheikh say that they are interested in explaining aggregate union growth, not its structure, but it is very doubtful that this can be done successfully without some explicit reference to the changing composition of the labour force. Another way of making this point is to say that their model has no obvious micro-economic or disaggregated equivalent.

Apart from compositional effects, the authors ignore other structural arguments that may be significant for aggregate union growth. For example, one influence on union growth might be the changing occupational earnings structure, but the authors do not consider it, surprising as this omission might be from so perceptive a writer on white-collar unions as Professor Bain. It is true that some (but not all) of these structural arguments are difficult to specify and measure, but that is not a good reason to ignore them in a theoretical discussion.

Reference

BAIN, G.S., and F. ELSHEIKH (1976), *Union Growth and the Business Cycle: An Econometric Analysis*, Blackwell.

19 G. S. Bain and Farouk Elsheikh

A Reply to Ray Richardson

From G. S. Bain and Farouk Elsheikh, 'Trade Union Growth: A Reply', *British Journal of Industrial Relations*, vol. 16, no. 1, March 1978, pp. 99–101.

In a review article in the July 1977 issue of the *British Journal of Industrial Relations*, Ray Richardson assesses our recently published work, *Union Growth and the Business Cycle: An Econometric Analysis* (Blackwell, 1976). Although he has some favourable things to say about it, he raises several critical points which we wish to answer.

Richardson's first criticism is that our theoretical analysis is 'shallow and *ad hoc*'. We disagree. We specified our explanatory variables within an analytical framework which sees changes in union membership as being determined by changes in both the *propensity* and the *opportunity* to unionize. The same set of variables could have been specified within the framework of conventional economic analysis which views unions as 'firms' and employees as 'customers' operating in a market where 'union services' are the commodity being sold and bought at a given price (membership subscription). We preferred our analytical framework, as we mentioned in the book, because it is more methodologically neutral than that of supply-and-demand analysis and because it is compatible not only with economics but also with the other disciplines upon which the wider study draws. It should, therefore, more readily enable us in the final volume of the study to integrate into a comprehensive general theory the insights which several disciplines have to offer into the process of union growth.

Richardson goes on to criticize us for ignoring what he regards as relevant explanatory variables. In particular, he argues that we should have considered the impact on aggregate union growth of such factors as the changing composition of the labour force. As we indicated in the book (p. 116), however, such variables as the industrial and occupational composition of the labour force exhibit little annual variation because they are dominated by their time trends, and hence they are irrelevant in a rate of change model such as ours. More generally, we suggested that factors which are unique to particular industries, occupations and regions are unlikely to be relevant to the explanation of aggregate union growth. This does not mean that these factors should be ignored, but only that they should be considered in a disaggregated analysis of union growth. We are currently undertaking such an analysis.

Richardson also criticizes some of the variables which we do include in the model. He claims that we give 'no reason' for the non-linear relationship between changes in union membership and changes in prices. This is not true, as an inspection of pp. 84 and 108 will reveal. Although he grants that our theoretical arguments on behalf of prices, wages, and unemployment may be true, he thinks that they require a more detailed defence. In our view, the theoretical defence presented in the book is strong enough as it stands, and it is supported by the results which the model produces not only for the United Kingdom but also for those countries which Richardson ignores in his review: Australia, Sweden and the United States.

Another charge which Richardson directs against the model is that of simultaneity. He says that 'the authors presumably believe that union growth has no impact on unemployment, wage changes, etc.', and suggests that this 'strong and unusual position, together with its implications, might have been considered at some length'. Perhaps we should have discussed this point at greater length, but Richardson does not seem to have understood the two pages (pp. 117–18) which we did write on the subject. If there is a two-way relationship between changes in union membership and changes in prices, wages and unemployment, presumably the implication is that we should have built a simultaneous model. Even if we had built such a model, there would still have been good arguments (see p. 118, n. 9) for estimating it by the ordinary least-squares technique rather than by a simultaneous technique. This is not the place to list these arguments, but after reviewing them all Theil concludes that 'although the method of ordinary least squares can no longer claim to have the brilliant properties which earlier econometricians thought it had, it can be regarded as one of the few one-eyed men who are eligible for king in the country of the blind' (Theil, 1961). In short, even if we had built a simultaneous model, in this case we would still have preferred to estimate it by ordinary least squares, and hence the results for the unionization equations would be the same as those cited in the book. [. . .]

Finally, Richardson attempts to test our model by disaggregating the data by sex and running the equations separately for males and females for the period 1950–74. He claims that the results are not particularly good. This may be a fortunate or unfortunate finding, depending upon your point of view, but it hardly constitutes a refutation of our model. Leaving aside the fact that this work cannot be properly evaluated because, in contrast to the standards which he applies to us, he cites not a single result and says not a single word about how he disaggregated the data, these equations for males and females are, as we argued above about the aggregate equations for 1950–70, likely to suffer from severe multicollinearity.

Even if they do not, they are not an appropriate test of our model. Our model attempts to explain aggregate union growth, and hence any test of it must be undertaken on aggregate data. Nowhere in the book did we pretend that the model necessarily explained disaggregated patterns of union growth. On the contrary, we pointed out (pp. 21 and 116) that some of the factors which explain disaggregated patterns of union growth may be different from those which explain aggregate patterns. Even at the aggregate level, we demonstrated that the model could not be mechanically applied to different countries, but had to be modified to take into account differences in their industrial-relations systems. If we believed that the model could be mechanically applied, we would not have bothered to undertake this comparative analysis. Nor would we have invested several man-years of labour to obtain data on disaggregated patterns of union growth in the United Kingdom and other countries and, as we mentioned in the book, be presently analysing them in an attempt to develop a more comprehensive and general theory of union growth.

Richardson does not think that we have travelled very far towards this 'ambitious goal' in this book. But we have built a model which is satisfactory when judged in terms of the classical statistical criteria and in terms of its sensitivity to the addition of observations, its structural stability and its predictive ability. And, as far as we are aware, it is unique in being able to explain aggregate union growth not only in the United Kingdom but also in Australia, Sweden and the United States.

Reference

THEIL, H. (1961), *Economic Forecasts and Policy*, 2nd edn, North-Holland.

20 Ray Richardson

A Rejoinder to Bain and Elsheikh

From Ray Richardson. 'Trade Union Growth: A Rejoinder', *British Journal of Industrial Relations*, vol. 16, no. 1, March 1978, pp. 103–5.

In my rejoinder I will follow the order of the comments in Elsheikh and Bain.

First, there is their disagreement with my view that the analysis in their book is 'shallow and *ad hoc*'. They express their disagreement, not by replying to my specific points, but by reproducing the rather vague assertions to be found in their book, assertions which do not bear on my criticisms.

Let us consider, as an example, the argument given by Bain and Elsheikh in their book that people join unions when wages are rising because they believe that it is union activity which has caused the higher wages. Why should non-unionized workers attribute to union activity a generalized increase in wages, i.e. one which they are, presumably, sharing? One could see an argument if the union/non-union wage structure were changing, but Bain and Elsheikh do not make this point. In reviewing the book, it seemed to me that their argument was *ad hoc*, and as in their reply they are completely silent on this point, I see no reason to change my mind. The same is true, in my opinion, of their arguments on some of their other variables, where there is too great a reliance on crude assertions about the behaviour of workers and employers. [. . .]

Of course it may be true that the final volume of the series will present a satisfactory general treatment of these matters that is also consistent with the presently *ad hoc* one, but I was not reviewing the final volume.

Secondly, there is my criticism of their omission of explicit compositional or structural variables. In my review it is clear that what worried me here were the larger compositional changes that have taken place over the last seventy-five years, e.g. the rising importance in the labour force of women, white-collar workers and the public sector. In their reply, Elsheikh and Bain repeat the view expressed in their book that these changes are sufficiently steady for their omission not to affect anything of importance. That such changes have trends is not in doubt; that they are all 'dominated' by their trends is much more questionable. As support for their view, Bain and Elsheikh in their book refer us to p. 193 of Bain's *The Growth of White Collar Unionism*, where there are estimates of white-collar workers as a percentage of all workers, for manufacturing, 1948–64. Inspection of the data shows that the standard deviation of the annual changes in the percentage (roughly 0·35) is nearly as great as the mean change, or trend (slightly more than 0·4). This cannot reasonably be said to be a series dominated by its trend. It may be that such compositional variations are not related to union growth, but elementary reasoning and an examination of the raw data both suggest that they should be considered at greater length than was done in the book.

Thirdly, there is their reaction to my criticism of their treatment of the non-linear relationship between inflation and union growth. I have looked again at p. 84 and p. 108, but still cannot find any reason for this interesting empirical result. What I saw again was a restatement of the result masquerading as an explanation. Thus, on p. 84 we read 'high rates of inflation tend to numb people's sensitivity to price rises'. It is difficult to see how this is an explanation of workers' diminishing responsiveness in the face of increasing inflation. Similarly, on p. 104 we read that British (and Swedish) workers, having experienced more of it, are 'more blase' and 'less sensitive' to inflation than are American workers. This is nothing more than a verbal expression of the empirical finding; it is certainly not an explanation of it.

Fourthly, there is my unease about the problem of simultaneity. Here, Elsheikh and Bain are inferring more than I suggested. All I wanted, and all I asked for, was that simultaneity 'might have been considered at some length', which Elsheikh and Bain do acknowledge. They are wrong to suggest that I did not understand pp. 117–18, and that I was unaware that more complex techniques than ordinary least squares raise their own problems. Whether, on balance, one uses ordinary least squares or another technique is a nice question, but making the choice does not necessarily eliminate the problem, and the consequences of possible simultaneity bias still need to be considered. For this study I can see difficulties with alternative techniques, but I would have preferred a more extended defence and more discussion of the implications for statistical inference of using OLS than Bain and Elsheikh provide. [. . .]

On the disaggregations by sex, I must first deal with the proposition that it is not legitimate to evaluate aggregate models by certain

279

disaggregations. This, as a general argument, seems to me to be wholly without foundation. For Elsheikh and Bain to use it is particularly surprising because the analysis in their book is in terms of individual reactions to particular events, e.g. unemployment or inflation. Thus, it begins as a highly disaggregated model. It is clear that for very narrow sections of the labour force, specific circumstances might have an overwhelming influence, thus making an unamended aggregate model work badly in explaining behaviour. If, however, one considers groups of eight or thirteen million workers, widely dispersed throughout the economy, there is no obvious reason why the general arguments of a successful aggregate model should not have explanatory power. In my view, such a disaggregation is legitimate and helps one to assess the robustness of the approach. To put it another way, if I have one theory to explain union growth among females and a second one to explain it among males, how do I arrive at a unified aggregate theory for the whole labour force? [. . .]

Overall my view of the book is not changed by Elsheikh and Bain's reply; it is an interesting but flawed work, having an unsatisfactory theoretical basis, an inadequate discussion of the consequences of (UK) data imperfections and empirical results that are on the surface satisfactory but less convincing when analysed further.

21 R. Undy, V. Ellis, W. E. J. McCarthy and A. M. Halmos

The Role of Union Leadership in Membership Growth: Further Criticisms of Bain's Theory

From R. Undy, V. Ellis, W. E. J. McCarthy and A. M. Halmos, *Change in Trade Unions: The Development of UK Unions Since 1960*, Hutchinson, 1981, pp. 163–6 and 349–50.

The conditions of natural growth

It can be seen that individual union growth was clearly affected by both external and internal factors in the period studied. Some unions' patterns of growth were therefore influenced by whether or not they had an historical presence in industries and/or among occupations that became more inclined to join unions in the 1960s and 1970s.

However, it cannot be said that a union necessarily grew faster than any other union just because it had an historical presence in areas favourable to growth. Unions in such areas, such as the 'open' TGWU and the GMWU, had quite different growth rates. Moreover, even unions with a near monopoly in favourable areas, such as NALGO and the POEU, were not just receivers of new members. It was thus only the exceptional NUM that found its size largely, if not solely, determined by external factors.

Unions generally affected their growth, in both multi-union and single-union job territories, by engaging or not engaging in the activities identified above as producing growth. The fact that some unions in the early part of the period did not undertake these activities on a national scale gave other more consistently growth-oriented unions major advantages. Thus the restrictionist–passive GMWU's initial 'benefit oriented' approach to membership provided their main competitor, the positive–expansionist TGWU, with the opportunity fully to exploit its organizational advantages.

One of the primary conditions for achieving relatively high union growth was thus a national leadership oriented and committed to growth as a priority. However, commitment alone was not a sufficient condition. Those committed to expansion had to have control of the means of acquiring a high rate of national growth if they were to realize their ambitions. The internal system of decision-making in the TGWU and ASTMS provided such opportunities.

Both the bifurcated TGWU and ASTMS provided their general secretaries with a concentrated and centralized (in the non-bargaining channel) government eminently suitable for the purpose of influencing growth. The general secretaries dominated the general policy-making channels and thus easily spread their growth ethic throughout the bureaucracy and into the lay ranks. They could virtually guarantee that the appointed full-time officers followed the national policy on expansion. Moreover, the national leadership in both unions was firmly in favour of using more militant and local bargaining policies to identify the union with the domestic needs of its actual and potential members. They believed in the service rather than the benefit-oriented approach to membership. The image projected by their unions was therefore in sharp contrast to that of some of their less demonstrative competitors.

It is not surprising therefore that the pattern of growth was uneven between unions recruiting in similar circumstances. Unions differed according to whether or not the national or regional leadership made growth a priority. They also differed in the degree to which their centralized–decentralized and concentrated–diffused systems of government allowed the leadership to achieve their goals – Jones in the GMWU, for example, would not have achieved the same growth effect as he did in the TGWU. Unions themselves therefore to a great degree shaped the conditions for growth between 1960 and 1975.

We turn now to the implications our findings have for aggregate union growth. The emphasis in recent theories (e.g. Bain, 1970) has tended to be on external factors as the key, and only, variable influencing aggregate union growth. For instance, in examining white-collar union growth it was concluded that 'No significant relationship was found between the growth of aggregate white-collar unionism and any of the following factors (including such aspects of trade unions as their public image, recruitment policies and structures)'[1]; and similar conclusions were reached regarding total union growth when it was claimed that such 'indirect and secondary factors as union leadership are largely dependent upon and hence captured by the explanatory variables (that is, rate of change of prices, rate of change of wages, the level and/or rate of change of unemployment and the level of union density)'.[2]

1. Bain (1970), p. 183.
2. Bain and Elsheikh (1976), p. 117.

There are, of course, some important differences in the method we used to assess the causes of disaggregated growth and those used by the above theorists to identify the causes of aggregated growth of unions. At the disaggregated level, we asked different questions. We did not, as can be clearly seen above, rely on the statistical methods employed in the aggregate studies. Further, we chose a different length and period of time and concentrated on the British situation to the exclusion of international comparisons. Nevertheless, despite these methodological and other differences, it would seem to us that there is *prima facie* a conflict between the Bain *et al.* general theory of growth and our more limited findings regarding the factors that influence disaggregated growth. It would seem from our research, to put it no stronger, that unions' structure, government, policy and leadership significantly affect disaggregated and aggregated union growth.

Our analysis of disaggregated growth challenges the above aggregate theory in the following manner. If those individual unions that influenced their own growth rates did not do so at the expense of the 'received' expansion of their own or other unions, trade union variables can be said to have influenced aggregate growth. It is, moreover, highly unlikely that all or most of the achieved growth mentioned above occurred at the expense of received growth. Indeed, it was more often than not at the expense of continuing non-unionism. For instance, NALGO's recruitment of additional members in local government through the adoption of a closed shop policy was definitely not at their own or any other union's expense. There were no other unions in local government capable of recruiting these non-unionized workers. Similarly, the extension of the 100 per cent shop by the POEU directly affected its size. Furthermore, the general development by virtually all unions studied of the check-off system and consequent reduction in union turnover can be quite confidently claimed to have been largely at the expense of continuing non-unionism. Also, ASTMS's and the TGWU's selective recruitment efforts in areas of non-unionism, and the extension of the shop steward system in the TGWU and certain regions of the GMWU and UCATT, almost certainly positively affected their membership growth without depriving other unions of an immediate membership increase.

Growth associated with strike action was also generally at the expense of non-unionism. Moreover, the extension of the closed shop and the check off meant that the sudden leap in membership often associated with strike action could be consolidated in many cases into a more long-term membership gain.

And, as explained above, underlying this aggressive recruitment activity was the advent of a new growth-conscious leadership. This leadership, for instance, Jones of the TGWU and Jenkins of ASTMS, was also willing to accelerate local and shop steward involvement in the bargaining process. This resulted in the enhancement of the role of the most effective recruiting agent – the shop steward. Moreover, in the most flexible union, ASTMS, highly selective recruitment campaigns were used to attract into membership members who previously found it extremely difficult to associate themselves with trade unionism. It is difficult to believe that these combinations of activities did not help ASTMS to acquire members by more effectively penetrating parts of the non-unionized workforce normally adverse to unionism.

Thus, although our examination of various kinds of disaggregated growth in a limited number of unions cannot be used as conclusive evidence as to the factors affecting total union growth, it can be used to suggest that growth in the UK over the period examined was to some significant extent influenced by union leadership and other facets of union organization. This suggests that aggregate theories that discount internal factors may be oversimplifying the causes of union growth.

Finally, the above arguments regarding the influence of unions over aggregate growth are somewhat strengthened when the activities of the TGWU and ASTMS are placed within the wider context of unions' general attitudes and practices vis-à-vis membership in the 1970s. Because both the TGWU and ASTMS were relatively 'open' and recruited in exposed territories, they disturbed the inter-union status quo. This stimulated a competitive recruitment contest, similar and related to that in the merger movement intended to restore the numerical balance. Furthermore, the advent of a more growth-conscious leadership in the GMWU – both nationally and regionally – also fed inter-union rivalries; and unions' needs for more representative (numerical) muscle in the TUC, for example, during discussions in the Social Contract, further heightened the membership contest. Also, inflation and other developments adversely affected some unions' financial standing and hence forced them to adopt a more effective means of retaining and acquiring members.

Thus individual unions' initial success in creating the conditions for their own growth caused others to emulate their self-help activities.

Out of this concern for comparative numerical strength a growth spiral developed which, it can be very reasonably suggested, made a significant contribution to aggregate growth. It also, no doubt, brought home to a number of union leaders the advantages that their counterparts in the more concentrated and centralized (in the non-bargaining channel) unions enjoyed. [. . .]

Bain's data are drawn from many different countries and his time spans are much longer than ours – sometimes stretching back into the nineteenth century. More importantly, his methodology is totally different and his concentration on the quantitative necessarily means that his results and inferences cannot easily be compared with ours. Nevertheless, we find it impossible to accept the clear implication in much of his work that unions are relatively powerless to affect the aggregate level of unionization by positive and deliberate action. Above all, we cannot square his verdict on the role of union leadership with our evidence. As he puts it, 'union leadership is dependent upon and constrained by the same socioeconomic forces which motivate or enable workers to join trade unions. As such it is very much a secondary or derivative determinant of aggregate union growth.'

The evidence of our study is that unions are able to 'achieve' a substantial increase in membership through their own efforts. We also cannot agree that several of Bain's external factors work in the unselective way he suggests – at least not at our level of analysis. For example, he considers that inflation acts as a general inducement or 'threat' – driving workers into unions to protect standards, and making employers more willing to recognize them. We would rather emphasize the different ways in which inflation can affect particular unions – most obviously UCATT, which found it difficult to maintain services or increase subscriptions in a period of rising prices. But in contrast to UCATT we would cite the experience of NALGO, where inflation contributed to a more aggressive bargaining and recruitment policy; or the TGWU, where it helped to strengthen the case for relying on servicing by shop stewards, because they were relatively cheap. Yet in other unions – for instance, the GMWU – inflation was easily absorbed, and appears to have made little impact on attitudes to growth for some considerable time.

Similarly, Bain argues that the rate of growth in money wages has an overall or 'credit effect' on union membership – since would-be members credit unions with general money increases, and so hurry to join them. This may happen in some instances, but our research indicates that in respect of UCATT, for example, higher money wages actually undermined unionization. Most building workers came to feel that in periods of rapidly rising prices they did not need organization and were better placed if they sought to negotiate individual 'lump' contracts with non-union employers. It was not until the leadership of UCATT became convinced of the need to undertake militant action to combat this process that membership stabilized.

In sum, then, we would argue that our studies throw doubt on how far macro-statistical analysis can provide a full explanation for the complex of factors that affect union growth, both at the level of trade union movement as a whole and in relative terms. As Bain admits in his latest contribution to the subject, his is a theory that stresses both the 'propensity and the opportunity to organize'. What it fails to do is to find sufficient room for the determination and the will to organize, and the critical role of leadership.

What we think is needed, at this stage, is not a more developed or refined analytical framework, including further macro-variables, but a study that seeks to combine our kind of evidence with Bain's kind of data – perhaps carried out at an intermediate level, where it is possible to distinguish between the relative impact of internal and external factors in contrasting situations.

References

BAIN, G. S. (1970), *The Growth of White Collar Unionism*, Oxford University Press.
BAIN, G. S., and F. ELSHEIKH (1976), *Union Growth and the Business Cycle*, Blackwell.

Part Six

The Economic Effects of Trade Unionism

The following nine extracts are concerned with three different issues. The first three consider the adequacy of the conventional tools of economic theory when used to describe trade union behaviour in the labour market. The next two summarize some of the results of studies designed to establish how far unions can be said to have influenced both the general level of wages and the wages of their members. The last four are all contributions to the highly topical debate about the impact of trade unions on the economy.

Reading 22 comprises the latest attempt of a well-informed neoclassicist to argue the case for the retention of economic theory. Arthur Rees fully appreciates that union goals are not the same as those of firms or the individual entrepreneur assumed by traditional economic theory. He explains how a union's relations with its members and potential members are unlike those between a company and its shareholders or customers. Yet he remains convinced that economic notions such as 'marginal analysis' and 'monopoly rent' can still be employed to construct a meaningful 'model' of union wage policy. He believes that 'the value of the concept of profit maximization as a point of departure is very great'.

Arthur Ross will have none of this in his seminal contribution to the debate. The concepts of traditional theory, with their focus on the attainment of 'equilibrium' and their assumption of the 'maximization' of benefits, confuse rather than illuminate. The central fact to grasp is that unions are 'political' institutions that happen to operate in an economic environment. Consequently, the considerations that determine their actions in relation to wage settlements are themselves political: i.e. the maintenance of the leadership in office and the organizational survival of the union. Pursuit of these objectives undoubtedly has an economic impact, but this is not primarily the concern of the union or its members.

No short extract can do justice to the subtlety and persuasiveness of Ross; serious students of the subject can be divided into those who take his point, and those who never quite appreciate what he is trying to say. More often than not he has been ignored by the great majority of economists – some of whom are represented here. He is now out of print, but remains as relevant as ever.

Reading 24 contains the doubts of a distinguished economic historian. Peter Mathias surveys the inability of 'economists down the years' to 'test what effect trade unions have in practice had on wages'. He includes in his list such names as Smith, Marx, Marshall and Keynes. He also doubts whether the methods of contemporary econometricians can be expected to produce more convincing, or precise, results. The problem lies in the number of variables to be taken into account, and the obstinate way the labour market has of not responding as it should to changes in supply, demand or price. Yet we cannot assume from this that unions have no significant disadvantageous effects, or that nothing should be done about them.

In Reading 25 Henry Phelps Brown, the doyen of labour economists, summarizes what is known about general movements in pay and variations in union power and strength in a number of comparable economies. His contribution is also one that is retained from the first edition, since in compression and scope it has not been improved upon. Studies show that in periods of relative union strength the general level of wages has risen significantly more than might be expected 'under the influence of the trade cycle and the market environment alone'. Yet the ability of unions to influence money wages in general has not usually entailed a similar impact on real wages. These have continued to be 'governed by productivity'.

In Reading 26 Charles Mulvey summarizes the evidence for a similar impact of unions on relative wages – in particular, 'whether or not, and in what degree, trade unions have raised the wages of their members above those paid to similar non-union workers'. The conclusions are that there is usually a positive union wage differential, but that it has been calculated as varying 'in the region of 0–40 per cent'. Mulvey discusses the many measurement problems that could explain some or most of these differences.

The next two readings are from well-known general economists who believe that union power is the sole or main factor preventing the labour market from 'clearing' as other markets are supposed to do. In effect, union wage bargaining is said to prevent the price of labour from falling to a level where employers can be persuaded to take on additional workers, thus eliminating or reducing the existing surplus.

In Reading 27 F. A. Hayek asserts that union power has under-

The Economic Effects of Trade Unionism

mined competitiveness and destroyed full employment in post-war Britain. For 'full employment cannot be maintained by preserving a conventional, outdated wage structure, but only by adjusting wages in each sector to changing demands – raising some wages by lowering others'.

It is to be noted that Hayek makes no mention of the multiplicity of other influences which combine to prevent labour markets clearing even where there are no trade unions. He also assumes that the collective strength of different groups of workers has little or nothing to do with their importance in the production process, so that the effectiveness of strike action to support wage claims varies from group to group. His view is that power reposes with trade union leaders who 'owe their power precisely to the scope for abusing privileges which the law has granted them'. (This notion is discussed further in Part Seven of the readings.)

In Reading 28 Patrick Minford adopts a slightly more complex theory of causation, but comes to the same conclusion. The responsiveness of the labour market to changes in price is also said to be affected by the existence of flat-rate unemployment benefit, which prevents unemployed non-unionists from accepting jobs at rates that are profitable to employers. But despite this influence Minford argues that it is still the increase in union power which has led to 'an 8·5 per cent reduction in output and the destruction of a million jobs since 1963'.

Minford's measure of union power is the percentage of the labour force unionized. He calculates that this rose by 13 per cent between 1963 and 1979, during which time unemployment rose by more than a million. It is as well to remember that since the early eighties unions have been losing members and have faced declining densities; yet over the same period unemployment has risen by more than two million.

In Reading 29 Brian Burkitt presents a very different view to that of Hayek or Minford. In so far as workers have power this is the result of a variety of factors present in their work situation. Effective power is confined to those who 'perform crucial tasks and are supported by cohesive organizations'. In general, unions 'are weaker than employers, whose possession of the means of production enables them to command decision-making procedures'. It follows that attempts to reduce union power by law are based on 'a severely flawed analysis' which cannot hope to achieve its long-term objectives. Any 'temporary achievements are likely to be gained at the expense of the less privileged'.

Finally, in Reading 30, Karel Williams and others summarize the findings of numerous field studies dealing with the factors that have contributed to Britain's poor economic performance since the war, with a view to forming an estimate of the relative importance of 'bloody-minded workers and their unions'. They conclude that while there may well have been a lack of 'management control over the labour process', this need not have been the result of union action. It also does not follow that imperfect labour input has resulted in 'significant penalties in terms of cost, output or quality'. On the contrary, most studies suggest that in Britain relatively ineffectual managers failed to overcome a series of much more important obstacles which had nothing whatever to do with cost and price advantages, in the labour market or elsewhere: e.g. the policies of British banks, the consequence of the merger boom of the fifties and the fragmentation of the domestic product market.

22 A. Rees

Economic Functions and Objectives

From A. Rees, *The Economics of Work and Pay*, Harper & Row, 1973, pp. 125–37.

Formal models of union objectives

Unions and collective bargaining now play a central role in the determination of wage levels and wage structures, as well as in many other aspects of the employment relation. About 30 per cent of non-agricultural employees have been union members in recent years, and the effects of collective bargaining extend beyond the limits of its coverage.

Our discussion will focus on the economic functions of the trade union to the exclusion of its role as a social and political institution. Even within the area of collective bargaining, nothing will be said about such topics as grievance machinery and seniority. The omitted areas are extremely important, of course, but the kind of analysis useful in dealing with them is very different from the somewhat formal economic analysis used here.

What is left to consider is the role of unions in determining wages and the level of employment. A union's concern with the total amount of employment is part of its broader concern with job scarcity and job security. The term *job security* includes the union's concern for the distribution of employment among members and for the job tenure of the individual members. In formal models, however, the focus is limited to the less inclusive goals of increasing total employment and expanding union membership; thus the models represent what may be an excessively narrow view of the union's concern with employment. But even in the narrowed field remaining, the formal models are not always successful.

In discussing the demand for labor in Part II, we used as a starting point the model of the profit-maximizing firm. This model must sometimes be modified, especially for large firms whose policies are directed by managers rather than by owners. Nevertheless, the value of the concept of profit maximization as a point of departure for analysis is very great.

It is much more difficult, if not impossible, to analyze union behavior by constructing a simple model of a trade union as a maximizer of anything, which implies a single goal common to the entire organization. Far more than the firm, the union is both an economic and a political entity. Though ultimate power nominally rests with stockholders in the corporation and with members in the union, both corporate management and union leadership play critical roles in determining policy. But in many unions wage bargains must be taken back to the membership for ratification, and leadership decisions are not always routinely endorsed. As a tactic in negotiation with management, leaders may sometimes send agreements back for ratification knowing that they are unacceptable; at other times they are genuinely surprised by the repudiation of a bargain they firmly believed to be the best obtainable. In contrast, corporate management and directors have full authority to negotiate wages without consulting the stockholders. In the long run they may suffer if they make a bad bargain, but in the short run their decisions will not be challenged.

Furthermore, the union leader faces greater risks than the corporate director when he seeks re-election. In corporations the rule of one share, one vote makes it very expensive to challenge management by soliciting proxies where management controls large blocks of stock. In contrast, the one man, one vote rule of unions, though it does not eliminate the advantages of incumbents, poses greater potential threats. In recent years three major American national unions have had their presidents replaced in contested elections in which the incumbent lost: the United Steelworkers; the International Union of Electrical Workers; and the State, County, and Municipal Workers.

The sharing of power in the union between leadership and membership creates difficulties in constructing a formal model of union behavior because there may be differences in aims or emphasis between leaders and the rank and file. The leader wants to head a large and stable organization and to expand its membership; he may become interested in extending his personal influence in the larger labor movement or on the national political scene. The members, on the other hand, are interested primarily in job security, higher wages, and good working conditions. And union leaders pursue these goals as well as their personal goals – both because they believe in them and because their own jobs may be threatened if they do not.

A second source of difficulty in constructing a formal model of union behavior is that the gains won by unions in collective bargaining do not go to the organization as such but to the individual members

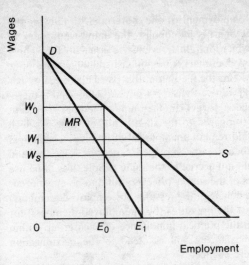

Figure 1 Two maximizing models of union wages goals.

directly, and there is no mechanism for the secondary redistribution of these gains. This is in sharp contrast with the corporation, where profits go to the firm before there is any distribution to stockholders. Some profits – often a major part of the total – are not distributed at all, and profits made in one establishment or activity within the corporation can be used in expanding another.

Keeping these difficulties in mind, we can now consider possible formal models of union wage policy. It is sometimes suggested that a union should behave like a product-market monopolist. Figure 1 illustrates such behavior. The curve D is the downward-sloping demand curve for union labor. Where all the firms producing for a given market are organized, the demand curve for union labor is determined by the factors that were considered in Part II. Where some of the firms in a product market are not organized, an increase in wages in the organized sector will enlarge the share of the non-union firms in total sales of the product, and this indirect substitution of non-union for union labor will make the demand for union labor more elastic than in the case of complete organization. The line labelled S is a horizontal supply curve of union labor to one firm, and MR is the *marginal revenue* curve corresponding to D, which shows the addition to the total wage bill produced by lowering the wage just

293

enough to permit the employment of one more man.[1] Following the analogue of the product-market monopolist, the union would seek to set the wage W_0, at which marginal revenue is equal to the supply price of labor. For a product-market monopolist, the analogous price would maximize profit. But for the union, this particular equality has no meaning. Wage W_0 is above the supply price of labor and is therefore more than is needed to get another union member to accept employment. But, as compared to the slightly higher wage at which one more member would remain unemployed, it involves a small loss in wages to each member already employed. Since the wage loss and the employment gain do not accrue to the same people, it is of no use to treat wages in excess of the supply price as a fund to be maximized. The union leader must balance the pressures (by employed members) for higher wages against the pressures (by unemployed members) for work, keeping in mind the political importance of each group within the union – and this balancing will not lead to the maximization solution, except by mere chance.

The rule sometimes suggested that unions should try to maximize the wage bill is even worse. This would involve setting employment at E_1 where MR is zero; if the demand for union labor is elastic at the non-union wage, the corresponding wage, W_1, will be below the wage W_s that would prevail with no union. It is impossible to see why any union membership or honest union leadership would want such a solution. Nor would the employer want it, since he would be unable to recruit labor.

The difficulties of a maximization model can be illustrated more clearly by considering the case of an industrial union that includes two distinct classes of members – a small group of craftsmen and a large group of operatives. We assume that the demand for craftsmen is very inelastic and that the demand for operatives is quite elastic. The product-market analogue is the case of the discriminating monopolist selling the same product in two separate markets. Here the solution that maximizes profit is to have marginal revenue in each market equal to the common marginal cost or supply price, which implies a higher price in the market where demand is less elastic. But if the union makes large wage gains for its craft members and small ones

1. This diagram has been adapted from Cartter (1959), p. 80. The slope of the supply curve has been changed for simplicity. It should be emphasized that Cartter presents the model only for discussion and does not believe it to be the most plausible one.

or none for the more numerous operatives, it has no way to channel part of the craft gains to the others. Such a policy will therefore put the union leaders in severe political trouble. They are forced to settle for a smaller total gain more equitably distributed, and there is good evidence that for this reason the craft members of industrial unions sometimes fare badly (see Rees and Schultz, 1970, ch. 10).

A more promising way to look at the formation of union wage goals is to regard them as influenced by at least two separate elements: the size of union membership and the wage level. The goals in question here are those for which the union is prepared to strike if necessary, as distinguished from initial bargaining demands, which may far exceed what the union expects to get. The relative weights to be attached to membership and wages will vary from union to union, with more weight given to the size of the membership in industrial unions than is given in craft unions, and more weight given to size of membership in unions that are interested in social and political reform than is given in so-called business unions interested largely in advancing the position of their own present members.

If we had chosen wages and employment, rather than wages and membership, as the two principal elements in the formation of union goals, we could have assumed from the downward slope of the demand curve for union labor that they were negatively related, and we could then have drawn a preference function like an indifference curve expressing the rate at which the union is willing to trade one of these goals for the other (such functions are drawn in Cartter, 1959, pp. 86–94). However, when a union has not organized its entire potential jurisdiction, the potential gains in membership from a policy of high wages, which is helpful in extending organization, could in some cases more than offset the contraction of employment among present members. In such a case the national leadership of the union (though not necessarily the local leadership) would prefer the high-wage strategy on both counts.

An interesting example of different choices made by two national unions facing apparently similar circumstances is afforded by events in the meat-packing industry in the early 1960s. Some major firms in the industry threatened to close a number of unprofitable unionized plants unless the unions agreed to wage reductions. The local unions concerned reacted differently to these threats, depending on local labor-market conditions. However, the Amalgamated Meat Cutters and Butcher Workmen persuaded its local unions to accept wage reductions, because it had organized many small plants, especially in the South, that faced competition from low-wage, non-union firms. It felt that it could grow only through a wage policy of moderation. In contrast, the United Packinghouse Workers influenced its locals to refuse the wage cuts and to accept the plant shutdowns. It was interested in organizing large new independent packing companies in the Midwest and felt that it could best do so by a policy of militance.[2] If the case of the United Packinghouse Workers were analyzed as a choice between wages and employment, it would appear that employment had no weight in the union's preference function. When employment is replaced by membership as the second element of the preference function, both elements play a role.

Factors influencing wage policy

One important feature of union wage policy is the critical role of the current money wage. A union will almost always insist on maintaining the current wage even at the cost of severe contraction in employment, whereas it would not insist on increasing the money wage if the consequences for employment were anything like as severe. In other words, the weight given to the size of membership or employment is much smaller for wage cuts than for wage increases. This downward rigidity of the money wage now extends to non-union portions of the economy as well, perhaps in part because non-union employers have feared that wage reductions would encourage unionization. There have been no general reductions in money wages in any important industry since the early 1930s, though there have been several moderately severe recessions and a number of major industries have had declining employment.

Unions have occasionally agreed to wage reductions at the firm or establishment level, when there has been a threat that an establishment would shut down or be relocated combined with the promise that a wage reduction would avert this. Such a position will seem credible only when taken by a management with whom the union has had good relations. Even in such cases, the union can agree only if the concession to one firm does not provide an occasion for other unionized employers to demand similar treatment. For this reason, a union cannot make wage concessions to one employer in a group engaged in multi-employer bargaining. However, it can try to help one

---

2. This paragraph is based on the unpublished doctoral dissertation of Hervey Juris, Graduate School of Business, University of Chicago.

employer improve productivity, which is a much less visible kind of concession.

As Keynes pointed out in the *General Theory*, union resistance to cuts in real wages that arise from increases in the level of consumer prices is much less rapid and less complete than resistance to cuts in money wages. A money wage cut initiated or proposed by an employer is a direct affront, because it always involves cutting wages relative to wages elsewhere. In contrast, a fall in real wages produced by an increase in the price level is impersonal, because it affects everyone. Moreover, it is not immediately perceived. This does not mean that unions or their members are so much the victims of money illusion that they will not respond to prolonged or severe rises in consumer prices. Once they have passed some threshold, such price rises will strengthen union demands for wage increases and may also assist unions in organizing new industries and areas (see Ashenfelter and Johnson, 1969, and Hamermesh, 1970).

The wage demands of any one union are strongly influenced by comparisons with other groups of workers with whom there have been traditional parities or differentials. The logic of such comparisons is often open to question – for any group, wage comparisons can be made in many directions. The unions will, of course, try to make those most favorable to a wage increase, while the management will make those least favorable. But once a particular comparison has been long accepted as equitable, it becomes very difficult to change. For example, in both the United States and Great Britain there are cities with a long tradition that policemen and firemen receive the same salary. At this equal salary it has sometimes been very difficult to recruit policemen, while there has been a long waiting list of candidates for posts in the fire department. Some public employers have reacted to this by trying to give a differential increase to policemen, but in several cases they have eventually been forced to extend the wage increase to firemen as well. The shortage of policemen could be alleviated only by increasing the excess supply of firemen (see Turner, 1964, p. 124, and Devine, 1969, p. 543).

Nevertheless, established wage relationships sometimes change even among unionized workers. Where a traditional differential has been established in absolute terms (cents per hour) rather than in percentage terms, its relative value is eroded by rises in the general level of money wages until it no longer is sufficient compensation for the extra training or responsibility of the more skilled group, while its real value in terms of purchasing power is eroded by rises in the price level. In such cases, the more highly-paid group may exert pressure to widen the absolute differential. Where the situation arises within one union, these efforts may take the form of attempts or threats to form a separate union. The special increases given to skilled craftsmen in some general wage settlements in the automobile industry are cases in point.

Demands of a particular group of union workers to achieve parity with a more highly-paid group doing comparable work often have particular force because worker sentiment is mobilized around a concrete goal rather than simply a demand for 'more'. The force of such definitions of equity in wage structures in forming union goals should be contrasted with the outcome of maximization models, in which there is no room for concepts of equity. The successful drive of Canadian automobile workers for wage parity with the American employees of the same companies is an example of such a goal (where parity was defined as the same number of dollars per hour in the two national currencies for the same work).

In the long run, the weight given by employers, the public, and other unions to claims for relative wage increases are likely to be influenced by labor market conditions. The claim of organized nurses or schoolteachers that their pay is inadequate to compensate them for their long training will clearly be more convincing when there is a shortage of labor in these professions than when there is not. But it is also true that a rather wide range of relative wages may be consistent with adequate supplies of workers to each of the trades concerned.

Employment goals and featherbedding

We have been assuming thus far that the union formulates its wage demands in collective bargaining on the expectation that the employer will be free to adjust his employment in response to whatever wage is agreed on. This amounts to assuming that the final position will lie on the demand curve for labor. Some unions, however, succeed in imposing rules that force the employer to use more labor than he would like to at the union wage; in other words, the employer is forced off the demand curve to the right. This possibility greatly enlarges the area of union choice in the formulation of its goals.

The practices by which unions create additional employment are called *restrictive working practices* or, more commonly, *featherbedding*. Such practices are formalized into rules largely among craft unions, though informal equivalents may exist at the plant level in some industrial unions. Featherbedding takes a number of closely related forms. The union may require the employment of men who do no work (for example, musicians' unions may require the employment of a local 'standby' band when a well-known traveling band is engaged).[3] In other cases unions require unnecessary work to be performed; for example, the 'bogus' rules of the typographical union make necessary the subsequent resetting of advertising material printed by newspapers from papier-mâché matrices received from outside.[4]

In other cases a union may refuse to permit the introduction of technological changes; thus most locals of the typographers' union have not allowed the setting of type by computers. Finally, the union may require that more men be used to do particular work than the employer thinks are needed. This is perhaps the most general form of restrictive work practice; an example is the musicians' unions' rules on the minimum size of orchestras.

The case of requiring a minimum number of men for a task is analyzed in Figure 2, using as an example the requirement once enforced by the Chicago local of the musicians that an orchestra for a musical show must consist of at least 18 men (see Countryman, 1948, p. 31, n. 43). The diagram shows the number of men who would be employed at each performance of a musical show at various wage rates. It is assumed that the musical would not be produced with an orchestra of fewer than 10 men; the demand curve is broken line ABC, which is vertical at an employment of 10 when the wage is $45 per performance or higher. The supply curve of competent musicians to any one producer in the absence of the union is assumed to be perfectly elastic at a wage of $15 per performance. In the non-union case the producer would choose point X, using an orchestra of 20 men. If the union simply imposed a wage of $30 per performance, with no further requirements, the producer would choose point Y, using only 15 men in the orchestra. By combining a union wage of $30 with the requirement that the orchestra consist of at least 18 men, the union forces the producer to point Z, which lies to the right of the demand curve.

3. For a discussion of working rules of the American Federation of Musicians as of 1948, see Countryman (1948), pt 1, pp. 56–8, and pt 2, pp. 239–97; reprinted in Weinstein (1965).

4. For a classic discussion of this long-standing practice, see Barnett (1909), pp. 435–819.

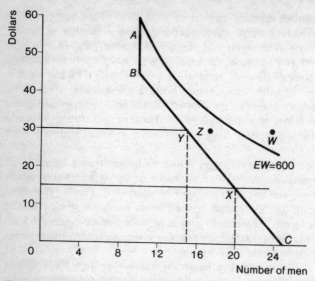

Figure 2 A hypothetical example of a featherbedding rule.

The union's ability to force the employer to spend more on his orchestra by a combination of wage demands and working practices must have a limit. At some point, the show would not be produced at all. In the diagram this limit is represented as a budget constraint consisting of a portion of the rectangular hyperbola $EW = \$600$, where E is employment and W is the wage. The producer would accept any point to the left of this rather than not produce the show; to the right, the cost of the orchestra would consume such a large portion of his expected gross revenue that the production would be unprofitable. Thus if the producer were confronted by a requirement that he use 24 men at $30 a performance (point W), he would not produce the show. The area above the supply curve lying between the demand curve and the budget-constraint hyperbola is the area in which the union can choose a wage–employment combination that would be accepted. Since the demand curve and budget constraint will differ from producer to producer and will not be known exactly to the union, the point chosen by the union does not necessarily lie on the budget constraint of any one producer.

It is important to note that by specifying employment per task, the union does not determine the total amount of employment of its members either for the industry or for the individual employer. Neither does the union specify the ratio of employment of its members to all other inputs.[5] In general, the union requires that its members be employed in fixed proportion to some *subset* of other inputs, and there may be substitution against this whole subset. At the industry level the union's employment requirement will raise costs and prices and will therefore lower output (the quantity of product demanded). In our example above, these forces can be represented both by a reduction in the number of shows produced and by a shortening of runs (number of performances), since a larger proportion of seats must be filled to justify extending a run. There will be a tendency to use larger houses for musical shows (a change in factor proportions), which will also contribute to shorter runs. For these reasons, a requirement of a specified number of men per performance is not guaranteed to increase total employment. If the requirement were set too high, it could depress total employment at any wage below what it would be in its absence. A clearer case of the failure of a union work rule to fix factor proportions is represented by the rules of railroad unions on the size of train crews, which specify the number of men per train. The ratio of capital to labor can be increased (and has been) by having more and larger cars per train.

Since true featherbedding represents a conspicuous waste of resources, it is understandably condemned by management, economists and the general public. In some cases, however, unions defend practices that appear to be featherbedding as necessary to protect the safety of workers or the public. The protection of union members from work hazards is an entirely legitimate union objective, and practices that in fact provide such protection should not be called featherbedding. An economist would nevertheless be inclined to insist that the added safety produced by these practices be obtained at reasonable cost – that is, it should meet the test of a careful benefit–cost analysis. The union is more likely to argue that life and health are priceless, to be guarded at any cost.

Featherbedding often has its origin in technical change that sharply reduces the employment of a particular craft. Such changes in employment may occur either because of new production processes in the

5. This suggests that much of the diagrammatic analysis of cases in which the union is said to specify either the level of employment or the ratio of employment to all other inputs represents wasted ingenuity. For example, see the articles by Weinstein and by N. S. Simler in Weinstein (1965).

industry where the craft is used or through the expansion of a competing industry. Thus television has reduced employment in the motion picture industry and the automobile and airplane have increasingly reduced employment in railroad passenger service, and unions in the declining industries have struggled to maintain employment. Union resistance to labor-saving technical change within an industry can often be moderated by careful management of change, which will minimize its effect in creating unemployment. This is much more difficult in the case of inter-industry effects, since an enterprise in one industry is unlikely to be concerned with the effects of its decisions on employment in another industry. Technical change often produces losses for investors who have invested in equipment and skills that are made obsolete. Where the investment is embodied in people rather than in machines, the human problems it causes are more severe and less tractable. Those outside the union movement cannot condone a position that blocks technical progress, but they can approve one that uses some of the fruits of progress to give reasonable compensation to workers for the loss of their livelihood.

References

ASHENFELTER, O., and G. E. JOHNSON (1969), 'Bargaining Theory, Trade Unions, and Industrial Strike Activity', *American Economic Review*, 59, March.

BARNETT, G. E. (1909), 'The Printers', *American Economic Association Quarterly*, third series, 10, no. 3, October.

CARTTER, A. M. (1959), *The Theory of Wages and Employment*, Irwin.

COUNTRYMAN, V. (1948), 'The Organized Musicians', *Chicago Law Review*, 16.

DEVINE, E. J. (1969), 'Manpower Shortages in Local Government Employment', *American Economic Review*, 59, May.

HAMERMESH, D. (1970), 'Wage Bargains, Threshold Effects and the Phillips Curve', *Quarterly Journal of Economics*, August.

REES, A., and G. P. SCHULTZ (1970), *Workers and Wages in an Urban Labor Market*, University of Chicago Press.

TURNER, H. A. (1964), 'Inflation and Wage Differentials in Great Britain', *The Theory of Wage Determination*, ed. J. T. Dunlop, Macmillan.

WEINSTEIN, P. A. (1965), ed., *Featherbedding and Technological Change*, Heath.

23 Arthur M. Ross

Trade Unions and the Theory of Wages

From Arthur M. Ross, *Trade Union Wage Policy*, University of California Press, 1948, pp. 294–311.

If it is good procedure to move from the known to the unknown, the best point of departure for the present study is a familiar and well-accepted fact: we no longer have a satisfactory theory of wages.

Two generations ago, economists were assured that they had, in the marginal productivity theory, not only an explanation of the way in which wages are determined, but also a description of a natural and harmonious system of distributive justice (Clark, 1899). Wages were the price of labor, fixed through the interaction of supply and demand in the labor market. Labor was apportioned among various lines of employment in such a manner as to maximize total output and was compensated in accordance with its marginal contribution.

Even then there were skeptics – socialists, institutionalists and proponents of the 'bargain theory of wages' – yet the doctrine was not seriously challenged in academic halls. Early modifications were made handily and appeared to be in the nature of refinements and improvements. It was readily conceded that the long-run labor supply, in Western societies at least, is governed by social customs regarding the size of the family and the employment of women and children. To account for the conspicuous absence of a single price, various compartments were described, within which mobility was regarded as great, and between which, as little. Thus, occupational differentials were explained by the existence of non-competing groups. Geographical differentials were explained by the immobility of labor between nations, regions and labor market areas. [. . .]

Among the obstrusive facts of industrial life, the trade union has been perhaps the most difficult to absorb into the theory of wages. In order to fit the union into a supply-and-demand theory, we have had to regard it as a seller in the market dispensing labor supply. The wage objectives of the union as a seller of labor have been variously dealt with. Marshall (1890, p. 627 of 8th edn) regarded the upper limit of the wage bargain as established by the necessity of retaining a sufficient supply of 'capital and business power' in the industry. Some authors describe union strategy as essentially defensive, designed to redress the unequal bargaining power of the individual worker and to restore the wage rate more nearly to the level which would have prevailed in a competitive market. Others, following the Webbs, conceive a union policy as the establishment of a 'standard rate' as a bulwark against the 'higgling of the market'. In Hicks's *Theory of Wages* (1932, p. 154), the union strives to obtain the highest wage rate possible, in view of the relative withholding power of workers and employers, without substantial concern over the danger of unemployment. More elaborate systems have been constructed by such authors as Edgeworth, Pigou, Hicks and Tintner, who deal with union and employer wage policy as an exercise in bilateral monopoly (see Edgeworth, 1881, pt 2, pp. 15–56; Hicks, 1935; Pigou, 1905, pp. 210–27; Tintner, 1939). The union is concerned with quantity sold as well as with price and pursues the objective of maximum total wage income.[1] Upper and lower limits of the wage bargain are represented; the final wage rate lies indeterminately within these limits and rests upon the balance of bargaining power. Perhaps the most complete of the purely economic formulations has been made by Dunlop (1944), who surveys a number of possible objects of maximization, considers a variety of competitive situations in addition to bilateral monopoly and analyses the determinants of bargaining power.

Thus, the treatment of union wage policy in economic literature presents a congeries of hazily related themes, operating under different assumptions and influenced by different social and economic preconceptions. We are reminded of the complaint by Hamilton and May (1923, p. 103) that 'there are just as many theories of wages, reputable and disreputable, as there are books and articles on the subject'. Nevertheless, we find in each instance a rudimentary concept of a labor monopoly seeking to achieve some single, quantitative objective.

Each of the listed objectives is open to serious doubt. It is clear from the situation in the coal and railroad industries that unions do not regard it as their obligation under all circumstances to protect the supply of 'capital and business power'; one often hears that 'a living wage is the first claim upon the proceeds of an industry'. To describe the objective as reducing inequalities and restoring a

---

1. Professor William Fellner (1947) has a formulation in which the union strives for the highest rate rather than the highest wage income.

competitive wage rate offers no clue to union behavior in the usual situation in which there is no competitive rate. Similarly, emphasis upon the standard rate as a bulwark against wage cutting is more in the nature of espousal than explanation. Many unions do not have a standard rate, but prefer to charge what the market will bear by classifying employers according to their ability to pay; and almost all unions are more interested in the process of achieving uniformity than in uniformity itself. In any case, the doctrine of the standard rate does not explain the particular level which is chosen as a standard.

To state that the union seeks the highest possible wage is true in a formal sense, but does not define the limited objectives established in particular cases nor explain the practical decisions made in the bargaining process. It does not permit us to analyse the behavior of many unions which are virtually in a position to set wage rates unilaterally. As already mentioned, the bilateral monopoly approach will be criticized in detail in a later chapter. It will suffice at this point to say that the union is not a seller of labor and is not mechanically concerned with the quantity sold and that the upper and lower limits of bilateral monopoly theory have no more than a superficial correspondence with the union's initial demand and the employer's initial offer in collective bargaining. As a matter of fact, many of the most interesting questions concerning union behavior cannot be answered by any strictly economic analysis – why the most compelling wage comparisons often have so little to do with labor market competition, why unions strike over small differences, why some wage differentials are ignored although others are attacked, why it is important to unions that they achieve higher real wages through higher money wages, and so on. [. . .]

It is commonplace that wage rates are now determined by conscious human decision rather than by impersonal market forces. In a formal sense, this has always been true; even the most impersonal forces can operate only through human agencies. A more significant question is whether the human agencies are the servants or the masters of the market forces. In an unorganized economic society, they are likely to be the servants. But there is a persistent tendency toward rational organization in sufficient strength to achieve a degree of mastery. Prominent in many spheres of economic life, rational organization operates not only through private associations, but also through the coercive authority of the State.

Mastery of market forces requires the power of consolidated decision. A little decision is merely the choice to be swept along in a stream; a big decision can redirect the stream itself. Hence the large business unit, which endeavors to control supply, creates demand and shapes the institutional environment in which it does business. Hence also the labor union and the other evidences of consolidated decision-making power over the 'terms and conditions of employment'.

There is real decision-making power in collective bargaining today. Negotiated wages vitally affect the allocation of labor and other productive resources, the level of prices and the size of national income. It is not necessary to look back to Marshall's day to appreciate the change which has taken place. Until recently, the specter of non-union competition hovered over the bargaining table and severely limited the extent to which union wages could rise without disastrous consequences; this was a major theme of Slichter's *Union Policies and Industrial Management*, which was published in 1941 and was based primarily on the experience of the 1920s and 1930s. By 1946 more than 80 per cent of the wage earners were covered by union agreement in each of the following industries (among others): agricultural equipment, aircraft, aluminum, cement, men's clothing, women's clothing, glass and glassware, leather tanning, meat packing, newspapers, non-ferrous metals, rubber, shipbuilding, basic steel, local transit, coalmining, construction, long-shoring, maritime, metal mining, motion-picture production, railroads and trucking. The unionization of one industry does not eliminate the competition of substitute products or services; however, the substitute products themselves may well be produced in an organized industry. The steel, aluminum and non-ferrous metals industries are all more than 80 per cent organized; the same is true of the railroad, maritime, trucking and airline industries (*Monthly Labour Review*, vol. 64, 1947, pp. 765–70). [. . .]

What is most needed is an informed prediction of union behavior in the economic and political circumstances of a full-employment policy, based upon an adequate understanding of the major controlling influences.

The major influences controlling union wage policy are largely the same as the major influences controlling union behavior in general. To understand them, we must understand the union itself – what kind of organism it is, how it functions and what is the role of leadership. Where should we turn for such an understanding?

Among all the participants in economic life, the trade union is probably least suited to purely economic analysis. It may be that the particular form of rationality assumed in traditional economic theory can properly be assigned to the individual entrepreneur and even to the corporation, which after all is a legal individual. In any case it is not necessary to argue that point here. But a trade union is pre-eminently a group, a collectivity. Psychologists have been insisting for more than half a century that group behavior is fundamentally different from individual behavior. The trade union is not only a group, but an institution as well; it leads a life of its own, separate and distinct from the lives of its members. Its problems are not merely those of the particular individuals it happens to represent at one point of time.

If we still wish to make a theoretical analysis of union behavior, we must operate within a broader frame of reference. Even the most primitive cliches of politics, sociology and psychology throw a good deal of light on the problem. This is not to suggest, however, that economic analysis be supplanted by political, sociological or psychological analysis. What is needed is to break down the walls between the separate disciplines of social science which have hitherto dealt with separate aspects of social behavior. When society was more loosely constituted and social forces were organized on a small scale, these various aspects of behavior could operate more or less independently in their own spheres. It was possible to talk about such fictions as the economic man and the political man. But today it must seriously be doubted whether there is any such thing as purely economic activity, purely political activity or even purely religious activity. No group can maintain significant economic power in present-day society without political influence. To acquire political influence, psychological techniques are indispensable. Effective psychological techniques are directed toward manipulating sociological relations and tensions. And so on. If different aspects of social behavior have now become integrated, does it not follow that the separate disciplines of social study must be brought together correspondingly? Otherwise, we have partial sciences, compared by Ruskin with a science of gymnastics which assumed that men had no skeletons (quoted in Beard, 1945, p. 6).

However, it does not require any profound theoretical analysis to understand union wage policy, or employer wage policy, for that matter. Walter Savage Landor has said that 'the seeds of great events lie near to the surface'. Intelligent union and management representatives understand well enough why their decisions are what they are. They could not succeed without a fairly good notion why the opposing party behaves as he does. This understanding is accessible to the

307

student of industrial relations, if only he is willing to accept it on its own terms and refrain from imposing an alien logic upon what he finds. The greatest danger is that the union and employer representatives will attempt to supply an answer in the economist's terms rather than to identify and describe the controlling pressures as really experienced. This is not deception but self-delusion. Both parties are anxious to appear farsighted and responsible; it is all too easy to look back upon a previous wage decision and ascribe it in one's own mind to the competitive situation in the industry or to the elasticity of demand for labor. The union leader, not yet fully accepted as a useful citizen, is peculiarly addicted to reverence toward the canons of conventional business morality. This is why mailed questionnaires, hypothetical questions and other devices of large-scale investigation have been avoided in this study. Research of this kind cannot feasibly be conducted wholesale.

Where is the wage policy of unions to be found? We have already suggested that it is not to be found in the mechanical application of any maximization principle. It might be best to dispose of some additional false leads which are inviting at first blush but not rich in explanatory value.

1. Wage policy is not explained by the hortatory slogans of the labor movement – a fair day's pay for a fair day's work, a living wage, a health and decency wage, a productivity wage, and so forth. These are the slogans under which the 'men of labor' are mobilized in disciplined ranks and led into battle and by means of which their general aspirations are explained to the outside world; they are no guide, however, to the strategy and tactics which are adopted in pursuing these aspirations, or to the limited objectives which are staked out at particular times and places. Samuel Gompers's remark that labor is seeking 'more and more and more' has often been quoted as the epitome of union wage policy. The remark is undoubtedly correct, but again it is no clue to the eminently pragmatic decisions which are made in the day-to-day conduct of union affairs. Nor is any clue to be found in various public pronouncements made in a 'responsible' vein: e.g. that the real objective is a fair distribution of income; or that the only true source of higher wages is greater production. These are equivalent to defining 'service' as the objective of business enterprise. An occasional result should not be confused with an underlying purpose.

2. An attractive expedient is to approach the problem through the formal arguments and documents of wage determination. Preliminary briefs, supplementary briefs, concluding briefs, rebuttals and surre-buttals, transcripts of hearings and negotiations, supporting statistical studies, fact-finding reports and arbitration awards are available in great quantity. They are constructed with much care and elaboration, are pitched on a high ethical level, and ostensibly are designed to focus the soundest principles of economic policy upon the problem at hand. Generally the arguments are cast in terms of a standard group of 'wage-determining factors', including changes in the cost of living, budgetary requirements of a living wage, the 'going rate' in comparable establishments, trends in productivity and the employer's ability to pay. These criteria have changed very little since before the First World War.[2] They have been incorporated in legislative and administrative regulations governing the adjustment of wages, such as the Railway Labor Act of 1920 and the wage stablization standards of the National War Labor Board.

One is tempted to conceive of trade union wage policy as the application of these customary criteria of wage determination. If this formulation were adopted, the union's primary objectives would be listed as maintaining the real wage, securing a fair living wage, insisting on the going rate, sharing in the benefits of increased efficiency, and so on.

However, there are several difficulties with a formulation of this kind. The 'wage-determining factors' are often mutually contradictory; for example, the budgetary requirements of a living wage may be incompatible with the employer's ability to pay. A given criterion, such as the cost of living, will be emphasized by the union at one stage in the business cycle and by the employer at the opposite stage. In specific cases, all the conventional standards are generally invoked; but some have a real weight in the resulting determination, whereas others have no weight at all. The most elaborate logical and statistical demonstrations are presented in support of arguments which are wholly devoid of effect; but often the crucial factor has no place in the oral arguments and written documents of the proceeding – including the arbitrator's award. In fact, there is probably no field of social inquiry in which the written word is more misleading than the

2. See Dickinson (1941), Feis·(1921), Soule (1928) and Storkelt (1918). In recent years aggregative analysis has been employed to demonstrate the requirements of a national wage policy compatible with full employment at stable prices.

negotiation and adjudication of wage rates. The limited relevance of formal exposition in wage determination is well recognized by union and employer representatives, as well as by many impartial arbitrators.

It is not contended that the customary criteria have no significance in the wage setting process. They serve as vehicles for the transmission of pressures, channels for the communication of facts, and symbols of allegiance to high ethical standards and sound economic principles. But it would be naive to suppose that they can be taken as the starting-point for examining wage policy.

3. Union wage policy in the United States is not substantially affected by anti-capitalist ideologies. Ideological differences exist among unions, of course, and particularly among union leaders and the minority of articulate members; there are right and left wings, Democrats and Republicans, communists and anti-communists. These differences give rise to a certain amount of factional conflict and occasionally provide a motive for employers to favor one union over another. They affect wage determination in the same manner as union leadership rivalries of any kind affect it. However, it does not follow, and is not generally true, that variations in ideology are associated with differences in wage policy. As a matter of fact, the Amalgamated Clothing Workers, with a strong socialist tradition, have shown more concern for the healthy survival of private enterprise in the clothing industry than the United Mine Workers, with arch-Republican leadership, have shown in the coal industry. The 'left-wing' leadership of the United Electrical Workers embarrassed the 'right-wing' leadership of the United Automobile Workers in 1946 by settling with the General Motors Corporation for a wage increase of $18\frac{1}{2}$ cents when the Auto-Workers were holding out for $19\frac{1}{2}$ cents. During the same year, the 'left-wing' National Maritime Union agreed to a wage increase of $17.50 per month, but the 'right-wing' Sailors' Union of the Pacific went on strike in order to force approval of larger increases by the National Wage Stabilization Board. The fact is that all important American trade unions should be classified as 'business unions' (see Hoxie, 1917, pp. 45–6) in the sense that their practical wage decisions are predicated upon indefinite prolongation of capitalistic economic organization. If capitalism is supplanted in the United States, it will not be over the wage issue.

There is also a political contest between unions and management, turning on the possession of certain disputed areas of sovereignty in the control of the employment relationship. This controversy over 'managerial prerogatives' and 'union rights' undoubtedly affects the wage bargain, because wages are often manipulated in order to attach the loyalty of the rank-and-file workers and the approval of the general public. Here again, however, the contest is carried on within the framework of a private enterprise system. What is more, those unions which have most successfully invaded the disputed areas of sovereignty (through acquiring the closed shop, control over technological change, and so forth) have also become the most prominent centers of political conservatism in the labor movement. This fact sheds a great deal of doubt over the assertion that the capitalistic order is threatened by the controversy over 'prerogatives'.[3]

American trade unions are business unions and their chief business is collective bargaining. The union at work is the union negotiating a contract. If this be true, then union wage policy can best be understood by examining the operating decisions which are reached in the course of the bargaining process. These decisions are the proof of the pudding. They are made 'when the chips are down' and reflect, more than anything else, the real determinants of policy.

Operating decisions are required at various points in the bargaining process. Should the wage provision of the agreement be reopened? What should be the union's initial demand? Should the employer's initial offer be accepted? What should be the union's compromise demand and should the employer's compromise offer be accepted? Should the union consent to arbitrate? Should a strike be called? Should the strike be terminated on the basis of a mediated settlement, or should it be carried on until the employer capitulates or the union disintegrates? Union wage policy is found in bargaining decisions; determinants of policy are the influences bearing upon these decisions.

To be sure, this is not a lofty definition of policy. Collective bargaining, we are frequently told, is essentially a 'pressure game'; and so it is. Let us accept it as a pressure game, recognizing that it

3. 'If unions are permitted to participate in management without responsibility for sharing losses, demands will know no limit. This will lead to profitless business operations and the closing of plants. In order to secure the needed production, the next step would naturally be "socialization" with government operating the business. In fact, some of the demands for labor sharing in management are undoubtedly made for the purpose of preventing the functioning of the present economic system' (National Association of Manufacturers, 1946, p. 21).

is not very different from numerous other phenomena in economic and political life. If our definition is not exalted, at least it is realistic; in the present state of affairs, it is difficult to see how any more pretentious definition of policy could have much meaning.

The American trade union, being essentially pragmatic and having no well-defined role in society as yet, is peculiarly subject to pressures. The task of the union leader is to reconcile these pressures in such a manner as to serve the paramount objective of 'building the union'. The following chapters [not included here] attempt to identify the major controlling influences and describe the union leader at work in the fascinating process of collective bargaining.

It is hoped that this approach will not seem unfair to the union leader. Of course, he has other ambitions for himself aside from political advancement and other hopes for the union aside from institutional survival. He believes in unionism as an organ of democracy and as an instrument of social justice. He hopes that the process of collective bargaining will secure for the workers a larger proportion of the national product and facilitate high levels of employment and real income. But these things are not within his control. His job is to make an agreement with a particular employer, or group of employers, covering a particular group of workers for a certain short period of time. When the time comes to negotiate and sign the agreement, the total national product and the total volume of employment are pretty remote, but the surrounding political pressures are urgent and immediate. The case might be different if we had a master wage bargain covering the whole economy; but even the largest and most influential bargains are applicable over only a minor segment of the economy. If union wage policy is parochial and particularistic, it is not because of any lack of enlightenment on the part of leaders, nor can it be cured by any amount of homiletic preachment.

The central proposition, then, is that a trade union is a political agency operating in an economic environment. In the following five chapters [not included here] I have tried to establish this proposition and to investigate some of its implications. These chapters are essentially a group of essays rather than a balanced theory of wage determination. It seemed advisable at this stage to concentrate on some of the factors which have received too little attention in our thinking about industrial relations, exploring them in this preliminary fashion and reserving until later the task of constructing a 'model' which would give proper and proportionate weight to all the factors. If the impression is given that labor supply and demand in a quantitative sense are regarded as having no bearing upon collective wage determination, this is the reason. It goes without saying that a purely political formulation would be just as unsatisfactory as a purely economic formulation and that just as many unanswered questions would have to be explained away as the result of irrational behavior and other imperfections.

In other words, the union as a political agency has been emphasized at the expense of the economic environment in which it operates, not because economic influences are considered unimportant – for they are highly important – but because they have been dealt with more extensively by other writers.[4] [. . .]

It might be advisable, however, to indicate briefly at this point the connection which I conceive to exist between the underlying economic influences present in every case and the political pressures focused upon the union leaders in the bargaining process. A number of influences are described in the literature: labor cost as a percentage of total cost; competitive conditions in markets for the product and for complementary and competitive factors of production; the extent of non-union competition; the profit position of employers; shifts in consumer demand; technological changes; and cyclical fluctuations in prices, output and employment. These are frequently listed as determinants of the union's economic bargaining strength.

That they do affect the union's bargaining strength, in the sense of its ability to win concessions from employers, is clear enough. Any full-blown theory of collective wage determination would have to give major emphasis to an analysis of bargaining power as defined in this sense. But the term is often used in another sense, as being principally affected by the elasticity of demand for labor. For example, Shister (1943, p. 530) states that '"bargaining power" may be divided into three elements: (a) the elasticity of demand for the union labor, (b) the quality of union representatives, (c) the ability to strike successfully'. He discusses importance of labor cost, elasticity of substitution of capital for labor, and price rigidity in the product market as affecting elasticity of demand for labor.

4. See Barkin (1940), Bronfenbrenner (1939), Coleman (1943), Dickinson (1941), Dunlop (1944), Dunlop and Higgins (1942), Haber (1930), Hill (1942), Lahne (1944), Lester (1942), Lester and Robie (1946), McPherson (1940), Millis (1942), Palmer (1932), Schmidt (1937), Shister (1943, 1944, 1946), Slichter (1941), Taylor (1931) and many other works on collective bargaining in particular industries.

'Elasticity of demand' expresses a price–quantity relationship. When the term is used as a blanket designation for a multitude of economic influences, it carries the inference that these influences are important to the union because they determine the amount of labor it can sell at various rates of pay. This implies, in turn, that the wage–employment relationship is the crucial criterion of union bargaining decisions and that the wage bargain is essentially a wage–employment bargain. It will be argued later, however, that the union is not automatically or continuously concerned with the quantity of labor sold; and further that the typical wage bargain (with certain significant exceptions) is necessarily made without consideration of its employment effect.

The real significance of the economic influences, I am convinced, is to be found elsewhere than in a continuous functional relationship between wage rate and employment level in the bargaining unit. (It is not necessary to decide here whether or not such a relationship does exist.) The economic environment is important to the unions at the second remove: because it generates political pressures which have to be reckoned with by the union leader. The effect of any given change depends upon how it fits into the general constellation of pressures. Such economic changes as a shift in consumer demand and a contraction of economic activity are particularly influential upon the relationship with the employer because they condition his attitude: how strongly he will oppose a wage increase, how vigorously he will insist on a wage cut, under what circumstances he will accede to a strike with its attendant losses, or make an attempt to break the union, or move into another area, or leave the industry altogether.

The much-debated question of union wage policy during a depression will serve as an example. Whether a cut in wages will raise the level of employment or mitigate the decline in employment need not be decided here, because ordinarily the question is not considered in these terms by the union leader. It may be virtually taken for granted that the employed members will oppose a cut and will have greater weight in the union than the unemployed.[5] What becomes important is the extent to which the employer insists on it. As Dunlop has shown, the employer is likely to be most insistent in that sector of the economy where employment has declined the least. Summarizing his analysis of wage reductions in the 1929–33 depression, Dunlop (1944, pp. 145, 146 and 148) states:

5. However, in some industries it is common for union members to work below the scale by secret agreement with the employer.

The net result is that in the sector of the economy in which wage reductions typically take place first, two separate pressures must be identified. Not only are labor costs relatively more important, but price declines in the product market (attributed largely to the character of competitive conditions) tend to force wage decreases. The decline in product prices is the more important influence . . . The central theme is that declines in product prices and not unemployment constitute the effective downward pressure on wage structures . . . Wages fell last (and probably least) . . . in the sector of the economy in which unemployment was clearly relatively greatest . . .

Thus, it is the employer rather than the unemployed or potentially unemployed worker who forces the decision in the normal case. From the standpoint of the union, the purpose of agreeing to the cut is to maintain the bargaining relationship on as satisfactory a basis as possible. What appears as a danger is not that employment will fall off but that the employer will become hostile. It is the loss of friendly relationships, bargaining units and collective agreements, rather than the loss of jobs, which is most to be avoided. Noting that many unions accepted wage cuts in the 1921–2 depression, Wyckoff (1924, p. 99) remarks: 'The question however arises as to whether the wage reductions were not more the result of a policy of buying union security with wage cuts, rather than a calculating concern for the general economic situation in the industry.'

It is submitted that these considerations can be compressed into 'elasticity of demand' only if the term is stripped of its essential quantitative content. As seen by the union leader, the problem of depression wage policy is qualitative rather than quantitative.

Much the same can be said for other aspects of the economic environment which affect union wage policy at the second remove. For example, a union's economic bargaining power may vary considerably between one group of employers and another, because of differences in the strategic position of union workers, the profit rates of employers and the importance of wages as an element in costs. Should corresponding variations in wage rates be introduced? In casual industries, such as long-shoring and construction, the union is likely to insist upon a standard wage. Workers move frequently from one employer to another and would object to continual changes in their hourly rates of pay. The problem of assigning workers through the union's hiring hall would be greatly complicated. Where the employment relationship is more stable, however, the union is likely to classify employers on the basis of differences in ability to pay. Thus, printing tradesmen in the San Francisco Bay area (as elsewhere) receive higher rates of pay in newspaper plants than in job shops. Milk-wagon drivers receive more than ice-wagon drivers. Theater janitors are better paid than hotel and restaurant janitors. If the different groups of employers are included in the coverage of a single master agreement (as in the coal industry or in the West Coast pulp and paper industry), the pressure for uniformity is likely to be strong.

The policy of union–management cooperation is often represented as an indication of concern for labor demand, but Ware (1937, p. 13) states that when 'confronted by new challenges (the welfare offensive, etc.) the labor unions turned to trade union–employer cooperation in order to encourage employers to deal with them'. Different unions have reacted in very different ways to non-union competition and to shifts in consumer demand, depending on what seems to be the most workable expedient for maintaining the union as a going concern. The problem of technological change, although somewhat removed from wages, offers a close parallel. Slichter has shown that the union may adopt a policy of obstruction, a policy of competition or a policy of control. The policies adopted by particular unions do not represent different degrees of enlightenment, but different ranges of choice, and cannot be understood until we recognize the primary importance of organizational survival as the central aim of the leadership.

References

BARKIN, S. (1940), 'Industrial union wage policies', *Plan Age*, vol. 1, pp. 1–15.

BEARD, C. A. (1945), *The Economic Basis of Politics*.

BEVERIDGE, W. H. (1945), *Full Employment in a Free Society*, Norton.

BRAUNTHAL, A. (1946), 'Wage policy and full employment', *Int. Postwar Prob.*, vol. 3, pp. 31–50.

BRONFENBRENNER, M. (1939), 'Economics of collective bargaining', *Quarterly Journal of Economics*, vol. 53, pp. 535–68.

CLARK, J. B. (1899), *The Distribution of Wealth*, Macmillan Co.

COLEMAN, M. (1943), *Men and Coal*, Farrar & Rinehart.

DICKINSON, Z. C. (1941), *Collective Wage Determination*, Ronald Press.

DUNLOP, J. T. (1944), *Wage Determination under Trade Unions*, Macmillan Co.

DUNLOP, J. T., and B. HIGGINS (1942), 'Bargaining power and market structures', *Journal of Political Economy*, vol. 50, pp. 1–26.

EDGEWORTH, F. Y. (1881), *Mathematical Physics*.

EDGEWORTH, F. Y. (1881), *Mathematical Psychics*.

FEIS, H. (1921), *The Settlement of Wage Disputes*, Macmillan Co.

FELLNER, W. (1947), 'Prices and wages under bilateral monopoly', *Quarterly Journal of Economics*, vol. 61, pp. 503–32.

FORCEY, E. (1946), 'Trade union policy under full employment', *Canadian Journal of Economics and Political Science*, vol. 2, pp. 343–55.

HABER, W. (1930), *Industrial Relations in the Building Industry*, Harvard University Press.

HAMILTON, W. H., and S. MAY (1923), *The Control of Wages*, Pitman.

HANSEN, A. H. (1946), *Economic Policy and Full Employment*, McGraw-Hill.

HICKS, J. R. (1932), *The Theory of Wages*, Macmillan Co.

HICKS, J. R. (1935), 'Bilateral monopoly', in 'Annual survey of economic theory: the theory of monopoly', *Econometrica*, vol. 3, pp. 1–20.

HILL, S. E. (1942), *Teamsters and Transportation*.

HOXIE, R. F. (1917), *Trade Unionism in the United States*, Appleton-Century-Crofts.

LAHNE, H. J. (1944), *The Cotton Mill Workers*, Farrar & Rinehart.

LESTER, R. A. (1942), *Economics of Labor*, Macmillan Co., 2nd edn, 1964.

LESTER, R. A., and ROBIE, E. A. (1946), *Wages under Regional and National Collective Bargaining*.

MACHLUP, F. (1946), 'Marginal analysis and economic research', *American Economic Review*, vol. 36, pp. 519–54.

MCPHERSON, W. H. (1940), *Labor Relations in the Automobile Industry*, Brookings Institution, Washington.

MARSHALL, A. (1890), *Principles of Economics*, Macmillan, 8th edn, 1930.

MILLIS, H. A. (ed.) (1942), *How Collective Bargaining Works*, Twentieth Century Fund.

NATIONAL ASSOCIATION OF MANUFACTURERS (1946), *Should Labor be Given a Direct Share in the Management of Industry?*

PALMER, G. L. (1932), *Union Tactics and Economic Change*.

PIGOU, A. C. (1905), *Principles and Methods of Industrial Peace*, Macmillan.

PIGOU, A. C. (1945), *Lapses from Full Employment*, Macmillan.

ROBERTSON, D. H. (1931), 'Wage grumbles', *Economic Fragments*, P. S. King, pp. 42–57.

SCHMIDT, E. (1937), *Industrial Relations in Urban Transportation*, University of Minnesota Press.

SHISTER, J. (1943), 'The theory of trade union wage rigidity', *Quarterly Journal of Economics*, vol. 57, pp. 522–42.

SHISTER, J. (1944), 'A note on cyclical wage rigidity', *American Economic Review*, vol. 34, pp. 111–16.

SHISTER, J. (1946), 'The locus of union control in collective bargaining', *Quarterly Journal of Economics*, vol. 60, pp. 513–45.

SLICHTER, S. H. (1941), *Union Policies and Industrial Management*, Institute of Economics, Washington.

SLICHTER, S. H. (1947), *The Challenge of Industrial Relations*, Cornell University Press.

SOULE, G. (1928), *Wage Arbitration*.

STORKELT, J. N., Jr (1918), *The Arbitral Determination of Railway Wages*.

TAYLOR, G. W. (1931), *The Full-Fashioned Hosiery Workers*.

TINTNER, G. (1939), 'A note on the problem of bilateral monopoly', Journal of Political Economy, vol. 47, pp. 263–70.

WARE, N. J. (1937), 'Trade Unions: United States and Canada', *Encyclopaedia of the Social Sciences*, vol. 15, New York.

WILLIAMSON, S. T., and HARRIS, H. (1945), *Trends in Collective Bargaining: A Survey of Recent Experience*, Twentieth Century Fund, New York.

WORSWICH, G. D. N. (1944), 'The stability and flexibility of full employment', *The Economics of Full Employment*, pp. 59–84.

WYCKOFF, V. J. (1924), *Wage Policies of Labor Organizations in a Period of Industrial Depression*, Johns Hopkins University Press.

24 Peter Mathias

Economists, Trade Unions and Wages

From Peter Mathias, *Trade Unions: Public Goods or Public Bads?* Institute of Economic Affairs, 1978, pp. 13–16.

The main reason for the existence of trade unions, and their continuing principal objective, is to defend the position of their members – in particular by increasing wages. This being so, and with the trade unions having grown to be one of the great estates of the realm in the twentieth century, it seems to me remarkable that economists down the years have offered so little theoretical analysis to test what effects trade unions have had in practice upon the level of wages. In a perverse way, this seems almost to operate in inverse ratio to the extent of popular public belief in the power of trade unions in this respect.

Historians of trade unions (a well-represented branch of historiography) are, if anything, even more prone to ignore this central issue than economists: the books on trade union history are dominated by institutional narrative, dramatized by industrial and political conflicts, but with scarcely an attempt to make an assessment of the central issue about how effective the union concerned has been over the years in influencing the wages received by its members.

General theories of wages unconvincing

All propositions by economists for a general theory of wages seem to offer no convincing explanation of reality – whether theories of subsistence-level wages (whether determined according to the minimum physical level of consumption or building in conventional requirements and levels of expectation into the concept of a 'minimum'); iron laws about a 'wages fund' linking wage levels inescapably to ratios between the growth of capital and population; or even those theories determining wage levels according to differential productivity. Classical economists in the nineteenth century and neoclassical economists in the twentieth have made basic assumptions about the economy and the labour market being in a state of competitive equilibrium, nationally or internationally. Prices, including the price of labour, tend towards marginal costs; profits are 'normal'; monopoly payments and quasi-rents are distortions – and such interferences in the market can only be temporary distortions – explained by external factors which, by definition, lie outside the variables encompassed by economic theory. One of the attributes of a competitive market is that prices become equalized.

On the other hand, socialist theorizing, particularly by Marxist writers in the nineteenth century, also made basic assumptions which denied much leverage to unions on wage levels. Marx, indeed, incorporated conventional levels of expectation into his views about what subsistence standards included (which offers scope for the collective expression of such expectations) but, at the same time, powerful forces for *minimizing* wages were also built into his assumptions about the dynamics of capitalism – the reserve army of labour, a falling rate of profit, the flight of capital, labour-economizing innovation, crises and depressions, etc. The voice of Keynes on all this was also silent in the *General Theory*.

Short-run/sectoral effects: nothing new since Marshall?

Of course, the short-run and/or sectoral redistribution effects of unions on wages have been acknowledged as long as their long-run macro-economic (aggregate) effects have been denied or ignored – at least since Adam Smith. Even here, however, has anything much been said which is new since Marshall spelled out in 1890 and 1892 the nature of the elasticities, substitutabilities, possibilities of technical change, competition in product markets and the like which governed – in the abstract – the degree of leverage which a union could exert? Public sector analysis seems even less responsive to economic theory, being without the parameters of unemployment, bankruptcy, the flight of capital and enterprise which set overall limits for redistribution within a competitive (but how competitive?) commercial context. And how rigidly are 'cash limits' in practice going to impose a 'trade off' between wage rates and unemployment in the public sector? (The classical economists spoke very clearly of the advantages a union could bring to its efforts to improve wage rates for its members by reducing the amount of labour competing in the market.)

In short, are the variables too many, the 'frictions' too great, the elasticities so indeterminate, the competitive forces so lax, the public sector and public influence so powerful, reasons of equity so persuasive, exogenous factors so numerous and heterogeneous that economic theory can *never* say anything useful or operational about the influence of trade unions on the general levels of wages? Or at least anything beyond the vital tautology that pushing 'significantly' beyond the limit set by the market will soon bring its own retribution by inflation, unemployment or both?

I am aware that there is some recent econometric analysis which seeks to measure the differential in wage rates produced by unionization – based on a comparison between wage levels in unionized and non-unionized sectors. In large measure this sort of analysis assumes (and has to assume) that *correlation* implies *causation* – which begs many vital questions. Why should we always assume that unionization brings higher wages and never that higher wages induce unionization? Of course, this analysis concerns only redistributive effects and implies the paradox that, with unionization universal throughout the economy, its effects on wages would be zero. In fact, the important issue is the *difference* in leverage effects between different unions. The analysis also tends to ignore the implications of competitive forces within different sectors of the market, product competition and substitutability, countervailing powers by organized consumers of the products or services in question, and a host of other issues which affect the real dynamics of the market.

The perspective of dynamic analysis

A prime weakness of this sort of analysis is that it is based on static, short-run analysis. Longer-term dynamic analysis can give a sharply different perspective. For example, it can also be argued that a high degree of unionization is associated with a fall in productivity and output. By reducing the potential efficiency of the economy, this effect of unionization would reduce the potential level of real earnings (which would not be eliminated by 100 per cent unionization). The alternative thesis is that, if unionization affects wage levels significantly, this will induce greater technical change to economize on labour and offset the other leverage effects of unions. Thus econometric analysis which seeks to 'put the numbers into the equations' contains difficulties in operational utility as great in their own way as those of pure theory.

This whole tradition of economic analysis has wider consequences, of which I mention only two. It may be tempting to conclude from the general agnosticism of economists that unions cannot do much to influence the general level of wages in the long run; that we need not worry – the going rate is still set by the market. Such a signal for inaction would be truly disastrous: the going rate will indeed be re-established, but only after a terrible retribution by inflation and unemployment, with political if not economic crisis.

An even greater liability of this mode of analysis, in my view, is that it encourages concentration almost exclusively upon the *division* of the national income rather than its creation. It needs to be said – loudly and clearly – that the greatest and only significant long-run gains for the mass of the nation have come from *enlarging* the national cake rather than redistributing it. Indeed, concentration upon redistribution may be seen as the consequence of economic stagnation – the economics of a siege economy. We all stand to prosper much more from the economics of expanding the national income than from the politics of envy – wholly concerned with its distribution.

25 E. H. Phelps Brown

The Influence of Trade Unions and Collective Bargaining on Pay Levels and Real Wages

From E. H. Phelps Brown, *Minutes of Evidence 38 to the Royal Commission on Trade Unions and Employers' Associations*, HMSO, 1966, pp. 313–30.

The influence of collective bargaining on the movements of the general level of pay

1. To assess the consequences of collective bargaining with certainty we should have to be able to compare what happens in its presence with what happens when some other method of regulating pay is used in societies otherwise the same. The actual course of events gives us little chance to do this. There are differences in plenty, it is true, between the ways in which pay has been regulated in different countries, periods or industries, but much else has been different at the same time. Nor can we very well make the needed comparison by way of what the physicist calls an 'ideal experiment', and ask what we can see happening, in the mind's eye, when a given society changes its ways of regulating pay. The trouble is that these ways are an organic part of the society. Their working depends on attitudes and traditions which they in turn help to mould: even in imagination we cannot lift them out and install others in their place as we might change the carburettor in a car.

2. None the less, if we are to reach any verdict on proposals for improving them we are bound to base it on some judgement of the effect they take, of what would come about differently if they were different. Ultimately this judgement must be intuitive, but it can also be informed. Comparisons are possible which, though far from controlled experiments, do throw light on the probability of different judgements. In a number of Western economies, for instance, we can compare the movements of rates of pay before and after the extension of collective bargaining. Where collective bargaining is established, we can compare the movements of rates of pay in different phases of the economy. Within any one country, again, we can sometimes compare different industries, or different regions of the same industry, some of which bargain collectively while others as yet do

not; or we can compare the course of events in one industry before and after it adopts collective bargaining. None of these comparisons is rigorous: other things always vary at the same time. But we can often judge how far it is to these other things that any differences in the movements of pay are likely to have been due; and then we are left with an estimate of the consequences specific to collective bargaining. We can also ask whether such estimates agree with the expectations created by an analysis of bargaining power.

3. It is the purpose of this note to give an account of these materials and the conclusions to which they lead. For the sake of brevity the account will be summary and the conclusions will be stated baldly. In a fuller account there would be more qualifications, but also more marshalling of evidence.

4. The United Kingdom is one of a number of Western countries in which we can follow the movements of pay and other incomes over the last hundred years. Figure 1 shows the course of the average earnings in money of manual workers, mainly in industry, in France, Germany, Sweden, the UK and the USA, since 1860. Only in the UK was collective bargaining of much account in the earlier years of this period and even here it was less extensive than trade unionism and was effective only for a small minority of the country's wage-earners. Between 1890 and the First World War, however, there was a remarkable growth of trade unionism in all five countries and this brought with it a substantial though intermittent development of collective bargaining. The number of trade union members over 10,000 of the occupied population in industry rose as in Table 1. We thus have an opportunity to see how money wages behaved in some Western economies in the comparative absence of collective bargaining, and also to ask whether the early development of collective bargaining seems to have made a difference.

5. The salient feature of the general level of money wages in all five countries, before ever collective bargaining could have taken much effect, is that it rose cumulatively. Earlier records show that, even excluding years of war, this tendency had been present from the early years of industrialism. How did it arise? Except in France, most of the rise – indeed, more than all the net rise – came about within only about half the total number of years. A cycle ran through the business activity of all these countries, with a period on the average of about eight years. It was in the four years or so in which activity was rising

or near its crest that money wages rose. The other four years in which activity was falling or near its trough brought no change in money wages or some cuts. These cuts, however, were smaller than the immediately preceding rises, so that on balance each cycle raised money wages. So far it looks as though the source of the cumulative rise of money wages lay in the cycle. If, moreover, the size of the rise in each prosperous phase depended on its intensity, the differences between the rates at which money wages rose in various periods and countries might be due simply to the different intensities of their cycles. But though some systematic dependence of this kind appears in Germany, the UK and the USA, there is too much variation about it for us to take it as a sufficient explanation of the rate at which money wages rose from time to time. From the mid-1890s onwards, for instance, money wages rose a good deal faster in Germany, Sweden and the USA than they had done through the twenty years before, but there was no corresponding intensification of the cycles in those countries. What explanation, then, can we offer? One account which is not incompatible with the evidence runs as follows.

Table 1

	France	Germany	Sweden	UK	USA
About 1890	220	440	210	810	510
About 1913	1440	2520	3300*	2690	1830

* This was in 1907, a high point reached after membership had more than doubled since 1904; through 1910–12 membership averaged nearly 20 per cent less.

6. We think of the labour market as a gravitational field, in which the force of gravity has been a pressure exerted from the side of labour towards wage rises and against wage cuts. This force has been present at all times, though in varying strength. Its action has not depended on labour being unionized, though union militancy intensified it.

7. The balance of supply and demand in the labour market operated in some times and places to reinforce what we have called the force of gravity, in others to counteract it. In the successive phases of the trade cycle the demand for labour rose now faster and now slower than the supply. This supply itself rose at a rate which, especially through the changing number of migrants, varied significantly from time to time. When it was the demand for labour that was extending

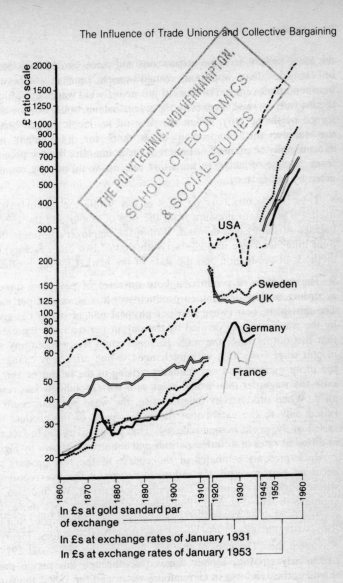

Figure 1 Average annual wage earnings (mainly industrial) in five countries 1860–1960

the more rapidly, in some occupations and places an absolute excess of vacancies over applicants would appear, and if competition between employers for labour did not actively bid wages up, at least the pressure to raise them from the side of labour would now be reinforced by the scarcity. When the demand for labour lagged behind the supply, the competition of workers for jobs might only exceptionally be allowed to underbid the going rate, but the pressure from the side of labour to keep that rate up would now be counteracted by redundancy.

8. Thus two factors bore on rates of pay within the labour market itself – a persistent pressure from the side of labour and the varying balance of supply and demand. Within the employer's business their joint influence came into contact with that of two other factors, the methods of production and the state of the market for the product.

9. The methods of production bore on rates of pay most directly according as they determined productivity, that is, output per man. The unit wage cost (wage cost per physical unit of output) is given by the wage per man divided by the output per man. To the extent that this output rose, the wage per man could rise without any rise in unit wage costs and, with unchanged selling price, any change in the profit margin; and any tendency arising in the labour market to raise the wage per man would meet with correspondingly less resistance. When productivity failed to rise, the wage per man could be raised only to the extent that the selling price of the product was raised or the profit margin reduced. That productivity did in fact rise at different rates in different periods and countries is shown by Figure 2 which presents estimates of the course of the real product per occupied person within the industrial sectors of the five economies whose wage movements we have already surveyed. We find also, by comparison with Figure 1, that where productivity rose more, the general level of money wages usually rose faster. This implies that the course of unit wage costs varied less than that of wages. Figure 3 illustrates this. The case of the UK between the 1890s and 1914 is particularly striking. Money wages rose through this period more slowly in the UK than in Germany, Sweden and the USA; industrial productivity also rose less at this time in the UK than in those other countries – indeed, in the UK it hardly rose at all, while in the others it rose rapidly: so that unit wage costs by no means rose less in British industry than among its competitors. We may suppose that international competition would have prevented any trading country from

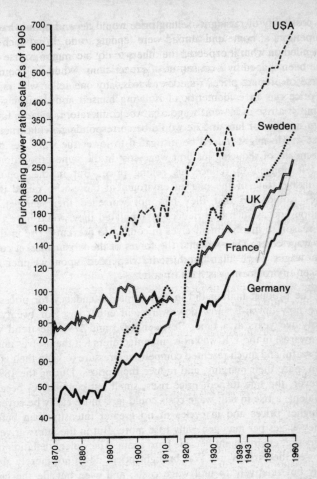

Figure 2 Productivity (physical output per occupied person expressed in £s of 1905 purchasing power) in the industrial sector of five countries 1870–1960

letting its unit wage costs rise much more than its competitors', or from failing to reduce its own costs if they were reducing theirs.

10. On the other hand, all countries could let their unit wage costs rise and cover them by higher prices, if all moved together. Here appears the second influence we noted on business decisions – the state of the market for the product. For any one firm at any one time,

the possibility of raising its selling price would depend upon what its competitors at home and abroad were tending to do. What each did depended on what it expected the others to do: a common course will have been shaped by a consensus of expectations. When the common course of product prices was downwards, any one seller who raised his price ran an evident risk of isolating himself and damaging his business: a rise in his unit wage cost would, therefore, mean a lower profit margin for him and he would be correspondingly concerned to resist it. He might indeed be instigated to lower the wage per man as a means of reducing his unit wage cost in the same proportion as he felt obliged to reduce his selling price. But in the opposite permissive state of the market environment those who raised their prices would find that they had not worsened their competitive position and as such experiences accumulated they would have ever less reason to involve themselves in conflict to prevent a rise in their unit wage costs. Thus whether the forces of the labour market could raise wages more than productivity depended upon whether the market environment was hard or soft.

11. The product market did in fact evince a tendency for prices to move now upwards, now downwards, in either case for twenty or twenty-five years at a time. Between 1873 and 1896 the trend was downwards: in the UK we know, manufacturers felt themselves under a powerful and much resented competitive pressure to keep their costs down, pare their margins, and reduce their prices. During the 1890s, however, the tide turned; price rises, small but cumulative, became prevalent; a rise in unit wage costs could now more easily be covered by higher prices and in cycles of no greater intensity than before money wages per man generally rose more. But in the interwar years the market environment became hard again. The violent deflation that followed the First World War brought prices down not merely absolutely but relatively to unit wage costs; and even outside the great depression that began in 1929, few manufacturers could expect that a rise in their own prices would not lose them business. In this period accordingly unit wage costs in industry were not allowed to rise; and the considerable rise of productivity that came about at the same time was used more to reduce prices than to raise wages.

12. But since the Second World War the market environment has been entirely different. Though old apprehensions about the bad effects of higher costs may have persisted at first, experience began to show that prices and real output could rise together year after year

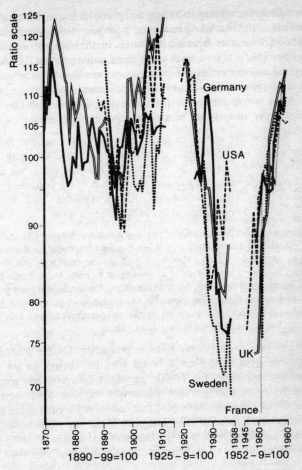

Figure 3 Indices of unit wage costs within industry in five countries 1870–1960

and profits increase in the same proportion as wages and salaries. The soft market environment *par excellence* now developed. It was conditioned not merely by the experience of the opening years, but by knowledge of governments' commitments to full employment – if employers made wage settlements that raised unit wage costs, governments would not in the event deny them the flow of monetary demand needed to keep their capacity fully occupied at the new level of costs.

In such a setting, resistance by any one group of employers to a wage settlement of the prevailing size came to be seen as equally futile and needless. Differences between countries in the rate of rise of unit wage costs still, it is true, took their effect on international trade and in any one country the rise of money wages would tend to be checked in so far as productivity did not advance enough to keep the rise in costs down to something like the international trend. But this trend still rose more steeply and persistently than ever before.

13. If this was the system of forces bearing on the general level of money wages, what difference should we expect collective bargaining to make and what if any do we find? In the first place, we might expect collective bargaining to give more effect to the persistent pressure to raise wages and resist cuts. Alfred Marshall (1892, book 6, ch. 13, section 5) noted the claim of the trade unions

to receive an earlier rise, a greater rise and a more prolonged rise than they could get without combination . . . When the time has come for the trade to reap the harvest for which it has been waiting, the employers will be very unwilling to let it slip; and even if an agreement to resist the demands of the men is made, it will not easily be maintained . . . Unions further hold that the threat of a strike, though less powerful when the tide of prosperity is falling than when it is rising, may yet avail for the comparatively easy task of slackening the fall in the high wages they have gained.

The stress here is on greater gains in prosperity. On the other hand it has been held that when a boom goes far enough to set up a competitive scramble for labour among employers, an accepted procedure for regulating wages collectively will slow down their rate of rise. Other observers have held that collective bargaining has taken most effect in depression. The historian of the rise of Swedish trade unions (Lindblom, 1938, p. 73), discussing the strikes of 1880–85 in which unions played an effective part for the first time, observed that

rises in wages won by unorganized strikes were easily taken away from the workers in times of depression . . . if they could not offer an organized resistance. The unorganized strike was a way of gaining momentary improvements in specially favourable circumstances. But only through organization could these improvements be made lasting.

In similar terms the historians of British trade unions from 1889 to 1910 have written: 'Unorganized or weakly organized workers frequently strike in years of good trade, but they lack the resources to sustain a defensive struggle during depression' (Clegg, Fox and Thompson, 1964, p. 362).

14. To see how far if at all these possibilities were realized we must ask whether, as collective bargaining extended, money wages departed from the course they are likely to have followed under the influence of the trade cycle and the market environment alone. In a number of ways they do seem to have done so, ways moreover that collective bargaining will account for. That the swing of money wages both up and down was generally narrower in later cycles than it had been in those of the 1860s and 1870s, without a corresponding difference in the cycles' own amplitude, supports the view that collective bargaining exerted some steadying influence on wages in boom as well as slump. The much smaller cut in wages in the unionized sector than in the rest of the US economy in 1929–32 also suggests that collective bargaining reduced the movement of wages under cyclical pressure. In a number of instances a phase of exceptional trade union vigour was associated with a bigger rise or smaller fall in wages than we should have expected from the level of business activity of the time. In the UK, for instance, rises in wages even greater than were to be expected from the rising phase of the cycle at the time were associated with the New Unionism of 1889, the release of the unions in 1906 from the constraint of Taff Vale judgement, and the growth of union membership and militancy in 1911–12. In the USA the fall of wages was exceptionally small during the depression of 1884–5 when the Knights of Labor were in their heyday; and in France wages actually rose during the depression of 1909, when trade union membership had increased by more than half over the six preceding years and the number of strikes had nearly doubled. There are instances also that suggest the effect of trade union weakness – in the UK, the smallness of the rise of wages during the increasing business activity of 1880–83, after what the Webbs (1894, p. 345 of 1920 edn) called 'a general rout of the trade union forces' in 1879, and the bigness of the wage cuts in 1901–2, when the cyclical recession was mild but the unions lay under the shadow of Taff Vale; in the USA, the smallness of the wage rises of 1905–8, when union membership that had increased perhaps fourfold between 1898 and 1904 suddenly ceased to grow and the unions came under organized attack by the employers and were increasingly subjected to court injunctions.

15. These instances all indicate some difference made by collective bargaining to wage movements and a positive association between those movements and the strength of trade unionism. But there are also negative indications. In two instances money wages rose

exceptionally fast at a time of exceptional weakness of the trade unions – in France, in 1874–9, when every sort of workers' organization lay crushed beneath a regime of surveillance and repression; and in Sweden, when after the defeat of the unions in the general strike of 1909 their membership fell by nearly a half, yet within three years the average earnings of men in industry rose by more than 12 per cent. But more remarkable than these particular indications is the general and prevailing absence before the Second World War of any marked and systematic change in the course of money wages that could be cited as an effect of the extension of collective bargaining. It is true that in the 1890s, when trade unionism in a number of countries began to grow to its present proportions, the trend of money wages in Germany, Sweden and the USA turned upwards; but there was no such turning-point in France and the UK; nor did the much wider extension of collective bargaining from the end of the First World War bring any upward trend at all. Whether we look into the changes in wages year by year in the course of business fluctuations or stand back and survey the trends over the longer run down to 1939, we see no discontinuity in any country that would imply the entry on the scene of some new factor in wage determination.

16. So far we have been concerned with the effects of collective bargaining as those may appear on the surface of the movements of money wages. We may look below to see whether any effects appear on the rise of productivity. Such effects might conceivably be various. On the one hand, the extension of trade union membership could give more effect to wage-earners' existing understandings about stints and norms of output, their dislike of changes in working practices and especially their resistance to labour-saving innovations. On the other hand, the enforcement of the union rate throughout a district would prevent inefficient managements from surviving by paying low wages; and in a hard market environment that did not allow of higher unit wage costs being simply covered by higher selling prices, a stronger drive for wage rises and resistance to wage cuts would put management under greater pressure to realize economies. In point of fact, the record of Figure 2 shows many differences in the rate at which productivity rose in various periods or economies, but none that suggests a systematic relation with the extension of collective bargaining. It is true that in the UK this extension at the end of the nineteenth century was accompanied by the virtual cessation of the rise of productivity, a change that was soon seized on by contempor-

aries and, under the title of 'the crisis in British industry', laid at the door of the New Unionism. But in Germany, Sweden and the USA the no less rapid extension of unionism at this time went with an accelerated rise of productivity. In the UK itself the rise was resumed and maintained through the interwar years, when the coverage of collective bargaining was far wider than it had been in the years of stagnation before the war. The years since the Second World War, in which the coverage of collective bargaining and the strength of the unions have been greater than ever, have seen an advance of productivity no less rapid than in any earlier period, in Germany, the UK and the USA. Any effect that collective bargaining may have taken on the rate of that advance must be small in comparison with that of other factors.

17. We may also ask whether collective bargaining seems to have taken any effect on the trends of money incomes and product prices that characterize different market environments. It might have done so because in a number of ways it induced a greater concentration of decisions affecting costs and prices. It gave wider publicity to particular claims and settlements. Though the unions engaged in bargaining still did little to concert their actions formally, the timing as well as the vigour of the moves each made to seize its own opportunities would be strengthened by the sight of others on the move. Employers for their part, aware that the claims confronting them were part of a general movement, would have less reason to fear that a settlement which raised their costs would worsen their relative position. Especially within any one industry, or at least within the district that bargaining covered, each firm would know that any pressure it was being put under to raise its prices was being exerted at the same time on its competitors. To bring wages and prices under collective control together was indeed the explicit aim of the 'Birmingham alliances' in the 1890s and the Royal Commission of Trade Unions was led to consider the possibility of collective bargaining becoming generally linked with price controls in this way. There is thus some reason to expect that the extension of collective bargaining would tend to raise the trend of money incomes and product prices. The course of that trend from its turning point in the 1890s down to the First World War does not conflict with that expectation. But then come the interwar years, with more collective bargaining than before, but a hard market environment and a downward trend of prices. Evidently more factors went to make the market environment than collective bargaining

alone: this could function as a price cartel only if those other factors permitted. But after the Second World War they did permit. Though the course of money incomes and product prices through these last twenty years has been unprecedented, we do not have to suppose that any new mechanism has been at work, only that a constraint on the mechanism has been removed. Proximately, this constraint was the expectation of employers that wage settlements which raised their unit costs would get them into trouble; ultimately, it was the absence of public policy to ensure that total monetary demand would not lag behind unit costs. Once public policy stood committed to ensure this, employers generally could reckon on being able to cover higher costs by higher prices without loss of business. It then became the function of collective bargaining to determine the movement of prices as well as of pay.

18. One way in which collective bargaining might make a difference to wage movements remains to be examined. With a given level of productivity and a price for the product that cannot be put up to cover a higher unit cost, the wage can still be raised if the profit margin is narrowed. It has been an aim of trade unionism to gain for the worker a larger share in the product. How has that share in fact behaved? There has been much discussion of the share of wages in the whole national product, but this share is too much of an amalgam to tell us much. In a labour-intensive industry like coal-mining the share of wages is naturally higher than in a capital-intensive industry like electricity supply, and the national aggregate of all such shares will vary with the relative sizes of different industries. What we need to follow is the division of the product per man between pay and profits in each industry by itself, and even here the amount of capital per worker will be increasing over time. The evidence at this level is complex and does not allow of a broad comparative presentation. It tends, however, towards three general conclusions. First, the share of pay in the product fluctuated widely in the course of the trade cycle because of the inverse fluctuation of profits. But, second, the level around which these fluctuations occurred showed no sustained trend upwards or downwards. In some instances the level may have been displaced through one or both of the two Great Wars, but otherwise what is remarkable is the absence of permanent change in the ratio between two quantities which themselves changed so much. Third, the share of pay has been able to follow a level trend through periods which have brought a progressive increase in the amount of capital

per worker and, therefore, in the amount due for the remuneration of capital, because in practice the output per worker has risen in the same proportion as the capital per worker.

19. This third finding is worth developing in more detail because it brings together the main elements of the distributive system on which collective bargaining has impinged. Let us take as typical the manufacture of a given product in two periods, I and II, in the second of which the amount of capital per worker was twice as great as in the first. We suppose for simplicity that the pound has the same purchasing power throughout. How the situations have in fact tended to compare is indicated in Table 2.

Table 2 *Typical changes in output and in incomes of labour and capital that have in practice been associated with an increase in capital per worker*

	Period I	Period II
1. Capital per worker	£300	£600
2. Net physical product per worker	50 tons	100 tons
3. Net value product per worker at price of £2 a ton	£100	£200
4. Annual earnings per worker	£79	£158
5. Profit at 7% on 1	£21	£42
6. Unit wage cost 4 ÷ 2	£1·58	£1·58

While capital per worker has doubled (row 1), output per worker has also doubled (row 2). The shares in the product have remained the same, so that the annual earnings per worker (row 4) and the total profit (row 5) have both doubled; but the rate of profit (row 5) and the unit wage cost (row 6) have remained the same. With constant purchasing power of money, the doubling of earnings in money represents a doubling of real earnings and these have risen in the same proportion as the physical product per worker.

20. In this system there are three relations, constancy in any two of which implies constancy in the third[1]: the ratio of capital to output (in our example, 3 to 1); the division of the product between earnings and profits (79 and 21 per cent) and the rate of profit (7 per cent).

1. They form the identity:
Share of earnings $= 1 -$ rate of profit $\times$ capital/output ratio,
or here, $0·79 = 1 - (0·07 \times 3)$.

335

We need not ask which have been the governing relations or why any of them should be stable. For our present purpose the essential is that the available estimates of the relevant magnitudes in the course of the development of some Western economies indicate that predominantly these relations have in fact been stable. The most significant of them for us here is the division of the product. If earnings per worker have tended to be a constant proportion of the product per worker, real earnings must have risen in proportion to productivity.

21. That this relation has held through periods in which there have been many and various changes in the course of money rates of pay and product prices implies a running adjustment between them. In fact this seems to have been made through the linking of product prices and unit wage costs. If in a given period money wages rose at 5 per cent a year, but productivity at only 3 per cent, and real wages correspondingly at only 3 per cent, prices must have risen at the rate of 2 per cent a year; but this they would have done if they were kept at a constant mark-up over unit wage costs, which themselves must have been rising by 2 per cent a year, the excess of the rise in money wages over that in productivity. Alternatively, if with productivity rising at 3 per cent money wages did not rise at all (as they did not, for instance, in the UK as between 1874 and 1889 or 1923 and 1937) real wages would still rise at the same rate as productivity if prices fell at 3 per cent a year, as they would do if they keep a constant ratio to unit labour costs.

22. In a system that behaves like this, power to raise the general level of money wages has not been power to raise real wages. If collective bargaining makes the general level of money wages rise more than it would otherwise have done, it will raise real wages only where prices cannot be adjusted so as to retain their previous relation to unit wage costs. But usually the circumstances in which money wages are most readily raised are those in which prices are most readily raised too; and at other times, when the price level is pinned down, rises in money wages in excess of the current rise in productivity are hard to wrest from employers. Generally, a difference made to the rate at which general level of money wages rises affects the rate of rise of prices but not that of real wages. Much more enters into the welfare and status of the wage-earner than the size of the basketful of goods that his wage will buy and there are many benefits not included in this basket that collective bargaining has gained for him. But the basketful itself remains a principal component of his material welfare and a

comparative study of different periods and countries strongly suggests that only occasionally has collective bargaining taken much effect upon its growth. This has been governed by the rise of productivity. [...]

23. It remains to be noted that collective bargaining has been the channel, and probably the indispensable channel, through which the form that advances in real wages should take has been decided – how much should be taken out in the pay packet and how much in shorter hours or fringe benefits. The institutions of collective bargaining provide for the formation of a common policy on these issues from time to time and for the administration of changes, some of which have to be made collectively if they are to be made at all. As productivity and standards of living continue to rise, these issues are likely to be of increasing importance in shaping the whole way of life of the working community.

References

CLEGG, H. A., A. FOX, and A. F. THOMPSON (1964), *A History of British Trade Unions since 1889*, vol. 1, Clarendon Press.

CREGG LEWIS, H. (1963), *Unionism and Relative Wages in the United States: An Empirical Inquiry*, University of Chicago Press.

LINDBLOM, T. (1938), *Den Svenska Fackföreningsrorelsens Uppkomst*.

MARSHALL, A. (1892), *Elements of Economics of Industry*.

WEBB, S., and B. WEBB (1894), *The History of Trade Unionism*, Longman, 1920.

26 Charles Mulvey

Union Influence on Relative Wage Levels

From Charles Mulvey, *The Economic Analysis of Trade Unions*, Martin Robertson, 1978, pp. 104–18.

This chapter is mainly devoted to a review of the empirical evidence on the effect of trade unions on relative wages. Essentially, we are concerned to discover whether or not, and in what degree, trade unions have raised the wages of their members above those paid to similar non-union workers.

The concept of a union relative wage effect

Throughout this book we have so far emphasized that if unions are to provide a positive economic return to their members – which is an important element in the demand for union services – they must do so by raising their members' wages above the rate which their members would receive in the absence of unions. In more practical terms, unions would probably go out of business if they were unable to achieve a positive union/non-union wage differential. Note that the non-union wage is *not* the same as the wage which would prevail in the absence of unions so long as union activity affects non-union wages – which it probably does – but, as we shall see shortly, the only practical measure of union wage effects available is the union/non-union wage differential.

We have already considered the special case of monopsony in the labour market – it is only 'special' in economic analysis; some variant of it is typical of the real world. The first task of a union in a labour market characterized by a positively-sloped supply curve of labour is to raise the wage to the competitive level. To do so involves the union in no costs in the form of employment foregone. The net result of a general union wage effect which everywhere and only countered monopsony power would be to establish a perfectly elastic supply of labour at the competitive wage to each monopsonistic employer in the economy. This would yield the same set of wages as would a perfectly competitive market. Empirically we have no way of knowing the degree or extent of union success in countering monopsony, although

338

it would hardly be outrageous to venture the opinion that monopsony-type power has probably been largely eliminated by trade union action.

Unions are most unlikely to be satisfied with merely countering monopsony power, even supposing that they knew at which point they had achieved just that. The whole concept of the union's wage policy being reflected in an internal trade off between wages and employment suggests that unions are concerned with increasing their members' wages to levels in excess of the competitive rate.

The differential and the state of the labour market

The implication of our assumption that unions will wish to establish a union wage in excess of the competitive rate is that a union/non-union wage differential will result. This differential will comprise both the (positive) wage premium which unions are able to extract from employers and any (negative) depressive effects on the non-union wage which result. We normally measure the differential as the percentage of the non-union wage represented by the union wage premium, i.e. $(W_u - W_n)/W_n$. 100.

Now, there is reason to suppose that the union/non-union wage differential will vary according to the state of the labour market. In general, when the labour market is tight we would expect the differential to be relatively small, and when the market is slack we would expect the differential to be relatively large. This follows from the analysis (in chapter 6) [not included here] of the relative importance of quit-and-strike threats under different labour market conditions. When the labour market is tight, the quit/cost ratio is high relative to the strike/cost ratio, and vice versa when the market is slack. Empirical evidence strongly supports this hypothesis (see Lewis, 1963). The importance of this observation is that we must be careful to take account of the state of the labour market at the point in time for which we are estimating the magnitude of the union/non-union wage differential. At certain points in time when the labour market was very tight, we might find that the estimated union/non-union differential was either zero or negligible. This does not mean, however, that unions generally have a negligible relative wage effect since estimates made when the labour market is very slack normally indicate a large and significant union/non-union wage differential. See Table 3 below for an illustration of this effect.

339

Unionism and relative wages – some conceptual problems

There are some important conceptual problems in attempting to identify the effects of unions on relative wages. Mostly they relate to situations in which the demand for unionism varies according to the characteristics of workers or those of their employment. For example, it is known that the extent of unionism among skilled manual workers is higher than among unskilled manual workers. Skilled workers tend both to be more highly paid than unskilled workers and to demand the services of unions more (and be more attractive potential members from the point of view of unions). How are we to untangle cause and effect in such a case? One might argue that the relatively high wages of skilled workers are not caused by a high degree of unionization, but are instead *the cause* of a high degree of unionization. One might also argue that the two features are simultaneously determined – relatively high wages for skilled workers are *both* a cause *and* an effect of a high degree of unionism. Again, one might argue that high wages are simply a consequence of a high degree of unionization. All of these are possible hypotheses, and economic theory does not help to discriminate between them.

Similar problems arise with a wide range of worker and employment characteristics. Plant size, industry concentration, sex mix, educational attainment, labour quality, race, geographical location, training characteristics, propensity to quit and labour turnover are all factors which might be jointly determined by both wages and unionism. Since we cannot sort these matters out on theoretical grounds alone – although the interested reader who wishes to study the many theoretical considerations involved will be enlightened by Johnson (1975), Reder (1965), Levinson (1967) and Ashenfelter and Johnson (1972) – we must bear them in mind in our examination of the empirical work on estimates of effect of unions on relative wages. In general, a failure to take account of the joint determination of wages, unionization and any of the factors listed above – if they are indeed *economically* jointly determined – will tend to attribute to trade unions a greater effect on relative wages than is the case.

Empirical estimates of the effect of unions on relative wages

Empirical estimates of the union/non-union wage differential are made by regression analysis. There are a great many detailed statistical problems involved in such analysis but it would not be appropriate to deal with these in this book. Lewis (1963) provides the most detailed and thorough account of the econometric methods involved in estimating union relative wage effects, but his exposition is hard to follow for non-econometricians. A simpler treatment may be found in Metcalf (1977, Appendix 2). We shall avoid getting into the complexities of estimating techniques by confining ourselves to some explanatory comments.

The basic equation which is employed in empirical estimates of the union/non-union wage differential is equation (1)

$$ln\ W_i = ln\ W_{ni} + \alpha_i \bar{M}$$

where $ln\ W_i$ is the natural logarithm of the average wage of an industry or occupation i, W_{ni} is the non-union wage in i, α_i is the proportion of the labour force in i who are paid the union wage, and $\bar{M}$ is the average union/non-union differential. In some studies the estimates are made for a sample of individual workers, rather than industry or occupation groups, and in those cases the is stand for the ith individual and α_i takes a value of 1 if the individual is paid the union rate and 0 if he is not. $\bar{M}$ provides an estimate of the union/non-union differential if we take its antilogarithm and subtract 1.

There are two important points to be clear about in the use of this estimating technique. Firstly, the method is really a very simple exploitation of the fact that any weighted average is dependent for its value on its weights. Hence the average wage is treated as a weighted average of the union wage and the non-union wage, the weights being the proportions who are paid the union and the non-union wage respectively. Estimation simply dismembers the average wage into its union and non-union components by applying the appropriate weights to it. Care must be taken to recognize that equation (1) is *not* based on the idea that *union power* is somehow proxied by the inclusion of the proportion unionized in the equation – a trap which many who ought to know better often fall into. Secondly, the non-union wage, W_{ni}, appears as an independent variable in equation (1), but is obviously not directly observable. If we could directly observe the non-union wage, all that would be required in order to know the union/non-union differential would be to subtract the non-union wage from the average wage. In estimation, therefore, it is necessary to replace the non-union wage term by a number of variables which we hypothesize will determine the non-union wage. In practice, in the case of a regression across industries, individuals or occupations at a single point in time – a cross-section regression – all that we require is a series of variables which may reasonably be supposed to account for variations in the non-union wage across the sample of industries, individuals or occupations. Care must be taken to ensure that the variables included for this purpose remove as much as possible of the variation in the dependent variable which is due to factors other than unionism. The intention therefore is to end up with an estimate of the union/non-union differential which indicates the difference in the wages of those paid the union rate and those paid the non-union rate by removing all sources of potential differences in wages other than that of union status.

The adjustment vector

The variables chosen to replace the non-union wage in estimation are often called 'the adjustment vector'. It comprises as many variables as economic theory suggests will give rise to variations in wages independent of unionism. Hence we know, for example, that economic theory predicts that the degree of skill possessed by an individual (his 'human capital') affects his wages since his wages include a return to the investments he has made in himself by way of education, training, etc. (the rate of return on investments in human capital). Now if we are estimating equation (1) across a sample of industries, we must take account of the fact that there may be differences in the skill composition of the labour forces in each industry and that this will be reflected in differences in the average wages in the sample. In order to avoid attributing wage differences arising from skill compositions to the effects of unions, we need to enter a variable in the adjustment vector specifically to take account of inter-industry variations in skill composition. Hence we would normally use a skill-mix variable specified as the proportion of the labour force in each industry who are classed as skilled and the proportion classed as unskilled.

Similarly, in aggregated studies, we would wish to enter a variable which removed variance in the dependent variable due to industry concentration, plant size, sex mix, labour quality, race or colour, age, experience, education, geographical location, marital status, and so on. All of these factors are capable of giving rise to variations in wages independent of union status, and their influence must be taken account of if accurate estimates of the union/non-union wage differential are to be made. In individual sample studies, additional variables relating to individual characteristics such as health, number of jobs held and so on may be included in the analysis. Since a wider range of such variables are normally available where individual samples can be obtained, the estimate of the differential ought to be more accurate.

Note that a number of variables suggested as appropriate for the adjustment vector have already been cited as potentially determined simultaneously with unionism – where this is the case, the estimated differential will tend to be biased upwards. However, since there is little agreement on the problem of simultaneous determination we must proceed, with caution, on the assumption that these variables are legitimate. We shall in any case soon return briefly to the problem of simultaneous determination in an empirical context.

Estimates of the union/non-union wage differential

The first estimates of the impact of unions on relative wages were made in the USA around 1950. Some were estimates of the union wage effect in individual industries and occupations, and some were economy-wide estimates. During the period 1950–60, over twenty such studies were published and most are reviewed in great detail in Lewis (1963). Around the middle of the 1960s individual samples became available in the USA owing to changes in the form of the population census, and a number of studies based on this information have subsequently appeared. In Britain the first attempt to estimate the union/non-union differential was made in 1974, but a good deal of work has been done since then. For the rest, there is the occasional study, but very little from outside the USA and Britain.

The US studies published in 1950–60

The various studies reviewed in Lewis (1963) differ in their methodologies but most are essentially based on a technique similar to that involved in estimating equation (1). Lewis has in fact reworked a number of the studies to standardize methodology to some extent. It would be tedious simply to repeat his summary of results (Lewis, 1963, pp. 184–6), so we report only the more interesting cases.

The earliest recorded estimate of a union/non-union wage differential was made for coalminers in the bituminous coal industry in the USA for the period 1909–13. Greenslade (reported in Lewis, 1963) estimated that the union/non-union differential in that industry was in the range of 38–43 per cent. Greenslade further estimated the differential for subsequent years – up to 1957 – and his estimates show that it was extremely erratic over time, jumping from around 0 per cent to around 40 per cent in a matter of two years. In general, Greenslade's results appear to show that the differential was at its highest when the economy was in deep recession ($M = 120$ per cent in 1922 and 57 per cent in 1933) and lowest when the economy was booming ($M = 0$ in 1945). Most of the other industry and occupation studies carried out at this time indicate that the differential was invariably positive although it was normally estimated to be less than the sort of figure estimated for miners by Greenslade. Take two representative years, 1922 as a slump year and 1939 as a boom year, and compare estimates made for different workgroups. Table 1 sets out the data and shows that the general order of magnitude of union relative wage effects was under 25 per cent in the inter-war period (although Greenslade's estimates are exceptional) and also that the estimated differential tended to be higher in 1922 than in 1939.

Table 1 Selected estimates of the differential for industries and occupations in the USA

Researcher	Sample studied	Estimated differential (%)	
		1922	1939
Greenslade	Bituminous coal miners	120	30
Sobotka	Unskilled construction labour	–	5
Sobotka	Skilled construction labour	>25	25
Rayack	Production workers (clothing)	20	17
Lurie	Motormen (local transport)	17	12
Scherer	Hotel workers		0

Source: Lewis (1963) Table 49, pp 194–6. All figures are approximate; in each case in which a range is quoted, I have taken a simple average of the high and low figures. All the studies cited are referred to in detail by Lewis.

Now, the studies cited above do not provide a very good basis for generalizations about the impact of unions on relative wages, since they refer to specific employments which will be characterized by special factors – such as differences in the elasticity of demand. Hence a number of attempts were made to estimate economy-wide union/non-union differentials. Again the methodology is similar to estimating equation (1). Table 2 gives the estimated differential at various dates. It is not possible to follow the procedure in Table 1 and pick out two dates, but I have tried to select dates as close as possible to each other.

Table 2 *Estimates of the differential for the US economy prior to 1960*

Researcher	Sample studied	M(%)	Date of estimate
Ross	Manufacturing and mining	10	1945
Ross and Goldner	Manufacturing and utilities	4	1946
Garbarino	Manufacturing	15	1940
Tullock	All workers	<25	1948/52
Tullock	All workers	<30	1953/57

Source: as for Table 1

As may be seen from Table 2, we are confronted with a range of estimates which appear to place the union/non-union differential for the USA in the immediate post-war years in the range of 4–25 per cent. Lewis himself has set out his own general estimates of the differential for the USA for the period 1920–58 on the basis of the studies cited above and his own work (see Table 3). Lewis reports his results in natural logarithms, and I have simply computed a percentage effect by taking the antilog − 1. Again, his estimates as presented in Table 3 appear to vary inversely with the level of economic activity – we shall return to this shortly. For the rest, the results show that the differential changes quite substantially from period to period and that, with the exception of periods of very high levels of economic activity, unions appear to have had a significant positive effect on relative wages. It should be noted at this stage that some economists have speculated that unions may have had an 'impact effect' on relative wages rather than a continuing effect. The argument is that unions, when they first become established, have a once-and-for-all effect on relative wages but thereafter do not subsequently affect them. (This would be in line with the notion that unions do little more than counter monopsony power.) This is not borne out by a casual glance at the data on the extent of unionism in relation to the estimates in Table 3. Unionism fell from about 15 per cent in 1920 to about 9 per cent in 1929, while the differential increased over the period; between 1930 and 1939 unionism increased from about 10 per cent to 19 per cent and, while the differential jumped in the first half of the period, it fell back sharply in the second half, which was

345

the half in which the extent of unionism grew most rapidly; from 1940 to 1958 unionism grew steadily from 20 per cent to 30 per cent and the differential rose, fell and then crept up again during that period. Hence there does not, at this impressionistic level, appear to be much support for the 'impact' hypothesis. Much more appealing is the apparent relation between the differential and the state of the economy.

Table 3 *Lewis's estimates of the union/non-union differential for the USA 1920–58*

Period	Estimated differential (%)	Period	Estimated differential (%)
1920–24	17	1940–44	6
1925–9	26	1945–9	2
1930–34	46	1950–54	12
1935–9	22	1955–8	16

Source: Lewis (1963), Table 64, p. 222

Since Lewis wrote his book there have been a number of economy-wide studies which tend to estimate a differential for the early 1960s of around 30 per cent (see, e.g., Throop, 1968; Rosen, 1969). However, a major advance in data availability which permitted estimates of the differential to be made on the basis of very large samples of individuals occurred during the 1960s, and estimates based on such samples are thought to be more reliable than those based on aggregates because of the scope provided for constructing a superior adjustment vector. Early estimates using this type of data tended to yield relatively low estimates of the differential. Weiss (1966) estimated a differential for 1960 of 20 per cent, and Stafford (1968) a range of 18–52 per cent for 1966. More reliable estimates have been made by Ashenfelter (1976). He estimates the differential for all workers for 1967 to be 12 per cent; for 1973 to be 16 per cent; and for 1975 to be 18 per cent. These estimates suggest that differentials estimated from aggregate data may contain a significant upward bias, since such estimates for the years covered by Ashenfelter yield higher estimates of the differential.

The spillover problem

In chapter 6 we noted there are likely to be significant spillover effects – that is, wages in the non-union sector of the economy will be influenced by wages in the union sector through such mechanisms as threat effects. Virtually all the US studies of the differential that we have considered above are unable to take account of such spillovers since the data used in estimation identify *union members* rather than *workers paid the union rate*. Although certain of the studies cited use data on collective agreement coverage, these data are unsatisfactory in many of the same respects as straightforward union membership data. In particular, the method of determining 'collective agreement coverage' used by the Bureau of Labor Statistics (BLS) is to count all those employed in an establishment with more than 50 per cent unionization as 'covered' and all those in establishments with less than 50 per cent unionization as 'uncovered'. If spillovers are significant, this implies that the estimates of the differential which do not take account of them will understate the true differential, since they will include in the 'non-union' category some workers who are paid the union wage. Rosen (1969) made an ingenious attempt to overcome this problem in a very complex study which cannot usefully be discussed here. Theoretical methods are, however, unlikely ever to overcome satisfactorily what is essentially a data problem. Fortunately, in both the USA and Britain significant advances have been made in recent years as regards the data.

The spillover effect simply means that some non-union workers are paid the union wage. This can arise by threat effects, by convention, by the criteria of third parties for non-union wage fixing, and so on. The full effect of unions on relative wages can only be identified if the union sector is defined in such a way as to include all or most of the spillover effect. The way in which the data have recently made this definition possible is by inquiry in the standard surveys as to whether a worker's wage is determined by the terms of a collective agreement or not, rather than whether he is a union member or not. In the USA the union/non-union status information was collected in a supplement to the US Current Population Survey. Since 1975 the survey has inquired whether the worker's wage was covered by a collective bargaining contract or not. If these data include most of the spillover category, then they would immediately overcome the problem of spillovers in estimating the differential. However, William Bailey of the BLS is reported by Ashenfelter (1976) to have estimated that the 'union' category formed 90 per cent of the 'covered' category – which implies that spillovers are only 10 per cent. In view of the fact that the 'union' category forms only about 69 per cent of the 'covered' category in Britain, the US data seem somewhat unlikely. There is no way of determining whether the US data understate the extent of the spillover, whether the British data overstate its extent or whether it is really only 10 per cent in the USA and 31 per cent in Britain.

Estimates of the union/non-union differential for Britain

In Britain the first attempt to estimate a union/non-union differential was made by Pencavel (1974), whose estimate refers to 1964. Pencavel used 'union' data and estimated that union workers in industries which did not engage in a significant degree of plant bargaining had a zero differential over non-union workers, but that workers in industries which did engage in a significant degree of plant bargaining enjoyed a differential of about 14 per cent over non-union workers. These estimates seemed to indicate that British unions affected relative wages to a significantly lower degree than US unions did. However, after Pencavel's study had been completed, new data on the coverage of collective agreements were published in the *New Earnings Survey* carried out by the Department of Employment for 1973. These data did not simply indicate the extent of union wage coverage, but also the extent of coverage of: national agreements only; national plus supplementary agreements; local and company agreements; and no collective agreement. Since these data did appear to capture a significant element of the spillover effect, a number of estimates of the union/non-union differential, as well as the differentials associated with each type of agreement coverage, were quickly made. The studies differ in the samples used and in the components of the adjustment vector; we list the estimates made by each with an indication of differences in sample used but neglect differences in adjustment vectors. The full range of British studies to date is given in Table 4.

Table 4 reveals a reasonably tight range of estimates of the differential and its components by agreement type with the exception of Stewart's estimate. If we leave Stewart's estimate aside for the moment the differential ranges from 16 per cent to 26 per cent for samples which variously include men, women and manual and non-manual labour. There is, however, some reason to suppose that these estimates may be too high, and further work is being undertaken which ought to clarify this matter. (See Thomson, Mulvey and Farbman, 1977, for some evidence which suggests that the differential may be lower than the estimates in Table 4.) Stewart's estimate is based on an adjustment vector which utilizes data on personal characteristics taken from the General Household Survey and also employs gross *weekly* earnings as the dependent variable. Certainly this latter feature of his study is known to result in relatively high estimates of the differential (as compared with those made with gross hourly earnings as the dependent variable), and it may be that the personal characteristics data also tend to inflate the estimate.

Table 4 Estimates of the union/non-union differential for Britain

Researcher	Sample	Date	Estimate (%)*			
			M	NO	NPLUS	CB
Pencavel (1974)	All manual workers	1964	8	0		14
Mulvey (1976)	Manufacturing male manual	1973	26	0	41	46
Mulvey and Foster (1976)	All industries male	1973	22	–	–	–
Nickell (1977)	All manual males	1972	18	0	22	20
	All manual females	1972	19	20	9·2	44
Stewart (reported in Metcalf, 1977)	Manual manufacturing workers	1971	40	Not known		

* M is the differential for all 'covered' workers over 'uncovered'; NO is the differential of those covered by national agreements only over uncovered workers; NPLUS is the differential of those covered by national plus supplementary agreements over uncovered workers, and CB is the differential of those covered by local and company agreements over uncovered workers.

Dependent variable is gross hourly earnings in Mulvey and Foster and in Stewart, where the dependent variable is gross weekly earnings.

An interesting feature of the estimates in Table 4 is that manual males whose wages are subject only to a national agreement appear to derive no wage premium over the non-union wage. This suggests that national bargaining alone is not sufficiently potent to yield a union wage in excess of the competitive rate or that the 'non-union' wage is determined by reference to national agreements. It is worth reflecting, though, that one quarter of all men in manufacturing industry in Britain are covered by national agreements only and appear to obtain no wage benefit in return. A positive wage premium from collective agreement coverage is confined to the 60 per cent of male manual workers in manufacturing, who are covered by national plus supplementary agreements or by company, local, etc., agreements. However, in the case of women this does not apply.

The Pencavel study, as has already been noted, was based on unionization rather than wage coverage data and that provides a ready explanation of the relatively low estimate made. However, Pencavel's estimate refers to 1964 – something of a boom year – while the other estimates all refer to 1973 – something of a slump year. Hence it may be that his estimate reflects the association between the differential and the level of economic activity which is evident in the USA.

Finally, Layard, Metcalf and Nickell (1977) have made estimates of the differential for Britain on a year-by-year basis between 1961 and 1975. These are rather *ad hoc,* since the coverage variable employed in each year's estimate is the data for 1973 – the only available series. Hence these estimates require the assumption that agreement coverage did not vary significantly over the period 1961–75. With that caution in mind, the estimates are set out in Table 5.

In a regression of the differential on unemployment for the period 1961–75, it does appear that the differential varies directly with unemployment, which confirms that the US evidence of this relation is supported on this limited basis for Britain too.

Some sub-hypotheses concerning the differential

We would expect the union/non-union wage differential to vary according to certain specific characteristics of different workgroups. Theoretical considerations would suggest:

(*a*) that skilled workers would obtain a higher differential than unskilled workers because the elasticity of demand is lower for skilled than unskilled workers (Rosen, 1970);

(*b*) that women would, other things being equal, secure a lower differential than men because women are less skilled than men and because unions may discriminate against women;

(*c*) that workers from racial minorities would obtain a lower differential than white workers because they possess less skill on average than white workers and because unions may discriminate against them.

Skill and the differential

In Table 6 we report estimates of the differential made for skilled and unskilled men in the USA for 1973. The evidence afforded by Table 6 shows that our hypothesis that skilled workers would obtain larger

Table 5 Estimates of the union/non-union differential for Britain 1961–75

Year	Estimate (%)	Year	Estimate (%)
1961	18·5	1968	22·1
1962	21·0	1969	23·4 (15·0)
1963	16·2	1970	29·7 (17·3)
1964	17·3	1971	29·7 (18·5)
1965	16·2	1972	36·3 (20·9)
1966	18·5	1973	36·3 (20·9)
1967	18·5	1974	28·4 (20·9)
		1975	36·3 (29·7)

Source: Layard, Metcalf and Nickell (1977). Figures in brackets are based on 1968 SIC classifications; all other figures are based on 1958 SIC classification.

wage differentials than less-skilled workers is not supported. In fact the reverse is apparently the case. Possible reasons for this are that skilled workers may lose any special advantage deriving from a low elasticity of demand when they bargain in collaboration with other workers, a practice that is normal in industrial unions and increasingly the case in many other situations, or that unions have deliberately pursued egalitarian policies to advance the cause of the lower-paid or, again, that non-union skilled workers are operating in a relatively more favourable market environment than less-skilled workers. Moreover, the quit threat of skilled non-union workers is likely to be relatively more potent than that of less-skilled workers.

Table 6 Estimates of the union/non-union differential for males in construction and manufacturing by skill classes for the USA 1973

	Manufacturing[†] USA	Construction USA
Skilled*	7	35
Semi-skilled*	14	52
Unskilled*	21	57

* These categories are labelled 'craftsmen', 'operatives' and 'laborers' in the US study.
[†] The data are unweighted averages of durable and non-durable manufacturing estimates.
Sources: data are taken from Ashenfelter (1976), Table 3.

Women, race and the differential

In Table 7 we report estimates of the differential made for men and for women in 1973 for the USA and in 1972 for Britain, and for race in the USA in 1973.

Our hypothesis that blacks would have a lower union/non-union differential than whites is not supported by the US evidence in Table 7 – the reverse is evidently the case. Since, as we have already seen, skill apparently confers no positive benefits to union workers – indeed the reverse – the lower average skill of black workers may account for the unexpectedly high relative differential, and also unions may, in the Equal Opportunities environment, have positively discriminated in favour of blacks. Ashenfelter (1976, Table 2) reports some evidence which suggests that the differential enjoyed by black trade unionists increased from near equality in 1967 with the white differential to its 1973 level and increased again (for men) in 1975.

The hypothesis that women would have a lower differential than men is supported by the US but not by the British evidence. The latter suggests an almost indentical differential for both men and women. The British result is hard to explain but may be connected with the growing influence of women in trade unions and also the effects of the Equal Pay Act.

Table 7 *The union/non-union differential by sex and race for the USA in 1973 and by sex for Britain in 1972* (%)

	Men White	Black	Women White	Black
USA	17	25	13·5	14
Britain		18		19

Sources: US data from Ashenfelter, 1976, Table 2, referring to all men and women workers; data for Britain from Nickell, 1977, Table 3, referring to manual workers

Some further empirical findings

One aspect of union policy which we have already discussed concerns the desire of unions to establish uniform wage rates and conditions throughout their jurisdictions. Unions are generally motivated to pursue this objective in order to protect their most vulnerable members and to restrict the scope for product substitution within the union sector. Empirical studies show that unions have apparently been successful in reducing interpersonal wage differentials (see Lewis, 1963, for evidence on the USA, and Thomson, Mulvey and Farbman, 1977, for Britain). In general the dispersion of wages within the union sector is considerably less than in the non-union sector, and on that basis one may infer that unions have reduced interpersonal differentials.

A variety of evidence tends to show that unions have been inclined to reduce geographical, industrial and inter-firm wage differentials, and this is again generally explicable in terms of a desire on their part to protect their weakest members and to limit the potential for competition within the union sector. Little is known about union effects on inter-occupational differentials, but it has been argued (Turner, 1957) that the growth of mass unionism with its emphasis on egalitarianism and a policy of flat-rate money wage increases for all has contributed to a narrowing of occupational differentials.

Table 8 Union/non-union differentials by components of gross weekly earnings in Britain 1973

Component of pay	Union/non-union differential (%)	
	Manual men	Manual women
Gross weekly earnings	+ 13·2	+ 19·0
Overtime	+ 37·4	+ 45·6
Incentive pay	+112·7	+ 65·7
Shift premium	+232·4	+400·0
Residual pay	0·5	+ 11·1

Source: Thomson, Mulvey and Farbman (1977), Table 4

Finally, there is evidence to suggest that unions do not significantly affect union/non-union earnings differentials for hours worked within the standard or basic work-week, but instead make all their influence felt regarding overtime rates, shift premiums, bonus pay, and so on. In Table 8 the gross weekly earnings of those covered by collective agreements are broken down into their main components and expressed as a set of percentage union/non-union differentials.

Since total hours worked by both the union and non-union workers were similar, the data suggest a union effect which influences the allocation of hours between premium and non-premium rates. Hence the standard work-week for union workers may be shorter than for non-union workers, so that a higher proportion of the union workers' hours are paid at overtime rates. However, no complete explanation of these curious and unexpected findings is yet available, although a number of possible hypotheses are advanced in Thomson, Mulvey and Farbman (1977). The effects of trade unions on relative wages are evidently not as straightforward as the conventional theory suggests!

Conclusion

There is one crucial matter which we must not lose sight of in considering estimates of union/non-union wage differentials, and that is the possibility that wages and unionism are simultaneously determined or that the extent of unionism is determined by the wage. If either of these possibilities were in fact true, then we could not regard estimated union/non-union differentials as an indicator of the magnitude of the effects of unions on relative wages. The conventional view is that estimated union/non-union differentials are indicators of the effects of unions on relative wages, and a number of those who have proposed alternative views have nevertheless continued to publish estimates of the differential on the conventional basis. Ashenfelter and Johnson (1972), Johnson (1975) and Pencavel (1971) have all advanced alternative hypotheses about the relation between unionism and wages, but have all been prepared to accept the conventional assumption in empirical work. The existing state of knowledge does not permit us to go further than that. We assume that unions have a unicausal influence on wages, while recognizing that this may not be the case and may some time be shown not to be the case.

On that basis we may conclude that unions do influence relative wages and that the magnitude of the union/non-union differential is in the region of 0–40 per cent. Unions affect relative wages to a greater extent when aggregate demand is low (unemployment is high) than when aggregate demand is high (unemployment is low). Unions appear to influence relative wages to a greater extent for less-skilled workers than for skilled workers, to a greater extent for blacks than whites in the USA, and to a greater extent for men than women in the USA and about the same for men and women in Britain. The type of agreement coverage also apparently affects the degree to which unions affect relative wages in Britain.

These general conclusions must be tempered by noting that the evidence also suggests that there are wide differences in estimated differentials as between occupations and industries for which we cannot at present account. In view of this, it would be wrong to put too much faith in the precise numerical estimates of the differential presented in this chapter.

Summary

We began this chapter by discussing the way in which a union/non-union wage differential will be established. In general, we would expect increases in union wages to cause a displacement of union labour into the 'non-union sector' of the economy and to depress the non-union wage as a result. Hence the union/non-union wage differential will comprise the union-won wage increase and the union-caused fall in the non-union wage. Unions, however, also affect non-union wages in the opposite way through spillover effects. The main spillover effect is likely to be due to the threat responses of non-union firms who pay wages sufficiently high to prevent a demand for unionization arising. The net effects of unions on non-union wages depends on the ease of substitution of non-union and union labour, the flexibility of relative wages, and on the extent of spillovers.

A simple statistical method of estimating union/non-union differentials exists, and depends for its validity on the assumption that unions affect relative wages in a unicausal way. We considered some of the evidence on the effects of unions on relative wages that have been made for the USA and for Britain at various points in time and for various sub-groups. These results and their implications are summarized in the 'Conclusions' section above.

References

ASHENFELTER, O. (1976), 'Union relative wage effects: new evidence and a survey of their implications for wage inflation', *Working Paper 89*, Industrial Relations Section, Princeton University.

JOHNSON, G. E. (1975), 'Economic analysis of trade unions', *American Economic Review*, Papers and Poceedings.

LEWIS, H. G. (1963), *Unionism and Relative Wages in the United States*, Chicago University Press.

METCALF, D. (1977), 'Unions, incomes policy and relative wages in Britain', *British Journal of Industrial Relations*, July.

MULVEY, C. (1976), 'Collective agreements and relative earnings in UK manufacturing in 1973', *Economica*, November.

REDER, M. W. (1965), 'Unions and Wages: The Problem of Measurement', *Journal of Political Economy*.

STAFFORD, F. P. (1968), 'Concentration and Labor earnings: comment', *American Economic Review*.

THOMSON, A., C. MULVEY and M. FARBMAN (1977), 'Bargaining structure and relative earnings in Great Britain', *British Journal of Industrial Relations*, July.

THROOP, A. (1972), 'The union–non-union wage differential and cost-push inflation', *American Economic Review*.

TOSEN, S. (1969), 'Trade union power: threat effects and the extent of organisation', *Review of Economic Studies*.

TURNER, H. A. (1957), 'Inflation and Wage Differentials in Great Britain', *The Theory of Wage Determination*, ed. J. T. Dunlop, Macmillan.

WEISS, L. W. (1966), 'Concentration and Labor Earnings', *American Economic Review*.

27 F. A. Hayek

The Trade Unions and Britain's Economic Decline

From F. A. Hayek, *Unemployment and the Unions, 1980s: The Distortion of Relative Wages by Monopoly in the Labour Market*, Institute of Economic Affairs, pp. 51-8.

I now turn to what is widely recognized as the crucial debility in Britain's economic future, but which is usually regarded as politically insoluble.

Trade unions, in their present form, have become part of the British way of life, and their power has become politically sacrosanct. But economic decline has also become part of the British way of life, and few people are willing to accept that as sacrosanct. Many British people are beginning to see the connection between the two. Yet this insight is in such conflict with what most of them believe the trade unions have achieved for the mass of wage-earners that they cannot see a remedy. This dilemma overlooks the unique privileges the unions enjoy in Britain, which have placed them in a position where they are forced to be anti-social, as even one of their friends, Baroness Wootton, has had to admit.

False claims to benefit the population as a whole

Unions have gained the public support they still enjoy by their pretence of benefiting the working population at large. They probably did achieve this aim in their early years when more or less immobile workers sometimes faced a single factory-owner. I do not, of course, deny the trade unions their historical merits or question their right to exist as voluntary organizations. Indeed, I believe that everybody, unless he has voluntarily renounced it, ought to have the right to join a trade union. But neither ought anyone to have the right to force others to do so. I am even prepared to agree that *everybody* ought to have the *right* to strike, so far as he does not thereby break a contract or the law has not conferred a monopoly on the enterprise in which he is engaged. But I am convinced that nobody ought to have the right to *force* others to strike.

Trade unions' legal privileges obstruct working-class prosperity

Such would be the position if the general principles of law applicable to all other citizens applied also to the trade unions and their members. But in 1906, in a typical act of buying the swing-vote of a minority, the then Liberal Government passed the Trade Disputes Act which, as A. V. Dicey justly put it (in *Law and Public Opinion in England*, 1914), conferred

upon a trade union a freedom from civil liability for the commission of even the most heinous wrong by the union or its servant, and in short confer[red] upon every trade union a privilege and protection not possessed by any other person or body of persons, whether corporate or incorporate . . . [it] makes the trade union a privileged body exempted from the ordinary law of the land. No such privileged body has ever before been created by an English Parliament [and] it stimulates among workmen the fatal illusion that [they] should aim at the attainment not of equality, but of privilege.

These legalized powers of the unions have become the biggest obstacle to raising the living standards of the working class as a whole. They are the chief cause of the unnecessarily big differences between the best- and the worst-paid workers. They are the prime source of unemployment. They are the main reason for the decline of the British economy in general.

Trade union members gain by exploiting other workers

The crucial truth, which is not generally understood, is that all the powers employed by individual trade unions to raise the remuneration of their members rest on depriving other workers of opportunities. This truth was apparently understood, in the past, by the more reasonable trade union leaders. Twenty-three years ago, the then chairman of the Trades Union Congress could still say that he did

not believe that the trade union movement of Great Britain can live for much longer on the basis of compulsion. Must people belong to us or starve, whether they like our policies or not? No. I believe the trade union card is an honour to be conferred, not a badge which signifies that you have got to do something whether you like it or not. We want the right to exclude people from our union if necessary, and we cannot do this on the basis of 'Belong or Starve'.

Thus Mr Charles (now Lord) Geddes.

There has evidently been a complete change. The present ability of any trade union to obtain better terms for its members rests chiefly on its legalized power to *prevent other workers from earning as good an income as they otherwise might*. It is thus maintained, literally, by the exploitation of those not permitted to do work that they would like to do. The elite of the British working class may still profit as a result, although even this has now become doubtful. But they certainly derive their relative advantage by keeping workers who are *worse* off from improving their position. These groups acquire their advantage, at the expense of those they prevent from bettering themselves, by doing work in which they could earn more – though somewhat less than those who claim a monopoly.

Free society threatened by union curtailment of access to jobs

If a free society is to continue, no monopoly can be allowed to use physical force to maintain its privileged position and to threaten to deprive the public of essential services that other workers are able and willing to render. Yet all the most harmful practices of British trade unions derive from their being allowed forcefully to prevent outsiders from offering their services to the public on their own terms. The chief instances of such legal powers are intimidatory picketing, preventing non-members from doing particular kinds of jobs such as 'demarcation' rules, and the closed shop. Yet all these restrictive practices are prohibited in most of the more prosperous Western countries.

Union restrictive practices have hurt the working man

It is more than doubtful, however, whether in the long run these selfish practices have improved the real wages of even those workers whose unions have been most successful in driving up their relative wages – compared with what they would have been in the absence of trade unions. It is certain, and could not be otherwise, that the average level of attainable real wages of British workers as a whole has thereby been substantially lowered. Such practices have substantially reduced the productivity potential of British labour generally. They have turned Britain, which at one time had the highest wages in Europe, into a relatively low-wage economy.

British price structure paralysed by political wage determination

A large economy can be prosperous only if it relies on competitive prices to coordinate individual effort by condensing all the information fed into the market by many thousands of individuals. The effect of the present system of wage determination in Britain is that the country no longer has an internal price structure to guide the economic use of resources. This is almost entirely due to the rigidity of politically determined wages. If it is no longer possible to know the most efficient use of the natural talents of the British people, it is because relative wages no longer reflect the relative scarcity of skills. Even their relative scarcity is no longer determined by objective facts about the real conditions of supply and demand, but by an artificial product of the arbitrary decisions of legally tolerated monopolies.

Impersonal nature of market decisions makes them acceptable

Prices or wages cannot be a matter of 'justice' if the economic system is to function. Whether it is necessary for maintaining or increasing the national income to draw people into tool-making or services, or to discourage entry into entertainment or sociological research, has nothing to do with the 'justice' or the merits or the 'needs' of those affected. In the real world, nobody can know where people are required but the market, which absorbs and digests the myriad bits of information possessed by all who buy or sell in it. And it is precisely because the decision is not the opinion of an identifiable person (like a Minister or Commissar) or a group of men (like a Cabinet or Politbureau), but results from impersonal signals in a process that no individual or group can control, that it can be tolerated. It would be unbearable if it were the decision of some authority which assigned everyone to his job and determined his reward.

British governments have supported union coercion

I would be prepared to predict that the average worker's income would rise fastest in a country where relative wages are flexible, and where the exploitation of workers by monopolistic trade union organizations of specialized groups of workers are effectively outlawed. Such exploitation is, however, the chief source of power of individual labour unions in Britain. The result of thus freeing the labour market would inevitably be a structure of relative wages very different from the traditional one now preserved by union power. This result will have to come about if the British economy is to stop decaying.

While a functioning market and trade unions with coercive powers cannot coexist, yet it is only in the free system of the market that the unions can survive. Yet the unions are destroying the free market through their legalized use of coercion. The widespread use of force to gain at the expense of others has not only been tolerated but also supported by British governments, on the false pretence that it enhances justice and benefits the most needy. Not only is the opposite true; the effect of this tolerance and support of union coercion is to reduce everybody's potential income – except that of trade union officials.

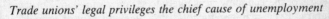

Trade unions' legal privileges the chief cause of unemployment

Impeding increases in productivity and hence real wage growth is not the worst effect of current trade union practices. Even more serious is the extent to which they have become the chief cause of unemployment, for which the market economy is then blamed.

The volume of employment is not a function of the *general* wage level but of the structure of *relative* wages. The contrary belief, still widely held in Britain by economists and politicians, is due to a unique experience of this country. It arose after Britain returned to the gold standard in 1925 at the pre-war parity between sterling and gold, when wages, which had risen considerably during the wartime inflation, proved generally too high for the country to maintain its exports. It was in that very special atmosphere that discussion about the relationship between wages and unemployment started, and the belief came to be held that the crucial factor was the general level of wages. The writings of Keynes unfortunately seemed to support this error.

The situation after 1925 was entirely exceptional. The normal cause of recurrent waves of widespread unemployment is rather a discrepancy between the way in which demand is distributed between products and services, and the proportions in which resources are devoted to producing them. Unemployment is the result of divergent changes in the direction of demand and the techniques of production. If labour is not deployed according to demand for products, there is unemployment. But the most common cause is that, because of excessive credit expansion, over-investment has been encouraged and too many resources have been drawn into the production of capital goods, where they can be employed only so long as the expansion continues or even accelerates. And credit is expanded to appease trade unions that fear their members will lose their jobs, even though it is they themselves who forced wages too high to enable the workers to find jobs at these excessive rates of pay.

Full employment requires continual changes in relative wages

Once such a misdirection of resources has taken place, tolerably full employment can be restored only by redirecting some of them to other uses. This is, of necessity, a slow process, even when wages are flexible. And so long as substantial unemployment prevails in such a large sector of the economy, it is likely to set up a cumulative process of deflation. Even maintaining total final demand cannot provide a cure, because it will not create employment in the over-expanded capital industries. The unemployment there will continue to operate as a persistent drain on the income stream. It cannot be stopped, or lastingly compensated for, by the expenditure of new paper money printed for the purpose or created in other ways. The attempt to cure it by adding to the supply of money must lead to accelerating inflation. Yet this has been the futile policy of recent British governments.

Such unemployment can be effectively cured only by redirecting workers to jobs where they can be lastingly employed. In a free society, this redirection requires a change in relative wages to make prospects less attractive in occupations or industries where labour is in surplus and more attractive where the demand for labour is expanding. This is *the essential mechanism which alone can correct a misdirection of labour* once it has occurred in a society where workers are free to choose their jobs.

Short of very special circumstances such as those after 1925, there is no reason why it should ever be necessary for the general level of wages to fall. But it is not possible to keep a market economy working *at full speed*, which is what the workers would like, without *some* wages occasionally falling while others rise. Full employment cannot be maintained by preserving a conventional, outdated wage structure, but only by adjusting wages in each sector to changing demands – raising some wages by lowering others.

Keynes's responsibility for 'the final disaster'

The final disaster we owe mainly to Lord Keynes. His erroneous conception that employment could be directly controlled by regulating aggregate demand through monetary policy shifted responsibility for employment from the trade unions to government. This error relieved trade unions of the responsibility to adjust their wage demands so as to sell as much work as possible, and misrepresented full employment entirely as a function of government monetary policy. For forty years it has thus made the price mechanism ineffective in the labour market by preventing wages from acting as a signal to workers and employers. As a result, there is divided responsibility: the trade unions are allowed to enforce their wage demands without regard to the effect on employment and government is expected to create the demand at which the available supply of work can be sold at the prevailing (or even higher) wages. Inevitably the consequence is continuous and accelerating inflation.

Futility of negotiating reform with union leaders until deprived of legal privileges

It is an illusion to imagine that the problems Britain now faces can be solved by negotiation with the present trade union leaders. They owe their power precisely to the scope for abusing the privileges which the law has granted them. It is the rank and file of the workers, including many trade union members, who ultimately suffer from this abuse. I believe they could be helped to understand this cause of their suffering. Their support must be obtained if the system that is destroying Britain's wealth and well-being is to be changed.

One of the more recent general secretaries of the Trades Union Congress, the late George Woodcock, wrote about 'the fear and dislike in which many of our own people seem to hold our own trade unions'. A political party in which trade unions have a major constitutional role cannot strike at the source of their power. If I were responsible for the policy of the Conservative Party, I would rather be defeated at the polls than be charged with policy without a clear mandate to remove the legal sources of excessive trade union power. This a trade union party, of course, can never do. The only hope is that an appeal to a large number of workers over the heads of their present leaders will lead to the demand for a reduction in their powers.

No salvation for Britain until union privileges are revoked

There can be no salvation for Britain until the special privileges granted to the trade unions three-quarters of a century ago are revoked. Average real wages of British workers would undoubtedly be higher, and their chances of finding employment better, if the wages paid in different occupations were again determined by the market and if all limitations on the work an individual is allowed to do were removed.

Britain can improve her position in the world market, and hence the price in work effort at which her population can be fed, only by allowing the market to bring about a restructuring of her whole internal price system. What is ossified in Britain is not the skill of her entrepreneurs or workers, but the price structure and the indispensable discipline it imposes. The present British economic system no longer signals what has to be done and no longer rewards those who do it or penalizes those who fail to do it.

28 Patrick Minford

Trade Unions Destroy a Million Jobs

From Patrick Minford, 'Trade Unions Destroy a Million Jobs', *Journal of Economic Affairs*, no. 2, January 1982, pp. 73–9.

Part I The central analysis and argument

It is not original to suggest that unions create unemployment. It has been a widespread claim by economists – including many associated with the IEA [Institute of Economic Affairs] – who have urged more freedom for market forces. What they have generally had in mind was that unions raise wages for *unionized* workers, some of whom as a consequence will lose their jobs (or equivalently other *non*-unionized workers will fail to get jobs in unionized industries). The workers displaced will find it hard to gain employment in the non-union sectors because of the limited opportunities there and will for the most part be unemployed.

What has been lacking in this argument is two-fold. First, there has been some vagueness about why workers would not find jobs in the non-union sector, since there they would drive non-union wages down until there was full employment. Second, the order of magnitude of the unemployment which could result from union power has not been indicated; this is obviously very important because if the magnitudes are trivial, the ordeal by fire required to reduce union power would not be politically attractive.

In the course of our researches at Liverpool we have devoted considerable effort to examining these two matters.[1] This article describes our examination. Our first conclusion has been that the operation of the tax and benefit system prevents wages in the non-union sector from dropping much, because benefits are 'flat rate' (i.e. regardless of previous earnings) after six months, and that for low-income jobs they may be so close to net earnings that the jobs would become unviable and unattractive for workers if wages fell very far. Hence the non-union sector has only a small ability to absorb workers displaced by the union sector.

1. Financial support for this work from the Social Science Research Council is gratefully acknowledged.

Upon estimating relationships which incorporate the role of the tax and benefits system, our second conclusion has been that *the substantial rise in union power since the early 1960s has raised unemployment by about one million*. This is a round number probably at the upper end of what politicians and practical men may have suspected, but, if correct, it must weigh heavily in the political scales against the fuss involved in reducing union power.

Challenge to wishful thinking

Our work is bound to be controversial at this stage because it challenges much wishful thinking. But it will be a long time before all the additional evidence has been sifted – particularly the immense amount of potential information in the Family Expenditure Survey – which may settle all the interlocking issues involved. But by the time such research has been done, it may be too late to take the necessary action. Already the tide of union power has swept in irresistibly. Some recent events have suggested it may temporarily be receding. But who can tell what access of strength it may gain in the next economic upturn and beyond? Now may be the last major opportunity available to politicians to push the tide out once and for all. To lose such an opportunity on the chance that our estimate of the effect of union power may be much too high would be a dangerous gamble. Compared with it, the risk that the highly unpopular union movement will be able to resist successfully and damagingly the necessary legislation to cut their powers seems a risk substantially less to be feared.

Union monopoly and unemployment

The basic ideas in our work are simple enough. A union exists to raise the wages of its members to an 'optimal' amount, given, first, that higher union wages means fewer union jobs, and, second, the wages their members could get in the non-union sector. The union typically determines an optimal union wage which is some way above the non-union wage. A monopolist raises his price to the point at which his profits are maximized; this point will be above that which would have been set by free competition and will reduce the size of the market. So with a union monopoly.

Workers who lose their jobs as a result of their monopoly power will then seek jobs in the non-union sector. These additional supplies of labour force wages down there, until supply is equal to demand.

But at this point we note that the social security system guarantees a minimum income regardless of work and that taxes apply to workers with very low incomes. As wages in the non-union sector fall, they become progressively less attractive (after tax) to workers forced out of the union sector; some, perhaps many, will not be prepared to take the jobs on offer for such rewards. They will go on the dole. The major way in which supply is equated to demand in the non-union sector by falling wages is through the contraction of supply. Demand rises as wages fall, but the tax and social security system imparts a 'floor' to wages, which causes major withdrawals from the labour market as wages get too close to this critical level. Consequently, *wages cannot fall enough to create much additional demand*.

This analysis is sometimes criticized on the grounds that the resulting unemployment is labelled as 'voluntary'. Many people feel, rightly, that unemployment is a tragic misfortune and cannot be regarded in any meaningful sense as voluntary. Consequently they feel inclined to dismiss the analysis.

But such a feeling is inspired by a complete misconception. There is nothing in the analysis to suggest otherwise than that unemployment is unpleasant and degrading. The point of the analysis is that *the alternatives to unemployment, non-union jobs at non-union wages, are even less attractive*. What is more, workers who take the jobs in the non-union sector would, of course, prefer to work in the better-paid union sector. It is a technical convention in economics to call the decisions of these people 'voluntary', because they are doing their best even in poor circumstances, but they could just as well be described as involuntarily forced out of the union sector.

No amount of relabelling, however, will avoid the basic problem society faces: how to create permanent jobs for pay that people will accept. The analysis clearly indicates that one major way to do this is to *reduce the power of unions to raise union wages*. As union wages fall, the demand for union labour rises, people are withdrawn from the non-union sector, non-union wages rise and more people are prepared to work in it.

The estimated effects of union power

In Part II we detail our analysis. It is basically that during the 1960s the world environment was kind to Britain, world trade grew fast and our terms of trade were favourable. British governments raised both social security benefits and taxation on labour substantially. Further-

367

more, union power increased sharply towards 1970. During the 1970s we have had a substantial worsening of the world environment, a slow-down in world trade, and a deterioration of our terms of trade (if to a modest extent offset by North Sea oil). Yet union power has continued to increase, though more slowly. And though real benefits have stabilized, labour tax rates have continued to rise. The opposite – a reversal of the trends in the 1960s – was required to prevent unemployment from rising as it has done in the 1970s.

We can inspect the effect of union power in various dimensions. The unionization rate in 1963 was 43 per cent; by 1979 it has risen to 56 per cent. Our estimates indicate this would have raised total real wages, once fully worked through, by 13 per cent compared with what they would otherwise have been. The effect on output would be to reduce it by $-8\frac{1}{2}$ per cent. The effect on the PSBR is correspondingly severe: an increase of $-£6\frac{1}{2}$ bn at 1981 prices. The effect on unemployment, coming both through the increased substitution of mechanization for labour (about 650,000) and through the contraction of output (about 350,000), would be about 1 million.

To produce such a rise in unemployment our equations suggest that non-union real wages would have been depressed by about 13 per cent. Hence the increased union power would have had its effect by reducing the living standards both of non-unionized workers and of those becoming unemployed and deciding to sign on rather than take non-union employment.

Conclusions

Even if our estimates are remotely near the truth, it would seem clear that *union power, even if only a modest nuisance in the 1960s, has become a major obstruction by the early 1980s*.

Monopoly power in the labour market from the union side now rates as a major allocational issue. Monopoly power in goods markets was the major allocational issue in the post-war period, resulting in important legislation such as the Restrictive Trade Practices Act of 1956, new institutions such as the Monopolies Commission and tax changes like the successive tariff-cutting 'rounds'.

In British history the trade unions have been the instigators of major social reforms. Once they were a 'countervailing force' in an economy where major employers held the whip hand in negotiations. But their historical role as social reformer is no longer relevant. The need for countervailing force has disappeared in an economy where employers' monopoly power has been heavily curtailed by the stronger competition in goods markets and the emergence of industrial relations institutions such as the industrial courts. It is hard to escape the conclusion that the public interest requires measures to deal with labour market monopoly power in an analogous way to goods market monopoly power. A corollary is that, since the power is vested in the unions by exceptionally favourable laws, *it is no use hoping that non-legal measures – such as incomes policies, 'confrontations' or exhortations – will have any effect on the problem*. Only changes in laws and institutions which take away union power will remove its effects on unemployment, output and the interests of non-unionized workers.

To my untutored legal mind it seems a simple and attractive course to abolish the 1906 (Immunities) Act, except for the peaceful picketing clause (a suggestion I owe to a prominent economic journalist, Andreas Whittam Smith), to abolish the closed shop, and to institute a Labour Monopolies Commission. Good legal minds can probably do better; but the essential is that *only the law can take away a force that the law has strengthened* to the point of inflicting severe damage on the British economy and our working people, *especially the poorer*.

Part II The assumptions, calculations and equations

The issues we are examining are not short-term matters; in the UK both the rise in unemployment and the rise in union power have taken place over two decades, in the course of five economic cycles. While it may be defensible to suppose that, in the short term of a year or two, there can be excess supply or excess demand in the markets for goods and labour, it is extraordinarily hard to defend such a supposition for longer periods.

Our analysis is concerned primarily with the long-run determination of employment, unemployment and real wages, and we assume that in the long run there is no excess supply or demand for labour or goods. Our long-run assumptions are captured in Figure 1. It shows, first, a supply curve of labour to the UK economy associated with the average real non-union wage, Wc/P on the vertical axis; the quantity of labour is on the horizontal axis. The supply curve is drawn flat at low wages because the ratio of real benefits (shown as B/P) to real wages becomes critically high for a large section of the population, but at high wages the benefit/wage ratios drop to irrelevance for the vast majority so that the only effect of benefits is to raise somewhat the length of time spent between jobs in 'search'. At these high wages the supply of labour approximates to what we may call the 'labour force' shown as $\bar{L}$; those capable of working would wish to do so under appropriate terms, and would mostly register as desiring work at unemployment benefit offices.

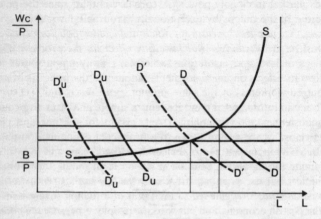

Figure 1 The effects of an increase in union power (*dashed lines represent situation after rise in union mark-up*)

This supply curve of labour shifts to the left if real benefits rise or if income tax rates (T_L) rise (reducing disposable wages corresponding to the gross wage shown on the vertical axis), or if the labour force is reduced. We must also allow for the rigidity of the housing market and the dispersion of employment opportunities; a mismatch between population centres and opportunities will shift the SS curve to the left if mobility is obstructed by housing.

The demand side of the diagram is drawn up on the simplifying assumption that there is a constant 'union mark-up' (the percentage by which unions raise unionized workers' wages above non-union wages) at all levels of non-union wages and other relevant variables. The expositional advantage of this (clear over-) simplification is that it allows union and non-union firms' demand curves for labour to be put on a single diagram. With union real wages uniquely related to non-union real wages, the demand for union labour, though truly related to union real wages, will also be uniquely related to the non-union real wage, as shown by the D_uD_u curve. The demand for non-union labour will be related straightforwardly to the non-union real wage. We can add the two demands for labour together to obtain the total demand curve, DD.

The position of these demand curves – the 'level of demand' – depends on four groups of factors. First, there are the international ones: world trade (WT), and our terms of trade (π), which together dictate what domestic demand and output will be consistent with current account balance at given non-union real wages. An expansion in world trade, for example, would increase demand for British goods from abroad; if these are supplied at higher real wages, the additional export earnings will be available for domestic demand to increase also, raising imports by the same amount. Both $D_u D_u$ and DD curves shift to the right, and real wages will rise, as will labour supply and employment.

Secondly, there are technological factors (k) which determine the productivity of labour and other costs. A rise in other costs, such as raw material or capital, both of which we assume to be set in international markets, will shift the DD curve to the left. A rise in the marginal product of labour will shift it to the right.

Thirdly, taxes on labour paid by firms and other implicit labour costs levied on employers (such as sickness benefits and redundancy costs), which we denote by T_F, will shift the DD curve to the left.

Finally, we come to the union mark-up. A rise will shift the $D_u D_u$ curve to the left, since a given non-union real wage will now correspond to a higher union real wage. The DD curve will be shifted to the left by the same amount (there will be no change in non-union labour demand at given real non-union wages).

What determines the union mark-up? Our analysis is straightforward enough: each union is a maximizing monopoly which faces the problem of working out an optimal time-path of real wages for its members, given that actions it takes today will have effects far into the future. In principle, therefore, all the factors determining the demand for labour in both sectors and the total supply of labour will come indirectly into each union's analysis. Complicated as this problem is, the essentials of the solution are clear enough; in particular, the mark-up will rise the less easy the employer finds it to substitute other factors of production including non-union labour for union labour. 'Union power' is measured in principle by the difficulty of this substitution, but this is not helpful in practice since this difficulty is unobservable. In practice, we resort to the only available index of union power, the proportion of the labour force which is unionized, and suppose that it is likely to bear some rough relationship to the true measure.

We can put this whole framework together easily enough. Employment and real non-union wages are determined in the long run at the intersection of the supply curve, SS, and the demand curve, DD. Unemployment is the difference between workers who register, $\bar{L}$, and those who are employed. This again is an oversimplification because not all in the labour force register for a variety of reasons – especially lack of eligibility and dislike of the unemployment status. But registered unemployment will be highly correlated with the difference between $\bar{L}$ and employment.

The mechanics of estimation

In the *short* run, the economy will not jump quickly to any new long-run equilibrium, for the traditional reason that there are costs of adjusting labour demands (and possibly also labour supplies, though we do not find them important). These costs of adjustment cause both employment and union real wages (so also average real wages) to move relatively sluggishly; our estimates suggest that adjustment takes between 2 years (quarterly data) and 4 years (annual) for 90 per cent to come through.

It is convenient for us to assume that in the non-union sector day-to-day (as opposed to *long*-run) supply is always equal to day-to-day demand; hence our model assumes 'continuous labour market equilibrium' in the sense that this residual market always clears and there is no excess supply. However, this is less important than it seems. Our analysis still has the conventional economic characteristic: that it takes time to get to the long run. Other analyses which would share our long-run framework but assumed 'short-run disequilibrium' (excess supply or demand) could well produce similar results. So our analysis does not appear to rest crucially on the assumption of continuous market equilibrium.

What our analysis gives us is two basic equations and one group of equations.

(1) An equation for total average wages (union and non-union) which, using real wages as the supply price of labour, says it depends on the volume of unemployment, real benefits grossed up for direct taxes, the size of the labour force, and the unionization rate. To allow for one-year nominal wage contracts over a proportion of employees,

the size of inflation-forecasting errors also enters the calculations; unexpected inflation causes workers who contracted in advance to suffer an unexpected drop in real wages. Finally, the last period's real wages enter because of the adjustment costs noted earlier. This is the 'supply equation' in the analysis.[2]

(2) An equation for unemployment, regarded as depending on the demand for labour; this is the demand equation in the analysis. Unemployment is related inversely to real wages grossed up for labour taxes on the employer, technological progress, the volume of output, and lagged unemployment.

(3) A group of equations determining the level of output. These are the equations of the Liverpool macro-economic model. They have the property that in the long run output must be such that there is current account balance; hence long-run output (and so employment) will depend, as in the diagram, on world trade, and the terms of trade, as well as all the other factors entering the SS and DD curves. Output in the short run depends on the fiscal, monetary and international shocks hitting the economy which cause fluctuations around the long-run equilibrium (discussed in our other reports and not important here).

These equations follow in summary form. They have been successfully tested for stability, autocorrelation and sensitivity to differently weighted benefit and tax series; the inclusion of a time trend in the wage equation and of the labour force in the unemployment equation also makes no difference to the other coefficients of these equations, both variables being quite insignificant.

Statistical appendix

Full details of the wage and unemployment equations are in A. P. L. Minford, 'Labour Market Equilibrium in an Open Economy', *SSRC Project Working Paper 8103*, University of Liverpool, 1981.

The wage and unemployment equations were estimated for quarterly data from 1964:2 to 1979:2, and also for annual data from 1955 to 1979.

2. The unionization rate (and so the union mark-up) enters the supply equation though it entered the demand curves in the diagram, because the diagram is in terms of the non-union wage, whereas the estimation is in terms of the (observable) total wage over all sectors.

Quarterly equations (t-values in brackets, constant and seasonal dummies not shown; Two Stage Least Squares):

$$w = - \cdot 28P^{ue} \quad - \cdot 027u \quad + \cdot 125(b + T_L) + \cdot 46UNR$$
$$\quad (0 \cdot 9) \qquad (2 \cdot 1) \qquad (3 \cdot 1) \qquad\qquad (2 \cdot 4)$$
$$\quad - \cdot 03N \quad + \cdot 77w$$
$$\quad (0 \cdot 1) \qquad (11 \cdot 8)^1$$
$$\bar{R}^2 = \cdot 98 \quad DW = 1 \cdot 77 \quad BP(16) = 15$$

$$u = - 2 \cdot 3Q + 1 \cdot 1(w + T_F) \quad + \cdot 01T \quad + \cdot 7u$$
$$\quad (4 \cdot 1) \quad (2 \cdot 8) \qquad\qquad (2 \cdot 8) \quad (9 \cdot 5)^{-1}$$
$$\bar{R}^2 = \cdot 96 \quad DW = 1 \cdot 95 \quad B\bar{P}(16) = 13$$

Annual equations (t-values in brackets; Three Stage Least Squares):

$$w = 3 \cdot 95 \quad - \cdot 034u \quad + \cdot 12(b + T_L) \quad + \cdot 95UNR$$
$$\quad (0 \cdot 8) \qquad (0 \cdot 9) \qquad (3 \cdot 0) \qquad\qquad (2 \cdot 8)$$
$$\quad - \cdot 6N \quad + \cdot 72w$$
$$\quad (1 \cdot 3) \quad (4 \cdot 5)^{-1}$$
$$\bar{R}^2 = \cdot 97 \quad DW = 2 \cdot 47 \quad BP(6) = 2 \cdot 3$$

$$u = 49 \cdot 1 \quad - 3 \cdot 4Q \quad + 1 \cdot 8(w + T_F) + \cdot 08T + \cdot 53u$$
$$\quad (2 \cdot 4) \quad (1 \cdot 7) \qquad (1 \cdot 1) \qquad\qquad (1 \cdot 2) \quad (2 \cdot 9)^{-1}$$
$$\bar{R}^2 = \cdot 87 \qquad DW = 1 \cdot 5 \qquad BP(6) = 11 \cdot 2$$

The output equations for the Liverpool model are set out in A. P. L. Minford, 'A rational expectations model of the UK under fixed and floating exchange rates', *The State of Macroeconomics*, Carnegie-Rochester Conference Series on Public Policy, vol. 12, 1980. The implied *long*-run equation for output is:

$$Q = 0 \cdot 3WT + 0 \cdot 3\pi - 0 \cdot 6(w + T_F) + \cdot 0026T$$

Putting the quarterly wage/unemployment equations together with the long-run output equation yields the following long-run equation for unemployment and real wages in terms of the exogenous variables (union power, taxes, benefits, etc.):

$$u = - 1 \cdot 2(WT + \pi) + 4 \cdot 1T_F + 2(b + T_L) + 8 \cdot 2UNR + \cdot 006T$$
$$\quad - \cdot 5N$$
$$w = \cdot 13(WT + \pi) - \cdot 5T_F + \cdot 25(b + T_L) + 1 \cdot 0UNR - \cdot 001T$$
$$\quad - \cdot 06N$$

Brief definitions of variables – all are natural logarithms unless otherwise indicated:

	w	= wages as defined above, deflated by prices (retail price index)
	P^{ue}	= unexpected inflation (fraction p.a.)
	u	= wholly unemployed (UK)
for married man with two children wife not working	b	= unemployment benefits including other allowances (·3 weight on earnings related, ·7 on flat rate)
	T_L	= average income tax rate (including child benefits and employee's National Insurance) – fraction
	T_F	= average employer's National Insurance – fraction
	Q	= real GDP
	T	= time (quarter and years); a proxy fork
	WT	= volume of world trade
	π	= terms of trade
	N	= labour force
	UNR	= unionized proportion of labour force (fraction)
	$\bar{R}^2$	= R – squared corrected for degrees of freedom
	DW	= Durbin Watson statistic
	BP	= Box Pierce statistic (degrees of freedom in brackets).

Excessive Trade Union Power: Existing Reality or Contemporary Myth?

From Brian Burkitt, 'Excessive Trade Union Power: Existing Reality or Contemporary Myth?', *Industrial Relations Journal*, vol. 12, No. 3, May–June 1981, pp. 65–71.

British trade unions are currently under siege. Public opinion polls demonstrate a popular belief that unions are 'too powerful', while many economists argue that their strength is used to the detriment of the economy. It is now widely held that unions have acquired sufficient power to become the dominant force in collective bargaining and in the formation of government policy. The present administration seeks to 'redress' the balance of power between employers and unions on the grounds that trade unions are 'over-mighty subjects'. Its Employment Act was designed to deal with various 'abuses' of union actions and to make them more 'responsible'; hence it reflects concern over the closed shop, secondary picketing and the nature of union decision-making. In view of the widespread appeal of this approach, its detailed scrutiny seems overdue.

The 'over-mighty subject' thesis

Many economists, e.g. Hanson (1978), argue that over the last generation the balance of market advantage in collective bargaining has moved in favour of trade unions. A number of socio-economic developments favourable to labour occurred:

(1) The principle of unconditional legal privilege for unions, accepted since 1875, has become increasingly significant with union growth and the development of state social security provisions that lower the cost of strikes to individual workers. Hutt (1975) argued these privileges provide unions with legal protection for what would be criminal acts if perpetrated by others, namely a form of coercion through the threat and actuality of strikes that is analogous to other types of extortion, such as the use of hostages, blackmail, hijacking and kidnapping. Hayek (1967) supplied justification for these assertions; the present power of unions rests on the coercion of other workers

who are deprived of the opportunity to offer their labour on their own terms. The coercion of enterprise is always secondary and operates through this deprivation.

(2) The growth in the size of firms and their increasing interdependence provides greater scope for those workers who control the provision of necessities to impose heavy costs upon the economy as a whole by withdrawing their labour. Where a monopoly supplies an essential service, the power of unions may prove almost irresistible.

(3) The State is now the employer, directly and indirectly, of around seven million workers. It is less likely to resist union demands since the commercial pressure upon it is lower, while governments are transitory, desire electoral popularity and must combat the tactics of pressure groups and the parliamentary opposition.

Many economists believe that trade unions have taken advantage of these developments in a way that is detrimental to economic efficiency. Thus Burton (1978) argued that unions gain benefit for their members, but impose costs upon society. These costs result from:

(1) Allocative inefficiencies due to distortions in relative wages.

(2) The use of inefficient productive methods to secure an 'easier working life', thus weakening the impetus to minimize costs.

(3) The example of an effective union which obtains benefits for its members creates an incentive to unionize in other sectors. Output is thereby lower as resources become diverted to the socially unproductive task of union organization.

(4) The impact of industrial disputes, which extends beyond the immediate loss of output to the build-up of larger stocks to circumvent the effect on sales of an interruption to production and the use of more flexible but more costly work methods.

(5) Beyond their direct incidence, these costs reduce the economy's future growth potential.

Many economists therefore regard trade union activity as an impoverishing influence that frustrates managerial and technological potentialities. Moreover, the extension of closed shops following the legislation of the last Labour government increased union monopoly power and its associated distortions, leading to a larger loss of potential output.

The policy prescriptions derived from this analysis centre on the withdrawal of the legal privileges that form the basis of union hegemony. Rowley (1978) listed these as the rights to conspire, establish a closed shop, impose union negotiated contracts upon all workers, coerce unionists by secondary strikes and boycotts, employment protection, state-financed benefits during strikes and exemption from the general rules applying to corporate bodies. Such a withdrawal, Rowley believed, would restore a balance of power between employers and unions. His minimum requirement was a curb upon the right to strike and a removal of the closed shop provisions from the Employment Protection Act. Policies with an indirect yet beneficial impact on union activity include the encouragement of product market competition and the development of simulated competitive pricing in nationalized industries, both of which induce greater efficiency.

The case that unions have become 'over-mighty subjects' has gained considerable support among economists and articulated public opinion, while a curtailment of trade union activities is an essential part of the present government's overall economic strategy. However, when this conventional wisdom is subject to detailed scrutiny, a sharply contrasting reality emerges.

The formation and growth of trade unions

The development of trade union organization is a feature of all advanced capitalist economies, except those in which their existence is banned by law. Perhaps, therefore, the starting-point for an analysis of the 'over-mighty subject' thesis is to consider the factors that promote the formation of unions and their subsequent growth.

Workers own only their labour power which they must sell to maintain themselves and their families, but capitalists possess funds that enable them to command man-made means of production and so enjoy bargaining advantages when negotiating terms of employment with individual workers. They enjoy a greater ability to withhold completing a contract due to their larger financial resources, are fewer in number, possess more information and are accustomed to exerting authority[1]. When the economic circumstances of the parties to a bargain are unequal, legal freedom of contract enables the stronger to dictate terms. Because only employers can exercise power in

1. Burkitt (1975) discussed the operation of these factors in greater detail.

unorganized markets, conflict is minimized. Workers are legally free yet effectively powerless.

Since the analysis of Robinson (1933), the possible existence of monopsonistic labour markets has been widely recognized. However, the significance attached to them is lessened by insistence on the rarity of pure monopsony, i.e. it is difficult to discover many instances with only one buyer of a particular type of worker. However, employers usually possess bargaining advantages over unorganized workmen which create partial rather than complete monopsony power, analogous to the more familiar concept of imperfectly competitive product markets.

Because workers are in an inferior negotiating position and are subject to a continuous and flexible structure of discipline once they have agreed the terms of employment, they seek to overcome their disadvantages by bargaining collectively. The history of trade union formation and subsequent growth is of the attempt to redress the inequality of power in unorganized markets. The effects of an initial market position tend to accelerate over time, since every unfavourable bargain currently reached implies a weaker position in future negotiations. Therefore unequal bargaining strength and the resulting market imperfections are normal rather than isolated occurrences when workers are unorganized.

Trade union achievements

Employers and workers, although ultimately dependent upon each other for an income, are never equally so in the short run, while certain conditions must be fulfilled before workers exercise any influence upon managerial decisions. First, workers must act as an organized group; a worker depends for his livelihood upon retaining a particular job, but capital relies for its profit not upon the employment of an individual but of the labour force as a whole. Second, labour needs the ability to impose costs upon its employer in the event of any disagreement. Such an ability implies the existence of effective trade unions capable of remedying to some varying extent the weakness of individual workers. Unions can articulate claims with more skill, aggression and knowledge than individual workers, because they possess greater resources and specialized bargaining expertise. Thus they are more likely to identify opportune circumstances and present claims persuasively.

Trade unions also attempt to restrict management's deployment of labour after it has been hired. They thereby introduce an element of democracy into an otherwise autocratic workplace by replacing unilateral employers' control with jointly agreed rules that regulate their members' wages and working conditions. Leijnse (1980, pp. 58–69) argued that shop-floor negotiations restrict the range of policy alternatives that management possesses, whether through formal negotiation or informal permission to manipulate the system. Trade unions can thus get employers 'to do some things they would not otherwise do', while involving the labour force through elected representatives in the determination of its job environment.

Unions have become the accepted vehicle to most manual workers for the defence and improvement of their living standards and working conditions. They therefore reject, if only implicitly, the basic premise of most economists critical of unions, i.e. that the life chances of individuals are most appropriately determined by supply-and-demand conditions. In this context, certain unions are currently endeavouring to extend the sphere of collective bargaining to rights in production, e.g. to a job and to participation in industrial decision-making, which conflict with the concept of labour as a commodity.

The limitations of trade union achievements

Despite their achievements, union influence remains severely circumscribed and is far from the all-powerful force frequently depicted. Unions represent workers more effectively, but they cannot offset all their members' bargaining disadvantages, because capitalists continue to control the revenue from which wages are paid and the distribution of property remains unequal. The socio-economic environment within which collective bargaining occurs, restricts the scope for union gains.

Leijnse observed that trade unions may restrict managerial options without being able to extend their own. Workers have secured some power at the level of fragmented job-control, but the structure of industrial authority at higher levels remains intact. Collective bargaining takes place within a framework created by previous interlocking employer decisions on such items as corporate strategy, the level and direction of investment, profit allocation and financing. Moreover, in a slow-growth economy fragmented job-controls come to be regarded as merely restrictive, while workers' remoteness from the locus of industrial decision-making inevitably leaves them suspicious of authority. Capital demands 'responsible' unions in the sense that they exercise restraint and appreciate employers' problems, but resists any actual sharing of responsibility. The hostility of the CBI to the recommendations of the Bullock Report demonstrated no willingness to share the power to make those decisions that determine the environment within which 'moderation' is required.

The motive for granting legal immunities in trade disputes is not that governments desire strong unions, but to ensure that they exist at all. If legal immunities were removed, unions could not survive as effective bodies. Employers would be able to take them to court for damages in breach of any commercial or employment contracts and thus destroy the right to strike. The series of laws passed between 1974 and 1978 for the most part did little more than restore the pre-1971 status quo, and extend to workers certain basic minimum individual rights, but without sanctions on employers to ensure that these become widely established. Far from being satiated with legal privileges, unions feel that existing legislation is usually ineffective in the face of determined employers. British law remains primarily concerned with individual rather than collective rights, while judges never cease to display insensitivity to the purposes and methods of trade unionism.

The nature of economic power

Many of the deficiencies of the 'over-mighty subject' thesis stem from a misunderstanding of the nature of economic power. Most critics of unions see power as essentially external to competitive markets, resting upon individual or group manipulation of monopoly or organizational advantages to secure additional resources. Its possession is reflected in the distortion of market forces, whose outcome provides the norm against which the exercise of power is assessed.

In reality, power derives not only from collective organization imposing costs upon other parties, but also from acquisitive ability within markets measured by the rewards that individuals can obtain when acting independently. If the latter type of power is often overlooked, that is a reflection of its secure establishment. Because union bargaining weapons are deployed in full public view, their critics concentrate upon them to the neglect of differential individual advantages arising from the inherent nature of market operations in a society characterized by inequality. Power resides in anonymous social institutions as well as in identifiable individuals and groups, and derives more from the routine application of effectively unchallenged assumptions than from domination after public conflict.

381

Economic power can be defined as the aggregation of influences determining the pressure that individuals and groups can exert, so that the earnings capacity of claims arising from property rights becomes crucial, whatever the degree of organization in the market where they are exercised. The crucial item for analysis is not the distinction between, but the combination of, individual and collective acquisitive ability. Therefore it is unrealistic to distinguish power exerted through union organization from that flowing from market opportunities, while it is one-sided to advocate restraint of organized strength without similar control of individual manoeuvring. Yet such a bias lies at the heart of the thinking of trade union critics.

Hutt argued that power exercised through unions is an unacceptable exploitation of monopoly, but such an argument rests on the value judgment that collective exercise of the power of individuals in themselves relatively weak should be condemned, while individual exercise of power by the independently strong need not be. Many fail to realize that power is an integral feature of labour market operations, made explicit by the development of collective bargaining. Contrary to the widely held view that strikes result from excessive union power, conflict is likely to be greatest when the power of each party is approximately equal and the perceived costs of disagreement are insufficient to deter.

Economists wedded to conventional neoclassical assumptions find it hard to accept that individual optimization and group organization are both methods of waging distributive conflict in a capitalist economy and that each is legitimated by the primacy accorded to the pursuit of self-interest. Nor is the description of union activities as 'monopolistic' convincing. Unions do not create a privileged position among otherwise equal parties, but seek to develop the bargaining strength of individuals who alone are relatively weak.

The distribution of income

The distribution of income in capitalist economies is largely determined by three interrelated influences: the private ownership of property, the operation of the labour market and the activity of the State. In 1970 the richest 1 per cent of the British population owned at least 25 per cent, and the richest 5 per cent at least 50 per cent, of total personal wealth. The distribution of income derived from the ownership of property was even more unequal; 5 per cent of adults received 92 per cent of property income, while 93 per cent of adults owned no shares or government bonds. This degree of inequality is not easily reconciled to the thesis that unions are 'over-mighty subjects'.

Within the complex of influences determining income distribution, the actions of capitalists are more significant than those of unions. Unions protect their members from insecurities that threaten the unorganized, but they find it difficult to eat into profits, since firms can react to higher wages by adjusting prices, product quality, production techniques and manpower requirements. Consequently, unions often fail to alter distributive shares when they push up money wages; for instance, the unprecedented acceleration of money wages between 1969 and 1973 raised the proportion of the national income accruing to labour by 1·35 per cent (Burkitt and Bowers, 1979, provided the relevant figures). Union claims were not self-defeating, but their impact on distribution was hardly substantial. As trade unions exercise no direct control over the price levels, this is not surprising.

In a largely private enterprise economy, only slight inroads into capitalist consumption are possible without reducing the rate of accumulation and hence long-run living standards. Glyn and Sutcliffe (1972) found that national rankings on the one basis of investment and profitability levels were almost identical. The determination of incomes is not even-handed; capital assets accrue from the joint abstinence of capitalists (in the form of saving) and workers (in the form of lower consumption than would otherwise be possible), but even in the presence of strong unions, the ownership and control of these assets belong to capitalists alone. Workers forego income not only to provide the profit and interest required to induce the owners of property to part with their liquidity, but also to finance the consumption standards they develop.

Trade union influence within the process of production

The contract of employment differs from other contracts in at least two ways. The owners of labour power cannot be dissociated physically from the services it renders, while the conditions under which it is supplied vary between a multiplicity of decentralized establishments, so that employers determine the job environment. Workers cannot change conditions without managerial consent, but employers can initiate change unilaterally by issuing orders that they expect to be obeyed. Therefore, once signed, the employment contract is inherently one-sided; because large-scale production is only efficient with a disciplined labour force, the individual worker finds the character of his job, hours of work and behaviour in the factory prescribed to him.

Trade unions respond by attempting to create a code of industrial rights which protects their members in some degree from market fluctuations, technical change and employer decisions. However, these rights remain limited. Union participation in the regulation of working conditions is essentially defensive, as it occurs within an environment determined by policies that capitalists have already formulated on the scale of production, the location of industry, investment technology, manpower levels, safety and welfare. Even the minority of unions which acquired substantial job-controls (e.g. newspaper printing) largely react to employers' decisions. Power gains by shop-floor groups can easily be eroded by management action or developments outside their influence. Indeed, such groups are often too small and isolated to obtain the information necessary to make an effective bargaining stand. Moreover, collective agreements are in practice implemented by representatives of the employer, who draws up financial accounts that unions have no independent means of checking. The need for business flexibility when interpreting general rules creates the personal and continuous character of authority in firms. To date, therefore, the industrial power structure has yielded little to union activity, which takes place against a background of continuing inequality, reflected in lifetime earnings, conditions of work and the intrinsic character of jobs. Organized labour has secured an increase in bargaining power without any change in its subordinate status as a group alienated from a share in the control of economic organizations.

Trade unions and national economic policy

The popular belief used to be that Jack Jones was more powerful than the Prime Minister. In fact, the ability to influence government policy is distributed between various interests, which together constitute a power structure. The British economy is currently dominated by three groups:

(1) Large, increasingly multinational corporations whose viability depends on earning sufficient profits to sustain investment and future growth, and which therefore seek conditions that enable such profits to be earned.

(2) Financial institutions geared to the private ownership of the means of production and the free international movement of commodities and currencies.

(3) Organized labour seeking to obtain improvements in real wages, job security and its control of the work environment.

All governments require at least the passive acquiescence of these pressure groups,[2] but in an economy based on private ownership the power of industrial and financial capitalists is greater than that of any other class, since their needs determine the conditions on which economic growth can be achieved. Governments have to pursue policies conducive to business confidence or face a shrinkage in output and employment. The requirements of profit-seeking enterprises limit the number of policy options and structure the framework within which they operate. Thus Leijnse noted that the growth in the size and scope of workplace bargaining during the 1970s in Britain coexisted with an incapacity of unions to negotiate on a national level either a more satisfactory employment situation or adequate wage compensation for inflation.

All governments managing a capitalist economy seek to create an environment in which profits flourish and managerial hierarchies remain unfettered. Keynes (1936) remarked that 'economic prosperity is excessively dependent on a political and social atmosphere that is conducive to the average businessman'. Prevailing economic orthodoxy is partly created by economists, but mainly reflects the current views of the strongest institutions concerning their own and the State's functions. These represent a power block that no government challenges lightly, since to do so risks the threat of retaliation from a concentration of industrial and financial strength whose cooperation and commercial viability is essential to the prosperity of an economy based upon private ownership.

The opinions and instincts of moneyed interests register automatically through financial markets. Stock exchange slumps dry up the source of new funds for industry and government, while panic in the foreign market drains away reserves under a fixed exchange rate or inaugurates a downward spiral in a flexible rate. Since 'confidence' is

2. To the extent that trade unions infiltrate decision-making structures, they increase the potential value of their cooperation. They thus exert, through nuisance value, countervailing power to the extra-parliamentary influence commanded by business and finance through market responses and extra-market contacts.

necessarily diminished by state actions which transgress the standards set by financial interests, a powerful indirect sanction against such actions is in permanent existence. Thus governments that antagonize business and finance usually encounter a capital strike; the ensuing economic difficulties lead with equal regularity to a relaxation of the offending policies. The essence of a capital strike lies in its unorganized, spontaneous character, rooted in the requirements of an economy operating under mainly capitalist auspices.

Interest groups acquire power through a competitive struggle, but they compete on unequal terms because some possess more potent sanctions than others. In this world of imperfect political competition, the existence of private ownership ensures that the greatest leverage over governments is enjoyed by industrial and financial capital. This dominance is strengthened by international pressures. The role of financial markets as a potential source of resistance to government policies could be curtailed by regulations requiring funds to be channelled in some prescribed manner, but the impact of such regulations is weakened by external influences, which provide an outlet for domestic capital and help to determine foreign capital flows. Insulation from international influences is difficult for any national economy to achieve with the growing interpenetration of business and banking interests, which renders control over capital movements hard to enforce without corresponding direction of trade and payments for current services. Consequently, the protection from financial pressure available to governments favouring trade union interests is limited.

In these ways, the scope of state economic activity is restricted by a silent veto belonging to business and money interests that determine financial confidence and so hold the key to credit-flows. Trade unions possess no comparable source of power.

Conclusion

An analysis of economic power reveals a very different state of affairs to the frequently expressed opinion that unions are too powerful. Such an opinion focuses upon symptoms and ignores causes. In reality, unions are weaker than employers, whose possession of the means of production enables them to command decision-making procedures. Some groups of workers exert considerable bargaining power, because they perform crucial industrial tasks and are supported by cohesive organizations, while over a wide spectrum of industry, unions have accumulated a greater degree of job control over the last forty years. However, employers remain dominant and control the crucial productive decisions subject to only limited restraints. For the most part unions remain insecure bodies reacting to, rather than initiating, labour market developments and possessing little ability to influence wider economic events.

These facts currently stand in danger of neglect; thus much of the recent discussion of industrial disputes is ill-focused, since strikes can only be realistically perceived against a background of unequal strength. On such a perspective, those economists who tend to see stoppages of work as a 'labour problem' are guilty of simplification, because collective action, or its threat, is essential to check the unilateral exercise of employers' authority.

If trade unions are to shape economic events rather than merely react to them, they must be able to define their own reality through controlling, as opposed to being incorporated into, decision-making procedures. Many unions obstruct employers' policies without the authority over command structures that would enable them to undertake initiatives on their members' behalf. This stalemate can be broken only by:

(1) Reducing trade union bargaining power.

(2) Extending the degree of union influence over, and responsibility for, key industrial decisions.

The first of these alternatives is currently part of a comprehensive government programme to reverse Britain's relative decline. The argument developed in this paper suggests that the evidence supporting such a policy, the 'over-mighty subject' thesis, is severely flawed when subject to rigorous scrutiny. The possibility of its long-term success therefore seems remote, while its temporary achievements are likely to be gained at the expense of the less privileged. Pursuit of the second alternative is therefore clearly indicated. The shackles upon trade unions created by current organizational imperatives (labour's subordination to capital) and by constraints on the scope of collective bargaining within these imperatives may be transcended by extending unions' effective activity to the organization of production and the formulation of general economic policy.

References

BURKITT, B. (1975), *Trade Unions and Wages: Implications for Economic Theory*, Crosby Lockwood Staples.

BURKITT, B., and D. BOWERS (1979), *Trade Unions and the Economy*, Macmillan.

BURTON, J. (1978), 'Are Trade Unions a Public Good/Bad?: The Economics of the Closed Shop', *Trade Unions: Public Goods or Public Bads?*, Institute of Economic Affairs.

GLYN, A., and B. SUTCLIFFE (1972), *British Capitalism, Workers and the Profits Squeeze*, Penguin.

HANSON, C. G. (1978), 'Collective Bargaining: the Balance of Market Advantage', *Trade Unions: Public Goods or Public Bads?*, Institute of Economic Affairs.

HAYEK, F. A. (1967), *Studies in Philosophy, Politics and Economics*, Routledge and Kegan Paul.

HUTT, W. H. (1975), *The Theory of Collective Bargaining*, Institute of Economic Affairs.

KEYNES, J. M. (1936), *The General Theory of Employment, Interest and Money*, Macmillan.

LEIJNSE, F. (1980), 'Workplace Bargaining and Trade Union Power', *Industrial Relations Journal*, vol. 11, no. 2.

ROBINSON, J. (1933), *Economics of Imperfect Competition*, Macmillan.

ROWLEY, C. K. (1978), 'The Economics and Politics of Extortion', *Trade Unions: Public Goods or Public Bads?*, Institute of Economic Affairs.

30 Karel Williams, John Williams and Dennis Thomas

The Relative Importance of Union Power as a Factor in Britain's Poor Manufacturing Performance

From Karel Williams, *Why are the British Bad at Manufacturing?* Routledge and Kegan Paul, 1983, pp. 34–47.

Every pub and club in Britain contains at least one drinker who will tell you that 'it's the bloody-minded workers and their unions who have ruined British industry'. If this argument is to be considered seriously, we must define the nature of the labour problem and its conditioning effects on manufacturing capital. We can begin by challenging the popular non-academic definition of the problem which focuses on strikes and lost working days; on this view the problem is that the British worker will not work and downs tools for trivial reasons. This view may be confirmed by the media presentation of news, but it is decisively contradicted by statistical evidence on strikes and industrial disputes.

The available statistical evidence does not show that Britain has had an unusually severe strike problem, and this conclusion stands even if we include the industrially troubled years of the early 1970s which culminated politically in the coal miners' strike of 1974. Relatively, even in the period 1967–76, Britain came somewhere near the middle of the developed countries' strike league table in terms of days lost per 1,000 workers (Smith, 1980). Absolutely, most manufacturing plants have not lost a large number of working days through stoppages; the Department of Employment calculated that, in the years 1971–5, 98 per cent of manufacturing establishments employing about 80 per cent of manufacturing employees experienced no work stoppages in an average year (Department of Employment, 1978). The official statistics understate the extent of the strike problem because they do not record the small unofficial stoppages which are particularly prevalent in Britain. It must also be admitted that there are general problems where plant size is large; as Prais (1981) has shown, in Britain strike frequency is almost directly proportional to size of plant. Nevertheless, when all these qualifications have been noted, it would be hard to argue that lost working days are a major condition of poor manufacturing performance.

If there is a labour problem in Britain, it arises from what British workers do when they *are* working. The descriptive literature on British manufacturing since 1945 has clearly documented a variety of bad work-practices. Across a broad range of British industries, machines, installations and assembly lines have been affected by several factors:

(1) They are *overmanned* by the standards achieved in manning comparable equipment in other countries. Unnecessary semi-skilled operatives are retained or demarcation rules about 'who does what' artificially maintain jobs for craftsmen and their mates.

(2) They are *run slowly* so that the equipment habitually works at speeds below those which it is technically capable of and does sustain in other countries.

(3) They are *poorly used* in other ways so that process throughput suffers. For example, the absence of effective preventive maintenance can lead to frequent breakdowns and excessive downtime, or machines may regularly turn out defective products which require expensive rectification further down the line.

At any moment of time, the existence of such work-practices reflects past union success in defending custom and practice when new technology is introduced.

If we put these observations about work-practices into a more formal framework, it could be argued that in British manufacturing over the past thirty years there has been a general failure of management control over the labour process. This failure could be a significant constraint on enterprise calculation. We can begin to examine whether this is so by considering Kilpatrick and Lawson's (1980) argument that poor control of the labour process is a major factor in our 'industrial decline' since the late nineteenth century.

Kilpatrick and Lawson's article must be welcomed as a progressive problem shift in applied economics. They problematize the important question of the struggle between management and labour over the organization (and reorganization) of the labour process within which labour power is expended. This is a necessary corrective to the orthodox neoclassical concept of production as a process combining factors in variable proportions rather like the ingredients in a cake mix. Neoclassical analysis ignores the central point that the efficacy of labour power is variably determined by micro-institutional conditions in the labour process. If they are right to reconceptualize production in this way, Kilpatrick and Lawson are wrong in trying so single-mindedly to relate our industrial decline to the labour process; they end up providing one more single-factor explanation of Britain's poor manufacturing performance. This line of argument is not only methodologically dubious, it also cannot be brought to a decisive conclusion. Kilpatrick and Lawson positively demonstrate that British employers have long accepted union prerogatives and they cite mainly nineteenth-century instances where the introduction of new technology was delayed and obstructed by organized groups of workers. But they never systematically confront the issue of the extent to which resistance to new technology and the resulting bad work-practices imposed significant penalties in terms of cost, output or quality.

From our point of view, this neglect of effects is a crucial weakness. If we are interested in the question of how the observed failure to control the labour process conditions enterprise calculation, it is not enough to show that bad work-practices exist. It is necessary to show that bad work-practices had damaging consequences which manufacturing firms had to suffer as constraints on their operations. Before we can examine this crucial issue, it is necessary to specify what these consequences might be. We will suppose that the direct adverse effects of bad work-practices would be low physical output and/or high costs. The indirect effects could include low product quality and other non-price deficiencies because, for example, poor assembly and quality control compromises reliability. We will not ignore these indirect effects, but to begin with we will concentrate on the direct effects of bad work-practices on output and costs. There are two reasons for starting here. First, orthodox economic theory incorporates strong presuppositions that price and cost disadvantages can decisively handicap a national manufacturing sector. Second, Thatcherism politically privileges industrial problems of low output and high costs; the government gives priority to reducing inflation and holding down wage rises because it presupposes that we must become more competitive in cost terms. Against all this it will be argued that there is little evidence that we have been seriously handicapped by low output and high costs and there is little reason to suppose that, in so far as British manufacturing has such a problem, it is either caused by bad work-practices or could be resolved by their abolition. Low output and high costs may be important for particular enterprises and segments of capital, but it is not the crucial constraint on manufacturing as a whole.

If we are concerned with low output and its relation to work-practices, the evidence on labour productivity is immediately relevant. The available measures here relate a physical quantum of manufacturing output expressed in value terms as value-added to the quantity of labour input expressed in person years. As a point of reference, we can consider the productivity achievements of France and Germany. The measures show that, when post-war reconstruction was largely completed in the mid 1950s, labour productivity in Britain was higher than in France or Germany. But for the past twenty years there has been a productivity gap with Britain lagging behind France and Germany; as Table 1 shows, by 1970, output per employee in manufacturing was over 50 per cent higher in France and Germany. 50 per cent seems to be a large gap, so it is worth remembering that, in dynamic terms, the gap is not all that large. By 1973, Britain had attained the levels of value-added per man hour which France and Germany had attained in 1965–6 (Jones, 1976). So Britain was behind by less than a decade.

Table 1 Gross value-added per person employed in year 1970 (on purchasing-power parity basis)

Belgium	155
France	164
Germany	155
Italy	105
Netherlands	183
EEC	147
Britain	100

Source: Jones (1976)

Furthermore, if absolute levels of output per man were lower in British manufacturing, the gap was not increasing dramatically by the later 1960s because the British rate of growth of labour productivity had accelerated towards the European norm. Back in the 1950s, the British trend rate of labour productivity growth was well below that achieved by our European competitors. But, as Jones (1976) shows, labour productivity in the UK grew faster in each sub-period from 1955–60 to 1963–73, and by the early 1970s the British rate of productivity growth had more or less doubled and reached the 4 per cent per annum level which France and West Germany had maintained since the early 1950s.

Table 2 Per cent per annum increase in output per person employed in manufacturing

	1955–60	1969–73
France	4·40	4·58
Germany	4·92	4·37
UK	2·1	4·46

Source: Jones (1976)

Other studies (Wragg and Robertson, 1978; Wenban-Smith, 1981), give slightly different results but confirm the overall picture of rising British rates of productivity increase which reached 3–4 per cent levels in the 1960s. Wragg and Robertson (1978) bring out the point that the rising rate of productivity increase was particularly commendable because it was an intra-industry achievement. Very little of the British productivity increase was obtained the easy way by redeployment of labour from low to high productivity industries; from 1954 to 1973, 90 per cent of the productivity growth was achieved within industries.

Longstanding international differences in physical output levels must also be set in the context of substantial international differences in labour cost levels. If we look at prevailing national levels of labour costs, by the 1970s the UK had become a low-wage economy.

Table 3 International comparison of labour costs*

Germany	231
USA	194
France	138
Italy	138
Japan	125
Britain	100

Source: Blackaby, (1979)
* Total cost of labour involved in manufacturing production at current exchange rates

If physical output levels were lower in Britain, suitably modest wage levels provided enterprises with some compensation. And, as we have already argued in our discussion of trade performance, there was never a secular problem about the rate of increase of labour costs in Britain. By the early 1970s, Britain had settled down into a kind of equilibrium as a low-wage, low-productivity-level economy.

In so far as Britain is a low-wage economy, perhaps labour's low physical output is a characteristic rather than a fault. In orthodox theory, there is no reason why all national manufacturing sectors should converge on one productivity level if the size of national market and the relative cost of labour and capital varies. Firms are supposed to adjust their production techniques according to differences in the relative prices of inputs, and, if labour is relatively cheaper, then larger quantities of labour should be used to produce a given quantum of labour. The relative cheapness of labour in Britain does make labour-saving investment very much less attractive. Pratten (1976) shows that in 1972, given a payback period of three years, expenditure of about £12,000 could be justified if it saved one employee in the USA; in the UK the equivalent figure was £5,000. It would be wrong to put too much emphasis on this neoclassical line of reasoning; the debate on Habakkuk's thesis about British and American technology in the nineteenth century shows that you cannot read choice of technology off a difference in wage level. Nevertheless, it is important to recognize that orthodox theory does not support the conclusion that a high level of labour productivity is invariably good and that a low level is invariably bad.

So far, we have concentrated on the labour productivity record up to 1973, and it must be admitted that the record afterwards is somewhat confusing. After 1973, there was a slow-down in the British rate of growth of labour productivity. But, with the oil crisis and the subsequent rolling recession, this trend was to some extent apparent in all the industrial countries. Almost all British industries experienced declining rates of productivity growth and this suggests an underlying conjunctural problem of demand deficiency (Wenban-Smith, 1981); cyclical down-savings in post-war Britain have classically depressed output growth, which in turn feeds through to reduce growth of output per person. Paradoxically, however, when demand fell away precipitously in the major downturn after mid-1979, productivity growth rates improved; by the end of 1981, output per person in manufacturing had increased by 3 per cent, while manufacturing output had declined by 15 per cent (*Economic Progress Report*,

January 1982). It may be that rates of labour productivity increase are returning to the relatively high levels of the 1960s. But the significance of 3 per cent per annum growth of labour productivity is now entirely different. In the 1960s, faster productivity growth was part of a virtuous cycle of expansion in the economy. In the early 1980s, with no signs of genuine recovery in manufacturing output, faster growth seems to be an effect of a permanent contraction in our manufacturing base. If that appears melodramatic, we should remember that major British industries like steel-making are clearly in a vicious circle of decline with ever lower levels of output associated with ever more remarkable improvements in labour productivity.

If we exclude this kind of 'achievement', the slow-down in productivity growth after 1973 must mainly serve to focus our attention more generally on the connection between the rate of output growth and the rate of productivity growth. Verdoorn's law postulates, and studies of the British economy (Wragg and Robertson, 1978; Wenban-Smith, 1981) confirm, that there is a strong positive relation between rate of growth of output and rate of growth of labour productivity. We know that, through the long boom of the 1950s and 1960s, output in British manufacturing grew relatively slowly. According to Jones (1976), British manufacturing output grew at about 3 per cent per annum, while in five other EEC countries it increased at about 6·5 per cent. If manufacturing output growth was independently constrained in the British economy, then this would excuse low rates of productivity increase and make the 1960s achievement all the more commendable. The problem, of course, is to know whether low output growth was an independent constraint or a symptom and result of low productivity growth. On this point, the argument in the later sections of this essay [not included here] is relevant; we will argue that British manufacturing faces demand problems about market limitations which were not surmounted because financial institutions and government were unhelpful. The implication of our argument is that output growth was independently constrained.

At this stage in our discussion of productivity, we can establish the basic contrast between British manufacturing's marketplace performance and its workplace performance. Our international marketplace performance is very bad; the evidence on trade share and import penetration is depressing and it is very difficult to find extenuating circumstances. But, after our review of the evidence and arguments about labour productivity and costs, we could conclude that British industry's workplace performance is quite reasonable. The evidence shows that labour productivity performance is respectable in relative international terms. Furthermore, our argument suggests that there are extenuating circumstances (such as wage levels and slow output growth) which could explain the observed deficit in labour's output. Even if this interpretation and argument about 'low' productivity were to be completely rejected, one thing is certain: there is no way in which existing labour productivity measures can be used to justify the inference that bad work-practices are the cause of low labour productivity. This crucial point will now be established.

Ultimately, the problem with all measures of labour productivity is one of attribution. Labour productivity measures relate a quantity of output to a quantity of labour input. Any deficiency in output could be attributed either to poor-quality labour inputs or to deficiencies in the quantity and quality of other inputs, especially capital. But, given the heterogeneity of capital goods, it is very difficult to measure the input of capital into the production process. We have some crude indications about the quantity and quality of capital in British manufacturing. For example, the proportion of manufacturing output which is re-invested is not much lower in Britain than in Germany or the USA. And if there is a capital equipment problem it is not simply a matter of vintage; in the key area of machine tools, British capital equipment is not older than that in use elsewhere. But we do not have any aggregate measure of productivity which reliably discloses whether a difference in the quantity and quality of capital equipment explains part or all of the observed deficit in national output. If we were able to resolve these problems and show that British capital equipment was not inferior, that might suggest the problem was poor-quality labour input. But, in this case, available measures of labour productivity would still not allow us to determine whether the poor quality of labour input was primarily caused by bad work-practices. There may be other significant causes of national differences in the quality of labour input. We know, for example, that technical and vocational education is very variably developed in different advanced capitalist countries. In Germany, vocational training is legally obligatory for all fifteen- to eighteen-year-olds not otherwise in full-time education; whereas in 1973 in Britain, 60 per cent of those aged sixteen to nineteen were undergoing no form of further education whatsoever (Prais, 1981). We simply cannot assess the impact of this kind of difference on quality of labour input; attempts such as those of Denison to weight labour input by years of education and age/sex characteristics remain controversial and unconvincing.

The uncertainties about attribution are so great that we must finally conclude that the privileged status of the labour problem in British manufacturing may simply reflect a measurement illusion. Economic discourse may privilege the labour problem because the quantum of labour input is all that can be measured easily and related to the quantum of output. Here, as elsewhere, economic science may be diversionary as well as dismal. No doubt, an uneasy awareness of this point explains the recent interest in process comparisons rather than orthodox productivity measures. From an empiricist point of view, the central problem with orthodox productivity measures is that they do not hold other factors constant so that we can isolate the variation in output attributable to different quantity and quality of labour input. But this *ceteris paribus* condition is approximately satisfied if analysis focuses on one manufacturing process which is undertaken using similar or identical capital equipment in different countries in two plants which are perhaps managed by one multinational company. This does not completely solve the problem because differences of plant layout may complicate matters where production processes are continuous and interlinked. And the quasi-solution is obtained, as always in this kind of control-the-variables empiricism, by narrowing down the frame of reference so that it is difficult to ascend to generalization. Nevertheless, the precision of attribution is such that it is worth taking process comparisons seriously.

By way of illustration, we can consider the widely cited process comparisons given in the 1975 Central Policy Review Staff Report on the British car industry which examined the whole process of final assembly and some specific operations such as body framing and door production. On final assembly the CPRS (1975) concluded that 'even with the same capital equipment, plant lay-out and working procedures, it takes almost twice as many labour hours to assemble a car in the UK as it does to assemble the same or a very similar car on the continent'. In single-process comparisons it was again a case of divide by two to find the output of the British worker; in door production using identical machines British output of doors per shift was approximately half the continental output. A follow-up investigation by the *Sunday Times* into Ford's British and European operations showed clearly that bad work-practices explained larger labour input and/or smaller process output. In Britain, output was lower because lines and machines stopped more often; the main assembly line routinely stopped when shifts changed over and press machines and welding gear broke down more often because of poor preventive maintenance.

Here, at last, we have a definite link between bad work-practices and lower output in one of Britian's problem industries. But when we consider the repercussions for costs and feed-through from labour cost penalties the picture is complex, and the evidence from process comparisons does not support popular economic prejudices about the damaging consequences of bad work-practices. Alarm about these consequences rests on a failure to interpret the evidence of process comparisons and specifically on a failure to discriminate the very variable repercussions of bad work-practices for manufacturing capital at different levels. First, it is important to register a systematic discrepancy between (a) the major importance of cost control problems in the labour process to the individual enterprise, and (b) the often minor importance of such problems to the industry. Second, it is important to register another systematic discrepancy between (a) the motivating force of national labour cost variations for some segments of manufacturing capital such as American-owned multinational companies, and (b) the minor importance of labour cost (or total cost) variation for national manufacturing capital as a whole.

We can first consider the enterprise/industry opposition by examining the case of motor cars. From the enterprise point of view, control of bad work-practices could reduce labour costs and dramatically increase profits for Ford or control losses by changing the break-even point for British Leyland. In 1975, when a family car cost £1,500, the total net cost penalty from using British labour was £25. This was a glittering prize in a low-margin volume-sale operation and it was the only no-investment change which could transform enterprise profitability. On the other hand, control of bad work-practices is not necessarily crucial to the industry, because industries where bad work-practices impose cost penalties often have larger cost-handicaps arising from other causes. This was true of cars because in 1975 average sales per British model were just over half the continental levels, so the high fixed costs of new model development had to be spread over a small volume of output. In 1975, the cost penalty arising from low-volume production was estimated at £90 per car, or nearly four times as large as the £25 penalty arising from bad work-practices. At the industry level, control of bad work-practices was an irrelevance because their abolition would not have turned the industry into a low-cost producer. The British industry's major problem was not work-practices but the fragmented structure of the industry and its failure to win volume in export markets.

The argument so far already suggests that control of costs through the elimination of bad work-practices may not be very important for national manufacturing capital as a whole. This interim conclusion is qualified and reinforced when we analyse the opposition between the segment of capital and national manufacturing capital as a whole. Relatively high labour costs arising from bad work-practices may be important in the calculations of some segments of capital. Even if, as we have already argued, multinationals are not generally retreating to low-wage developing countries, it may still be the case that labour cost considerations influence American multinational decisions as to where they site the subsidiaries which will supply the EEC countries. There is anecdotal evidence that American multinationals have switched some kinds of consumer good production to mainland Europe because they can source more profitably from non-British factories with superior work-practices. This no doubt explains why Ford is not only market leader in the British car market, but also Britain's leading car importer. More subtly, in other cases, British plants have been increasingly used to assemble for the British domestic market rather than to manufacture for British and overseas markets; this is the history of General Motors' British subsidiary (Vauxhall Cars) over the past ten years.

The aggregate impact of such production-switching changes on export performance and import penetration is obscure. If we consider exports, American multinational subsidiaries are often used as export platforms from which several markets are served. It is not surprising therefore that Dunning finds that the subsidiaries of American multinationals in Britain generally have a higher propensity to export than British companies. However, this is not altogether reassuring, because the subsidiaries of American multinationals are heavily concentrated in some sectors of British industry; in 1970–71, American-owned multinationals made 60 per cent of their sales in seven industrial sectors (food, tobacco, minerals, oil refining, instrument engineering, other electronic apparatus and motor vehicle manufacture) which accounted for only 38 per cent of the sales of all UK companies (Dunning, 1973). This industrial distribution may explain the apparently high propensity to export in British subsidiaries of American multinationals. Solomon and Ingham (1977) have shown that *within* the mechanical engineering sector, British subsidiaries of American multinationals have a significantly lower propensity to export than indigenous companies. At the end of this argument we can only conclude that significant production switching *may* have taken place. However, it is certain that this effect cannot be the central or single cause of poor British trade performance because the American-owned MNC segment simply is not large enough. Even if it does account for a larger proportion of exports, a segment which since the early 1950s accounts for 10–15 per cent of output can only act as one depressive influence on trade performance. Production switching can only be part of our overall explanation and more empirical work would have to be done before we could determine its exact importance.

Furthermore, we must emphasize that relatively high labour costs (arising from bad work-practices or any other cause) do not have great significance for national manufacturing capital. The predictions of classical theory in this matter are decisively contradicted by the empirical evidence which shows that, over the past thirty years, changes in relative cost competitiveness do not explain national success and failure in the international trade in manufactures. The Fetherston et al. (1977) analysis of the 1960 to 1976 period shows that a 40 per cent rise in relative unit labour costs did not prevent West Germany's share of world trade in manufactures increasing. By way of contrast, the USA lost share dramatically despite an almost 50 per cent reduction in relative costs, and Britain again lost share dramatically despite fairly stable relative unit labour costs. The implication is that non-price factors are crucial to success in the international trade in manufactures. And the knock-on effects of bad work-practices for labour costs cannot be crucial for national manufacturing capital as a whole.

If this conclusion is accepted, there is only one way in which bad work-practices could be important for national manufacturing capital as a whole; it would have to be demonstrated that the non-price considerations which account for our poor export performance were primarily caused by bad work-practices. Such work-practices can only directly explain a small proportion of the quality deficiencies of British manufactures. Strikes can cause late delivery and frequent plant breakdowns can lower assembly standards and thus cause reliability problems. But management is responsible for poor design or weak marketing and it is necessary therefore to specify a mechanism whereby management's poor performance in these areas is indirectly determined by bad work-practices. We know that junior and middle management in British problem industries often spends a disproportionate amount of time sorting out labour problems; plant managers in the British car industry claim to spend almost half their time dealing with labour disputes while their counterparts in Belgium and

Germany spend 10–15 per cent of their time on such problems (CPRS, 1975). Do bad work-practices and labour disputes distract British managers with damaging consequences for non-price competitiveness?

Our arguments in the later sections of this essay [not included here] suggest that this distraction effect is less important than is commonly supposed. Ineffectual management is immediately responsible for the non-price deficiencies of British manufactures. But in the 1960s the effectiveness of management was being undermined by a variety of developments. The relation to financial institutions conditioned a merger boom in big business which created large and unwieldy organizations with long spans of control. If such developments made the task of management objectively more difficult, is it necessary to invoke a subjective distraction effect as a major cause of ineffective management? In any case, the work-practice distraction effect must be limited since it primarily affects junior and middle-line management which is responsible for production at the factory. But the non-price deficiencies of British manufactures are not simply a matter of the quality of the product which leaves the factory gate; the deficiencies are at least as much a matter of marketing. If marketing failure stems from managment ineffectiveness, the culprits are senior managers with their development and marketing staffs who are all well away from the factory floor. Furthermore, in marketing, from the 1950s onwards, the problems facing management had nothing to do with the British worker, because there were difficulties about market limitations.

References

AARONOVITCH, A., and M. C. SAWYER (1975), *Big Business: Theoretical and Empirical Aspects of Concentrations and Mergers in the UK*, Macmillan.

BLACKABY, F. T., ed. (1979), *De-industrialisation*, Heinemann.

CARRINGTON, J. C., and G. T. EDWARDS (1979), *Financing Industrial Investment*, Macmillan.

CENTRAL POLICY REVIEW STAFF (1975), *The Future of the Car Industry*, HMSO.

CHANNON, D. F. (1962), *The Strategy and Structure of British Enterprise*, Cambridge, Mass.

CLARK, T. A., and N. P. WILLIAMS (1978), 'Measures of Real Profitability', *Bank of England Quarterly Bulletin*, December.

COWLING, K., *et al.* (1980), *Mergers and Economic Performance*, Cambridge.

ECONOMIC PROGRESS REPORT (1982), *Measures of Competitiveness in British Manufacturing Industry*, June, HMSO.

ECONOMIC PROGRESS REPORT (1982), *Recent Trends in Labour Productivity*, January, HMSO.

FETHERSTON, M., *et al.* (1977), 'Manufacturing, Export Shares and Cost Competitiveness in Advanced Industrial Countries', *Economic Policy Review*, no. 3, Cambridge.

JONES, D. T. (1976), 'Output, Employment and Labour Productivity in Europe since 1955', *National Institute Economic Review*, no. 77, August.

KILPATRICK, A., and T. LAWSON (1980), 'On the Nature of Industrial Decline in the UK', *Cambridge Journal of Economics*, vol. 4, no. 1, March.

KUEHN, D., (1975), *Takeovers and the Theory of a Firm: An Empirical Analysis for the UK*, Macmillan.

PRAIS, S. J. (1981), *Productivity and Industrial Structure: A Statistical Study of Manufacturing Industry in Britain, Germany and the US*, Cambridge.

PRATTEN, C. F. (1976), *Labour Productivity Differentials within International Companies*, Cambridge.

SMITH, D. C. (1980), 'Trade Union Growth and Industrial Disputes', *Britain's Economic Performance*, ed. R. E. Caves and L. B. Krause, Brookings Institute.

STOUT, D. (1977), 'International Price Competitiveness, Non-Price Factors and Export Performance', *National Economic Development Office*, 1977.

WENBAN-SMITH, G. (1981), 'A Study of the Movements of Productivity in Individual Industries in the UK', *1968–79 National Institute Economic Review*, August.

WRAGG, R., and J. ROBERTSON (1978), 'Britain's Industrial Performance since the War', *Department of Employment Gazette*, May.

Part Seven

Trade Unions and the State

The eight contributors to this part of the readings are for the most part concerned with three related questions. First, what ought to be the relationship between trade unions and the government of the day? Second, what should be their status in law? Third, what limits should the state set to the boundaries of lawful strike action? The first three readings deal mainly with the first question, while the remainder are focused on legal issues and problems.

Reading 31, by Joe England and Brian Weekes, contains a useful summary of the attitude adopted by successive governments towards trade unionism. It is shown that this has been mainly determined by the view taken of the impact of collective bargaining on the economy. In recent years the trouble has been that governments have blamed 'free collective bargaining' for assisting inflation, preventing industrial efficiency and contributing to unemployment. They have also felt that powerful groups in the public sector were making unjustifiable use of industrial action, causing considerable public inconvenience. As a result a crisis has arisen in government–union relations which is likely to continue until 'sectional demands and strife provoke increasing forms of state control'.

In Reading 32, Colin Crouch is concerned with the options available to government in this crisis. In the case of contemporary Britain, two effective alternatives are available: *neo-laisser-faire* and *bargained corporatism*. The first is very much the policy of the Thatcher government. Crouch makes a case for the alternative since it offers 'chances for the extension of real democracy in the management of economic affairs'. But it would require overcoming many obstacles, and he is 'not optimistic about the capacity of British institutions to achieve changes of this order'.

L. J. McFarlane, in Reading 33, considers the moral and social justifiability of various kinds of industrial action directed against the government – from attempts to improve the pay of government employees to political general strikes designed to force a change of government. Much is found to turn on the aims, of strikes of this kind and the absence of alternatives.

The Employment Acts of 1980 and 1982 have significantly narrowed the legal boundaries of lawful strike action and the right to organize industrial action of various kinds, most notably in areas such as secondary strike action, picketing and action, to enforce union membership as a condition of employment. The liability of individuals for actions in tort has also been extended as a result of the decision to narrow the definition of a lawful trade dispute. Additional restrictions and penalties have been included in the 1984 Trade Union Act, which imposes specified election procedures on unions and limit the freedom to organize official strikes.

But it is arguable that the most far-reaching change in recent years will turn out to be the provision of the 1982 Act which removes the general immunity for union funds against actions in tort. This was known as the 'belt and braces clause', and had existed, in one form or another, since 1906. Its aim was to limit the extent of union liability if and when the decisions of judges were found to narrow the intended immunities of other parts of the 1906 Act. (This actually happened during the sixties and seventies, most notably in the case of *Rookes* v. *Barnard*.)

The case for and against making this major change in the legal status of trade unions is discussed in Reading 34. This is taken from the government's 1981 Green Paper on trade union immunities, which led to the 1982 Act.

Reading 35 is from the same Green Paper. It reviews the case for and against an alternative system of trade union law based on 'positive rights' rather than 'negative immunities'. These are best seen as different ways of stating the degree of freedom the state has decided to accord to trade unions: definitions of the extent to which they can carry out their functions without giving rise to legal claims against them. Corporate bodies, such as limited companies, already enjoy a framework of positive rights, e.g. the right to limited liability. The question is, should existing trade union immunities be rewritten in the language of positive rights?

The extract reviews the case for and against such a change, providing a useful explanation of how Britain came to adopt its unusual system of negative immunities, which is refreshingly non-legal. In the event the government decided not to make a move of this kind, but the debate continues and it is discussed further in Reading 37.

Readings 36 and 37 contain the opposed views of two labour lawyers. In the first, Richard Tur accepts the validity of Hayek's argument that union power must be curbed by law. His view is that recent employment legislation is justified. Stripped of their legal immunities, unions will be forced to 'adopt a more limited and responsible role within a free market economy'.

In the second, Bill Wedderburn argues that the 1906 immunities, clarified and strengthened to set aside the effect of judicial 'interpretation', represent the minimum degree of protection required to 'support and promote collective bargaining'. Though different in form from systems of 'positive rights' in most other countries, they do not represent an unusual and unjustified degree of 'privilege'. On this view, the employment legislation of the government is seen as a major departure from the assumptions governing British labour law for almost three-quarters of a century. The aim being to 'restrict the social power of unions' and 'increase the power of employers'.

In Reading 38 the present writer provides a short account of the reasons why employment legislation since 1980 is bound to involve unions and their members in breaches of the law. Whether this will result in much litigation, and if it does what the consequences will be for union funds, nobody can say.

31 Joe England and Brian Weekes

Trade Unions and the State: A Review of the Crisis

From Joe England and Brian Weekes, 'Trade Unions and the State: A Review of the Crisis', *Industrial Relations Journal*, vol. 12, no. 1, 1981, pp. 11–26.

For more than two decades it has been popular to blame the problems of the British economy upon the state of British industrial relations. Central to much of the criticism has been the view that British trade unions are greedy, irresponsible and too powerful. They enjoy, it is held, a position of legal privilege which places them above the law. In the workplace they exercise a power which inhibits technological and economic progress; in society at large they have shown themselves capable of bringing down democratically elected governments. Consequently, the State must curb their power before irretrievable damage is done to the economy and to democracy. Such views as these are widely held and by members of all classes. But it is an indication of the confused and contradictory nature of the present crisis in industrial relations that other views are expounded with considerable force. One recently fashionable view is that trade unions for much of the post-war period have been enmeshed with employers and the State in a tripartite system which signifies the arrival of the Corporate State and which involves trade union leaders in 'selling out' the ordinary members, especially during periods of wage restraint. Another, heard frequently from the unions themselves, but also from certain employers, is that the traditionally voluntaristic nature of British industrial relations has been undermined by precipitate labour legislation and that the law with its inbuilt rigidities plays too great a part in current industrial-relations practice. Underlying these apparently contradictory views are divergent assumptions about the nature of power *within* trade unions, the legitimacy of the trade union challenge to management, and the basis of parliamentary sovereignty. To understand the source of these assumptions it is necessary to review the characteristics of that industrial-relations system and approach to labour law which stood largely unchallenged for the first sixty years of this century.

By 1910, certain distinctive characteristics of the British industrial-relations system had been firmly established. One was that collective bargaining between trade unions and employers was accepted as the principal method of determining wages and other working conditions; although in some industries the traditional controls unilaterally exercised by craftsmen continued alongside the more recent collective bargaining arrangements. Legal regulation of conditions of work was largely limited to matters of health and safety, and the range of topics covered by protective statutes was relatively narrow, despite the introduction in 1909 of trade boards for four specified trades. Indeed, since 1871 the major impact of statute law had been in granting the unions certain immunities from common law obligations. These were reinforced by the Trade Disputes Act of 1906. This Act gave trade unions a blanket immunity by prohibiting legal actions in tort against them, and for persons acting 'in contemplation or furtherance of a trade dispute' it provided immunities from liability for the torts of simple conspiracy, inducing a breach of employment contract and interference, as well as apparently confirming their right to picket peacefully. An alternative to granting these immunities would have been to bestow positive legal rights and obligations upon the unions, perhaps in the form of a comprehensive labour law code as can be found in France or Germany. That Conservative and Liberal governments chose instead to protect trade unions through statutory immunities from common law liabilities, a method which the unions appear to have preferred, raises questions about relations between organized workers, employers and the State at that time which have yet to be answered satisfactorily.

It is perhaps obvious why the trade unions, who had learned from long experience to fear the intervention of the courts, and whose demands were pragmatic rather than ideological, should welcome a system which sought to place their activities for the most part outside the law. It is less obvious why employers should have agreed to this and, indeed, they viewed the granting of these immunities or 'privileges' with considerable unease. Yet their opposition was softened by three considerations. First, the development of collective bargaining was itself an indication that employers increasingly saw advantages in such arrangements and in working with the trade unions. One advantage was that it prevented wage-cutting competition among themselves. Another was that it provided a more acceptable method of determining wages and conditions than the customary regulation by the members of craft unions at the point of production. Indeed, some of the agreements concluded in the first years of the century 'represented a joint victory for employers and trade union leaders over the hostility of a rank and file which was still wedded to the traditions of unilateral regulations' (Clegg, Fox and Thompson (1964), p. 471). The desire of employers to assert their 'right to manage' in the face of increasing international competition affected their attitude toward the immunities in another way. For while the common law immunities gave certain limited protection to workers and unions, they provided no legal basis for a trade challenge to the right of the employer to manage in his own workplace. The common law employment contract, which in the guise of 'freedom of contract' masked the subjection of the individual worker to the power of management, remained unaffected. Immunities were consequently for the employer a lesser evil than the alternative of a code which bestowed positive legal rights upon the unions, or which allowed forms of state intervention, either of which might have impinged upon the prerogatives of management. Finally, despite the spread of collective bargaining machinery, the vast majority of workers were not covered by it. In 1910, total trade union membership was 2,565,000, or only 17 per cent of those who were potential members. Consequently, many employers were only rarely, if ever, affected by trade union action.

The effect of these three factors can be seen in the years after the Taff Vale case in 1901, when the Law Lords laid trade union funds open to attack in the courts. The unions rapidly became involved in the nascent Labour Party and worked to secure a legal framework which would provide a satisfactory status for the movement. The employers by contrast were insufficiently concerned either to weaken or destroy the unions during the period (1902–5) when the Taff Vale decision operated, or to mount an effective political campaign to prevent the passage of the 1906 Act, or to seek its repeal after 1910.

As for the State, the common law immunities corresponded precisely with the presumptions of the liberal economic system which held that the economy was self-regulating and that prices, levels of economic activity and employment were, in general, decided by market forces. Trade unions were either irrelevant to the workings of the system or, at the most, their economic effects were minimal compared with those of the market. Employers and trade unions were therefore left to work out their own rules and arrangements and devise their own machinery for enforcing them. The immunities in this light were no more than a device by which obstacles to industrial autonomy could be removed. This attitude was embodied in the Conciliation Act of 1896, which assigned to the State only the role of a conciliator, helping employers and trade unions to reach agreement with the minimum of friction. But there was no coercion and the parties were free to refuse state assistance, although arbitration was available if the parties wished.

There was another reason for the legitimation and acceptance of the unions. Collective bargaining was not a challenge to the values of capitalism but an accommodation to them. If employers maintained that labour was a commodity to be bought at the lowest possible price, then it was no more than logical for workers to sell that labour at the highest possible price. It followed naturally from this that trade unionism was predominantly concerned with a narrow range of bread-and-butter issues rather than those of social and political control. It followed too that 'politics' were divorced from trade unionism, confined by tradition to Parliament and other constitutional channels. Even when, in response to the Taff Vale decision and the failure of the existing parties to adopt working-class candidates, the unions (or some of them) set up the separate Labour Party, it functioned as little more than an adjunct of the Liberal Party. Before 1918, its programme in no way sought to challenge the presumptions of the liberal economy.

Here then were the roots of 'voluntaryism' as the system became known. Individualistic laisser-faire gave way to a collective laisser-faire which, in due course, induced in its practitioners an almost ideological belief in 'free' collective bargaining. But the roots were put down when the Empire flourished and sterling was strong, when late-Victorian Britain was successful enough in its creation of wealth and liberal enough in its ideology to accommodate trade union 'bargainers' of respectable character.

Beneath the emerging consensus, however, were attitudes and aspirations which were to break through again and again in succeeding years. On the employers' side there remained an unyielding attachment to 'the right to manage'. Although collective agreements were acceptable for regulating certain market relationships, they were not allowed to impinge upon managerial decision-making within the firm over such issues as discipline, manning, technological innovation, payment systems or redundancies. In 1897 the engineering employers imposed a national lock-out for thirty weeks on just this issue of managerial prerogatives.

On the workers' side there were three sources of reservation about collective bargaining. One was the obverse of the employers' 'right to manage'. The desire to control unilaterally many of the issues over which employers asserted their right to manage remained strong among craftsmen, among whom it was legitimized by custom, but was also present among many other groups of workers. Collective bargaining was regarded with suspicion if it threatened unilateral controls and customary practices. Secondly, there was a small minority of workers who advocated the revolutionary transformation of society through direct industrial action. For these syndicalists neither peaceful collective bargaining nor parliamentary government were acceptable. Thirdly, while collective bargaining had obvious advantages for trade union leaders and for unions as organizations, providing status to one and greater stability to the other, the ordinary members judged it by the results in their pay packets. When real wages fell, as they did after 1905, there was an increasing resort to industrial action by both organised and unorganized workers; this was especially so in the period of high employment after 1910. In these struggles, the syndicalists played a prominent part and exerted an influence beyond their numbers. Working days lost through strikes between 1910–14 rose to an annual total of 10 million or more. Police were stoned, strikers were fired upon, crowds were bayonet-charged at Llanelli and Chesterfield. Trade union membership increased from 2,565,000 in 1910 to 4,145,000 in 1914. A sense of class antagonism transcended the various specific grievances and demands. It was a dramatic illustration that the apparent integration of the working class into 'responsible' modes of behaviour was by no means an accomplished fact.

The First World War and after

The unprecedented strife of the years immediately before 1914 meant that industrial relations were no longer peripheral but a major concern of the State. The First World War confirmed that change but also marked a major evolution in the industrial-relations system. It brought what the Webbs called 'a revolutionary transformation of the social and political standing of the official representatives of the trade union world'. Without the cooperation of labour the war could not be won. In return for certain promises, most of which were subsequently broken, and in a high spirit of patriotism, trade union executives agreed to a ban on strikes, the introduction of compulsory arbitration, the suspension of all craft union controls, and the implementation of elaborate schemes of 'dilution' under which semi-skilled and unskilled labour were brought into the factories. But the collaboration of labour was required in many other ways and trade union leaders found themselves consulted on a wide range of economic and political issues. Three served in the War Cabinet. The Webbs, in a contemporary judgment, believed that, by 1920, trade unionism had won 'distinct recognition as part of the social machinery of the State, its members being thus allowed to give – like the Clergy in Convocation – not only their votes as citizens, but also their concurrence as an order or estate' (Webb and Webb, 1920, p. 635).

While it was the union leaders who had entered into these agreements, it was the munitions and engineering workers who were subject to their consequences. Important developments in trade unionism followed. Shop stewards, who before the war had occupied a relatively minor role, now grew rapidly in numbers as the problems caused by 'dilution' and other changes multiplied. They became the de facto workshop spokesmen for the workers, sometimes without official recognition from their union. In 1917 and 1919 they did receive formal recognition in the engineering industry when national agreements were signed between the unions and the Employers' Federation which provided for the recognition of stewards and workshop committees. For the first time, the right to establish trade union machinery in the workshops was explicitly recognized and collective workshop bargaining affirmed. Twenty years later, this agreement was to be a launching-pad for a new generation of shop stewards.

In addition to the considerable growth in the number of shop stewards who fulfilled the role of workplace bargainers, a separate, but linked, wartime phenomenon was the rise of the Shop Stewards' Movement. This was an explicitly revolutionary movement which inherited the syndicalist ideas of overthrowing capitalism through direct action and its replacement by a society based entirely on industrial organizations. It was centred mainly on the Clyde and a few other major centres of engineering. After the war, in very different economic conditions, the Movement melted away, many of its leaders finding a home in the Communist Party of Great Britain formed in 1920–21.

The absorption of trade union leaders into the social machinery of the State and the growth of shop stewards, each in part a reaction to the other, were new developments in the system. A third development took place in collective bargaining where, before the war, settlements had largely been on a district basis. The arbitration system and government control of certain industries encouraged industry-wide settlements: the railways in 1915, coal in 1916, the engineering industry in 1917. By 1918, industry-wide pay awards had also been achieved for carters, dockers, tram and bus workers, and employees in the chemical, aluminium and aircraft industries, gas undertakings, brick-making and flour-milling. The great majority of these arrangements endured after the war. Industry-wide bargaining was promoted too by the reports of the Whitley Committee 1917, set up in response to the shop steward unrest. These recommended that within each industry joint councils representative of employers and unions should be set up at various levels. By 1921, seventy-three joint industrial councils had been formed. Many failed to survive the post-war slump and the majority which remained became national negotiating bodies. By 1926, there were forty-seven JICs, in 1938 there were forty-five. The Whitley Committee's recommendations thus played a large part in extending industry-wide collective bargaining far beyond its pre-war confines. In the public service, after initial hesitations, the Government implemented the scheme in full and the acceptance of trade union organization and negotiation in this sector was to have wide significance with the extension of nationalization and public control after 1945.

The war strengthened and the inter-war period confirmed, therefore, the system of voluntary collective bargaining. The Whitley institutions were designed to promote trade union recognition and the growth of collective bargaining machinery and, through that machinery the achievement and maintenance of industrial peace. Collective bargaining was the approved method by which industrial disorder would be contained and industrial peace was the touchstone by which the State judged the industrial-relations system. In the aftermath of the war, with all the dislocations caused by the transition from a wartime to a peacetime economy, with the heightened expectation, soon to be dashed, of a 'land fit for heroes', with customary differentials upset by wartime wage awards and with rapid fluctuations in the price level, industrial militancy ran high. During the years 1919–25, an annual average of nearly 28 million working days were lost through strikes and lockouts. But then came the economic crisis of the 1920s which weakened the militants, decimated union membership from a peak of 8 million in 1920 to under 4·5 million in 1933, and enabled wages to be forced down in the unsheltered staple trades. In these circumstances, union leaders conducted a lengthy rearguard action in the JICs to obtain uniform rates of wages. Eventually they were successful in convincing employers that industry-wide wage agreements and price agreements rather than cut-throat competition were the best way of combating the depression. The achievement of trade union recognition and industry-wide bargaining under the prevailing conditions was seen by union leaders, particularly those of the two large general workers' unions formed by amalgamations in the early 1920s, the Transport and General Workers' Union and the General and Municipal Workers' Union, as significant steps in promoting trade union aims.

While the respectable bargainers were consolidating their relationships with the employers, unemployment ensured that rank-and-file activity was largely dormant. Workplace wage bargaining apparently faded away. The General Strike of 1926, reluctantly led by the General Council of the TUC in aid of the miners, was a defeat for all militants and the final spasm of the syndicalist urge for direct action. Yet the old traditions of job control and ca'canny were not abandoned. Indeed, from the workers' point of view, the economic situation required that jobs should be protected with greater intensity. The struggles over dilution during the 1914–18 war had confirmed the effective limitations of managerial power. Dilution during the war was about the employers' right, as a result of an agreement with the Government and national trade union officials, to employ non-skilled people on jobs previously treated as skilled. Yet the right to place any engineering worker on any job had been a management right since the agreement of 1898 which had ended the thirty-week lockout. Again, in 1922, the engineering employers locked out their workers and the settlement reasserted the pre-war authority of 'managerial functions'. Yet even in periods of heavy unemployment, employers found that a degree of pragmatic give and take was necessary at the point of production, whatever the legal norms and the nature of formal national agreements. The problem of how to achieve efficient production from an alienated workforce remained.

One other development must be mentioned. The inter-war years saw a growth in the influence of the TUC. In 1921, it widened its powers and increased its resources and staff. More and more, the General Council's decisions came to be based on information supplied by specialists. After 1926, Walter Citrine, as general secretary, guided the TUC into the Mond Turner talks and, after their failure, into greater consultation with employers' federations and the Government. Although frequently excluded from formal consultation on issues which they believed affected them, the General Council members nonetheless acquired new representative functions (as well as honours), and cooperation with the State gradually grew.

The inter-war period was consequently one in which the predominantly voluntary system of collective bargaining was strengthened and institutionalised. While unemployment held in check shop-floor demands and the TUC became more statesmanlike, the rituals of joint national negotiations appeased class antagonisms and protected the organizational interests of trade unions and employers. The State, now intervening more in economic affairs, but in a piecemeal fashion, uninformed by any set of general principles, was content to support the autonomous evolution of the system.

Full employment in a managed economy

After 1940 the context was transformed. The autonomous system of 'free' collective bargaining which had been initiated in the spirit of Victorian laisser-faire and developed during the inter-war depression now entered its maturity within a managed economy with full employment. The consequences for relations between trade unions and the State were momentous and have not yet been fully worked out. But, at first, the war confirmed previous trends. Collective bargaining was further strengthened. The appointment of Ernest Bevin as Minister of Labour and National Service ensured that, while the unions were required to make similar concessions to those of 1914–18, they did so in exchange for tangible benefits guaranteed to continue after the war. Bevin insisted that trade union sacrifices should be matched by the extension of collective bargaining or, in weakly organized trades, by statutory regulation of conditions. Altogether, fifty-six JICs or similar bodies were revived or newly established in 1939–46, and, by 1950, 80 per cent of employees were covered either by joint voluntary negotiating machinery or by statutory machinery. Trade union membership increased from 30·5 per cent of the labour force in 1938 to 45 per cent in 1948.

At the same time, the TUC General Council and the leaders of other influential unions were incorporated into the machinery of government decision-making and consultation. As Pelling remarks, 'the annual reports of the TUC General Council began to read like the records of some special government department, responsible for coordinating policy in the social and industrial spheres' (Pelling, 1963, p. 215). This major enhancement of the political status and influence of trade union leaders (Citrine alone served on thirty different public or industrial bodies) was again a development of the corporate bias in the political system first discernible in 1914–18 and resurgent in the 1930s. After the war, the relationships between the trade union leadership and the leading figures in the Labour Government continued to be strong and were, for the most part, usually cordial. These close relationships reflected a possibly unique consensus between politicians, civil servants and trade unions about the form of the post-war political settlement. In particular, state planning and controls were to be relaxed only gradually and, above all, the Government was firmly committed to improving standards of social welfare, and, following the famous 1944 White Paper, to maintain a 'high and stable level of employment'. The advent of Conservative governments in the 1950s did very little to change this fundamental consensus. On an ever-widening range of topics, the TUC's collective advice was sought after and listened to.

The third change brought about by the war, large-scale intervention in the economy, did not end in 1945. The Keynesian revolution, the nationalization of key industries and services, the growth of the Welfare State and a continuing concern with 'planning' of various kinds ensured that the economic influence of the Government remained powerful and far-ranging. Not least it became the employer of more than a quarter of the labour force.

Finally, the war brought a return of shop steward organization. Now, as in 1914–18, they were mainly workplace bargainers (but legitimized by the agreements of 1917 and 1919). Unlike the earlier period, there was no explicitly political 'Movement' of shop stewards. And unlike the earlier period, they did not go into a decline when the war ended. The continuance of full employment enhanced the power of work groups, and bargaining between shop stewards and management developed on a scale previously unknown. This bargaining was not only over money but about those matters which management still declared to be, in theory, within their own prerogative: discipline and redundancy, working arrangements, overtime and manning. From the mid 1950s, the number of stewards grew considerably and modern British trade unionism became grounded in workplace power bases with their own institutional arrangements and expectations. It was a form of trade unionism which, in its emphasis upon workplace autonomy, echoed an older tradition which had become overlaid in the twentieth century by the development of national bargaining. But whereas the older tradition had been largely confined to craftsmen and those with a strong sense of occupational identity, it was the unskilled and semi-skilled who in the fifties and sixties developed, and through organization exercised, controls over their work processes. This qualitative change in the nature of trade unionism was of great significance and, in conditions of high employment, one with which management had to make accommodation. When employment deteriorated during the 1970s, workplace organization remained strong. Just as employer recognition had sustained unions nationally during the 1930s, so it did again, but at shopfloor level, in the 1970s.

From this sketch of the development of trade unions and collective bargaining we can see more clearly the nature of the contradictions which have emerged over the past twenty years. The essence of the British industrial-relations system as it developed from the late Victorian era was one of industrial autonomy within a market economy. The parties were free to conclude the best available bargains. The State's only concern was for industrial peace. The post-1945 role of the State as regulator of the economy and principal employer was bound to conflict with this traditional system. The new economic objectives inevitably undermined the assumption that governments were indifferent to the consequences of collective bargaining. But the contradictions between government economic policy and trade union activity were not at first apparent. In the early years after the war, both trade union leaders and employers operated within the pre-war system of industry-wide bargaining with which they were familiar. The larger trade unions were known for their non-militancy, political conservatism, and the exercise of highly central-ized autocratic power. Wage demands were moderated by loyalty to the Labour Government and a recognition of the serious problems of post-war reconstruction.

From the mid-fifties, the complaints about 'trade union power' which were later to swell in volume began to appear. This historical survey enables us to see that apart from a substantial increase in the number of trade unionists there are three levels at which British unions have exercised power since 1945. One is at shop-floor level; another is in industry-wide negotiations which remain the rule in the public sector but have a much diminished influence elsewhere; and the third is at the level of the TUC and its relations with the State. (The unions' relationship with the Labour Party is taken here to be an aspect of this third level of power and will be discussed presently.) The ability to exercise power at these three different levels is what makes the British trade union movement one of the most powerful in the world (although the occasions on which power has been exer-cised on all three levels *at the same time* are rare).

The aspect that was new in post-war Britain was strong shop-floor organization, particularly in engineering, which challenged managerial rights and pursued short-term, sectional objectives by disorderly, even disruptive, methods. This jostling for advantage between groups of workers, paralleled in many cases by employers who competed for labour by bidding up earnings above the nationally-agreed basic rates, resulted in wage drift, inflationary pressures, and a sharp increase in the number of strikes, the great majority of which were unofficial. The annual average number of strikes rose from 1,791 in 1945–54 to 2,521 in 1955–64. As the peaceful resolution of conflict had been the major criterion for judging the system, this was particularly disturbing to the authorities. At the same time, the basic problems of British capitalism were becoming clear. Large sections of industry were under-capitalized, inefficient, and finding it increasingly difficult to compete in international markets. As a result, the economy grew more slowly than its competitors and there were recurrent balance of payments crises. Shop-floor unionism with its protection of restrictive practices and interruptions to production was seen as contributing to the problems of manufacturing industry. It also had an effect upon the relationship between trade union leaders and members. As work-place organization developed in extent and resources the full-time official found he was likely to be dealing with a membership that had thrown off the passivity of pre-war years and was now less willing to accept the advice and instructions of national leaders. With the dispersal of bargaining and the existence within unions of more self-confident, articulate (and better educated) lay officials, the economic, political and industrial coherence of trade unions as national insti-tutions declined. Thus many of those who declared the unions to be too powerful, at the same time berated them for not being strong enough to control their own members. The 'outmoded' structure of the unions, the inadequacies of collective bargaining machinery, and the general efficacy of the whole system were more and more called into question. From the early sixties, a whole range of reforms was initiated by the State.

The State intervenes

The motives for intervention were several and overlapping, while the methods chosen did not always lead to compatible results. The major motives were the comparatively slow growth of the economy, the rate of inflation, a growing perception that the narrow concerns of tradi-tional collective bargaining were failing to meet urgent social and economic problems, and a recognition that a political response was required to the increasingly popular view that unions were the major factor in the country's misfortunes.

Concern with the overall state of the economy led to a revived interest in planning; concern over inflation led to a search for a viable incomes policy. Both strategies involved close cooperation with individual trade unions and the TUC. Planning machinery was created by the Conservative Government in 1962, when they set up the tripartite National Economic Development Council (NEDC), on which sat six senior trade unionists as TUC representatives, supported by the National Economic Development Office (NEDO). Throughout most of the sixties and seventies, trade unionists were involved in all the other layers of planning machinery – the so-called 'little Neddies' at industry level, regional development councils, and industrial strategy working parties. The almost constant use of incomes policies was conterminous with these developments. A wage freeze in 1961 was followed by the setting up of the National Incomes Commission in 1962 and this was succeeded by the National Board for Prices and Incomes in 1965. In 1966, the Prices and Incomes Act significantly breached the voluntarist tradition by giving the Secretary of State discretionary powers to compel the reporting of claims, settlements, prices and charges and to impose a legal standstill on them; and defined criminal sanctions for 'breach of standstill'. The following years up to 1979 saw both Conservative and Labour governments applying incomes policies, sometimes with and sometimes without statutory controls. Until Mrs Thatcher's Government broke radically with the post-war Keynesian consensus, changes of government made little difference to the pursuit of these policies. The Labour Party under Wilson and Callaghan was consciously a party of social integration and of 'national' government. Although trade union leaders were pushed on to the defensive by government intervention in 'free' collective bargaining, they participated, to a greater or lesser degree, in framing incomes policies and in administering them. In this way, they salvaged what they could of the voluntary principle.

By the early sixties, the deficiencies of collective bargaining as a method for tackling specific problems in the labour market were also being recognized, as was the uneven application of standards created by fragmented workplace bargaining. Thus there followed a gathering tide of legislation which began with the Contracts for Employment Act 1963 and continued through the Industrial Training Act 1964, Redundancy Payments Act 1965, Race Relations Act 1968, Equal Pay

Act 1970, Employment and Training Act 1973, Health and Safety at Work Act 1974, Employment Protection Act 1975, Sex Discrimination Act 1975, and the Race Relations Act 1976. Most of these statutes mark concerns common to both governing parties; in particular, an expectation that the industrial-relations system should provide trained and mobile labour and that there should be a floor of rights available to all employees with special protection for those liable to suffer discrimination by race or sex. But the Employment Protection Act (and the Trade Union and Labour Relations Act 1974 and as amended 1976) combined an extension of individual rights with measures designed to strengthen the rights of trade unions as organizations and the rights of union representatives in the workplace. These measures included the encouragement of trade union recognition and the establishment of the closed shop, the right to disclosure of information necessary for effective collective bargaining, and the right of union representatives to advance consultation and information and to take time off for trade union or public duties. That these provisions should be enacted after so long an outcry that 'something must be done' to *curb* union power is a dramatic illustration of the political power of the unions. Before discussing the nature of that power however we must first consider the State's efforts during the sixties and seventies to use the law against the unions.

As on so many other occasions, it was the judiciary which made the first move. Since the 1920s judges had largely abstained from developing new common law liabilities to evade the Trade Disputes Act 1906. But the anxieties aroused by the alleged excessive power of unions and workgroups brought a number of verdicts in the sixties which threatened union immunities. The most noteworthy was the Lords' verdict in *Rookes* v. *Barnard* which held that the threat of industrial action in breach of employment contracts could provide the ingredients for the obscure tort of 'intimidation'. The protection given by the 1906 Act appeared to have been stripped away. One of the first acts of the new Labour Government was to introduce the Trade Disputes Act 1965 which gave a degree of immunity from the tort of intimidation. But, at the same time, the Government announced the establishment under Lord Donovan of a Royal Commission to inquire into trade unions and employers' associations. No one doubted that trade unions were intended to be the main target for investigation. When the Commission reported three years later they acknowledged that there were many defects in British industrial relations but they did not identify trade unions as the main cause. Rather, they pointed

419

to the autonomy and fragmentation of informal workplace bargaining and blamed employers and managers for not having effective personnel policies and for responding in *ad hoc* fashion to shop-floor pressures. The Commission did not believe that the law could be the primary instrument for reform and argued instead for properly negotiated 'factory-wide agreements' which would formalize bargaining arrangements and restore order in the workplace. The Government recognized the Commission's underlying strategy but was dismayed by their long-term perspective. It felt that the public was looking for swift action in the form of legal sanctions against unofficial strikers. The subsequent White Paper *In Place of Strife* was forthrightly interventionist and included a compulsory conciliation pause under which unconstitutional strikers might be legally ordered back to work; a compulsory strike ballot; and a recognition procedure for inter-union disputes whereby the Secretary of State could enforce solutions. After fierce opposition from the TUC, these 'penal' clauses were eventually withdrawn. The 1970 election enabled the Conservatives to enact their own proposals for reform.

The Conservative Government's Industrial Relations Act 1971 broke much more comprehensively than *In Place of Strife* the tripartite consensus about British industrial relations which had existed since the late twenties. The break was not only in the substance of the Act but also in the manner it was presented. For a generation, trade union leaders had become accustomed to their views on legislation receiving careful consideration, above all when it affected the unions. The newly elected government largely cast aside this constitutional development, stood firm on its mandate, turned a deaf ear to the TUC's objections to the principles of the proposed Act, and proceeded with its passage. The Act set out to replace collectivist laisser-faire with a comprehensive legal framework which would restrict conflict, reform collective bargaining and promote individual liberties. Individual workers were given the right not to belong to a trade union, thus placing closed shops outside the protection of the law. Unlike the Donovan Commission, the Government believed that law could be the main instrument for their actions. Consequently, one of the principles of the Act was the promotion of 'effective' and 'responsible' trade unions. Among the many provisions of this complex Act, a Registrar of Trade Unions and Employers' Associations was established with whom organizations had to register in order to bring themselves within the legal definition of a 'trade union'. As an inducement to register, certain legal rights and protections were reserved for registered unions only. A number of aspects of industrial relations behaviour were classified as 'unfair industrial practices', most of them forms of trade union action. Those who felt that they had been unfairly treated could press their claims in the newly created National Industrial Relations Court (NIRC). In addition, the Government gave itself the power to apply to the NIRC for restraining orders under 'national emergency' injunction and ballot procedures.

The Act was a failure. The TUC instructed its affiliates not to register and the great majority complied. Twenty unions which did register were expelled and one resigned. Rank-and-file activists joined with trade union leaders in opposition to the Act, thus bringing about one of those rare occasions when all levels of union power were operating in the same direction at the same time. Employers were almost as reluctant as unions to apply the law. Many did not see their own industrial relations as a problem and they frequently combined with the unions to protect the closed shop and other bargaining practices built up over many years. The number of days lost through strike action rose dramatically. From an average of less than four million days a year during 1964–70, 24 million were lost in 1972 alone, the worst total since 1926. When Labour returned to office in 1974, the Act was immediately repealed.

The results of intervention

What then were the results of state intervention in industrial relations during the sixties and seventies? Two reactions to intervention were mentioned at the beginning of this essay – the allegations of corporatism and legal interference. The considerable involvement of trade union officials in economic planning bodies and in supporting, to a lesser or greater degree, incomes policies account for the charges of corporatism. The essence of these charges is that the trade unions have been induced, via incomes policies, to act as agents of state control over their members. Such charges are simplistic. The immense diversity of traditions and governmental forms of British unionism ensures that generalizations about internal systems of social control encounter innumerable exceptions. More specifically, the existence of strong shop-floor organizations has made it impossible for leaders to become far out of step with their members. No phase of incomes policy has managed to withstand shop-floor pressure for more than two years. Such pressure may also be seen as a resource which strengthens the capacity of trade union leaders to resist state press-ures. In this way, shop steward power has made it much more possible for the corporate bias which undoubtedly exists within the system – and which, as we have seen, has long antecedents – to be one in which bargains may be struck between the State and trade unions rather than one in which the State, through trade unions, imposes decisions made in the interests of the existing order. Two decades of attempts at incomes policies suggest therefore the *limits* of corporatism, defined as a method of social control. It was partly for this reason that the Heath and Thatcher Governments in their initial phases both drew back from corporatist strategies and turned instead to legal regulation of the unions, and why the Labour Government of 1974–9 entered into a bargain with the unions in the form of the 'social contract'.

The spate of legislation, whether designed to provide a floor of rights for workers or to curb union power, explains the complaints heard from both employers and trade unions about legal 'inter-ference'. Laws which suit one party often annoy the other, judicial interpretations are sometimes unexpected, and there may be unin-tended consequences to legislation which neither side welcomes. But the central conclusion must be that the sheer volume of legislation is disturbing to those brought up in the voluntarist tradition. Over the past two decades, there has been a marked trend towards legal regulation in the British system of industrial relations. Although collective bargaining remains the dominant method of determining terms and conditions of employment and of resolving disputes, its contents and procedures are more and more influenced by legal norms and machinery. Increasingly, that machinery, as it operates through industrial tribunals, offers an alternative to collective bargaining.

Despite this trend, another lesson to emerge from the past two decades is that there are limits to what the law can achieve. Compul-sory strike ballots may harden opinion for industrial action rather than prevent it, as in the railway dispute of 1972. The continuance of the closed shop during the period of the Industrial Relations Act illus-trates that legal sanctions are not in themselves an effective means of changing popular conduct which is motivated by deep-seated convictions. It also illustrates the fact that laws which seek to interfere with workplace arrangements are often ignored by managements and unions who are satisfied with the arrangements. Collective bargaining is itself a regulative process which commands an authority within its bargaining unit which may be at least as strong as parliamentary laws. Legislation which seeks to establish rules at variance with the social mores of significant sections of the population have a limited chance of success.

Finally, a clear result of two decades of state intervention was a much strengthened TUC. Largely this was directly due to government encouragement. When governments desired the union viewpoint on economic planning, incomes policy or legislation it was inevitably to the TUC that they turned. Unions outside the TUC were largely ignored by government. Consequently, many unions which had remained aloof from the TUC, particularly those organizing professional workers, affiliated in order to have their voice heard. In the past twenty years, the organizations of teachers, local government officials, university dons and middle- and senior-grade civil servants have been among those which have affiliated. More authoritatively than ever before, the TUC stands as the representative body of British trade unionism with its affiliated unions representing more than 90 per cent of union members. The TUC gained authority too from its successful stand against the Industrial Relations Act. Besides demonstrating its ability to frustrate that legislation, the degree of discipline it maintained over affiliates at that time was notable. The influence of government planning machinery and legislation was also reflected within the TUC by the development of its industry committees, regional councils, a vigorous expansion of provisions for trade union training, and the publication of its distinctive annual economic reviews. Yet this accession of authority to the TUC was not at the expense of shop-floor activists. More industries and services have shop-floor organization today than ever before; the number of workplace representatives almost doubled between 1960 and 1980; and the range of issues bargained over within the workplace has widened rather than diminished. In addition, it should be noted that total union membership increased from 9·8 million in 1960 to 13 million in 1978. Overall, two decades of intervention did not achieve the result that many were seeking.

The unions and the Labour Party

State intervention in industrial relations has increased the power of the unions in a different and more direct way. It has always been a traditional role of the Labour Party to promote legislation favourable to the unions, particularly when statute law was required to redress judicial encroachments upon union rights. Examples may be found in 1906, 1913, 1946 and in 1965. But this role was developed when

Labour was a minority party and, more importantly, when governments played little part in regulating industrial relations. During the sixties, both these factors changed. Government intervention became the norm and Labour was in power during 1964–70 and 1974–9. The unions' capacity to influence legislation was thereby considerably increased, although there was a time lag before this was fully understood either by the Party or by the unions. The Wilson Governments in the sixties, during their reformist stage, identified the unions, like the House of Lords, as institutions that would have to be brought up to date. The unions, while agreeing with some reluctance to the setting up of the Donovan Commission, ensured that its composition was broadly favourable and included George Woodcock, general secretary of the TUC. It was not until 1969 that government proposals for trade union reform were formulated in *In Place of Strife*. They were aborted when it became clear that the proposals were unacceptable to the union interests within the Party and within the House of Commons.

. The unions' power within the Labour Party can be briefly stated. Over 90 per cent of the votes cast at Labour's policy-making annual conference come from trade union delegates. Twelve of the twenty-seven members of the Party's national executive committee are trade union representatives. The unions also have a dominant voice, through the block vote, in the election of the five women members and the Party treasurer who also sit on the executive. Thus, eighteen of the twenty-seven places are controlled by the unions.[1] Within the Parliamentary Labour Party, anything from a third to almost a half of the members (48 per cent in 1979) are sponsored by trade unions. Most of the Party's finances come from the unions. Even so, the unions do not dominate the Party in quite the way all this suggests, for on many issues trade union votes are split. But rarely is this the case on legislation affecting themselves. In 1969 a substantial number of the trade union group of MPs made it clear that they would not allow the Wilson Government's bill for union reform to go through. This more than anything else killed the bill. A year later when Labour lost the general election, it seemed to many that this was partly a consequence of abstentions by activists upset by the Government's attitude to the unions.

The 1970 election defeat was followed by the Industrial Relations Act. Their combined effect was to draw the Labour Party and the unions closer together than ever before despite the ill-feeling left by

---

1. Since 1980 unions have also been involved in the election of the leader and deputy leader of the Party.

In Place of Strife. After its attempts to impose incomes policies and labour legislation upon the unions the Labour Party recognized both the impracticability and the electorally damaging consequences of such strategies. The unions desired the repeal of the Industrial Relations Act as soon as possible. In January 1972 the TUC Labour Party liaison committee met for the first time, composed of six members of the shadow cabinet, six members of the Party's national executive and six representatives of the TUC. It met at regular two-monthly intervals thereafter and produced policy statements not merely on industrial relations but also on economic and social policy. In this way, the 'social contract' was born. In the present context, the social contract was significant in three ways. First, the Labour Party pledge to repeal the Industrial Relations Act passed a death sentence on the Act and greatly strengthened the TUC's opposition to it. Secondly, the unions' influence over a wide area of state policy was made explicit. The old distinction between industrial and political questions, which had long been blurred, now became largely meaningless. Thirdly, just as the Industrial Relations Act had broken the old consensus and sought to tilt the balance of power away from the unions, so the legislation envisaged by the social contract and enacted by Labour when it came to power, principally in the Employment Protection Act 1975, was deliberately intended to increase the rights of individual workers, trade union representatives and unions as organizations vis-à-vis employers.

The unions' position within the Labour Party therefore adds another dimension to the increase in union influence noted in the previous section. State intervention in the industrial relations system has enhanced the unions' role as rule-makers: the more legislation affecting industrial relations, the greater the role for the unions within Party policy making. When Labour is in power, this role may be exercised negatively, as when the 'short sharp bill' based on *In Place of Strife* was killed in 1969, or positively as in the example of the Employment Protection Act 1975, which was largely drafted by the TUC. Even when Labour is in opposition, the expectation that the Party will gain power within a few years provides the unions with a powerful sanction against anti-union legislation passed by the Government of the day, as was the case with the Industrial Relations Act.

The limits and value of union power

During the twentieth century, the development of union power in both its industrial and political dimensions has been formidable. But it would be wrong to exaggerate this power. A major characteristic of contemporary trade unionism is its fragmented nature. The existence of three levels of power – workplace, industry and national – provides opportunities for disunity as well as strength. Under the influence of persistent inflation, sectionalism has grown rather than diminished. The growth of autonomous workplace organizations has encouraged a 'factory chauvinism' rather than a class consciousness. Union rivalries undermine concerted action, as the steel strike of 1980 demonstrated. Divisions between national leaders and shop stewards, between the leaders of different unions, between shop stewards and rank-and-file members, and between the workers in different factories have been successfully exploited by employers and governments in recent years. The changing composition of the labour force is significant here. It is by no means certain that the unions of widely dispersed professionals – teachers, civil servants, technicians and managers – which are now much larger than the unions intimately based in local communities – mining, steel, docks, shipbuilding – possess the same strength of purpose.

Nor has the union movement always used in its own narrow interests the power it has. Much of the past twenty years has been characterized by voluntary wage restraint 'in the national interest'. However unreal this behaviour may seem to those who view industrial relations in crude conflictual terms, it is highly significant that union leaders and their members have shown themselves susceptible time and again to appeals based upon community spirit and the homogeneity of British society. Such appeals tap a deep-rooted tradition within British working-class life. Wage militancy has only been reasserted when workers have experienced restraint to be materially self-defeating and when politicians have failed to proceed with social reforms commensurate with their rhetoric of community based upon shared experience.

But, above all, it is absurdly partial to discuss union power and to overlook the enormous growth during the twentieth century of the power of the State and of multinational firms. It remains true, as Flanders pointed out, that 'trade unions cannot determine the greater part of the experience to which their members react' (Flanders, 1975, p. 293). Trade unions do not control exchange rates or interest rates or the levels of taxation; they do not decide marketing strategies or when and where investment will take place; they do not determine the price of oil or the supply of housing. The central levers of economic power are not in their hands. It is as a countervailing power to the decisions made by the State and by capital that trade union strength now, as in the past, can best be understood. It remains by comparison, even in the best of times, defensive and opportunistic. Whatever the attitude toward unions adopted by particular governments there are agents of the State with considerable power and wide areas of discretion, such as civil servants, judges, the police, intelligence services and military who favour the established order and regard the growth of trade union power with distaste. Much of the mass media shares this view and energetically purveys it.

Assertions that trade unions are 'holding the country to ransom' or that they override the sovereignty of Parliament have therefore to be seen in a wider perspective. The fact that trade unions may oppose the objectives of government, even by failing to obey or accept the law, is no more than the prerogative exercised by religious and political groups for centuries. Parliamentary sovereignty has never implied, in this country, parliamentary dictatorship. In a free society, individuals and groups will oppose authority and, if necessary, accept the legal consequences. In this way, new freedoms have been won and old freedoms maintained. Shop-floor organization during this century has been an essential element in the resistance to further centralization of power and control in modern society. Similarly, the freedom to strike is an essential safeguard of democracy and recognized as such in the United Nations International Covenant on Economic, Social and Cultural Rights. A society which grows intolerant of workers who exercise the essential freedom to withdraw their labour should therefore weigh carefully the implications of curbing this freedom.

The drawn-out crisis

Nonetheless, the demand that 'something should be done' remains at the centre of British politics. In part, the demand arises from employers who, under increasingly severe economic pressures, believe that only by recovering their prerogative to manage can industry be made efficient. In part, it arises from middle-class dismay at the deterioration of collective bargaining as a method of social control. 'Ugly scenes' on picket lines feed a widespread unease among the professional classes about social stability. Both these perceptions are in response to the qualitative as well as quantitative changes in post-war unionism. But the widespread nature of the demand has another source. A major feature of contemporary industrial action is that it often adversely affects the public at large, either as workers or as consumers. A strike in a small component factory may result in thousands of car workers being laid off. A strike in a service such as gas, electricity or transport may affect the whole country. The grievance may be real, the strike legitimate and taken only as a last resort. But structural and technological changes in the economy, the concentration of ownership and the rise of mass consumption ensure that its adverse effects are felt far beyond the immediate parties in dispute. The social consequences of strike action, which in the nineteenth century were largely confined to local labour and product markets, may now be generalized throughout the economy. From this springs much anti-union sentiment.

At a deeper level are the contradictions in the unions' ideological position. The material conditions which made collective laisser-faire possible – a successful market economy at the centre of a great empire – long ago ceased to exist, yet the unions adhere to free collective bargaining as a preferred model of behaviour, even while they advocate state intervention in numerous other areas of economic policy. At the same time, it is impossible for the Government as the major employer and overseer of the economy to ignore the industrial and economic consequences of the wage-bargaining process. Faced with strong shop-floor organizations, rising working-class aspirations and confidence, and a decline in deference, the State in the past twenty years sought to replace the discipline exercised by mass unemployment in the thirties with incomes policies and legal restraints. Neither was conspicuously successful, for unions were able to exert power at various industrial and political levels and thwart attempts to control them. Meanwhile, the British economy became progressively vulnerable to overseas competition, with unemployment and inflation at uncomfortably high levels. The 'winter of discontent' in 1979 gave further strength to the view that legal compulsion and authoritarian state regulation were necessary in order to restore order.

The Thatcher Government, pledged to a return to monetary disciplines and a head-on attack on trade union power, was returned to office. Its programme included the curtailment of trade union legal immunities, in some cases taking the legal position back to before 1906; a reduction in the level of social security benefits paid to the dependants of strikers; the constraint of pay increases through tight monetary policy; and an acceptance of a high and rising level of unemployment. Employers were encouraged to reassert their prerogatives. It is a programme which enjoys the influential support of international finance capital and which (with the backing of North

Sea oil revenues) has some chance of success. The factors which have served to increase union power have deliberately been put into reverse. But it is a programme that will require great political courage to carry through and which has already entailed large-scale economic disruption and growing social bitterness. The level of unemployment required to restrain wage settlements to within even hailing distance of the rate of productivity increase may be of catastrophic proportions. It is a programme for those who put their trust in the coercion of trade unionists through a return to the discipline of mass unemployment and an increase in the powers of the police and the courts.

The strategy faces obvious difficulties within the short term. If it succeeds on the economic front and the economy moves out of recession and into expansion, an embittered trade union movement will be waiting to launch a wage offensive. The next Labour Government will be under great union pressure to restore the legal immunities. And a movement that has developed through 200 years is unlikely to change its character in the face of what, in a parliamentary democracy, must be a necessarily brief period of authoritarianism. Yet the failure of the strategy, combined with increasingly aggressive foreign competition in manufactures and 'unreformed' union behaviour, could well *itself* lead to further demands for even stronger state action to reduce union power. If this weight of public opinion were to be combined, as seems likely in the 1980s, with generally high levels of unemployment, then there may indeed, in the medium term, be a fundamental reduction of union power and expectations conterminous with a significant increase in state-imposed limitations upon union activities. An onslaught upon working-class aspirations in this way would represent a major change in political values in Britain. However, in the present climate, this is easier to envisage than a revolutionary transformation of the economic system in favour of the working class. The corporate power of domestic and international capital in combination with the coercive forces of the State, the constitutionalism of the TUC, above all the lack of present commitment to radical class struggle among British workers, remove this option from the political agenda in any foreseeable future.

While these scenarios may appear extreme, they illustrate that the breakdown of the post-war consensus inevitably opens the door to the polarization of opinions and that a new accommodation is likely to be built on ground some way to the left or right of the old one. The 'trade union question' raises fundamental political issues and no settlement will be lightly achieved. The development of workers' organizations in this century suggests four characteristics which need to be recognized before a settlement can be reached. One is that trade unionism is a permanent feature of British capitalism, giving institutional form to a mass of deep-seated reservations, disagreements, and outright rejections of the prevailing organization of production, and the inequalities of wealth and power which arise from it in the workplace and subsequently in society at large. Secondly, wherever possible workers seek control over the work processes which affect them and thus present a direct challenge to notions of managerial prerogatives. Thirdly, capital cannot survive without the cooperation of labour. It was for this reason that in both world wars labour was drawn at all levels into the war effort. Finally, and germane to the previous point, there is the proven willingness of the trade union movement to respond to national crises and to enter into 'social contracts' or 'concordats' with a government sympathetic to its aspirations.

It is this last point which is most commonly seized upon by those who reject the moves toward legal restriction of the trade unions and yet who accept the need for a change in behaviour. An incomes policy, voluntarily agreed between the unions and the government, is seen as an essential element in future economic and social stability. That may be so. But such a policy is far from an easy option, for it requires a government to adopt policies acceptable to the trade unions and their members, yet which convince the electorate and the interests of capital that such policies are necessary for industrial success. This is not made easier by the fact that trade union strength, and the experience of the Social Contract, make it highly probable that in any future agreement a government would have to give specific commitments to meet the TUC's views on economic and industrial policy as well as labour legislation. Even if such an agreement could be reached between trade union leaders and a government, the difficulties of achieving shop floor compliance would remain. Two aspects of this in particular demand attention.

The first is the largely apolitical nature of many shop floor activists whose horizons are bounded by struggles over job control and wage bargaining. The development of a wider consciousness, resting upon greater knowledge of macro-economic problems and social responsibilities, will be necessary if any future incomes policy is to last longer than the customary two years. Secondly, there is the struggle for job control itself. In the face of employer resistance, this struggle has failed to develop into anything more positive than a capacity to weaken the competitiveness of British Industry.[2] Yet the need to raise productivity will be vital if any future incomes policy is not to be just another device for lowering real wages. The issue of job control may therefore have to be confronted and, in the political circumstances of a new social contract, legislative backing given to a significant increase in industrial democracy (by various means). This would require a greater shift in power *and* responsibility to workers and their representatives than anything so far attempted in this country.

Before the 'social contract option' could be envisaged, therefore, as the basis for a new consensus of any lasting value, two conditions would have to be met. One is a climate of opinion quite different from that currently prevailing. In that climate it would be recognized that trade unions are not an alien force but important democratic institutions which represent a major cultural achievement by the British people in the course of industrialization. Also that as products of this society, they reflect rather than determine the prevailing values. When people are constantly urged to consume, and have their expectations stimulated by mass advertising, it is pointless, for example, to attack the unions for being 'greedy'. Thirdly, that the subordinate position of employees within the enterprise, and the importance attached to managerial prerogatives, stifle creative abilities. How can responsibility be demanded from those to whom responsibility is not given? Finally, that trade unionism represents a force to be worked with rather than to be subjugated. In their turn, the unions would have to admit openly that free collective bargaining evolved in very different circumstances to those of today; that governments now have a legitimate and necessary interest in the outcome of pay bargaining; and that strikes often impose unwelcome costs upon the community at large. From these perceptions, a start could be made to build a common sense of obligation and responsibility. The moral basis for this lies in those principles of citizenship, fellowship and equality which have deep roots in the British democratic tradition. During and after the Second World War these ideals sustained a highly productive economy and significant social advances.

But, as this example reminds us, rhetoric is not enough. It must be allied with an honest application to the nuts and bolts of policy. The manner in which the Social Contract was conceived during 1972–4 is

2. The corporate plan produced by the Lucas Aerospace Combine Committee is an example of the remarkable creativity which at present is being frustrated.

431

instructive here. During the meetings of the Labour Party-TUC liaison committee the union members would not contemplate an incomes policy and therefore did not have to consider the ways in which such a policy might be administered. In particular, the extent to which a plausible policy implied greater TUC power over affiliated unions was not faced. The parliamentary leadership in their turn were not required to think through the details of their industrial; financial and economic policies. It is little wonder then that the unions were disappointed with the Government's economic policies; that an incomes policy was inevitably cobbled together, in 1975, in the midst of a crisis; and that the whole venture fell apart in the winter of 1978–9 amid recriminations. The advances of the 1940s were not merely based upon a sense of moral obligation and of moral outrage against mass unemployment and social deprivation. They also resulted from the determination of trade union and Labour Party leaders to face up to difficult problems and produce practical yet far-reaching solutions.

The present divisions within both the Labour Party and the trade union movement cast doubt upon the capacity of the present generation to emulate their predecessors of forty years ago. But the alternative is that the long-drawn-out crisis will continue, until sectional demands and strife provoke increasing forms of state control.

References

CLEGG, H. A., A. FOX and A. F. THOMPSON (1964), *A History of British Trade Unions since 1889*, vol. 1, Oxford.

FLANDERS, A. (1975), *Management and Unions*, London.

PELLING, H. (1963), *A History of British Trade Unionism*, Harmondsworth.

WEBB, S., and B. WEBB (1920), *A History of Trade Unionism*, London.

Alternative Policy Developments

From Colin Crouch, *The Politics of Industrial Relations*, Fontana, 1979, ch. 8, pp. 177–96.

The main alternatives available to Britain in the politics of industrial relations emerge from the analysis in previous chapters [not included here]. There are two separate choices, each of which opens up two alternatives: are trade unions to remain autonomous, decentralized and powerful, or not? And is the system to develop in a liberal or in a corporatist direction? The available options can be combined to give the following:[1]

Table 1

Nature of system	Position of trade unions	
	Strong	Weak
Liberal	1. Free collective bargaining	2. Neo-laisser-faire
Corporatist	4. Bargained corporatism	3. Corporatism

Both liberalism and corporatism can only work in their pure form if labour is subordinated. Under classic economic liberalism, labour is weak because unorganized; under corporatism, it is weak because its organizations are controlled from above and outside. In the table above, the two right-hand boxes constitute the pure models; both left-hand boxes involve compromises with workers' rights to form and control their own powerful organizations. Obviously, the different options have very different political and economic implications, and some of these can now be explored.

Free collective bargaining

This is the model least likely to dominate in the foreseeable future, though it was the predominant pattern of the 1950s and early 1960s.

1. Further discussion of this theme will be found in Crouch (1977), pp. 262ff.

It is the preferred model of trade unions and especially of the union left. Liberal political economy and strong trade unions being ultimately incompatible, such an option can only survive if there is some external support. A major task of Chapters 1 and 2 [not included here] was to show how in the post-war period, when free collective bargaining flourished, support was provided, first by a certain element of corporatism arising out of the war-time situation, and second (as that gave way) by growing national prosperity. Now that the particular combination of circumstances which constituted the 'age of affluence' is no longer with us, while the distinctive corporatism of the earlier years has all but vanished, the free collective bargaining option no longer appears viable. It is always possible that there will be a new advance in national prosperity; the idea of wealth bubbling up out of the sea is, after all (surprisingly), less of a pipe dream than one might in the past have supposed. But even so, this wealth would be coming into a society very different from that of the 1950s. There was then a working class whose historical experience had been two world wars and the biggest recession since the industrial revolution. Prosperity was unexpected and thus, for many people and for several years, in excess of expectations. The working class of the 1980s will be one which takes for granted continual advances in real incomes, as provided in the 1950s, 1960s and indeed much of the 1970s. While there has probably been some check to expectations in the past five years, it is most doubtful whether this would be enough to make people respond as passively as they did during the 1950s and early 1960s. It would need a really spectacular increase in national prosperity fully to absorb popular expectations for an improved standard of living.[2]

In the absence of such unlikely developments, continued free collective bargaining in conditions of trade union strength is a most uncertain prospect. A condition of union strength is a low overall level of unemployment. (There is just one possible exception to this: a small, unionized sector with low unemployment within a wider economy of weak labour and high unemployment; but this would not be a *system* of free collective bargaining, just islands of it, and anyway in Britain union strength is too evenly distributed throughout the economy for this to be a really likely development.) Now, in the

2. There is a considerable sociological literature on the importance of expectations. For a good account relating it to themes similar to those discussed here, see Hirsch and Goldthorpe (1978).

circumstances of the current British and world economies, there is no way that free collective bargaining can be maintained alongside full employment without a high rate of inflation. Even if governments are prepared to accept this for a while, international economic forces will soon impose a change of direction; inflation will lead to speculation against the currency, threatening the country's terms of trade and raising the real possibility of economic collapse. This must sooner or later lead to counter-inflationary action. The pattern of events described is not just hypothetical; it is what happened to Britain in 1976.

The government response is almost certain to be action to restrict demand, and this brings unemployment, especially if wages are rising fast. And of course a major consequence of rising unemployment is a check to trade union strength and thus to the free collective bargaining option itself. Something similar to this happened in West Germany in 1974–5.

There may well be some scope for expanding the economy at the present time; some wage increases may lead to productivity improvements and thus have no effect on prices; or wage rises by some groups may simply be at the expense of other groups, again without an overall price effect. There is therefore some room for manoeuvre in the pursuit of free collective bargaining, but all this is of limited scope. It is sometimes argued by advocates of this option that Britain could insulate itself from international economic forces though protectionist measures, such as import controls and limits on the movement of capital.[3] It may well be that policies of this kind would be in Britain's economic interest; but they would not make unrestrained free collective bargaining a viable policy – rather the reverse. It is inconceivable that a government could control nearly all variables in the economy except wages and salaries, for this could only mean high inflation.

Inflation is not necessarily the ultimate economic evil that must be avoided at all costs; a certain rate of inflation may be more acceptable to many people than the consequences of certain policies for controlling it, such as very high unemployment or the suspension of certain basic freedoms. But there is considerable debate over the conditions under which inflation can be contained at relatively low levels. Once

3. The most elaborate version of such a policy is Holland (1975). He does not face squarely the likely implications for collective bargaining, but he does include a high level of worker participation within his proposals, which, it might be argued, would in the long run amount to something similar to income restraint.

it reaches those levels experienced in Britain and elsewhere in the wake of the oil crisis of the mid 1970s, it is doubtful whether anyone is content with it – and as far as collective bargaining is concerned, all it does is erode its achievements. It is therefore naive in the extreme to pretend that a return to unrestrained collective bargaining alongside full employment is a viable option in itself. Unions may want to retain the *threat* of trying to return to it, in order to strengthen their bargaining position under some of the other options, and that is a sound enough strategy. And shop-floor workers may well advocate it on the grounds that it is only at that level that they can effect anything, while they are in no position to control the economy as a whole – an understandable position, some of the implications of which will be considered below. Finally, some groups may advocate this option not because they believe in it as such but because they believe it will hasten the collapse of the Western economic system, from which they expect a new social order to arise. To adopt such a position is to express a confidence in the human capacity to extract something good out of chaos and disarray which many will find rather unconvincing, especially in the light of twentieth-century history.

Neo-laisser-faire

There are superficial resemblances between free collective bargaining and this second option. Some Conservatives join such figures of the union left as Arthur Scargill, leader of the Yorkshire miners,[4] in calling for the government to keep out of relations between employers and workers. The difference is that while the union left assumes a government commitment to full employment, Conservatives would regulate demand so that wage increases beyond those which the market would have anyway provided lead directly to unemployment. This would be achieved by tight control of the money supply and the regulation of public spending. This is not advocacy of free collective bargaining in any commonly understood sense.

Involved is not just a policy of demand control. There would also be tax cuts and a reduction in public spending (apart from the armed forces and police, where expenditure would be increased). It could be that reductions in taxation would have some effect in limiting wage demands: in Chapter 4 the activities of the 1974 Labour government in this area were discussed and explained. This might provide something of a dilemma for the unions, given not only their long-term

4. Now President of the National Union of Mineworkers.

political commitment to public spending on the social services but also the considerable weight of public sector unions who have a clear and obvious interest in a high level of public expenditure. It is in fact unlikely that unions would be happy with such a situation, while public spending cuts would bring conflict in other areas of society over deteriorating education, health services, roads and housing conditions.

It is further claimed for the neo-laisser-faire option that tax cuts, increased social inequality and a reduction in government intervention would liberate enterprise, leading to greatly increased prosperity for all and, in the long run, the chances of true free collective bargaining combined with low unemployment, as in the first option.[5] The doubts that exist over the capacity for prosperity again to have the implications it did in the 1950s have already been expressed. More generally, the chain of reasoning that starts with tax cuts and ends with a great increase in economic growth stemming from released entrepreneurial energies involves several very large and untestable assumptions, and, in its unsubstantiated optimism, does not fall very far short of the argument that high inflation might lead, via chaos, to a new social order.

However, a major strength of this option lies in the support it enjoys from international and finance capital. A continuing problem for laisser-faire is that it has to try to put economic decisions beyond the reach of democratic politics – not beyond *all* politics, because it will be important that government takes political measures necessary to sustain the laisser-faire system, but beyond democratic pressures for full employment and social services. Several advocates of this strategy have therefore spoken of the need to roll back democracy, or to elevate some institution, such as the central bank, which cannot be 'interfered with' by politics (for example, see Brittan, 1978). To some extent finance capital and the international monetary system provide such a possibility. It emerged from the discussion in Chapter 6 that these are the only sectors of capital which have a fairly clear means of avoiding compromise and pressure from labour. Finance capital can move at will between countries, rejecting those with strong labour movements, and it does not get bogged down in the horse-trading of either collective bargaining or tripartitism which is the lot of industrial capital. Furthermore, democracy and trade unions do not operate internationally. A government dependent on international capital will therefore be subject to strong pressures to withstand

5. See the speeches of Sir Keith Joseph, especially Joseph (1978).

437

domestic labour pressure. The recent role of the IMF in the British economy provides a very clear instance of how this operates.

Neo-laisser-faire is therefore a major force to reckon with as a likely future development, but it has distincts costs and certain snags. The continued high unemployment on which it depends in the short and possibly medium term means postponing for some time any real recovery of the British industrial economy. And as recovery eventually began there would be a particular tricky moment, with unions realizing their strength was increasing and workers eager to make up for the deprivations of the years of recession at a time before the economy was in fact in a position to produce widespread new wealth. This is a highly vulnerable moment for an economy which is restraining collective bargaining through demand management alone, and it could well result in continued postponement of the recovery. Furthermore, the strongest groups in the labour market are among the least likely to be hit by unemployment. Union strength being high among skilled workers whose work is vital to the economy – for example, miners, power engineers, certain sectors of engineering – unions are likely to continue to be powerful at certain crucial points. One of three courses of action must be pursued: (i) constant concessions would have to be made to these groups (as has in fact been advocated by some Conservatives), leading to distortions in the labour market and considerable resentment elsewhere; (ii) unemployment would have to bite very deep indeed in order to affect even these groups; or (iii) there would have to be considerable coercion, using the police and the armed forces, to break strikes in these powerful sectors.

Overall, the laisser-faire option means pushing back trade union strength by means other than compromises and agreements, neutralizing various democratic pressures on economic policy and cutting back severely on public services. That laisser-faire was not a matter of economic policy alone was recognized by the Conservative Party when it last adopted a stance of this kind in the late 1960s. The machinery then advocated for buttressing economic by political control was legislation of the kind that eventually became the Industrial Relations Act, combining a degree of corporatism with straightforward legal limitation of trade union freedoms. In the light of the experience of that Act the emphasis has now shifted. Strict demand regulation would now be accompanied by some kind of corporatist understanding with the unions and/or a new emphasis on the role of the police and the army.

Both aspects of this new emphasis are paradoxical. One of the purposes of neo-laisser-faire is, according to its advocates, to stop the growth of corporatism; the possibility that it may in fact be *dependent* on corporatist strategies will be considered below. Reliance on police and army may seem paradoxical in that a party which stresses its dedication to freedom and opposition to state interference finds itself, precisely as a result of having dismantled means of government intervention, relying more on the most coercive and least democratically responsible arms of the state. The paradox is not the result of any muddled thinking among contemporary Conservatives; it lies deep in the classic liberal model of the state. Economic liberalism does not imply a weak state; it is merely opposed to detailed government interference with the rights of property owners, and if the cost of doing that is considerable interference with other kinds of liberty, then so be it. It is very important to grasp this point, and in particular not to label the exercise of just any kind of state power as corporatist.

Corporatism

There have been distinct signs of corporatist developments in Britain, as has been discussed in previous chapters. But these have had very limited success, because the base for corporatism within British society is poorly developed owing to the strength of the liberal legacy. The trade union movement is very decentralized, with strong shop-floor roots; civil liberties are deeply entrenched; industrial organizations like the CBI have few powers of coordination; the financial sector is large, powerful and external to the structure of organized interests; there is a strong sense of the autonomy of society from the state; and there has been a decline in social and moral cohesion. These characteristics of Britain emerge from any comparison between it and those countries in which corporatism of various kinds has been more prominent – such as West Germany, Japan, Sweden and the Netherlands.[6] On the other hand, in a comparison with such countries as France or Italy[7] one is struck by certain features favourable to corporatism: the long-standing unity of the nation; a certain surviving legacy of cohe-

6. See, on Britain and Japan especially, Dore (1973); and, more generally, C. J. Crouch, 'The Changing Role of the State in Industrial Relations in Western Europe', in Crouch and Pizzorno (1978).

7. See, on Britain and France in particular, Gallie (1978); and, more generally, Crouch, as in n.6.

sion from the 1940s and a much more recent acceleration in the pace of organization of economic interests. The United Kingdom is thus interestingly poised between various kinds of liberal and corporatist elements. In recent years this balance has mainly taken the form of corporatist attempts; but there have been few successes, an important stumbling block being the continuing strength of organized labour.

Corporatism and laisser-faire are opposed models of social organization, and in some respects they constitute the main political alteratives being 'offered' to Britain at the present time. However, as has already been hinted, they may now actually be complementary. An example has been Britain since 1976; a combination of monetarism with more or less cooperative trade unions offering wage restraint. This alliance can be explained in terms of the position of labour. Where there is a strong labour movement, a liberal economy cannot work because labour's power goes beyond the purely economic, so corporatist measures are introduced to regulate labour at the level of organizations. But how is this possible if labour has such a high degree of autonomous strength? By weakening that strength through high unemployment and monetarism.

This is the important fact overlooked by those advocates of neolaisser-faire who see themselves as opposed to the corporate state. A distinct pattern is emerging in the Western world, of domestic corporatism disciplined by international monetarism. The UK and West Germany are probably the most outstanding cases, but there have been notable attempts in Italy, the Netherlands and elsewhere. If Keynesianism characterized much of the post-war world, this new combination seems to characterize the political economy of the late 1970s. It may well be 'successful' in controlling inflation, but it is a rather unattractive option, combining the restrictions of both economic liberalism and corporatism without the compensating attractions of either. There is also some doubt over how long it could last, largely because of characteristics of the union movement which will now be considered further.

Bargained corporatism

As is argued in a recent study of the West German trade union movement – probably the most cooperative in Western Europe – no trade union can cooperate indefinitely with employers and government without doing something to represent its members' immediate interests, at least not in a free society (Bergmann, Jacobi and Müller-

Jentsch, 1976). In fascist and communist countries where non-cooperative unions can be liquidated and membership of cooperative ones made compulsory, the same rule might not apply, though even there unions probably have to play some role in limited grievance representation in order to stem the development of incipient rival channels. The problem is that unions will become unable to deliver their members' consent to restraint if they never offer them anything to make acceptance of coordination by the union leadership worthwhile. Legal sanctions imposing certain kinds of discipline over workers who act outside formal union channels may alleviate this difficulty to some extent; the German legal system does so at several points, the Industrial Relations Act tried unsuccessfully to do so in Britain. But this kind of compulsion, even if it can be introduced, is unlikely completely to relieve representative organizations of the need to represent. The consequence of this is a continual slippage away from corporatist arrangements to free collective bargaining on the part of union leaderships. This means that union consent to participation in corporatist relations has to be continually regained by governments through concessions – either concessions to compensate unions for the difficult time they will have at the hands of their members, or concessions that will be experienced as such by the members. This makes possible what I have elsewhere described as 'bargained corporatism':

It involves acceptance by unions of several strategies which, compared with liberal collectivism [free collective bargaining], constitute a set-back for [workers'] interests. But it also holds out the chance of advances. Unions are tempted – and frightened – by corporatist developments to sacrifice some of their entrenched but narrow and unambitious achievements in exchange for the possibility of greater political influence and more and broader power for their members in the work-place, but at the same time to accept more restraint, a more obvious role for the unions in restraining their members, more state interference and fuller acceptance of the industrial order and its priorities (Crouch and Pizzorno, 1978).

The possibility of unions undertaking this kind of bargaining in exchange for their commitments under corporatism opens up a chink of light in what is otherwise a tight, closed system. Unions accept periods of wage restraint, the relaxation of protective practices and similar measures, in the interests of improving efficiency; but on the conditions that they receive in return (i) certain other gains for their members and themselves and (ii) a share in making the economic policy of which the efficiency measures are a part. The former opens up interesting possibilities. In incomes policy the government interposes itself between the unions and their normal bargaining partner, the employer, but in so doing becomes itself their bargaining partner; and the government is able to offer several things which cannot be achieved in bargaining – and which may be less self-defeating than wage claims often are – such as social policy reforms, workers' rights, changes in economic and fiscal policy. A share in making economic policy is necessary if unions are to have any genuine confidence that the restraints and concessions which they offer are necessary and are being matched by changes elsewhere in society for the same ends of efficiency.

These possibilities raise several difficult problems. First, there is the relationship between the emerging political role of unions and employers' organizations and that of parliament. Historically, parliament has been associated with liberal political economy, which minimizes the role of organized economic interests. In his recent study, M. Moran (1977) shows effectively how Conservatives have come to believe that they are at a disadvantage in this kind of interest representation; as a result, they are both loud in their advocacy of the central role of parliament and of monetarism as the only economic policy which might (though not according to the arguments I have developed here) free the state from economic activity. (It should be noted that the 'sovereignty of parliament' refers only to its relationship to certain, that is labour, pressures; closely allied to monetarism is the idea of the central bank being autonomous and thus *not* subordinate to parliament.) As Moran points out, Conservatives have also turned their minds to an alternative to parliament which would serve the real aim, which is to reduce the political weight of unions. This is the idea of the plebiscite, or referendum, perhaps to be used during a major national strike in order to wield public opinion against the unions. The strategy is presumably based on the fairly sound grounds that, since Conservative interests have effective control over mass communications, they are more likely to succeed through a populist appeal than by trying to come to terms with organized interests.

En route, Conservatives find themselves jettisoning a very weighty old Tory doctrine about the importance of government working in harmony with the great vested interests of the society, which has curiously become a Labour Party doctrine instead.[8] On the other hand

8. For a discussion of this aspect of traditional Toryism and its relation to corporatism, see Beer (1965).

quasi-corporatist organization is very vulnerable to criticism. Unlike parliament, it is based on no universal representation comparable to 'one man, one vote', and there are real possibilities of whole sections of the community being left out of consideration. However, this does not in practice follow as automatically as might seem to be the case in theory. For example, Moran cites retirement pensioners as a group which parliament will care for but which will be left out of account in state–union bargaining. In reality pensioners in Britain, long neglected by parliament, have seen a major improvement in their relative income position since the trade unions adopted their cause when bargaining with government (largely, but not entirely, through the personal concern of Jack Jones).

The issue is not a simple one. Of course, if one believes that parliament is the effective decision-making body of our national affairs, or that it is only prevented from being so by the power of trade unions, then one can adopt a clearcut view. If, on the other hand, one sees the management of a modern economy, with its inevitably organized interests, as something which will always be beyond the control of parliament, and which will be controlled through the interchange of government bureaucracy, international monetary institutions and domestic organized interests, then one may well come to see the scope for some autonomous action by the unions within that framework as the best hope for an element of pluralism in our emerging political economy. One weakness of recent developments has been their *ad hoc* nature, and eventually there would need to be some established institutional embodiment. However, it is premature to try, as some have recently done, to follow the Webbs in drawing up blueprints for an 'industrial parliament' or similar body. For the time being it is best that governments, unions, employers and everybody else become practised in and accustomed to the substance of the process, working out its possibilities and limitations. In many areas of policy this country has recently had a surfeit of institutional innovation, of attempts at solving deep-seated problems by the creation of empty, cosmetic (and often expensive and bureaucratic) formal bodies as substitutes for real answers.

A second and probably greater problem recalls certain problems outlined in Chapter 7 [not included here]: often the issues which might be up for negotiation are of little interest to unions' shop-floor members, because ordinary workers have little opportunity to affect anything beyond their own money wage and therefore cannot be expected to perform as though they were actors on any wider stage. It is at this point that several observers have developed the case for a major increase in workers' participation. If shop stewards are to be expected to act in some wider company – or even national – interest in their activities, then they must be able to share fully in decision-making at the company level, and through their unions be closely involved in problems of national economic policy-making; and, it might be added, it will no longer be adequate for companies to be legally limited to the protection of shareholders' interests alone, with workers regarded as simply one of the commodities which the company uses. It is thinking along these lines which has generated, with different degrees of radicalism, the British Leyland and Chrysler participation experiments, the Bullock Report and wider plans for giving unions a say in the investment decisions of financial institutions (especially of their members' insurance funds). It is all very well telling workers that their actions will threaten investment and the position of the firm, but how do they know all this to be true unless their representatives are involved in the relevant decision-making? Employers resort to bluff and exaggeration frequently enough for scepticism to be justified.

It is usually employers' representatives who bemoan the idea of 'two sides of industry' and who call upon workers to cooperate in the common good. But it was not workers who instituted the rigorous distinction between those who make decisions and those who receive instructions. Or, to put it another way, how can responsibility be demanded from those to whom responsibility is not given? The changes needed to induce more cooperation in British industry will have to be at the level of power and structure before they can be expected in workers' attitudes.[9] The same might not be true in countries with a less well developed, less decentralized trade union movement. It might then be possible for deals and understandings between capital and labour to be limited, on the labour side, to the leaders of formal organizations rather than to the workers themselves. Such was the case in Britain from about 1940 until 1950, and again over the past few years. But it could have no permanency unless something were to be done to destroy finally the base of shop-floor power. The achievement of this task would involve a major interference with both democracy and liberty.

Those who reject such a course of action, but who also realize the

9. The theme of the preconditions for trust in work relations is discussed at length in Fox (1974). For an analysis of some of the implications of a powerful, decentralized labour movement, see Fox (1978).

futility of labour persisting with the pursuit of free collective bargaining as its chief end in life, must take seriously the implications of the bargained corporatism option. Superficially, it seems a convenient compromise, half-way between collective bargaining and the incorporation of unions, and in some senses it would constitute yet another compromise between the forces of order and freedom, or between capital and labour. But it is not a compromise in the same sense of being the easy way out, the line of least resistance. To be really serious about labour being in a position to bargain knowledgeably about the terms on which it would offer collaboration in the pursuit of efficiency means to contemplate radical changes, not just at the national political level, but also within industry. It means, for example, the extension of industrial democracy on lines at least as radical as the Bullock majority report. At the industrial level it means a major extension of the economic development committee system within NEDC, so that unions are technically equipped to engage in a debate about real planning with the employers, leading to the negotiated introduction of agreed changes. This may not seem too remote a possibility, but it is problematic. Such an extension of unions' activity would involve the growth of their own expert officialdom, working on technical tasks of industrial development, probably at the expense of more direct services to members. Some German unions are beginning to experience this problem. It could only be overcome if the unions were able to involve and interest shop-floor activists in such issues; this would not be easy, though it would be less difficult once a system of industrial democracy has been established.

A further problem of all these reforms would occur if Britain were to move in this direction in isolation – though whether it would in fact be doing so is another matter. Earlier chapters have drawn attention to the international constraints imposed on our political economy at the present time. The warnings sounded by the CBI as to the likely implications for overseas investment in this country if the government had gone ahead with Bullock may be taken as a reliable guide to the response which other similar moves would invoke. In the foreseeable future there is going to be some competition in attracting investment between, on the one hand, all those countries professing a degree of ordinary democracy and, on the other hand, such nations as Brazil, South Africa, South Korea and possibly eventually Iran and Saudi Arabia, which are able to offer capital an environment less threatened by civil rights and freedoms. The position of a country extending democracy further into the industrial arena would be more vulnerable still. All this indicates further implications of bargained corporatism, in terms of policy on freedom of capital movements and on the international coordination of labour-movement policies – to date, not an area boasting of impressive achievements.

As this brief review indicates, bargained corporatism taken seriously is uncomfortably uncertain and radical. But to set against these points which may seem to remove it from the area of reality is the fact that, at the more humble levels, several developments identifiable as part of bargained corporatism have begun to occur, in Britain and elsewhere. First and foremost, there has been the need to offer unions something at the national political level in exchange for restraint. The extension of workers' rights at work, and various fiscal changes of the past few years, would probably not have occurred if governments had not been engaged in this bargaining process, and they did not occur during earlier phases of incomes policy. Similarly, the discussion with union leadership of major parameters of the country's economic development by governments and the CBI has been extended considerably since the foundation of the NEDC in 1962 and especially since Edward Heath's programme of tripartite talks ten years later. At the level of individual industries or large companies there are now many cases of shop stewards being taken into some kind of confidence over investment plans, and (sometimes as part of the same process) major new experiments in industrial democracy.

How likely is it that these openings will develop into the more radical possibilities? It is my view that further developments along the lines of bargained corporatism constitute the most attractive opportunities presented to this country by the recent turmoil around industrial relations, offering chances for the extension of real democracy in the management of economic affairs which has always eluded us. But overall, as perhaps the above discussion of obstacles has suggested, I am not optimistic about the capacity of British institutions to achieve changes of this order. Some combination of monetarism and attempts at straightforward corporatism are more likely to be the order of the day; in which case occasional union bargaining triumphs for shop steward consultation over investment plans, or for reforms in some area of social policy in exchange for a limited programme of wage restraint, are likely to be the most encouraging outcomes that we can expect.

References

BEER, S. H. (1965), *Modern British Politics*, Faber & Faber.

BERGMAN, J., O. JACOBI AND W. MÜLLER-JENTSCH (1976), *Gewerkschaften in der Bundesrepublik*, vol. 1, Aspekte Verlag.

CROUCH, C. (1977), *Class Conflict and the Industrial Relations Crisis*, Heinemann.

CROUCH, C., and A. PIZZORNO, ed. (1978), *The Resurgence of Class Conflict in Western Europe since 1968*, vol. 2, Macmillan.

DORE, R. P. (1973), *British Factory – Japanese Factory*, Allen & Unwin.

FOX, A. (1974), *Beyond Contract: Work, Power and Trust Relations*, Faber & Faber.

FOX, A. (1978), *Socialism and Shop-Floor Power*, Fabian Society.

GALLIE, D. (1978), *In Search of the New Working Class*, Cambridge University Press.

HIRSCH, F., and H. GOLDTHORPE (1978), *The Political Economy of Inflation*, Martin Robertson.

HOLLAND, S. (1975), *The Socialist Challenge*, Quartet.

JOSEPH, SIR KEITH (1978), *Monetarism is Not Enough*, Conservative Centre for Policy Studies.

MORAN, M. (1977), *The Politics of Industrial Relations*, Macmillan.

33 L. J. McFarlane

The Right to Strike against the Government

From L. J. McFarlane, *The Right to Strike*, Penguin, 1981, pp. 151–65.

Economic strikes against the government

For analytical purposes it is helpful to start by looking at general strikes called for economic purposes, since we are able to discuss the issue against the most celebrated of all general strikes, the 1926 General Strike called by the TUC in support of the miners. No British Government since the Baldwin Government in 1926 has faced the threat of a general strike. The TUC rejected calls for strike action against the Trades Disputes Act 1927, and the Industrial Relations Act 1971, and its response to the imprisonment of the 'Pentonville Five' in 1972 was a call for a one-day national protest strike, which never materialized as the men were released before the date fell due. It is apparent that only the most extreme and extraordinary situation would now persuade the British trade union movement to call a coercive general strike. Since the credibility of such a serious venture turns on the prospect of securing overwhelming support, the issue can only arise where there is already a deep and widespread sense of intense grievance. Moreover, given the controversy and disquiet surrounding general strikes, British trade unions would only consider embarking on such a course with the greatest reluctance and for the sole purpose of securing the remedy of the grievance concerned. The last thing Western trade union leaders want is embroilment in a political or constitutional crisis.[1] A brief glance at the British General Strike of May 1926 is revealing in this respect. The positions taken up by the various parties on the eve of the strike turned on their attitude to the Report of the Samuel Commission set up by the Government in 1925 to inquire into the coal industry, and were roughly as follows:

---

1. This would not necessarily be true of the Communist leaders of the French and Italian trade union movements; but such movements are both weaker than, and different in many ways from, the British trade union movement.

Table 1 1926 General Strike – positions of parties to the dispute

Samuel Commission	Owners	Miners	Government
Agreement on reorganization of coal industry *then* wage cuts*	No reorganization	Reorganization of industry	Reorganization of industry
	Immediate wage cuts	No wage cuts	Immediate wage cuts
Maintenance of national wage agreements	District wage agreements	National wage agreements	National wage agreements
No increase in hours (fixed by law)	Increase in hours	No increase in hours	Increase in hours

* Miners's wages had been subsidized since August 1925 by the Government at a cost of £23 million.

The TUC accepted that some wage cuts would almost certainly be necessary and were prepared to negotiate a settlement based on the Samuel Commission Report. The cost of avoiding the General Strike, or of meeting the TUC's requirements once it had started, can be represented as follows:

Table 2 *1926 General Strike – cost of meeting TUC minimum requirements*

Cost to Government	Cost to coal-owners	Cost to miners
Payment of temporary subsidy during period of negotiations	No immediate reduction in wages. Likelihood that negotiated wage cuts would be less than the owners could impose. Retention of national wage rates	Likelihood that wages would be cut within a few months
Abandonment of proposal to increase hours of work	No increase in hours of work	
Forcing owners to accept reorganization of industry Forcing owners to withdraw lock-out notices*	Imposition of reorganization	

* The coal-owners had locked out the miners before the General Strike began.

Given the close association of the Government with the mining industry, the intransigent attitude of the coal-owners, and the suffering which would result from the imposition of the owners' lock-out terms on the already depressed miners, the decision of the TUC to intervene in the dispute was fully justified and its proposals were moderate. Indeed, it can be argued that they were too moderate, or at least too limited, and that, both in terms of social justice and of expediency (the need to secure the miners' support for TUC proposals), they should have included a demand for a continuance of the Government subsidy until such time as the reorganized industry was itself able to meet the cost of paying reasonable wages. Even with such a provision the proposals would not have placed an unreasonably heavy or impossible charge on the country's financial resources.[2]

The only question at issue is whether the TUC were justified in threatening, or in undertaking, a general strike to secure their moderate proposals. The issue was and still is a matter of contention, where judgement is made more difficult by the complexities of the developing situation and the ineptitude and confusion of the actors on all sides. At one level one may argue that the Government's failure to provide a ready response to the TUC's proposals, and its precipitate breaking off of negotiations justified the strike action taken. There was no threat to democratic or constitutional government, since those who led the strike had no intentions beyond the realization of their limited proposals for the coal industry. The implementation of these proposals would not have imposed an impossibly heavy burden on the Exchequer, nor would they have undermined the ability of the Government to realize its policy objectives, or constitute a radically new and unwarranted interference with the rights of private industry. Against this, it may be asserted that the authority of the Government was seriously challenged by the threat of strike action on a national scale, involving as it did the assertion by the unions of quasi-governmental authority during the course of the strike. Only the capitulation of the TUC had prevented this challenge from assuming

2. Mr Churchill's 1925 Budget (drawn up before any question of coal subsidy had arisen) showed a projected surplus of income over expenditure of £26 million – £24 million of which he devoted to reducing the standard rate of income tax, by 6d in the £ (costing £32 million in a full year). He was able to meet the cost of the coal subsidy without increasing taxes, or dipping into the sinking fund for the redemption of the National Debt, by using £10,000,000 of his projected surplus for 1926–7 to replace the £10,000,000 borrowed from the supply fund for subsidy purposes. (*The Annual Register*, 1925 and 1926).

the form of open confrontation. Even if the TUC's proposals were reasonable, and the Government's response open to severe criticism, that did not mean that the trade unions were entitled to bring the country to a halt in order to force the Government to adopt policies to which it was opposed.

In terms of democratic theory, as distinct from Marxist theory, the case for the 1926 General Strike is at best a doubtful one. That example shows that a sympathetic strike by the whole trade union movement will necessarily assume for the Government the form of a challenge to its authority, irrespective of the limited purposes of the strike leaders themselves. That is not to say that a general strike is in principle unjustified (still less that it should be legally proscribed as in the Trades Disputes Act 1927), but only that, given the necessarily political nature of the challenge it would require a direct political threat to democratic practices or to the rights of trade unions to exist and operate to be justifiable. The strict requirements of the latter can be gauged from the fact that the trade unions themselves did not regard the restrictions imposed on their activities by either the Trade Disputes Act 1927 or the Industrial Relations Act 1971 as grounds for general coercive industrial action.

The great difference between an economic general strike and an ordinary economic strike directed against the government is that the latter is not in itself a direct challenge to the government's authority to run the country or a possible threat to the constitution. On the other hand strikes of this character, unlike general strikes, are a quite familiar feature of the modern industrial scene. Before discussing specific problems it is necessary to touch on the situation created by the emergence of the government as both the largest single employer of labour directly on the one hand and the indirect controller and financier of much of the public sector of employment on the other. In general it is accepted and acceptable that labour relations in the public sector should be treated on the same basis as those in private industry with regard to the exercise of the right to strike. However, the fact that the money to meet the cost of strike-backed union demands has to come directly from public funds (i.e. in large part from the taxes levied on other workers) does mean that there is a moral obligation on the part of public service unions not to use the threat of sanctions to secure a privileged position for themselves at the expense of other groups of workers. It also means that a particularly strong case can be made that public sector unions should submit their claims to arbitration in the event of inability to reach agreement.

Strike action against public authorities needs specific justification in terms of substantiated grievance, especially in periods when the government is seeking to give effect to a policy of voluntary wage restraint. It might, for example, be justified if that policy had a built-in discrimination against public sector workers, or if the authorities had deliberately held back, or drawn out, negotiations to ensure that major claims were caught in the wage-restraint or wage-freeze net – situations which public sector unions have experienced in the past.

In discussing the justification for economic strike action directed against the government, it is important again to stress the distinction between protest strikes designed to draw the government's attention to the strength of feeling that exists, and coercive strikes designed to force the government's hand. To be coercive a strike must be more than a mere inconvenience that can be put up with even for a long period. It must impose a substantial burden or cost which the government will feel under an urgent obligation to remove as soon as possible. It is clear, therefore, that unions vary greatly in their ability to mount a coercive strike against the government, as well as in their readiness to do so. Unions are unlikely to challenge the government unless (a) they have failed to achieve their objectives through negotiation and (b) they believe they are in a strong position to secure their demands or extract major concessions. No union will lightly 'take on' the government and any union doing so will feel required to justify its challenge. The government thus invariably finds itself faced not with a precipitate strike, but with the *threat* of strike action in support of clearly defined demands. The threat itself will assume different forms according to the ability of the specific groups of union members concerned to take strike action that would seriously disrupt (a) the working of the machinery of government, (b) the lives of wide or vulnerable sections of the public, and (c) the working or condition of the economy as a whole.

The government's attitude to such threats will turn on four factors:

(1) Its assessment of the seriousness of the threat in terms of:
   (a) the ability of the union to mount and sustain a major stoppage;
   (b) the ability of the government to take counter measures to reduce the disturbance to manageable proportions.

(2) The financial and political cost, both immediate and consequential, of meeting the union's minimum demands or providing minimum concessions necessary for a negotiated settlement.

(3) The extent to which the government is committed *in principle* to:
    (*a*) its existing policies and position;
    (*b*) *not* giving in to threats of strike action.

(4) The possibility of 'heading off' or delaying strike action by offering to submit the dispute to some independent investigating body.

It is apparent that the chances of union success will be strongest when the 'cost' of making concessions, as seen by the government, is appreciably less than the 'cost' of facing a protracted strike on an issue to which it is not strongly opposed in principle. Thus there was a much greater chance in 1919 of the miners extracting at strike-point the promise of legislation to reduce the hours of working, than of securing their demand for the nationalization of the mines. No government could have secured nationalization legislation from a Conservative-dominated House of Commons. Indeed many would go further and question whether, in the early wake of a general election which had overwhelmingly returned candidates of parties opposed to nationalization, the Miners' Federation was justified in threatening coercive strike action to secure what was an essentially political demand. If a case is to be mounted in terms which do not challenge the authority of the government to govern, it would have to be on the basis that successive governments had increasingly found it necessary to regulate conditions in the coal industry and that what was then at stake was the return of this strike-torn industry from government to private control – a reversion which threatened the interests and livelihood of over a million miners.

From the above discussion one might perhaps draw the general conclusion that a trade union is entitled to threaten coercive economic industrial action against the government only if:

(1) It is acting in pursuance of an ordinary trade union objective (which of course would include strikes against government action which threatened members' jobs).

(2) The granting of the union's demands would not be incompatible with the maintenance of the government's political authority and credibility, unless the government can reasonably be held directly responsible for the crisis the union faces.

(3) The dispute will be conducted in such a fashion as not to cause deep and serious harm to vulnerable sections of the population.

The case for union action will be further strengthened if:

(4) The union states its willingness to withdraw its strike threat in return for an independent inquiry, whose findings the government pledges itself to accept.

(5) If any claim to be a special case deserving to be treated as an exception (e.g. in relation to wages policy), has the support of other unions who might otherwise make the same kind of claim on their own behalf.

Political strikes against the government

Coercive strikes in support of strictly political demands can only be assessed in the context of the political system and political situation in which they occur, and the purpose for which they are called. If one is dealing with a highly repressive or autocratic regime it is not difficult, in terms of democratic theory, to justify the use of the strike weapon to secure the overthrow of the government or major changes in the constitution. It was the widespread strikes in Russia in October 1905 which led the frightened Czar to issue his manifesto promising a constitution, civil liberties and universal suffrage. Conversely, democratic theory would condemn strikes, or the threat of strikes, designed to prevent the granting of basic political or human rights to underprivileged or deprived sections of the population, e.g. the threat of strike action by white trade unions in South Africa against the government's proposals to lift restrictions on blacks working in many fields of employment. The issue is rather different if one is dealing with a strike, not against an authoritarian or inherently repressive regime, but against a constitutional State which refuses to grant basic rights to all its working-class citizens. Thus the Belgian trade unions called general strikes in 1893, 1902 and 1913 in support of the demand for universal manhood suffrage. The use of the strike weapon to secure the right to vote seems fully justified where, as in Belgium in 1893, the authorities stubbornly refuse to grant universal suffrage and fail to agree on any measures to reform and extend the very narrow franchise then existing. The decision to call the Belgian General Strike of 1893 was also justified by events, since within five days the Assembly agreed to a scheme which increased the number of voters tenfold. The strike of 1902, on the other hand, was ill-timed and failed, while that of 1913 was probably unnecessary (Kossman, 1978, ch. 6, 1, and ch. 8, 3).

If one turns to the modern democratic State based on universal suffrage, the only valid grounds in democratic theory for coercive political strike action that could be made would be that such action was essential to preserve the democratic State itself against (*a*) internal subversion, (*b*) government subversion of democracy, or (*c*) the catastrophic effects of a morally indefensible government policy. Whether any case can be made will, of course, depend on the particulars. The following examples may serve to illustrate the kind of considerations involved.

(1) *Saving the democratic State from internal subversion*. In 1920 a successful monarchist–military *Putsch*, lead by Dr Kapp against the new democratic Weimar Republic, was defeated by the combination of the refusal of collaboration by higher civil servants and a highly successful general strike called by the Social Democratic Party.

(2) *Saving democracy from government subversion*. Following the Nazi victory at the polls in 1933, and the attacks on democratic rights which followed on the burning of the Reichstag, a government decree was issued providing severe penalties against anyone seeking to provoke a general strike. It is just conceivable that a strike then called jointly by the Social Democrats and Communists might have forced the Nazis from office.

(3) *Saving the community from the catastrophic effects of a morally indefensible government policy*. In August 1920 the Labour Party and the TUC set up a National Council of Action pledged to call a general strike if the Government sent troops or munitions to aid the Poles in the war against Soviet Russia which the Poles had initiated.

The third example is the one most open to dispute, but as I have argued elsewhere, given the past record of military intervention against Soviet Russia, the British Labour Movement had strong grounds for believing that the Government would only be deterred from embarking on further intervention to secure the overthrow of the Bolshevik regime by the threat of industrial action (see McFarlane, 1967). The validity of taking strike action in this case turns on whether, and if so in what terms, one can establish that one's own government is preparing to embark on an unjust war which ought to be resisted.[3] Even if such a case can be established, the question

3. This is the subject of Michael Walzer's thoughtful book, *Just and Unjust Wars: A Moral Argument with Historical Illustrations*, Allen Lane, 1978.

still remains as to whether there is sufficient support amongst union members to justify issuing a strike call. While both the British attack on Egypt over Suez and the United States war in Vietnam are strong candidates for moral condemnation, in neither case was industrial action contemplated because union members were very far from united in strongly opposing these military adventures. Similarly, while adequate grounds might be adduced for saying that strike action against McCarthyism would have been justified in the early fifties to protect the democratic rights of American citizens, there was a marked absence of condemnation, indeed a marked degree of support for McCarthyism among trade unionists in the United States. There seems no reason, therefore, to expect an excess of commitment to the protection of democratic principles by trade unions through strike action – possibly the reverse.

It is striking that the close association of the trade unions with the Labour Party in Britain has never resulted in any attempt to harness union industrial action to further Labour's political demands or policies. This reflects the constitutional character of both the Labour Party and the trade unions, made possible by the development of the parliamentary democratic system. But, while the Labour Party has consistently adhered to constitutional principles (subject to an implicit recognition that in an extreme emergency coercive political action might be necessary to protect the democratic system itself), there are indications that individual trade unions, or groups of unions, are increasingly prepared to consider undertaking industrial action to force through changes in government policy in their own immediate area of concern. This may take the form either of seeking to impose a policy on the government, or more commonly of seeking to prevent the government giving effect to its declared policies.

A striking illustration is to be found in the dispute over private pay beds in National Health Service hospitals, which had been agreed to by the Labour Government when the Service was set up in 1946. In its election manifesto of October 1974 the Labour Party announced that it 'has started its attack on queue-jumping by increasing the charges for private pay-beds in NHS hospitals and is now working out a scheme for phasing private beds out of these hospitals' (Craig, 1975, p. 460). In March 1975 the Conference of the Confederation of Health Service Employees (COHSE) threatened the Labour Government with industrial action in the hospitals unless a clear timetable for phasing out pay-beds was drawn up by early May. The Government quickly responded by putting up private bed charges by nearly fifty per cent and by announcing that 400 pay-beds would be axed by July. It followed this up in August with proposals to abolish all 4,000 remaining private pay-beds in NHS hospitals, but providing for new licensing laws for private nursing-homes which would permit a comparable increase in the number of acute-case beds in the private sector to offset those to be lost in the NHS hospitals. The National and Local Government Officers Union in September announced its opposition to all private practice and advised its branches how to thwart planning applications for the building of private hospitals. For their part hospital consultants in various hospitals up and down the country decided to treat only emergency cases in order to put pressure on the Government to amend its proposals. In October the Conservative spokesman in the Commons urged doctors to stop this disruptive action, while promising that the Conservatives would restore private beds when returned to office. In January 1976 the British Medical Association balloted hospital consultants on a compromise plan which provided for the early elimination of 1,000 beds; but for the creation of a board representing doctors and other health service staff to supervise the phasing out of the remaining 3,000 beds, without time limit, and in step with the reasonable availability of alternative facilities for private hospital practice. This proposal was accepted by the consultants.[4] The Government's compromise proposals, with some minor amendments made by the Lords, became law in October 1976, and steps were gradually taken to implement them. In May 1979, however, the Conservatives won the general election on a programme which included a promise 'to allow pay beds to be provided [in NHS hospitals], where there is a demand for them and end Labour's vendetta against the private health sector and restore tax relief on employer/employee medical insurance schemes'.[5] Within a few weeks COHSE was threatening industrial action and the annual conference of the National Union of Public Employees (NUPE), in face of executive opposition, passed a resolution instructing 'all NUPE members to provide no further services to private patients' if the Government had not set a firm date for the removal of all remaining private beds by 1 January 1980.[6]

The issue of private pay-beds in NHS hospitals is without question a major political issue on which the two main parties sharply differ.

4. *The Annual Register*, 1975 and 1976.
5. *Conservative Party Election Manifesto*, May 1979 General Election.
6. The *Guardian*, 21 May 1979.

It is also an issue on which there is a sharp division of opinion on the principle of private medicine between the unions representing hospital workers and the professional bodies representing hospital doctors: but with this difference that, whereas the latter have a direct financial interest in maintaining private pay-beds, the former has no direct interest in getting them removed. I have already argued that members of the medical profession are *never* entitled to engage in industrial action. In this case the action of the consultants was especially open to objection since it was taken by highly-paid persons, in the claimed interests of patients and the principles of the medical profession, when in practice the action served to further their own self-interest and sought to frustrate the Government's political programme for the hospital service. While the unwarranted action of the consultants does not constitute a moral justification for union counter-attacks against pay-beds (moreover the initial COHSE threats preceded the consultants' action), it will be readily apparent that once doctors cross the crucial line of sacrificing their patients' interests to what lowly-paid union members see as a sordid combination of self-interest and political prejudice, it becomes virtually impossible to persuade such members to themselves refrain from threatening action in support of the opposite political policy on pay-beds, based on egalitarian principles.

The unpalatable truth that needs to be asserted is that coercive industrial action against the government in furtherance of directly political objectives is a danger to the democratic political system. It is dangerous precisely because it constitutes a direct challenge to the right of an elected government to give effect to its policies, even where there is no question of such policies involving interference with basic union rights or interests, the fundamental rights of citizens or the maintenance of the democratic system itself. This was clearly brought out in the Protestant 1974 Ulster Workers' Council strike. That strike had as its aim the break-up of the 'power-sharing' Executive of Protestants and Catholics, set up after the June 1973 Ulster Assembly Elections, and the forcing of new elections. Such elections, it was confidently expected, would return a majority of Protestants pledged to end power-sharing and the Sunningdale Agreement which had provided for a Council of Ireland, representing the Ulster, Eirean and British governments, to deal with a limited range of issues of common concern. A combination of good organization, extensive intimidation and a weak response from the British authorities ensured success for the strike and the collapse of the hopeful experiment of power-sharing.[7] As far as the present Conservative Government is concerned there was the possible danger that the NUPE example might be followed by other unions – the teachers might threaten strikes unless the commitments to abolish compulsory comprehensive education were withdrawn, and the local government officers unless the proposals for facilitating council house sales were dropped. If such a situation had arisen, or arises in the future, then the issue of severely curbing the right to strike would come to the forefront of the political scene, with the strong possibility of dire consequences for both the unions and the British political system. Only those suffering from romantic illusions or revolutionary pretensions have any cause for viewing such a prospect with equanimity or hope.

7. It must be admitted, however, that the Ulster Workers' Council had substantial grounds for their assertion that the Protestant majority, led by Faulkner, no longer represented Protestant opinion. In the February 1974 General Election in Britain the Faulknerites failed to win a single Ulster seat. The Protestant militants, led by William Craig and the Rev. Ian Paisley, swept the board except in Belfast West which was won by Gerry Fitt, leader of the predominantly Catholic Social Democratic and Labour Party.

References

CRAIG, F. W. S (1975), *British General Election Manifestos 1900–1974*, Macmillan.
KOSSMAN, E. H. (1978), *The Low Countries 1780–1940*, Oxford.
MCFARLANE, L. J. (1967), 'Hands off Russia – British Labour and the Russo-Polish War, 1920', *Past and Present*, December.
WALZNER, M. (1978), *Just and Unjust Wars: A Moral Argument with Historical Illustrations*, Allen Lane.

Do Trade Unions Need Immunity for Their Funds for Actions in Tort?[1]

From the Dept of Employment Green Paper on Trade Union Immunities, HMSO, 1981, pp. 27–37.

Chapter 2 described how, since the Trade Disputes Act 1906, trade unions as such have had a more comprehensive immunity than that conferred upon their officials and other persons acting in contemplation or furtherance of a trade dispute. This immunity is contained in Section 14 of the Trade Union and Labour Relations Act 1974. It was unaffected by the changes to the law on immunities made by the Employment Act 1980.

Section 14 gives immunity to trade unions from actions in tort (with certain minor exceptions[2]) for *all* acts, whether or not they are done in contemplation or furtherance of a trade dispute. It thereby prevents trade unions, as opposed to individuals, from being sued in tort for an injunction or damages either for their own acts or, more important, for acts done on their behalf by their officials or members.

The immunity therefore differs in two important respects from that conferred on individuals by Section 13 of the Trade Union and Labour Relations Acts 1974 and 1976:

(i) first, it applies to *all* torts (e.g. nuisance or negligence) and not simply to those involving interference with contracts specified in Section 13; and

(ii) secondly, it is not limited by the formula 'in contemplation or

1. It should be noted that subsequent to the proposals in the Green Paper the 1982 Employment Act has repealed Section 14 of the 1974 Act and made unions liable in tort. See Reading 37 for a review of the present position. – Ed.
2. Under Section 14(2), a trade union is liable to be sued in tort for negligence, nuisance or breach of duty resulting in personal injury or for breach of duty relating to the ownership, occupation, possession, control or use of any property, where the act is not done in contemplation or furtherance of a trade dispute.

furtherance of a trade dispute' and so extends to torts committed by trade unions outside trade disputes.

In this way the law gives to British trade unions a status for which there is no parallel in other countries.

If Section 14 were removed altogether, trade unions would still be protected by Section 13 and would, therefore, have the same immunity as a person for acts done in contemplation or furtherance of a trade dispute.[3] Without the sort of immunity conferred by Section 13 it would be impossible for trade unions to operate without a constant and potentially destructive threat to their existence from actions for damages such as there was between 1901 and 1906. But how far is the wider immunity for trade unions provided by Section 14 necessary to enable trade unions effectively to represent the interests of their members?

How wide should the immunity for trade union funds be?

The legislators of 1906 believed that the House of Lords' judgement in the Taff Vale case of 1901 had threatened the very existence of the trade union movement by putting trade union funds at risk as a result of almost any industrial action undertaken by their officials or members. They decided that so unacceptable a threat could only be avoided by conferring on trade unions an immunity from virtually all actions in tort.

Looking at the extent of this immunity in 1968, the Donovan Commission recommended that it should be limited to 'torts' committed in contemplation or furtherance of a trade dispute'. It commented:

Whatever may happen in a trade dispute, it is not the case that trade unions frequently commit torts when no trade dispute is involved, or that they need to do so. Their officials remain liable at all times to be sued for any torts they commit: and when these are committed while acting in the course of their employment as trade union officials the union sometimes pays any damages which may be awarded out of its own funds. To that extent the immunity conferred by Section 4(1) [of the 1906 Act: now S.14(1) of the 1974 Act] is waived ... [paragraph 908]. In all the circumstances we think it would be right and proper to confine the immunity of trade unions so that it applies as regards

3. This is because Section 13 confers immunity on 'any person' which, in legal terms, covers an unincorporated body of persons such as a trade union as well as an individual: but to ensure that trade unions were subject to Section 13, it might be necessary to have a declaratory provision to this effect.

461

torts committed *in contemplation or furtherance of a trade dispute* but not as regards any other tort ... [paragraph 909] [our italics].

However, the reasons adduced by the Commission for amending the immunity in this way make it clear that they regarded the practical effect of such a change as very limited. Since trade unions have not sought to avoid liability for torts committed outside a trade dispute, the withdrawal of the immunity from such torts would be little more than a recognition of existing practice.

In recent years interest has focused on the more radical suggestion of bringing the Section 14 immunity for trade unions fully into line with the Section 13 immunity for individuals. This would mean that a trade union itself could be sued for an injunction or damages and its funds would be at risk if the officials, or even members, of that trade union committed torts – for example organizing secondary action beyond the limits laid down in Section 17 of the Employment Act 1980 – for which there is no immunity under Section 13.

Four main arguments have been advanced for such a narrowing of the Section 14 immunity: first, that it is right in principle that trade unions should be held financially responsible for the unlawful acts of their officials; secondly, that if trade unions were made financially responsible in this way they could be expected in their own interest to exert greater internal discipline over their officials and members, particularly in respect of unofficial action; thirdly, that it would enable employers to gain proper redress from trade unions for damage done to them by unlawful industrial action, whereas at present they can only sue individuals who are not usually in a position to pay substantial damages; and finally, that it would remove the risk of individual trade unionists adopting the role of 'martyrs' if they were sued for acting unlawfully in the course of an industrial dispute.

A number of arguments are advanced against such a narrowing of the Section 14 immunity: first, that because so much industrial action is unofficial it would often be uncertain whether trade unions could in fact be held to be legally responsible for the unlawful acts of their officials and members; secondly, that because of this uncertainty, bringing the Section 13 and Section 14 immunities into line would not itself be a significant deterrent to unlawful industrial action and that, for the same reason, it would not significantly reduce the risk of 'martyrdom'; thirdly, that employers are in any case more concerned to get unlawful industrial action stopped quickly than to claim compensation for the damage it causes; and, finally, that because of the way British trade unions are organized and disputes arise, the effect of putting union funds at risk, far from making unions more disciplined organizations, would be to encourage internal dissension, to weaken their internal authority and therefore to threaten an increase in unofficial action.

The argument of principle has always been closely bound up with arguments of practical effect. As described in paragraphs 47–53 there was considerable controversy between 1901 and 1906 over the extent of the immunity trade unions needed and should be allowed. The immunity ultimately conferred by Section 4 of the 1906 Act was wider than that recommended by the Royal Commission which had been appointed to consider the whole subject following the Taff Vale case. It can be argued that it was unnecessary and anomalous from the outset for trade unions to have a wider immunity than their officials and that it has become more evidently anomalous as the bargaining power of trade unions has increased. Against this it is argued that the immunity for trade unions, now contained in Section 14 of the 1974 Act, has acquired immense symbolic and psychological significance for the trade union movement, so that the practical consequences of any change which put union funds at risk need to be weighed very carefully.

If the Section 13 and Section 14 immunities were brought into line, how likely is it that unions would be held liable for the unlawful actions of their officials or members? Would the trade unions do more to discipline their officials and members who took unlawful action if such action put union funds at risk? Would employers make use of the ability to seek compensation for the damage caused by unlawful action? These are the issues which are considered in the following paragraphs.

Vicarious liability[4]

It is not always easy to determine when any organization is to be held legally responsible for action done on its behalf and it is particularly difficult to determine this in the case of unincorporated bodies such as trade unions. In general terms the law holds a person (which in this case includes a trade union) liable, not only for torts committed by

4. Vicarious liability means that one person takes the place of another so far as liability is concerned.

himself, but – subject to certain conditions – for torts committed by persons acting or purporting to act on his behalf. Where the relationship of master and servant exists, as in the case of a union and its employees, the master is liable for the torts of the servant if – but only if – they are committed in the course of the servant's employment in the context of industrial action. In recent years, trade unions have been penalized as a result of this relationship only when they refused to register under the Industrial Relations Act 1971, thereby rendering themselves and their officials' liable for an unfair industrial practice if, for example, in contemplation or furtherance of an industrial dispute, they induced or threatened a breach of contract. It was left to the courts to decide, using the common law concept of vicarious liability, when unions which had refused to register under the Act were responsible for acts done by their officials. The cases in which this issue was involved raised many questions and by the time the 1971 Act was repealed there was considerable uncertainty about when a trade union might or might not be held responsible for the actions of its officials.

The first case to reach the House of Lords was *Heatons Transport* v. *TGWU*, involving blacking at the Liverpool and Hull docks. In this case the House of Lords, unanimously overruling a unanimous Court of Appeal, established the vicarious liability of a union which was unregistered under the 1971 Act for 'unfair industrial practices' committed by shop stewards acting within scope of a 'general implied authority' to take industrial action at their workplace in furtherance of union policy which included the 'blacking' of haulier firms. The authority of an official of a trade union, including a shop steward, to bind the union was found to depend on two sources: the written rule-book of the union and the custom and practice of the union. The House of Lords held that:

If the authority to take a particular type of action is not excluded by the rules, and if such authority is reasonably to be implied from custom and practice, such authority will continue to exist until unequivocally withdrawn.

(The TGWU subsequently issued shop stewards with credentials which limited their authority in relation to organizing industrial action). Moreover, in the same case the House of Lords ruled that it was not enough for a union to draw attention to a court order restraining the industrial action or to advise their members to desist.

They should take some positive steps to stop the action, if necessary, withdrawing a shop steward's credentials to act on the union's behalf.

The case of Heatons involved issues, such as 'implied authority' and 'custom and practice', which were inherently imprecise. In another case which reached the House of Lords, *General Aviation Services (UK) Ltd* v. *TGWU*, a majority of the House of Lords found that the circumstances of the Heatons case – particularly the local situation at the Liverpool and Hull docks and the evidence of a union policy on containerization – were not repeated and that shop stewards at Heathrow airport were not acting with the authority of the defendant union.

No cases involving trade union liability for unlawful action by individual *members*, rather than officials, arose under the 1971 Act but of course such action – perhaps organized by self-appointed leaders – is far from unknown. Such cases would be likely to pose less difficulty for the courts: it seems improbable that they would hold a trade union responsible for action which was so clearly unauthorized.

The experience of the 1971 Act suggests that it would be unsatisfactory to remove the Section 14 immunity without attempting to deal specifically with the issue of vicarious responsibility. It would leave the courts a wide discretion if, as in 1971, only general principles were stated. For example, a requirement that trade unions should use their 'best endeavours' to bring unlawful action by their officials and members to an end or to take 'all reasonable steps' (the current Australian model) would still leave the courts with the difficulty of determining what constituted 'best endeavours' or 'reasonable steps' in each case. It may be that a more particular definition would be required for a tolerable degree of accuracy to be achieved. But the problem is more than a matter of devising a satisfactory definition of vicarious liability. A definition which in its application compelled a trade union to expel members who had acted unlawfully in order to satisfy the courts that it had used its 'best endeavours' to bring that unlawful action to an end could have very serious consequences for trade union authority and collective bargaining arrangements. The effect, it can be argued, might well be to strengthen the power of unofficial, shop-floor leaders and to cause the fragmentation of existing unions and the formation of small splinter unions. Equally, to make unions automatically responsible for all unlawful acts carried out by their members, whether or not they have authorized or ratified them, would stretch the concept of vicarious liability well beyond any application it has ever had under common law and might be seen to deprive it of its moral validity. As Lord Scarman said in the case of *General Aviation Services (UK) Ltd* v. *TGWU*:

Justice would appear to demand that to establish liability against the union . . . there should be some evidence that some person or committee claiming to represent the union had authorised or ratified the action complained of.

Furthermore, the experience of the 1971 Act suggests that it would be no easy task to define in legislation such concepts as delegated authority within a trade union. Section 167(9) of the Act, for example, said:

Any reference in this Act to a person taking any action within the scope of his authority on behalf of an organization shall be construed as a reference to his taking that action in his capacity as an official or agent of the organization in circumstances where he is authorized, by or under the rules of the organization or by virtue of an office in the organization which he holds or otherwise, to take that action on its behalf.

Commenting on this Section in his judgement in the Heatons case, Lord Wilberforce said that it showed the wide range of matters which must be taken into account in determining the scope of authority conferred by a union on its officials:

The authority may be conferred (1) by the rules expressly or by implication, (2) under the rules, presumably by express or implied delegation, (3) by virtue of the office held – in this case the office of shop steward, (4) 'or otherwise', which must include custom and practice, the course of dealing and the series of events which have happened in the particular case.

Three conclusions may be drawn from this analysis:

(i) to establish effective trade union liability for the unlawful actions of officials and members would require detailed legislative definition of the vicarious responsibility of trade unions or it would mean leaving a wide discretion to the courts;[5]

(ii) given the variety and, sometimes, the lack of clarity of union rule-books, the very different structures unions have adopted and the historical overlay of custom and practice in relation to delegated authority, any definition would be likely still to leave

5. Section 15 of the 1982 Act in fact adopts the first alternative: a detailed statutory definition of who is to count as a 'responsible' person. – Ed.

the courts with considerable problems of interpretation in individual cases; and

(iii) given this uncertainty, it is unlikely that the courts would hold that trade unions were responsible in some – perhaps many – cases of unlawful, unofficial industrial action.

Possible effects on trade unions

The next question to be considered is to what extent a narrowing of the present immunity for trade union funds would encourage changes in trade union structure and behaviour which might reduce the impact of these difficulties.

As has been seen above, the only recent experience in this country of the effects of withdrawing the immunity for trade union funds was in the period 1972 to 1974 when the 1971 Act was in operation. That was of course too short a time to gauge the long-term effectiveness of such a change in terms of modifying attitudes and behaviour. Two points, however, became clear. The first, as already noted, was the uncertainty about when unions would or would not be held responsible in law for the actions of their officials or of their members. The second was the deep significance for trade unions of the immunity – first established by the Trade Disputes Act 1906, following the Taff Vale case – which safeguards them from potentially destructive claims for damages arising from the calling of strikes and other forms of industrial action. Any judgement of the likely industrial relations consequences of removing the immunity of union funds must take account of both these factors.

More than 90 per cent of strikes are unofficial. This has been a constant feature of British industrial relations since the 1950s. The desire to see trade unions exert much greater authority and discipline over their officials and members who organize and take part in unofficial action lies at the root of many of the arguments for removing immunity from union funds. If trade union funds were at risk of payments for damages because of unlawful actions by their officials and members at shop-floor level, trade unions would, it is argued, take more effective steps to restrain such action than they have hitherto. They would be more ready to exercise authority and to discipline those involved, if necessary by expelling them from the union. Such a change in the law would, it is suggested, induce unions to reform their structures and rule-books and to turn themselves into more authoritarian organizations, reversing the trend towards the increasing authority of the shop steward and power of the working group at the expense of the authority of branch and national officials.

The changes in the nature of trade union internal authority which have accompanied the growth of unofficial action were noted in Chapter 1. They are not the result of changes in the law but reflect developments in the structure of industry and employment, in the increased bargaining power of employees themselves and in social attitudes and expectations generally. There is no evidence that the direction of those developments has changed significantly in recent years. It is a matter of judgement how far, in the absence of much wider changes in industry and society, an alteration in the law alone could reverse the tendency for industrial power to be concentrated in the hands of employees and their local leaders and deployed at shop-floor level.

Furthermore, some of the factors already noted might reduce the impact of a change in the law on trade unions. To the extent that it was necessary as a matter of justice for the law to continue to treat unofficial action as beyond the responsibility of trade unions, the existing pressures which lead unions to seek to control those taking such action could be reduced. To the extent that it was uncertain when the courts would and would not hold unions responsible for unlawful, unofficial action,[6] trade unions might be inclined to avoid making any internal changes and to resist the application of the law, as they did between 1972 and 1974. The deep-rooted sensitivity of trade unions to any interference with their internal arrangements would tend to reinforce this inclination. Much would also depend on the view the trade unions took of the prospects of an early reinstatement of the previous immunity.

Opponents of change in the immunity for trade union funds argue that it is fallacious to assume that the trade unions could or would turn themselves into more authoritarian structures under the threat of having to pay out large sums in damages. In their view, the shift in the balance of power within trade unions to the shop floor has gone too far to be reversed by a change in the law. It is said that some of those who organize unofficial action at plant or shop-floor level have

6. Trade unions would, of course, still have immunity in cases of unofficial action which was lawful under Section 13.

come to have little or no regard for their union leaders at national level and would be unmoved by any threat to the central funds of their unions, not least because, while a strike is unofficial, a union's financial support is withheld. Thus the more likely effect of putting union funds at risk would be a further weakening of the authority of national leaders and even the breakdown or splintering of some unions under the threat, or as a result, of large-scale expulsions. Far from reducing the incidence of unofficial action, they argue, the ultimate result might be to increase it. The existing system of industrial relations, whatever its many damaging imperfections, could be imperilled.

On the other hand, proponents of change point out that trade unions can, and in certain circumstances already do, exercise control over their members. They therefore argue that if the funds of trade unions were at risk they would find ways of safeguarding them by exerting greater control over their members. Britain is unique in the nature and extent of the immunity the law confers on trade unions as such and trade unions in other countries operate effectively within a framework of law under which they can be sued if their officials or members act unlawfully or in breach of a legally enforceable collective agreement. If trade unions were prepared to adjust their internal organization so that they exercised greater control over their members, the problems of deciding when a union was vicariously responsible for the acts of its members would be considerably reduced.

Nature and extent of damages

Another advantage claimed for the removal of the Section 14 immunity is that it would enable employers to sue trade unions for damages incurred as a result of unlawful industrial action. At present, it is argued, an employer has no prospect of gaining financial redress because he can only sue the individual organizers of unlawful action. This raises two issues:

(i) the amount of damages which might be available to an employer;

(ii) the extent to which employers would wish to sue for damages.

Experience of cases which arose under the 1971 Act shows that, even in the smallest disputes, claims for damages can be very large. General Aviation Services Ltd, for example, in a localized dispute with the TGWU claimed damages of £2 million against the union.

It would, of course, be possible to fix by legislation a limit on the amount of damages which could be awarded in a particular case: for example, by putting a ceiling on the damages which could be claimed by an individual employer or alternatively by all the employers involved in a particular dispute. Such a limit could be related to the size of a union's membership although this would necessarily be very arbitrary in effect. The experience of the 1971 Act (and, indeed, of the Taff Vale case) suggests that, without a limit of some kind, a union could be bankrupted by a relatively minor instance of unlawful industrial action. On the other hand, any arbitrary limit on the amount of damages might prevent an employer from gaining full compensation for the loss he had suffered as a result of unlawful action and would thus run counter to one of the purposes of narrowing the immunity.[7]

Narrowing the Section 14 immunity for trade union funds would have little or no impact unless employers were prepared to sue trade unions for damages in cases of unlawful industrial action. Those who are opposed to a change in the Section 14 immunity argue that an employer's primary concern is to get industrial action stopped quickly and that an injunction to restrain the organizer of the unlawful action provides an effective means of achieving this. An action for damages against the union, which would often be heard long after the dispute was over, would once more sour industrial relations and might threaten continuing or renewed disruption.[8]

Between 1972 and 1974 only one out of the thirty-three applications by employers for relief from industrial action reached a full hearing of a complaint for damages. In that case the AUEW was ordered to pay £47,000 compensation to the Con-Mech engineering company for losses resulting from the union's unfair industrial practices. The union refused to pay and the court ordered the sequestration of all its assets. When the AUEW then threatened to call a strike throughout the engineering industry, anonymous donors offered to discharge the union's liabilities. The court, while making clear that this did not involve any surrender of its authority, accepted the offer and the sequestrated funds were returned to the union. Employers' behaviour

7. Section 16 of the 1982 Act contains specified damages 'limits' which are related to size of membership. – Ed.

8. Even when the question of liability to pay damages has been decided in the courts, the assessment of the amount could take considerably longer. In the Taff Vale case damages were assessed a year after judgement was given in the House of Lords.

today might not be the same as in the early 1970s. Nevertheless, the experience of the operation of the 1971 Act must raise doubts about the extent to which employers might exercise a right to claim damages from unions.

The 'martyrdom' of individual union officials

In the event of unlawful industrial action – or the threat of it – the employer whose business has been, or may be, damaged is already able to bring civil proceedings against the union official (or unofficial leader) who is organizing the action. The employer normally applies for an injunction requiring the official to call off the action. If the official refuses to obey an injunction he is liable for contempt and may be fined and ultimately, if the contempt continues, imprisoned. This procedure carries the risk that individuals may be moved to seek martyrdom by deliberately ignoring an injunction, with the risk that new and emotive grounds might then be provided to widen and prolong the dispute. It is sometimes argued that this risk could be reduced if Section 14 of the Trade Union and Labour Relations Act 1974 were amended to enable the courts to issue injunctions against the union itself and fine the union for non-observance of the injunction. In the event of the failure of the union to pay such a fine, the assets of the union might be sequestrated.

However, quite apart from the other implications of removing the Section 14 immunity already discussed, it is far from certain that this procedure would be as effective as that which now exists or that it would significantly diminish the risks of self-inflicted martyrdom. It could be a less certain and speedy means of getting unlawful action stopped, particularly in the case of unofficial industrial action which is carried on without a union's authority or in defiance of its instructions. Certainly, where the courts held that a trade union was not responsible or that it had done all it could reasonably be expected to do to stop such unofficial action, the law would be powerless to help an injured employer if he could not then seek an injunction against the individual organizing the unofficial action. In practice, if civil proceedings could be taken against both individuals *and* trade unions, it is likely that employers would seek injunctions against individuals where the unlawful action was unofficial and against both named union officials and the union itself where the unlawful action was official. In such circumstances, the opportunities for individuals to seek martyrdom might be reduced, but would not be eliminated.

471

Conclusion

Great Britain is unique in the extent of the immunity from legal action which it affords to trade unions as such. Whereas in most other countries the legal liability of trade unions is deeply rooted in the legal system and has shaped their growth and development, the trade unions in this country have grown up within a legal system which has since 1906 protected them from legal action for the unlawful acts of their members. Industrial relations have undergone great changes since the present immunity was introduced in 1906 and it must now be considered whether the extent of immunity then thought necessary to safeguard the existence and operation of trade unions is still appropriate seventy-five years later. In particular, it is often questioned whether the law should continue to provide trade unions with a wider immunity than it provides for individuals who organize industrial action. The arguments for and against bringing these immunities into line with each other go to the heart of the debate on the failings of our industrial-relations system and practices, and on the role the law can reasonably be expected to play in improving them. Consideration of these arguments has to take account of the movement of bargaining power to the shop floor and the implication of this development for the concept of 'trade union power'.

The Government would welcome views on the issues discussed in this chapter. In particular, if the Section 14 immunity for trade unions were narrowed to bring it fully into line with the Section 13 immunity for individuals, thus putting union funds at risk for the unlawful acts of union officials and members:

(i) would the change result in more responsible behaviour by trade unions themselves and by their officials and members?

(ii) to what extent would employers in practice make use of the ability to sue trade unions for injunctions and damages in cases of unlawful action?

References

Employment Act, 1980, HMSO.
ROYAL COMMISSION ON TRADE UNIONS AND EMPLOYERS' ASSOCIATIONS (The Donovan Commission) (1968), *1965–8 Report*, HMSO.
Trade Union and Labour Relations' Act, 1974–6, HMSO.

35 Government Green Paper on Trade Union Immunities

Should a System of Positive Rights Replace the Present System of Immunities?

From the Department of Employment Green Paper on Trade Union Immunities, HMSO, 1981, pp. 83–91.

The last chapter [not included here] discussed possible changes in the law which might be made to the existing system of immunities which provides the legal framework for industrial relations in this country. This chapter considers whether and how the immunities could be converted into a system of positive rights, similar to those operating in a number of other countries.

The chapter is concerned primarily with the law as it relates to strikes and other industrial action. It concentrates, therefore, on the possibility of replacing the immunities provided by Sections 13 and 14 of the Trade Union and Labour Relations Acts 1974 and 1976, and by the Employment Act 1980, by a positive rights equivalent.[1] It is not primarily concerned with other rights, such as the right to associate and to join a trade union which are common features of other systems, except in so far as they may be considered an essential adjunct to a positive right to strike.

The chapter discusses the main characteristics of an alternative system based on the positive right to strike and in so doing identifies the main decisions that would be required and difficulties to be resolved. Its purpose is of a legal character: to discuss what would be involved in changing from our present system based on immunities to a system based on a positive right to strike. To provide a background for this discussion the chapter first considers how far the concept of positive legal rights is already present in the system of labour law in this country.

1. Section 14 of the 1976 Act has been repealed by Section 15 of the 1982 Employment Act. See Readings 34 and 37. – Ed.

Positive rights in British labour law

The common law itself, which provides the guiding precepts for our whole legal system, comprises in fact a series of fundamental rights and duties which, unless abrogated by legislation or sometimes by contract, govern all relationships including those at the workplace. As has been seen, however, these fundamental rights are not sufficient to guarantee the legality of trade union activity. It is because the common law operated to make associations of workers and concerted industrial action unlawful, that a system of immunities from legal processes at common law has developed. Indeed, simply to repeal the immunities and to return to the common law could make it virtually impossible for trade unions to exist and operate lawfully at all.

Positive legal rights have also been introduced into British labour law by statute. Three examples may be cited:

(i) a number of Acts of Parliament, particularly during the last decade, have conferred positive employment rights on individuals. Some of these have simply strengthened or confirmed rights recognized at common law (e.g. the right to notice before termination of contract); others have introduced new rights on which the common law is silent (e.g. rights in relation to guaranteed pay and maternity);

(ii) the Employment Protection Act 1975 established a number of trade union rights (e.g. the right to information for collective bargaining purposes, the right to be consulted about a redundancy), again in areas where the common law was silent;

(iii) the Industrial Relations Act 1971 established a number of legal rights including, for the first time, the right to join and not to join a trade union; Section 1 also contained a description of the 'guiding principles' on which the provisions of the Act were based. These included the principle of free association of workers in independent trade unions and the principle of collective bargaining 'freely conducted on behalf of workers and employers and with due regard to the general interests of the community'. The Act was repealed in 1974.

In addition, a number of international conventions and treaties to which the United Kingdom is a party have established basic employment rights. The European Convention for the Protection of Human Rights and Fundamental Freedom, for example, guarantees an employee's right to freedom of association, including in particular the right to join or form a trade union.

However, these examples of existing positive rights provide only limited practical guidance on how to convert a system of immunities into a system of positive rights. There are two reasons for this. First, none of these rights is concerned directly with the law as it relates to industrial action. Secondly, none of these rights has been introduced in areas where there has previously existed an immunity from the operation of the common law. In general, they have dealt only with areas where there are already common law rights which needed enlarging or where the common law is silent altogether.

In short, the introduction of positive rights into the law relating to strikes and industrial action in Great Britain would be an entirely novel step. It would represent a fundamental change from the legal system based on immunities which has developed over the last 100 years. This raises major issues which cannot, logically, be isolated from the question whether there should be some general form of Bill of Rights. This is, of course, a wider question than the subject matter of this Green Paper.

Main characteristics of a positive right in relation to strikes

The following would appear to be the main matters to be resolved in adopting a system of positive rights.

(i) A right to strike or a right to organize a strike?

Most legal systems based on positive rights start with a statement of fundamental rights which forms the basis for all subsequent labour law. These basic rights are sometimes contained in the Constitution itself; sometimes they are to be found in statute. They almost all include in one form or another the right of employees to strike though, as will be seen, this right has usually been limited by subsequent legislation.[2]

As the previous chapter showed, the nearest equivalent to the right to strike in Great Britain is the immunities from actions in tort under

2. An exception is West Germany, where the Constitution of 1949 is silent on the subject of the right to strike. The courts and subsequent legislation seem, however, to operate on the basis that a *de facto* right to strike exists.

475

Sections 13 or 14 of the Trade Union and Labour Relations Acts 1974 and 1976 as restricted by the Employment Act 1980. These immunities, however, protect the *organizers* of industrial action, whether they be individuals, trade unions or employer's associations. There is no immunity for the employees who actually take the industrial action; if they do so in breach of their contracts of employment they may be sued in contract.

The exact equivalent of the current immunity in a positive rights system would not, therefore, be a right to strike, but a right to organize a strike. This is not a concept which is recognized in other countries; in most countries the right to organize a strike is held to be implicit in the right to strike itself and other protective rights such as the right to take part in trade union activities. If, therefore, there were to be a positive right in relation to industrial action in Great Britain, it is arguable that it should be a right to strike rather than a right to organize a strike.

It would also be necessary to decide whether such a right should override the law of contract and enable those who go on strike in breach of their contracts of employment to do so without fear of being sued by their employers or being dismissed. French law, for example, regards a strike as suspending the individual contract of employment. In contrast, US law states that a strike during the renegotiation of a collective agreement breaks the employment contract and allows the employer to dismiss the strikers and to take on replacement workers.

There is also the question of whether a right to strike implies a right not to strike. This does not appear to be an issue in other countries, but it would be relevant to the situation in this country where unions discipline members for refusing to follow their instructions to strike. If there were a right not to strike the question would arise whether such disciplinary action was legal.

(ii) *The right to lock-out*

The immunities apply equally to employers and employers' associations who organize a lock-out. This suggests that in a positive rights system the right to strike might need to be matched with a corresponding right to lock-out.

The right of an employer to lock-out his employees is recognized in most countries, though often as a result of judicial decision rather than in the Constitution or in statute. An exception is Sweden where the right to strike and to lock-out appear alongside each other in Article 5 of the Swedish Constitution:

Any trade union and any employer or association of employers shall have the right to take strike or lock-out actions or any similar measures, except as otherwise provided by law or ensuing from a contract.

The same questions as those described above would arise in relation to a right to lock-out. Should there, for example, be a right to lock-out or a right to *organize* a lock-out? Should an employer exercising the right of lock-out be liable for breaking employment contracts?

(iii) Definition and limitation of the right to strike

A right to strike or lock-out by itself would leave almost unlimited scope for industrial action. It would therefore be necessary to limit that right in a number of ways.

In most other countries the basic right to strike has been limited by subsequent legislation. These limitations fall into six main categories, five of which have parallels in the existing law in Great Britain. As part of a change to a positive rights system it would be necessary to determine precisely what restrictions should be placed on the right to strike in respect of:

(a) secondary action (Section B of Chapter 3);
(b) picketing (Section C);
(c) political strikes (Section D);
(d) strikes in breach of contract (Section E); and
(e) special groups of essential workers (Section H).

The sixth category of limitation of the basic right to strike relates to the legality of industrial action short of a strike. In most systems the right to take action short of a strike (e.g. a work to rule or 'go slow') derives from the right to strike itself and is not specified separately. In some countries (such as Sweden) action short of a strike is covered by a formula such as 'strike action or other similar measures'. In others (e. g. France) it has been specifically declared unlawful. British law recognizes no such distinctions: either the contract of employment is broken or it is not.

In respect of each of these restrictions it would be necessary to decide whether it should be defined so as precisely to reproduce present British law or whether any changes should be made.

This is not an exhaustive list of the decisions and problems which would be involved in limiting a right to strike. But it illustrates the extent to which a positive right to strike would need detailed definition and limitation in legislation. It is important to note that, wherever the law was silent on a particular point, the right to strike would apply and, wherever this created uncertainty in the law, it would be for the courts to decide what the right to strike meant.

(iv) Corresponding obligations

Another way in which rights may be defined or circumscribed is by the obligations which are placed on others not to interfere with them. In other systems this question arises most clearly in relation to rights other than the right to strike. The right to join a trade union, for example, is usually supported by an obligation on an employer not to prevent someone from joining a union. Equally the right of employees to bargain which is written into some systems imposes a correlative duty on an employer to bargain in good faith with representatives of employees.

There are not many circumstances in which interference with the right to strike is likely to occur and, in consequence, the right to strike has not generally led to corresponding legal duties being imposed on others. Italy, however, provides an example of how the right to strike enshrined in the Constitution can lead to specific statutory obligations on others not to interfere with that right. There the right to strike has been reflected in the law relating to unfair dismissal in a provision requiring an employer not to discriminate against or dismiss an employee simply because he has participated in a strike.

If, of course, a system of positive rights for Great Britain were to cover other rights (e.g. the right to associate or to bargain collectively) the problem of corresponding obligations would be enlarged.

(v) Whose rights?

If there were to be a positive right to strike (or lock-out) the intention would be for it to be exercised by individual employees (and employers). If there were a right to organize a strike, it would have to apply both to individuals and to trade unions if it were to correspond to the existing legal position.

This raises the question of whether there would need to be special treatment of trade unions and employers' associations. Section 14 of the Trade Union and Labour Relations Act 1974 grants much wider immunity to trade unions and employers' associations than does Section 13 to individuals.[3] If the aim were to leave this position unchanged, this would have to be carried through into a system of positive rights. It is difficult to see how a right corresponding to the existing Section 14 immunity might be formulated since it operates essentially as a means of protecting unions against actions for damages or injunctions for torts (not just those committed in contemplation or furtherance of a trade dispute). In other words, it is not a means of enabling unions to take positive action but rather, of its nature, a 'negative' right. If it were desired to achieve the same position as in existing law, the solution might be to retain something like the present immunity which prevents trade unions and employers' associations from being sued for any wrongful act. This would, of course, mean that the law would consist of a mixture of positive rights and immunities.

Enforcement

A system of positive rights, has, in most countries, been accompanied by its own procedures for enforcement. This has meant devising sanctions for those who infringe or overstep the right to strike and deciding which courts are to administer and enforce those sanctions.

The nature of sanctions depends to a large extent on how the positive rights are defined and limited. For example, if, as in Italy, the right to strike were supported by a corresponding duty on an employer not to dismiss an employee for going on strike, then the remedy for an aggrieved employee might more naturally be an application to an industrial tribunal as in other cases of unfair dismissal.

The main consideration, however, is the sanction to be applied to those who overstep the right to strike by taking unlawful industrial action. There are three main questions which would need to be

First, what is to be the nature of the wrong? At present, those who are not protected by the legal immunities are liable at common law for actions in tort for interfering with contracts. In an alternative

3. Section 14 of the 1974 Act has been repealed by Section 15 of the 1982 Employment Act. See Readings 34 and 37. – Ed.

system there would need to be some new grounds for legal action to replace the common law remedies. The US legislators of the 1930s and 1940s solved this problem by creating a new offence – the 'unfair labor practice'. This idea was adopted in this country by the Industrial Relations Act 1971. Under that Act it became possible to bring an action for an unfair industrial practice against the organizers of a strike declared unlawful by the Act; and this remedy was intended to replace the actions in tort available at common law. It is likely that something similar would be needed to complement a legal right to strike (or lock-out).

The second question is what remedies should be available to someone who is suffering from unlawful industrial action? In particular, should the main remedies continue to be an injunction and an action for damages? These are the main remedies in most other countries, though in some cases restrictions are placed on the amount of damages which can be awarded. Under the American system, the decision whether to seek an injunction against unlawful industrial action rests, not with the employer, but with the General Counsel of the National Labor Relations Board who then takes up the case on behalf of the aggrieved party.

Third, which courts are to administer and enforce the law? One option is simply to leave the existing civil courts to administer and enforce labour law. A feature of several positive rights systems, however, is the labour court, with a separate and distinct jurisdiction. In some systems this is almost completely insulated from the rest of the legal system. In West Germany, for example, there are three tiers of labour courts, with the Federal Labour Court providing the court of final appeal. In other systems the jurisdictions of the labour courts and civil courts overlap. This is particularly marked in the United States, where the National Labor Relations Board hears complaints of unfair industrial practice, with a right of appeal to the Federal Appeal and Supreme Courts. In addition, an employer can of his own accord pursue an action for damages in the district court.

It is noteworthy that where positive rights have been introduced by legislation in Great Britain separate labour courts have developed to administer them. Most of the individual employment rights, for example, are in the jurisdiction of the industrial tribunals and the Employment Appeal Tribunal (although appeals from the latter go into the ordinary legal system); some collective rights are enforced through the Central Arbitration Committee.

Positive rights and the common law

Another important consideration is the relationship between a positive rights system and the common law. The common law, as has been seen, provides the basic rights and principles which underlie our legal system. It is, therefore, essential that any new system of positive rights takes account of the common law, and vice versa. To fail to do so would leave the law in a state of great uncertainty.

Difficulties could arise, for example, from the relationship between a positive right to strike and the law of tort. Replacing the existing immunities by an alternative right to strike would, without special provision to the contrary, restore the common law remedies in tort available against the organizers of unlawful industrial action. This would mean that two parallel courses would be open to those damaged by an unlawful strike: either to seek redress through whatever sanctions and penalties were devised for the system of positive rights or to sue in tort for unlawful interference with contract. The existence of statutory and common law rights alongside each other would clearly be a source of confusion. The courts might be expected to decide that a positive right overrode the remedy available at common law; but, of course, if they did not do so the positive right to strike could be nullified by the continuing remedies available in tort.

Another area of difficulty, already referred to, would be in relation to the law of contract. Without specific guidance, the courts would have to decide whether a right to strike or lock-out released an individual from his obligations not to break his contract of employment. If it did not do so then, in spite of the right to strike, a person would be liable to be sued for damages if he took industrial action in breach of his contract.

Finally, in the absence of specific provision to the contrary, the creation of a positive right to strike could itself give rise to common law as well as statutory remedies. This is because of the common law maxim '*ubi ius, ibi remedium*', which expresses the general principle that whenever there exists a 'right' recognized at law there exists also a remedy for an infringement of that right, even though no remedy appears to be provided by statute. This could mean, for example, that even if the law were silent on the sanctions available for interference with the right to strike (e.g. by discriminating against an employee for going on strike), there might nevertheless be a remedy in the civil courts where such interference occurred or where those concerned combined to cause such interference.

This suggests that there would be a need to insulate any legal right to strike from the common law and to make it clear that the only remedies available against unlawful industrial action are those enacted by the legislation which establishes the right and not otherwise. This could mean developing a completely separate system of law with its own sanctions and with separate courts to administer and enforce those sanctions. Moreover, the remedies for infringement of the right to strike would presumably have to exclude action taken by the employer in pursuance of his right to lock-out referred to above.

Advantages and disadvantages of a positive rights system

It is apparent from this analysis that there would be a number of complex legal and technical questions to be resolved in switching from immunities to a system of legal rights. In particular, there could be special difficulty in insulating a right to strike from the common law; a difficulty which could be compounded if some elements of immunity (e.g. Section 14 of the Trade Union and Labour Relations Act 1974: see above) had to coexist with positive rights. To a certain extent, the success of a positive rights system would depend on how successfully these problems could be overcome.

In considering the merits of a positive rights system it can be misleading to suppose that the provision of a positive right to strike would necessarily impose further restrictions on union power. Many who favour such restrictions are attracted by a legal system based on positive rights. There is, however, nothing in a positive rights system which is inherently more restrictive of trade union power than the present system. As experience of other countries shows, positive rights can accommodate a whole range of different approaches. Whatever legal system is adopted, the policy issues raised in the previous chapter remain to be settled.

The more narrow question considered here is whether a legal system based on positive rights is a more effective way of defining the legal protections and obligations of employees and trade unions than one based on immunities. The advantages which are generally seen in a positive rights system are ones of simplicity and clarity. It is argued that positive rights enable the law to be framed in terms which relate more directly to industrial experience. It is believed that a lot of the misunderstanding about the present law stems from the inherent complexity of the torts concerned and that laymen have difficulty in applying concepts based on the common law of contract and tort to the reality of industrial disputes. To the extent that a positive rights system succeeded in moving the language and concepts of the law on industrial conflict away from immunities against tortious liability, it might be easier to understand and more straightforward to apply, not just for unions and management but for the courts as well. Indeed, it is possible that a system of positive rights would help remove the unions' traditional suspicion of the courts. The latter have often been seen as anti-union because their function has been to uphold the common law which is based on individual rights. To the extent that a system of positive rights changed that function into one of defending collective rights, the courts might seem more neutral in interpreting the rights of management, unions and workers.

It is a matter of judgement how far these benefits could be achieved. But three points seem to emerge from the examination of a positive rights system undertaken in this chapter. First, though the language of positive rights can be more easily related to industrial reality, this does not necessarily make for a simpler legislative provision. There appears to be no escape from a detailed provision which carefully defines and constrains the application of a right to strike. Secondly, however carefully defined, there would always remain under this and under any other system some uncertainty at the margin about whether a particular action was lawful or not. Thirdly, there is no indication that a positive rights system would be any less open to judicial interpretation than a system of immunities. There would always be difficult cases for the courts to decide. Indeed, an entirely new legal framework would be likely to open up new areas of uncertainty until a corpus of judicial interpretation had developed.

It should be added finally that, of course, the success or failure of a positive rights system would not be judged solely by the clarity of the drafting or the ease of application. It would depend to a large extent on the nature of the rights it established and on the success with which it resolved the conflicting considerations discussed in the previous chapter.

Conclusion

It would undoubtedly be a formidable task to formulate a legal system of positive rights to replace the present law. The whole question would need to be expertly examined. But it would first need to be decided whether there was a positive advantage in the establishment of a new system. The Government would therefore welcome views on the above analysis and, in particular, on the following points:

(i) would it be desirable to make the fundamental change from the present system based on immunities to one based on positive rights?

(ii) would a system of positive rights contribute to an improvement in industrial relations?

(iii) would it be clearer, more easily understood and less complex as a system of law?

(iv) would both employers and unions welcome the obligations that would be involved?

References

Employment Act, 1980, HMSO.
Trade Union and Labour Relations Act, 1974–6, HMSO.

The Legitimacy of Industrial Action: Trade Unionism at the Crossroads

From Richard Tur, *Labour Law and the Community: Prospects for the 1980s*, ed. K. W. Wedderburn and W. T. Murphy, University of London, Institute of Advanced Legal Studies, 1982, pp. 155–64.

The assumptions underlying the legislation of the seventies and indeed the labour legislation of the preceding century seem already of a different age and cast of thought. It was assumed that the extension of free collective bargaining and therefore of the influence and power of trade unions was beneficial to industrial relations and to society at large, both in terms of justice and of efficiency. It was further assumed that trade unions required protection from the full force of hostile common law and an unsympathetic judiciary. This led to blanket immunity for unions from actions sounding in tort, and unionists were protected provided they acted 'in contemplation or furtherance of a trade dispute'. The scope of 'trade dispute' was very widely drawn in that any connection, no matter how minimal, with items listed in Section 29, TULRA [Trade Union and Labour Relations Act], 1974, fell within the protected zone. Further, Section 17(2) imposed or reaffirmed a special regime relating to 'labour injunctions'. By contrast, the legislation of the early eighties is founded upon the radically individualistic principles of political economy associated with Adam Smith and resurrected by Hayek; it represents a serious challenge to the assumptions of a century, and therefore calls into question the role of trade unions and the legitimacy of industrial action.

It is, of course, possible to join with one strand of contemporary thought in believing that the current legislation is but a temporary phenomenon to be seen not as a radical attack upon the unions but merely as a piece of fine-tuning, readjusting the limits of permissible industrial action. However, it is arguable that 1976 merely marked a restoration of the *status quo ante* in the face of judicial erosion of the effect and scope of existing immunities. Just as the Trade Disputes Act, 1965, was an obvious reaction to judicial creativity,[1] so the 1976 amendment, though less obviously, was a reaction to the creeping

1. *Rookes* v. *Barnard* [1964] AC 1129.

erosion of the threshold of liability for the tort of inducing a breach of contract.[2] If so, the legislation of the early eighties cannot properly be assessed or explained as a local reaction to recent excesses, but must be regarded as a fundamental attack on the position established as early as 1906. The question of the justification of union powers and privileges is, therefore, in part a historical question which calls into play consideration of the political, social and economic context to trade unionism at the turn of the century. It might readily be shown that the 1906 immunities were wholly justifiable against the posture of the common law, judicial hostility, inequalities of bargaining power, differential access to information and to the institutions of government, the organizational weaknesses of trade unions and the imperfectly developed consequences of the extension of the franchise. But even if it was proved conclusively that the legislation of 1906 was, in 1906, wholly justifiable, it cannot follow that it remains wholly justifiable in 1982, unless it can be shown that the justifying conditions still obtain.

It is a mistake to believe, for example, that judicial hostility has been a constant feature throughout the period in question. Since 1906, albeit gradually, the judicial mood appears to have changed, and there are dicta and decisions sympathetic to trade unions and their objectives,[3] so much so that learned commentators can rightly suppose that the statutory immunity from the tort of civil conspiracy may have made little practical difference simply because here at least the judges were prepared to regard certain types of industrial action as 'justified', such justification providing a defence to actions sounding in tort (Elias, Napier and Wallington, 1980, pp. 232–6; cf. Davies and Freedland, 1979, p. 629). There was, indeed, a resurgence of judicial hostility in the mid-sixties,[4] but such hostility after a period of considerable judicial tolerance may itself reflect a wider discontent in society rather than the frequently-alleged class bias of the judiciary. In any event, the political, social and economic context of 1982 is so emphatically different from that of 1906 that it is appropriate to face the issue of the justification of industrial action afresh.

2. *Thomson* v. *Deakin* [1952] Ch. 646; cf. *Stratford* v. *Lindley* [1965] AC 269, *Torquay Hotels* v. *Cousins* [1969] 2 Ch. 106, *Emerald Construction* v. *Lowthian* [1966] 1 WLR 691.

3. *Reynolds* v. *The Shipping Federation* [1924] 1 Ch. 28; *Crofter Hand Woven Harris Tweed* v. *Veitch* [1942] AC 435; *Thomson* v. *Deakin* [1952] Ch. 646; *Pete's Towing Services* v. *NIUW* [1970] NZLR 32.

4. e.g. *Rookes* v. *Barnard* [1964] AC 1129, *Stratford* v. *Lindley* [1965] AC 269.

Kahn-Freund and Hepple (1972, p. 6) have usefully listed four main arguments which seek to justify the legal freedom to resort to industrial action; 'These are . . . the equilibrium argument, the autonomy argument, the voluntary labour (or Benthamite) argument and the psychological argument.' This list may be supplemented by the human rights argument which affirms that it is a fundamental human right to withdraw one's labour. This is, in effect, Bentham's voluntary labour argument couched in the terminology of natural law and natural rights which Bentham himself did so much to excise, stigmatizing natural rights as 'simple nonsense' and natural and imprescriptible rights as 'nonsense upon stilts' (Bentham, 1973, p. 269). In any event, apart from pious affirmations in social charters and international conventions, there is no legal basis for the assertion of a *right* to strike; rather there is what one might, with Kelsen, style a 'negative permission' to strike (Kelsen, 1967, p. 16). Even if a right to strike were part of our law, and such might be the appropriate way forward, it does not follow that such a right must be either absolute (cf. Kahn-Freund, 1977, p. 240) or inalienable (Hayek, 1960, p. 269). Very few 'rights' declared in charters and constitutions are established absolutely. Rather, the declaration of such a 'right' creates a presumption against its denial or dilution. But such a presumption is rebuttable. Thus it is open to an American state or a member of the Council of Europe to show that its legislation, which admittedly encroaches upon a right protected in the controlling instrument, is necessary in a democratic society *and* that the encroachment is the minimum possible to achieve a legitimate objective. Both the contempt of court case[5] and the closed shop case[6] exhibited precisely this mode of argumentation. Further, even if a right to strike were part of our law, it does not follow without further argument that such a right cannot be bargained away either temporarily, for example, in a no-strike clause, or permanently denied on the grounds that the function of the workers concerned is simply too vital to allow of striking as, for example, is the case with the armed forces and the police. None of these justifications, however, focus upon the issue in hand, which is not *is*, but *to what extent* is industrial action justified?

Prior to the current legislation, the definition of 'trade dispute' was very widely drawn and the resultant immunity comprehensive. The 'two disputes' argument canvassed in the Court of Appeal in *Duport*

5. (1979) 2 EHRR 245.
6. *Young, James and Webster* (1981) Council of Europe Press Release, 13 August.

Steel[7] fell upon deaf or unsympathetic ears in the House of Lords and only if a dispute was purely political as in *BBC* v. *Hearn*[8] did the industrial action fall out with the statutory immunities. Consequently, it was no new discovery of the House that the shape of the law left unionists virtually free to pursue their objectives irrespective of the general disutility thus occasioned. In *Duport Steel* the House stressed the full extent of the immunities and insisted that its only function was to apply the law according to its meaning. But their Lordships also emphasized that the law was far too widely drawn and even explained how it might be amended. Despite protestations of judicial impotence in the face of such intolerable union activity as preventing heating oil reaching hospitals during bitter winter weather, the House had previously been at pains to assert that the special 'labour injunction' provisions which defused the potentially far-reaching impact of *Ethicon*[9] were *not* paramount and that there remained an ultimate discretion in the court to grant an injunction if the consequences of not granting it would be extremely serious, even if there was some likelihood of the trade dispute defence being made out at the ultimate trial.[10] Doubtless judges would be unwilling readily to invoke such a power, which in effect determines the trade dispute without ever reaching to the legal merits of the case. If, however, such a power exists, then much of the basis for the current legislation which assumes judicial impotence in the face of union excess is eroded.

Doubtless, too, a reluctance to become embroiled in the politics of industry and an unwillingness to act as back-seat drivers in trade disputes constrain judges further, but what is primarily in issue is not the resolution of the trade dispute or even the effectiveness of the tactics adopted but the policing of the outer limits of legitimate industrial action. If the courts cannot police such outer limits, who can? It falls foursquare within the judicial enterprise to protect innocent third parties remote from trade disputes and powerless to influence their outcome injured in property rights or legitimate expectations. An irony of the current situation is that having by their self-denying ordinance in relation to trade disputes laid bare the unaccountability of unions and unionists even for excessive injury and disruption, the legislation thus fomented places squarely upon the judiciary the business of determining whether or not there is a trade dispute on the

7. [1980] 1 WLR 142.
8. [1977] ICR 685.
9. [1975] AC 396.
10. *NWL* v. *Woods* [1979] 1 WLR 1294.

much narrower definition, and, if not, whether an unjustifiable tortious act has been committed, a determination all the more crucial as it will now relate not only to injunctions but also to damages, awards of which against unions, especially where there are several plaintiffs, could seriously interfere with a wide range of union functions to which no one, least of all Hayek, could take exception (cf. Hayek, 1960, pp. 275–7).

The political economy which informs the current legislation is simplicity itself. Presupposed are rational individuals bent upon optimizing individual utilities, constrained only by the hidden hand of market forces. Individual employees can seek to maximize wages, but if they seek more than an employer is willing or able to pay then they must either settle for less or seek employment elsewhere. If another employer is willing to pay more, then either he is at a competitive disadvantage as against the first employer and his goods will price themselves out of the market with the resultant loss of the better-paid jobs, or the first employer, paying less than market rates, will find his workforce evaporating and will either go out of business or raise wages to retain his workforce. Therefore both employers and employees are constrained to operate within the limits determined by the market. Further, this laisser-faire model is defended as being administratively efficient or economically optimal because industry or society does not have to carry the additional costs of bureaucratic machinery established to determine 'just' wage settlements and police their operation. Further still, since 'social justice' is a mirage because no absolute standard of just wages exists from which the correct wage may be read off, the hidden-hand mechanism appears no more unjust than its rivals. Again, the hidden hand adjusts wages and prices constantly in accordance with variations in supply and demand.

There is little wrong with the model as a model, but in real life competition is imperfect; individuals have imprecise awareness of supply-and-demand curves, and in any event are not solely rational optimizers of utilities. Family commitments, personal loyalties, the transaction costs of changing jobs and perhaps moving house, and the opportunity costs of retraining all suggest that the model is not susceptible of implementation in social reality. Further, even if the hidden hand ultimately adjusts prices and wages, it is a crude and harsh mechanism which reacts slowly enough and thus subjects those whose skills are plentiful but in little demand to severe economic disadvantage. Equally, those with skills in short supply but much in demand are advantaged. Again, the much-vaunted 'freedom' which the model incorporates may be illusory, especially in the eyes of those victimized by the market at times of change. The conflict between the competing values of economic security and freedom is ultimately irresolvable and the model retains a seductive charm, appealing particularly to those confident in their own ability to adapt. Such appeal is heightened if one accepts the impossibility of rationally constructing a blueprint for the organization of society and the distribution of burdens and benefits (Hayek, 1973, ch. 1). Imperfections of knowledge and indeterminacy of aim preclude the construction of such a scheme.

On such a view the primary role of government is to free the economy from forces which obstruct or distort the operation of the hidden-hand mechanism. Thus restrictive practices, *unreasonable* restraint of trade, job protectionism and 'artificially' high wage settlements, born of union power and privilege, all contribute to the inefficiency of the economy and to imperfect competition. Such obstructions must therefore be eliminated. Viewed in this light, trade unions must be under severe attack because they inevitably distort the operation of the hidden-hand mechanism.

Again, if primacy is given to controlling inflation, even at the expense of savage unemployment (cf. Hayek, 1960, pp. 281–2), unions must be under even greater attack on the political economy just recounted. Allow free collective bargaining full operation and the artificial powers, privileges and immunities of the unions will so distort the operation of the market that wages will be artificially high, manufacturers will require higher prices and an inflationary spiral will be set in motion, at least in so far as one cleaves to the Keynesian ideal of 'full' employment. Free collective bargaining will in such circumstances operate as a ratchet to inflation. Abandon full employment as a goal, refuse to print more money, deny 'new money' to the negotiators, and unemployment will steadily rise. In the face of massive unemployment, a new 'realism' may pervade collective bargaining, but such are the artificial powers of unions that the tightly limited money supply will be disproportionately distributed; in this Hobbesian war of each against all, the apparent and perhaps real short-term gains go to those who are most powerful, most determined and most unscrupulous. Only by the substitution of true market forces for the anarchy of collective bargaining can the injustices of union power be constrained. Consequently, the privileged position of unions must be reassessed in the name of distributive justice.

Such economic arguments can be further developed. For example, it is by no means clear that even the sectional interests of the members of dominant trade unions are well served by industrial action. Not only do strikes entail loss of wages, but wages can be raised above what would obtain in a free market only by limiting the labour supply. Limiting the labour supply means creating unemployment by keeping people who want to work at market rates out of work, so that those in jobs can earn more than the market rate for the job. Consequently, the success of unions in bettering the conditions of working men may be illusory and any real gains by one group inevitably at the expense of another group of workers. This aspect of unionism, namely the closed shop whereby unions may control the labour supply and thereby push wages beyond market rates for those who have jobs, must, in any comprehensive economic strategy, be under attack. The provisions in the current legislation do not merely reflect a long-standing ideological objection to the 'unfreedom' of the closed shop, but also a necessary element in the battle against inflation.

Unions have also adopted an aggressively political stance, claiming with some success a say in the governance of the country and the 'right' to make or unmake governments or governmental policies. Protest, persuasion and participation are, of course, permissible, but in a democracy the interests of all need consulting rather than the sectional interests of one group. Organized coercion, for example, a denial of transport or hospital services until the government yields, is an anti-democratic, non-parliamentary mode of social decision-making. Judges are frequently criticized as being unelected and unaccountable for their decisions, but their mission as shown by their oath is general whereas 'elected' trade union leaders are elected only by the members whose sectional interest they represent and their mission is specific. Consequently the disproportionate influence of unions upon government is democratically suspect.

The disparity in power, influence and organization between unionists and consumers reflected, for example, in *Hubbard* v. *Pitt*[11] is such that every strike quite irrespective of the pressure brought to bear upon the employer and the government occasions considerable inconvenience to innocent third parties 'remote' from the dispute and powerless to affect its outcome. By what right and to what end do unionists subject millions of innocent bystanders to inconvenience, financial loss and emotional distress? Since many of those consumers are also in employment a strike is all too often an implement with a

11. [1975] ICR 308.

worker at each end. Government, of course, seeks to prevent such disruption by emergency powers and contingency planning, but more attractive from the consumer viewpoint are 'no-strike employments' such as the police or armed forces. The extension of such a regime to major public services and utilities would go a long way towards serving the legitimate interest of consumers in the continuity of such services and utilities. So long as unions enjoy their privileged position such that the powerful may profit any attempt to reach no-strike agreements is vain simply because it asks unionists to give up something of great value and effect. Once, however, trade unions stand in a like position to all other actors on the economic stage, a no-strike arrangement will be that much more attractive to employees to the betterment of the condition of consumers.

Unionists have a full hand of responses to such arguments, though few of the cards which they can play are obvious 'masters' unless, as Hobbes shrewdly observed long ago, in such matters 'clubs are trumps'. To the cluster of economic arguments unionists may reply that they presuppose an antiquated and erroneous atomist model of society and that the collective power of capital can only be countered by the collective power of unions, which in their inevitably unequal struggle need all the assistance which their powers, privileges and immunities give them. But unions, too, advocate *free* collective bargaining, though the freedom involved has hitherto included a freedom from the legal restraints of the ordinary law of the land which had allowed unions to achieve their ends at almost any cost to others. If one is seriously to reject the laisser-faire economic model, wages will have to be determined by regulation, be it statutory or non-statutory incomes policy or 'national economic assessment', and that entails a curtailment of the freedom of unions greater than anything immanent in the current round of legislation. Either one allows market forces to determine wages or one seeks to regulate wages. One cannot reconcile wages regulation and *free* collective bargaining. Consequently, unions must become mere arms of government in a corporate state or accept what free collective bargaining entails, namely that they appear in the market place on like terms to all other economic actors. Only Orwellian double-think allows politicians the luxury of proclaiming a commitment both to a planned economy and to free collective bargaining.

To the near-blasphemous accusation that union pressure may of itself cause unemployment and worsen the position of some employees, the unionist may seek to deny that the wages round is a zero-sum game. Clearly if it is then gains for some promote corresponding losses for others. Of course the wages round is not a zero-sum game; 'new money' is always available through renegotiating the distribution of consumption and investment, by forcing prices up, or by obtaining government finance. But such new money is not obtained without cost; curtailing investment ultimately costs jobs and erodes productivity, and since many enterprises operate at the margins such erosion of investment cannot be long sustained. Passing wage rises off either directly in prices or indirectly in taxes simply redistributes wealth to the benefit of the strong and unscrupulous and to the detriment of the weak and unorganized, who cannot avail themselves of the tactics secured to the beneficiaries by the absence of normal legal restraints. So evident is this even to unionists that they frequently resort to the productivity argument, which in effect postulates new money without costs. But even this argument is vulnerable; first, it cannot apply universally because not all workers are productively employed; secondly, no guarantees secure increased productivity throughout the period to which an agreement relates; thirdly, increases in productivity may flow as much from increased investment or refined technology as from additional labour, and then investors having foregone consumption or those financing research have as colourable a claim as the workforce.

To the democratic argument unionists may reply that our democratic institutions are so imperfect that direct action, civil disobedience, demonstrations and wholly political strikes are legitimate modes of activity in pursuit of change. But even in a democracy as imperfect as ours such arguments require considerable refinement to carry conviction and could bear the weight of extreme disruption only as a last resort, if at all. In any event, the correct response to imperfections in our democratic institutions is not selective benefit born of anarchy but universal benefit flowing from the reform of defective institutions. Again, it may be argued that such tactics are the necessary prerequisite of the inevitable social revolution and that one might as readily seek to stop history itself as to stop a necessary incident thereto. But this response depends upon considerable theoretical underpinning, not universally approved, and so supportive of the interests of those who espouse it as to be at least suspect as self-serving.

To the social arguments the near-universal response is one of sorrow for the inconvenience caused together with an imputation that the true cause is the employer's recalcitrance. But employers operating at the margins simply cannot meet the demands made of them. Does anyone, for example, believe that the employers could meet the miners' 21 per cent wage claim? And if employers are 'reasonable' and meet the demands, inevitably it is the consumer who foots the bill.

Even allowing due weight to these counter-arguments, the case against unions on the political economy recounted is very strong. What justification can there be for the unique legal position enjoyed by unions and unionists? The only intellectually respectable answer appears to be Marxism. Society, that is capitalist society, is ineradicably ridden with conflict, exploitation and injustice. Unions are a vehicle of the inevitable social revolution. The present plight of victims of union power is but a staging post in the intensification of the contradictions of capitalism and, as in all revolutions, the end justifies the means. But if one regards the impressive intellectual edifice erected by Marx as philosophically and methodologically implausible, for all its pregnant insights, and the social revolution heralded therein as improbable, and if one rejects the monolithic conflict model in favour of a conception of society which acknowledges not only conflicts of interest between workers and employers and workers and consumers, but also the possibility, indeed the necessity, of consensus and compromise, then the case against the unions is formidable indeed.

The challenge facing contemporary society is the creation of mechanisms which will temper the necessary conflict and protect bystanders from injury. It is sometimes argued that the total exclusion of tort law from the industrial arena is much to be applauded because it would be irrational to allow the accidents and happenstances of that branch of the law to determine the outcome of industrial disputes, a task for which it was not designed and for which it is totally unsuited (see Davies and Freedland, 1979, pp. 624ff.). Two points can be made in response to this; first, a significant part of tort law originates in trade disputes litigation; secondly, the role of tort law here is not the resolution of trade disputes but the definition of the outer limits of legitimate industrial action for the protection of the property and legitimate interests of innocent third parties. For this function the law of tort is a wholly appropriate mechanism. By declaring a boundary the courts are not determining the dispute. Rather, they say to the parties: 'Reach whatever resolution you please, but you must not seek to make an outcome more likely by doing X', where X may represent a wider or narrower range of harmful activities. To this extent tort operates like crime. Although it is for the parties to settle the dispute they may not resort to assault or criminal damage to promote a favoured outcome. The correct analogy is not back-seat driving but border patrols.[12] The courts are singularly ill-equipped to second-guess industrial dispute strategy, but they are particularly well placed to rank conflicting interests and to protect vested rights and legitimate expectations. On this analysis the abolition of trade union immunities is wholly appropriate and may even be seen as of itself a modest step against the backdrop of the political economy which informs the current legislation.

The furore occasioned by the current legislation might suggest that trade unions were being abolished and their leaders marched off to prison, whereas all that is being proposed is that trade unions are now big enough boys to stand equally under the ordinary law along with the rest of society. The protest may bespeak a ready realization of just how favourably placed unions currently are and just how much power and influence they stand to lose. But the protest may also bespeak confusion and uncertainty wholly understandable in the face of the complexity of labour law, the rapidity of social transformation and the covert falsification of assumptions so long-standing as to be 'self-evident'. In particular, even experienced trade unionists may be unable to visualize life after the immunities have disappeared. It may be thought that the absence of a defence of 'justification' will expose unions to serious judicial incursions, but the absence is exaggerated[13] and explicable by reference to the extent of trade union immunities which, in effect, pre-empted any question of justification. Life without immunities will visit upon the judiciary the delicate and difficult role of determining the outer limits of legitimate industrial action and labour law in the eighties, at least in this regard, will become a chapter in the law of tort.

Trade unions stand today at the crossroads. Either they accept that they are subject to the same legal pains and penalties as the rest of society and adopt a more limited and responsible role within a free market economy, ultimately the only economy which can sustain them, or they accept the only possible alternative, namely the determination of wages by government which leaves no room for free

12. *Express Newspapers* v. *McShane* [1980] 2 WLR 82, 104, per Lord Scarman.

13. Elias, Napier and Wallington (1980), p. 235, and see *Reynolds* v. *The Shipping Federation* [1924] 1 Ch. 28 and *Pete's Towing Services* v. *NIUW* [1970] NZLR 32; cf. *South Wales Miners' Federation* v. *Glamorgan Coal Co.* [1905] AC 239, a decision on the facts which might call for reconsideration hereafter.

collective bargaining, nor for *free* unions. Inflicting economic loss should be regarded as *prima facie* tortious but susceptible of justification (see Davies and Freedland, 1979, p. 629). Life without immunities offers unions an honourable and responsible role as *voluntary* associations active within the limits of the ordinary law of the land to secure the interests of their members. A 'national economic assessment' together with some latter-day version of the social contract is but the shadow of corporatism wherein trade unions ultimately lose their identity within the organs of government, even though their leaders may enjoy more personal prestige and patronage through their association with government, at least for a time, than that which the free market economy can ever offer them. They will, however, ultimately be able to do less for the members whose interests they purport to serve.

References

BENTHAM, J. (1973), 'A Critical Examination of the Declaration of Rights', *Bentham's Political Thought*, ed. B. C. Parekh, Croom Helm.

DAVIES, P., and M. R. FREEDLAND (1979), *Labour Law*, Weidenfeld & Nicolson.

ELIAS, P., B. NAPIER and P. WALLINGTON (1980), *Labour Law, Cases and Materials*, Butterworth.

HAYEK, F. A. (1960), *The Constitution of Liberty*, Routledge & Kegan Paul.

HAYEK, F. A. (1973), *Law, Legislation and Liberty*, vol. 1, Routledge & Kegan Paul.

KAHN-FREUND, O. (1977), *Labour and the Law*, 2nd ed., Stevens & Sons.

KAHN-FREUND, O., and B. A. HEPPLE (1972), *Law Against Strikes*, Fabian Society.

KELSEN, H. (1967), *Pure Theory of Law*, Cambridge University Press.

The New Politics of Labour Law

From Lord Wedderburn, *Occasional Paper No. 1*, University of Durham Industrial Relations Group, 1983, pp. 2–29.

The public policy of labour law

There can be little doubt that a continuity of public policy which persisted for nearly three-quarters of a century has now been ruptured. There was such a policy. Some governments paid lip-service to it; others embraced it; but none jettisoned it as this administration has done since 1979. The change may be measured by attempting to guess the date of a Ministerial pronouncement on labour law policy:

A great argument upon which we rely . . . is decent provision for industrial workers. 'General low wages,' said Mill, 'never caused any country to undersell its rivals'; nor did high wages ever hinder it.

In the 'great staple trades . . . powerful organization on both sides' promotes 'healthy bargaining', and increases 'competitive power':

But where you have what we call sweated trades, you have no organization, no parity of bargaining, the good employer is undercut by the bad, and the bad employer is undercut by the worst . . . and ignorance generally renders the worker an easy prey to the tyranny of the masters and middle men.

That was not an Opposition speech against the Employment Bill 1982, but – as perhaps the words 'sweated trades' reveal – Winston Churchill, President of the Board of Trade, introducing the Trade Boards Bill in 1909, from which sprang today's Wages Councils.[1] Measures to support and to promote collective bargaining (but *not* to regulate or control it) were already becoming an accepted feature of the system as far back as the Fair Wages Resolution 1891 and the Conciliation Act 1896 – the *fons et origo* of ACAS.[2] After the Reports of the Whitley Committee 1917 consultation between employers and workers organized collectively became acceptable to, and even favoured by, government as a method of resolving industrial

1. Parl. Deb. HC 28 April 1909, cols, 387–8; see now Wages Councils Act 1979.
2. See, on the clause, Kahn-Freund (1948), pp. 269 and 429; on conciliation, Wedderburn and Davies (1969); and Davies (1978).

disputes. It was, of course, no accident that the same year saw the last reports of the Commissioners on Industrial Unrest.

This was the system of industrial relations which Kahn-Freund ultimately rationalized as one based on 'abstention' of the law or as 'collective laisser-faire', a structure to which, in his brilliant descriptions in the 1950s, he ascribed the virtues of 'a state of maturity' through non-reliance on the State or legal sanction.[3] This was (at any rate in peace-time) the supreme 'voluntary' system. His analysis and his influence – for example, on the law affecting collective agreements – is well recognized, by every labour law scholar, to have been 'brilliant and compelling'.[4] True, we begin now to see more confidently what may prove to be the transitional character of this system, with its insistence upon the primacy of collective bargaining; to acknowledge that the stability and 'equilibrium' so vital to Kahn-Freund rested often upon 'a middle-class acquiescence in the current balance of industrial power'.[5] Even so, it was a long transition, from the Trade Disputes Act 1906 to the new policies of 1979. Even the vindictive little statute passed in 1927 to punish the unions defeated in the General Strike the year before looked little more than a sidewind; Baldwin after all refused to abolish trade union 'legal immunities' as the employers demanded.[6]

Kahn-Freund saw the Industrial Relations Act 1971 as an event in which:

The law has now – to some extent – abandoned the previous policy [of 'abstention'] . . . we shall see whether legal compulsion or its threat is capable of remoulding industrial relations.[7]

The failure of the Act to achieve its objectives before its repeal in 1974 is well documented.[8] More to my present purpose, it is important to stress that the abandonment was intended only *'to some extent'*. For the authors and protagonists of the 1971 Act believed that it would produce:

The improvement of industrial relations in Britain [which could] only be secured by collective effort on the part of Government, managements, unions

3. See, respectively, Ginsberg (1959), p. 224; Flanders and Clegg (1954), p. 43.
4. See Lord Wedderburn, 'Otto Kahn-Freund and British Labour Law', in Wedderburn *et al.* (1983), ch. 3.
5. Wedderburn (1972), p. 270.
6. See the Special Study by G. McDonald in Morris (1976), p. 289 *et seq.*
7. Kahn-Freund (1972), p. 270; contrast 2nd edn, 1977, p. 276, after the repeal of the Act in 1974.
8. Weekes *et al.* (1975); Thomson and Engleman (1975).

and workers within a new framework of law which (i) sets national standards for good industrial relations; (ii) safeguards those who conform to them; (iii) protects industrial rights .... and (iv) provides new methods of resolving disputes.[9]

The Government desired 'collective bargaining between employers and strong representative trade unions supported by orderly procedures';[10] unions had only to register and accept the new National Industrial Relations Court in order to participate. Moreover, the Act was, they claimed, in line of descent not only from the Conservative Party's *Fair Deal at Work* (1968), but, in great measure, from the Labour Government's *In Place of Strife*, and from the great Donovan Report itself.[11] The Act was, of course, meant to clip the wings of the trade unions, and in that it carried the seeds of the strife to come. Even so, it was an ambiguous statute; it appeared to have two 'phantom draftsmen': one concerned with reform to produce greater 'order'; the other obsessed with 'individual rights'.[12] But it could be, and was, presented – not altogether without legitimacy – as pursuing the politics of 'reform', even if that meant greater elements of 'corporatism'.[13] Indeed, some radical commentators saw the 1971 Act as a 'Tory approach to reform', and thought more generally that 'reformism', by the mid-1970s, stood 'at something of an impasse'.[14] I could not myself agree that the 'reformism' of the 1971 Act had much in common with the Social Contract legislation of 1974–6; but it is obvious that both appealed, though in very different ways, to sentiments of the traditional politics in a manner not shared by the legislation of 1979–82.

The new policy of restriction

Jon Clark and I have recently suggested that the old traditional public policy which was partly replaced in 1971 has now been 'ruptured' and

9. *Consultative Document Industrial Relations Bill*, Department of Employment, 5 October 1970.
10. R. Carr, Secretary of State for Employment, Preface to Draft *Code of Industrial Relations Practice*, June 1971. The CBI believed the legislation would 'have a major influence on the future development of our industrial relations system' and stressed 'the importance of employers and their organizations taking the initiative' for reform: *Guidance to Employers on the Industrial Relations Bill* (1971), pp. 1 and 3.
11. Respectively Cmnd 3888, 1969, and Cmnd 3623, 1968.
12. Wedderburn (1972), p. 282.
13. See Crouch (1977), pts 3 and 4.
14. Goldthorpe in Clarke and Clements (1978), p. 215.

largely replaced by a new policy of 'restriction'. The *essence* here is to 'restrict the social power of trade unions', and

as part of a wider strategy to increase the power of employers and strengthen managerial control in industrial relations as a means of promoting greater efficiency and productivity in the economy

in a policy which considers that

trade unions are a distortion of the market relation between employer and employee, and trade union aspirations to regulate jobs and labour markets, even by way of *joint* regulation, are incompatible with individual liberty [my italics].[15]

By 1980, the new policy had been seen by others as one of 'coercion' of trade unions;[16] and recently Davies and Freedland, in a tentative but fascinating analysis of labour law through the window of 'anti-wage inflation strategies', see the 'policy of restriction' as complemented by that of 'Control by the Market', i.e.

direct attack upon the economic conditions which create union strength, rather than by use of positive law.[17]

It is clear that the new policy relies upon economic forces in what Professor Kaldor has called its aim 'to break real wage resistance'.[18] The doctrines of Professor Hayek are central to it: there can be 'no salvation for Britain until the special privileges granted to the trade unions three-quarters of a century ago are revoked': such nostrums have been adopted as part of a policy for a substitute 'incomes policy', where the policies of reform offered little to satisfy conventional wisdom which is convinced of the root evil of 'wage-push'.[19] But the 'free market' element operates mainly in the private sector; and the policy of 'restriction' must, in my view, lead inevitably to legal restrictions bordering on the authoritarian against the industrial rights of

15. J. Clark and Lord Wedderburn, 'Modern Labour Law: Problems, Functions and Policies', in Wedderburn *et al.* (1983), pp. 130–31 and 135. See that chapter for elaboration of these and other points in what follows.

16. Lewis and Simpson (1981).

17. P. Davies and M. Freedland, 'Labour Law and the Public Interest – Collective Bargaining and Economic Policy', in Wedderburn and Murphy (1983), ch. 2, pp. 17–18.

18. Kaldor (1983), p. 9 (reprint of his speech in the House of Lords on 16 April 1980).

19. Hayek (1980), p. 58; see also the discussion by Bill Wedderburn, 'Introduction: A 1912 Overture', in Wedderburn and Murphy (1983), ch. 1, pp. 4–7.

workers and effective, autonomous trade unionism in the *public* sector. To this we return later.

What, after all, have we seen in these four extraordinary years since 1979?[20] Let us look at the five headings.

First, the protective legislation for individual employees was severely restricted by adjusting the qualifying period and other rules about unfair dismissal and by narrowing maternity rights for women, restrictions often put forward on grounds which research had shown to be unfounded (such as the idea that, especially in small firms, employers refused to hire workers because of such legislation).[21] Secondly, the traditional policy of favouring union organization has been discarded. The non-unionist, secure in the knowledge that if dismissed as such he can claim the new minimum £12,000 from either his employer or, in the case of industrial pressure, from the union or its officials has been promoted to a legal status equal, if not superior, to that of the trade union member. The 1982 Act completed, the Secretary of State declared

the most comprehensive and the most effective statutory protection for non-union employees that we have ever had in this country,

and he followed through by asserting not only that requirements for work to be done by 'union labour only' are 'deliberately stifling competition', leading to 'loss of jobs' (another statement short on proof), but that 'the lump' is, if 'properly managed . . . a very effective institution'.[22]

Thirdly, the 1982 Act creates a new statutory tort in respect of employers' commercial pressure or trade union industrial pressure – pressure which is otherwise in every respect lawful – if *one* of the grounds for such pressure upon another employer party to a contract for goods or services is that the latter does not or is not likely to

20. What follows summarizes the main effects of the Unfair Dismissal (Variation of Qualifying Period) Order SI 1979 no. 959; Employment Act 1980 ss. 4–19; Employment Act ss. 2–19. On the 1980 Act see Lewis and Simpson (1981); on the 1982 Act, Lewis and Simpson (1982); Ewing (1982); Lord Wedderburn in Clerk and Lindsell (1982), ch. 15, pt 5; and J. Clark and Lord Wedderburn, in Wedderburn *et al.* (1983), ch. 6.

21. See Daniel and Stilgoe (1978), and Daniel (1981). The Department of Employment was widely believed to be in part responsible for non-publication of an authoritative survey of the closed shop by a research team led by Prof. J. Gennard during the passage of the Employment Bill 1982.

22. Parl. Deb. HC 8 February 1982, cols. 742–4.

recognize, negotiate or consult with a trade union. Pressure on another employer *not* to bargain is lawful. Pressure upon him to bargain, or even to consult with unions, is unlawful. And the ban remains even if he is under a legal duty to consult recognized union representatives – as in the case of safety committees or impending redundancies. Moreover, anyone 'adversely affected' can sue for an injunction and for damages the miscreant business or trade union which has thereby tried to extend the range of collective bargaining. Naturally, the trade unions and their officials are stripped of their normal 'immunities' in trade disputes in such cases. These sections are the clearest illustration of the reversal of the public policy favouring collective bargaining normally followed since 1917.[23] The statute declared a policy not even of neutrality. It is *against* the extension of collective consultation.

Fourthly, a great range of 'auxiliary' laws which have traditionally been 'props' or 'encouragements' for collective bargaining has now been swept away. These include the right of a union to unilateral arbitration for low-paid workers which (in some form) has existed since 1940, and the right of ACAS to require recognition of a union by an employer. Convention 94 of the ILO has been denounced and the Fair Wages Resolution rescinded – the first time since 1891 that contractors with government are not required to observe minimum conditions of employment. The 'fair wages' protection in the Road Haulage Wages Act 1938 is repealed. The government has declared that, when it can review its ILO obligations in 1985, we can expect the role of Wages Councils to be 'slimmed down'.[24] It has reduced the implementation of the EEC 'Transfer of Undertakings' Directive on employment protection to farcical Regulations[25] and is known to be bitterly opposed to the 'Vredeling' draft directive which aims to improve union rights to information and consultation in large and, especially transnational, enterprises in the Community.

23. For further discussion see Clark and Wedderburn, in Wedderburn *et al.* (1983), ch. 6, esp. pp. 162–3, 210 and n. 379; Lewis and Simpson (1982), pp. 228–33; Lord Wedderburn in Clerk and Lindsell (1982), ch. 15, para. 15–29(2).

24. See Parl. Deb. HL. 22 March 1982, col. 892. Within a fortnight of this lecture being given, the Secretary of State showed that he was determined to prevent the traditional operation of Wages Councils when, in an unprecedented intervention, he objected to an 8 per cent increase proposed by the Non-Food Wages Council for shop workers (raising the minimum wage to £67.50 per week), and was instrumental in securing the Council's agreement to only a 6 per cent rise: *Financial Times*, 12 March 1983.

25. See Davies and Freedland (1982); Hepple (1982).

As for industrial action – the fifth area – a new legislative technique has now been employed. Traditionally it has been the judges who have 'eroded' the immunities or (to use Davies and Freedland's happy phrasing) diminished 'the exclusion of common law regulation'[26] which Parliament has attempted to impose via the 'immunities'. Indeed, in many respects, the 'immunities' from civil liability in trade disputes (on which alone rests the legality of workers' withdrawal of their labour in whole or in part) are in many ways narrower now than under the Trade Disputes Act 1906. That is incontrovertibly the case with picketing. The uncertain protection in regard to 'interference with trade or business' has been repealed. The right of the strong to aid the weak has been emasculated, first by restoration of common law liabilities for so-called 'secondary action' in 1980, and then in 1982 by the redefinition of 'trade dispute' and especially of the term 'worker'. Even the traditional aid rendered altruistically by British workers to the enslaved crews of 'flag of convenience' ships is now regularly dubbed unlawful in our courts.[27] The new definition will also cause some disputes to be seen by the courts not as 'trade' but as 'political' disputes, for example, disputes about government 'privatization' of nationalized enterprises. In 1982, furthermore, common law liability in tort was reimposed upon the trade union itself, a very real threat to the depleted funds of contemporary unions (despite the ceiling on damages in a particular 'proceeding') and one reinforced by the imposition of a special statutory code in place of the common law principles of vicarious liability when an 'industrial' or 'economic' tort is alleged. The union and its officials are also threatened by new liabilities for industrial pressure by way of 'joinder' in the tribunals when non-unionists sue for unfair dismissal.

Similar though it may be to the policy of 1971 in its desire to reduce the influence of trade unions and of workers' collective action and to increase the rights of a somewhat reified 'individual', the new policy is nevertheless startlingly different from that of 1971. There is on the table no corporatist 'offer' of a 'deal' to trade unions. No new structure is envisaged into which they might be 'integrated'. Instead, the

26. Davies and Freedland (1979), p. 596. On what follows see especially ss. 16, 17 of the 1980 Act and ss. 7, 11 and 15–19 of the 1982 Act.

27. As to the illusory nature of the much-vaunted 'exceptions' in s. 17(3)(4), Employment Act 1980, see *Marina Shipping Ltd* v. *Laughton* [1982] QB 1127, CA; *Merkur Island Shipping* v. *Laughton* [1983] 2 AC 570 HL; see Wedderburn (1982), and *Industrial Law Journal*, 10 (1981), p. 113; Benedictus and Newell, *Industrial Law Journal*, 11 (1982), p. 111.

effect of the statutes of 1980 and 1982 has been to whittle away the right to withdraw labour to a level below that which is acceptable in most pluralist democracies today.

Indeed, it has become 'difficult to define the natural boundaries of the new strategy'.[28] Events have moved too fast for the ink to dry. In 1982, no sooner did one think that the Fair Wages Resolution might be rescinded than it was abruptly swept away with little apology. As one wondered whether the 1913 compromise on political funds of trade unions would 'still be sacred', up popped a Green Paper to show that the Government was out to scrap that too.[29] No sooner had the logic of the market sunk in than it was made clear that it would indeed apply to the 'sweated trades' and Wages Councils. In 1982 we asked: 'Will the restriction strategy lead inevitably to legislation on the maintenance of "public" or "essential services"?' Now that the legislature had 'learned from the judges the central technique of "modifying" the immunities' and of manipulating 'non-interventionist' institutions in the service of restricting trade union activity, it seemed logical that it should use the new weapon of removing 'immunities' (coupled perhaps with compulsory arbitration, or even an 'up to date' version of criminal liabilities) against workers in the public sector or in 'essential services'. To government eyes they would no doubt appear to be using their 'monopoly powers' to obstruct the economic and social market, and especially to hinder the proper 'pricing' of jobs.[30] Such developments go hand in hand with

the deliberate policy, since 1979, of taking government off its pedestal as a model for progressive labour-relations policies.[31]

Even in industrial training the record of government in the last three years has been one of dismantling tripartite machinery set up by law.

28. Clark and Wedderburn, in Wedderburn *et al.* (1983), ch. 6, p. 210; on the importance of s. 15 of the 1982 Act and the lack of a 'command structure' in the trade unions upon which vicarious liability can be structured, see pp. 199–206, and on 'joinder' crossing a 'legal and ideological Rubicon', p. 207.

29. Clark and Wedderburn, in Wedderburn *et al.* (1983), Ch. 6, p. 211; *Democracy in Trade Unions*, Cmnd 8778, ch. 4 [and now Trade Union Bill 1984].

30. Clark and Wedderburn, in Wedderburn *et al.* (1983), ch. 6, pp. 211–4 (where the role of the media is also mentioned); and see G. Morris, 'Essential Services, the Law and the Community', in Wedderburn and Murphy (1983), esp. pp. 25–6 on s. 5, Conspiracy and Protection of Property Act 1875 and the proposals of the Centre for Policy Studies.

31. B. Hepple, 'Labour Law and Public Employees', in Wedderburn and Murphy (1983), ch. 7, p. 78.

Today one finds that both the Prime Minister and the Secretary of State do indeed have in mind new legal measures against workers in the public sector, the natural drift of the policy of 'restriction' – legislation in relation to such 'abuse of monopoly power' as was evinced in the 1983 national strike by water-workers, possibly to enforce arbitration agreements, or (since these can be broken or not concluded) to impose 'a statutory duty to continue the supply of essential services'.[32] At this point, there are present the seeds of a dangerously illiberal, even authoritarian, thread in the skein of the market-orientated restriction policy. The services that are 'essential' to a modern community are hard to define; they clearly range from power-stations, electrical and nuclear, through fire-stations, gasworks and ambulance-stations on to doctors, nurses, police and sewerage workers.[33] But why end there? The Government observed in 1981:

[The] interdependent nature of industry means that a case can now be made for regarding a strike by most groups of workers as threatening essential services or supplies.[34]

A statutory duty to ensure services entails, of course, the risk of introducing forced labour.

Other writers have adverted to the dangers of authoritarianism that lurk both in the Government's ill-defined powers to use troops and in the demands of new (especially nuclear) technology.[35] Ironically, it was the Heath Government that repealed the special and 'selective'

32. Margaret Thatcher, Prime Minister, Parl. Deb. HC 24 February 1983; N. Tebbit, Secretary of State for Employment, Evidence to HC Employment Committee, *The Times*, 17 February 1983 (referring to the proposals in the Green Paper, *Trade Union Immunities*, Cmnd 8128, 1981).

33. All these are named by the Centre for Policy Studies, which has recommended a ban on strikes in essential services with rights of action for those suffering (including next of kin) and for the Attorney General: see *The Times* and the *Guardian*, 19 February 1982. (See now the Centre's *The Right to Strike in a Free Society*, March 1983.)

34. *Trade Union Immunities*, Cmnd 8128, 1981, para. 334. Most legal systems do differentiate in respect of 'essential service' workers: cf. G. Morris, in Wedderburn and Murphy (1983), ch. 3, citing Pankert, 'Settlement of Labour Disputes in Essential Services' *International Labour Review*, November 1980, p. 723. The SDP proposes legislation on 'life and limb' risks, to impose a pause for arbitration: SDP, *Reforming the Unions*, p. 27.

35. See e.g. C. Whelan, in Wedderburn and Murphy (1983), ch. 4, and *Industrial Law Journal*, 8 (1979), p. 222, on troops; on the police G. Morris, *Industrial Law Journal*, 9 (1980), p. 1; and on nuclear power workers R. Lewis, *Industrial Law Journal*, 7 (1978), p. 1. See, too, Elias *et al.* (1980), pp. 290–93.

criminal sanctions under the 1875 Act applicable to gas, water and electricity workers, because it believed that 'the necessary safeguard against action leading to serious harm is provided by section 5', – the section of that Act which makes it criminal to strike in breach of contract causing risk to life or property.[36] No doubt it is instructive that no prosecution has apparently ever been launched under that section. But recent experience suggests we should not rely on that. Certainly it is increasingly difficult to designate just what is an 'essential' service or industry, or even which disputes may create an 'emergency', in our type of society.[37] It seems inevitable that, if continued, the policy of restriction will feel compelled to use special legal weapons, which it has so far kept largely in reserve, to abate 'real wage resistance' to its policies by public sector workers. Yet it is more than fifty years since Harold Laski rejected Leon Duguit's claim that the State may and must make strikes illegal where stoppages would dislocate enterprises 'at the very heart of social organization'. Not only would such a law be futile; Laski added, in words which Kahn-Freund echoed even in his last pessimistic years: 'I do not think the right to strike can be denied to any vocation.'[38] Even more worrying, in terms of liberty and democracy, is the character of the debate promoted in the 1983 Green Paper. This carries various traits of authoritarianism; it accuses the trade union movement of fraud and malpractice in general terms, which history will show to be false; and it is prepared to consider legal measures that go to any lengths to compel trade unions to submit, such as providing, for unions which fail to comply with new statutory provisions on rule-books, 'for the taking over by an outside authority of the running of the business of the trade union in the interest of its members'.[39] If that sanction applied in respect of failure to meet standards set for the rules, it would *a fortiori* be logical to apply it in respect of breaches of other parts of the restrictive legislation. The plan seems to be for the State, having shackled political activities and industrial action by trade unions, to be ready with a team of Trade Union Receivers to take

36. *Industrial Relations Bill Consultative Document*, Dept of Employment, 5 October 1970.

37. For a comparison of different systems see Aaron and Wedderburn (1972), ch. 6; and on North America S. Anderman, in Wedderburn and Murphy (1983), ch. 7. On the British experience 1971–4, Weekes *et al.* (1975), pp. 213–8; *Sec. of State* v. *ASLEF* (No. 2) [1972] ICR 19, CA.

38. Laski (1925), pp. 254–5, 515. See Kahn-Freund (1979), pp. 75–88.

39. *Democracy in Trade Unions*, Cmnd 8778, 1983.

over any that refuse to submit. One wonders what the response would be to parallel proposals for the seizure of companies formed by capital. No doubt, the army of consultants who have recently arrived from the United States to advise employers how to *resist* unionization would prosper in this framework – especially in the absence even of statutory reporting provisions.[40] More important, one is reminded of one of the last sentences written by Kahn-Freund – for a German audience:

> The German reader of this book, who is acquainted to some extent with the history of Germany over the last half century, will not need to be reminded of the immense general political significance of the maintenance of internally active trade unions.[41]

Alternative policies

There are alternative policies. If one envisages a general change or deflection of direction, what is the lawyer likely to contribute? It is no part of my purpose to place this question here in the context of particular party-political programmes. But most alternatives to the market economics and labour law policy of restriction now on offer by government have certain features in common: they would operate a more 'managed', less market-orientated economic policy, above all in order to fight unemployment; and to that end, and in seeking to rediscover wider areas of social *consensus*, they would attempt to involve the trade unions in a common effort. 'Tripartitism' would find renewed favour; more, at any rate, than it now receives in Whitehall. Of course, the political programmes which would require extensive legislation in favour of rights of consultation and participation for workpeople and their trade unions necessarily rely, in the current crisis, on tripartite structures. Such policies diverge, too, (though not always explicitly) from the 'individualist' ethic of current policies. In particular, both 'corporatist' forms of 'tripartitism' and policies which aim to reduce 'corporatism' by maintaining decentralized, direct democratic structures acknowledge that individual workers gain freedom largely by collective organization. More radical attitudes perceive the *individual* employment relationship, as Kahn-Freund

40. See Craver (1978).
41. O. Kahn-Freund, in Wedderburn *et al.* (1983), ch. 1, p. 7 (translated after his death from the German). See, too, Kahn-Freund (1979), p. 20, for a similar statement.

thought, to be a relation of *subordination* and *submission* concealed by the 'figment' of a contract.[42] It would be inevitable (to put it at its lowest) that in the presence of such policies the price of trade union cooperation would be the revision, if not the total repeal, of the statutory measures of 1980 and 1982 and a return to something more like traditional labour law policy. No doubt the return cannot resurrect the old 'abstentionist' system. But there must be a return to the acceptance of collective organization and strong trade unionism. But a return in what legal form? To the 'immunities'? It is my belief that we are witnessing the beginnings of an unhappily formalistic debate on that question. My objective here is to suggest that a formalistic debate on that issue will be counter-productive and may even obscure the real problems.

Some aspects of the issues can be dealt with quickly. For example, it is sometimes suggested that the laws of 1974–6, simply by being enacted, in some way 'caused' the retrogressive legislation of 1980 and 1982. This mistakes the place of law, its 'secondary force in human affairs, and especially in labour relations'.[43] I have, for example, heard it said that section 23(1)(c) of the Employment Protection (Consolidation) Act 1978 somehow 'facilitated' the law enacted by the Employment Act 1980 section 15(1), which by repealing four words of the 1978 section totally changed its meaning and function. It seems hardly likely that the draftsmen of 1980 would have been incapable of composing the laws they wished to have even if there had never been a 1978 Act. Of course, precisely what the *social* effect of the individual 'employment protection' legislation had and is having is not clear, not least in the ways it has affected industrial bargaining and behaviour. The evidence so far does not suggest that it has 'juridified' the system to the disadvantage of trade unions; and it has certainly not had any effect remotely comparable with the forces of the labour market.[44]

But let us return to the 'immunities'. It is now widely accepted that they too were the product not of legal, but of social causes. The difference between Britain's legal 'immunities' and the legal 'rights'

42. Kahn-Freund (2nd edn, 1977), p. 6. On plans for future tripartitism and rights of unions on a decentralized basis see the joint TUC/Labour Party *Economic Planning and Industrial Democracy* (1982).

43. Kahn-Freund (2nd edn, 1977), p. 2.

44. See Clark and Wedderburn, in Wedderburn *et al.* (1983), ch. 6, pp. 184–98, for the arguments on the effects of the 'Social Contract' legislation. B. Simpson has suggested that such a framework could 'easily be amended in pursuit of policies contrary to those for which it was envisaged': *Industrial Law Journal*, 8 (1979), p. 83.

available to French, German or Austrian trade unions, said Kahn-Freund, 'reflects the histories of the various working-class move-ments'.[45] Our 'unique legal solution to the common problem of trade union illegality' rested upon the unique conjunction of three *social* events in Britain's industrial revolution: comparatively strong unions at an early date; the absence in the formative period of a working-class political party; and the absence of universal male franchise – all emerging in a laisser-faire society.[46] The legal protections – it is now generally agreed, even by the 1981 Green Paper *Trade Union Immun-ities*[47] – were the British method of providing the elementary social 'rights' which in other legal systems are sometimes – not always and not all – provided by legal rights (and obligations): especially in three rights always claimed by trade unionists – the rights to combine, to be recognized by employers for bargaining and to withdraw labour.[48] Of course, the form of our general law did play a role in this history, not least the absence of a written constitution; it contributed, but it was relatively minor cause. The critical factors that gave to share-holders *rights* to associate in limited liability companies after 1855, but provided the right to associate collectively to trade unionists after 1871 primarily by way of *immunities*, were not legal but social. The nature of these statutory 'immunities' must never be misunderstood, and the problems inherent in their form are well known:

In substance, behind the form, the statute provides liberties or rights which the common law would deny to unions. The 'immunity' is mere form . . . One of the problems inherent in this way of doing things is that the judges remain in a strategically very powerful position.[49]

The question remains, of course, as to how far a change of form might affect their powers.

Judging the immunities

Recently, writers on labour law have once again suggested that the 'immunities' should be scrapped in favour of a system of statutory

45. Kahn-Freund (1949), p. 172, n. 154. Later he slightly changed the emphasis; see Kahn-Freund (1977), p. 39.

46. See Wedderburn *et al.* (1983), ch. 3, pp. 36–9; and Wedderburn (1980).

47. *Trade Union Immunities*, Cmnd 8128, 1981, ch. 5.

48. The three rights claimed by the TUC in 1982 with which Mr Tebbit, Secretary of State, said he had 'no quarrel', as his 1982 Bill did not interfere with them: Parl. Deb. HC 8 February 1982, col. 744.

49. Wedderburn (2nd edn, 1971), p. 314.

'positive' rights. The Donovan Committee considered the point – not a new one even in 1968 – but it believed that nothing would be 'improved by granting the right to strike in express terms'.[50] Indeed, the fact is that proposals for positive rights to strike, etc., have normally been put forward in recent times by those who have wished to see a more legally regulated system of collective bargaining; and, of course, the right should be subject to 'reasonable limitations' as a CBI report put it.[51] Such limitations are now, we should note at once, less likely to find agreement in our society in the 1980s than twenty years ago.[52]

But this is not a sufficient answer to those who, having worked hard to master the techniques of a complex system of law and watched the judiciary time and again subvert its very purposes, conclude that 'over seventy years' experience has shown that no amount of legislative tinkering with the "golden formula" will remedy the imbalance of industrial power', and who call for the 'total exclusion of industrial relations' (or at least of interlocutory processes) from injunctive relief.[53] So, too, a policy of:

legislative pirouettes attempting to circumvent the legal perspective by stipulating immunity in defined circumstances is inadequate . . . A statute which in principle prohibited the employer from carrying on his operation in the circumstances of a trade dispute would resolve the problems of picketing to a very large extent.[54]

One can readily understand and share the emotions raised by the century or more of legal struggle for effective trade union rights. Moreover, much of this writing approaches the issue pragmatically, asking after the effect of the law on particular industrial power relationships. This is surely right. The debate about 'immunities' or 'positive rights' must be neither wholly technical nor theological. Secondly, however, such propositions, if put into legislative form,

50. *Report*, Cmnd 3623, 1968, para. 935. For early proposals of 'positive rights' by trade unionists, see Jenkins and Mortimer (1968).

51. *Trade Unions in a Changing World; The Challenge for Management* (discussion document; CBI 'Steering Group', 1980), p. 22.

52. Wedderburn (1980), pp. 82–3; (2nd edn, 1971), p. 401.

53. B. Doyle, *Modern Law Review*, 42 (1979), p. 462; to the same effect, K. Ewing, *Industrial Law Journal*, 11 (1982), p. 218.

54. Bercusson (1977), p. 292. See, too, his interesting 'Labour Law and the Public Interest: A Policy Appraisal', in Wedderburn and Murphy (1983), ch. 18; and *Industrial Law Journal*, 9 (1980), p. 232.

would still require a *definition* of 'industrial relations' or 'trade dispute'. To this we return. Such definitions of basic concepts of labour law constitute 'limiting factors' determining the scope of rights available to employer, workers and trade unions.

Thirdly, one can sympathize with the impatience that shines through much modern commentary at the role of our judges for over a century in labour law. The invention of special doctrines on criminal conspiracy in 1872; on civil liability and conspiracy in 1901; *ultra vires* and political activity in 1910; the apparent conversion of the judges to an understanding of 'non-intervention' when 'Labour says: "Where are your impartial Judges?"', and when the balance of power lay with employers, or later synthesized in a war effort; the re-emergence of judicial erosion of the 'immunities' in the 1950s and 1960s, above all, by way of the economic torts; the invention of new torts such as 'intimidation' in 1964 (a 'frontal attack', Kahn-Freund held, 'on the right to strike'); the granting of labour injunctions not only in inter-locutory proceedings but even *ex parte* – this is a small part of a tale well known and often told.[55] So too, the statutory protection of peaceful picketing was approached by judges determined to decide rights of workers in the law of nuisance and obstruction as though they were on a par with persons 'carrying banners advertising some patent medicine or advocating some political reform' in 1967; or with hitch-hikers in 1974; implicitly confirming the pronouncement of Lindley L. J. in 1896: 'You cannot make a strike effective without doing more than is lawful.'[56] Those who doubt whether 'many judges have yet learned the simple historical truth' that immunities are not *ipso facto* 'privileges'[57] must then ask how many of today's judicial hearts do not still beat in rhythm with the robust and masterly declar-ation of Lord Bramwell in 1891 in the legislature:

55. See respectively *Quinn* v. *Leathem* [1901] AC 495, HL; *Taff Vale Rlwy Co.* v. *Amal. Soc. of Rlwy Servants* [1901] AC 426, HL; *Amal. Soc. of Rlwy Servants* v. *Osborne* [1910] AC 87, HL; Scrutton L. J., *Cambridge Law Journal* (1923), p. 8; *Crofter Hand Woven Harris Tweed Co.* v. *Veitch* [1942] AC 435, HL; *Cunard SS* v. *Stacey* [1955] 2 Lloyd's Rep. 245, CA; *Torquay Hotel Ltd* v. *Cousins* [1969] 2 Ch. 106, CA; *Square Corp. Reinforcement Ltd* v. *MacDonald* [1968] SLT 65; O. Kahn-Freund *Federation News*, 14 (1964), p. 41; Wedderburn, (2nd edn, 1971) ch. 8.

56. Respectively *Tynan* v. *Balmer* [1967] 1 QB 91; *Broome* v. *DPP* [1974] AC 587, 597; *Lyons* v. *Wilkins* [1896] 1 Ch. 811, 825.

57. Clark and Wedderburn *et al.* (1983), ch. 6, p. 168. See too Davies and Freedland (1982), chs. 8 and 9; Griffith (1981), ch. 3; Wedderburn (2nd edn, 1971), chs. 1, 7 and 8; Lewis and Simpson (1981), chs. 9 and 10; Wedderburn (1980).

I have said and do say there is nothing unlawful in picketing, provided that it is lawfully practised, but that is what it never is.[58]

In three quick strokes, game set and match to the common law.

Even when they were rectifying a line of cases in the Court of Appeal that were little less than outrageous distortions of the 'golden formula',[59] most of the Law Lords in the famous modern trilogy of decisions of 1979–80 took the occasion to state that, properly interpreted, the immunities (which, as Lord Scarman demonstrated, effectively reproduced the 1906 protections) were 'intrinsically repugnant'; tending 'to stick in judicial gorges' – 'unpalatable'; and above all 'privileges'; and when Lord Salmon said: 'surely the time has come for it [the law on trade disputes] to be altered', he knew that Government proposals to do just that were on their way to the statute book.[60] Indeed, the 'emotively charged illustrations' of what might be within the 'golden formula' (driving an employer out of business, or demands fierce enough 'to bring down the fabric of the present economic system') led some commentators understandably to see these ostensibly liberal decisions as 'thinly disguised justifications for changing the law, if not an invitation to the government to propose changes to Parliament'.[61]

Moreover, even when one examines those English decisions on civil conspiracy which are thought to prove that 'judicial hostility' has not always been a constant feature,[62] one finds that even these decisions favoured 'the big battalions of labour and capital' standing against the

58. Debate on the 'Scotch Railway Strike', Parl. Deb. HL 6 March 1891, col. 371. Nobody could object if 'the picketers . . . had merely met their fellow workmen in a friendly way and asked them to join, with nothing but a kind persuasiveness in their manner'. The parallel in tone with the 1981 *Code* on picketing is remarkable.

59. See, on the Court of Appeal cases, Ewing (1979) concluding that, if unions' rights were established, 'the present formula will need major revisions or . . . a fresh statutory initiative will have to be offered' (p. 146). The Court of Appeal went to the brink of unconstitutional behaviour in its insistence upon making union officials liable: *Duport Steels Ltd* v. *Sirs* [1980] 1 All ER 541.

60. See *Express Newspapers Ltd* v. *McShane* [1980] AC 672, 687 (Lord Diplock), 690 (Lord Salmon); *Duport Steels Ltd* v. *Sirs* [1980] ICR 161, 177, 184 (Lord Diplock), 186 (Lord Edmund-Davies), 188 (Lord Keith). Contrast Lord Scarman's analyses in [1980] ICR 189–93; and in *NWL* v. *Woods* [1979] ICR 867, 885–9; and see Lord Wedderburn, *Modern Law Review*, 45 (1980), p. 319.

61. R. Simpson, *Modern Law Review*, 45 (1980), pp. 335–6, especially on Lord Diplock's opinion *NWL* v. *Woods* [1979] ICR, p. 878.

62. See R. Tur, 'The Legitimacy of Industrial Action', in Wedderburn and Murphy (1983), Ch. 16, p. 156, offering *Reynolds* v. *Shipping Fedn* [1924] 1 Ch. 28; the *Crofter* case, *supra*, n. 55; above, Reading 36.

small militant union or small producers: corporatist, not radical, decisions.[63] Indeed, it is scarcely possible to discover in the long history of the 'golden formula' an important reported judgment which advanced the collective interests as such of workers effectively and unequivocally on a critical point of law. Even the two decisions in which Lord Scarman's thoughtfully informed opinion on industrial relations led the Law Lords to that attitude in judgment were made in the context of the repeal of the relevant legislation, – a posthumous endorsement of a more liberal stance.[64] Even the refusal of the Law Lords in 1982 to adopt the most draconian view of remaining trade union freedoms left commentators doubtful,[65] especially when a majority of the Law Lords subsequently refused to include a world-wide trade union industrial practice as giving rise to a 'trade dispute', preferring in the classical style to equate a trade union demand for payments to a workers' welfare fund to a demand for payment to guerrillas in El Salvador (a view that Lord Scarman found little less than 'cynicism').[66] That decision, it is to be remembered, was rendered under the old definition before the 1982 Act's changes in the definition of 'trade dispute'. And to rub the point home, it is always open for the judges to say with Lord Denning MR, and with Hohfeldian accuracy:

[When] Parliament granted immunities to the leaders of trade unions, it did not give them any *rights*. It did not give them a *right* to break the law or to do wrong by inducing people to break contracts. It only gave them immunity if they did.[67]

63. See Wedderburn (2nd edn, 1971), p. 30.
64. *UKAPE* v. *ACAS* [1981] AC 424, HL; *EMA* v. *ACAS* [1980] ICR 215, HL, on ss. 11–16 of the 1975 Act, repealed by s. 19(*b*) Employment Act 1980. Compare too the posthumous relations of *GAS* v. *TGWU* [1976] IRLR 224, HL, with *Heatons Transport* v. *TGWU* [1973] AC 15 HL.
65. *Hadmor Production Ltd* v. *Hamilton* [1982] 2 WLR 322, HL; Simpson, *Modern Law Review*, 45 (1982), p. 454, doubts whether 'the integrity of [the legal non-interventionist] framework could ever be restored'.
66. *Universe Tankships of Monrovia Inc.* v. *ITWF* [1982] 2 WLR 803, HL; see Wedderburn (1982); Lord Diplock felt it necessary to apologize (pp. 818–9) to the lower courts for his formulation of the law on the golden formula in the *NWL* case, *supra*, thereby again evincing the unpredictability of judicial temperament in this area. See below, n. 103.
67. *Express Newspapers Ltd* v. *McShane* [1979] ICR 210, 218 CA. Oddly, in jurisprudential terms this view was inconsistent with Lord Denning's view that acts rendered 'not actionable' by the immunities were 'lawful' (see e.g. *Stratford* v. *Lindley* [1965] AC 269, 285), contrary to Lord Pearce's view (*ibid.* p. 336), which was later held to be 'wrong' in the *Hadmor* case, *supra*.

The language of 'immunities' gives judges easy, semantic points of entry. But that is the beginning, not the end, of our inquiry. Some judges never lack points of entry to ground they mean to occupy.

Unavoidable problems

So it is perhaps an understandable feeling of impotence in the face of this century of obstructive interpretation (now joined by the Parliamentary policy of restriction) that has caused some commentators recently to declare that 'the present immunities represent a very insecure foundation for the freedom to strike'. Such writers advance the argument that the best method of guaranteeing 'the freedom to strike' today may be by way of 'a positive right to strike', a method 'which has a number of virtues though they should not be exaggerated'. The method is, however, thought to be virtuous enough to reverse the burden of proof: 'So whatever may be the arguments against a right to strike they have yet to be convincingly made.'[68]

One objective in choosing 'positive rights' is of course to secure the clear formulation of minimum standards for the rights to associate, to bargain and to strike – as well as the semantic advantages of 'rights' over 'immunities'. The facts of economic recession do not necessarily preclude such progressive measures. The great labour law reforms in France illustrated that last year.[69] But rights cannot be discussed in the abstract. The arguments *for* 'positive rights' must themselves meet certain standards if they are on the agenda. It is not clear that this has yet been achieved.

For example, what is to be the definition of a 'strike'? That very definition is a limiting factor in any labour law system. The Donovan Report in 1968 asked whether it would apply to 'unofficial' or 'unconstitutional' strikes?[70] The 'golden formula' has always applied to *any person* acting in furtherance of a trade dispute, a very liberal tradition that has avoided the granting of industrial rights to 'official' action,

68. Elias and Ewing (1982), pp. 356–8 (who summarize the case which other writers have supported). Their account of the torts was overtaken by some later developments: see Wedderburn (1983).

69. See J. M. Verdier, 'Les Réformes et le Droit Syndical', *Droit Social* (1982) 291; J. C. Javillier, Y. Delamotte and C. Morel, 'Les Projets de Loi Auroux', *Regards Sur L'Actualité*, Juillet-Août 1982, 3, 11 and 19; J. C. Javillier, *Les Réformes du Droit du Travail Depuis le 10 Mai 1981*, (1982). The French reforms introduce a new right to bargain.

70. *Report*, Cmnd 3623, para. 943 (in the context of 'suspension' of employment contracts). References below are to this paragraph of the Report.

or to unions approved by the State. In this respect, it is not the case that an explicit decision is made 'in any legal system' on the status of 'unofficial' action,[71] or at least not in the traditional British system. One of the rocks on which the 1971 Act foundered was its insistence that only official action by state-licensed trade unions could be lawful. We want no more positive rights of that sort.

So, too, the traditional formula applies to lesser forms of industrial action, to a 'go slow', to a 'work to rule', to 'working without enthusiasm'. Would the new positive right? Existing British legislation refrains from defining generally the phrase 'strike or other industrial action'; but the courts have held (to the detriment of workers' rights) that it includes an overtime ban which is *not* a breach of workers' employment contracts, because that is a 'combined application of pressure' on the employer.[72] There is no obvious or common international meaning even for these basic concepts. As for concepts, the French constitutional 'right to strike' sees a 'go slow' or a 'work to rule' as not a 'strike' at all; it is only 'defective execution of work' and not a 'concerted cessation'. German law accepts a 'work to rule' as a 'strike'. Swedish law accepts a stoppage by even one worker as a 'strike' if he acts on union instruction. As for legality, the Italian constitutional 'right to strike' extends to strikes for political objectives, but the French does not, except for 'demonstration' strikes. An Italian 'strike' requires a concerted stoppage for common ends, but permits as lawful 'rolling', intermittent or 'hiccup' strikes by groups of workers (*sciopero articolato* or *a singhiozzo*); these are within the pale in France only so long as they *are* real stoppages (*grèves tournantes*) rather than *débrayage répété* (repeated short-term disengagements) except in respect of public sector workers for whom rolling strikes are forbidden.[73]

These matters are not technicalities. The concepts of 'strike' and the legality provided by each system reflect the social and historical roots of its own labour law and its own society. It is, therefore, quite

71. Elias and Ewing (1982) p. 357. It is of course true that the extent of a positive right to strike 'would depend to a very large extent on the government in power'.

72. *Power Packing Casemakers Ltd* v. *Faust*, [1983] 2 WLR 439, CA (no jurisdiction therefore in respect of unfair dismissal). The definitions in Employment Protection (Consolidation) Act 1978, Sched. 13, para. 24(1) of 'lock-out' and 'strike' are for the purposes only of determining 'continuous employment' (s. 151). Then have been used, however, as guidance generally: *Coates* v. *Modern Methods and Materials Ltd* [1980] IRLR 318, 321; *McCormick* v. *Horsepower Ltd* [1980] ICR 278, 281. But contrast *Rasool* v. *Hepworth Pipe* [1980] ICR 494, 509 (definition no help on 'other industrial action').

pointless to propose a discussion of a 'positive right to strike' *in principle*. Discussion can be meaningful only if the proponents make clear what kind of *right*, what kinds of *strikes*, what extent of *legality*, they have in mind.

I note in parenthesis that it is highly arguable that the central core of these legal concepts on industrial conflict tends to be established at a time or over a period of strong consensus when a labour movement is strong, as in Italy in the years following the constitution of 1948, or when the labour movement is too weak to oppose a system which it later comes to accept, as happened with the Labour Court and binding collective agreements in Sweden in 1928 and did not happen here in 1971–4. Perhaps our unwillingness or our inability in Britain to achieve a shared definition of 'strike or other industrial action' in 1974–8 says something about the continuing social division which followed the defeated attempt to impose alien labour law concepts on trade unions in 1971. It may also be a reason why, with our society fragmented as never before in the post-war period, today – or even tomorrow – may not be the right moment to make another attempt.

But protagonists of 'positive rights' have no choice. One must define the rights which one proposes. This is particularly true if one argues (as perhaps one should) that:

> The essence of a *right* to strike as opposed to a liberty to strike is that those exercising the right are protected against any prejudice or detriment in consequence of having struck, particularly at the hands of their employer.[74]

This raises, *inter alia*, the issue of the effect of industrial action upon individual employment contracts. Whether or not notice is

---

74. P. O'Higgins, 'The Right to Strike – Some International Reflections', in Carby-Hall (1976), ch. 3, relying especially upon the European Social Charter, Art. 6, of which both the Industrial Relations Act 1971 and TULRA 1974, he alleged, were in breach: p. 117.

---

73. See H. Sinay, *La Grève* (1966, Mise A Jour 1979, Dalloz), paras. 60–65, 74–5, 85–91; G. Camerlynck and G. Lyon-Caen, *Droit du Travail* (10th edn, 1980), paras. 691–712, 735–40; J. C. Javillier, *Droit du Travail* (1981, Mis A Jour 1982), paras. 635–69; G. Giugni, *Diritto Sindacale* (1979), pp. 179–213; G. Ghezzi and U. Romagnoli, *Il Diritto Sindacali* (1982), paras. 321–41; G. Halback, A. Martins, R. Schwedes, O. Wlotzke Ubersicht, *Recht der Arbeit* (1981) p. 236; W. Däubler, *Das Arbeitsrecht* (1976), ch. 5; Folke Schmidt, *Law and Industrial Relations in Sweden* (1977), ch. 11, esp. pp. 164–6; see, too, the different understandings in these systems of the term 'lock-out'; cf. on Britain B. Hepple, 'Lock-outs in Great Britain' (1980), *Recht der Arbeit*, s. 25.

given, English law regards a strike and most other forms of industrial action as a breach of the relevant employment contracts.[75] The failure of Lord Denning's attempt to introduce a doctrine of 'suspension' resulted not only from the clear precedents against it, but also from his failure to answer most of the major questions posed on this matter in 1968 by the Donovan Report: was a strike notice required? If so, of what length to bring about suspension? Could the employer dismiss or discipline the workers during suspension? Could the suspended strikers take other jobs? How could we know when the strike had terminated? Suppose it went on for years? Or for ever? Could the parties 'contract out' of the doctrine, either individually or through collective agreements?[76] It is well known that in French law (as in many other systems) a strike does not *per se* break the employee's contract, but that the employer can dismiss for *faute lourde* (grave misconduct); less is known about the complex case law concerning *faute lourde individuelle*, *faute lourde collective* (let alone *faute grave* and *faute légère*).[77] What would English judges make of all that?

The problem of dismissal by the employer goes to the root of the issue. Our employment protection legislation has long provided that the tribunals shall have no jurisdiction if the employer dismisses without discrimination *all* the workers taking part in the industrial action.[78] Though this provision has now been greatly amended so as to favour the managerial interests of the employer[79] the primary reason for this odd legal structure remains unchanged. If dismissal by reason of a strike without victimization were made justifiable, the principles by which a strike is to be accounted 'reasonable' would be placed squarely into the hands of the tribunals, and before long therefore into the hands of the judges of the Court of Appeal and House of Lords. How do proponents of 'positive rights' deal with that issue?

75. *Simmons* v. *Hoover Ltd* [1977] 1 QB 284; see Davies and Freedland (1982), pp. 246, 651–9.

76. *Report*, para. 943; see Lord Denning MR, *Morgan* v. *Fry* [1968]2 QB 710, 728–30. In rare cases the notice may be the basis of a variation of the terms of employment: see Davies L. J., *Morgan* v. *Fry*, *supra*, p. 731; but contrast Lord Donovan in *Stratford* v. *Lindley* [1965] AC, p. 342. Lord Denning MR, op. cit did suggest an answer on the length of the notice required, i.e. the same as that needed to terminate the employment contract. It is not obvious that the two periods should necessarily be the same.

77. See J. C. Javillier, op. cit., paras. 346–8; 634; Camerlynck and Lyon-Caen, op. cit., paras. 727–8.

78. Now s. 62 Employment Protection (Consolidation) Act 1978.

79. See s. 9 Employment Act 1982; Wallington (1983).

How should – or could – the legislation effectively guide the courts on that issue? How far would judicial principles on 'reasonable strike' invade the rest of labour law? And what is to happen to the employment contract – and the power to dismiss – in a lock-out? Would the current equivalence of strikes and lock-outs be continued? Many would argue that withdrawal of labour should be treated with more liberality than a withdrawal of the opportunity to work. If so, would a 'positive rights' system distinguish the two rights in its approach?

I am not suggesting that these questions might not be satisfactorily answered. But proposals that fail to confront them do not contribute to the debate. Instead, the introduction of 'rights' without thinking through such questions in detail could result in handing to judges who so often call for greater 'clarity' in labour law[80] an easier opportunity to control the legality of industrial action by way of *a priori* concepts of 'fault'. The concepts are ready to hand; and part of the judiciary is eager to apply them, so as to say who is 'right' in a dispute.

> The public suffers from every industrial dispute. Ought they not to know who is right? Adopting this new approach they *would* know, for the court which investigated the dispute would tell them.[81]

We have a good comparative example to hand of a modern labour law system in which a 'right' to strike has been limited by judicial concepts of 'social adequacy' or 'disproportionality' (i.e. the judges' view of who is socially 'right'). German labour law illustrates the manner in which the right can be reduced to the narrow range of judicially moulded 'ultima ratio', exercisable by official trade unions alone in a narrow compass.

> Thus the court fills the gap which exists through the lack of compulsory settlement or even of statutory settlement procedures in German law.[82]

Nothing is worse than the assumption that 'positive rights' *necessarily* afford a wider area of industrial legality than a statutory 'immunity'. Both the historical and the comparative study of labour law systems prove any such assumption to be false.

80. See Sir John Donaldson MR, *Merkur Island Shipping Corpn* v. *Laughton* [1983] 2 WLR 45, 66. The objectives of Lord Scarman were different in that he did not wish to be made a 'back seat driver' in trade disputes, *Duport Steels Ltd* v. *Sirs* [1980] ICR, p. 193; *Express Newspapers Ltd* v. *McShane* [1980] AC, p. 694.

81. Donaldson (1975), p. 192.

82. T. Ramm, 'Federal Republic of Germany', *International Encyclopaedia for Labour Law and Industrial Relations*, ed. R. Blanpain, 1979, para. 617.

Moreover, the problem of 'suspension' of employment contracts cannot be relegated to a footnote as something which may or may not be 'desirable'.[83] No one familiar with the brilliant analysis of the effect of industrial action upon individual employment rights by Professor Blanc-Jouvan in 1972[84] can fail to recognize the subtly diverse answers which can be given in comparable legal systems to this problem. Such scholarship imposes an obligation to come forward with a specific, concrete answer on the point for British proposals. The same study shows that these issues concern not only the employee's interface with his employer; social security law (at the very least unemployment benefit law) must be confronted. Again, is a 'right to strike' to be subrogated to the right of trade unions and employers to extinguish or modify it in collective agreements and their 'peace clauses'? If one relies upon the European Social Charter, Art. 6, as an international source of the 'right to strike', it must be noted that that Article specifically makes the right to strike subject to 'obligations that might arise out of collective agreements', and applies it only to 'conflicts of interest' – in both respects a less liberal doctrine than the traditional British formula. Foreign systems vary enormously, of course, on this point. Swedish law is based upon the binding force of the negotiated peace obligation; in both France and Italy some clauses of this kind risk being unconstitutional; while German law relies on them at collective level, but traditionally does not incorporate them into individual contracts of employment.[85] When should English courts incorporate from the collective agreement a 'procedure' or 'no-strike' clause into the individual employment contract of (say) a non-union worker whose terms and conditions otherwise stem from that agreement, as they so often do? Would the requirements of s. 18(4), TULRA, 1974, be varied?

These are just a few of the items on the agenda. The Green Paper of 1981, for all the poverty of its intellectual quality, raised others. No doubt it would be true that 'a positive rights system' might succeed in changing the 'language and concepts' of industrial conflict law so

83. See Elias and Ewing (1982), p. 358, n. 58.

84. X. Blanc-Jouvan, 'The Effect of Industrial Action on the Status of the Individual Employee', in Aaron and Wedderburn (1972), ch. 4, written when the 'suspensory' s. 147 Industrial Relations Act 1971 was in force, on which see especially pp. 198–210.

85. See G. Aubert's useful study of seven systems, L'Obligation de Paix du Travail (1981), and especially on Germany pp. 98–100. See too G. Giugni, 'The Peace Obligation', in Aaron and Wedderburn (1972), ch. 3.

that the law would be easier, superficially at least, to understand.[86] But would that in itself stop the misrepresentation of trade unionists' rights to 'privileges' – a process which has reached a new peak in the 1983 Green Paper?[87] The 1981 Green Paper gave good reason for the belief that in practice, 'a positive rights system could be at least as restrictive as the immunities and possibly more so'.[88]

It opened up, for example, the prospect of a prohibition on unions' disciplining members who refuse to strike, on the basis of the fallacy that a positive 'right to strike' implies the negative 'right not to strike'. This consideration poses the question of the relationship with a 'Bill of Rights'. Here the 'positive rights' argument intersects with the 'shallow legalism' that equates the right to associate in unions with the right to dissociate as a non-unionist[89] and with the unsatisfactory character of the European Convention on Human Rights (which establishes no right to strike at all).[90] These and other international sources have sometimes led even those judges who are sensitive to industrial relations to declare that the 'negative' right is part of English law.[91] Other judges have exulted in its application in Britain to protect individual rights: 'even though it could result in industrial chaos'.[92] If some 'Bill of Rights' is to be part of a 'positive rights' system, there seems on present experience little reason to believe that it will 'help remove the unions' traditional suspicion of the courts' or that 'the courts might seem more neutral in interpreting the rights of management, unions and workers', as the Green Paper stated. In any

86. *Trade Union Immunities*, Cmnd 8128, 1981, para. 379. The quotations that follow are also from paras. 351, 345, 376. The parallel problems of labour courts (paras. 365–71) are not discussed here.

87. *Democracy in Trade Unions*, Cmnd 8778, 1983, especially para. 52(*d*). See generally Wedderburn (1980).

88. Lewis and Simpson (1981), p. 226, who point out the relevance of the Code of Practice on Closed Shops, para. 54.

89. Kahn-Freund (2nd edn, 1977), p. 196; and see Lord Wedderburn in Schmidt (1978), ch. 6.

90. For the unsatisfactory application of Article 11(1) (after the withdrawal by the UK of a defence under Art. 11(2)), see *Young, James and Webster* v. *UK* [1981] IRLR 408 (ECHR).

91. See Lord Scarman, *Report of a Court of Inquiry ... Into a Dispute (at) Grunwick Processing Laboratories Ltd*, Cmnd 6922, 1977, paras. 56–8 (where he recognizes '*all* rights and freedoms for which each side contends').

92. Lord Denning MR, *Cheall* v. *APEX* [1982] ICR 543, 557 (the CA decision was reversed by the HL [1983] 2 AC 180). Compare reliance by Lord Denning and Lord Scarman on the Convention in *UKAPE* v. *ACAS* [1979] ICR, pp. 316–7; [1980] ICR, p. 214.

event, if trade union rights are not to be restored or enlarged, why *should* such suspicion be removed other than as part of a confidence trick?

Quis custodiet opificibus leges?

The truth is that a formal switch from 'immunities' to 'positive rights' cannot by itself produce judicial 'neutrality'. The root problem is not the form of the law. It is its administration: 'A change in its semantic presentation does not alter the fundamental problem.'[93]

This is an issue, however, which has been joined by advocates of positive rights. Sometimes they give the impression of believing that they can, as the Green Paper put it, 'insulate [the] legal right to strike from the common law'. The claim seems to be that, whereas the 'immunities', even in 'more sophisticated and complex terms', cannot halt the 'relentless march and new liabilities' of the common law, now:

The advantage of a rights-based system is that the right could exist regardless of common law developments. So even if the judges developed new causes of action, this would be largely irrelevant in the labour field because they would always be secondary to the primary statutory rights . . . it may be that the development of the common law would come to a virtual standstill.[94]

This is a bold pronouncement. If it were correct, it could hold the key to the format of an alternative strategy. The ability to regulate developments of the common law has been long sought in various areas of our law. But some questions arise. What is the definition to be, in precise terms, of this '*labour field*' into which common law will not now venture? Will it be that of 'trade disputes'? How is it to be made more judge-proof than a revised 'golden formula'?

Secondly, does the historical evidence suggest that the semantics of 'positive' rights secure workers' rights from judicial novelty or incursion like St George from the dragon? From 1906 to 1971 and 1974 to 1983 we have had one basic right expressed in positive form, even though its content since the 1980 Act has been restricted to a minimum ambit. The right to picket peacefully, which stemmed from the proviso to the crime of watching and besetting in the Conspiracy and Protection of Property Act 1875, section 7 – a proviso at once interpreted in a customarily hostile manner by the courts – was

93. Clark and Wedderburn, in Wedderburn *et al.* (1983), ch. 6, p. 157.
94. Elias and Ewing (1982), p. 358.

521

subsequently enunciated in the 1906 Act in different, *positive* form. '*It shall be lawful . . .*' said the statute (and later statutes said the same), to attend in furtherance of a trade dispute at or near a place (now, of course, the place) of work merely for the purpose of informing, or of persuading not to work. Yet the judges regularly turned the flanks of this positive provision just as easily as they had restricted the proviso; pickets who committed nuisance or obstruction on the highway were placed, as we have seen, outside the bounds of attendance declared to be 'lawful', equated to hitch-hikers or to persons carrying banners advertising patent medicines.[95] Even Kahn-Freund saw some of these judicial limitations as 'obvious', for example, in 'mass'-picketing on which, in the words of one chief constable, one sometimes gets 'a very jaundiced picture from the news media'.[96] The judicial attitude to the positive right to picket in fact incorporated the old tradition that *effective* demonstrations by workers are presumptively wrong. That attitude was not materially affected by the change from immunity in 1896 (*Lyons* v. *Wilkins*) to right in 1967 (*Tynan* v. *Balmer*). What is more, the House of Lords made it quite clear in dealing with the 'mixed' form of the statutory picketing section in the Industrial Relations Act 1971 (section 134, which can be seen as part 'immunity', part 'right') that the form was immaterial.[97] Indeed, faced with Parliament's desire to create an effective 'right' of peaceful picketing, it remained true in face of all forms of statutory expression that: 'the courts have adopted the curious approach of hunting for some minimal activity that the section protects and then reasoning that Parliament can have intended to create no greater protection'.[98]

This approach is indeed the normal judicial approach to the social rights of trade unionists whenever they infringe the contractual or property rights of others or invade the realm perceived by judges to be that of 'public order', both areas on which workers' collective action

95. Trade Disputes Act 1906 s. 2; TULRA s. 15 (also in form as substituted in 1980); Employment Act 1980, s. 16. See the cases in n. 56 above; and recently on 'nuisance'. *Mersey Dock and Harbour Co.* v. *Verrinder* [1982] IRLR 152; *Norbrook Labs. Ltd* v. *King* [1982] IRLR 456 (NL).

96. Chief Constable of South Wales, J. Woodcock, Evidence to HC Employment Committee, 27 February 1980. See Kahn-Freund (2nd edn, 1977), pp. 261–2 and *Industrial Law Journal*, 3 (1974), p. 200.

97. *Broome* v. *DPP* [1974] AC 587; *ante* n. 56.

98. Davies and Freedland (1979), p. 677; cf. Clark and Wedderburn, in Wedderburn *et al.* (1983), pp. 58–9 and 168–9; Bercusson (1977).

must trespass to be effective. (Indeed, on occasions when they have been unable to discover any such minimal activity to be protected, judges have even been prepared to declare the entire statutory provision to be 'unnecessary', 'pointless' or 'nugatory'.)[99] Given a century of interpretation, though, of the positive right to picket peacefully, what ground is there to believe that a right to strike would fare materially better?

Again, the apparent 'right' to recognition hardly modified the application of the power of judicial review in respect of ss. 11–27 of the Employment Protection Act 1975.[100] Equally, consider more generally the treatment of the limiting factor of 'recognition' itself in our modern labour law. A number of positive rights for trade unions, their officials and members require that the union be 'recognized', the rights to information, for example, or to time off or to undertake trade union activity. The statutory definition of 'recognition' has remained broadly the same since 1975;[101] but few would claim that they foresaw the restrictions placed upon it by the courts, by such devices as inflating the distinction between 'representations' and negotiations, or, most of all, by placing ponderous weight upon the subjective intention of managers (representing the 'employer').[102]

The approach of our judges to limiting factors that are required in any system of industrial jurisprudence is unlikely to change. Their minds will turn naturally to the needs of management, of property, of capital, and of the hypothetical 'individual' long before they consider those of trade unionists. Indeed, one is compelled to inquire further and ask what magical quality of draftsmanship will by the enactment of positive rather than negative phrases immediately halt relentless developments in 'economic duress'. True, in that case a majority of the Law Lords indicated that they would not (probably) allow the new common law doctrine to invade the territory of labour

99. See *Rookes* v. *Barnard* [1964] AC 1129, 1177, 1192, 1236, in respect of s. 3 (second limb) of the 1906 Act, the same provision as s. 13(2) TULRA 1974, now repealed by s. 19, Employment Act 1982.

100. As in the *Grunwick* case ([1978] AC 655, HL); see the invaluable case study in Elias, Napier and Wallington (1980), ch. 1.

101. See now Employment Act 1980, sched. 1, para. 6; Employment Protection Act 1975 s. 126; s. 29 TULRA 1974 (as amended now, however, by s. 18 Employment Act 1982, especially subsection (6)).

102. *USDAW* v. *Sketchley* [1981] ICR 644, EAT; *NUGSAT* v. *Albury Bros.* [1979] ICR 84, CA: *R* v. *CAC ex parte Tioxide* [1981] ICR 843, EAT; and cf. *NALGO* v. *National Travel* [1978] ICR 598.

relations that is guarded from tort liability – by the immunities.[103] Could a 'positive right' have hoped to fare better? It might have fared worse. In the same case, would a 'positive right' have stood a better or worse chance of resisting the decision that this was not a 'trade dispute' (or the *'labour field'*), or of pacifying the desire of some of the judges to encumber labour law with the mysteries of resulting trusts?[104] Why would a new doctrine of 'economic duress' necessarily be 'irrelevant' to a right to strike and payments made in connection with its exercise?

It is, of course, difficult to assess precisely how a 'positive rights' system would fare. But the agenda demands some elaboration. Would a new format prevent a judge from ever again perceiving the law giving workers the right to bargain collectively as one which, like some compulsory purchase order, snatched away their right to bargain individually?[105] Indeed, the mere mention of experiments of this sort in the 1975 legislation reminds us that no proposal has yet advanced a solution to the fearsome problems inherent in a 'right to collective bargaining' – with the morass of difficulties illustrated by the huge corpus of American litigation on the 'duty to bargain in good faith' – a formulation rightly said to raise 'as many problems as it solves'.[106] Does the proposal of a positive right to strike not require an attendant, positive 'right to bargain' – with at least a tentative description of its character? The difficulties encountered by the 'duty to bargain' have very little to do with the literary form of the legislation, and much, perhaps everything, to do with industrial reality and, in Britain at least, with the judiciary.

A simple return to the classical tradition of the 'voluntary' industrial-relations system is hardly possible in the 1980s. But if a new policy is to replace the current policy of restriction, its greatest challenge will be the construction of an adequate and positive role for effective and autonomous trade unions. Such a policy should use whatever drafting format is appropriate to particular problems. That would not exclude 'positive rights', any more than the use, where

103. *Universe Tankships of Monrovia Inc.* v. *ITWF* [1982] 2 WLR 803; see the doubts of Lord Brandon, p. 833; and the extraordinary majority decision trade dispute; Wedderburn ('Economic Duress', *Modern Law Review*, 45 (1982), p. 556. For the view that unions should not be protected against 'economic duress' when statutory protection applies only to tort, see G. Jones, *Cambridge Law Journal* (1983), pp. 47–8.
104. See B. Green, *Modern Law Review*, 45 (1982), p. 564, and 46 (1983), p. 361.
105. Browne-Wilkinson J., *Powley* v. *ACAS* [1978] ICR, p. 135.
106. Davies and Freedland (1979), p. 103.

beneficial, of negative rights, freedoms, liberties, or, where appropriate, immunities. New ventures in democracy generally in industrial relations may make use (may have to make use) of legislation with rights blended as far as possible into the system. There we stand on the frontier of the wider debate which must be for another occasion.

But whatever 'formula' is chosen, the common law – that means the judges – will have to be excluded from certain areas of industrial life. They, as John Griffith has put it, are 'concerned to preserve and to protect the existing order'. If they move with the times, 'their function in our society is to do so belatedly'.[107] Demands that trade unions must be placed under 'the rule of law' (meaning the common law) 'are not legal demands. They are ideological demands.'[108] The ideology of the common law is stronger than that of most statutes; and it is more dangerous because of the mystifying pretence that it does not exist. There can be no *a priori* assumption that judges will abstain or be less 'jealous' of their jurisdiction because a statute tells them that their common law is 'secondary' to a primary statutory right. Proponents must demonstrate just what the statutory form of words would *be* to establish that the primary right prevails against all doctrines (existing and yet to be discovered) of the common law and judicial review? For many years our colleagues in public and administrative law have been telling us that such control of the judiciary is difficult, if not impossible[109] – unless perhaps we can dress up the union as David facing Goliath (and avoid its being perceived as a 'troublemaker').[110]

Judges (whatever they may say) are not 'jealous' of their jurisdiction primarily because of the form of immunities. Misunderstanding as to their nature as 'privileges' at most compounds the 'jealousy' carried in the very blood of the common law towards collective organizations by workpeople who had to fight their way to legality against its civil and criminal liabilities. The 'insecure foundation' for the freedom to strike in our society today is *not* primarily

107. Griffith (1981), p. 241.

108. Bill Wedderburn, in Wedderburn and Murphy (1983), p. 6. Oddly, the greatest exception to judicial interference was a case which involved no statutory rights or immunities at all: *Ford Motor Co.* v. *AUEFW* [1969] 2 QB 303.

109. See the contrasts in Griffith (1981), ch. 10.

110. Lord Denning MR saw the parties as 'David and Goliath' in *UKAPE* v. *ACAS* [1979] ICR 303, 310 and *PO* v. *Crouch* [1973] ICR 366, 375; but he turned against the small group confronting the TGWU in *Morgan* v. *Fry* [1968] 2 QB 710, 729, because they were 'troublemakers who fomented discord in the docks'.

the form of the present immunities. It is the attitude of the courts and of the common law – now ably reinforced by the mass media and the myths of 'trade union power' in a powerfully projected market analysis.

In truth, a philosophical confrontation between doctrines of 'immunities' and 'positive rights' is no more useful today as a contribution to the politics of labour law than a dispute about the number of shop stewards able to dance on the head of a pin. The approach to drafting should be pragmatic. No doubt, wherever it is advantageous, a form of words will be chosen which cannot easily allow a fundamental human freedom to be misrepresented as a 'privilege', whether in Grimsby or in Gdansk. Perhaps, at times in the past, draftsmen did not always keep that point adequately in mind. But, by itself, consideration of the statutory *form* of the law is secondary – a matter not of strategy but of tactics.

More important are the substantive liabilities of the common law. Should the approach to these be bolder? It was suggested in 1965 in connection with the new tort of intimidation:

> Instead of creating what looks like another privilege for trade disputes . . . it might be preferable . . . for the statute to repeal the novel doctrine . . . for the law of tort.[111]

That is to say, some areas of common law liability might simply be abolished. Similarly, Davies and Freedland think there would 'seem a lot to be said for restructuring s. 13 (TULRA) on the model of s. 14',[112] though the difficulties in respect of torts that cover violence, assault and other similar acts are obvious.[113] We should certainly think about the repeal of certain common law doctrines altogether, leaving it to Parliament to revive such parts of the liability as are needed for commercial, family or property transactions. That is roughly what we did with the common law crime of conspiracy in 1977. It is arguable that the same technique should be used as an antidote to some parts of the poison which the common law brings to its treatment of trade unions and industrial action. But we should not be surprised if we find a need to utilize the limiting factor of 'trade disputes', as the 1977 legislation did on certain minor issues.

The right to strike is always expressed, in practice, in the legal

111. K. W. Wedderburn, in Kahn-Freund (1965), p. 153n., proposing an answer to *Rookes* v. *Barnard* [1964] AC 1129.
112. Davies and Freedland (1979), p. 607; cited by Elias and Ewing (1982), p. 356.
113. Elias and Ewing (1982), p. 356.

systems of societies comparable to ours, by reference to some limiting factors. These may *interets professionels* as in France, or, as has been the case in Germany, 'social adequacy' or 'proportionality'. Even in Italy, when the right is perhaps at its widest, it is confined to actions which are: 'not aimed at subverting constitutional order nor at hindering or obstructing the free exercise of the legal powers in which popular sovereignty is expressed'.[114]

Unless one goes that far – and British labour law seems unlikely to do so – one is left with the hard task of drawing a new line between 'State' and 'society', in the full knowledge that in any such edifice of law (as Kahn-Freund concluded in 1954) 'the foundations are shaky'. But whether or not they are wholly defensible philosophically, they are drawn because they represent 'the social and political convictions on which all law-making rests'.[115] A 'trade dispute' may not exist, like God; but, perhaps, like Him, it needs to be invented.

Social substance and forms of law

The task of building a new labour law will be difficult. The difficulties do have a little, but relatively only a little, to do with the form of 'rights' and 'immunities'. They have more to do with practical enforcement of areas of legality for effective and autonomous trade unionism as part of a transition to social advance, the re-establishment of opportunities for employment, and industrial participation and democracy. At the level of the courts, particular attention must be paid to ending – whether by positive rights, immunities or (perhaps more important than either) procedural adjustments – the preposterous practice of interlocutory labour injunctions (an area where our judges still claim indefensible rights of jurisdiction).[116] Most of all it has to do with finding a new boundary, sufficiently based upon social *consensus* but sufficiently broad in its class terms, which will prevent the ideology of the common law torpedoing the trade union contribution. What is more, that structure must face a world of internationalized trade, where localized trade unions face transnational

114. *Public Prosecutor* v. *Antenaci*, Constitutional Court, 1974, *International Labour Law Report*, vol. 1, p. 54 [see now *Industrial Law Journal*, 12 (1983), p. 253].

115. O. Kahn-Freund, in Flanders and Clegg (1954), p. 127; see Clark and Wedderburn, in Wedderburn *et al.* (1983), pp. 155–65 and 198–206.

116. See *Express Newspapers* v. *McShane*, *supra*; *NWL* v. *Woods*, *supra*; Wedderburn, *Modern Law Review*, 45 (1982), pp. 325–7; B. Simpson, *Modern Law Review*, 45 (1982), pp. 330–32.

capital. We must ask: what role can national law play in promoting the development of effective trade unionism on an international plane?

Perhaps, too, it is time to inquire anew into the nature and functions of our specialized system of labour courts, not least the role of the lay members of the tribunals, and ask whether the 'wing persons' should be invested, in French fashion, more directly with a representative character.[117] We certainly cannot wait for the problems of the judiciary (and the profession from which it comes) to fade away in face of a 'new generation of lawyers', trained to a new sensitivity of 'industrial relations', which was the hope of both Donovan and Kahn-Freund.[118] We must do our best with the judges we have and utilize whatever shape of statute seems most suitable to the time. Perhaps we have spent so long trying to explain to them the true nature of the 'immunities' that we failed to realize that all along it was not the form but the substance that mattered to them.

There may well be a case for more positive rights in areas of our labour law. But arguments for them will be convincing only if based upon something more concrete than their idealized virtues. The critical issue for 'rights' and for 'immunities' is: how will they fare in court and on the shop floor? Judges in courts determine the meaning of the law in action. And the law will have some effect – though one much more difficult to determine – upon bargaining and industrial behaviour. Moreover, comparative study which goes beyond the form of foreign laws will demonstrate why we must not be led astray by the functioning of positive rights in *other* systems to assume that those rights must produce the same results here. Comparison with Italy is particularly useful. No British court could produce the judgment of the Italian Constitutional Court on 'political' strikes unless specifically directed by Parliament to do so – and who knows even then? On the other hand, the 'right' not to be unfairly dismissed in Italy does, in very many cases, lead to re-engagement. In Britain that remedy is notoriously rare. Why has the British 'right' fared so much worse?[119] Equally important, the interplay of the industrial and social forces does not always produce qualitatively similar results out of parallel

117. On the industrial tribunals, see Clark and Wedderburn, in Wedderburn *et al.* (1983), pp. 173–84.

118. *Report*, Cmnd 3623, 1968, para. 583; Kahn-Freund (1969), p. 316. See on this problem Clark and Wedderburn, in Wedderburn *et al.* (1983), pp. 166–73.

119. See Clark and Wedderburn, in Wedderburn *et al.* (1983), p. 208, and authorities cited in nn. 364–9.

pressures. It has, for instance, been said of Italian trade unions that their 'general weakness' tends to nurture hopes of 'long-term goals', and

> leads the unions to link themselves to and depend upon political parties. From this, as from the ideological propensity to be orientated towards long-term ends, the predominance of political action or of political aspirations over narrowly union ones is born.[120]

Most observers would make the very opposite judgment of tendencies in British trade unions over the last decade. This has direct relevance for legal developments; for there can be no doubt that judicial cognisance and understanding of the political dimension of the labour movement has at times been a critical factor in the interpretation of the Constitution by Italian courts. No such cultural influence would be felt in Britain. British judges do not always recognize that a democratic trade union movement cannot, in a free society, be excluded from the 'politics' from which capital does not abstain. Comparative legal inquiry must take account of such factors, therefore, in considering the forms of foreign law, and recognize the need to judge the meaning of law primarily by reference, not to its formal drafting but to the entire social and cultural context that determines its meaning and effect in application.

Finally, to those who are not lawyers I add this: these are not merely technical issues, delights savoured only by the sharp tastes of academics or in the briefs of their brethren in professional practice. The role of lawyers remains limited; as Otto Kahn-Freund put it in 1954: 'The first duty of a lawyer about to discuss the legal framework of industrial relations is to warn his readers not to overestimate its importance.'[121] But the procedure, the substance and the very concepts of the law frequently reflect the dissonance or harmony of the social substructure. Where there is industrial dissonance, you must not expect the lawyer to solve problems beyond the law's competence. In his turn, the lawyer must not present the technicalities of his craft, the mysteries of 'rights' and 'immunities', as if they are primary rather than subsidiary items on the agenda of social and legal reform, as if the form determined the substance. For the politics of his laws are

120. A. Pizzorno, 'Azione di classe e sistemi corporativi', in *I Soggetti del Pluralismo*, 1980, p. 198; quoted and discussed in P. Lange, G. Ross and M. Vannicelli, *Unions, Change and Crisis, French and Italian Union Strategy 1945–1980*, 1982, pp. 268–86.

121. Flanders and Clegg (1954), p. 43.

the politics of the wider society and his laws cannot as such solve political confrontations. Nor could anything be more absurd today than that lawyers should impede the urgent, concrete debate about such priorities of the crisis as unemployment with some alien, abstract argument on juridical formalities.[122] The law is, in the last resort, never a substitute for politics.[123]

122. In Italy, the leading labour lawyer Professor Gino Giugni said recently, in the context of his role as chairman of an expert committee which helped to negotiate the new social compact amending the 1975 agreements on the *scala mobile* (indexation of wages), that each epoch has its own 'model' for labour law: 'In the sixties, with an economic boom, it was right to concentrate on a system of collective bargaining to increase wages. Today, with unemployment and crisis, objective number one in industrial relations must be the defence of employment' (*Panorama*, 31 January 1983, p. 95). Compare the conclusion of Clark and Wedderburn, in Wedderburn *et al.* (1983), p. 219 and 220, that labour law must, 'so long as the democratic principle of maintaining effective, independent trade unions remains paramount', now be based upon policies addressed to 'low incomes and, especially, to mass unemployment. The policy for labour law must find its appropriate place in that immediate enterprise'.

123. The message is, of course, best spelled out in Griffith (1979) and Griffith (1981).

References

AARON, B., and K. W. WEDDERBURN, ed. (1972), *Industrial Conflict – A Comparative Survey*, Longman.

BERCUSSON, B. (1977), 'One Hundred Years of Conspiracy and Protection of Property', *Modern Law Review*, 40.

CARBY-HALL, J., ed. (1976), *Studies in Labour Law*, MCB Books.

CLARKE, J., and L. CLEMENTS (1978), *Trade Unions Under Capitalism*, Fontana.

CLERK, G. F., and W. H. B. LINDSELL (1982), *Law of Torts*, 15th edn, Sweet & Maxwell.

CRAVER, C. (1978), 'The Application of the LMRDA "Labour Consultant" Reporting Requirements to Management Attorneys', *Northwestern University Law Review*, 73.

CROUCH, C. (1977), *Class Conflict and the Industrial Relations Crisis*, Heinemann.

DANIEL, W. (1981), 'A Clash of Symbols: The Case of Maternity Legislation', *Policy Studies Journal*, 2.

DANIEL, W., and E. FREEDLAND (1979), *Labour Law, Text and Materials*, Weidenfeld & Nicolson.

DANIEL, W., and E. STILGOE (1978), *The Impact of Employment Protection Laws*, Policy Studies Institute.

DAVIES, P. L. (1978), 'Arbitration and the Role of Courts', *UK National Report to the Ninth International Congress of the International Society for Labour Law*, Heidelberg.

DAVIES, P. L., and M. FREEDLAND (1979) *Labour Law, Text and Materials*, Weidenfeld & Nicolson.

DAVIES, P. L., and M. FREEDLAND (1982), *Transfer of Employment*, Weidenfeld & Nicolson.

DONALDSON, SIR JOHN (1975), 'Lessons from the Industrial Court', *Law Quarterly Review*, 91.

ELIAS, P. and K. EWING (1982), 'Economic Torts and Labour Law', *Cambridge Law Journal*, 32.

ELIAS, P., B. NAPIER and P. WALLINGTON (1980), *Labour Law, Cases and Materials*, Butterworth.

EWING, K. (1979), 'The Golden Formula, Some Recent Developments', *Industrial Law Journal*, 8.

EWING, K. (1982), 'Industrial Action: Another Step in the "Right" Direction', *Industrial Law Journal*, 11.

FLANDERS, A., and H. CLEGG, ed. (1954), *The System of Industrial Relations in Great Britain*, Blackwell.

GINSBERG, M., ed. (1959), *Law and Opinion in England in the 20th Century*, Stevens & Sons.

GRIFFITH, J. A. C. (1979), 'The Political Constitution', *Modern Law Review*, 42.

GRIFFITH, J. A. C. (1981), *The Politics of the Judiciary*, 2nd edn, Fontana.

HAYEK, F. (1980), *1980s Unemployment and the Unions*, Institute of Economic Affairs.

HEPPLE, B. (1982), 'The Transfer of Undertakings (Protection of Employment) Regulations' *Industrial Law Journal*, 11.

JENKINS, C., and J. MORTIMER (1968), *The Kind of Laws Unions Ought to Want*, Pergamon Press.

KAHN-FREUND, O. (1948), 'Legislation through Adjudication', *Modern Law Review*, 11.

KAHN-FREUND, O., ed. (1949), *(Renner) The Institutions of Private Law and Their Social Functions*, Routledge & Kegan Paul.

KAHN-FREUND, O., ed. (1065), *Labour Relations and the Law: A Comparative Study*, Stevens & Sons.

KAHN-FREUND, O., ed. (1965), *Labour Relations and the Law: A Comparative Study*, *British Journal of Industrial Relations*, 7.

KAHN-FREUND, O. (1972; 2nd edn, 1977), *Labour and the Law*, Stevens & Sons.

KAHN-FREUND, O. (1979), *Labour Relations, Heritage and Adjustment*, British Academy.

KALDOR, LORD NICHOLAS (1983), 'The Economic Consequences of Mrs Thatcher', *Fabian Tract 486*.

LANGE, P., G. ROSS and M. VANNICELLI (1982), *Unions, Change and Crisis, French and Italian Union Strategy 1945–1980*, Allen & Unwin.

LASKI, H. (1925), *A Grammar of Politics*, Allen & Unwin.

LEWIS, R., and SIMPSON, B. (1982), 'Disorganizing Industrial Relations', *Industrial Law Journal*, 11.

MORRIS, M. (1976), *General Strike*, Penguin.

SCHMIDT, F., ed. (1978), *Discrimination in Employment*, Almqvist and Wiksell.

THOMPSON, A. W. J., and S. R. ENGLEMAN (1975), *Industrial Relations Act: A Review and Analysis*, Martin Robertson.

WALLINGTON, P. (1983), 'Section 9 of the Employment Act 1982 – A Recipe for Victimization?', *Modern Law Review*, 46, May.

WEDDERBURN, K. W. (1965; 2nd edn, 1971), *The Worker and the Law*, Penguin.

WEDDERBURN, K. W. (1972), 'Labour Law and Labour Relations in Britain', *British Journal of Industrial Relations*, 10.

WEDDERBURN, Lord (1980), 'Industrial Relations and the Courts', *Industrial Law Journal*, 9.

WEDDERBURN, Lord (1982), 'Secondary Action and Primary Values', *Modern Law Journal*, 45.

WEDDERBURN, K. W. and P. L. DAVIES (1969), *Employment Grievances and Disputes Procedures in Britain*, University of California Press.

WEDDERBURN, K. W., R. LEWIS and J. CLARK, ed. (1983), *Labour Law and Industrial Relations: Building on Kahn-Freund*, Oxford University Press.

WEDDERBURN, K. W., and W. T. MURPHY, ed. (1983), *Labour Law and the Community*, University of London, Institute of Advanced Legal Studies.

WEEKES, B., M. MELLISH, L. DICKENS and J. LLOYD (1975), *Industrial Relations and the Limits of Law*, Blackwell.

Trade Unions and the Limits of the Law

From W. E. J. McCarthy, 'Trade Unions and the Limits of the Law', *New Society*, 21 April 1983.

I interrupted her speculations . . . 'Have you no respect at all for the law?'
'It depends, dear, to which law you refer. Like the ten commandments. I can't take very seriously the one about the ox and the ass.'

Graham Greene, *Travels with my Aunt*

Since the 'day of action' in September 1982 the TUC has organized various forms of 'sympathetic action' in support of the pay claims of member unions. It is freely admitted that this has often involved breaches of the 1980 Employment Act – most notably Section 17. But this is only the beginning. A number of individual unions have taken secondary action to support other workers in dispute and found themselves faced with the threat of an interlocutory injunction. Failure to respond to such an injunction could involve an action for contempt of court. Both the National Graphical Association and the National Union of Journalists have refused to assist non-union printers. Such action is almost certainly unlawful under section 14 of the 1982 Employment Act.

The fact is that the 1980 Act rendered unlawful a wide range of union practices, including most sympathetic strikes, all 'off site' picketing and action to enforce the closed shop. When it was followed by the Act of 1982, trade unions found themselves exposed to the risk of actions for damages or compensation over a much wider area and with more serious consequences for their funds.

But even this is not the end. The government is introducing a third Trade Union Bill, which is likely to reach the statute book some time in 1984. This will impose penalties and liabilities on unions that fail to conduct elections for a wide variety of offices; and in most cases conformity with the law will involve significant changes in union rule-books and current practices. The scope for official strike action will also be restricted. Finally, beyond the third Act there looms the hazy spectre of a fourth, or even a fifth. The Prime Minister has said that legislation may have to continue 'until we get it right'. The purpose of this article is to discuss the options available to unions in this situation.

The approach is that of a non-lawyer whose main claim to be heard is that of a specialist in the academic study of industrial relations. The intention is to be as objective as possible, in a subject where this is notoriously difficult and frequently misunderstood. The chosen method is to explore the implications and practicality of the frequently expressed view that trade unions should at all times ensure that they 'remain within the limits of the law'. The argument advanced is that, given their position, advice of this kind is of very little help.

The first problem with this approach is to discover what the law is. As supporters of the Government admitted during the passage of the 1982 Bill, there are now many areas where the legal limits of industrial action are far from clear. Thus, while it is accepted by all that Section 17 of the 1980 Act seriously narrowed the boundaries of lawful secondary action, it is not universally agreed that it made it impossible in all its forms. Some labour lawyers are convinced that this is so, others equally distinguished disagree. Many believe that there is no way of finding out until there are more leading cases.

Then again, in my own area of relative expertise, I would argue that virtually all of the customary ways of enforcing the closed shop are now of doubtful legality. But not all students of the subject agree with me. What is clear is that nobody can say how far Section 18 of the 1982 Act will turn out to modify Section 29 of the 1974 Trade Union and Labour Relations Act. As a result we have little idea what are the present legal limits of a trade dispute. It is also impossible to say whether the effect of repealing Section 14 of the 1974 Act will be unimportant or disastrous from the viewpoint of union funds.

Thus it can be said that already the combined effect of the existing legislation has been to narrow the so-called 'immunities' of unions in a radical but indeterminate way. In the end, the judges may tell us what it all means, if they are asked to decide enough cases. Meanwhile, presumably, even Walter Goldsmith does not expect unions to seek out lawyers who take the most limited and pessimistic view of their rights, so that they can follow their advice. This is not the way the rest of us react to the news that some of the things we have been doing for years are on the margin of legal liability. We take the best advice we can afford from the most friendly lawyer we can find, and hope for the best. As a result, we sometimes find that we have misjudged and misunderstood the law. If there is to be litigation on any scale as a result of both Acts I do not see how trade unions can be expected to avoid breaking the law from time to time. Unless and until there are enough leading cases, they will be quite unable to determine the consequences of acting in any other way. Since most of us would do the same I hope their reactions will not be regarded as all that reprehensible. But I am not very hopeful.

However, it may be said that there are circumstances where the excuse of uncertainty will not serve – e.g. in respect of many of the more extended and indirect forms of secondary actions, or 'off site' picketing, or the dismissal of existing employees from new closed shops. What options are available to trade unions in these areas?

The first point to make is that what will usually be involved is the creation of a civil liability. Apart from the sensitive area of so-called 'militant picketing', or refusals to obey interlocutory or final injunctions, no question of a crime or misdemeanour will normally arise. This means that it will be open to any individual or organization to discharge liability by the simple expedient of agreeing to pay any damages, compensation or costs awarded against them.

The second point worth stressing is that most of us regard the discharge of liabilities by payments of this kind as a perfectly reasonable response to a wide variety of existing illegalities. Thus in the field of labour law it is common for small employers to justify their failure to observe the more restrictive provisions of the Health and Safety at Work Act by pointing to the fact that their employees are free to report them to the factory inspector. Similar justifications are often employed to excuse the non-observance or evasion of race and sex discrimination laws. One is told that those who think they have rights can always take them to Industrial Tribunals.

What evidence there is suggests that since the wage inspectorate was reduced, as part of the Government's drive to reduce public expenditure, there has been a significant increase in the numbers employed at illegal rates of pay. Doubtless this tendency has been encouraged by recent statements that the Government thinks all forms of minimum wage legislation are unnecessary, and intends to abolish them in the not-too-distant future.

But perhaps the closest parallel to the position which trade unions now face has existed for employers since 1971, as a result of 'unfair dismissal' legislation. Since there is no absolute right to reinstatement, employers have always had the option of dismissing 'unfairly' if they were prepared to pay the appropriate level of compensation. Outside the special area of dismissal on grounds of union membership or non-membership, where the 1982 Act has quadrupled the level of compensation, this will continue to average out at a few hundred pounds per person dismissed. Employers can even arrange for such payments to be made out of court – indeed, any competent lawyer would advise them to act in this way.

Even officials of the Advisory Conciliation and Arbitration Service, who are involved as conciliators in cases of alleged unfair dismissal, normally suggest some kind of payment of this sort where there is reason to believe that an employee might sustain an action before a Tribunal. Of course, there is nothing illegal in all this; although the employer may openly admit that he intends to break the law to rid himself of some undesirable worker or 'trouble-maker'.

Moreover, outside the field of labour law there are many other groups who think they have a right to break the law if they are willing to pay the price. We all know motorists who take this attitude to parking on double yellow lines. (Some countries actually encourage the belief that you can 'pay your way out' in circumstances of this kind by providing more or less friendly traffic wardens who impose on-the-spot fines.)

More generally, in the field of civil liability, a willingness to pay is often regarded as a sufficient justification for embarking on a course of action that may well lay one open to action for breach of commercial contract. What matters is thought to be the balance of advantage and disadvantage, rather than the abstract principle of 'sanctity of contract'. What lawyers are asked to calculate is the cost of bringing an action, or mounting a defence, as against the prospects for a settlement out of court.

I conclude from all this that if trade unions were to adopt the option of carrying on as usual and 'paying their way out' where necessary, they would not be doing anything novel or reprehensible. Many employers, and most of us, ought to be able to see their point. Nevertheless, I doubt if they will be all that ready to adopt such an expedient, for four excellent reasons.

First, largely as a result of the 1982 Act, the payments required may be ruinous. Thus Sections 4 and 5 of the new Act increase the scale of compensation available to those dismissed on grounds of non-unionism, making it possible for individuals to receive as much as £31,000 each. Similarly, Section 15 allows unions to be sued in their own name and Section 16 specifies a wide range of penalties linked to the size of organizations. As a result, for unions of 100,000 members or more, a single action may involve a penalty of a quarter of a million pounds, and in addition to this there may be substantial costs awarded against them.

When provisions of this kind are taken in conjunction with the new definition of a trade dispute in Section 18, it seems clear that even the biggest and most prosperous union could face bankruptcy if they were to lose several contested cases.

Second, even where union leaders might well favour payment, their members could disagree. It is one thing to say, in answer to the man from the Gallup Poll, that unions are 'too powerful' or that 'the closed shop should be abolished'. It is quite another to agree that compensation should be paid from union funds because the branch decided not to work on orders diverted from a factory down the road, where other members are on strike. It may be even more difficult to accept the need to pay £20,000 or so to an ex-member who has developed a 'deeply held personal conviction' which prevents him from paying up his arrears.

Third, one of the most remarkable developments of the last few years has been the relative absence of actions against trade unionists arising out of the new legislation. Nobody is certain why this is, but unions naturally believe that it has something to do with the fact that they are known to be violently opposed to both Acts and take a poor view of any employer who invokes their provisions. As a result, it is thought, employers are reinforced in their belief that taking their workers to court will not help to improve their industrial relations. Meanwhile, union leaders take the view that an openly expressed willingness to cooperate and pay up may be seen as an encouragement to litigation – not least among suppliers and non-unionists.

But, much more important than this, the trade union movement has become convinced that over-ready acceptance of this option would be interpreted by the Government as capitulation in a campaign that has far from run its course. The debate over the precise form and effects of the 1984 Act has not been completed, and it could be that when it is, further legislation will be introduced which is equally menacing and just as imprecise.

It follows that from the point of view of trade unions, no clear and generally acceptable option presents itself. Simple observance of legality, or a cheerful willingness to pay up, is not really a practical solution. Yet they dare not abandon the field to the Government, and the situation is too serious to merely carry on as before and hope for the best.

In any case, the eleven million workers who belong to British unions have no more wish to break the law than the rest of us. Even the half million or so activists who run them are for the most part respectable people, who pay their taxes and final demand notes and have been known to help old ladies across the road. Their few thousand full-time officials are not looking for the way to Cary Street, or a period in Wormwood Scrubs. The great majority of them will do their level best to stay out of the clutches of the law, although none of us can say how far they will succeed.

Much could depend on how far a determined and concerted attempt is made to use the legislation as part of a general campaign to change the balance of industrial power. So far there are few signs of this. More may turn on how far third parties are induced to demand their rights against particular groups – e.g. contractors excluded from a printing union's 'fair list', or suppliers obstructed by a miners' flying picket.

If the legislation lasts long enough, and is made even more comprehensive, the most important factor could be the direction taken by the economy. If there is a significant and sustained economic revival, which actually reduces the level of unemployment, shortages of labour will arise – say among skilled workers. In these circumstances, many more trade unionists might be willing to defy the law to gain a little of what they have lost during the recession – e.g. a restoration of real wage levels. But in the long run the most important single factor may be a handful of judicial decisions, including one or two from the new Master of the Rolls. These could surprise us all.

Further Reading

The inclusion of a work under one or another of the headings below should not be taken to imply that it has nothing to contribute to other aspects of the subject.

Union objectives and methods

ALLEN, V. L., *Militant Trade Unionism*, 1966, Merlin.

BAIN, G., D. COATES and V. ELLIS, *Social Stratification and Trade Unionism*, 1973, Heinemann.

BLACKBURN, R., *Union Character and Social Class*, 1967, Batsford.

CLARKE, T., and L. CLEMENTS, *Trade Unions Under Capitalism*, 1977, Fontana.

GOODRICH, G., *The Frontier of Control*, 1920, G. Bell.

HYMAN, R., and I. BROUGH, *Social Values and Industrial Relations*, 1975, Blackwell.

LOZOVSKY, A., *Marx and the Trade Unions*, 1935, Martin Lawrence.

OLSON, M., *The Logic of Collective Action*, 1965, Harvard University Press.

PEDLER, M., 'Shop Stewards as Leaders', *Industrial Relations Journal*, vol. 4, 1973–4.

PERLMAN, S., *A Theory of the Labour Movement*, 1928, Macmillan.

POOLE, M., 'Towards a Sociology of Shop Stewards', *Sociological Review*, vol. 22, 1974.

VAN DER VAL, M., *Labour Organisations*, 1970, Cambridge University Press.

WEBB, S., and B. WEBB, *Industrial Democracy*, 1894, Longman.

WILLMAN, P., 'Leadership and Trade Union Principles', *Industrial Relations Journal*, 11, 1981, p. 39.

Trade unions and industrial democracy

BATSTONE, E., and P. DAVIES, *Industrial Democracy: European Experience*, 1977, HMSO.

BRANNEN, P., E. BATSTONE, D. FATCHETT and P. WHITE, *The Worker Directors: A Sociology of Participation*, 1976, Hutchinson.

CLEGG, H. A., *A New Approach to Industrial Democracy*, 1960, Blackwell.

COATES, K., and T. TOPHAM, *Industrial Democracy in Great Britain: A Book of Readings and Witnesses for Workers' Control*, 1968, MacGibbon & Kee.

COLE, G. D. H., *Self Government in Industry*, 1919, G. Bell.

CREESEY, P. *et al.*, *Industrial Democracy and Participation: A Scottish Survey*, Dept of Employment Research Paper no. 1., 1981, HMSO.

ELLIOT, J., *Conflict or Co-operation: The Growth of Industrial Democracy*, 1978, Kogan Page.

STURMTHAL, A., *Workers' Councils: A Study of Workplace Organisation on Both Sides of the Iron Curtain*, 1964, Harvard University Press.

TOWERS, B., E. CHELL and D. COX, 'Worker Directors in Private Industry in Britain,' *Dept of Employment Research Paper*, December 1983.

WALL, T., and J. A. LISCHESON, *Workers' Participation: A Critique of the Literature and Some Fresh Evidence*, 1977, McGraw-Hill.

Trade union structure and government

ALLEN, V. L., *The Militancy of British Miners*, 1981, Moor Press.

BANKS, J. A., *Trade Unionism*, 1974, Collier Macmillan.

BATSTONE, E., I. BORASTON and S. FRANKEL, *The Social Organisation of Strikes*, 1978, Blackwell.

BORASTON, I., H. CLEGG and M. RIMMER, *Workplace and Union: A Study of Local Relationships in Fourteen Unions*, 1975, Heinemann.

BOSTON, S., *Women Workers and the Trade Union Movement*, 1980, Davis-Poynter.

BURAWOY, M., *Manufacturing Consensus: Changes in the Labor Process under Monopoly Capitalism*, 1979, University of Chicago Press.

EBSWORTH, R., and M. TERRY, 'Factors Shaping Shop Steward Organisation in Britain,' *British Journal of Industrial Relations*, vol. 16, 1978, p. 139.

EDELSTEIN, J. D., and M. WARNER, *Comparative Union Democracy: Organisation and Opposition in British and American Unions*, 1975, Allen & Unwin.

EDWARDS, P., and H. SCULLION, *The Social Organisation of Industrial Conflict: Control and Resistance in the Workplace*, 1982, Blackwell.

ELIAS, P., 'Trade Union Amalgamations: Patterns and Procedures', *Industrial Law Journal*, II, 1973, p. 125.

ESTEY, M., *The Unions: Structure, Development and Management*, 1967, Harcourt, Brace & World.

HEMINGWAY, J., *Conflict and Democracy: Studies in Trade Union Government*, 1978, Oxford University Press.

HERDING, R. G., *Job Control and Union Structure*, 1972, Rotterdam University Press.

LEWENHAK, S., *Women and Trade Unions*, 1977, Benn.

SAYLES, L. R., and G. STRAUSS, *The Local Union*, 1957, Harcourt, Brace & World.

TURNER, H. A., *Trade Union Growth, Structure and Policy*, 1962, Allen & Unwin.

WEBB, S., and B. WEBB, *Industrial Democracy*, 1894, 1902, Longman.

Factors affecting union growth

ADAMS, R., 'Bain's Theory of White Collar Union Growth: A Conceptual Critique', *British Journal of Industrial Relations*, November 1977.

BAIN, G. S., *The Growth of White Collar Unionism*, 1970, Oxford, University Press.

BAIN, G. S., and FAROUK ELSHEIKH, *Union Growth and the Business Cycle*, 1976, Blackwell.

BAIN, G. S., and ROBERT PRICE, *Profiles of Union Growth: A Comparative Statistical Portrait of Eight Countries*, 1980, Blackwell.

BLUM, A. A., 'Why Unions Grow', *Labour History*, Winter 1968.

CLEGG, H. A., *Trade Unions Under Collective Bargaining*, Blackwell, 1976, ch. 2.

DAVIES, H. B., 'The Theory of Union Growth', *Quarterly Journal of Economics*, vol. 55, 1941, p. 611.

DUNLOP, J. T., in *Insights into Labour Issues*, ed. R. A. Lester and T. Schister, 1949, Macmillan Co.

LIPSET, S. M., and J. GORDON, in *Class Status and Power*, ed. R. Bendox and S. M. Lipset, 1954, Routledge & Kegan Paul.

MOORE, J., and R. J. NEWMAN, 'On the Prospects for American Union Growth', *Review of Economics and Statistics*, 1974, p. 435.

PERLMAN, M., *Labour Union Theories in America*, 1958, Row, Peterson.

RICHARDSON, R., and S. CATLIN, 'Trade Union Density and Collective Agreement Patterns in Britain', *British Journal of Industrial Relations*, XCIII, 1979, p. 376.

SHISTER, J., 'The Logic of Union Growth', *Journal of Political Economy*, LXI, 1953, p. 413.

STURMTHAL, A., *White Collar Unions*, 1966, University of Illinois Press.

The economic effects of trade unionism

BAILY, M., and A. OKON (eds.), *The Battle against Unemployment and Inflation*, 3rd edn, 1982.

BECKER, G., *Human Capital*, 1971, Chicago University Press.

BLACKABY, FRANK (ed.), *The Future of Pay Bargaining*, 1980, Heinemann.

BLACKBURN, R. M., and M. MANN, *The Working Class in the Labour Market*, 1979, Macmillan.

BOSANQUET, N., and P. DOERINGER, 'Is There a Dual Labour Market in Great Britain?', *Economic Journal*, 1973, p. 421.

BRITTAN, S., 'The Political Economy of British Union Monopoly', *Three Banks Review*, September 1976.

BROWN, W. A., *Piecework Bargaining*, 1973, Heinemann.

BROWN, W., and K. SISSON, 'The Use of Comparisons in Workplace Wage Determination', *British Journal of Industrial Relations*, March 1975.

CHATER, R., A. DEAN and R. ELLIOT, *Incomes Policy*, 1982, Oxford University Press.

CLARK, COLIN, 'Do Trade Unions Raise Wages?', *Journal of Economic Affairs*, July 1981.

CREEDY J. (ed.), *The Economics of Unemployment in Britain*, 1982, Butterworth.

DOERINGER, P. B., and M. J. PAINE, *Internal Labour Markets and Manpower Analysis*, 1971, Lexington Heath.

DUNLOP, J. T., *Wage Determination under Trade Unions*, 1950, Blackwell.

First Report and General Report of the Standing Committee on Pay Comparability, 1980, HMSO.

FISHER, M., *The Measurement of Unemployment*, 1980, Blac

FISHER, M., *The Economic Analysis of Labour*, 1971, Weidenfeld & Nicolson.

GARSIDE, W., *The Measurement of Unemployment*, 1980, Blackwell.

HILL, S., 'Norms, Groups and Power', *British Journal of Industrial Relations*, July 1974.

HUNTER, L., and C. MULVEY, *The Economics of Wages and Labour*, 1982, Macmillan.

JACKSON, D., H. A. TURNER and F. WILKINSON, *Do Trade Unions Cause Inflation?*, 1972, Cambridge University Press.

MACKAY, D. *et al.*, *Labour Markets Under Different Employment Conditions*, 1981, Allen & Unwin.

Megaw Report of an Inquiry into Civil Service Pay, vols. 1 and 2, 1982, HMSO.

METCALF, D., 'Unions, Incomes Policies and Relative Wages in Britain', *British Journal of Industrial Relations*, July 1977.

MILLER, R., and J. WOOF, 'What Price Unemployment?: An Alternative Approach', *Hobart Paper 92*, 1982, Institute of Economic Affairs.

MINFORD, PATRICK, *Unemployment, Causes and Cure*, 1983, Martin Robertson.

MULVEY, C., and J. TREVITHICK, 'Some Evidence on the Wage Leadership Hypothesis', *Scottish Journal of Political Economy*, February 1974.

PERCIVAL, J., 'The Distributional and Efficiency Effects of Trade Unions in Britain', *British Journal of Industrial Relations*, no. 21, 1977.

PHELPS BROWN, E. H., *The Inequality of Pay*, 1977, Oxford University Press.

PHELPS BROWN, E. H., and M. H. BROWNE, *A Century of Pay*, 1957, Macmillan.

REDDAWAY, W. B., 'Wage Flexibility and the Distribution of Labour', *Lloyds Bank Review*, October 1959.

ROBINSON, D. (ed.), *Local Labour Markets and Wage Structures*, 1970, Gower Press.

ROUTH, G., 'Industrial Relations, Unemployment and Inflation: A Review Article', *British Journal of Industrial Relations* (forthcoming, 1984).

ROUTH, G., *Occupation and Pay in Great Britain*, 1980, Macmillan.

SMITH, A. D., *The Labour Market and Inflation*, 1968, Macmillan.

THIRWELL, A. P., 'Keynesian Employment Theory is Not Defunct', *Three Banks Review*, no. 131, 1981, p. 14.

THOMAS, B., and D. DEATON, *Labour Shortage and Economic Analysis*, 1977, Blackwell.

WILKINSON, F. (ed.), *The Dynamics of Labour Market Segmentation Theory*, 1980, Academic Press.

WOOD, A., *A Theory of Pay*, 1978, Cambridge University Press.

WOOTON, B., *Social Foundations of Wages Policy*, 1955, Allen & Unwin.

Trade unions and the State

ALLEN, V. L., *Trade Unions and the Government*, 1980, Allen & Unwin.

BALFOUR, C., *Incomes Policy and the Public Sector*, 1972, Routledge & Kegan Paul.

CROUCH, C., *Class Conflict and Industrial Relations*, 1977, Heinemann.

DAVIES, P., and M. FREEDLAND, *Labour Law, Text and Materials*, 1979, Weidenfeld & Nicolson.

DORFMAN, G. A., *Wage Politics in Britain, 1945–67*, 1973, Amest Iowa University Press.

ELLIOT, R. F., and J. L. FALLICK, *Pay in the Public Sector*, 1981, Macmillan.

GRIFFITHS, J. A. C., *The Politics of the Judiciary*, 1981, Fontana.

HEPPLE, B. A., and P. O'HIGGINS, *Employment Law*, 4th edn, 1981, Sweet & Maxwell.

HIRSCH, F., and J. GOLDTHORPE (eds.), *The Political Economy of Inflation*, 1978, Martin Robertson.

KAHN-FREUND, O., *Labour and the Law*, 2nd edn, 1977.

KAHN-FREUND, O., *Labour Relations: Heritage and Adjustment*, 1979, Oxford University Press.

LEWIS, R., and B. SIMPSON, *Striking a Balance*, 1981, Martin Robertson.

LOVELL, J., and B. C. ROBERTS, *A Short History of the TUC*, 1968, Macmillan.

MARTIN, R., *TUC: The Growth of a Pressure Group 1878–1976*, 1980, Oxford University Press.

PANITCH, L., 'Recent Theorisations of Corporatism', *British Journal of Sociology*, XXXI, no. 2.

PANITCH, L., *Social Democracy and Industrial Militancy*, 1976, Cambridge University Press.

RITCHTER, I., *Political Purpose in Trade Unions*, 1973, Allen & Unwin.

WEDDERBURN, K. W., R. LEWIS and J. CLARK, *Labour Law and Industrial Relations: Building on Kahn-Freund*, 1983, Oxford University Press.

WEEKES, B., M. MELLISH, L. DICKENS and J. LLOYD, *Industrial Relations and the Limits of the Law*, 1975, Blackwell.

Acknowledgements

The author and publisher would like to acknowledge
the following sources:

1 Faber & Faber
2 Prentice-Hall
3 Macmillan
4 Basil Blackwell
5 Bell & Hyman Ltd
6 Basil Blackwell
7 Constable
8 HMSO
9 Basil Blackwell
10 Basil Blackwell
11 *Industrial Relations Journal*
12 Hutchinson
13 Hutchinson
14 HMSO
15 Simon & Schuster
16 *Sociology*
17 Basil Blackwell
18 *British Journal of Industrial Relations*
19 *British Journal of Industrial Relations*
20 *British Journal of Industrial Relations*
21 Hutchinson
22 Harper & Row
23 University of California Press
24 Institute of Economic Affairs
25 HMSO
26 Martin Robertson
27 Institute of Economic Affairs
28 Institute of Economic Affairs
29 *Industrial Relations Journal*
30 Routledge & Kegan Paul
31 *Industrial Relations Journal*
32 Fontana

34 HMSO
35 HMSO
36 Institute of Advanced Legal Studies
37 University of Durham Industrial Relations Group
38 *New Society*

Index

rules, 193–215
  of admission to membership, 194, 195,
    196, 198–203
  disciplinary, 194–5, 196–7, 203–11, 467
  legal requirements, 194
  TUC initiatives, 196–7
Russell, B., 217

safety, 38, 39
Sailors' Union, 310
Salmon, Lord, 512
Samuel Commission, 448–9
sanctions, internal, 30
sanitation, 38, 39
Scanlon, H., 188
Scargill, A., 436
Scarman, Lord, 466, 512, 513
Schregle, J., 97
Schultz, G. P., 295
Scottish Associated Tilefixers, 140
Scottish Commercial Motormen, 144
Scottish Plasterers Union, 143
Scottish Transport and General Workers,
  144
secondary action, 502, 533, 534
sectionalism, 426
Seltzer, G., 138n.
Selznick, P., 118
Sex Discrimination Act, 1975, 419
Shanks, M., 27–8
Sheet Metal Workers Union
  admission of members, 198
  disciplinary rules, 204
Ship Constructors and Shipwrights, 143
Shipbuilding and Allied Industries
  Management Association, 146
Shister, J., 265, 266–7, 285, 313
shop convenors, and role of stewards, 64
Shop Distributive and Allied Workers, 130
shop-floor organization, growth of, 416–17
shop stewards, 32, 43
  and board representation, 100
  and corporatism, 422, 444
  'cowboys', 65–6, 67
  growth of movement, 98, 411, 415
  nascent leaders, 65–6, 67
  populists, 66, 67, 68, 69, 70
  and promotion, 65
  relations with members, 60–63
  representative or delegate role, 69–71

  role definition, 63–7
  and staff stewards, 59–60
  and union principles, 59–71
Shop Stewards' Movement, 411
Silbertson, A., 117
Simler, N. S., 301n.
Simpson, B., 255
Simpson, D. H., 154n.
size of workplace, 263–4, 377
skilled workers
  union membership, 262
  wage levels, 340, 350–52
Slichter, S. H., 316
small firms, 263–4
Smith, A., 485
Smith, A. W., 369
Smith, D. C., 389
social contract, 422, 425, 430, 431–2, 499
social goals, unionism and, 52, 54
social security benefits, 365–6, 367, 428
socialism
  guild, 81–2, 92
  and role of unions, 26–7
socialization of unions, 53
society, unions and, 28
Society of Civil and Public Servants
  (SCPS), 145, 164
Society of Graphical and Allied Trades
  (SOGAT)
  disciplinary rules, 207
  exclusion from areas, 211–12
  mergers, 139, 143, 152, 164
solidarity, 43, 45
Solomon, 399
staff conveners, and role of stewards, 64
staff stewards
  relations with members, 61–3
  role definition, 63–7
  and union principles , 59–60
Stalker, G. M., 117
Stamford Mutual, 144
standards, uniformity and, 41–4
state
  attitude to unions, 406–32
  coercive strikes against, 452–4, 491
  as employer, 415, 451; see also
    nationalized industries; public sector
  intervention, 417–21, 433–46
  Labour Party and unions, 423–5
  political strikes against, 454–9

MORE ABOUT PENGUINS, PELICANS
AND PUFFINS

For further information about books available from Penguins please write to Dept EP, Penguin Books Ltd, Harmondsworth, Middlesex UB7 0DA.

In the U.S.A.: For a complete list of books available from Penguins in the United States write to Dept DG, Penguin Books, 299 Murray Hill Parkway, East Rutherford, New Jersey 07073.

In Canada: For a complete list of books available from Penguins in Canada write to Penguin Books Canada Limited, 2801 John Street, Markham, Ontario L3R 1B4.

In Australia: For a complete list of books available from Penguins in Australia write to the Marketing Department, Penguin Books Australia Ltd, P.O. Box 257, Ringwood, Victoria 3134.

In New Zealand: For a complete list of books available from Penguins in New Zealand write to the Marketing Department, Penguin Books (N.Z.) Ltd, Private Bag, Takapuna, Auckland 9.

In India: For a complete list of books available from Penguins in India write to Penguin Overseas Ltd, 706 Eros Apartments, 56 Nehru Place, New Delhi 110019.

Also published by Penguins

A HISTORY OF BRITISH TRADE UNIONISM

Henry Pelling

'A genuine and worthwhile addition to the growing literature on trade unionism' – George Woodcock in the *Sunday Times*

Today trade unionism plays a more important part in the nation's economy than ever before, and its problems of internal reform and its relations with the government and the public are constantly under discussion. But its present structure can only be understood in relation to its long history.

Henry Pelling, a Fellow of St John's College, Cambridge, and author of *The Origins of the Labour Party*, leads the reader through a vivid story of struggle and development covering more than four centuries: from the medieval guilds and early craftsmen's and labourers' associations to the dramatic growth of trade unionism in Britain in the nineteenth and twentieth centuries.

He shows how powerful personalities such as Robert Applegarth, Henry Broadhurst, Tom Mann, Ernest Bevin, and Walter Citrine have helped to shape the pattern of present-day unionism; and for this edition Henry Pelling has added a chapter 'The Industrial Relations Act and After (1971–6)'.

'Readable and intelligent' – *The Times Educational Supplement*

Third Edition

Also published by Penguins

TOWARDS 2000

Raymond Williams

What sort of world will we have in 2000 AD?

Mass unemployment and nuclear war are two of the crises which may darken an uncertain future. Here, the radical thinker Raymond Williams examines our current predicament and points the way forward. Taking his essay on Britain in the sixties as a starting point, Williams reassesses and extends the arguments of *The Long Revolution* (a book which set the guidelines for the socialist debate). In discussing the major changes within British society, he raises proposals for fresh political structures which take account of true equality and revitalized socialism.

'The nearest thing the British New Left has to a sage' – *Observer*

Also published by Penguins

POVERTY IN THE UNITED KINGDOM

Peter Townsend

The definitive contemporary study

'This momentous book will rank as the contemporary successor to the classic works of Booth and Rowntree: its case histories alone should put paid to those who still assert that there is no longer poverty in Britain' – Barbara Wootton

Also published by Penguins

THE MAKING OF THE ENGLISH WORKING CLASS

E. P. Thompson

The Making of the English Working Class, now published as the thousandth Pelican, is probably the greatest and most imaginative post-war work of English social history. This account of artisan and working-class society in its formative years, 1780 to 1832, adds an important dimension to our understanding of the nineteenth century, for Edward Thompson sees the ordinary people of England not as statistical fodder, nor merely as passive victims of political repression and industrial alienation. He shows that the working class took part in its own making. In their religious movements, their political struggles and their growing community organizations, working people in very different walks of life gradually developed an identity of interests which was expressed in a vigorous and democratic popular culture.

Within the conventional framework of English history in the Industrial Revolution, Mr Thompson gives controversial assessments of the popular traditions of the eighteenth century, the cost-of-living controversy, the role of Methodism and the genesis of parliamentary reform. He also includes radically new interpretations of underground traditions usually ignored by historians, from clandestine Jacobin societies and millenarian movements to the Luddites.

But the most impressive feature of this exceptional book is its re-creation of the whole life-experience of people who suffered loss of status and freedom, who underwent degradation, and who yet created a culture and political consciousness of great vitality.

Also published by Penguins

UNEMPLOYMENT

Kevin Hawkins

A new, up-to-date edition of Kevin Hawkins's major survey on unemployment in Britain.

As Britain's 'unemployment problem' escalates, arguments about it grow in fervour and complexity. But just who believes what? What are facts and what mere opinions and prophecies? Above all, what is being *done* about the problem?

Here Kevin Hawkins provides us with a full briefing on all the major theories and courses of action – current and proposed. Into a coherent context go the Phillips Curve, Bacon and Eltis, Lord Keynes and Professor Friedman, the 'welfare scroungers' theory, the Manpower Service Commission, the balance of payments, youth employment schemes, job-sharing and much else besides.

There are many unemployment problems and no single solution; but, as the author shows, some – if not all – *could* be solved.

Second Edition

Also published by Penguins

POLITICAL IDEAS

Edited by David Thompson

This Pelican introduces the most significant and fundamental ideas of eminent European political thinkers in the last five hundred years – those who have had a lasting influence on history. The theme of the book, which is the work of a team of specialists, falls into four consecutive but overlapping parts. The discussion of Machiavelli, Luther and Hobbes deals ultimately with the creation of political sovereignty; the essays on Locke, Paine, Montesquieu and Rousseau, on the other hand, are more concerned with the relationship between government and the governed, and from their ideas sprang the great liberal and constitutional tradition of politics; Burke, Hegel, and Mazzini represent the concept of the Nation-State; and Mill reasserts the claims of individual personality against excessive government authority, whilst Marx is evolving his theory of revolutionary communism.

These political thinkers nevertheless defy classification: all are concerned with the complex human problems from which we cannot escape in our own lives – the problems of human freedom, the grounds of obligation, the limits of obedience, the basis of law and loyalty. And if, as David Thomson suggests in his conclusion, the emphasis in future political ideas is on Equality, rather than on Liberty, it will be seen that the great political debate, highlighted in this book, is a continuing one.

Also published by Penguins

THE PELICAN ECONOMIC HISTORY OF BRITAIN   VOLUME 3

INDUSTRY AND EMPIRE
E. J. Hobsbawm

The industrial revolution marks the most fundamental transformation in the history of the world recorded in written documents. For a brief period it coincided with the history of a single country, Great Britain. This book describes and accounts for Britain's rise as the world's first industrial world power, its decline from the temporary dominance of the pioneer, its rather special relationship with the rest of the world (notably the underdeveloped countries), and the effects of all these on the life of the British people.

'When a brilliantly gifted and learned man impatiently sets about the lesser people who profess his subject, he writes a book that attracts and deserves attention. Eric Hobsbawm, by far the most gifted economic historian now writing, has done just this. Under the guise of a textbook he has produced an original and masterly reinterpretation of Western economic (not to speak of social and political) history' – John Vaizey in the *Listener*

'A masterly survey of the major economic developments and changes of the last 200 years, sharply and ironically observed, elegantly written and, for the statistically undernourished, illustrated by a host of excellent diagrams and maps' – *Guardian*

VOLUME 1: MEDIEVAL ECONOMY OF SOCIETY   *M. M. Postan*

VOLUME 2: REFORMATION TO INDUSTRIAL REVOLUTION   *Christopher Hill*

THE WINNING STREAK

Walter Goldsmith and David Clutterbuck

Marks & Spencer, Saatchi & Saatchi, United Biscuits, Plessey, GEC ...

What gives these and other British companies their *winning streak*?

Drawing on exclusive interviews with Britain's leading company directors and executives, Goldsmith and Clutterbuck set out to analyse the hows and whys of the UK's most successful companies. The result is a book that no British manager can afford to ignore. For the authors' conclusions, highlighted by comparison with other, unsuccessful businesses, provide detailed guidelines that could very profitably be adopted by *all* companies in Britain.

The Winning Streak will have the major impact on management in Britain that its bestselling precursor, *In Search of Excellence*, had in the United States. If companies are prepared to learn from this book, the authors point out, 'the only economic problems Britain would have would be problems of success'.

A CHOICE OF
PELICANS AND PEREGRINES

☐ **The Knight, the Lady and the Priest**
Georges Duby   £6.95

The acclaimed study of the making of modern marriage in medieval France. 'He has traced this story – sometimes amusing, often horrifying, always startling – in a series of brilliant vignettes' – *Observer*

☐ **The Limits of Soviet Power** Jonathan Steele   £3.95

The Kremlin's foreign policy – Brezhnev to Chernenko, is discussed in this informed, informative 'wholly invaluable and extraordinarily timely study' – *Guardian*

☐ **Understanding Organizations** Charles B. Handy   £4.95

Third Edition. Designed as a practical source-book for managers, this Pelican looks at the concepts, key issues and current fashions in tackling organizational problems.

☐ **The Pelican Freud Library: Volume 12**   £5.95

Containing the major essays: *Civilization, Society and Religion, Group Psychology* and *Civilization and Its Discontents*, plus other works.

☐ **Windows on the Mind** Erich Harth   £4.95

Is there a physical explanation for the various phenomena that we call 'mind'? Professor Harth takes in age-old philosophers as well as the latest neuroscientific theories in his masterly study of memory, perception, free will, selfhood, sensation and other richly controversial fields.

☐ **The Pelican History of the World**
J. M. Roberts   £5.95

'A stupendous achievement . . . This is the unrivalled World History for our day' – A. J. P. Taylor

A CHOICE OF
PELICANS AND PEREGRINES

☐ *A Question of Economics* **Peter Donaldson** £4.95

Twenty key issues – from the City and big business to trades unions – clarified and discussed by Peter Donaldson, author of *10 × Economics* and one of our greatest popularizers of economics.

☐ *Inside the Inner City* **Paul Harrison** £4.95

A report on urban poverty and conflict by the author of *Inside the Third World*. 'A major piece of evidence' – *Sunday Times*. 'A classic: it tells us what it is really like to be poor, and why' – *Time Out*

☐ *What Philosophy Is* **Anthony O'Hear** £4.95

What are human beings? How should people act? How do our thoughts and words relate to reality? Contemporary attitudes to these age-old questions are discussed in this new study, an eloquent and brilliant introduction to philosophy today.

☐ *The Arabs* **Peter Mansfield** £4.95

New Edition. 'Should be studied by anyone who wants to know about the Arab world and how the Arabs have become what they are today' – *Sunday Times*

☐ *Religion and the Rise of Capitalism*
  R. H. Tawney £3.95

The classic study of religious thought of social and economic issues from the later middle ages to the early eighteenth century.

☐ *The Mathematical Experience*
  Philip J. Davis and Reuben Hersh £7.95

Not since *Gödel, Escher, Bach* has such an entertaining book been written on the relationship of mathematics to the arts and sciences. 'It deserves to be read by everyone ... an instant classic' – *New Scientist*

A CHOICE OF
PELICANS AND PEREGRINES

☐ *Crowds and Power* **Elias Canetti**   £4.95

'Marvellous . . . an immensely interesting, often profound reflection
about the nature of society, in particular the nature of violence' –
Susan Sontag in *The New York Review of Books*

☐ *The Death and Life of Great American Cities*
Jane Jacobs   £5.95

One of the most exciting and wittily written attacks on contemporary
city planning to have appeared in recent years – thought-provoking
reading and, as one critic noted, 'extremely apposite to conditions in
the UK'.

☐ *Computer Power and Human Reason*
Joseph Weizenbaum   £3.95

Internationally acclaimed by scientists and humanists alike: 'This is
the best book I have read on the impact of computers on society, and
on technology and on man's image of himself' – *Psychology Today*

These books should be available at all good bookshops or newsagents, but if
you live in the UK or the Republic of Ireland and have difficulty in getting to
a bookshop, they can be ordered by post. Please indicate the titles required
and fill in the form below.

NAME _____ BLOCK CAPITALS

ADDRESS _____

_____

Enclose a cheque or postal order payable to The Penguin Bookshop to cover
the total price of books ordered, plus 50p for postage. Readers in the Republic
of Ireland should send £1R equivalent to the sterling prices, plus 67p for postage. Send to: The Penguin Bookshop, 54/56 Bridlesmith Gate, Nottingham,
NG1 2GP.

You can also order by phoning (0602) 599295, and quoting your Barclaycard
or Access number.

Every effort is made to ensure the accuracy of the price and availability of
books at the time of going to press, but it is sometimes necessary to increase
prices and in these circumstances retail prices may be shown on the covers of
books which may differ from the prices shown in this list or elsewhere. This list
is not an offer to supply any book.

**This order service is only available to residents in the UK and the Republic of
Ireland.**